THE NEW YORK TOMBS

PATTERSON SMITH SERIES IN
CRIMINOLOGY, LAW ENFORCEMENT & SOCIAL PROBLEMS
A listing of publications in the Series *will be found at rear of volume*

PUBLICATION No. 178: PATTERSON SMITH SERIES IN
CRIMINOLOGY, LAW ENFORCEMENT & SOCIAL PROBLEMS

THE
NEW YORK TOMBS

ITS SECRETS AND ITS MYSTERIES

BY

CHARLES SUTTON

EDITED BY

JAMES B. MIX & SAMUEL A. MACKEEVER

REPRINTED WITH THE ADDITION OF
A NEW INTRODUCTION BY THOMAS M. McDADE

Illustrated

MONTCLAIR, NEW JERSEY
PATTERSON SMITH
1973

First published 1874 by the
United States Publishing Company, New York

Reprinted 1973 by Patterson Smith Publishing Corporation
Montclair, New Jersey 07042

Library of Congress Cataloging in Publication Data

Sutton, Charles.
    The New York Tombs: its secrets and its mysteries.

    (Patterson Smith series in criminology, law enforcement
& social problems. Publication no. 178)
    Reprint of the 1874 ed. with a new introduction.
    1. New York (City). Tombs Prison. 2. Crime and
criminals — New York (City). I. Title.

HV9481.N62T68 1973   365'.9747'1   76-172588
                ISBN 0-87585-178-9

This book is printed on
permanent/durable paper

INTRODUCTION TO THE
REPRINT EDITION

I

IT was a cliché of the early writers on crime in its more florid phases to excuse their seemingly morbid interest by describing their purpose as one of moral enlightenment. Thus the Philadelphia publisher, Mathew Carey in 1810, in a work full of heinous and bloody crime, can recommend it to the guardians of children for bringing home to "thoughtless childhood and unreflecting youth" the dire consequences of a misguided life. The present volume, a half-century later, likewise pays obeisance to this convention.

> If the reader takes up this book with the idea that we have unrolled a record of violence, crime and blood, to gratify a depraved taste for the horrible; or because we are fond of writing about such scenes; or exult in the barbarism of strangling human beings to death on the gallows, he will make one of the biggest blunders of his life.

The reader of *The New York Tombs* will not be misled. But today the reporting of crime is so pervasive in newspapers, novels, the cinema and television that we accept the part it plays in our culture. What the nineteenth century viewed as an unhealthy preoccupation with crime, a morbid interest that it must excuse, explain and justify on a moral basis, the twentieth recognizes as merely an enlightened interest in one part of the whole social scene.

We need not take too seriously the statement of the high moral purpose of the book. Charles Sutton, warden of the county jail of New York County, uses this book to tell about the notorious characters to whom he played host. In so doing he has given a vivid picture not only of crime in a large city but of how society dealt with it in that period. As our laws and the manner in which they are enforced are merely reflections of the mores and social customs of the times, the significance of what is here reported is not what the criminal did but how society reacted to it.

II

The jail of which Sutton writes was known as the Tombs from the style of its architecture. In 1837 the American traveler John L. Stephens (whom Sutton misspells in the text) published an illustrated book on his travels in the Middle East. The resemblance of the New York structure to an Egyptian tomb depicted in Stephens' work suggested the name for the new jail. Since its opening in 1838, all the jails in New York County (of which the present one is the third) have been known as the Tombs.

The new jail was not only a vast improvement over the jails which had preceded it but it was eminently superior to the local jails and lock-ups used to confine prisoners awaiting trial in smaller communities. Nevertheless, it was still a cold, dirty, vermin-ridden place, where the wealthy could still procure the privileges always attendant on money and the poor suffered even more indignities for lack of it.

The ready acceptance of the inequality of the classes is nowhere more evident than in the description of how a well-to-do prisoner charged with murder might live.

In a patent extension chair he lolls, smoking an aromatic Havana, while he reads the proceedings of his trial the day previous in the morning papers. He has an elegant dressing gown on, faced with cherry colored silk, and his feet are encased in delicately worked slippers. . . . his lunch [is] not cooked in the prison but brought in from a hotel. It consists of a variety of dishes, such as quail on toast, game patés, reed birds, ortolans, fowl, the newest vegetables, coffee [and] cognac.

This description is made, not by some muck-raking journalist unmasking privilege, but by the warden of the jail. Sutton merely reflected the conviction of the times that poverty was necessarily a result of sloth and indolence, and that riches were the rewards of perseverance and industry. The American dream that everyone was in control of his own destiny had not yet tarnished—so that there was nothing improper in permitting the possessors of wealth to purchase privileges despite their confinement in jail on serious charges. Still, in the perspective of time, we might wish now that Sutton had devoted more room to the homely details of prison life—the food the ordinary prisoners were served, the other social classes of jail life (it is burglars who are generally considered part of the elite in a prison population); and also such mundane details as the procedures for processing prisoners, the kinds of records maintained on each, and the presence or absence of problems of dope, sex and segregation.

For Sutton's tenants in the prison did come from a broad spectrum of the criminal element and the descriptions of their offenses provide an education in crime of the period. The famous and the infamous spent brief or longer periods in the Tombs' cells. E. Z. C. Judson, popularly known as Ned Buntline, writer of dime novels and adventure stories, was there before his conviction for his part in the notorious Astor Place Riots. Madame Restell, the abortionist who maintained a twenty-five-room chateau on Fifth Avenue and catered to the rich, ran afoul of the law more by chance—and when she had served her term she returned to her mansion and practice. Edward Stokes, who killed Jim Fisk in a dispute involving the beautiful Josie Mansfield and a struggle for control of the Erie Railroad, was a royal guest of Sutton, who devotes a whole chapter to the case, a *cause célèbre* of the period.

It is this broad sweep of cases which lends color and tone to the period and the book. In some instances there is only enough about the case to rouse the interest of the reader to find out more about it. In other cases the treatment is almost complete. One of the fascinating murder puzzles of the period involved the death of a dentist, Harvey Burdell, on a rainy, foggy night in 1857. An essential element of greatness in any criminal case is that last remaining mystery which is never resolved. It might be the identity of the murderer; or it might involve the motive or the means. It is that last dark corner for which there is no answer and around which students may add their own conjectures to those of the investigators who tried to resolve the problem.

On the morning of January 31, 1857, much as some novelist might plot it, a boy taking a scuttle of coal from the cellar to Dr. Burdell's second-floor bedroom had to push rather hard against some resisting object to get the bedroom door open. The object was a very badly battered Dr. Burdell, whose blood was splashed all about the room, furniture and walls, as well as the hall, the stairs and even the front door. Fifteen stab-wounds had brought about his death. Living in the remainder of the house, under the aegis of the landlady, Mrs. Cunningham, were a total of eight other persons, none of whom seem to have been disturbed by the violence that had overtaken the good dentist sometime the previous evening. Suffice it to say that the law saw fit to elect Mrs. Cunningham as its chief suspect and that when brought to trial for murder she was defended by Henry L. Clinton, a leader of the New York trial bar. The ramifications of the case would do credit to Agatha Christie; all the elements of a ready-made detective novel are there. Mrs. Cunningham's alleged secret marriage to Dr. Burdell three months before the murder, for instance, or the correspondence between Mrs. Cunningham's left-handedness and the doctors' conclusion that the blows were delivered by a left-handed person.

For all that, the case against the good Mrs. Cunningham was inconclusive, and the jury had no trouble acquitting her. The matter did not end there, however. She claimed to be pregnant by the dead doctor, and in the fullness of time produced a child, though there was considerable doubt that she was the mother of the infant exhibited—which in fact she had "borrowed" from Bellevue Hospital. This attempted fraud brought new charges against Mrs. Cunningham, but these too she eventually defeated. P. T. Barnum, ever alert to a good thing, rented this fraudulent offspring and its genuine mother and exhibited them at his Broadway museum, undoubtedly profiting more than anyone else from the case.

To give a larger view of the kinds of places used for the confinement of prisoners at that period, the book also includes sketches of Sing Sing and the penitentiary on Blackwell's (now Welfare) Island. Because we know something of the conditions of the modern prison, the description of the conditions at Sing Sing at that time, including the manner of its construction and the kinds of punishments then used, furnishes a shocking contrast. The prisoner was then in effect the slave of the state, used, except when his product tended to compete with the free market, as a machine for labor: now prisoners frequently have a freedom of action and a series of rights which give them access to books, education and training. For those who may wonder where to look for signs of social progress, who may despair that things will ever be better, a reading of the prison conditions in the nineteenth century must surely suggest that there has been improvement in the social order.

III

The declining interest in the execution of criminals may make both the science and the ritual of such an event a lost art. While Sutton describes some executions in the Tombs, they already had lost much of the ceremony of an earlier day. Here we are reminded that the hanging of a miscreant was not only a frequent but also a public event. It was not necessary in this period, as it was in earlier days, to pardon a condemned man under terms which required him to act as the public executioner for a term of years. Apparently there were enough candidates for this lucrative, if slightly gruesome, job. Before 1832 executions of state prisoners were performed in public, presumably to deter others from following their example. The great concourse of people who turned out for these events led the authorities to try to conceal the place of execution until the last moment.

When John Johnson was to be hanged for murder in 1824 the scaffold was moved by boat to a farm on 13th Street and Second Avenue, but word quickly spread throughout the city. The parade of the prisoner from the jail, then at City Hall Park, was a semi-military event. A troop of cavalry formed an enclosed square, within which a company of infantry formed a further guard around the principals who occupied the core. A band of music followed the front line of foot soldiers; next came a wagon bearing the prisoner, already dressed in a shroud, sitting on the coffin which rode with him, and accompanied by two clergymen. Police, sheriff and coroner added official dignity to the conclave, which took an hour to move a mile through the throngs lining the roads.

After 1832 all executions in the city took place within the jail and the usual practice (unlike the English one of burying the executed man within the jail yard) was to deliver the body to relatives for burial. In the case of some criminals the court might order the body delivered to doctors for anatomical purposes, and in a few bizarre episodes attempts were made to restore the executed man to life.

The great debate over capital punishment which has raged for the past hundred years was much a part of Sutton's time. While New York State has now abolished the death penalty for virtually all offenses except the slaying of a police officer performing his duty, the road to this abrogation was long and hard fought. Bills providing for the abolition of the death penalty were repeatedly brought before the legislature during the nineteenth century, although, except for a few hiatuses, executions continued.

What is startling about many of the capital cases reported in the book is that the act for which the accused was condemned would sustain no more than a charge of manslaughter today. A man who lashed out and killed someone in the heat of passion or under momentary provocation, or tormented by a neighbor, or engaged in a drunken brawl, might well nevertheless end up on the gallows. Sutton reports the case of a citizen who was attacked by loafers and who overreacted to their taunts and stabbed one of them to death. He was hanged despite popular efforts to obtain a commutation of sentence. The stern code of our Puritan fathers held sway for a long time in our criminal courts.

IV

Every period likes to believe that its problems are unique. "Here in New York, in the nineteenth century, the air blatant with church chimes, murder runs riot and flaunts its gory banner in the face of the law." In the latter half of the twentieth century, we find that neither the variety nor the volume of crime has diminished, but that the social context is vastly different.

In 1806 a young man traveling across Massachusetts was set upon by robbers and beaten to death and his body dropped in the Chicopee River. Overtaken a few days later at Cos Cob, Connecticut, the assailants, Daley and Halligan, were found in possession of the victim's money: a five-dollar bill of the Nantucket bank, a seven-dollar bill of the Saco bank, a three-dollar bill of the Newburyport bank, and a one-dollar bill of the Bristol bank.

At their trial, to show their hasty flight from the scene of the crime, it was testified that while they had walked from Boston to Wilbraham, a distance of 85 miles, in four days, it had taken them but three days to cover the 120 miles from Wilbraham to Cos Cob. In his plea to the jury their counsel, mindful of the prejudice of the times, could ask, "Do not therefore believe them guilty because they are Irishmen." In this brief vignette we see how the threads of social history—the local, haphazard banking practices, the prevailing means and rate of travel, and the then current religious or national prejudice—all combine to make a pattern in and around an event which has so many counterparts today.

Some years ago Herbert Asbury, a New York newspaper reporter, wrote a series of crime books on the major cities of America. These books are minor classics in their field: *Gem of the Prairie* (on Chicago), *The Barbary Coast* (on San Francisco), and of course *The Gangs of New York*. It is books such as Sutton's that are the major source of Asbury's compilations, that made it possible to construct a criminal history of a city. In our study of history today, however, we continually go back to the sources for both content and flavor. This is what distinguishes even undergraduate work today from that of the past.

What original sources such as Sutton's possess in genuineness and authenticity they often lack in style, organization and balance. Thus he dwells at excessive length on some cases, such as the MacFarland–Richardson killing or the case of Stokes (where the defendant is furnished with a whole appendix to devote to *his* explanation of the tragedy). Undoubtedly the case was at that time still a sensation in the daily press and reader interest would have been high. Parts of Sutton's work were indeed quite obviously assembled by means of scissors and paste from newspapers, broadsides and pamphlets of the period. Were one assembling this material today, better selections might be made, with perhaps more dramatic illustrations. But something would also be lost, for only the eye of the times can take in the experience of the period.

In fact what is continuously surprising in perusing an old work such as Sutton's is the sudden relevance of material old in time and use. Women's liberation may seem new, but most of it was foreshadowed by Victoria Woodhull a hundred years ago. Whether or not it was her outrageous accusations which caused the public prosecutor to overreact, arrest her and keep her in jail, as well as to try to suppress her publication, she knew the value of publicity and soon became a martyr in the battle between the sexes. Even her attorney, George Francis Train, got into the spirit of the act, and when he was arrested and borne to the Tombs he organized a club in Murderers' Row which irritated and confounded the authorities. Meanwhile "The Woodhull," as she was known, traveled, lectured, published, ran a brokerage house, entered politics, and all in all received endless publicity from the combination of "the piquant and the prurient," as her talks were characterized.

To the student of this period books such as Sutton's supply the minutiae of detail—the color, the flavor and dimensions of crime then, as well as an indication of the attitude of society as a whole toward criminal behavior. The omnivorous collecting we see today on all sides, not only of valuable and superior works of art, but of all the mass of trivia such as buttons, playing cards, tools, trade flyers, public notices, regimental badges, postcards, railroad timetables, yes, even barbed wire, attests to an enormous interest in period cultural history. Not every collector is cognizant of the value of the material to a social historian, but in the fullness of time it all assumes its place and value in the source material for a period.

The rise of reconstructed villages, not all with the magnificence of a colonial Williamsburg, yet each with its specimen general store, church, print shop, tavern and blacksmith's shop, attests to our growing interest in our past. In each there is a natural adjunct to give evidence of our criminal past, be it stocks, pillory, ducking stool or town jail. A popular picture for the camera enthusiast is of someone posed with head and hands clamped in the frame of the pillory, a culprit on display. If our social history is thus a little brighter, a little less grim than the actuality of the period—a remoter time, when the body of the executed murderer might be preserved with a coat of tar and hung in chains (to keep it intact) at some crossroad as a warning to the populace—at least there is the urge to know something of the past.

That past is thus the sum of all the experiences of the times, the good, the great, the bad, the inspired, the mad, and the ordinary. Though a man may go through his life without ever having spent a night in a prison cell, he must, if he claims to be a man of his times, know what such a cell is like, how hard the bed, how cold the room. And if he would know what imprisonment meant in earlier centuries, he must also bear in mind what life outside was like then: a New England whaler could accept the stern conditions of the confined fo'c's'le of his vessel for a year at a time, for he was mindful that the life of the New England farmer was hardly less rigorous.

Historians are becoming more aware of the interrelation of all the parts of our society. Many of them, too, are actively collecting and collating the ephemera of their own day for the light it will throw on people and events when that time is long past. Peace marchers, black militants, conscientious objectors, campus revolutionaries, "hash" users—all have languages, media and scenes of their own. Some of the items printed to tell their stories today will one day be reprinted as this book has been to recapture a small piece of the period. The stories are not always complete nor necessarily well told, but they will be told with the voices of our twentieth century, just as this book speaks to us from the nineteenth.

THOMAS M. MCDADE

Purchase, New York
January, 1973

THE NEW YORK TOMBS

Respectfully,

Yours,

Chas Sutton.

THE NEW YORK TOMBS;

ITS

SECRETS AND ITS MYSTERIES.

BEING A

HISTORY OF NOTED CRIMINALS, WITH NARRATIVES OF THEIR CRIMES,

AS GATHERED BY

CHARLES SUTTON,

WARDEN OF THE PRISON.

EDITED BY

JAMES B. MIX AND SAMUEL A. MACKEEVER.

———

" *Those Dreadful walls of Newgate.*"—DICKENS.

———

SPLENDIDLY ILLUSTRATED FROM ORIGINAL DESIGNS.

———

SOLD ONLY BY SUBSCRIPTION.

———

New York:

UNITED STATES PUBLISHING COMPANY,

11 & 13 UNIVERSITY PLACE.

———

1874.

[*facsimile of the original title page*]

CONTENTS.

CHAPTER I.

PAGE

INTRODUCTORY... 17

CHAPTER II.

Prisons of New York.—Stadt Huys.—Old City Hall.—New Jail.—Bridewell.—Bellevue Penitentiary.—State Prison at Greenwich.—Ludlow
Street Jail.—House of Refuge..................................... 20

CHAPTER III.

Modes of Punishment.—The Whipping Post.—The Pillory.—The Ducking
Stool.—The Stocks.—The Wooden Horse.—The Treadmill............ 35

CHAPTER IV.

The Tombs.—The Collect.—Incidents in its early History.—Progress of Improvements.—Erection of the Tombs................................ 44

CHAPTER V.

A Treatise on Gambling.—An Essay by a Convict.—The Strange and Re-
markable Career of Mulligan.—Shot down in San Francisco.—The
Desperate Fight preceding his Death.—The Beau Brummel of the
Gamblers at that time.. 53

CHAPTER VI.

Colt's Case.—The Murder of Samuel Adams.—The Death Grapple in Colt's
Office.—Shipping the Body to New Orleans.—Detection.—Arrest.—The
Tombs.—The Wedding in the Cell.—Suicide of Colt................. 64

CHAPTER VII.

PAGE

The Driftwood in the Current of Metropolitan Life.—Vagrants—Bummers—
Drunkards—Revolvers—Misers.................................... 81

CHAPTER VIII.

Humorous and Pathetic Incidents.—Benevolence of the late Simeon Draper.
—A Practical Joke.—What Happened in an Omnibus.—How a State
Room was Secured... 87

CHAPTER IX.

Murderers' Row.—Assassins of the Period.—How they Live in the New
York Tombs.—Murder at a Premium.—Flowers, Canary Birds and Kid-
derminster Carpets.—Gentlemen of Elegant Leisure.—Rose-Colored
Life in the Prison Cell... 93

CHAPTER X.

Helen Jewett, the Queen of the Demi-monde.—Her Early Life.—Correspond-
ence.—Acquaintance with Prominent Statesmen, Artists and Actors of
the Day.—Her Youthful Lover, Richard P. Robinson.—Her Murder.—
Attempt to Burn the Body.—James Gordon Bennett's Description of
the Charred Corpse, as viewed the next Morning.—Excitement at the
Trial.—Eloquence of Robinson's Counsel, Hon. Ogden Hoffman.—
Murder of a Witness.—Bribery of a Juror.—Perjury of a Witness.—
Acquittal of Robinson —Flight to Texas.—A Strange Sequel.......... 97

CHAPTER XI.

The Stanwix Hall Tragedy.—Native American Party.—Tom Hyer.—Bill
Poole.—John Morrissey.—Lewis Baker.—Paudeen.—Assassination of
Poole.—Fate of his Assailants.—Letter of John Morrissey on Retiring
from the Prize Ring... 137

CHAPTER XII.

Executions in the City and County of New York.................... 148

CHAPTER XIII.

The Bond Street Tragedy.—The Murder of Dr. Harvey Burdell.—Stabbed
to Death in his own Office.—Who did it? Was it a Left-Handed
Woman? Arrest and Trial of Mrs. Cunningham.—Not Guilty.—That
Wonderful Baby... 156

CHAPTER XIV.

PAGE

The Story of the Frenchman who did not witness the Execution, and how it happened.. 168

CHAPTER XV.

John Mahony, the American Jack Sheppard.—An account of his Adventurous Life, written by Himself.—His Career of Crime, and his Remarkable Escapes... 170

CHAPTER XVI.

Murder most Foul.—Entrance to the Chamber of Horrors.—Hicks the Pirate.—His Bloody Deeds on board an Oyster Sloop.—Execution on Bedloe's Island.. 209

CHAPTER XVII.

Charles Walters Murders his Faithless Wife, while mad with Rum.—The Death Sentence.—Efforts of Judge Stewart.—Commutation of Sentence to Imprisonment for Life..................................... 216

CHAPTER XVIII.

Wife Murder by Arsenic.—The Case of John Stephens.—Persecution of his Wife's Niece.—Her Brother Attempts to shoot Him.—The Finger of Suspicion.—Exhuming the Body.—Traces of Arsenic Found.—The Trial, the Cell and the Rope...................................... 222

CHAPTER XIX.

Murder of a Mistress.—Shocking Tragedy on the Steps of the Brandreth House.—Robert C. Macdonald shoots the beautiful Virginia Stewart.— Rum, Rage and Jealousy... 232

CHAPTER XX.

Confidence Men.—Romantic Adventures of Eugene Mickiweez, the Russian Count.—The Diamond Ring.—Colonel Marmaduke Reeves.—How he cut off a Cossack's Head.—His Erratic Career........................ 236

CHAPTER XXI.

Burglary.—A Mercantile Transaction.—Chauncey Johnson............... 250

CHAPTER XXII.

PAGE

Counterfeiting.—Forgery.—Spencer Pettis.—Monroe Edwards.—Canter.—
Redman.—The Webb-Marshall Duel............................... 258

CHAPTER XXIII.

The Haunted Cell... 273

CHAPTER XXIV.

Burdett the Lunatic.—An Incident of Bummer's Hall.................... 280

CHAPTER XXV.

Piracy and Privateering.—Baker and his Confederate Crew.—Babe the
Pirate.—The Doomed Unknown.—Anecdote of the Elder Booth.—What
Mrs. Ann S. Stephens did. 285

CHAPTER XXVI.

Escapes from the Tombs.. 289

CHAPTER XXVII.

Captain Gordon, the Slave-Trader.—His Crime, his Trial and his Execution.—The Attempt at Suicide...................................... 295

CHAPTER XXVIII.

"Hanging is Played Out."—The Case of Jack Reynolds.—A Bloody Murder
on a quiet Sunday Eve.—William Townsend Stabbed to the Heart.—
The Angry Mob.—His Execution.................................... 303

CHAPTER XXIX.

Ten Days in the Tombs.—A Bona Fide Personal Sketch.—A View from the
Inside.—How the Ten-Day Folks are Treated.—The Maniac.—Poor
Kate Golden.—The "Black Maria."—Off for the Island.............. 328

CHAPTER XXX.

The Astor Place Riot.—Edwin Forrest.—Charlotte Cushman.—Macready,
the English Tragedian. — Chevalier Wikoff. — "Workingmen, Shall
Americans or English Rule in this City."—The Riot and its Instigators.
—Arrest of E. Z. C. Judson, "Ned Buntline."—His Indictment, Trial,
Conviction and Sentence... 340

CHAPTER XXXI.

PAGE

Abortionists.—Madam Restell.—Her Crimes, Arrest, Trial, Conviction, Imprisonment in the Tombs, and on Blackwell's Island.—Her Fifth Avenue Palace.—Rosenzweig.—The Trunk Horror.—Alice Bowlsby's Melancholy Fate.—Quack Doctors and Doctresses.—Their Patrons and Patients.—Escape of Rosenzweig..................................... 359

CHAPTER XXXII.

Murder in the Tribune Office. — The Richardson-McFarland Tragedy.— Abby Sage Richardson's Sad History.—The Wedding at the Astor House.—Henry Ward Beecher.—Marriage Ceremony.—" So Long as You Two Both do Live."—Death as a Divorce Lawyer.—Trial of McFarland.—Not Guilty... 375

CHAPTER XXXIII.

The Case of Charles Jeffards.—He Kills His Step-father.—How the Crime was Traced to Him.— His Death in Prison.— Henry Carnell.—He Murders his Landlord.—The Unlucky Jump into the Area.—Four Years in the Tombs... 449

CHAPTER XXXIV.

Murders in Hot Blood.—The Car-hook Murder.—Foster's Crime, Trial and Fate.—Efforts to Secure Executive Clemency.—Is a Man Crazed with Rum Responsible for His Acts?—Felix Sanchez Stabs His Father-in-Law.— Murdered with a Bayonet.—Stabbed to Death with a Sword-Cane... 457

CHAPTER XXXV.

River Thieves.—The Birds of Prey who Prowl Nightly along the River Front of New York.—How they Operate.—The Shadowy Skiff Propelled by Muffled Oars.—The Dark-lantern of the River Police.—Revolver Practice, " My God ! I'm Shot."—The Howlett and Saul Case.—The Double Execution.—Haunts and Habits of the River-Gang.—Their Deeds.— Tragic End of " Socco the Bracer.".................................. 467

CHAPTER XXXVI.

Sharkey's Crime, Trial, and Escape.—" Stone-Walls do not a Prison Make, nor Iron Bars a Cage."—The Love of Maggie Jourdan.—That Famous Red Ticket.—The Veiled Lady who Passed out of the Gate.—Maggie's Trial and Devotion... 482

CHAPTER XXXVII.

PAGE

The Parricide.—Young Walworth Shoots his Father at the Sturtevant House.—Trial.—Efforts to Save.—Charles O'Conor as Counsel.—State Prison for Life.—A Mother's Devotion.............................. 499

CHAPTER XXXVIII.

The Adventurous Career of Mrs. Victoria C. Woodhull and Miss Tennie C. Claflin.—How they did the Clairvoyant Dodge in the West.—" Eastward the Star of Woodhull takes its Way."—Their Appearance in New York. —The Office on Broad Street and the Up-Town Residence.—Establishment of "Woodhull and Claflin's Weekly."—Free Love.—Gathering of the Storm.—Vicky's Lightning Flashes.—The Great Beecher Scandal.— "In the Tombs."—Geo. Francis Train.—Ludlow Street Jail.......... 506

CHAPTER XXXIX.

Mansfield, the Modern Cleopatra.—Her Life with the Prince of Erie.—Stokes on the Scene.—Speculation, Sin and Law. —Scene at the Grand Central Hotel.—Tragedy on the Stair-Case.—" There's a Man Shot at the Ladies' Entrance."—The Funeral.—Trial.—Conviction.—Death-Sentence.—New Trial.—Luxury in the Tombs.—Sing Sing.—Stokes' Statement... 520

CHAPTER XL.

The State Prison at Sing Sing.—Its Origin, Capacity, Discipline, Etc., Etc. 582

CHAPTER XLI.

Blackwell's Island as seen by a Lady, H. B............................. 610

CHAPTER XLII.

The New York Ring.—Its Extent, Influences, and Purposes.—The Great Ring Magnate, William Marcy Tweed.—His Confederates.—Buying the Legislature.—Ruling New York.—The Millions Stolen from the City Treasury.—Trials, Convictions, Sentences, Escapes.................. 629

APPENDIX.

Statement of Edward S. Stokes.. 649
Prison Management and Reformation.—Hubbell........................ 657
Prison Sunshine... 663

INDEX.

665

LIST OF ILLUSTRATIONS.

CHARLES SUTTON, facing title-page.
New York in 1640, 20
Stadt-Huys, 21
City Hall, Wall street, 22
The New Jail, or "Prevost," 23
State Prison at Greenwich, 26
Old Sugar-House, 28
Bridewell, City Hall Park, 29
Fly Market, 32
House of Refuge, 34
U. S. Treasury Building, former site of City Hall, 36
The Whipping Post, 38
Collect Pond, 45
The Tombs, 49
The Yard of the Tombs, 50
The Pillory, 52
Exterior of a Fashionable Gambling-hell, 55
A Gambling Saloon, 60
A Bar-Room Victim, 63
Finding the Body in the Box, 67
The Blood in the Gutter, 71
The Marriage in the Condemned Cell, 76
The Tombs, 78
Burning of the Tombs Cupola, 80
The Popular Idea, 94
Luxury in the Tombs, 95
Sing Sing versus the Tombs, 96
Helen Jewett, 98
Richard P. Robinson, 102
Robinson's Escape over the Fence, 113
The Body of Helen Jewett, 117
Court Scene, 132
Paying the Juryman, 133
Tom Hyer, 138
Bill Poole, 139
Stanwix Hall, 143
First Execution in New York, 149
Whipping Boys at the House of Refuge, 174
Bowery Theatre, 179
Escaping over the Cradle, 183
Mahony's Cell, 184
Escape of Mahony, 191
Mahony's Leap from a Car, 195
Ball and Chain, 196
Carrying Mahony to Sing Sing, 208
College of Physicians and Surgeons, 215
New York Tenement Houses, 217
John Stephens, 223
Felix Sanchez, 227
Warden Sutton's struggle with Stephens, 230
Jack Reynolds, 305
Murderer's Row, 334

Knife of the Dissecting Table, 337
Edwin Forrest, 341
Mercantile Library, formerly Opera House, 349
Ned Buntline, 353
The Astor Place Riot, 355
John McKeon, 357
Madame Restell, 362
David Graham, 364
Rosenzweig, 371
Alice Augusta Bowlsby, 373
Tribune Office Tragedy, 377
A. D. Richardson, 380
Hon. John Graham, 405
Col. Charles S. Spencer, 407
Hon. Noah Davis, 447
Elbridge T. Gerry, 448
Foster in his Cell, 461
Execution of Foster, 462
Murder of Avery D. Putnam, 466
Sharkey, 483
Maggie Jourdan, 484
The Escape of Sharkey, 486
Superintendent Matsell, 491
Wm. F. Howe, 493
Mansfield Tracy Walworth, 501
Frank H. Walworth, 504
Victoria C. Woodhull, 507
The Agitators in Ludlow-street Jail, 514
George Francis Train, 518
Col. James Fisk, Jr., 521
Edward S. Stokes, 522
The Position on the Stairs, 523
Joseph Dowling, 536
"Jay Gould's money has secured this conviction."—Stokes, 549
Stokes Receiving the Death-sentence, 550
Stokes Dines his Friends, 557
Benjamin K. Phelps, 559
Ludlow-street Jail, 562
Lyman Tremain, 574
The Social Glass at Daily's, 578
A Convict at the Hospital Window, 579
Map of Collect Pond, giving the present site of the Tombs, 580
The Cat-o'nine-tails, 591
The Shower-bath, 592
The Bishop's Mitre, 594
Boys Bound for the Island, 617
One more Unfortunate, 619
Wm. M. Tweed, 630
Blackwell's Island, 642
A. Oakey Hall, 644
The New Court-House, 648
Miss Flora Foster, 663
Miss Linda Gilbert, 664

ONE WORD AFTER YOU SEE THE TITLE.

IF the reader takes up this book with the idea that we have unrolled a record of violence, crime and blood, to gratify a depraved taste for the horrible; or because we are fond of writing about such scenes; or exult in the barbarism of strangling human beings to death on the gallows, he will make one of the biggest blunders of his life.

We abhor crime, and therefore we write its history in true colors, that we may deter our fellow-men from its perpetration—just as buoys are set over sunken rocks to keep other ships from going down—just as the reformed drunkard from the platform, curdles the blood of his hearers by painting the hell that burned in his own wretched soul, and the heart-broken sufferings he brought to his once happy fireside. His pictures of the degradation and foul beastliness which drink brings a man to are not likely to throw any enchantment around *delirium tremens*.

If we trace the road to murder, by drops of blood left in the slayer's track, are we planting flowers in the path of the young? If we report criminal trials, and show by what artifices advocates invoke the most subtle and desperate agencies to save deep-dyed villains from punishment; and how fearlessness in the prosecution, and uprightness on the bench and in the jury, strip off all disguises and drag the wrong-doer to his merited doom,—no matter how high, how rich, how popular, or how powerful the felon may be,—are we presenting any allurements to the young to take the downward road?

Above all, if by depicting the barbarism of legal murder—the brutalizing effect of making a community familiar with the shedding of human blood by judicial executions—if we show that blood-shedding is no antidote to blood-shedding—that because some besotted wretch, more likely than not crazed by rum, has committed *one* murder, therefore *another* must be committed—if we show how civilized men have at last become so sick of hanging their brother man that it takes four hundred citizens to strain out a jury, and even then, if there be no choice between hanging and not punishing at all, will generally bring in a verdict of not guilty; or disagree, and leave the same farce to be played over again, till it often takes two years, and one or two hundred thousand dollars of the tax-payers' money *not* to hang one poor wretch in cold blood, while scores of murderers walk with impunity the streets of every city in the land—if by exposing these fearful evils, the reader, be he young or old, does not rise from reading this book with the feeling that we have tried to do the cause of virtue and humanity some service, then we have indeed written in vain.

Make your laws so justly proportioned to crime, that every good citizen will aid in their inflexible execution. In this way alone will crime ever be abated.

In this Book we do not attempt to give a full record of the history of crime in New York, since our space will not admit of a hundredth of the cases. But we choose from the most prominent and striking. Nor do we find it advisable to adhere in every instance to chronological order. We have drawn our information from various sources, and during the progress of the work have kept open our chapters for suggestions from our numerous advisers, and this has necessarily disarranged the order. The facts we claim to give.—THE EDITORS.

* * * "As I saw no reason, when I wrote this book, why the *dregs of life* (so long as their speech did not offend the ear) should not serve the purpose of a *moral* as well as its *froth and cream,* * * * * * so I saw many strong reasons for pursuing my course. I had read of thieves by scores ; seductive fellows (amiable for the most part), faultless in dress, plump in pocket, choice in horse flesh, bold in bearing, fortunate in gallantry, great at a song, a bottle, pack of cards or dice box, and fit companions for the bravest. But I had never met (except in Hogarth) with the miserable reality. It appeared to me that to draw a knot of such *associates in crime as really did exist, to paint them in all their deformity, in all their wretchedness, in all the squalid misery of their lives; to show them as they really were, forever skulking uneasily through the dirtiest paths of life, with the great black, ghastly gallows closing up their prospect, turn them where they might ,* it appeared to me that to do this would be to attempt a something which was needed, and which would be a *service to society.* And I did it as best I could."

CHARLES DICKENS,
Preface to Oliver Twist.

CHAPTER I.

INTRODUCTORY.

" If great criminals told the truth—which, being great criminals, they do not—
they would very rarely tell of their struggles against crime. Their struggles are
towards it. They buffet with opposing waves to gain the bloody shore, not to re-
cede from it."—DICKENS, *in Our Mutual Friend.*

CRIME is almost coeval with the creation of the world. Drifting, as we are, toward the Millenium, man's vices have, nevertheless, generally gained the supremacy, and vanquished virtue in
the strife. In the rude and barbaric ages violence ruled the hour,
and murder stains the dismal records of those gloomy times. True
it is that the church spire has risen side by side with the frowning
jail, but still those of us who have the greatest faith in human
nature, and its ultimate perfection, cannot deny that the dangerous
classes preponderate in the world's population. The substratum of
society is seamed with sin. Beneath the sun-lit surface is a dark,
surging sea, tempest tossed by the winds of brutality, ignorance and
license ; a sea which rises with angry roar against the strong wall
which guards our social system. That wall is the law, its battle-
ments and turrets are the jails.

Murder has ever been one of the chief crimes, if not the chiefest
crime which man can commit. When the club of Cain went crashing through the skull of Abel, the virgin earth was dyed with the
first blood that cried for vengeance. He stands the head of the list
of assassins. From him down the line is a dreadful one—a blood
besmeared procession, skulking through the ages. The end is not
yet, and like that phantom throng which seared the brain of Macbeth, will, no doubt, stretch out to the crack of doom. Here in
New York, in the nineteenth century, the air blatant with church
chimes, murder runs riot, and flaunts its gory banner in the very
face of the law. The bludgeon has been superseded by the knife
and revolver, but the crime is just the same, and just as heinous.
But, heinous as it is, it would seem that the flight of time has
dulled the sensibilities of mankind. Murder has become so fright-

fully frequent that it is looked upon as a trivial affair, and the daily reports of assassinations are read with the same nonchalance with which the stock list is conned. A crimson flood threatens to submerge society, but scarcely any save those whose duty it is to stand as sentinels before the gates take heed of the rising of the fearful tide.

Despite the horror attached to the crime of murder, there is a great fascination surrounding the recital of its details. With what avidity the graphic reports of each deed of blood are consumed by the public ! How the morbid crowd loiters around the fatal house, peering with furtive glances at the windows of the room where some human being was ushered into the presence of his God by the act of his fellow man. And so with executions. The terrible gallows tree is a perfect loadstone, and the tragedy enacted beneath the black beam will always find an eager audience. It has ever been thus ; whether the malefactor be broken on the wheel, be drawn and quartered, left dangling on Tyburn hill, beheaded in the Tower, guillotined in the Place de la Corcorde, shot upon the fatal plain of Satory, thrown into the sea, hung from the yard arm : wherever, or in whatever manner one man suffers death at the hands of the law, there will be plenty of spectators. Happily for the effect upon the public, our executions are conducted in partial privacy. There are no more disgusting scenes, as in London of yore, when ladies bought chairs in convenient windows, as if they were stalls at the opera, to see some miserable wretch swung into eternity. If we have improved upon murder, it is no less true that we have improved upon the manner of our executions.

It being granted, then, that crime and its consequences are themes of universal interest, we have deemed it, upon mature reflection, not an unwise task to give these reminiscences to the public. In these pages will be found many strange and startling stories. It is a retrospective glance into the criminal history of our city. Men whose crimes have been forgotten will here enact again the dread dramas in which they played when alive. In the dim distance of departed years their forms are vague and shadowy. We shall endeavor to make them stand out once more in bold relief. We shall also tell of the romantic career of daring burglars, of noted forgers, of pretty shop-lifters, of all classes of thieves. Men of marvellous brain power, and women of miraculous beauty, who have given themselves up to crime, shall sit again for their pictures. The book will be an immense rogues gallery, for it is the history of the Tombs and its inmates for thirty years And if, in telling its secrets, we shall have shown the enormity of crime, the sure fate of the criminal, the downward career of all who once enter the fatal circle of vice, and the retributive justice that is sooner or later meted out to those who leave the paths of rectitude and virtue to beat about in the jungle of crime, we shall be more than repaid for the labor this work his cost us.

CHAPTER II.

PRISONS OF NEW YORK.—STADT HUYS.—OLD CITY HALL.—NEW JAIL.—BRIDEWELL.—BELLEVUE PENITENTIARY.—STATE PRISON AT GREENWICH.—LUDLOW STREET JAIL.—HOUSE OF REFUGE.

"As the captive men were faded and haggard so the iron was rusty, the stone was slimy, the wood was rotten, the air was faint, the light was dim. Like a well, like a vault, like a tomb, the prison had no knowledge of the brightness outside."— DICKENS, *in Little Dorrit.*

AMONG the earliest institutions of New York were Jails, Prisons, Bridewells and Houses of Correction; they existed a century and a half before the State, and were recognized in the most ancient charters. In the charter of 1730 the corporation was

NEW YORK IN 1640.

authorized to erect "one or more Bridewells, Houses of Correction and Workhouses." Power was also given to the Mayor, Recorder and Aldermen to arrest "Negroes, vagabonds, stragglers, and idle and suspicious persons." Provision was also made for "one or more Jails within the city limits."

It appears from the old Dutch records that there was a Prison, or a place for the confinement of prisoners, within the old fort, as early as 1640, but it is probable that this Prison consisted of little more than cells or apartments connected with the fort. It was of a temporary character, and on the building of the City Hall ceased to be used for that purpose.

STADT HUYS.

We now come down to the "Stadt Huys," the first building used for a Jail in the City of New York. It was built in 1642, at the corner of Pearl street and Coenties slip, fronting the slip. It was of stone, and three stories high. The West India Company furnished the means; and it was also called the "Stadt Herberg," the "Company's Tavern," or "City Tavern." Distinguished strangers were also entertained here, when not received by the Governor. Here the courts were held, and the first school was opened in one of its rooms. Near the close of the century it became so dilapidated that it was considered dangerous to longer hold the courts there. In 1698 it was decided by the authorities to build a new City Hall. In order to take care of the prisoners in the meantime, a committee was appointed to view the block house near the Governor's garden, for the purpose of seeing if it could be turned into a Prison until the new hall could be finished.

CITY HALL, WALL STREET.

The new City Hall was located at the head or north end of Broad street, and occupied the site of the present Treasury building. It cost about $6,000, and was looked upon in those primitive days as being rather a stylish building. It was completed during the year 1699, and on the 9th of August it was resolved that the old City Hall, and all belonging to it—the bell, king's arms, and iron work excepted—be sold at "publick outcry." It was not until

THE NEW JAIL, OR "PREVOST."

February 17, 1704, that the new City Hall was used as a Jail. On that date the Sheriff was ordered to have the City Jail made ready for the accommodation of felons. It was also arranged to place debtors in one of the upper stories, thus giving them, at least, the benefit of an attic philosophy.

But while the city was growing in commercial importance the

rogues were also improving in their line, in becoming both more numerous and more adroit. This condition of affairs necessitated a new Jail in 1758. It was built on what was then known as "the fields," the City Hall Park of the present day. It was a small stone building, nearly square, three stories in height, having its main entrance on the south side. The new Jail was not much of an improvement upon the old one, and frequent complaints were made of the barbarity with which the prisoners were treated.

The new Jail continued to be the Prison of the city until 1775, when the new Bridewell was erected, and on the occupation of the city by the British army they were both turned into military Prisons. The new Jail was then known as the "Prevost," or "Prevo," and became famous under the control of Capt. William Cunningham, Provost Marshal, who, by the appointment of Gen. Gage, was at the head of the police of the city. Lossing says of this man, "It makes the blood curdle to read of the sufferings of those who fell under the sway of that monster, so devilish in all his ways. The miseries of others seemed to give him the greatest delight, and often, in the sight of starving prisoners, would he kick over a pail of soup, or scatter a basket of fruit or cold victuals which some benevolent hand had placed upon the door step, with the hope that it might nourish the famished soldiers." It has been stated that he was hung at Newgate, England, but Mr. Bancroft examined the records without being able to find the name.

Such was the monster Cunningham, and we might remark, *en passant*, that it is to be hoped that the Newgate rumor was well founded.

Mr. John Pintard, one of the founders of the New York Historical Society, was an eye-witness to the scenes enacted in this Prison. He says: "The new Jail, or the 'Prevost,' was destined for the more notorious rebels, civil, naval and military. An admission into this modern bastile was enough to appal the stoutest heart. On the right hand of the main door was Capt. Cunningham's apartment, opposite to which was the guard room. Two sentinels stood at the entrance door day and night, and two more at the first and second barricades, which were grated, barred and chained. When a prisoner was led into the hall the whole guard was paraded, and he was delivered over in a high and solemn manner to Capt. Cunningham. What with the bristling of arms, unbolting of bars and locks, clanking of enormous iron chains, and a vestibule as dark as Erebus, the unfortunate captive might well shrink under this infernal sight, and parade of tyrannical power, as he crossed the threshold of that door which possibly closed on him for life. So closely were the prisoners packed, that when they lay down at night on the hard oak planks, they could not turn except at the word of command, being so wedged together as to form an almost solid mass of human bodies. In this gloomy abode were incarcerated at different periods many American officers and citizens of distinction, awaiting with sickening hope their liberation. Could these dismal walls speak what scenes of anguish might they not disclose! In the drunken orgies that usually terminated Cunningham's dinners he would order the rebel prisoners to turn out and parade for the amusement of his guests, pointing them out in this wise: 'This is the d—d rebel, Col. Ethan Allen;' 'that is a rebel judge,'" etc. Mr. Pintard conveyed to Gen. Jones a list of the grievances of the prisoners. They complained that they had but two pounds of hard biscuit and two pounds of raw pork per man per week, and without any fuel to dress it. Things are different now, when the inmates of Murderers' Row, in the Tombs, luxuriate in Kidderminster carpets and canary birds.

The Penitentiary at Bellevue was established shortly after the revolution. In 1816 a Penitentiary, then so first called, was opened in one of the new buildings of the recently completed almshouse at Bellevue. It is in part still standing on Twenty-sixth street, near First avenue, and is used as a dye house. The punishment of the tread mill was here first introduced, as will be elsewhere noticed. On the opening of this Penitentiary the Jail in the City Park was used as a Debtors' Prison until 1832, when it was converted into the present Hall of Records, now occupied by the Register. The Penitentiary at Bellevue was soon found to be too small, and about the year 1836 the present Penitentiary on Blackwell's Island was constructed. On the opening of this institution the Penitentiary at Bellevue was devoted to female prisoners, until the year 1838, when the Tombs was completed.

In 1796 the foundations of a State Prison were laid at Greenwich village, on the North river, about a mile and a half from the City Hall. It was completed in 1797, and occupied on the 28th of

STATE PRISON AT GREENWICH.

November of that year. The area covered by the building and its yard was about four acres. It was two stories high, built of free-stone, and surrounded by a stone wall. No convict was admitted to this Jail unless he was confined for three years or more. It was finally sold to the city by the State, after the completion of the State Prison at Sing Sing. It was also used for a time as a Bridewell.

I shall now speak of " The Bridewell," the history of which forms an important epoch in the Prison chronicles of the city. The name is of English origin—the first Prison of that kind, which was formerly a palace, being near St. Bridget's (St. Bride's) well. This was given to the City of London by Edward VI, in 1552. The gift was made at the request of Bishop Ridley, who solicited it " as a workhouse for the poor, and a house of correction for the strumpet and idle person, for the rioter that consumeth all, and for the vagabond that will abide in no place." It contained a portrait of the king with these lines :

> "This Edward, of Fair memory, the Sixt,
> In whom with greatness, goodness was commixt,
> Gave this Bridewell, a palace in olden times,
> For a chastening house of vagrant crimes."

One of the chief methods of punishment in vogue at the London Bridewell was flagellation, especially of unchaste women. The whipping was done on appointed days, and in the presence of the Governor. Parties were often made up to witness the operation, as if it were to be a pic-nic. The stripes were laid on the bare back of the culprit by a beadle, and were not discontinued until the President struck the table with his hammer. A common cry of the women was, " O, good Sir Robert, knock !" which passed among the lower classes as a popular slang phrase. Among the noted characters confined in this Prison was Madame Cresswell, a noted procuress of the time of Charles II. She was often whipped, and finally died in Bridewell. One of the conditions of her will was that a sermon was to be preached over her body, the minister to have £10, provided he said nothing but what was well of her. The sermon was accordingly delivered, the theme being Mortality. At the close the preacher said : " By the will of the deceased it is expected I should mention her, and say nothing but what was *well*

OLD SUGAR HOUSE.

of her. All that I shall say of her, therefore, is this—she was born well, she lived well, and she died well; for she was born to the name of Cresswell, she lived in Clerkenwell, and she died in Bridewell!"

The first Bridewell in New York was built as early as 1734, and continued to be occupied for many years as a house of correction. In 1773–5 a new Bridewell was built, which was located west of the

BRIDEWELL, CITY HALL PARK.

present City Hall, and between it and Broadway. The funds were raised by lottery. The ground on which it was erected was memorable as the site of the famous struggle of the "Sons of Liberty" to maintain a "mast," or liberty pole. Desperate battles took place between the citizens and the soldiers, the latter being incensed at the character of the banners thrown to the breeze by the "Sons of Liberty." Several poles were cut down or blown up by the soldiers, but eventually the pole was allowed to remain unmolested. It then became the rallying point of the people in the scenes of popular uprisings against the British misrule which

culminated in the revolution.   On this historic spot the new Bridewell was erected in 1775.   The corner stone, with this date upon
it, is in the possession of the New York Historical Society.   This
stone was laid by the Mayor, Whitehead Hicks.   The building was
of dark gray stone, two stories high above the basement.   It was
finished in 1775, just as the Revolutionary struggle began, and
almost the first use to which it was put was the imprisonment of the
patriots, and the captive soldiers of the American army.   The same
scenes of cruelty were enacted here as in the other British Prisons.
Oliver Woodruff, who was taken prisoner at Fort Washington, says :
" We were marched to New York, and went into different Prisons.
Eight hundred and sixteen went into the new Bridewell, I among the
rest ; some into the sugar house, and some into the Dutch Church.
On Thursday morning they brought us a little provision, which
was the first morsel we got to eat or drink since breakfast on the
previous Saturday.   We never drew as much provisions for three
days' allowance as a man would eat at a common meal.   I was
there three months during that inclement season, and never saw
any fire except what was in the lamps of the city.   There was no
glass in the windows, and nothing to keep out the cold except the
iron grating."   Another prisoner says : "All the fuel we had was one
cart load a week for eight hundred men !   At nine o'clock in the
evening the Hessian Guard would come in and put out the fire, and
lay on the poor prisoners with clubs for crowding around the
warmth.   The prisoners died like rotten sheep with cold, hunger
and dirt—and those who had good apparel, such as buckskin
breeches, or good coats, were necessitated to sell them to purchase
bread to keep themselves alive."

Like the Jail, the Bridewell was again used as a Prison, or house
of correction, on the close of the war.   By an Act of the Legislature, passed in 1814, it was provided " that the part of the Bridewell in the City of New York which is now established and used
as the Jail of the said city, for the confinement and safe keeping of
all persons charged with or convicted of any crime or misdemeanor,
except persons sentenced to imprisonment in the State Prison, shall,
after the above mentioned building at Bellevue becomes the Penitentiary of the said city, continue to be the Jail of the said city."
After the removal of the prisoners the " Bridewell " became the

Debtors' Jail. The Bridewell continued until 1838, when the Halls of Justice (Tombs) were erected, the stones of the former building being used in the construction of the latter. The Tombs is, in fact, the legitimate successor of the Bridewell, and a portion of it was, for a time, set apart as a city Bridewell.

Imprisonment for debt is an offshoot of English jurisprudence, and was early incorporated into our laws. Debtors were first confined in the attic rooms of the new City Hall, at the head of Broad street. When this building was no longer used as a Prison, these prisoners were removed to the new Jail, and subsequently to the Bridewell. Persons imprisoned for debt were always regarded by the public most charitably, and were the recipients of many favors. It is stated among the old chronicles that these prisoners, when confined in the old City Hall, were accustomed to suspend old shoes and bags from the dormer windows, as a hint to the charitable passer by. This became a fixed custom, and was encouraged by the community, as appears from a notice published in the winter of 1751, and dated at the City Hall. In it the prisoners make an appeal to the public, stating that they are without "firing, not having a stick of wood to burn." They also state that they are "most of them strangers in the country, and are destitute of the necessaries of life." That this appeal was responded to, we learn from a paper dated March 16th, in which the prisoners return thanks for the relief. From this petition for alms the prisoners seem to have been recent settlers in the country, and probably came to the city with scant means, which were soon exhausted; they then contracted debts which they were unable to pay, and as a punishment were seized and thrust into prison. If, at the termination of their sentence, they were still unable to satisfy the demands of their creditors, they were sold to pay their jail fees, as appears from notices as late as 1751.

The following acknowledgment of alms from the debtors, as late as 1772, shows that they still suffered great privations, and continued the custom of appealing to the public for assistance : " The debtors confined in the Gaol of the City of New York, impressed with a grateful sense of the obligations they are under to the respectable public, for the generous contribution that has been made for them. beg leave to return their sincere and hearty thanks for

the same, particularly to the worshipful the Corporation of the City
of New York; to the reverend the clergy of the English, Dutch
and Presbyterian Churches, and their respective congregations, by
whose generous donations they have been comfortably supported
during the last winter, and preserved from perishing in a dreary
prison with hunger and cold." In 1821 Mr. Gibbons, a noted
butcher, slaughtered twenty premium cattle, and two days after the
following card appeared, dated from the Debtors' Prison: "With
gratitude the prisoners in the Debtors' Jail acknowledge the receipt of a plentiful donation of 'premium beef' from Mr. Gibbons
and the 'Joint Society of Butchers of the Fly Market.'" In July,
1824, appeared the following notice: "The poor debtors render
their thanks to the good people of Fulton Market for the abundant

" FLY MARKET."

supply, for the 4th of July, of meats, fish, vegetables, lemons, sugar
and brandy. Their healths shall be drunk this day at 12 o'clock."
It was in 1812 that the Rev. John Stanford, D. D., a Baptist
clergyman of this city, suggested the necessity of establishing a
reformatory institution for juvenile offenders. He had been appointed by the City Government as its chaplain in 1811, and in the
following year began the outline of a plan for the establishment of
an asylum for vagrant youth, "with its promising advantages to
prevent pauperism and the commission of crime." He proposed,
also, that the boys should be trained as sailors, thus anticipating
our present "school ship" more than half a century. He proposed,
according to a recent writer, "to have navigation taught in the
asylum upon land, and by masts and rigging to give a general idea
of a sailor's duty." Dr. Stanford recommended the location of the

proposed asylum to be at the foot of the Bloomingdale Road and Old Post Road. This ground, now Madison Square Park, was then occupied by the United States Arsenal. His suggestion was subsequently carried out.

The House of Refuge grew out of this philanthropic purpose. It was incorporated in 1824, under the title of " The Managers of the Society for the Reformation of Juvenile Delinquents in the City of New York." This body took the place of the old society " For the Prevention of Pauperism." The Arsenal grounds were obtained on application to the Common Council. This location was then far out of town, in the midst of a rich farming district. It consisted of about four acres. The institution, consisting of the soldiers' barracks refitted, was formally opened on January 1st, 1825, with an address by Hugh Maxwell, Esq., then the District Attorney. The inmates consisted of six girls and three boys, who had been brought in by the police. This proportion would seem to establish the fact that the women are twice as bad as the sterner sex, although we are too gallant to believe it.

The beneficial results following the opening of the House of Refuge were thus related by Mr. Maxwell, as early as October of the year of opening: "I am happy to state that the House of Refuge has had a most benign influence in diminishing the number of juvenile delinquents. The most depraved boys have been withdrawn from the haunts of vice, and the effect of the examples set them has in a great degree been destroyed."

The Refuge continued to occupy the site of its original location until 1839, when the improvements in that neighborhood required its removal. Three sites were suggested, all quite beyond the limits of population, viz : Murray Hill, between Fifth and Sixth avenues ; Hamilton Square, and the Bellevue Fever Hospital, between Twenty-third and Twenty-fourth streets, First avenue and avenue A. The latter was selected. The institution continued to occupy this site until 1848, when the question of its removal was again raised, owing to its crowded condition. It was not until 1850 that a new location was secured. The trustees selected ten acres of land on the southern portion of Ward's Island, the object being to secure a secluded site, which would not be again encroached upon by improvements. This property was exchanged the following year for about thirty acres on the southern extremity of Randall's Island, where the present buildings were erected. The cost was $470,000. The buildings are of brick, and consist of two principal structures, which front the river and form a façade nearly one thousand feet in length. The larger building is for the boys, the other for the girls. Other buildings are for the various purposes of the institution and are of the most substantial kind.

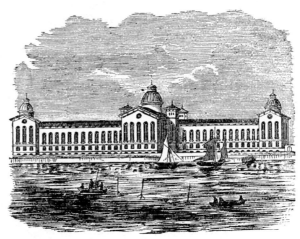

HOUSE OF REFUGE.

CHAPTER III.

MODES OF PUNISHMENT.—THE WHIPPING POST.—THE PILLORY.—
THE DUCKING STOOL.—THE STOCKS.—THE WOODEN HORSE.—
THE TREADMILL.

  *   *   *   " We shall do much better than by going down into the dark to grope
for the *whip* among the rusty fragments of the *rack*, and the *branding iron*, and the
chains and *gibbet* by the public roads, and the *weights* that pressed men to death in the
cells of Newgate."—DICKENS—" *Lying Awake.*"

THE early annals of New York constantly refer to the instruments by which punishment was inflicted upon criminals.
These instruments and methods are all unknown to the present
generation, and the very mention of them fills us with horror. In
numerous ordinances of the Common Council the list of instruments above given are mentioned generally together, as a part and
parcel of the established institutions of the city. They stood in
front of the City Hall, and were carefully kept in good repair.
The first instruments of this kind were erected in front of the old
City Hall, at Coenties slip, between it and the dock. Some time
after the new City Hall was built at the head of Broad, on Wall
street. It was ordered that these instruments be erected in front of
that building. This was on the 1st of November, 1703. If erected,
they must have stood in Wall street, at the head of Broad street,
but it appears that in 1710 it was again ordered that these instruments be removed to the upper end of Broad street, and a little
below the City Hall.

That they were frequently used we have sufficient evidence, from
the notices in the earliest papers of the appearance of prisoners
while suffering the different forms of punishment, and the whole
matter is treated as of almost daily occurrence. As examples, the
following may be given : " A woman was whipped at the whipping
post, and afforded much amusement to the spectators by her resistance. James Gain, pursuant to sentence, stood in the pillory,
near the City Hall, and was most severely pelted by great numbers
of the spectators ; a lad was also branded in the hand."

The public whipper was, in early times, an important officer, and his appointment is frequently noticed, and the amount of his salary is given. In 1713 Richard Cooper was appointed to this office, at a salary of five pounds. In later times the office would seem to have fallen somewhat into disrepute, though the salary was raised. On the 10th of November, 1756, it was ordered in Council that the Mayor issue his warrant " for the sum of three pounds, in order to

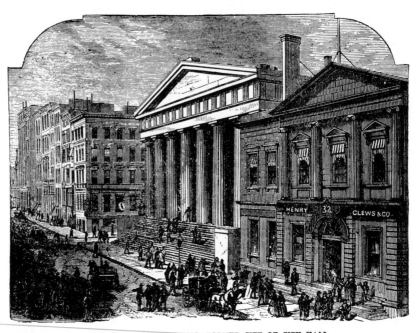

U. S. TREASURY BUILDING, FORMER SITE OF CITY HALL.

clothe John Duggan, the present public whipper, now in the poor house, and his salary to commence from this date," viz., twelve pounds.

It is quite impossible to realize that at the great centre of financial transactions of this continent, the junction of Wall and Broad streets, but a little more than a century ago stood a cage, a pillory, a whipping post, a ducking stool and the stocks, for the punishment of offenders against the then existing laws. At hours of the day when multitudes of men now meet on this ground, and eagerly discuss the fluctuations in the financial world, one hundred years ago as eager crowds gathered to jeer poor women struggling at the whipping post, or to throw missiles at criminals confined in the pillory. It is stated that at least one thousand persons assembled to witness these cruelties.

It can but interest every reader to learn the origin and nature of the instruments with which our forefathers punished criminals. While we shrink with disgust at the very mention of those modes of torture, we nevertheless find much in the history to palliate the seeming barbarity of the authorities of that early day. The early religious, political and social institutions of this country were in great part transplanted from Europe. Especially is this true of the forms of law, the judiciary systems, and all that pertained to the administration of justice. In our search, therefore, for an explanation of any peculiarity in matters relating to the punishments of criminals, we should naturally be led to examine the history of those countries of Europe from which the body of citizens emigrated. We have then two sources of information on this subject, viz., Holland and England, and it soon becomes apparent that from both of those sources the methods of punishing criminals were derived.

THE WHIPPING POST.—Punishment by whipping, or flagellation, is as old as the time of Moses. The Mosaic law prescribes the offence for which this form of punishment is to be inflicted, and the number of stripes in each case. It was in common practice by the Greeks and Romans, and in later times prevailed in all the European States.

The method of punishment in this country by whipping was introduced both from England and Holland. The ancient laws of Germany directed its employment, and the halls of justice and houses of correction contained every form of instrument—the whip, the cane and the birch. The magistrates had unlimited power in the infliction of the rod for crime. The whipping post in many towns stood in the market place, and the culprit was stripped and whipped by a regularly appointed officer, in the presence of large numbers of spectators.

In England, during the 17th and 18th centuries, the rod was the recognized mode of correction. The notorious Judge Jeffreys

THE WHIPPING POST.

condemned criminals, both men and women, to be whipped through the streets, with almost apparent pleasure and delight. " Hangman," he cried, on one occasion, " I charge you to pay particular attention to this lady! Scourge her soundly, man—scourge her till her blood runs down! It is Christmas—a cold time for Madam to strip in! See that you warm her shoulders thoroughly." The sentence of Titus Oates, tried for perjury in 1685, illustrates forcibly the peculiar severity of the punishments then in vogue, and which were brought to this country by the immigrants of that period. It ran as follows: " To pay on each indictment (two) a fine of 1,000 marks; to be stript of all his canonical habits; to be imprisoned for life; to stand in the pillory on the following Monday, with a paper on his head declaring his crime; next day to stand in the pillory at the Royal Exchange, with the same inscription; on Wednesday to be whipped from Aldgate to Newgate; on the Friday to be whipped from Newgate to Tyburn; upon the 24th of April, in every year during feil, to stand in the pillory at Tyburn, opposite the gallows; on the 9th of August in every year to stand in the pillory opposite Westminster Hall gate; on the 10th of August in every year to stand in the pillory at Charing Cross; and the like on the following day at Temple Bar; to be continued on 2d of September every year at the Royal Exchange." The Court expressed deep regret that they could not do more. Flogging was the ordinary punishment for all political misdemeanors.

The practice of whipping, and the appliances of the whipping post—the cane, the rod, the birch, &c., and the public whipper— were introduced into all the American colonies. In all the New England towns the whipping post was the recognized adjunct of the Courts, and flagellation was constantly resorted to for all forms of offences, whether religious, social or political. The Quakers were especially condemned to this form of punishment for their supposed heresies. Nor has this relic of barbarism, the whipping post, been banished from our soil, though it has disappeared from public view. The State of Delaware still cherishes this instrument of torture, and in public places it still stands a silent but most suggestive satire upon advancing civilization—the scene as represented on the preceding page being enacted November 20, 1873.

THE DUCKING STOOL.—This instrument came into use in the latter part of the fifteenth century, and continued until the early part of the eighteenth century. It was occasionally met with as late as the nineteenth century.

It consisted of a long pole or lever, to which was attached a stool, chair or basket—the lever being so attached as to allow of much perpendicular motion. It was placed by the water's edge, and the culprit was to be fixed to the chair or stool. The punishment consisted in ducking the offender in the water as frequently as the sentence required.

The ducking seems to have been used for the punishment of various classes of offenders. Howard, the great philanthropist, in the account of his visits to the Prisons of Germany, in 1778, makes the following statement in regard to this method of punishment: " The bakers of Vienna are punished for frauds by the severity and disgrace of the ducking stool. This machine of terror, fixed on the side of the Danube, is a kind of long pole or board, extending over the water, at one end of which the delinquent, being fastened in his basket, is immersed." He adds, " The bakers would gladly purchase a removal of this machine, but the punishment is continued, and inflicted on delinquents by order of the magistrates."

We have several accounts of its uses in this country, and in general it was designed to punish scolds and slanderers. Bishop Meade, of Virginia, says : " If a woman was convicted of slander her husband was made to pay five hundred weight of tobacco, but this law proving insufficient, the penalty was changed into ducking, and inflicted on the woman herself. Places for ducking were prepared at the doors of Court Houses. An instance is mentioned of a woman who was ordered to be ducked three times, from a vessel in the James River, near Bermuda Hundreds, for scolding."

The following letter, published in the *Am. Hist. Record* for May, 1872, gives a very complete account of the instrument and its uses, as early as 1634. It is dated " Hungar's Parish, Ackowmake, Virginia, June yᵉ 16th, 1634," and was written by Thomas Hartley, who was on a visit to Virginia, to Gov. Endicott, of Mass. He says : " It is undeniable yᵗ they endeavor to live amiably, keep yᵉ peace in families and communities, and by divers means try to have harmony and good will amongst themselves and with Strangers who may sojourn among them. For this they use a device which they learned in England, they say, to keep foul tongues, y^t make noise and mischief, silent, and of which I must fain tell you. They have a law which reades somewhat in this wise : ' Whereas it be a sinn and a shame for scolding and lying Tongues to be left to run loose, as is too often the way amongst women, be it therefore enacted y^t any woman who shall, after being warned three severall times by ye Church, persist in excessive scolding, or in backbiting her neighbors, shall be brought before ye Magistrate for examination, and if ye offence be fairly proved upon her, shee shall be taken by an Officer appointed for ye purpose, to ye nearest pond or deepe streame of water, and there, in the presence of said Magistrate, and of her accusors, be publicly ducked by said officers in ye waters of s^d pond or streame, until shee shall make a solemn promise y^t shee'l never sinn in like manner again.'

" The day afore yesterday, at two of ye clock in ye afternoon, I saw'this punishment given to one Betsy, wife of John Tucker, who, by ye violence of her tongue, had made his house and ye neighborhood uncomfortable. She was taken to ye pond near where I am sojourning by ye officer, who was joyned by ye Magistrate and ye Minister, Mr. Colton, who had frequently admonished her, and a large number of people. They had a Machine for y purpose, y^t belongs to ye Parish, and which I was tcld had been so used three times this Summer. It is a platform with 4 small rollers or wheels, and two upright posts, between which works a Lever by a Rope fastened to its shorter or heavier end. At ye end of ye longer arm is fixed a stool, upon which Betsy was fastened by cords, her gown tied fast around her feets. The Machine was then moved up to the edge of ye pond, ye Rope was slackened by ye officer, and ye woman was allowed to go down under ye water for the space of half a minute. Betsy had a stout stomach, and would not yield untill shee had allowed herself to be so ducked 5 severall times. At length she cried piteously, ' Let me go ! let me go ! by God's help I'll sinn no more.' Then they drew back ye Machine, untied ye Ropes, and let her walk home in her wetted clothes, a hopefully penitent woman.

" Methinks such a reformer of great scolds might be of use in some parts of Massachusetts Bay, for I've been troubled many times by yᵉ clatter of yᵉ scolding tongues of women, yᵗ, like yᵉ clack of y mill, seldom cease from morning till night."

THE TREADMILL.—The tread mill, stepping wheel, or stepping mill, as it was variously called, is a modern invention. It was introduced into this country from England, and was first employed in New York in 1822, during the Mayoralty of Stephen Allen, Esq. A building was erected at the Almshouse, Twenty-sixth street and East river, for that purpose. This building was of stone, thirty feet by sixty, and two stories high, with a garret. It is still standing on Twenty-sixth street near First avenue, and is now used as a dye house. On the ground floor was the part occupied by the wheels, on which the prisoners worked, the mill. The wheel house was separated from the mill by a stone wall, so that no communication was held between those who attended the mill and those who performed the labor on the wheels. On the second floor were the mill stones. The building was originally intended for three wheels, and three run of stones, but it was found by experience that the place was not sufficiently ventilated to admit a greater number of prisoners than could work on two wheels.

Each wheel was calculated to give employment to thirty-two prisoners—sixteen on each wheel at once. A bell was so arranged as to strike every half minute, when one of the prisoners on the wheel went off and and another went on, so that each man worked eight minutes and rested the same time.

The wheel on which the prisoners worked was a cylinder four feet in diameter and twenty feet long. The steps were formed on the outside of this wheel, with a rise of about eight inches, and run horizontally with the shafts, and there was a fixed rail extending the whole length of the wheel, which the prisoner grasped when at work. This rail was about breast high when a person stood on the centre or horizontal step; the weight of the body caused the step to fall and the wheel to rotate.

The mill was for the purpose of grinding the grain used for the food of the inmates of the Almshouse and Prisons, and consisted of two run of stones. The average quantity of grain ground per day was from forty to fifty bushels. The consumption of this ground grain by the inmates of the different institutions was about fifty bushels per day, the grinding of which cost the city formerly sixteen to twenty-two hundred dollars annually. The Treadmill system was therefore regarded as very economical, and was highly lauded by the Mayor.

The punishment by the Treadmill was not limited to male prisoners: females were also required to perform this kind of labor. It is an interesting fact that the women were found to endure the labor much better than the men, and were apparently much less fatigued.

This mode of punishment seems to have been much dreaded by prisoners. The keeper of this Prison, Arthur Burtis, reported that the men who worked out behaved better and worked more diligently after the mill was in operation than before, and there had been no attempt to escape, for they had been threatened with work on the wheel the remainder of their time if such attempt was made.

THE WOODEN HORSE.—This instrument was designed originally in Holland for the punishment of soldiers. It consisted of a wooden horse, having a sharp back. The soldier strode the instrument, and his body was forced down upon it by a chain and iron stirrup, or by a weight fastened to his legs (Watson's Old Time in N. Y., p. 29). There is a notice of the infliction of this punishment in New York on two soldiers in December, 1638.

CHAPTER IV.

THE TOMBS.—THE COLLECT.—INCIDENTS IN ITS EARLY HISTORY.—
PROGRESS OF IMPROVEMENTS.—ERECTION OF THE TOMBS.

" Elsewhere people are restless, worried, hurried about, anxious respecting one
thing, anxious respecting another. Nothing of this kind here, sir. We have done all'
that; we know the worst of it; we have got to the bottom; we can't fall: and what
have we found   Peace. That's the word for it—Peace."—DICKENS, *in Little
Dorritt.*

IT scarcely seems credible to the present generation, unfamiliar
with the original topography of "Beautiful Manahatta," that
there was once a lovely and picturesque lake, bounded by Canal
street on the north, Pearl street on the south, Mulberry street on the
east, and Centre street on the west; and yet such was the case.
This lake was surrounded by romantic hills, which, on the west, in
the vicinity of Broadway, rose to a considerable height. Its waters
were pure and fresh, and its depth, once thought to be unfathom-
able, was ultimately ascertained to be about fifty feet. It had a
navigable outlet into the North river, and abounded in a variety of
fish. The Indians made it their favorite resort, and built their villages on its shores. Long before the white man placed his foot
upon the island the savage here cultivated his rude arts, built his
simple wigwams in clusters around the quiet water, clove its calm
surface with his bark canoe, and drew from its crystal depths the
struggling fish. What scenes of rude and barbarous sport, of joy
and sorrow, of crime, cruelty and war, were here enacted long
before the days of Hudson!

In the early history of the island this collection of water was
called by the English "Fresh Water," and "Fresh Water Pond."
The Dutch called it "Kalchhook," or "Shell Point," from a large
deposit of decomposed shells, which formed a point on the western
shore. This name was afterwards abbreviated into "Kalch,"
"Callech," "Colleck," "Collect."

"The "Collect Pond" occupied almost the entire space which
is bounded on the north by White street, and on the south by

COLLECT POND.

Worth, Orange street (now Baxter), running along the eastern edge, with Elm street on the west of the pond. The outlet of this body of water was at the northerly end, about where Centre and White streets intersect. The stream took a northwesterly course, striking Broadway at the present Canal street, at which point a stone bridge was built over the stream, and thence along the line of Canal street—draining the adjacent property, which was known as Lispenard's meadows—into the north river. This fresh water pond remained one of the peculiar features of the natural scenery of the island for upwards of one hundred years after the first settlement. During that period it was the favorite resort of fishermen and sportsmen.

The following chronological incidents are of interest, as showing the progress of improvements in the vicinity of one of the most important business centres of New York. When the city limits began to extend above Wall street the lands adjacent to the pond attracted the settlers, and the pond itself became, if we may so speak, a landmark for surveyors. In 1732 Anthony Rutger obtained a grant of the swamp—a tract of land laying on either side of the outlet of the pond—which consisted of about seventy-five acres. This tract extended from the North river, on either side of Canal street, to the present site of the Tombs. He had represented the marsh as very unhealthy, and agreed to drain it within one year. He accordingly opened a drain from the river to the pond, and made it so deep that the people complained that he drained the pond too low. He was required to remedy this defect by filling up the drain for thirty feet from the pond. The city afterwards, in 1791, purchased the claim of the heirs of Mr. Rutger to the lands about the pond for £150. In 1732 an ordinance was passed forbidding the taking of fish from the pond with any form of net. In 1745 the tanners, who had been driven from their former situation, located their works on the shores of the pond. In 1747 a powder house was built on an island in the pond. In 1761 the Collect was set apart as a reservoir of water to be used for the extinguishment of fires, and for other purposes. In 1784 a committee was appointed to lay out the streets near the pond, and in 1787 the pond was reported as in a filthy condition, owing to the practice of throwing refuse into it. In 1790–3 a survey of the

pond was ordered, and the location of surrounding streets was recommended. In 1796 the committee on canals was ordered to
confer with the proprietors of the swamp in regard to constructing a
canal forty feet wide, as an outlet of the pond into the North river,
and to lay out streets on either side thirty feet wide. It is reported
that the first attempt at steam navigation was made on this pond,
in the summer of 1796 or 1797, by a man named Fitch, assisted by
a boy, John Hutchings. R. R. Livingston and Robert Fulton were
both present when the experiment was made, and enjoyed the pleasure of a sail around the pond on this novel craft—a common yawl
boat—the machinery of which was of rude construction, made by
Mr. Fitch. The motive instrument was a screw in the stern of the
boat. Mr. Fitch acted as engineer and fireman, while the boy,
Hutchings, stood in the stern of the boat and steered it with a
paddle.

On October 18, 1802, Mr. Jacob Brown, who at that time was
Street Commissioner, submitted a report to the city authorities
recommending the draining of the " Collect Pond " and adjacent
lands, by opening a canal from the East river through Roosevelt
street to the pond, and thence to the Hudson river, thereby redeeming some four hundred acres of land, which he foresaw would be of
immense value. This suggestion was not acted upon, however,
and the " Collect" remained a nuisance to the city.

The winter of 1807–8 was noted for the inclemency of the
weather. To add to the general misery occasioned by the severity
of the season, work was almost entirely suspended, owing to the unsettled condition of public affairs, and the laboring people were on
the verge of starvation. Owing to foreign troubles the maritime
trade was also entirely suspended. In January, 1808, a demonstration of sailors and others was made in the Park. They presented a petition to the authorities, and demanded bread for themselves and starving families. Appropriations were voted, and the
work of filling up the Collect was at once begun. The hills laying
to the west of the pond and near Broadway were levelled, the earth
being used in filling up the pond, thus affording employment to
many. At length the pond was filled in and streets were cut
through, Centre street (formerly called Collect street) running in a
direct line north and south through what was the middle of the

pond. A large sewer, beginning at Pearl street, running through
Centre street to Canal street, and thence to the river, following as
near as practicable the original water course, was then built. It
effectually drained the surrounding property, and thus added considerable to the available building space.

In 1830 the population of the city was 203,000. Crime had increased in proportion, and the need of a new Prison was keenly
felt. The old City Prison, or Bridewell, just west of the City Hall,
had become a nuisance, and was eventually torn down. The
Bellevue Jail was too far out of town, too distant from the Courts,
and accordingly, in 1833, it was resolved that a City Prison be
erected further down town. The old Collect grounds were selected
as the site of the new Prison, with a recommendation that it be
built so as to afford the necessary accommodations for court rooms
as well.

About this time there was published a book entitled "Stevens'
Travels." The author was John L. Stevens, Esq., of Hoboken,
who had recently returned from an extended tour through Asia
and the Holy Land. The book was full of interest, and contained
many illustrations of the rare and curious things he had seen.
Among these illustrations was one of an ancient Egyptian tomb,
accompanied by a full and accurate description.

The Committee appointed by the Common Council to decide
upon the necessary plans for the new Prison were impressed with
the idea of erecting a building whose general appearance and construction should correspond with the tomb described in Stevens'
book. They accordingly made their report, recommending the construction of such a building, suggesting, as a most fitting and
appropriate name, "The Tombs." The report was adopted, and
work was begun at once. The nature of the ground was such as
to render a good foundation for so massive a structure a matter of
difficulty, and it was found necessary to sink the piles on which the
building now stands. The "Tombs" was completed and ready for
occupation in 1838. We had hoped to give the name of the first
criminal committed to this Prison, but, owing to the loss or destruction of the records, we are unable to do so.

Originally the "Tombs," as were the other Prisons, was under
the control of the Sheriff, who appointed the keepers. Subse-

quently a commission was appointed to take the charge of the public institutions of the city, the "Tombs" and House of Correction coming under the supervision of this commission. In 1845 a change was again made, whereby the Tombs was placed under the control of one commissioner, and Mr. James II. Cook was appointed. He served for one year, and was succeeded by Moses G. Leonard, who continued in office until 1849. The Legislature of that year passed a law placing the Tombs and the other public institutions under the charge of a body of ten, who were known as

THE TOMBS.

the Board of the Ten Governors of the Almshouse—five being appointed from each of the two political parties, Whig and Democratic. The Board of Ten Governors was, in its turn, supplemented by the Commissioners of Public Charities and Corrections, appointed by the Comptroller of the city to serve for five years. This system continued in force until 1870, when the new Charter vested the appointment in the Mayor, and added one to the number of the commissioners, which had previously been four.

The officers attached to the Tombs are a Warden, two Deputy

Wardens, a Physician, a Record Clerk, a Steward, eleven Keepers, a Matron and two Deputy Matrons. The capacity of the Prison is for about 200 prisoners, allowing one to each cell, but as it frequently happens that there are more prisoners than cells—there having been as many as 500 prisoners at one time during 1870—it is found necessary sometimes to keep two and even three

THE YARD OF THE TOMBS.

in a cell. The Prison for males is wholly separated from that for females, and contains about 150 cells, ranged in four tiers. In a portion of the cells on the lower floor, or ground tier, are placed the convicts, *i. e.*, those under sentence. To the second tier are consigned such prisoners as are brought in charged with serious offences, such as murder, arson, etc. To the third tier prisoners brought in for grand larceny and burglary are sent. The cells on the upper tier are reserved for those charged with minor offences, such as petit larceny and the like. The lower tier cells are the largest, those on the upper tier the smallest. All are of the same width, but, owing to the manner in which the corridors are constructed, the cells on each tier are about two feet less in depth than those immediately underneath. The lower cells are quite commoious, but in the upper ones there is no room to spare.

On Franklin street there is a stone building, which was formerly used as a station for the police of the district. It has since been altered, the cells and offices being taken out, and the building converted into one large hall. In this hall are put the tramps, vagrants, vagabonds, and those found drunk in the streets, where they are kept until the next morning, when their cases are severally disposed of by the Commissioners—some being sent to the Penitentiary, others to the Workhouse, and others to the Almshouse. This building is known to the *attachés* and frequenters of the Tombs as " Bummers' Hall."

The location of the Tombs is not such as a commission of experts would recommend as the site of an hospital, situated as it is in the middle of what was once a deep fresh water pond, which was filled up with the dirt and rubbish of the city, and the drainage of which is anything but perfect; dampness pervades the entire structure, and it is not an uncommon thing for the cells to be overflowed with the water which is forced back through the drain pipes—yet the sanitary condition of the place compares favorably with that of any similar institution. During the cholera season of 1849 but few cases occurred in the Tombs, and none of them were contracted in the place. This circumstance must not be taken as evidence of the healthfulness of the locality. Nothing but the unceasing vigilance of the officers, and the strictest regard to cleanliness and known sanitary laws, preserved the general good health of the prisoners.

The Tombs has, on more than one occasion, been pronounced unsafe. The walls in several places are sunken to a considerable extent. Not many years since a crack, fully four inches in width, which extended from the top to the bottom, was discovered in one of the walls. It was occasioned by the sinking of some of the foundation stones. This crack was at the time repaired, making

the building look, to the eye, as good as ever. Some day the
people may be startled by the announcement that the City Prison
has become a Tomb indeed.

During the last year there were committed to this Prison alone
30,271 prisoners—a daily average of above 83. On the 31st of
December, 1872, there were remaining 517 prisoners in the Tombs.

THE PILLORY.

CHAPTER V.

"Jacques," said Defarge, "judiciously show a cat milk if you wish her to thirst for it—judiciously show a dog his natural prey if you wish him to bring it down one day."—DICKENS, *in Tale of Two Cities*.

EVER since the painted pasteboards were invented for the amusement of an indolent Spanish king, gambling has had a strong hold on humanity. The turn of a card has consequently been the turn in many a man's fortune, and more unwritten dramas have been enacted around the green baize than will be found in all of dramatic literature from Euripides down; and siren as is the voice of Fortune at any time, it is peculiarly beguiling when it comes in the shape of the rat-tat-tat of a roulette ball or the click-click of a faro check. We all feel this fascination for games of hazard at some time or other, and the fever in the blood will break out now and then in our tramp from the cradle to the grave. It makes no difference whether it be a toss of the dice on a sweat cloth or a flyer in Wall street, it is gambling all the same. The " tiger " is a chamelion beast, and roams the jungle of society in various shapes. We may meet him within the portal of a church, where some beautiful and devout young lady member, anxious to gain as many dollars as possible during the Fair, raffles off a kiss at a dollar a chance; but it is still the tiger, with the prayer book in its velvet paws. We see him also on the grand stand at the race course ; at the pool room during election times ; upon the Rialto, where his growl comes in the form of the gold indicator's click; everywhere, in fact, where men meet, can the tiger be seen. But whether the wager be a pair of kid gloves or a million dollars it is all gambling. It is a passion as universal as that of love.

This being the case, it is not at all unnatural that those who do not drop their money on the magic cards themselves, should nevertheless take an immense interest in all stories connected with the tiger. We find this the most interesting kind of literature ; it holds us as did the lurid eye of the Ancient Mariner the gaping listener to his fishy tale. Knowing this weakness of our common nature, we propose to introduce the reader into the chamber of horrors through the ante-room of gambling.

Perhaps as good a salute as any will be an essay on this particular vice from the pen of a convict—a man who, in his palmy days, had an intimate acquaintance with the tiger, and knew all the peculiarities of that wonderful animal. It was written by a graduate of the New York House of Refuge, and will be found, we trust, an entertaining screed:

A GAMBLER'S VIEW OF GAMBLING.

It has been said with truth that a great city is a conglomeration of forces, which, in their action on individuals, are as merciless as Niagara. We all know how that gigantic cataract rushes on to its dizzy edge. It makes no difference to it whether drift wood or human beings—whether boats or babies come within its power; its business is to pour on and roar on, and that it does without the slightest compunctions of conscience. So, too, does a great city roar on and rush on, without regard to the fate of individuals. What cares a great city whether this man or that is swept over the cataract of metropolitan vice, and then swallowed up in the great maëlstrom of destruction, which ever stretches its swirling gorge just below. Great cities like New York are crossed in every direction by rapids of vice, and are full of whirlpools of moral and physical destruction. I intend in this article to map out one of the most fearful maëlstroms that beset voyagers—especially the young—as they sail over the ocean of life. This monster vice is Gambling.

It is of such hideous mien that it would seem as if it only needed to be exposed to be shunned. Let the case be fairly stated, without exaggeration or any false color being given to the picture; let the youth know beforehand the consequences of indulging in this sin—its effects upon his character, habits and prospects; the deceits, stratagems and frauds connected with it; the kindred vices into which its victims inevitably fall—and he would no more enter a gambling hell for amusement than he would sport upon the crater of a raging volcano. Men are not so mad as to ruin themselves deliberately, and with their eyes open.

No man becomes a professed gambler with the expectation of

EXTERIOR OF A FASHIONABLE GAMBLING-HELL.

blasting his hopes, planting daggers in his breast, and bringing ruin upon his head. The youth who finds himself for the first time in a fashionable gambling saloon has no intention of shipwrecking his moral principles, disappointing the cherished hope of friends, filling a mother's heart with anguish, and bringing down a father's gray hairs with sorrow to the grave. Convince him that such will be the inevitable end of this night's beginning, and he will flee from that hall as he would from the jaws of death. But he has been enticed there, and he tarries under a fatal delusion. His attention is absorbed by the brilliancy of the scene the gay company, the exhilaration, the excitement connected with the thought that he may in a few moments win large sums of money. But he knows not where he stands. He knows not that *Hell* here lies in ambush, and nightly hundreds of young men are here offered up to the gigantic Moloch of Play. He knows not that he is breathing a deadly atmosphere—as deadly as that of the Upas valley ; that beneath the fair exterior and winning smiles of the company before him the fiercest passions are raging. He sees not the burning avarice which is all aflame in every heart, which has consumed to ashes all the virtues of humanity. All is bright now, the dark shadows are yet to come. Should this warning save but one youth from the snares and fascinations of this vice, it will not have been written in vain.

In treating the subject I will include under the term Gambling all games of hazard, whether played with cards, dice or billiard balls, for money or its equivalent. The objections to the system apply to every department of it, and every avenue that leads to it. It matters not how trivial is the amount that is staked, or how firm may be one's resolution not to risk large sums, and not to became an habitual player, the principle involved, and the dangers connected with the evil are the same. The most inveterate gambler, who is dead to all moral considerations and human feelings—whose swindling operations are carried on upon a gigantic scale—commenced his career by playing for a glass of wine or an oyster supper. He perhaps laughed at the idea that he should ever play, except occasionally for amusement. But once launched upon it, he was powerless to resist the force of the current which was sweeping him onward to the black sea of infamy.

When once the victim gives up the plea of playing for a small stake, merely to give a zest to the game, he takes up the more dangerous one of making a business of the matter. He never acquires the wealth he aims at, for, as dupe after dupe is caught in his net, and their gold falls rattling into his coffers, his cry is still *more—more!*

It is true that a few persons may amass wealth by games of chance, but every dollar is the fruit of some one's toil. It is covered with the poor man's sweat, the tears of orphans, the blood of broken hearts.

It is found that a gambler is rapidly qualified for every other species of villany. The fiery excitement to which he yields himself in the gaming room influences every other passion. It produces a state of mind that can be satisfied only with intense and forbidden pleasures. The gambler finds his amusement in the circus, the theatre, the lascivious dance, the race course, and in night revellings and Bacchanalian feasts. Ordinary excitements are insipid and stale in his estimation. He would gladly witness as a pastime bull fights, pugilistic encounters, and, perhaps, his craving for excitement could only be fully satisfied by scenes such as the pagan Romans formerly feasted their eyes upon, in which men and women were torn to pieces by wild beasts.

In this manner does this great vice make a Vandal of a man. Nor should the youth forget that, if he is once overtaken in its toils, the hope of extricating himself, or of realizing his visions of wealth and happiness, is exceedingly faint. If he does not become a bankrupt in property he is sure to become one in character. Would the gamester unlock the springs of his heart, that he has pressed down as with iron—would he suffer memory and reflection to do their work, what tragic pictures of life might they paint for him.

The first tableau in the series would be one of calm bliss and joy—not a cloud in the heavens, save that tinged and made beautiful by Hope. Then the scene changes. A tearful and deserted wife, with her sobbing child, keeping watch with her lone night lamp until the breaking of the morn. Again it changes, and haggard misery creeps into the picture. The tears of starved and shivering children embitter the cup which Fate presses to the lips of the gamester. Once again it changes and we see a grave—a green and lovely grave—where the faithful heart that loved him to the last sleeps its lone sleep of death.   Nature is more kind to this heaving mound than was the husband to the wife who lies beneath the daisies.   The singing bird builds its nest in the willow that lovingly bends o'er it ; the sunshine gilds the scene with its splendor, and the rains of heaven fall, like tears, upon the hallowed spot.

"Dark is the night! how dark! no light, no fire!
Cold on the hearth the last faint sparks expire.
Shivering she watches by the cradle side
For him who pledged her love, last year, a bride.

Hark! 'tis his footstep! No, 'tis past, it's gone.
Tick-tick! How wearily the time crawls on.
Why should he leave me thus ? He once was kind,
And I believed 'twould last. How mad! how blind!

Rest thee, my babe! rest on! 'Tis hunger's cry.
Sleep, for there is no food! the fount is dry.
Famine and cold their wearying work have done.
My heart must break! And thou! The clock strikes one.

Hush! 'tis the dice box; yes, he's there—he's there!
For this he leaves me to despair.
Leaves love! leaves truth! his wife! his child! for what?
The wanton's smile, the villain and the sot!

Yet I'll not curse him—no, 'tis all in vain ;
'Tis long to wait, but sure he'll come again.
And I could starve and bless him but for you,
My child—his child! Oh, fiend! The clock strikes two.

Hark! how the sign-board creaks! the blast howls by.
Moan! moan! A dirge swells through the cloudy sky.
Ha! 'tis his knock! He comes—he comes once more!
'Tis but the lattice flaps—the hope is o'er.

Can he desert me thus ? He knows I stay
Night after night in loneliness, to pray
For his return—yet he sees no tear !
No! no! It cannot be—he will be here.

Nestle more closely, dear one, to my heart;
Thou'rt cold! thou'rt freezing! but we will not part.
Husband, I die! Father! It is not he!
Oh, God protect my child! The clock strikes three.

They're gone—they're gone ! the glimmering spark has fled;
The wife and child are numbered with the dead !
On the cold floor, outstretched in solemn rest,
The babe lay frozen on its mother's breast!
The gambler came at last, but all was o'er.
Dread silence reigned around   The clock struck four."

Gambling leads to intemperance.   The intoxicating cup is the natural refuge of the gamester.   All the large gambling establishments are furnished with private bars.   Here many young men are induced, for the first time, to put the wine cup to their lips.   A delicious supper is also spread nightly.   The choicest viands, the rarest game, the most expensive liquors grace the board.   Tinted chandeliers throw a mellow light over the scene.   The foot falls noiselessly upon soft carpets, and the eye is enchanted with the superb pictures hung around the room.   There is no noise, save the muttered exclamations of the players and the clicking of the ivory chips.   Can it be wondered at that this scene should seem fascinating to the young man just entering upon his metropolitan life.

It was the boast of the famous Crockford, of London, who kept a magnificent gambling house, that *he ruined a nobleman every day*. May not the keepers of the gambling hells in New York and other large cities boast that they ruin some noble youth—some son of hope and promise—every day.

Most truly has the gaming *salon* been denominated a *hell*.   It is a hell of fierce passions, of wrecked hopes and agonizing tortures— a hell where fiends congregate, and foul deeds are plotted and accomplished.   Could the malice, rage, deceit, remorse and despair that are found within its walls be embodied in tangible shape, and their ghostly forms move around the table—could the spirit of departed victims but return and utter their wild execrations against the villains who ensnared them—could the cries of wives and starving children echo through the brilliant saloons, would not the gamesters be startled from their gayeties, and look with horror upon the spectal forms around them?   Would not the bloated inebriate, the hoary blasphemer, the keen swindler, the merciless destroyer of the innocent turn pale and tremble in view of the doom that awaited him?

They are indeed hells, and their keepers are indeed monsters— men who have been known to kick from their doors the unfortu-

nate from whom no more money could be fleeced, who have absolutely left those by whom they have been enriched to perish by
cold, hunger or suicide.

Gambling naturally leads to murder and suicide. Under this
head might be presented a long and dark catalogue of crimes. I
can point to no less than four of my boyish companions who became
murderers in their young manhood, because they were demoralized
by the vices and associations of the gambling room. Two of these
are serving out life sentences in State Prisons, and two of them

A GAMBLING SALOON.

were hanged—one in Pennsylvania and one in New York. I cannot think of one of the latter unfortunates without feelings of deep
grief Alas! poor Jerry. My best friend in my boyish days, at
the New York House of Refuge, studying in the same class, and
playing the same pranks on the tutor. He was a fine looking,
curly headed boy, and was an universal favorite with his young
companions. Graduating from the Refuge, he grew up, as a matter
of course, a wild young man; but he was as generous and kind
hearted as he was wild.

He was induced by a friend to visit a gambling hell, and from that day became a victim to the gaming table, and all the hellish passions and vices that are fostered by gamblers. When luck went against him he took to stealing, and so between gambling and stealing he spent his time.

About this time he became acquainted with a young woman, and she promised to marry him; but a fellow gambler and thief won the girl away from poor Jerry, and this was the blow which crushed him. Maddened by liquor, and chafing under the wrong done him by a man in whom he had confidence, he sought immediate revenge. Arming himself with a huge knife, he went to the man's room with the intention of killing him, but instead of finding him there he found his unfaithful sweetheart. His brain was all on fire with rum, and in a sudden burst of passion he stabbed the girl whom he had so sincerely loved. The girl died almost immediately, and poor Jerry was tried, convicted and hanged. He had a dear old mother, loving sisters, and many kind friends, but they were powerless to avert his doom. In the Tombs, on the morning of his execution, his mother and sisters came to take farewell of Jerry. He was still the cherished treasure of his mother's heart; still the idol of his sisters. They loved him none the less for his misfortunes. They clasped him closer to their breasts because he was condemned of the world. It is said the most affecting scene which ever took place in the Tombs happened then and there, when the mother and sisters were told they must bid him farewell. The very officials of the Tombs, who are used to such scenes, could not but weep like little children. Again and again did the mother embrace her curly headed boy and say farewell. The sisters' grief had made them dumb, and they stood weeping their very souls into their eyes. But the final moment came at last, and the women, blinded by tears, were almost carried away.

I could also mention many young men whose lives have been wrecked, and whose death has been that of the suicide; but why enlarge upon the dreadful story. I trust that enough has been said to bring vividly before the inexperienced youth the horrors of this dreadful vice. I could number, also, scores of men now dragging out felons' dreary lives in the State Prisons of the country. The wine cup slays its thousands, gambling its tens of thousands.

Yes, gambling destroys the soul—it breaks down the moral principles, deadens the conscience, and severs every tie that binds man to his Creator. It leaves him without hope and without God in the world—a poor outcast from the sympathies and promises of Heaven—a wanderer upon a bleak and desolate creation. No stars of hope light up his pathway through life. He neither seeks the joys of Paradise nor fears the fires of Hell. The approach of Death does not startle him—the darkness and silence of the grave do not terrify him.

As a fit *finale* to this gloomy chapter I will tell the story of Billy Mulligan's life, a noted gambler of this city, and his attempt at murder in a faro bank.

William, or Billy Mulligan, as he was commonly called, was a man of small stature, but as desperate a character as could be found among the rowdy element of New York. He was a professional blackleg, and, like the rest of his kidney, always dressed in clothes of the finest texture, although rather loud and flashy in their pattern, style and general appearance. At the breaking out of the gold fever he went to California, where he gave full play to his native ferocity, and was concerned in many brawls and bar room fights, during which he made free use of the knife and pistol, weapons which he would use on the slightest provocation, real or fancied. He soon earned an unenviable notoriety, and receiving a pressing invitation to leave the place, he returned to the city, where he engaged in the only pastime—gambling—for which he seemed to have any inclination. He one evening entered one of the most fashionable hells on Broadway, where, becoming involved in a dispute with one of the men of the house, he drew his pistol and attempted to shoot him. For this he was arrested and sent to the Tombs. He was tried for the offence, convicted, and was sent to the State Prison for two years.

During his incarceration in the Tombs he was frequently visited by a handsome young woman, who was possessed of some money and considerable jewelry—diamonds, etc.—which she sacrificed to meet the expenses of Mulligan's trial. On the evening preceding his departure for Sing Sing she called upon him, and in so many words offered to marry him. He consented. The knot was tied by Judge Brennan, who at that time was on the bench. The next day they started on their wedding tour for Sing Sing, the bride manifesting a devotion such as woman only knows. Mulligan did not remain long in prison. After he had been there about three months he was pardoned. In spite of the devotion of his wife, and all she had done for him, he deserted her on his release from jail and returned to California, where, getting into trouble, he was ordered to be arrested. He was pursued by the officers into a house, into which he barricaded himself. When the officers

A BAR ROOM VICTIM.

approached he made a desperate resistance, firing several shots through the window at the crowd below, one of which took effect. The door was forced only to find Mulligan at the head of the stairs with a revolver in his hand. He had evidently made up his mind not to be taken alive.

At length, seeing there was no other alternative, and really in self-defence, one of the officers drew his pistol and shot him, killing him instantly. Few mourned his loss.

CHAPTER VI.

COLT'S CASE.—THE MURDER OF SAMUEL ADAMS.—THE DEATH
GRAPPLE IN COLT'S OFFICE.—SHIPPING THE BODY TO NEW
ORLEANS.—DETECTION, ARREST, THE TOMBS.—THE WEDDING IN
THE CELL.—SUICIDE OF COLT.

"The hand had shut upon it tight, with that rigidity of grasp with which no
living man, in the full strength and energy of life, can clutch a prize he has won.
They dragged him out into the dark street, but jury, judge and hangman could have
done no more, and could do nothing now. Dead, dead, dead!"—DICKENS, *in Martin
Chuzzlewit.*

ON the afternoon of Friday, the 17th day of September, 1841,
Mr. John C. Colt, a professional book-keeper, and teacher of
ornamental penmanship, was sitting in his office, which was in the
granite building at the corner of Chambers street and Broadway.
The building still stands, and is occupied by Delmonico as a restaurant. Mr. Colt's office was on the second floor, looking out upon
Chambers street.

In an adjoining room a Mr. Wheeler, also a book-keeper, was
sitting at work. With him was a young lad, a pupil of his.

It was between three and four o'clock, and at that very moment
there was walking to the building a man who was walking to his
death. That man was Samuel Adams, a printer.

Colt was engaged in writing a work on book-keeping and Adams
was printing it. There was a balance of money due by the author
to the latter, and Adams was coming to see Colt about the accounts.

On he came—into the entrance, up the stairs, into the room.
He sat down on the opposite side of the table to Colt, and the two
began an argument about the amount of money due from one to
the other.

A small hammer, or axe, lay upon the table.

The different opinions held by the two about the debt led to ill
feeling. Argument became abuse.

"You are a liar!" This from Adams, followed by a blow.

They grappled; it was the struggle of death!

Adams held Colt by the neck, and shoved him up against the wall.

As quick as a flash Colt seized the hammer and rained blow after blow upon the head of his assailant. There was a groan, a heavy fall, and the fiend Murder had added another name to his crimson catalogue of votaries.

Mr. Wheeler, in the next room, looked up from his work, and said to his pupil, "Did you hear that? What was it?"

Stealthily he crept to Colt's door and peered through the key-hole, displacing the cover, which was down, with the handle of his pen.

What did he see? He saw a man, with his back to the door, stooping over *something*, and quietly raising it. There was no noise—all was still as the charnel house.

After the fatal blows Colt staggered into a chair, sick unto death, almost; but, although he looked out into the gay street, that form on the floor was always before him. Where the head rested there was a fearful, hideous stream, crawling out over the floor.

> "The deed was done, but one ugly fear
> Came over me now to touch this thing.
> There was nothing to struggle against me here
> In this lifeless heap. I wished it would spring
> And grasp me, and strike at me, as it did
> Only a moment or two before.
> I lifted the head, but it dropped, and slid
> From my grasp to its bed of gore.
>
> What will you do with this horrible thing?
> Down—and grub a grave in the ground!
> Grub with your nails! If you choose you may sing
> That song of his. Don't start and look round!
>
> Dig! How terribly slow you are!
> The dawn in the East begins to grow;
> The birds are all chirping; bury there
> That body at once, and for God's sake go!
> The world will be up in less than an hour,
> And rattle and ring along the road.
> Dig for your life! Ah, well, that's o'er,
> And he lies in his last abode!"

Something must be done. It wouldn't do to leave this dead man on the floor, with the blood soaking into the planks. But what?

First out into the open air. His brain was on fire, and he wanted the cool evening breeze. Noiselessly he opened the door and peered out on the landing. It was all dark and still. He crept down, turning pale when the stairs creaked. The street once reached he took a walk in the City Hall Park. It was a beautiful night, and the stars never looked more lovely; but to him their soft light was a baleful blaze. The round moon rose on the metropolis, but to the red handed man walking among the trees it looked as if it had come dripping from a sea of blood. That fearful pool in his room, that crimson snake, crawling along in the dark, had flooded the universe, and everything was incarnadine.

Colt walked down to the City Hotel, corner of Cedar street and Broadway, where a brother of his was stopping, with the intention of telling him about the deed he had done.

He looked through the window into the reading room. His brother was talking to a gentleman, and Colt retired.

He went back again to his room. On the way he thought of many things. First he determined to fire the building and burn the corpse up. This plan he gave up.

Once more he was alone with his dead. It lay there—that hideous corpse—limp, lifeless. The tongue would never again utter a word; but how eloquent that dead clay was! It spoke with a thousand tongues.

In a closet in that room was a box; in the box was a piece of cord and some canvas awning. He first tied the cord around the dead man's neck, for the purpose of stopping the flow of blood; then he wrapped the body up in the awning, and proceeded to pack it in the box. It was merchandise now, and he had determined to ship it away to some distant port, and after cramming it in he *salted* it.

Then he began to wash up the floor and the walls of the room. That done it was necessary to cleanse his shirt, which had certain fearful stains on it. This was done at the Washington Bath House, in Pearl street. From that establishment he went to his home, where his mistress, Caroline Henshaw, awaited him. He

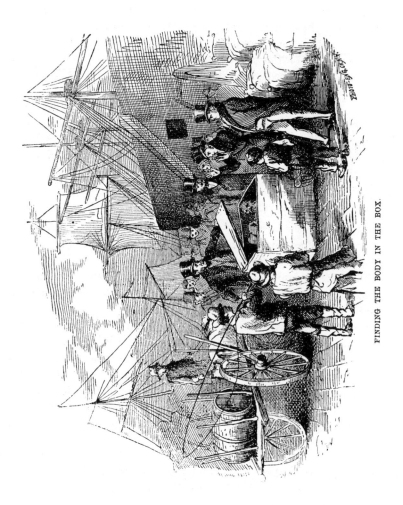

FINDING THE BODY IN THE BOX.

struck a light, undressed and went to bed. As Tom Hood says, in
his poem of " Eugene Aram," did " Death, the grim chamberlain,
light him to his couch?"

The next morning he shipped the body of Adams to New
Orleans, putting it on board a vessel lying at the foot of Maiden
lane. Fate held that vessel back. It was delayed a week. A
horrible stench came from the hold. " Break the cargo!" That
was the order of the skipper. They came upon this mysterious
box; it was opened, and there what remained of Adams was
found.

The Superintendent of Carts advertised for the carman who
brought the box to the ship. In the meantime the strange disappearance of Adams was the town talk. The carman appeared, and
told who gave him the box. Colt was immediately arrested and
locked up in the Tombs.

THE TRIAL.

While in prison Colt lived like a prince. His respectable connections and the wealth of his relatives made him an immense
sensation. The papers were full of the murder and the coming
trial. The case was the town talk.

The trial began, and lasted some ten days. Colt appeared unconcerned and careless. He was always neatly dressed, and created a favorable impression by his appearance.

District Attorney James R. Whiting conducted the prosecution.
Colt was defended by an array of the brightest legal talent of that
day. The line of defence determined upon was that of manslaughter in self-defence. At last the jury retired, and, after
being out several hours, brought in a verdict of " Murder in the
first degree."

Unusually strenuous exertions were made to save the doomed
man. The case was carried from court to court, but all in vain.
Money was also lavishly used, but it could not buy this man's life
from the outraged law. Eventually he was sentenced to be hanged
on the 18th day of November, 1842—over a year from the perpetration of the murder.

COLT'S CONFESSION.

Shortly after his arrest Colt wrote out the following confession:

"Samuel Adams called on Friday at my office, as near as I can recollect, between the hours of three and four o'clock. Whether he had any especial object in view in coming at that time or not I cannot say. When he entered my office I was sitting at my table, as usual, and was at that time engaged in looking over a manuscript account book, as I had been engaged in this work for one or two days previous—that is, I was reading over the entries, and reconsidering the arithmetical calculations belonging to the entries, etc. Mr. Adams seated himself in a chair near the table, and within an arm's length of myself—so near that had we both leaned our heads forward towards each other, I have no doubt but that they would have touched. I spoke of my account, which he had, at my request, handed to me ten or twelve days before. I stated to him that his account was wrong, and read to him at the same time the account, as I had made it out on another piece of paper, and requested him to alter his account as I had it. He objected to it at first, saying that I did not understand printing. He however altered his figures as I read them from my account, as I made the remark that I would give $10, or some such sum, if I was not right; after he had altered his figures, and on looking it over, he said he was right at first. He made the remark that I meant to cheat him. In the meantime we both had been figuring on separate papers parts of the account. Word followed word until we came to blows. The words 'you lie' were passed, and several slight blows, until I received a blow across my mouth, and more, which caused my nose slightly to bleed. I do not know that I felt like exerting myself to strong defence. I believe I then struck him violently with my fist. We grappled with each other at the time, and I was shoved against the wall, with my side next to the table. There was a hammer on the table, which I then immediately seized hold of, and instantly struck him over the head. At this time I think his hat was nearly in my face, and I think his face was downward. I do not think he saw me seize the hammer. The seizing of the hammer and the blow were instantaneous. I think this blow knocked his hat off, but will not be positive. At the time I only remember of his twisting my neck handkerchief so tight that it seemed to me as if I lost all power of reason, still I thought I was striking away with the hammer. Whether he attempted to get the hammer away from me or not I cannot say. I do not think he did. The first sense of thought was, it seems, as though his hand or something brushed from my neck downward. I cannot say that I had any sense or reflection until I heard a knock at the door, yet there is a faint idea remains that I shoved him off from me, so that he fell over, but of this I cannot say. When I heard the knock on the door I was instantly startled, and am fully conscious of going and turning the key so as to lock it. I then sat down, for I felt very weak and sick. After sitting for a few minutes, and seeing so much blood, I think I went and looked at poor Adams, who breathed quite loud for several minutes, threw his arms out, and was silent. I recollect at this time taking him by the hand, which seemed lifeless, and the horrid thrill came over me that I had killed him. About this time some noise startled me. I felt agitated and frightened, and I think I went to the door to see if I had fastened it, and took the key out and turned down the slide. I think I stood for a minute or two listening, to hear if the affray had caused any alarm. I believe I then took a seat near the window. It was a cold, damp day, and the window had been closed all day, except six or eight inches at the top, which I let down when I first went to the office, and which remained down all the time I occupied it. I remained in the same seat for at least half an hour without moving, unless it was to draw close the curtains of the window, which were within reach. My custom had been to leave the curtains about one third drawn from the side of the window towards Broadway. The blood at this time was spreading all over the floor. There was a great quantity, and I felt alarmed lest it should leak through into the apothecary store. I tried to stop it by tying my handkerchief around his neck tight. This appeared to do no good. I then looked about the room for a piece of twine, and found in a box which stood in the room, after partially pulling out some awning which was in it, a piece of cord, which I tied tight around his neck, after taking his handkerchief off, and his stock, too, I think. It was then I discovered so much blood, and the fear of its leaking through the floor caused me to take a towel and gather with it all I could, and rinse it in the pail which stood in the room. The pail was, I should think, at that time about one third full of water, and the blood filled

at least another third full. Previous to doing this I moved
the body towards the box and pulled out part of the awning to
rest it on, and covered it with the remainder. I never saw his
face afterward. After soaking up all the blood I could, which
I did as still and hastily as possible, I took my seat near the win-

THE BLOOD IN THE GUTTER.

dow and began to think what it was best to do. About this time
some one knocked at the door, to which, of course, I paid no atten
tion. My horrid situation remained at this time till dark—a silent
space of time, with still more horrid reflection. At dusk of the evening, and when some omnibuses were passing, I carefully opened
the door and went out as still as possible, and was, as I thought,

unheard. I crossed into the Park and went down to the City Hotel, my purpose being to relate the circumstance to a brother who was stopping at that house. I saw him in the front reading room, engaged in conversation with two gentlemen. I spoke to him; a few words passed between us, and, seeing that he was engaged, I returned to the Park. I walked up and down, thinking what was best to do. I thought of many things, among others of going to a magistrate and relating the circumstance to him. Then I thought of the horrors of the excitement, the trial, public censure, and false and foul reports that would be raised by the many that would stand ready to make the best appear worse than the worst for the sake of a paltry pittance, gained to them in the publication of perverted truth and original, false, foul, caluminating lies. All this, added to my then feelings, was more than I could bear. Besides, at this time, in addition to the blows given, there would be left the mark or evidence of a rope drawn tightly around the neck, which looked too deliberate for anything like death caused in an affray. Firing the building seemed first a happy thought, as all would be enveloped in flames and wafted into air and ashes; then the danger of causing the death of others, as there was quite a number who slept in the building, the destruction of property, etc., caused me to abandon the idea. I next thought of having a suitable box made, and having it leaded, so the blood would not run out, and then moving it off somewhere and burying it; then the delay of all this, and the great liability of being detected. After wandering in the Park for an hour or more I returned to my room and entered it as I had left it, and, as I supposed, unobserved. Wheeler's door was open, and he was talking to some one quite audibly. I went into my room, entering undetermined, and not knowing what to do. After I was seated in my room I waited silently until Wheeler's school was out and his lights were extinguished—and during this suspense it occurred to me that I might put the body in a cask or box and ship it somewhere. I litt'e thought at this time that the box that was in the room would answer; I thought it was too small, and short, and unsafe, as it was quite open. Wheeler's school being out I still heard some one in his room, and, as I then thought, whoever it was lay down on the benches. The noise did not appear exactly like a person going to bed; there was no rustling of bed clothing. I felt somewhat alarmed. The thought then occurred to me that it might be the person who Wheeler had stated was going to occupy the room which I then held as a sleeping room as soon as I gave it up, which was to be in about ten days. The party in question was temporarily occupying Wheeler's room. Relieving myself by this thought I soon lit a candle, knowing that something must be done; there was no time to lose. This was about nine o'clock, I should think. Having closed the shutters I went and examined the box to see if I could not crowd the body into it. I soon saw that there was a possibility of doing so, if I could bend the legs up so it would answer, and if I could keep some of the canvas around the body, so as to absorb the blood and keep it from running; this I was fearful of. It occurred to me, if I bury or send the body off, the clothes he had on would, from description, establish his identity. It became necessary to strip and dispose of the clothes, which I speedily accomplished by ripping up the coat sleeves, vest, etc. While doing so the money, keys, etc., which he had in his pocket, caused a rattling; I took them out and laid them on one side, and then pulled a part of the awning over the body to hide it; I then cut and tore a piece from the awning and laid it in the bottom of the box; then cut several pieces from the awning for the purpose of lessening its bulk, supposing it was too much to crowd into the box with the body; I then tied, as tight as I could, a portion of the awning about the head, having placed something like flax, which I found, in the box with the awning; I then drew a piece of rope around the legs at the joint of the knees and tied them together; I then connected a rope to the one about the shoulders or neck, and bent the knees towards the head of the body as much as I could, which brought it into a compact form. After several efforts I succeeded in raising the body to a chair, then to the top of the box, and, turning it around a little, let it into the box as easy as I could, back downward, with head raised. The head, knees and feet were still a little out, but by reaching down to the bottom of the box, and pulling the body a little towards me, I readily pushed the head and feet in. The knees still projected, and I had to stand upon them with all my weight before I could get them down. The awning was then all crowded into the box, excepting a piece or two, which I reserved to wipe the floor. There being still a portion of the box next to the feet not quite full, I took his coat and, after pulling up a portion of the awning, crowded it partially under him, and replaced the awning. The cover was at once put on the box and nailed down with four or five nails, which were broken, and of but little account. I then wrapped the remainder of his clothing up, and carried it down stairs to the privy and threw them into it, together with his keys, wallet, money, pencil cases, etc.; these latter things I took down in my hat and pockets, a part wrapped in paper and a part otherwise. In throwing them down I think they must have rattled out of the paper. I then returned to the room, carried down the pail which contained the blood, the contents of which I threw into the gutter—into the street. I pumped several pails of water and threw them in the same direction. The pump is nearly opposite the outer door of the building. I then carried a pail of water up stairs, and, after rinsing the pail, returned it clean, and two thirds full of water, to the room, opened the shutters as usual, drew a chair to the door, and leaned it against it on the inside as I closed it, locked the door, and went at once to the Washington Bath House, on Pearl street, near Broadway. On my way to the bath house I went to a hardware store, for the purpose of getting some nails to further secure the box. The store was closed. When I got to the bath house, I think, by the clock there it was eight minutes past ten o'clock. I washed out my shirt thoroughly in parts of the sleeves and bosom that were somewhat stained with blood from washing the floor; my pantaloons, in the knees, I also washed a little, and my neckhandkerchief in spots. I then went home. It wanted, when I got home, about five minutes of eleven o'clock. I lit a light as usual. Caroline wished to know why I came in so late. I made an excuse, saying I was with a friend from Philadelphia, I think, and that I should get up early in the morning to see him off. I went to the stand and pretended to write till she became quiet or went to sleep, then put out the light and undressed myself, spread my shirt, etc., out to dry, and went to bed. In the morning, about half past five, I got up, put my shirt and handkerchief, which were not yet quite dry, in the bottom of the clothes basket, under the bed. I always change my shirt on going to bed. In the morning put on a clean shirt and handkerchief, and was nearly dressed when Caroline woke up. I stated to her it was doubtful if I would return to breakfast; did not return; went to the office, and found all, apparently, as I had left it. I went after some nails and got them at Wood's store. The store was just opened. I returned to the office, nailed up the box on all sides, and went down to the East river to ascertain the first packet to New Orleans. I then returned to the room, marked the box, and moved it, with great difficulty, to the head of the stairs. I did not dare to let it down myself, but went to look for a carman. I saw a man passing the door as I was going out, and requested him to help me down with the box. He got it down without any assistance, preferring to do it himself, and I gave him ten or twelve cents. I then went down Chambers street for a carman whom I saw coming towards Broadway, and hired him to take the box to the ship at the foot of Maiden lane. I went with him. While he was loading the box I went to my office for a piece of paper to write a receipt on, and wrote the receipt to be signed by the captain on my way down the street. I did not offer the receipt to be signed; requested one, which the receiver of the box gave me. The clerk was by at the time, and objected to the form of the receipt, and took it and altered it, wishing to know if I wanted a bill of lading. I at first remarked, as there was but one box it was not very important, adding, however, that I would call at the office for one. I did not go for the bill of lading. I tore up the receipt before I was two squares from the ship. I returned to my office by way of Lovejoy's Hotel, opposite the Park. I went to the eating room and called for a hot roll and cup of coffee; I could not eat, but drank two cups of coffee. Went to my office, locked the door, and sat down for some time. I examined everything about the room, wiped the wall in one or two places, and then went home and to bed."

Caroline Henshaw, although not married to Colt, was true to him. During his incarceration she was a constant visitor to the Tombs. It was the doomed man's desire that he should marry her before he was hanged. Consent having been obtained, the marriage ceremony was performed at noon on the fatal day, the time of execution having been fixed four hours later.

The bride was at the cell at 11.30. She was attired in a straw bonnet, green shawl, claret colored cloak, trimmed with red cord, and a muff. She was accompanied by Colt's brother and John Howard Payne, the author of "Home, sweet home." The Rev. Mr. Anthon performed the ceremony. The mistress became by law the wife, and the same law had decreed that in four short hours she should be a widow. Colt bore up like a man, and was

THE MARRIAGE IN THE CONDEMNED CELL.

even cheerful and chatty. It was his wedding day, and when should a man be in good spirits if not then? The marriage was solemnized in presence of David Graham, Robert Emmett, Justice Merritt, the Sheriff, John Howard Payne and Colt's brother. After it was over the bride and groom were allowed to be alone one hour.

What could have been their conversation—what their thoughts? A husband of an hour, with his valet, Death, making his wedding toilet! a bride whose orange flowers would soon be cypress leaves, and whose trosseau was the weeds of widowhood!

FIRE! FIRE!

After his wife had gone, and the honeymoon of an hour was over, Colt requested to be left alone. His wish was respected.

In the meantime the excitement in and around the Tombs was tremendous. The gallows was erected—all the preparations were completed. The time was slipping away, and the dread hour was near at hand. Just as the clock trembled on the verge of four—the boundary moment between brief time and endless eternity—the cry of fire was raised. The greatest commotion immediately prevailed. It was found the cupola of the prison was all ablaze. Engines thundered down the street, the bells rang, and the light of the conflagration cast its lurid glare over the horrid scene.

"DEAD, FOR A DUCAT—DEAD!"

But the man must be hanged all the same. At a few minutes before four o'clock the Rev. Mr. Anthon went to the cell to notify Colt that all was ready. He opened the door and entered. In a moment he staggered out with a wild cry, and his face as white as the snow. The cell was crowded in a twinkling. There, dead upon the bed, with a knife in his heart, lay the man for whom the rope was waiting outside. His hands were composedly crossed upon his stomach. The gallows was cheated, and the ghastly execution in the prison yard was anticipated by the suicidal knife in the prison cell!

PUBLIC EXCITEMENT.

The excitement created by this remarkable and fearful affair was naturally great. In the *Herald*, the next morning, appeared the following editorial:

"THE LAST DAY OF JOHN C. COLT.—HIS EXTRAORDINARY SUICIDE AND DEATH.

In another part of this day's paper will be found the extraordinary suicide and death of John C. Colt, before the hour appointed by law for his execution, and the no less extraordinary circum-

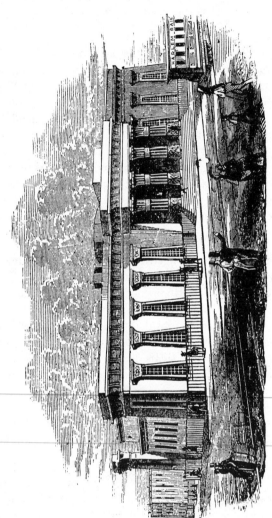

THE TOMBS.

stance of his marriage to Caroline Henshaw, his final separation, and the firing of the cupola of the Halls of Justice about the hour at which he committed the fatal act that closed his course on earth.

We hardly know where to begin, or how to express the feelings and thoughts which rise up in the mind in contemplating this awful, this unexampled, this stupendous, this most extraordinary and most horrible tragedy. The death of Adams, and the circum- stances attending that fatal deed, can only be paralleled by the trial, sentence and awful suicide of Colt. The history of the case cannot be equalled in its horror by that of any criminal trial on record.

Yet it will not probably end here. The public will demand a full investigation of the circumstances through which such a catas- trophe was permitted. How came Colt to ask for religious conso- lation from a clergyman and yet to commit suicide? The prayers said over him by the Rev. Mr. Anthon seem to have had little influ- ence upon his mind when we look at the horrible termination of his life. Christianity had not penetrated or pervaded the last mo- ments of his existence in the remotest degree. Taking all the horrid circumstances of his end into consideration, we have every reason to believe that Governor Seward will order an investigation into the facts, and ascertain that no one is to blame for such a death but the unfortunate being himself. Toward him that was, none can have any feeling but that of pity, commiseration, and deep anguish of heart. From the first moment of his trial to the last pulsation of his existence he seems to have been under the influence of a false system of morals, a perverted sense of human honor, and a sentiment that is at utter variance with the mysterious revelations of Christianity, or the sacred institutions of justice in civilized society. The perverted principles of honor and respectability that spring from modern philosophy and human pride have precipitated him upon the fatal precipice. These principles, arising from materialism in philosophy and unbelief in all revelation, are too rife in the world, and may be looked upon as the principal cause of all the licentiousness, private and public, which seems to overwhelm the whole institutions of civilized society in one mass of uproar, confusion and despair.

We cannot say more to-day, nor could we say less at this mo-

mentous crisis. We have no doubt Governor Seward will order
an investigation at once into this most unheard of—most unparalleled tragedy."

In a further allusion to the subject, the *Herald* says: " WHO
GAVE HIM THE KNIFE? Persons who were alone with him in his
cell yesterday: Rev. Mr. Anthon, Dudley Selden, Samuel Colt,
Caroline Henshaw, Sheriff Hart.

BURNING OF THE TOMBS CUPOLA.

" In addition to the above, David Graham and Robert Emmett
visited him together, when no other persons were present. Also,
John Howard Payne and Lewis Gaylord Clarke visited him with
Samuel Colt. Who gave him the knife?"

There were at the time, and are now, many persons who believe
that during the excitement consequent to the burning of the
Tombs cupola, Colt was allowed to escape, and a body substituted
by his friends to convey the impression of suicide.

CHAPTER VII.

THE DRIFTWOOD IN THE CURRENT OF METROPOLITAN LIFE.—VA-
GRANTS, BUMMERS, DRUNKARDS, REVOLVERS, MISERS.

"May I take this opportunity of remarking that it is scarcely delicate to look at vagrants with the attention that I have seen bestowed upon them by a very dear young friend of mine? They should not be looked at. Nothing disagreeable should ever be looked at."—DICKENS, *in Little Dorritt.*

THE tattered army of Vagrancy is fully as miserable a one, although a great deal larger than that crew of ragged militia which the doughty Falstaff commanded. These descendants of Ishmael are found all over the globe. Whether it is the diseased lazzaroni, sunning their sores in the streets of Naples, the dirty alms seeking wretch, who prowls through the fetid alleys of Constantinople, the stalwart sun burned gipsy, pitching his tent in the fragrant English lane, or the Irish beggar, who runs beside your jaunting car, turning somersaults in the mud for your amusement; whether it be any of these, or any of the thousand and one shapes in which Vagrancy manifests itself, its miserable votaries are all stamped with the unmistakable mark of vagabondism, and all march to a pauper's grave under the same ragged banner. Tramps abound in the country, where they eke out a precarious existence, but it is in the great city that destitution loves to hide itself. Down along the river front, and in the back slums of a metropolis like New York, can be seen at all times cases of hardship which would break the heart of a philanthropist to contemplate. There, where foul smells abound, where the pawn shop blossoms side by side with the bucket groggery, where dirty children play in the mud with dogs and pigs, where drunken men beat drunken wives, where battered hats are thrust into broken windows, where a sickly and polluted light gives all things a horrid glare, where disease, poverty and death stalk in fearful •shapes, there it is that the outcast lives a miserable life, and there it is whence the workhouse is liberally recruited. Such men and women are constantly drifting into the

Station Houses and into the Tombs, and it is of this class that we now intend to speak.

In the Tombs, at all times, there is a certain class of inmates, termed, in the slang of the police, " Revolvers," to whom the Tombs and the Penitentiary on Blackwell's Island are their only home. They are not regarded or treated in the same manner as criminals, their only offence being intoxication or disorderly conduct. Most of them are confirmed inebriates, but could they let rum alone they would in most instances make good and useful members of the community. Many of them are victims of some misfortune, and to drown their grief and forget their troubles they plunge in the terrible vortex of drunkenness. To them liquor is always more acceptable than food, and when without money they resort to every expedient to gratify their appetite. In most cases the drunkard travels from one grog shop to another, and, after having spent his last cent, is invariably turned into the street, to be taken up by the first policeman who may notice his demoralized condition. If without a friend to pay $10 for his release, the drunkard is classed under the head of " Bummer," and he is committed to the Tombs or the Island, whence he is discharged after having served out the prescribed time, only to return after a short interval to expiate a like offence.

Many of these unfortunate creatures are in their way quite interesting characters. Each one has his or her history of misery and woe, and longs ever so much for that sympathy which is always denied them. Philanthropists and humanitarians they rarely encounter, and they are seldom rescued from the atmosphere of squalor and wretchedness which surrounds them.

Of this class was a German named Peter—a large man, of powerful frame, and rugged, robust nature—by trade a mason. He was a good worker, who thoroughly understood his business, and when sober could command the highest wages. He was given many jobs while in the Prison, which were executed in the best and most workmanlike manner. Anything in his line that was to be done about the Prison was given him to do, and when it was necessary, as sometimes was the case, to employ extra help, he was given sole charge and direction of the men. He would see that the work was properly done, and would work himself as faithfully as any. There is, as may readily be conceived, plenty to do for a man of this kind in such an institution as the Tombs.

He would go to work as cheerfully as though especially hired. He would commence work at seven o'clock, work steadily and faithfully until noon, when he would quit. At one o'clock he would resume his labor and remain at his post until six in the evening—giving his full time as though it were a duty to be conscientiously done.

This man would remain in Prison for three months at a time, not wishing to go out. In the morning he would go about from cell to cell and gather the loose papers and rags which had been thrown in the dirt boxes by the prisoners, and carefully put them away in bags which he kept for the purpose, and after he had amassed a sufficient quantity, would take it out and sell it, often realizing a hundred dollars and more, with which he would go on one of his sprees, not unfrequently losing all of his money in one night, which would end, as usual, by his being brought to the Tombs in a beastly state of intoxication.

Peter led this sort of life for a number of years. On the breaking out of the rebellion he, with two grown up sons, enlisted in the Union army. He returned with a good record, leaving, however, the bodies of his two boys, who had fallen in the cause, behind him. He visited the Prison with fifteen hundred dollars in his possession. He had reformed—had given up the use of liquor, and had determined to lead a different life.

He has since bought himself a farm in the West and is doing well.

Another quite interesting subject is an Irishman, named Duffy, who had been in the Tombs, off and on, for upwards of twenty years—in fact he is still there, the writer having seen him and spoken to him on a recent visit to the institution.

He is a man of superior education—a good Greek and Latin scholar, and of excellent family and connections. He had in former years done a prosperous business in this city, but rum getting the better of him, he neglected his business, lost his self-respect, and chose the Tombs as a residence in preference to all other places. He had a brother at the South, who had repeatedly offered to send him the money to take him hence, should he conclude to reform, and who promised to assist him to the extent of his means in getting along respectably; but the offer was declined—Duffy preferring the life he was leading to being, as he termed it, under obligations, or accountable to any one for his conduct.

This man is one of the most useful about the Prison. It frequently happens that the soil pipes or drains become stopped up, causing the cells to overflow with water. To remedy this evil Duffy is always called upon, and willingly does he respond. He will, if necessary, thrust his hand and arm up to the shoulder in filth with as little concern as though brought up to a scavenger's life. He has made himself perfectly familiar with the various pipes through the Prison, and the drains and sewer in the cellar and yard. It frequently happens that the obstruction is in the cellar, where there is always more or less water. When this is the case he prepares himself for the job—puts on a pair of india rubber boots and overalls, and proceeds to explore the place. When the stoppage is ascertained he cuts a hole in the pipe and pulls out perhaps a tin cup, or pan, or old blanket, thrust down the sink by some prisoner in a spirit of maliciousness.

In consideration of these services he is allowed to reside in the Tombs, and serve the prisoners with papers, and do other little chores to turn a penny. Had this man been engaged at a stated salary to perform just such duties, it is doubtful if they would be done with the same cheerfulness, or that he would respond with the same alacrity to the calls made on him; but situated as he is, he seems to feel as though his being there at all, and the privileges (?) he enjoys, are a special favor which it is his duty to requite.

At times Duffy gets very drunk, but under no consideration will he tell where he got his liquor.

A MYSTERIOUS CASE.

One day there was brought to the Tombs, on a charge of vagrancy, an old man, who asked to see the Warden.

"What am I brought to prison for?" he asked, when brought before the Warden.

"For vagrancy," was the reply. "You are an old man, and unfit to roam about the city."

"What constitutes vagrancy?" resumed the old man.

"A vagrant is a person," responded the Warden, "without a home or visible means of support."

"That is not my case, then. I am no vagrant. I have at this moment two thousand dollars in my possession."

"If you have that amount of money about you," then said the Warden, "'twere better you hand it over to me. I will lock it up in the safe, and when you go out it will be returned to you. It is not safe for you to have this money about you; it may be stolen from you."

After considerable persuasion he was at length induced to hand it over. It was done up in a package, his name written on it, and put away in the safe.

That afternoon he was stricken down with a partial paralysis. On the following morning his case was brought to the notice of the Commissioners, to whom he stated he had a married daughter in Ohio, and that because she and her husband could not get him to give them this sum of money they had turned him out of the house, and in his wanderings he had reached this city. He further stated that he had had considerable means, which they had by degrees got from him, and now, when he found that they were seeking to get his last—his all he had on earth—he left rather than part with it.

The money was sent to the office of the Commissioners of Public Charities and Corrections and the old man to Bellevue Hospital.

The family was written to, and about three weeks afterward some one called at the Mayor's office making inquiries for him. The Mayor's Marshal was sent to the Tombs, where he learned that the old man had been sent to Bellevue Hospital, and that his money was in the hands of the Commissioners.

Inquiries were made at Bellevue Hospital, but no traces of the man could be discovered. No such man had been entered on their books, nor could any one remember a person answering his description.

Nothing was ever found out about the old man, and his money was sent to his heirs.

THE SICK BEGGAR.

A case illustrative of the various phases of degradation which came under the author's observation while connected with the

Tombs, was that of a miserable specimen of humanity who was one day brought in by an officer to be sent to the hospital, he having found her sick in the street.

She was a poor miserable wreck—a beggar—without shoes or stockings to her feet; her only clothing a dirty tow-cloth frock. She was given in charge of the kind Mrs. Foster, the Matron of the Female Prison, who at once exerted herself in the poor wretch's behalf, doing what she could to alleviate her sufferings.

On searching the miserable creature there was found tied round her waist an old piece of rope, with a bag attached, which on examination was found to contain about fourteen hundred dollars in gold, silver and copper coins, the weight of which, as may be supposed, was not inconsiderable, and which, being constantly carried thus, had ultimately made her sick.

The money was taken away from her and sent to the Commissioners' office for safe keeping, and she was sent to the Hospital. On her discharge the money was returned.

CHAPTER VIII.

HUMOROUS AND PATHETIC INCIDENTS. — BENEVOLENCE OF THE
LATE SIMEON DRAPER.—WHAT HAPPENED IN AN OMNIBUS.—
A PRACTICAL JOKE.—HOW A STATE ROOM WAS SECURED.

"There was a tiny blink of sun peeping in from the great street round the corner,
and the smoky sparrows hopped over it and back again, brightning as they passed—
or bathed in it like a stream, and became glorified sparrows, unconnected with
chimneys."—DICKENS, *in Domby & Son*.

THERE was one day brought in a poor German tailor, nearly
dead. He had a wife and family of five children, living in
Baxter street, near the Five Points. He had no work, nor the
means to supply his family with food. One of his children lay
dead on some straw in one corner of the room, sheer starvation
having been the cause of the child's death. He could not endure
the misery about him, and in a fit of despondency determined on
suicide as an end to his woes; he accordingly provided himself
with a rope, and fastening it to a bar across the window, attempted
to hang himself. He was discovered ere life was extinct, cut down
by the officer on the post and brought to the Tombs, where the
physician succeeded in restoring him to consciousness and his right
mind.

It is the custom of the Commissioners to call at the Tombs every
morning and dispose of those cases demanding their attention.
The attention of the late Mr. Draper, President of the Board of
Commissioners, was called to this man's case. Mr. Draper asked
what prompted him to such a terrible deed.

Tears rapidly chased each other down the poor wretch's cheeks,
and with a choking voice he informed the Commissioner that his
child had starved to death—that his wife and other children were
barely alive—being also in a state of complete starvation. He
could not beg, he said, nor would he steal; work it was impossible
to find. What could he do? And the man wept like a child.

Mr. Draper, whose heart was as big as himself, was moved by
the man's story. His eyes watered, and thrusting his hand into his

pocket he emptied the contents into the poor fellow's hand, telling him to go buy bread for the family first, and then to bring them to the Tombs, where he would see that they were properly cared for, and that the Warden would see to the interment of his dead infant.

Another instance of the large heartedness and kindly disposition of the late Simeon Draper, Esq., is shown in the following case :

One day he was examining some boys who had been brought in the day before. Among the number was a rather bad looking boy, to whom the usual question, as to " what had brought him there ?" was put.

" I ain't done nothin', sir," was the reply.

" O ! what a darned liar you are," spoke up a little urchin at his side, who scarcely reached to his shoulder. " You told me that you stole a pair of shoes, and that the Judge sent you to this gentleman for him to take care of you. I couldn't lie like that."

" Who is he ?" asked Mr. Draper of the writer.

" That, Mr. Draper," was the reply, " is one of your cares."

" Come here, my little fellow," he said, addressing the boy." " What brought you here ?"

" Well, now, I'll jest tell yer the hull truth. Yer see, I'm a livin' up in the country, back o' Catskill, with my mother ; an' my uncle, he went to the war. I heern that he was wounded and brought on to this city, an' I kinder thought I'd come down an' see if I couldn't find him out. When I left home I had jest fifty cents in my pocket. I got on the cars, an' when the conductor came along I told him how much money I had, and asked him to let me ride for nothin', 'cause I s'posed I'd want the money when I got to York. He wouldn't let me ride, though, and so I got off an' waited for the next train, an' that conductor let me ride free. When I got here I found I was pretty hungry, an' so I bought something to eat. I travelled 'round all day, but couldn't find out nothin' 'bout my uncle. Night was comin' on—I was very tired, and had only fifteen cents in my pocket, and didn't know what to do. Seein' an officer I went up an' spoke to him. He was very kind to me, and took me to the Station House, and from there I was brought here. That's the hull truth. I would like to find my uncle, but 'spose I'll have to go home without."

When the boy had concluded his story Mr. Draper instructed the Warden to see that he was furnished with a new straw hat and sent home—remarking that he expected yet to hear from him as the representative in Congress of the Catskill district.

The boy was supplied with the hat and sent on his way home that afternoon.

" What is that fine looking elderly man doing among that lot of bummers ?" one morning inquired Mr. Draper of the Warden, at the same time pointing to a man of about sixty years of age, who was one of the motley crew.

" That's a subject for you, sir," was the reply.

" How came you here and what can I do for you," asked the kind hearted Commissioner, as he called the man to him.

The man's eyes filled with tears as he told his story. He had brought up a family of children, and given them a fair education. He had been in business, and made some money, but it was all gone now. His children had, one after another, turned him away, and he was left, an old man and penniless, to get along as best he might.

" Well, my friend," said Mr. Draper, " I'll send you up to the Almshouse, where you will be well cared for."

" And has it finally come to this," sobbed the old man. " The last place on earth I thought to end my days in."

" Don't take it so to heart," said Mr. Draper. " You'll not find it such a terrible place. I'll call and see how you are getting along next Sunday." And he kept his word.

WHAT HAPPENED IN AN OMNIBUS.

Riding down town in one of the Broadway stages one day, the writer's pantaloons were soiled by mud from the boot of a passenger—a consequential looking dandy—who, in crossing his legs, rubbed his foot against them.

The man not seeming in the least concerned, nor offering any apology, the writer's feelings were a little ruffled, and laying his hand on his knee, pushed his legs away, remarking that he did not care to have his pantaloons used as a mat.

The dandy crossed his legs again, when they were again shoved off. Some words ensued, when the man, losing patience, exclaimed :

" Sir, I think I know you—I have seen you before."

" I have no doubt of it," was the reply, coolly uttered.   " Your face seems quite familiar to me, also.   I am, and have been for a number of years Warden of the Tombs down here," pointing down Franklin street, which the stage was at the moment crossing.

A loud laugh broke from the passengers, and the man, greatly annoyed, concluded to get out and walk, or take another stage.

A PRACTICAL JOKE.

It was about the holidays, a day or two before Christmas, and, as the author was in the habit of observing the time-honored custom of the season, of bestowing on " the loved ones at home" some *souvenir* of his regard and affection, he entered one of the jewelry stores on Broadway for the purpose of purchasing some articles of jewelry, to be given to his wife and daughter in honor of the occasion. He was politely waited upon by the proprietor of the establishment, who temptingly displayed quite an assortment of elegant rings, brooches, bracelets, etc., from which to make a selection.

Being wholly absorbed in the examination of the wares before him, the author did not take any particular notice of a gentleman who entered the store, and who, having signaled to the proprietor, held a short whispered conversation with him, at the conclusion of which he (the proprietor) at once commenced putting away his goods, leaving only two or three articles exposed, and quite changing in his demeanor towards his customer—not appearing so anxious to sell—in fact, acting as though he'd rather have him off his hands.

Without making a purchase the writer turned to leave the establishment, when the gentleman between whom and the proprietor the whispered conversation alluded to had taken place, saluted him :

" Hello! Charley; what are you doing here?"

Looking up the writer recognized an old friend, and quite a practical joker, to whom he stated the object of his visit to the store.

" Did you find what you wanted?" asked the gentleman.

On being answered in the negative, he assumed that a better assortment of goods, in his estimation, was not to be found, and that the proprietor was one of the best fellows in the trade, concluding his laudation by saying, "Let me introduce you to him," and, suiting the action to the word, formally introduced the writer as "Mr. Sutton, the Warden of the Tombs, who was daily in communication with thieves, gamblers and confidence men."

The proprietor was overwhelmed with confusion, and apologized as best he could, under the circumstances, for the shabby treatment of his customer, the cause of which was explained.

It seems that the gentleman was passing the store, and seeing the author with a lot of fine jewelry displayed before him, was seized with the idea of perpetrating one of his jokes. He accordingly entered the store, and beckoning the proprietor, with whom he was well acquainted, asked him if he knew the man who was looking at his goods. "No," was the answer. "Well," he resumed, "he is a man who is daily in communication with thieves, gamblers and confidence men." This was enough for the jeweller, who, no doubt, thinking that a man of such proclivities was not the most welcome customer in an establishment such as his, at once set about "putting things to rights," doing his utmost to get rid of him at the earliest possible moment.

The proprietor of the store at first naturally felt a little sore at having been made a victim of his friend's joke, but after a while that feeling passed off, and a very agreeable half hour was spent.

It is needless to add that the Christmas presents were bought at that establishment.

HOW A STATEROOM WAS SECURED.

The author had occasion, while Warden, to go to Boston, and accordingly took passage on one of the Fall River line of steamers. There was an unusually large number of passengers aboard, and the demand for staterooms was in excess of the supply. After the steamer had got under way the passengers' ears were saluted with the customary tintinabulations of a dinner bell, accompanied by the words, bawled forth by the steward, notifying "all passengers who had not yet paid their fare to step up to the captain's office and settle."

As the author was one of those for whose special benefit this entertainment was gotten up, hewended his way to the designated spot, and taking his place on the line, calmly awaited his turn.

Before his turn came, however, the few staterooms that had not been secured were all disposed of, and passengers were obliged to content themselves with berths in the lower saloon. The man just in advance on the line had been rather abruptly informed that "there were no more rooms." Nothing daunted, however, the writer coolly tendered the money for his fare and a stateroom, asking for the key.

"Didn't you hear me tell the gentleman just ahead of you that I had no more rooms?" impatiently asked the clerk.

"How's that?" was the reply. "A large steamer like this, and can't accommodate a man with a room. If you ever stop at my hotel you'll never find me so full that I'll not be able to give you a good and secure room."

"Do you keep a hotel?"

"I do."

"Where?"

"In New York."

"Whereabouts in New York?"

"On the corner of Centre and Franklin streets."

"Corner of Centre and Franklin streets?" hesitating, as if trying to locate it. "Why, that's the Tombs!"

"The very place."

"Stand aside a few minutes; I'd like to have a chat with you."

His duties were soon over, when he called the writer in, and expressed great satisfaction at making his acquaintance. He had, he said, got on a lark once, and had spent a night in the Tombs, and had to pay ten dollars on the next day in order to get out. He had since thought that he would like to know some of the officers of that institution.

The writer found him a man full of humor and a congenial spirit, in whose company he spent a very agreeable evening, and when, late in the night, he parted from him, he was handed the key to one of the best rooms aboard.

The author has lost all track of the clerk, but, wherever he may be, he has the best wishes of the man who once kept the hotel on the corner of Centre and Franklin streets.

CHAPTER IX.

MURDERER'S ROW.—ASSASSINS OF THE PERIOD.—HOW THEY LIVE IN THE NEW YORK TOMBS.—MURDER AT A PREMIUM.— FLOWERS, CANARY BIRDS AND KIDDERMINSTER CARPETS.— GENTLEMEN OF ELEGANT LEISURE.—ROSE COLORED LIFE IN THE PRISON CELL.

"There is something in his appearance quite——— – – – what do you call it when lords break off door knockers, and beat policemen, and play at coaches with other people's money, and all that sort of thing. Aristocratic? Ah! aristocratic—something very aristocratic about him, isn't there?"—DICKENS, *in "Nicholas Nickleby."*

WHEN from the flame crowned top of Sinai the Almighty thundered forth his mandate, "Thou shalt not kill," mankind considered the crime a heinous one, and punished it accordingly. In those dark days, into which the light of the historian's torch penetrates but dimly, the shrift of the murderer was dramatically short. It was an eye for an eye, a tooth for a tooth, a life for a life. But *nous avons changé tout cela.* This is the age of civilization, and as we have made progress in the sciences, arts and mechanics, so we have also in the treatment of our murderers; at least it is so in New York. Their path may or may not lead to the gallows, but it is certainly strewn with roses.

The popular idea of a murderer in his cell is a grave one. The fancy paints with sombre tints a cold, dark cell. A sickly shaft of light comes from the high barred window, and illuminates feebly the haggard face of the criminal, as he sits upon his wretched pallet of straw. Whenever he moves or presses his trembling hands to his hot brow we hear the clanking of huge chains. The fires of despair burn luridly in his bloodshot eyes. At intervals the iron door creaks harshly open, and the rough keeper hands him his coarse fare. There is no furniture save a crazy chair or two—no carpet, nothing but the damp stone flags of the cell; and here he lies until he is led out to be hung in chains, or executed in whatever manner may be in vogue.

Victor Hugo, in his "Last days of a Condemned Man," paints this picture superbly. The very thoughts of the miserable wretch are reproduced in his glowing language. We shrink with horror from the contemplation of the scene, and wonder, since such is the fate, how any man can commit murder. They may do those things better in France, but how is it in New York?

Let us take a stroll through Murderers' Row in the Tombs. Coming in from the pure air and warm sunshine you say, as you

THE POPULAR IDEA.

step upon the corridor, "Surely this is dismal enough!" And so it is; but this is only the exterior of the parlors.

As the keeper swings open the door of the first cell we come to the odor of sweet spring flowers strikes you. It is no delusion, for there they are in a delicate vase upon the centre table. That handsomely dressed lady, with the golden hair, whom we passed on the stairs, has just left them. To-morrow they will be replaced by fresh ones. The table itself is a pretty one—there is nothing handsomer on Fifth avenue. It is of exquisite workmanship, and is covered with a dainty cloth. In a gilt cage, hanging against the wall, is a canary, whose dulcet strain gushes out from his palpitating throat in a flood of melody.   A pretty set of swinging shelves, suspended by silken cords, catches the eye next.   Here are to be found the latest novel—the freshest magazine.   Pictures here and there break up the dull wall into gorgeous color.   You tread on roses, for the cold stones are concealed by a piece of rare kidderminster carpet.   And the murderer—how is it with him?

You see he is not sitting on any pallet of straw—not any.   In a patent extension chair he lolls, smoking an aromatic Havana, while he reads the proceedings of his trial the day previous in the morn-

LUXURY IN THE TOMBS.

ing's papers.   He has an elegant dressing gown on, faced with cherry colored silk, and his feet are encased in delicately worked slippers, the gift of one of his lady friends.   His clothes are neat, and up in style to the latest fashion plate.   He is cleanly shaven, and has a general air of high-tonedness about him which is quite refreshing.   To one side of him is his bed—a miracle of comfort.

When he is tired of reading, or smoking, or sleeping, he takes a stroll in the yard.   It is necessary to dress for this, and his toilet takes considerable time.   Finally he appears, booted and gloved. He may have his seal skin coat on, or he may appear in a light spring affair, of exquisite cut and softest tint.   In his hand is a gold headed switch, which he carelessly twirls during his morning promenade.

Then comes his lunch—not cooked in the prison, but brought in from a hotel. It consists of a variety of dishes, such as quail on toast, game patés, reed birds, ortolans, fowl, the newest vegetables, coffee, cognac, etc.; and then it is back again to easy chair, book and segar.

Such is life in Murderer's Row, and a merry-go-round it is. In some of the upper tiers it is just possible that some miserable varlet who stole a ham is paying the outraged law its full penalty. His cell is cold and cheerless enough. There are no flowers, no books, no birds, no carpet. But then it serves him right! He was fool enough to steal, and such an insignificant thing at that, too, as a ham, and therefore cannot expect anything better. When he gets out he will know how to proceed to have a furnished parlor in Murderer's Row, and lead the life of a prince.

SING SING *versus* THE TOMBS.

CHAPTER X.

HELEN JEWETT, THE QUEEN OF THE DEMI-MONDE.—HER EARLY
LIFE. — CORRESPONDENCE. — ACQUAINTANCE WITH PROMINENT
STATESMEN, ARTISTS AND ACTORS OF THE DAY.—HER YOUTH-
FUL LOVER, RICHARD P. ROBINSON.—HER MURDER.—ATTEMPT
TO BURN THE BODY.—JAMES GORDON BENNETT'S DESCRIPTION
OF THE CHARRED CORPSE, AS VIEWED THE NEXT MORNING.—
EXCITEMENT AT THE TRIAL.—ELOQUENCE OF ROBINSON'S COUN-
SEL, HON. OGDEN HOFFMAN.—MURDER OF A WITNESS.—BRIBERY
OF A JUROR.—PERJURY OF A WITNESS.—ACQUITTAL OF ROBIN-
SON.—FLIGHT TO TEXAS.—A STRANGE SEQUEL.

" Pause, you who read this, and think for a moment of the long chain of iron or
gold, of thorns or flowers, that would never have bound you but for the formation of
the first link on one memorable day."—DICKENS, *in Great Expectations.*

THE crimson volume of murder has no bloodier page than the
one whereon is written the brutal butchery of the lovely
Helen Jewett by her lover, Richard P. Robinson, which occurred
in this city on the night of the 11th of April, 1836. It was a most
damnable crime, and created a tremendous sensation. The comeli-
ness and intellect of the fair but frail Helen, her remarkable career
since first she embarked upon the treacherous sea of passion, and the
tragic fate that overtook her while yet the bloom was on her cheek
and the fire was in her eye, combined to interest every one in the
case, and made it the talk of the street, the store, the hotel and
the club. This interest was heightened by the youth and social
standing of the young man whose hands were most undoubtedly
dyed with her life-blood. The trial was the theme of the hour,
and was eagerly watched by all classes.

Thirty-seven years have elapsed since then, but there are many
yet among us who can recall the radiant Helen as she swept like a
silken meteor through Broadway, the acknowledged queen of the
promenade. The beauteous face and form have long since turned
to dust, but the moral of the story is as potent to-day as it was
when the tragedy was enacted. Let those, therefore, who would

know how sad a gift loveliness is, without virtue, and how the
stream of illicit love, fair as it may be to look upon, sooner or later
runs to the rapids of crime, listen to the legend of the unhappy
Helen.

Helen Jewett was but one of the many names borne by this
unfortunate girl. Her real name was Dorcas Doyen. She was

HELEN JEWETT.

born in the month of June, 1813, of Welsh parents, at Augusta,
Maine, and was therefore but twenty-three years old at the time of
her death. By nature she was impulsive, and she also displayed at
an early age a remarkable aptitude for learning. With such gifts
it is not remarkable that she became at a precocious age a lovely
and accomplished girl.

When Dorcas was thirteen years of age, and shortly after the
death of her father, she was adopted by a wealthy Judge, who
resided in the vicinity of her own home. It was about this time

that she made her first false step. It was an amour with a young sailor, who had been her youthful playmate; but the indulgence in stolen joys was doomed to end most lamentably. After her sweetheart's departure for the " raging main " she sought sweet consolation for her sorrow in the intimacy of a young banker of Portland. Grown bold by long continued immunity from exposure, she neglected to stop this side of flagrancy in her course, and eventually the rumors of the town made themselves audible to the family of the Judge. There was but one thing to do and it was done. Helen was turned from the house in disgrace.

We see her next at Portland, to which city she journeyed in hopes of finding her financial friend. Here she drifted steadily downward in the moral scale, but rose with corresponding grandeur in the realm of the *demi-monde*. The banker was found, and he, proud of her beautiful face and voluptuous form, dressed her like a duchess, and instated her in a mansion of palatial splendor. Here she gave champagne suppers to the gallants of the town, at which she presided as an Aspasia, her own laugh the merriest, her wit the most scintillating; but it couldn't last. As ladies often will, who occupy so questionable a position in society as did Helen, she quarrelled with her friend, by reason of being too generous in the dispensation of her favors, and was forced to leave the pleasant home of her protector. She went to Boston.

In Boston, and while under the name of Miss Stanley, she came very near being married to a member of one of the best families of the place. She was exposed, however, upon the wedding eve, and in a fit of rage and mortification she resolved to leave the militia of immorality and join the regular army. To do this she started for New York, and it is at this point that the prologue ends and the curtain rises upon the real play.

It was at a Mrs. Post's, in Howard street, that Helen made her first stop in New York. And now, since it was her personal attractions that wrought her destruction, it may be as well to inform the reader as to her appearance at that time—1832. She is thus described:

" She was a shade below the middle height, but of a form of exquisite symmetry, and which, though voluptuously turned in every perceptible point, was sufficiently dainty in its outline to give her the full advantage of a medium stature to the eye. Her complexion was that of a clear brown, bearing in it all the voluptuous ardor of that shade, without the dregs and specks which are too apt to muddy the coarser specimens of the brunette, and which, instead of the Promethean fervor, indicate no quality above mere grossness of the blood. Above a forehead of transparent smoothness, and beside a pair of ivory temples, in which might be dimly seen a delicate tracery of blue, she trained two heavy waves of glossy jet black hair, while on the top, that crown of female glory, reposed the richness of an abundant coil. Her features were not what might be termed regular, but there was a harmony in their expression which was inexpressibly more charming than mere mathematical agreement or a precise accord. The nose was rather small, which was a fault; the mouth was rather large, but the full richness of its satin lips, and the deep files of ivory infantry which crescented within their rosy lines, redeemed all of its latitudinal excess; while her large black steady eyes, streaming now with glances of precocious knowledge, and anon languishing with meditation or snapping with mischievousness, gave the whole picture a peculiar charm, which, despite its disagreements, entitled it to the renown of one of the most fascinating faces that ever imperiled a susceptible observer. Added to all these natural gifts she possessed a nice and discriminating taste for dress, which, aided by a graceful carriage, consisting of a sweet oscillation that seemed rather to woo than to force the air to give it place, served to display those blessings to the best advantage.

In disposition this lovely creature was equal to her form. She was frank and amiable. Her heart was kind to excess to all who required her assistance, though the ardor of her temperament rendered her amenable to the fiercest sentiments of passion. These bursts, however, were fitful, not malevolent, and though unscrupulous while in their first gush of rage, might be turned, by a single well directed touch into the viaduct of generous forgiveness. In manner she was vivacious and merry, though, like all intellectual persons of that description, she was subject to sudden and violent depressions. But these were brief, and the animal sparkle of her spirits soon triumphed and scintillated over all."

Helen did not stay long at Mrs. Post's. A slight unpleasantness which occurred in that abode of peace—which was no less than the surgical (?) murder of a beautiful girl, an inmate of the house—induced her to change her quarters. Upon the advice of a gentleman friend she removed herself and wardrobe to Mrs. Ann Weldon's hotel, No. 55 Leonard street. While in this establishment she amused herself by writing letters to a large number of noted people, the answers to be sent to the city Post-office. Almost any fine day she could be seen floating down Broadway, dressed in green silk, with a letter daintily held in her kidded hand. She came to be known by this "make-up," and, as she passed, both old and young would turn to have a look at Helen Jewett. As a sample of her letters we will give one, selected at random. It was addressed to a prominent theatrical artist of the city at that time.

"MY DEAR MR. —— :

I saw you in Othello last night, and I am going to be pert enough to say I did not like you. That is to say, I did not like to see you in such a guise and such a character. Your features are too noble to be so disfigured and covered up with grime. I would rather see you in Iago, for I think he is the best man of the two. Othello is, in my opinion, a great lout and a great fool, and has not half so much to cry about as Iago. Cassio was a white man, to say the least, which was not the case with the man who Iago suspected with Emelia. I should like to see you in Damon or in Romeo. I should like above all things to be your Juliet, or to rehearse the character with you in private at any rate. I have some notions on the philosophy of her character, and likewise on that of Romeo, which would perhaps amuse you. But never mind; I will not bother you upon the subject now; if, however, you ever have foolish curiosity enough to wish to know them, you can drop a line in the city post, directed to ATHELIA."

So far the stage of our story has been occupied only by Helen and those gad-flies who fluttered about the light of her beauty. It is now time to introduce Richard P. Robinson, the young man whom Fate had already decreed should be at once her lover and her executioner. When he made her acquaintance the lovely planet had shifted her position in the Heaven of Passion, and was then blazing with added splendor at the house of Mrs. Berry, in Duane street, known to the wild spirits of the town as the *Palais de Duchesse Berri*. Robinson, then a clerk in a Maiden lane store, first saw Helen in Broadway, and was at once entranced by her charms. But no acquaintance resulted at that time, although Helen herself was somewhat fascinated by the fresh and youthful beauty of the handsome boy. But a few evenings subsequently

RICHARD P. ROBINSON.

they met again at the theatre. Helen was subjected to some insult by a drunken ruffian, and Robinson took her part. That same evening he was handed a note, in which Helen requested him to call after the performance at the house in Duane street. It is needless to state that he did so, or to expatiate upon the fervor of the meeting. Helen felt that she had at last met her affinity—the one whom she could love with all the power of her passionate soul—and, as for Robinson, he was intoxicated with the beauty of his possession, and felt all the sweet delirium of delight.

Richard P. Robinson was the descendant of a highly respectable family in the interior of Connecticut. He was a bright, vivacious boy, of generally pleasing manners, but of fierce temper and resentful disposition. At the age of fourteen, at which time his father was dead, he took a desire to go to the City of New York, and though opposed by his remaining parent, he broke through all check, and put his wishes in progress of fulfilment by running away from home.

On arriving in this city he called upon a relation who kept a retail dry goods store, and who, finding the youth literally afloat in a great town and under his own shallow guidance, gave him a situation in his store. With the generosity usually evinced in such cases, however, the philanthropy was circumscribed by a salary too small for his subsistence; so he was driven to the usual alternatives of deriving the necessary deficit from home, or making it up after his own fashion, from the proceeds of the shelves or drawer. Which of these lines of policy he at that time embraced it is doubtful to determine, but the solution is much easier arrived at as to a later period, when his taste for frolic led him into all the extravagancies of city life, and caused him to become a frequent visitor to the billiard saloons and bowling alleys of the town.

At the time he met Helen, although but eighteen years of age, he had already run the gamut of vice, and was a well known visitor at every *maison de plaisir* in the city. In person he was strikingly handsome, having a frank, boyish face, that was well set off by curling hair of golden brown. He always dressed neatly, and was seldom seen, at least in cool weather, without a Spanish cloak, which he wore jauntily about his shapely person. This cloak became famous during his trial, and its like was known for a long time after as the " Robinson " cloak.

But though graceful in person he was dissolute in habits and unprincipled in mind. His reading was extensive, but it had a tendency to erotic literature that produced no good results. He was also singularly selfish, and devoid of sympathy for others—in a word, a cool, calculating philosopher of the extremest pagan school. He plunged into vice because it gratified his sensual nature—but he was devoid of the feeling of true love.

Such was the young man whom Helen thought was the *beau*

ideal of whom she had so fondly dreamed. On the night we have mentioned she received him with rapture in a room that would have done credit to the palace of Cleopatra. A pile of music lay upon the table. The most rare and gorgeously bound albums and keepsakes were sprinkled in all directions, and costly articles of *vertu* were arrayed upon the mantelpiece and marshalled on the dressing table. A superb gilt eagle held in his shining beak a canopy, which drifted its snowy sheets of film over a pampered couch, while on a luxurious crimson divan at its foot were cast the rich garments of the mistress of the chamber, in a loose disorder, which showed that they had relinquished all their duty of reserve.

For a time all went smoothly; but eventually Robinson, confident of the fealty of Helen, and yielding to the baser whisperings of his nature, began to reject her for every fresh beauty that struck his fancy. This enraged our lovely friend, and induced her one night, after he had been away from her longer than usual, to disguise herself as a young man and track him to wherever the new attraction was. Posting herself opposite the store in Maiden lane where he was employed, she waited for his appearance and then followed him, first to his boarding-house in Dey street and then to a house in Broome street. After he had entered she rang the bell, and being admitted, walked into the parlor and found her lover in company with a female whom she particularly despised. A lively scene ensued, for Helen, wild with fury, threw herself upon her rival and struck her repeatedly with her bediamonded hand, bringing the blood at every blow.

This little episode induced Robinson to widen still further the gap of separation. Day after day passed and the house in Duane street knew him not. Helen grew restless and at last repented. She really loved the boy, and this estrangement was torture to her, so she essayed to woo him back, and for that purpose wrote to him repeatedly. When her letters became really imploring the haughty youth unbent his dignity, and once more graced the *Palais de Duchesse Berri* with his presence. All was forgiven, and Helen was as happy as the bird that carols in the grove. Then he, always suspicious, began to test her, and, as an evidence of the artfulness and cunning of his disposition, we submit the following letter, which he wrote to her over an assumed name:

DEAR MISS :
" NEW YORK, July 7, 1834.

The author of the following epistle is a stranger to you, and common courtesy demands a perusal of his sentiments. I should have spoken freely what I here remark to your private ear, were it not I was of opinion you would suppose me guilty of trifling with your credulity and insulting your misfortune.   I am not ignorant of your present mode of life and your degraded situation, and you will excuse the plainness of both the language and remarks.   Acting with the impulse of nobler sentiments than those who have heretofore addressed you, I would present for your reflection the following proposal :

If the gifted and fascinating Helen will forsake the rough road on which she has previously been a traveller, and adopt one more in unison with her enlightened mind, with no other security than her own word, he who now presents this petition will greet her, not as heretofore she has been, as a mistress, but as one whom the laws of the land bid him protect, cherish and love.   I am sensible that the world would chide me for what they term folly, but the purity of my feelings, the genuine motives that inspire me, and the knowledge of your disposition and excellent qualifications that I have gleaned from the information of others, as well as my own observations, have instigated this request, which I solicit may be granted to your suitor, who respectfully subscribes himself,

Yours in esteem,   REUBEN JARVIS.

To MISS HELEN JEWETT,
  No. 3 Franklin St., N. Y."

It was a painful struggle for a woman in her position, but she was equal to it.   Here is the reply :

" NEW YORK, July 9, 1835.

DEAR SIR :
It would be of little use for me to deny to a person who seems to know me as well as you do, that an acceptance of your offer would be one of the most desirable things, as a social advantage, that my imagination could conceive.   I do not attempt to conceal that it would ; but, sir, I at the same time perceive that its acceptance would inevitably lead to the most unbounded actual misery to both of us hereafter.   You could never substantially respect me,

and, after the first season of your fancy, your fondness would give place to mistrust, and I would be suspected at a greater disadvantage than the numerous unblemished women who, notwithstanding the blamelessness of their early lives, are rendered miserable by the unfounded jealousy of their husbands every day, Give me leave to speak, sir, on this subject as if I knew something of it. Woman is the bauble of man's passions—always so when he has no deep respect for her purity of character or sentiment. You would be troubled with many unpleasant reflections, after the first season of your liking was over, and the check which you would continually find me to your intercourse with society would first manufacture regrets and then turn them into hate. Knowing this from the experience which I have personally had of the evanescent ardor of mere passion, it would be unjust in me not to undeceive you, or not to reject a bond of ultimate misery for both. There are other reasons, less magnanimous than those which I have stated, that induce me to respectfully refer your offer back to your reflections, but of these I need not speak. I find no fault with you for your frank estimation of the present degradation I am living under, but I am in a whirlpool from which I cannot rise by means of your proffer, and all I can do is to trim my bark to sail as decently as possible till I am eventually swallowed in its vortex.

For the compliments which you pay my qualities of heart and mind I feel grateful, of course; but I commend you, if you are sincere, to think as little of them as possible hereafter. What destiny I am reserved for I do not know, but I do know that I cannot eke it out in the current you propose. If, therefore, you see me again—for I have no doubt that you have been acquainted with me more intimately than you pretend—maintain your *incognito*, and do not encourage yourself that an appeal in person, under any circumstances, will alter the resolution which I have here set down. That you may not hope that this determination was founded in caprice, I repeat there are circumstances of a private and selfish nature, which, apart from any conclusion of philosophy, would oblige me to decide definitely against you.

Yours with respect,   H. J.

To REUBEN JARVIS,
     New York Post-office."

Shortly after this novel correspondence Helen had a serious quarrel with Robinson, and he, leaving the house in anger, swore he would never set foot in it again. For fear the oath would prevent her ever meeting him she left herself and took up her quarters at Mrs. Townsend's, No. 41 Thomas street. This house deserves more than a passing mention, as it was here that hate, fear and jealousy culminated at last in the commission of as dreadful a murder as the most sombre and extravagant imagination could picture. It stood upon the last square next to Hudson street, the centre of a row of dwellings of a pale yellow color, which occupied the middle of the block. It was an elegant two story dwelling, then modern in its build, and furnished in the inside with all the elegant improvements which characterized the latest style of metropolitan architecture. "This house," says a strong and graphic writer of the day, "was the centre of attraction for all the roystering spirits of town. In the rear was a garden decorated with arbors—picturesque retreats, covered in the summer season with lovely garlands, evergreens and flowers, and all the beauties of the vegetable world. Under the bright shining moon, climbing up the dark blue heaven during the soft summer months, these arbors would be filled with syrens and champagne, pineapples and pretty *filles de joie*, talking, chattering, signing and dancing, and throwing out all the blandishments their talents and qualities could muster. The woman who keeps this place is fitted for its mysteries. Her splendid establishment has long been the pride of the gay reprobates from one end of the Union to the other. She unites under the same flashing eye the manners of a lady, the elegance of a Lais, the passion of a fury, and the cunning of a serpent. In Greece and in Rome they had their celebrated women in a certain line; their Laises, their Aspasias, their goddesses, who united beauty, business, ambition and luxuriousness in the same person, and under the same roof. The profusion and extravagance of the celebrated Aspasia, ministered to by Pericles, the greatest ornament of Athens, was not greater than was nightly seen during the summer season at the hotel in Thomas street."

But Robinson kept his oath, and over a year had passed when he and Helen next met, and it was then by the purest accident. The lovely Augustan, piqued at his long continued absence, sought

to color her weariness with new amours, one of which took her to
Albany. On the morning that she returned to New York it so
happened that Robinson was at the wharf, all unconscious of the
fact that his former sweetheart was a passenger by the boat. She had
no sooner put her shapely foot upon the gang-plank, however, before there was an immediate recognition. To Helen it was a joy-
ful one, whatever it was to Robinson. She greeted him with
demonstrative rapture, and he received her caresses as of yore.
Once more the serpent was coiled about the fawn. This was in the
first week of October, 1835.

But this pleasantly murmuring stream of love did not long run
smoothly. Crimination and recrimination ensued as formerly, and
the flame of jéalousy flared up into a lurid blaze. Helen became
possessed of the information that Robinson had poisoned, or attempted to poison a young girl whom he had first ruined, and who
then stood in the way of his marriage with the daughter of his employer, to whom he was paying court. At any rate the girl died
under suspicious circumstances. Helen taunted Robinson with this
crime, and his rage and fear can easily be imagined. They had a
stormy interview, but the warm love of the beautiful woman thawed
her resentment eventually into a flow of tears. Robinson saw his
opportunity and seized it. Amid mutual embraces they resolved
to blot out the past and begin anew. This was particularly agreeable to Helen, as she had then formed the intention of coercing her
lover into marriage with her, and, on one particularly tender occasion, he promised her that it should be so. Nothing more was
wanting to make her happy, and each hour was saturated with sunshine.

But alas! the sunshine was but a delusion—only the golden
fringe of the dark cloud overhanging her. Robinson deliberately
lied in the promise he made, and before long Helen knew it. It
then became clear to her mind that his ultimate intention was to
discard her altogether, and when she was told more clearly of his
matrimonial prospects in another quarter, she was transformed from
a woman, naturally born to love and be loved, into a tigress. In a
gust of rage she left New York and went to Philadelphia, whence
she sent her deceitful paramour a threatening letter, containing
covert insinuations that should he dare to trifle with her, she would

not only balk his marriage scheme but would acquaint his employer whence came the money that had bought many of her rustling silks and gleaming bracelets.

Then it was that murder crept into the soul of Robinson and made its hideous lair there.   He felt that he *must* rid himself some- how of Helen or he was lost.   He was goaded on to the commis- sion of the bloody deed by an exposure of his licentious course to the lady he hoped to marry, made anonymously.   He attributed it at once to Helen, and hate turned the balance of his resolve.   It was settled—she should die !

Time had now drifted along as far as the month of April, 1836. In that fatal week of the murder, and on the day just preceding it, he received the following note :

" THURSDAY EVENING, 7 *o'clock.*

MY DEAR FRANK.—You have passed your promise by two nights, and you have not thought proper to send me a single line, even in the shape of an excuse.   Do you think I will endure this ? Shall *I*, who have rejected hundreds for your sake, sit contented under treatment which seems invented for my mortification—nay, for my destruction.   Pause, Frank, pause ere you drive me to madness.   Come to see me to-night, or to-morrow night if you do not receive this before 12 o'clock.   Come and see me and tell me how we may renew the sweetness of our earlier acquaintance, and forget all our past unhappiness in future joy.   Slight me no more. Trample on me no further.   Even the worm will turn under the heel.   You have known how I have loved—do not, oh do not pro- voke the experiment of seeing how I can hate.   But, in hate or in love,   Your HELEN."

The crafty Robinson answered as follows :

" FRIDAY MORNING, *half past one.*

I did not get your note till one o'clock, so that will excuse my not having come to you at once.   It so happens that I cannot come till Saturday night.   I cannot explain the reason why on paper, but try and be satisfied it is a good one, until I can assure you of it in person.   I shall come about nine o'clock, and I wish you would let me in yourself.   I have read your note with pain—I ought to say displeasure—nay anger. Women are never so foolish as when they threaten. You are never so foolish as when you threaten *me*. Keep quiet until I come on Saturday night, and then we will see if we cannot be better friends hereafter. Do not tell any person I shall come. Yours, ———."

This note, though without signature, is evidently in the hand-writing of Robinson. It was not so identified, however, and consequently was not produced at the time of the trial in the case.

It was the preliminary overture to the tragedy, and, acting on its text, Robinson on the next morning prepared to carry out his dire intent. He went about his business as usual; no one noticed from his manner that anything unusual weighed upon his soul; the same demeanor which had always characterized him was maintained, and he was as serene and unruffled as in his most listless and uninterested hours. Beneath the flowers which bloomed upon his cheek, however, there raged the pent up fires of hell, ready to burst forth like the volcano and strew everything with ruin.

At first he thought of accomplishing his purpose with poison, and, directed by that idea, went to the store of Dr. Chabert, better known by the title of the Fire King, and who kept a drug shop a door or two above Pearl street, in Broadway. He had been there before, and was slightly known to the clerk by the name of Douglass.

He asked for arsenic, but the clerk not liking his manner, refused the sale, and he went away without his object. Foiled in this aim, he dared not double his chances of detection by going to another druggist's, but returned to his store in Maiden lane with the endeavor to force his cogitations to some new issue. Arriving there, his sharpened senses sprung upon the means to accomplish his intent as soon as he entered, and the sight of the hatchet, which now hangs as a terrible memento in the office window of the New York *National Police Gazette*, determined instantly the horrid fashion of his crime.

When Robinson went home that evening he slipped the hatchet underneath his cloak and deposited it within his trunk. On the following night he tied it by the string, which is still seen upon its handle, to the tassel of his wrapper, and, thus prepared, set out to the residence of his unhappy mistress for the performance of a deed which was to electrify half a hemisphere with horror. The murder might now be said to be upon its feet.

Helen awaited him anxiously, as she still entertained some hopes of effecting a perfect reconciliation. All this while her fate was steadily marching upon her.

Black purposes sympathize with darkness, and Robinson, usually so fond of the spirit of Broadway, now turned down to the gloomy and narrow avenue that runs next to it on the North River side. Hurrying along he soon reached Thomas street, and drawing the folds of his wrapper well around him, that no chance observation should pierce his thick disguise, he in a few moments more stood upon Mrs. Townsend's stoop. Twice he impatiently rang the bell, and at the second summons the landlady came to the door. The cautious Rosina, however, did not open it merely because there was a summons of impatience on the outside. That was not her mode of doing business, and she was the more careful of her rule on this occasion, as her furniture and conscience had recently suffered from the irruption of some riotous characters, whom one of her girls had incautiously let in. Mrs. Townsend, therefore, under this combination of restrictive influences, inquired through the panel who was there, and being answered that the visitor was for Helen, and recognizing the voice, she let the comer in. It was then that she recognized the person in the cloak to be Richard P. Robinson, and, telling him to wait a moment, went to the parlor door to inform Helen that her lover had come.

Robinson answered not a word in reply to the landlady, but pulled his hat over his eyes to hide his face from the light, and drawing up his cloak for the same purpose, hurried through the entry to the stairs. As he passed the parlor door he turned upon his heel for a moment, as if he would wait for Helen to come out. While he paused, and while Mrs. Townsend's head was in the front room, Emma French and Maria Stevens, two of the girls, passed by and spoke to him. Robinson did not raise his head, or give other token that he heard the words, and as the speakers glided off he turned to go up stairs. At this moment Helen issued from the parlor, and catching him by the cloak, exclaimed, loud enough for Mrs. Townsend to hear, " Ah, my dear Frank, how glad I am you have come." Robinson made no reply, and they both went up stairs together.

It was between nine and ten o'clock on the night of the 11th of April, 1836, when Richard P. Robinson and Helen Jewett retired to their chamber at the house No. 41 Thomas street. For an hour neither of them issued from the room (except that Helen once ran down for a moment to receive a pair of shoes), but at eleven o'clock she made her appearance in *dishabille* at the head of the stairs and called for a bottle of champagne. She proposed to wait and take the salver of wine and glasses from Rosina at the head of the stairs, probably at Robinson's desire to prevent Mrs. Townsend from coming in the room; but it so happened that the demand for wine that night had been very great at No. 41 Thomas street, and that Mrs. T. was obliged to descend into the cellar. This occasioned a loss of considerable time, during which Helen's patience gave out; so, when Mrs. Townsend went up stairs with the salver, she found she was obliged to knock for admittance. Helen opened the door at her summons, and as the mistress of the house handed in the tray she saw Robinson lying on the bed, with his head on his arm and his face turned to the wall. The foot of the bed stood towards the door, the curtains being thrown back, and of the kind used with a French bedstead, it exposed the whole surface of the couch to any person standing at the entrance of the room. Helen, perceiving that the presence and position of her lover had been observed, asked the landlady, in the way of courtesy, if she would not come in and join her in a glass; but, alas for her! the landlady refused, and when the door closed upon her this poor creature virtually bade good night to the rest of the world forever. With the departure of Mrs. Townsend she looked her last upon a human face, save that of the demon on the bed, if his might so be called.

Gradually all the inmates of that house of sinful luxury retired, and with the rest the beautiful Augustan, still as blooming to the eye as when she left her home, sought in a serpent's arms the soft repose of sleep. At one o'clock everything was hushed within that Palace of the Passions. At two, or perhaps a little later, Maria Stevens, who lay directly opposite the room of Helen, and who was wakeful, heard in the opposite chamber the sound of a heavy blow, which, though it did not resound, seemed to shudder in the floor. It was followed by a long and heavy moan, which inspired her with a compassionate desire to know more. After whispering silence to her companion she got up out of bed and listened at her door; but nothing further followed, save two or three deep and broken sobs. Presently, and as she was about

ROBINSON'S ESCAPE OVER THE FENCE.

returning to her couch, she heard the door of Helen's chamber softly open and as softly close again, and in the next moment a person left it for the stairs. Turning her door knob gently she pulled it suddenly open, and saw a person going down. He was wrapped in a cloak, and bore in his hand a small glass globe lamp, while something which he held within his mantle seemed to engage the other arm. He was going swiftly but steadily down. Miss Stevens did not follow.

At three o'clock or thereabouts there came a knock at the front door, which aroused Mrs. Townsend, and she was obliged to let a person in. Before retiring to bed again, however, she was a little surprised at perceiving a lamp burning in the parlor in the rear. Such a thing being unusual she went to see about it, and there perceived upon a marble table the glass lamp which belonged to Helen Jewett's room. At the same moment Mrs. Townsend discovered that the back door was open, and the bar which fastened it stood by its side. Supposing that some person was in the yard who would soon return within the house, she returned to her own chamber and waited some ten minutes, when, hearing no one come in, she went to the rear again, and having called "Who's there?" twice, without avail, put up the bar and went up stairs to Helen's room. She found it on the latch, but as she pushed it open a dense volume of offensive and stupefying smoke rushed out and drove her back. Retiring over to Miss Stevens' room the terrified landlady beat against her door and aroused the house. First came out Maria, and leading the way she plunged into the burning chamber. Twice was she and Mrs. Townsend driven back by the stifling torrents, but the vent at length threw up the smother into flame, and there before their eyes, with her transparent forehead half divided with a butcher's stroke, and her silver skin burnt to a cinder where it was not laced with blood, lay all that was left of the mortal remains of the unfortunate Dorcas Doyen.

Robinson made his escape by means of the back yard. He clambered over the fence, losing the cloak he wore in the operation. That particular cloak was one that he had bought from a friend some time before. He had another one, also, of the same description, at his house. In scaling another fence he dropped the bloody hatchet, which he had intended to take with him. He was now directly in the rear of a two-story yellow frame house, in which lived a negress and her daughter. Robinson forced open the cellar door that opened into the yard, and soon burst through the door that opened into the street. The noise awakened the negress, who hailed him. By this time, also, the shrieks of the women in Mrs. Townsend's rang out appallingly upon the night. There was not a moment to be lost. He turned and fled down the street like a deer.

All was confusion and dismay in the Thomas street house. The inmates ran to and fro crazed with terror. Mrs. Townsend opened a front window and cried loudly for the " Watch !" Three or four came immediately, and with their assistance the fire was speedily extinguished. One of them, named Eldridge, found the hatchet, still wet with blood ; and another, named Palmer, found the cloak. Then came Coroner Schureman and a police officer named Brink. Acting upon the story told by Mrs. Townsend, Brink and a fellow officer immediately proceeded to the residence of Robinson, in Dey street. They did not expect to find him there, and were much surprised when they discovered him in bed with his room-mate, Tew, and apparently sound asleep. When he was told that Helen Jewett was murdered, and that he was wanted, he displayed no concern, but simply said " This is a bad business." As he dressed himself the officers noticed that the knees and seat of his pants were marked with whitewash, similar to that on the fence in the yard of Mrs. Townsend. Robinson requested his friend Tew to go with him, shrewdly seeing the necessity of enlisting his sympathy. When confronted with the corpse Robinson was as cold as a statue, and simply repeated, " This is a bad business."

The medical examination occupied the greater portion of the day, and resulted in the following opinion :

" The undersigned are of the opinion, and do certify and believe, first, that Helen Jewett came to her death by a blow inflicted on the head by the hand of some other person. Second, that the blow was inflicted with a heavy instrument, and with great force. Third, that the blow was unexpected, and that the force was such as to immediately destroy life, without a struggle ; and, fourth, that the burning was after the extinction of life.

DAVID L. ROGERS.
JAMES B. KISSAM.

NEW YORK, *April* 10*th*, 1836."

And the verdict of the Coroner's jury was given in the following words :

" It is the opinion of the jury, from the evidence before them, that Helen Jewett came to her death by a blow or blows, inflicted on the head with a hatchet, by the hand of Richard P. Robinson."

The most tremendous excitement followed this murder. The city thought of nothing else, and the papers were full of it. The following article is from the *New York Herald* of April 12, '36:

" VISIT TO THE SCENE.—Yesterday afternoon, about four o'clock, the sun broke out for a moment in splendor. I started on a visit to the scene at 41 Thomas street. On passing through Chapel street I came to the corner of Thomas street, which runs west from behind the Hospital yard to Hudson street. A large crowd of young men stood around the door, No. 41, and several groups along the streets in various directions. The excitement among the young men throughout the city was beginning to spread in all directions.

" The house is two stories and attic, large and elegant, painted yellow, and on the left hand side as you go to Hudson street. It is said to be one of the most splendid establishments devoted to infamous intercourse that the city can show. I knocked at the door; a police officer opened it stealthily. I told him who I was. 'Mr. B. you can enter,' said he, with great politeness. The crowd rushed from behind, seeking also an entrance.

" ' No more can come in,' said the police officer.

" ' Why do you let that man in?' asked one of the crowd.

" ' He is an editor—he is on public duty.'

" ' I entered—I pressed forward to the sitting room or parlor. There I found another police officer in charge of that apartment. The old lady of the house, Mrs. Townsend, was sitting on a sofa, talking to several young men, in a great state of excitement. She described what Helen had said—how she discovered the fire—how she made an alarm—how she called for the watch. The room was elegantly furnished with mirrors, splendid paintings, sofas, ottomans, and every variety of costly furniture. The police officer, when he saw me, said, 'Mr. B., would you like to see the place?'

" ' I would ' replied I.

" He immediately rose—I followed him. We mounted an elegant staircase, dark and gloomy. On reaching the second story the police officer took a key from his pocket and opened the door.

What a sight burst upon me! There stood an elegant double mahogany bed, all covered with burnt pieces of linen, blankets, pillows, black as cinders. I looked around for the object of my curiosity. On the carpet I saw a piece of linen sheet, covering something, as if carelessly flung over it.

THE BODY OF HELEN JEWETT.

" 'Here,' said the police officer, 'here is the poor creature.'

" He half uncovered the ghastly corpse; I could scarcely look at it for a moment or two. Slowly I began to discover the lineaments of the corpse, as one would the beauties of a statue of marble. It was the most remarkable sight I ever beheld—I never have, and never expect to see such another. 'My God!' exclaimed I, 'how like a statue! I can scarcely conceive that form to be a corpse.' Not a vein was to be seen. The body looked as white, as full, as polished as the purest Parian marble. The perfect figure, the exquisite limbs, the fine face, the full arms, the beautiful bust, all, all surpassed in every respect the Venus de Medici, according to the cast generally given of her.

" ' See,' said the police officer, ' she has assumed that appearance within an hour.'

" It was the first process of dust returning to dust. The countenance was calm and passionless—not the slightest appearance of emotion was there. An arm lay over her bosom; the other was inverted and hanging over her head. The left side, down to the waist, where the fire had touched, was bronzed like an antique statue. For a few moments I was lost in admiration at the extraordinary sight—a beautiful female corpse, that surpassed the finest statue of antiquity. I was recalled to her horrid destiny by seeing the dreadful bloody gashes on the right temple, which must have caused instantaneous dissolution.

"I then looked round the room. It was elegant, but wild and extravagant in its ornaments. On the drawers was a small library, composed of light novels, poetry and monthly periodicals. There hung on the wall a beautiful print of Lord Byron as the presiding genius of the place. The books were Byron, Scott, Bulwer's works and the Knickerbocker.

" A work table in a state of disorder stood near by. It was covered with fragments—pen, ink, paper, crayons, pamphlets, etc., etc. Above the mantelpiece hung several theatrical fancy sketches.

" I returned to take a last look at the corpse. What a melancholy sight for beauty, wit and talent, for it is said she possessed all, to come to such a fatal end!

" I came down stairs; the house looked dark and gloomy, all the windows being half shut, but it was throughout splendidly furnished. Such is the scene as it was seen yesterday afternoon.

" This extraordinary murder has caused a sensation in this city never before felt or known. I understand that a large number of fashionable young men, clerks and others, were caught in the various apartments by the police when the cry of fire was given. It was Saturday night. The murdered girl was one of the most beautiful of her degraded *caste*. She was a perfect Millwood. She has seduced by her beauty and blandishments more young men than any known in the police records. She was a remarkable character, and has come to a remarkable end. The house is in danger from the mob; let the authorities see to it. A morbid excitement pervades the city. It is said that she threatened to expose Robinson when she lived, having discovered that he was paying attention to a respectable young lady. This threat drove him to madness. On Saturday she walked up and down Broadway half the day, nodding to her acquaintances among the dissipated young men.

"Helen Jewett was well known to every pedestrian on Broadway. Last summer she was famous for parading Wall street in an elegant green dress, and generally with a letter in her hand. She used to look at the brokers with great boldness of demeanor— had a peculiar walk, something in the style of an English woman.

"During her residence here she carried on an extensive country correspondence with every part of the Union. We learn from the post-office that during last summer she usually received from three to eight letters a day. Her postage bill exceeded that of several brokers in Wall street. Her private correspondence is of a most remarkable character, resembling that of Abelard and Eloisa."

A strong effort was immediately made to save the life of Robinson. A friend of his, named Gray, was prominent in this attempt. No stone was left unturned. First of all it was sought to cast imputation upon the veracity of the women in Thomas street, founded upon their known character. Anonymous letters were written to the newspapers, insinuating that Helen had loaned Mrs. Townsend a considerable amount of money, and that it was quite likely that the deed was perpetrated by the debtor as an escape from the obligation. But, unfortunately for Robinson, just at this time Gray was detected in the commission of a crime and sent to jail.

On the 16th day of April, six days after the commission of the crime, Robinson was brought before a police magistrate, preparatory to his case being sent to the Grand Jury. Ogden Hoffman and William M. Price appeared as his counsel. The following was the result of the examination:

" *City of New York*, ss. : Richard P. Robinson, brought out of prison to be examined on a charge of having, on the night of Saturday, the 9th day of April, inst., caused the death of Helen Jewett by inflicting a blow or blows on the head with a hatchet, and having been informed by the magistrate that he was at liberty to refuse to answer any question that might be put to him, in the presence of his counsel answers as follows and says: That he is innocent of the charge brought against him, and, by the advice of counsel, declines answering any questions that may be put to him.

Taken the 16th day of April, A. D. 1836.

O. M. LOWNDS, *Special Justice.*"

The Grand Jury took the matter up on the 19th of April. They examined twenty-seven witnesses. A true bill for wilful murder was found against the prisoner. Robinson was immediately remanded for trial.

As might be expected, the churches took hold of the sensation and rang the moral changes on it. On the Sunday following the murder sermons were preached everywhere with crime as their text. In the Chatham Street Chapel, a famous place of Methodist revival, all young females were advised to reject every suitor who had ever been known to visit a house of evil repute. A noted divine, Dr. Brownlee, made an eloquent appeal for the murderer, and looked coolly upon the blotting out of Helen's young life as a deed to be commended. While all this was going on, and the day for the trial was approaching, public sentiment shaped itself into two popular expressions of opinion—one for and the other against the prisoner. The commisserative class was by far the most numerous—the sympathy for Robinson running so high that the fast young men of the day wore a fancy glazed cap like Robinson's, which was known as the " Frank Rivers Cap "—a name by which the young murderer was known in the parlors where he was wont to spend his evenings. On the day he was brought to the Court of Oyer and Terminer, at the City Hall, there was an immense representation of these caps, the owners of which cheered Robinson when he appeared, but reviled and hooted every " soiled dove " summoned to testify against him.

Just previous to the trial Robinson received a mysterious letter from his friend Gray, who was in the Bridewell, which was to the effect, in the main, that the negro woman through whose cellar Robinson made his way on the night of the murder would not appear against him. There was something else in the letter, but its nature can only be conjectured. After Robinson read it he thought a moment and then said, "I think I can get some one to do it." A few nights after Maria Stevens, the woman who saw Robinson stealing down the stairs, lamp in hand, was found dead in her bed! People wondered, and then forgot it.

Three days previous to the trial Robinson sent Gray the following letter, which is an admirable index of the cold-blooded nature of the assassin:

"W. D. G.—My pen is poor—I can't use it. It is worn off one side, like a crab. In my last note I perfectly recollect using the word conjointly. I see, however, you understood me and set me right. But the idea of partnership in keeping *her* is laughable. Grammercy! I liked to have split a laughing when I read it. And you gave *her* black eyes! Haven't these folks mistaken one girl for another? Does my journal edify you? Whether Mrs. Potter will be a witness or not I can't say—Mrs. M. probably will. It is no sign that you are not a witness because you didn't go down last week; only those, I believe, were subpœnaed whom they wished to give *recognizances*. They will try to injure my '*character*.' Don't be caught napping. *My trial commences to-morrow, Thursday.* Saturday night I'll either be free or *crazy;* and as soon afterwards I will pay you a visit as I possibly can. It's lucky it's cold, or how the court room would smell to-morrow. When do you have the doctors come to see you? They are with me a good deal, smoking and drinking, and a real clever, merry set. It's about dinner time, and I shall have to break off sudden, as soon as I hear the doors begin to open. One of the Drs. has just left me and gone for a couple of bottles of porter—will be back in five minutes or less. I am very busy to-day, fixing to go down to-morrow, and writing and poking names out of my sleepy head. Done 1 June. OLD PORT.

"Don't tell Jewell of our correspondence."

The trial began on the 2d day of June, 1836. The Court of

Oyer and Terminer was densely packed, while a large crowd of citizens surged around the exterior of the building. The prisoner was brought in by a squad of tipstaves, and looked, it is said, as bland and careless as a bridegroom. Messrs. Hoffman, Price and Maxwell, his counsel, accompanied him. He was dressed in a suit of blue, wore a light curly *wig*, and held in his hand a cap; whereas, on the night of the murder, he wore a black hat. This was a silent feature of the process toward proving an *alibi*—the line of defence determined upon.

It took five hours to get a jury, after which the District Attorney, Mr. Phœnix, made an impressive address, and called the first witness, Mrs. Rosina Townsend. The following testimony given by her, as well as the summary of the trial, is from the account written by the present Chief of Police, George Washington Matsell:

Mrs. Townsend described the occurrences of the fatal night. She mentioned the knock at the door at nine or half past nine; the entrance of Robinson, enveloped in a cloak, with a *hat* drawn over his eyes; his ascent into Helen's chamber, with Helen following from the parlor; the call by Helen, about 11 o'clock, for a bottle of champagne; Robinson's appearance as he lay in bed when witness took the bottle up, and her notice that his head, which now seemed covered with so full a suit of hair, was extremely thin on the back part where it was parted. At a quarter past twelve that night she locked up her house and went to bed. At three she was awakened by a knocking, and, having let a friend of one of the women in, she discovered a light in the back parlor, as if some person had gone into the yard. She called at the back door twice for the person to return, but, receiving no answer, she barred the door and went up to Helen's room, to which the light in the back parlor belonged. Helen's door was on the latch; she shoved it open, when the smoke rushed out so that it drove her back. She then gave the alarm of fire, upon which Miss Stevens came forth, rushed into the burning chamber and discovered the dead body. The testimony of Mrs. Townsend occupied the entire day; but, though she was subject to the most rigid cross-examination, she sustained the previous statements made by her, before the Coroner and Grand Jury, without departure or prevarication.

SECOND DAY.

The excitement which had filled the avenues of the City Hall on the first day of the trial of the young murderer had vastly increased on the morning of the second, and the instant the prisoner was taken into the court room the deluge poured behind him, so that he and his conductors were actually borne by the current into the further end of the apartment before they could resist its impulse. The flood swelled upwards even against the walls, and many spectators held their fortunate places by fixing their fingers in the mouldings of the doors and windows, while some, more fortunate still, stayed a precarious foothold with their handkerchiefs thrown round a column, or fixed to a supporting nail. The noise and confusion proceeding from this crammed and overflowing auditory were so great that it was impossible to proceed with the trial, and also impossible, under the circumstances, to correct it. The Court, therefore, after half an hour of vexation, were obliged to retire with the jury and the prisoner into the Common Council room opposite, until the room was cleared.

In the course of an hour the object was accomplished; the Court retook possession of the room, and the agitated elements were kept within restraint by the attendance of fifty additional marshals. The Court then commenced its business, and it was remarked, by certain close observers in attendance, that, during the previous excitement, the prisoner was the only person who did not seem to be the least flurried by the disturbance.

Doctor Rogers, who had held the post mortem on the body, recognized the bloody hatchet, found by the watchman in the yard, as an instrument fitted to the crashes in the skull of the deceased, and the *watchmen* and officers testified to the finding of the hatchet and the cloak in the rear yards; also as to the blood upon the weapon, and as to the string upon its handle being the separated half of that which still hung to the tassel of the cloak. The *porter* in Hoxie's store, in which Robinson was a clerk, then identified the hatchet as one which belonged to that establishment, and which had been missing therefrom ever since the day before the murder. Dennis Brink, the police officer who arrested Robinson, testified that the prisoner's pantaloons, on the morning of the arrest, bore the appearance of whitewash on the legs, as if he had got it in scrambling over the fences in his flight, and that the cloak, of which Robinson now denied the ownership, had also the same mark of whitewash on the tassel. In consequence of Robinson having denied possession of this cloak, Miss Elizabeth Salters was here called, who swore that she knew it, and that it belonged to the prisoner. She knew it, because, once when the prisoner visited her, the tassel had been broken off, and she had sewed it on for him. This 'witness further testified, that on the afternoon previous to the murder she had been out with Helen Jewett, and returned with her about six o'clock, at which time a gentleman who had followed them home went with Helen to her room. Charles Tyrrel, an acquaintance of the prisoner, had seen him, on the night of the murder, leave his boarding house about eight o'clock, dressed in a dark coat, and, as he thought, a cap. The witness thought, by the way the prisoner swung his cloak, he could not have had a hatchet under it. He left the prisoner at the corner of Beekman street. Emma French testified that she saw the prisoner enter Mrs. Townsend's house between nine and ten o'clock on the night of the murder, and that he wore a *hat* and cloak. There were two Frank Rivers who visited Helen, but this one was the prisoner.

It being now ten o'clock in the evening the court adjourned, and the prisoner was led back to jail.

THIRD DAY.

On this morning the Sheriff, with a *posse* of an hundred marshals, managed to preserve order about the Hall, and to prevent the scenes which had occurred the two previous days. Cordons of officers were stretched across all the avenues which led up stairs, and an auditory barely sufficient to fill the seats was let in. The prisoner, attended by Mr. Lyons, the prison keeper, and as special officer, took his seat within the bar some time before the opening, and appeared as collected and serene as before, and held a long consultation with his counsel, in which he exhibited much spirit and energy of manner.

The proceedings of this day commenced with the introduction of William Van Nest and Samuel Van Nest, two public porters, whose posts of business were in Maiden lane, near the prisoner's store, and who both testified to having carried letters to and fro between the prisoner and the deceased. Joseph Hoxie, Senior, identified one of a number of letters produced by the prosecution as the prisoner's, and his son identified some other portions of the prisoner's correspondence. Anthony Gilfert, a fellow-clerk of the prisoner, also identified nine more. Miss Elizabeth Salters was here recalled, and testified to having found a handkerchief beneath the pillow of the murdered body, marked with the initials of Bill Easy, whereupon a fine looking young man, named George T. Marsden, appeared upon the stand, to admit the title of Bill Easy, and to explain that he had given to Helen the handkerchief alluded to, in order that she should mark it with his initials. Sarah Dunscomb, the colored woman, who waited upon Helen's room, was here introduced, to state that the gentleman who came in with the deceased on the afternoon of the murder, at early candle light, was not Robinson, and that he went away at half past seven o'clock; after which the gentleman himself, whose name was Edward Strong, came forward and testified to the circumstances and duration of his visit; as they were of a very common character we need not give them. Frederick W. Gourgas, a clerk in the apothecary shop of Dr. Chabert, testified that he had seen the prisoner in the drug store some four or five times; that he gave his name there as Douglass, and some ten or twelve days previous to the murder had applied for the purchase of some poison. The description of poison which he asked for was arsenic, and his excuse in asking for it was that he wanted it to kill rats. The witness did not sell the prisoner the arsenic, as it was contrary to the rules of the store.

Elizabeth Stewart, the woman at whose house the prisoner had established a Miss Chancellor, under the name of Douglass, was next called to the stand. On being sworn, she testified that the prisoner at the bar had come to a house which she kept in Reade street, to engage a room for himself and a young female. At this point the witness was suddenly interrupted by Mr. Price, of counsel for the prisoner, who objected to the testimony, unless the District Attorney intended to show that the female in question was the deceased. The District Attorney replied that it was his object to show by the witness that the prisoner went by the name of Doug-

lass in other places as well as in Doctor Chabert's store.   Mr. Price
objected to this description of evidence, as being inadmissible and
illegal, and assumed that the circumstances of the prisoner attempting to obtain poison to kill Helen Jewett, or any other woman, was
not proper, under an indictment in which the date, the hour and
the weapon were specifically charged.   The Court agreed with the
views of Mr. Price, and the testimony of Gourgas was stricken
from the record, and Mrs. Stewart was informed that she might
leave the stand.

Mr. Robert Morris, who assisted the District Attorney, now
offered to read the letters of the prisoner to Helen, which had been
identified as his handwriting; but, on Mr. Hoffman objecting to
this course, the District Attorney, with a singular and indeed an
inexplicable liberality, arose and consented to waive their introduction in the case, informing the Court at the same time that the
prosecution would now rest their case.

A great bustle and whispering followed this announcement, and
the auditory, which had listened to the terrible amount of proof
against the prisoner, settled into breathless silence to hear what testimony could possibly be brought forward in his favor.

THE DEFENCE.

The audience seemed scarcely to draw a breath when Mr. Ogden
Hoffman rose to open for the defence.   To them it seemed that the
black portals of the case were shut against the introduction of any
rebutting fact, and the feeling which inclined all ears towards the
counsel was rather one of curiosity, as to how his ingenuity would
fence against defeat, than an expectation, ever so remote, that he
could disturb the proofs which had been adduced against the
prisoner.

Mr. Hoffman commenced with deploring the disadvantages under which the counsel for the prisoner labored, as compared with
the prosecution, in the procuration of witnesses for the defence, and
with great ingenuity assumed that the paucity of his testimony
would be rather the result of artificial obstacles in his way than
the fact that there was no evidence in existence in his behalf.
After considerable wandering eloquence, now directed against the
character of the frail women whom circumstances had made the

main witnesses for the law, and now extending to the boy at the bar in streams of spurious sympathy, he seized the enthusiasm which he had created while at its height, and suddenly developed that his defence was in the bold assumption that, at the time when the women of the house in Thomas street swore the prisoner was under that roof, he was more than a mile and a half away, and, consequently, could not have been the murderer who had crushed the skull of Helen Jewett with the hatchet, and who had fled across the fences for his escape. He promised to prove this by the testimony of a witness who, by himself, was worth a host of the polluted wantons who had brazened it out upon the stand against his client, and to further prove, by a watchman of the night, that Mrs. Townsend, who was the hinge and pivot of the prosecution, had admitted, on the morning after the murder, that it would be impossible for her to identify Mr. Robinson as the person who had been with the deceased. The former of these statements took not only the auditory but the opposing counsel by surprise, and with a sentiment that partook somewhat of the nature of confusion, they saw Robert Furlong, the grocer of Cedar and Nassau street, present himself as the champion of the crisis. All eyes were riveted upon this man as he took the stand ; but though a flush and an alternate pallor came once or twice upon his cheek as he moved forward, he soon conquered the agitation and became the picture of composure.

After being sworn, Furlong testified that he was thirty-three years of age ; that he kept a family grocery on the corner of Cedar and Nassau streets, and that he had been a grocer for twenty-six years. He knew the prisoner, from his having been frequently in his store to buy segars. The last time the prisoner had come to his store was at half past nine on the night of the murder ; he remained there until full fifteen minutes *past ten*, at which time, the store being closed up, he went away. He was sure of the time, because the prisoner and himself compared their watches together. The prisoner on that occasion wore a dark frock coat and a cap. It was more than a mile from his store to Mrs. Townsend's, in Thomas street, so the prisoner could not have reached there within an hour of the time stated. The witness, after the murder, had visited Robinson twice in his prison.

Though the manner of this witness showed plainly to all observers that he was bribed and perjured, his cross-examination, strange to say, was very light, and neither then, nor in the subsequent stages of the case, were any of the numerous accessible witnesses produced who could have shown that he was notorious as a liar, and entirely undeserving, even in the most trifling matters, of belief.* At the close of Furlong's evidence it was ten o'clock at night, and the court adjourned, and the spectators went home wondering and puzzled at the strange testimony which they had heard. Most of them, however, were not so much puzzled at the contradiction of the words of the last witness with the former testimony, as with the thought whence a mortal man could derive the satanic courage to oppose alone the entire artillery of Heaven's truth, in the hope to bear it down

FOURTH DAY.

More greedy still than ever did the excited multitude swarm round the avenues which led to the court room on the fourth day. The extraordinary testimony of Furlong was the common theme of every mouth, and thousands stood patiently in the nearer portions of the Park throughout the day, on the mere hope of hearing, from time to time, such fragments of new proof as might pass from the trial chamber to the outside crowd.

The proceedings in the case were renewed by calling, on the part of the defence, Peter Colyer, a watchman, to impeach the veracity of Mrs. Townsend in the case. Colyer was one of the watchmen who had answered the alarm by rushing into Mrs. Townsend's house on the night of the murder, and while in the parlor on the following morning, had held a conversation with a woman named Jones, who bore an extraordinary likeness to Mrs. Townsend, and whom it appears the witness supposed it to be. It was the conversation which thus took place that he was called upon to relate. Colyer swore, therefore, that Mrs. Townsend had told him that when Robinson had come to the house the night before he wore a *cap*, and that she did not think she would know him again if she should meet him in the street. He further stated that all the

* In a few weeks after the trial this man committed suicide by jumping from the deck of a vessel into the North River.

girls on that occasion, except one, said that they did not know the prisoner ; the one who said she did was named Maria Stevens.

Upon this witness leaving the stand, Mr. Maxwell, for the defence, with an assumption of great candor, inquired of the District Attorney if he had Maria Stevens in the court among the list of witnesses. Mr. Phœnix, however, replied very coolly that he had not, inasmuch as *she was dead*, and anticipated Mr. Maxwell's intended flourish by the remark that, were she alive, she would be a most important witness for the prosecution.

Mrs. Rosina Townsend was here recalled, and testified that Maria Stevens died at the house of Mrs. Gallagher, in Chapel street, on the Wednesday week previous to the trial. The witness also denied knowing the watchman Colyer, or of having held any such conversation with him as he had described. After she had retired a witness, named R. G. Moulton, identified the cloak found in the rear of Mrs. Townsend's premises on the morning of the murder as one which he had seen the prisoner wear, and which the prisoner told him he had torn at the tassel on a sleigh riding party.

James Tew, the room-mate of Robinson, testified that on the night of the murder the prisoner, Mr. Tyrrel, Moulton and himself, left their boarding house at 42 Dey street together, at about eight o'clock. He left the prisoner in Broadway and returned to Dey street at a quarter past eleven and went to bed. The prisoner was not in bed at that time ; but when the witness woke in the night he found Robinson by his side. He did not look at his watch when he woke, but supposed it was between one and two o'clock.

Wm. H. Lane, another watchman, was here called to corroborate the testimony of the watchman Colyer, as to the conversation of the latter with Mrs. Townsend.

Daniel Lyons, the head keeper of the Bellevue Prison, and Henry Burnham, a deputy keeper, next testified to the fact that Robinson had his head shaved while in prison and assumed a wig.

Here took place a debate as to whether the letters of the prisoner to the deceased should not now be put in evidence by the prosecution, notwithstanding their previous waiving, but as the argument ran as far into the night as ten o'clock, the court adjourned till the following day without hearing it to a close.

FIFTH DAY.

On this morning the argument as to the admission of the letters was resumed, but resulted in a compromise that one of the letters, to be selected by the District Attorney, should be read, and no more. A letter of the 14th November, 1835, directed to Helen at Mrs. Berry's, demanding the return of his miniature, and reproaching her for retaining in her possession evidence to effect his personal safety, was then selected and read; after which the list of witnesses was finished by Doctor Rogers being recalled to testify that he thought the stains upon the hatchet were those of blood instead of rust, and Joseph Hoxie, Jr., to state that his father's store was painted a few days preceding the murder, when both the prisoner and himself got paint upon their pantaloons.

Here ended the testimony of this extraordinary trial; and the District Attorney, after regretting that some witnesses for whom he had sent had not been captured or brought in, reluctantly consented that the evidence on both sides should be closed. The witnesses who had thus failed the prosecution were the colored women who had seen Robinson escape by the cellar door into the street, after the commission of the murder. They had kept out of the way at the instigation of Gray and other agents of the prisoner, and it was owing to this excellently managed portion of the business that his counsel were enabled to make a show for his defence.

At length, by the act of the District Attorney, the inquiry which had agitated the minds of the whole community, and which had been of such vital interest to the young prisoner at the bar, was brought to a close; and amid a silence to which all previous attention had been bustle, his counsel, Mr. Price, rose and commenced the summing up on the part of the defence. He was followed by Robert H. Morris, Esq., who, concluding his address at five o'clock, gave place to Ogden Hoffman.

The appeal of this gentleman in behalf of his youthful client has always been characterized as one of the most magnificent displays of forensic eloquence ever delivered at the bar; now vigorous, now touching, now vehement as fire, and again as tender as if pathos herself were speaking with the accents of a dove. The speech was most remarkable on the one side for its scathing derogation of the abandoned women who had testified against the prisoner,

and on the other for its impassioned and tender allusions to the
" innocent boy " whom these miserable witnesses sought to offer up
as a sacrifice to save one of themselves. From the first to the last
the audience and jury were held almost breathless by the charm,
and when the speaker stopped, the fever which it had bred in the
imaginations of those who heard it, could not be chilled back to
any degree of reason by the ordinary powers of the prosecuting
officer or the cold logic of the Judge. The jury retired at a late
hour in the evening, but, before the Court had concluded to leave
them for the night, a summons was received that they had agreed.

The whisper ran round the room like lightning, and each person
present stretched forward to catch the first glimpse of the foreman
as he entered, as if to tear the secret of the verdict from his looks.
The prisoner himself, who, through all the changes of the previous
acts, had sat so stony and so unimpassioned, now started involuntarily with the common impulse, and inclined his form towards the
door.

Solemnly the jury came in and took their places, but it could be
seen, as they rose to the summons of the clerk, that they were not
free from the prevailing agitation which betrayed itself in the manner of every person else. The eye of the prisoner, and a middle
aged man who sat near him, might at this moment have been seen
to be riveted upon one individual on the jury. They looked at
none other of the panel, but upon him they fixed a gaze of unut-
terable anxiety and peculiar meaning which could not be mistaken.
The person whom they thus stared upon was a man of some
twenty-eight or thirty years of age, with a florid face and dissipated
look, and whose slight shabbiness of attire evinced that he was not
altogether above dependence on the world. For a moment or two
the shabby juryman did not seem to recognize the appeal thus
made to him, but at length turning his eye slowly towards where
the prisoner sat, he gave him to understand, by a slight movement of the eyelid, that all was right.

Almost at the same moment, and before he could rejoice, the
prisoner found himself summoned to look upon the jury, and as he
rose the voice of the clerk made the regular inquiry :

" How say you, gentlemen, do you find the prisoner at the bar
guilty or not guilty ?"

There was a pause—a short and fearful pause—during which the prisoner swallowed his agitation as if to keep his life from escaping out of doors; but then the pause ended, and silence was broken by the reply, Not Guilty! spoken by the foreman in a steady voice.

All in the court room were amazed, and the prisoner, overcome at last, sank back in the arms of one of his counsel and burst into tears The glaze caps who had taken up his cause, and which were stowed away in all parts of the court room, burst out in ebullitions of ap-

COURT SCENE.

plause.   The Judge, of course, checked the exhibition, but perfect order could not be again restored, and the court adjourned in a buzz of confusion, leaving the prisoner to make headway through the throng of mistaken friends who crowded forward to congratulate him, as a swimmer stems the full power of a flood.

Robinson, however, did not receive these overtures with the equanimity which was to have been expected from his previous self-command; he seemed to be overcome with a sudden weakness, and evinced a solemnity of manner that he had not before displayed.   In short, the necessity for further deception was over;

he was free from the law and its power, and privileged to lay by
the dissimulation which had sustained him, and to feel, as near as
his nature would allow, like a man.

As he moved towards the door the crowd followed, and as he
passed along the hall to the main central staircase they pressed in

PAYING THE JURYMAN.

upon him on all sides, so that he and his attendants were obliged to
turn aside into a private chamber, and from thence, after the dis-
persion of the crowd, to leave the building by one of the subterranean doors.

There were five persons with the murderer when he issued in the
air. It was near midnight, and the departing moon had left the

heavens to the sovereignty of the stars. Still there was light sufficient to distinguish objects at considerable distance, and the middle aged friend of Robinson observed, under one of the heavy
sycamores which stand near the central gate at the head of Murray
street, the shabby juryman whom we have alluded to before.
Touching the arm of Robinson significantly, the middle aged person made his excuses to the rest of the party and moved towards
the figure. The person in waiting seemed to understand the action,
for he turned on his heel and walked slowly away, till coming to a
gloomy place, beneath a tree of heavy foliage, they paused. As
they stood there a person who had watched their movements drew
near through the trees behind, but though he could not overhear
the whispered language that passed between them, he observed the
middle aged person dive in his pocket and pass to the juryman a parcel of some description. They then separated—the juryman going
toward Chatham street, and the middle aged friend of the acquitted
murderer turning back towards Broadway.

Thus ended the famous trial, than which there has been no more
interesting one in the history of our courts. The curtain came
down upon the stage, the footlights were out, the play was over.
Robinson, the murderer, walked forth into the sunlight, while poor
Helen, the lovely, fair, frail, misguided girl, rested in her grave.

The young assassin shortly after left for Texas and never returned. But of late there has been a strange sequel to the tragedy, com-
prised in a lawsuit in an Illinois court about the ownership of some
lands which Robinson possessed at the time of the murder. It has
come about in this wise: Mr. Joseph Hoxie was Robinson's employer, and as it was strongly suspected at the time that Robinson's
accounts were not square, the latter gave the certificates of the lands
to Mr. Hoxie to hold as security until an examination should be
made of the books at the store. Robinson fled to Texas. Hoxie
never took any steps in the matter. A few years ago the land was
sold for taxes and bought by J. Y. Scammon. Then it was a mere
waste, but now it is worth $150,000. In the meantime a Mr. Geo.
W. Hill, a lawyer of Chicago, discovered, in going over the records,
the peculiar manner in which Hoxie obtained the certificates, and believing that the title was still vested in him, came on to New York
to investigate. He obtained a quit claim from Hoxie, also the

original certificates, and on his return opened a legal fire upon both Hoxie and his heirs and Robinson and his heirs.

In the meantime Robinson had died in Texas, and made a will leaving the property to a family named McKay, who had been kind to him in his exile. It came to the knowledge of a Texas lawyer that Hill had commenced suit to bar the Robinson heirs from claiming the property, and he informed the McKay family of it. The McKays employed this lawyer, Root by name, who wrote to the Second National Bank of Chicago, asking a reference to a competent solicitor to undertake the defence of their claims. The Second National Bank recommended its own lawyer, Mr. Joseph P. Clarkson. Mr. Clarkson's first concern was to ascertain whether the McKay heirs could prove that the transfer of Robinson's certificates of purchase of the Hyde Park property was in the nature of security, and not an absolute conveyance of the fee. It was remembered that Robinson had a sister, who had remained faithful to her brother during his trial, and who might have knowledge of his transactions with Hoxie. After considerable searching throughout the country this sister, Mrs. Still, was found in St. Louis, where she was a professed spiritualistic medium, though a well educated woman, and was practising as a physician and living in very straitened circumstances. When Mrs. Still was found she told a straightforward story, alleging that the property had been transferred to secure Mr. Hoxie against any loss that might occur from Robinson's suspected defalcations. She said that, after Robinson's acquittal of the charge of murder, Hoxie, Robinson and herself went to Connecticut. It was here that the transfer was made, immediately before Robinson left for Texas. Mrs. Still has a married daughter living in New York, Mrs. Brooks by name. The McKay heirs, conscious that they had no claim of blood relationship upon Robinson's property, and that the will cut off Mrs. Still and her daughter (his heirs-at-law), promised to give Mrs. Brooks $3,000 and five per cent. of the value of all the property of Robinson's which they might recover. There was nothing corrupt in this transaction in the eyes of the law, and it was a matter of simple justice in the eyes of humanity. The other side of the case, however, saw the necessity of impeaching Mrs. Still's evidence, and, with the help of the St. Louis Chief of Police, secured the services of a detective to work on Mrs. Still. This man, by feigning sympathy with her spiritualistic practices, ingratiated himself into her confidence, and persuaded her that the McKay heirs did not intend to keep faith with her, nor give her daughter any portion of the money offered. He then suggested to her to offer to sell out to the other side for $2,000 cash. She followed this suggestion. When Mr. Clarkson ascertained that his only witness had been tampered with, and that the other side could now break down the evidence she had previously given, he immediately withdrew from the case. Mr. McKay's heirs subsequently abandoned their defence for the same reason, and a decree was entered in favor of Hill. Hill afterward brought suit in ejectment against Scammon, who was holding under a tax deed, and secured a judgment in his favor. Mr. Scammon carried the case to the Supreme Court, where it is still pending.

CHAPTER XI.

THE STANWIX HALL TRAGEDY.—NATIVE AMERICAN PARTY.—TOM
HYER.—BILL POOLE.—JOHN MORRISSEY.—LEWIS BAKER.—PAU-
DEEN.—ASSASSINATION OF POOLE.—FATE OF HIS ASSAILANTS.—
LETTER OF JOHN MORRISSEY ON RETIRING FROM THE PRIZE RING.

" 'Murder!' said Nadgett, looking around on the astonished group. *Let no one
interfere.*' The sounding street repeated Murder! Barbarous and dreadful murder!
Murder! Murder! Murder! rolling on from house to house and echoing from stone
to stone, until the voices died away in the distant hum which seemed to mutter the
same word."—DICKENS, *in Martin Chuzzlewit.*

MURDER, violence and rowdyism were never more rampant in
this city than during the Know Nothing excitement, which
was at its zenith in the year 1855.

The growth of this secret political party was very rapid, and it
suddenly became a powerful element in the State. The intolerance
of the new party in New York provoked a hostile spirit among its
opponents which led to many acts of violence. The strongest par-
tizans and most active supporters of the two factions, the " Know
Nothings " and the " Democrats," were found among what is known
in the Metropolis as the " Sporting Fraternity." This class of the
body politic is not much given to industry, except in villany
and roguery, in which branch they excel. They embrace gamblers, prize fighters, ropers, counterfeiters, thieves, pickpockets and
cracksmen. Prominent among the American side of the " Sporting
Fraternity " were Thomas Hyer and William Poole. They were
regarded as the champions of the prize ring, and on account of their
prowess were always the centre of attraction wherever the " Fancy "
would congregate. There were not at that period two more perfectly formed or better physically developed men in the entire city.
" Native here and to the manner born," they felt their superiority, and
it was nothing unusal for their names to appear in the public prints
in connection with some porter house disturbance or street broil.
Tom Hyer, the champion of the American Prize Ring, stood six
feet two inches in height, and was as straight and athletic as an
Indian brave. With a small mouth, compressed lips, straight nose,

piercing black eyes and high forehead, he presented a perfect picture of manly beauty and strength. Faultless in his apparel,
modest in his demeanor, and possessing an innate refinement, he was,
notwithstanding his notoriety as a gambler, tolerated, if not welcomed in respectable circles of society.

Bill Poole was the champion of the rough-and-tumble fighters,
and was the leader of a large faction on the " West Side." Bold,

TOM HYER.

daring and aggressive, with broad shoulders, brawny arms, and a
frame of iron, he was the terror of every bruiser in the city. Both
Hyer and Poole were by trade butchers, and Poole followed his
calling to the last. Between these two men, representing the
American party, and John Morrissey, Lewis Baker and James
Turner, adherents of the Democrats, there was a bitter, relentless
animosity, which it was frequently asserted death only could end
—and how true the prophecy was subsequent events will prove.

Poole, with all his faults, had at least one redeeming trait—he loved his country—and his idea that to be an American was something to boast of, was a constant cause of many of his difficulties. In the early part of 1855 it was well known among the fast men of the city that it needed but the slightest altercation among these men to bring on a collision. Some time in January, Hyer was followed

BILL POOLE.

from Lafayette Hall to Platt's, under Wallack's Theatre, by James Turner and Lewis Baker. From what occurred it was evident they intended to kill him. Hyer was standing in front of the bar when Turner came up and extended his arm across his (Hyer's) face, at the same time uttering an expression which reflected on the legitimacy of Hyer's birth. Hyer expostulated, when Turner and Baker threw off their coats and drew their pistols. Turner discharged his revolver twice at Hyer, one ball grazing his neck. Hyer told Turner that he was armed, but did not want to kill him, and with that he turned around and discharged his pistol at the wall. Hyer detecting Turner in the act of again cocking his revolver, grasped him by the neck and threw him to the floor. While engaged in finishing Turner, Baker attacked Hyer from behind, using the butt of his revolver on his head. Hyer suddenly turned on Baker and served him the same as he had Turner. This lively encounter was witnessed by more than a dozen persons, a majority of whom were the friends of Turner and Baker, but not one showed any inclination to lend a hand. By this time an officer came down into the saloon, but seeing the situation of affairs, declined to interfere, notwithstanding he was ordered by Hyer to arrest Baker. Hyer thereupon took hold of Baker and dragged him from the saloon to the street. Baker struggled fiercely while Hyer was bringing him up stairs, and he managed to cut Hyer's fingers with a knife, but Hyer maintained his grip.

This affair created great excitement, happening as it did in a well known resort on Broadway, and pistols became everywhere in demand among the adherents of the contending parties.

John Morrissey, who has now sown his wild oats, then ranked high in the fistic arena. Between him and Poole there had for some time existed a bitter feud. Morrissey, who was about the equal of Poole, physically, was not beneath him in either courage, tenacity or endurance, and was always eager for the fray that would decide their superiority in the art of gouging, biting and kicking, and all the other phases of rough-and-tumble bar room fighting. Poole, desirous of accommodating Morrissey, offered to bet him $50 that he would name a place in New York where Morrissey would not dare to meet him and fight. Morrissey covered the money, and Poole named the Christopher street pier, which was within two blocks of Poole's residence. Morrissey seeing the utter uselessness of engaging with Poole under such circumstances, paid forfeit, but declared that Poole could not name another place. Again the $50 was put up and Poole named Amos street pier—only one square above the first named place—time, seven o'clock in the morning. Morrissey, nothing daunted, agreed to meet him. On arriving the next morning, accompanied by a dozen men, his carriage was surrounded by a crowd, numbering nearly two hundred persons. As he alighted he was knocked down and kicked unmercifully, and but for his friends,

would undoubtedly have been killed. Such treatment was not calculated to make Morrissey tractable or docile, and he nursed his
wrath until the evening of Feb. 24, 1855, at which time, while drinking with some boon companions in the back room of the newly opened Stanwix Hall, which was then located opposite the Metropolitan
Hotel, on Broadway, he recognized Poole's voice, who was standing
in front of the bar drinking with some of his companions. As
might be expected, they came together. Morrissey came toward
Poole and poured out a torrent of abuse. Parties surrounded
them and endeavored to prevent an encounter, when Morrissey drew
an Allen's revolver and snapped it three times while pointed at
Poole's head. Poole drew his revolver on Morrissey, and Morrissey
pleaded for another pistol, which was not forthcoming. Mark Maguire, king of the newsboys, here interfered, and asked Poole if he
was going to murder a man in cold blood. This only enraged
Poole the more, whereupon he seized two carving knives from off
the lunch counter, and throwing them down, invited Maguire to an
encounter, which Maguire declined. During the altercation Baker
came in, having been told by a messenger that Morrissey was quarrelling with Poole. Baker was quiet, he understanding the situation at a glance. Officers came in and arrested Morrissey and Poole.
The officer having Poole in charge took him to the station house.
After being discharged from arrest, Poole, accompanied by Charles
Lozier, his brother-in-law, and Charley Shay, returned to Stanwix
Hall, ostensibly to apologize to the proprietor, but really to talk
the matter over among his companions. Morrissey, who had but
recently married, and was then living with his father-in-law at 55
Hudson street, having promised the officer that he would not go
above Canal street again that evening, kept his word. He went
home, and while he may have been the primary and unthinking
cause of what subsequently occurred, he was in no way connected
with the tragedy by which his adversary met his death. Wherever
Morrissey's friends met that evening his altercation with Poole was
the only topic of conversation.

From testimony submitted at the trial it would appear that
Baker, Turner, Huyler, Van Pelt, Linn and McLaughlin, *alias*
" Paudeen," had determined to settle matters that evening. Be it
as it may, it was admitted at every trial of Lewis Baker that about

an hour after midnight the parties previously mentioned did, one after another, saunter into Stanwix Hall. The saloon was supposed to be closed, but the door had not been locked. Poole was standing by the bar, surrounded by Lozier, Shay and Harris. If Poole was intoxicated previous to this meeting, the danger that now threatened him was undoubtedly calculated to sober him. All present realized that there was to be bloodshed. Poole's antagonists stepped up to the bar and Turner called for drinks. Paudeen, the last to come in, had locked the door, and turning to Poole, remarked, " What are you looking at, your black muzzled —— ?"

The fact that murder was intended was so palpable that Turner pretended to quiet Poole's apprehensions. After Paudeen had clutched Poole by the coat lappel, spit in his face three times and dared him to an encounter, Poole, in a very undemonstrative manner, offered to wager $500 he could whip any of them. He put up five golden eagles, but disdained to notice Paudeen, remarking that he was not worth it. Turner, according to the testimony of Cornelius Campbell, becoming restive, said quickly, " Sail in," at which he threw off his Talma, drew from a holster strapped to his waist a large Colt revolver, swung it around his head, and, levelling it in the hollow of his arm, fired in the direction of Poole. The ball entered his own arm, and from weakness or some other cause he fell to the floor. The next shot entered Poole's leg, and he staggered towards Baker, who, as yet, had not moved. It has always been a question whether Poole meant to grapple in a struggle for life or death with Baker, or whether he tottered towards him while throwing out his hands to prevent his falling. Poole, however, fell, and while Baker was over him he drew his revolver, and exclaiming, " I guess I will take you any how," placed it close to Poole's breast and fired, driving the ball into his heart. It was never satisfactorily explained whether Lozier and Shay were attacking Baker while he was over Poole. Baker, after firing another shot into Poole's body, escaped from the saloon. Poole, through his great strength, was enabled to regain his feet, and seizing a knife endeavored to pursue his assassins, but he only reached the door when he fell in the arms of Shay.

The firing during the affray was very indiscriminate. Those present who were loth to indulge in the sport scampered for the

STANWIX HALL.

closet, which was soon crowded. It would seem that Shay and Lozier remained by Poole, and did their best to kill somebody. Turner dragged himself to the door. It is probable that Turner hugged the floor, having received all the fight he desired; however, he made his way out and reached a place of safety. Poole was taken to his home, where he lingered for fourteen days. Just before expiring he solemnly assured Dr. Putnam that he never fired a shot that evening, and died believing that Morrissey was the cause of the tragedy. There was no reason why Baker should feel any remorse for Poole's death. Poole, in company with a man named Johnstone, but a few weeks previous to the fatal tragedy, met Baker in the "Gem" during the middle of the day, and there, without any provocation, they both attacked Baker and attempted to gouge out his eyes. Poole had repeatedly notified Baker that he would "settle his hash," and Baker was armed night and day, prepared for the encounter. The shot that caused Poole's death penetrated his heart, and he is the only person that was ever known to live with half an ounce of lead imbedded in that portion of the body. His death created a profound excitement, and his funeral was one of the grandest pageants that ever took place in the City of New York. The casket containing his remains was wrapped in the Stars and Stripes, and Broadway was lined from Bleecker street to Whitehall with spectators. All implicated in this murder either gave themselves up or were arrested the same night, except Baker. Baker made his escape to Jersey City, where he was concealed until the 10th of March, on which day he took passage on the brig Isabella Jewett, which had already cleared for the Canary Islands. It was some time before it was ascertained in what direction Baker had gone; but, as soon as it was known, George Law placed his clipper yatch Grapeshot at the disposal of the authorities, and the officers who went in pursuit of Baker entered the port of Teneriffe two hours before the Isabella Jewett arrived, and, going on board, they arrested Baker, and returned with him to the City of New York.

Baker was indicted with James Turner, Cornelius Linn, Charles Van Pelt, John Huyler, John Morrissey, James Irving and Patrick McLaughlin, *alias* Paudeen, for having feloniously killed William Poole with a loaded pistol. The Attorney General, Ogden Hoffman, the District Attorney, A. Oakey Hall, and James R. Whiting, Judge elect of the Court, appeared for the prosecution. James T. Brady and Horace F. Clark defended Baker. Judge Roosevelt was on the bench. The trial occupied fifteen days, and, notwithstanding the jury were out over a day, they were unable to agree. It was reported in the papers that they stood nine for conviction of murder and three for acquittal. Those three were citizens of foreign birth. Baker was again placed at the bar for trial, and a third time at Newburgh, but in each case the jury failed to agree, and he was discharged on bail. Several of the principal actors in this affray have since died in a tragic manner—more than one of them having died with their boots on. No murder had ever occurred in New York that occasioned so much excitement. Commenting upon the trial a prominent paper said : " The trial is especially remarkable as having developed a state of crime and ruffianism in our city that is truly startling. The inefficiency of our present police system, the delays of justice, the frequent escapes from punishment of well known offenders, *as herein* manifest, calls loudly for reform—not a reform that will waste and spend itself in mere words, but for practical results."

THE " PAUDEEN " HOMICIDE.

Notwithstanding the parties implicated in the Poole murder were never molested by the law which they had offended, they nevertheless had the sword of Damocles suspended above their heads. Men of the same stamp gave them a wide berth, and always clutched their revolvers when in their presence. "Paudeen," who spat in Poole's face, and was the chief instigator of the Stanwix Hall tragedy, was a low, brutal ruffian, without one redeeming trait in his character. Part of his nose had been bitten off by a man named Murray, and his face always presented a repulsive appearance. His fate astonished no one, and his death was a genuine blessing. He roamed about Broadway like a wild tiger, always looking for prey, and at an early hour on the morning of March 20th, 1858, he came to his end in a dance house known as Butt Allen's, in Howard street. Daniel (*alias* Dad) Cunningham, who rendered the city such a great service, went into the dance house about midnight, in company with two or three friends, for the purpose of having a cotillion with some

of the girls who usually frequented the establishment. " Paudeen "
came in some time after, and, meeting Cunningham at the bar, began
abusing Morrissey, who was not present. Cunningham took excep-.
tions to " Paudeen's " remarks, being a friend of Morrissey, and for
his temerity received a good shaking at the hands of " Paudeen."
Cunningham, who was exceedingly small of stature, warned " Paudeen " to desist. " Paudeen " saw there was danger, and asked
Cunningham to drink. His invitation was refused. This only
incensed " Paudeen," and he offered to bet 25 cents he would slap
Cunningham's face the next day. Cunningham, at this juncture of
affairs, went behind the bar. " Paudeen " reached across and
attempted to draw Cunningham over the bar. While in the act
Cunningham shot him, and " Paudeen " died the following day at
the New York Hospital. His remains were scientifically carved
by the surgeons and then given to his friends. " Little Cunningham " remained in the Tombs until June following, when his trial
came off before Recorder Barnard. John Sedgwick appeared for
the prosecution, and James R. Whiting defended the prisoner.
His trial was of short duration, occupying only five days. The
jury were unable to agree, and, as in the case of Baker, were discharged after having been locked up twenty-four hours. Seven of
the jurymen were in favor of a verdict of manslaughter in the third
degree, one in the fourth degree, while the remainder where in
favor of the prisoner's acquittal.

LETTER FROM JOHN MORRISSEY ON RETIRING FROM THE PRIZE RING.

To the Editor of the N. Y. Tribune.

SIR : Previous to my recent engagement with Mr. Heenan I
publicly announced that it would be my last fight. At its conclusion I proclaimed the same determination. Circumstances, seeming
to me imperative, forced me into that contest. I considered myself,
in my position, obliged to make the match and fight it—determined
by it to vindicate my character for honor and manhood, and to relieve myself from the persecution and assaults of my foes. I consider the first of these objects accomplished. No one has or can

complain of the manner in which my friends or myself conducted the fight. I had hoped my second object would also have been secured. I have no desire for further contest with any man. My duties to my family and myself require me to devote my time and efforts to purposes more laudable and advantageous. I hope to be permitted to do so without further interference from my late antagonist or his friends. I am aware of his published challenge and threat. It seems to be the determination to force me to another match, or to assail me openly with violence. I now repeat that I shall never enter the prize ring again, and those who know me will not misapprehend the motives for this resolution. It arises from no fear of any man, but from an honest desire more becomingly to discharge my duties to my family and society; nor shall I be driven from this purpose by any threats of unlawful violence. I shall trust to the laws and to the just influence of public sentiment to preserve me in the enjoyment of the common privileges of an American citizen.

If assaulted, I have no fear of my ability to defend myself, unless overcome, as I have heretofore been, by cowardly combinations. I shall exercise the right of protecting myself, and trust to the countenance of all fair men to sustain me in my peaceable determination.

Before the fight with Mr. Heenan I declared publicly on the ground that, if he vanquished me, I would take him by the hand and acknowledge my defeat, without cherishing any animosity. My treatment of him and his friends after it was over is well understood. It certainly was not illiberal or unkind. It is not for me to proclaim or boast of it, but I am entitled to say that it ought at least to protect me from all abuse from him or them.

Yours respectfully,

JOHN MORRISSEY.

TROY, *October* 5, 1858.

CHAPTER XII.

EXECUTIONS IN THE CITY AND COUNTY OF NEW YORK.

" A great multitude had already assembled; the windows were filled with people
smoking and playing cards to beguile the time; the crowd were pushing, quarrelling
and joking; everything told of life and animation but one dark cluster of objects in the
very centre of all—the black stage, the cross beam, the rope, and all the hideous apparatus of death."—DICKENS, *in Oliver Twist.*

THERE are no official data of executions in the city and county
archives made during the period of the Dutch Government.
Here and there are found notes of executions, with the crimes
stated, but no reliable list is available.

The most notable in the early history of our city was the execution of Jacob Leisler and his son-in-law, Milbourne. The news of
the abdication of James II and the accession of William, Prince
of Orange, was received in Boston, April, 1689, when the people
seized Governor Andros and imprisoned him. The news reached
New York May 31st, and Capt. Jacob Leisler put himself at the
head of a party, seized the fort, and a Committee of Safety, which
convened in this city June 26, 1689, gave Leisler the superin-
tendence of affairs. In December the same year, a letter addressed
by the English Ministry, authorizing Col. Francis Nicholson to act
as Lieutenant-Governor, was received by Leisler during the former's
absence, and Leisler assumed the powers of that office. In 1691
Governor Henry Slaughter arrived, but Leisler persisted in holding
his power, and was, with his son-in-law, in consequence, tried for
treason before a special commission, found guilty and executed,
May, 1691.

From the time the government of the city became vested in the
citizens of the United States executions for capital offences (murder, manslaughter, highway robbery, forgery and arson) were legal
punishments, and were performed in public, until the enactment in
1834 of the law now in force, requiring all executions to be performed in private, in the presence of certain officials and a coroner's
jury of citizens. A correct list of all who have paid the death

penalty would be difficult to obtain, even by a search through the archives of the State Department in Albany. The list given, the author regrets, does not comprise those punished by the Federal Government, but simply catalogues those who were tried and punished under the State laws.

The negro plots of 1713, 1740-'41 were circumstances of great terror, and citizens watched night and day until the alarm subsided.

FIRST EXECUTION IN NEW YORK.

The negroes charged with participation therein were chained to a stake and burned to death in a valley between Windmill Hill (site of the old Chatham Theatre) and Pot Bakers' Hill, midway between Pearl and Barclay streets, where public executions were performed for some years after. John Hustan (white) who was one of the principals in the last outrages (1740-'41), was bound in chains on a gibbet at the southeast point of Rutger's farm—not ten yards from the present southeast corner of Cherry and Catharine streets. Carson, a negro, was also hanged in chains on a gibbet at the southeast corner of the old powder house in Magazine street. At this time a general alarm prevailed, and the scenes of arrest, trial and execution at the Collect Pond, where the Tombs now stands, kept up a continual feverish excitement.

During the great fire of 1776, which commenced late at night, September 21st, in a small wooden shed on the wharf, near White-hall, then used as a bagnio, and which burned both sides of Broadway to Harrison's brick house on the east, and St. Paul's Church on the west, down to the North river, a little beyond Bear market, Barclay street. Trinity Church was fired, but St. Paul's saved, and 493 houses were consumed. During that terrible time a respectable man named White, whilst inebriated, was hanged on a sign-post at the corner of Cherry and Roosevelt streets.

In 1700 the Assembly passed an act to hang every Popish priest, which remained in force for over fifty years; but there is but one recorded execution under the same.

There is found recorded the execution of John Higgins and John Anderson at "Fresh Water" (site of the present City Prison (Tombs), for passing counterfeit money. This pond was set aside in 1761 to be used as a means for extinguishing fires.

Andrews, the pirate, was hanged in chains just above the present site of Washington Market, in 1769, and his body transported and hanged on Gibbet Island. Since then there have been a number of executions on Government reservations—Gibbs, Wansley and others—for piracy and desertion from the army.

In 1816 Ishmael Frazer, a colored man, for arson; and Diana Silleck for murder, were hanged on a gallows at the intersection of Bleecker and Mercer streets, which location was then beyond the city limits.

In 1820 Rose Butler (negress) was executed for arson, in Potter's Field, near Washington Square. She was the last person hanged in this county for that crime. But few convictions for that crime have since been had. Alexander Jones, the last, was sent to State Prison for life.

On the 16th March, 1824, John Johnson was convicted of the murder of James Murray, and was executed, April 2d following, at the intersection of Second avenue and Thirteenth street. Murray was a stranger, and had taken board at Johnson's house on Front street. Johnson was arrested by " old Hayes," as he was coming out of Trinity Church.

A curious case of legal technicality arose as follows : In 1827 William Miller was sentenced to be executed, on a day fixed, for the murder of David Ackerman, but execution was stayed by Judge Ogden Edwards. Governor De Witt Clinton, having doubts as to the power to appoint another day for the execution, commuted the prisoner's sentence to imprisonment for life. After serving twenty years the prisoner was pardoned. His case was a peculiar one. As the captain of a North River sloop he punished a refractory sailor by towing him along in the wake of the vessel by means of a rope attached, diversifying the punishment by drawing him in and letting him go " with a run," which treatment resulted in the victim's death.

On the 7th May, 1829, Richard Johnson and Catharine Coshear, a black woman, were hanged on the northern end of Blackwell's Island, being taken from the Bridewell, in City Hall Park, and conveyed to the island on one of the Brooklyn Ferry boats. The former was hanged for the murder of Ursula Newman, the latter for that of Susan Saltus. Johnson became fascinated with Ursula Newman, who was obdurate. After a few words with her in the parlor, in the frenzy and excitement of the moment he shot her with a pistol. In his speech to the Court, before sentence was passed, Johnson said : " In life, the deceased was the object of my tenderest affection—an affection that her own unjust conduct seemed but to inflame. Baffled in my honorable purposes, reason was expelled from its throne, and, in its absence, I was led to the commission of the offence for which I am now to satisfy the offended community by my own life. Were I conscious of any moral guilt, at this result I should not repine. Accustomed throughout life to respect the law, I have not now to learn that the blood of the murderer is alike a propitiatory sacrifice to the laws of God and man. Convicted of the legal .crime, I know my fate. For the moral offence, I have to answer to my conscience and to my God—and that innate monitor tells me that I stand before this Court and this community a legal, but not a moral murderer."

On the 7th of January, 1832, Daniel Ransom was executed for wife murder at the City Prison at Bellevue.

In 1835 the first execution under the present law took place at
the same prison. Richard C. Jackson *alias* Manuel Fernandez, a
Portuguese seaman, was hanged. He took the matter with great
coolness and deliberation, smoked a cigar complacently, and asked
if he had not time to smoke another—his last words.

Nov. 18th, 1842, John C. Colt escaped the gallows through
suicide.

As to the pirates, the name of Capt. William Kidd stands out
prominently in the city's history. He was recommended to Lord
Bellamont (Richard Cook), Governor of New York, by Robert
Livingston, who solicited the English Government for a vessel to
suppress piracy; but all the fleet being required for the war with
France, the Duke of Shrewsbury, Lord Chancellor Somers, the
Earls of Romney and Oxford, and others, became sharers in the
enterprise with Livingston and Bellamont, who engaged Kidd. The
" Adventure," galley of 30 guns and 60 men, started from Ply-
mouth in April, 1696, and arrived in New York the following July.
Here Kidd was at home, having lived on a garden not remote from
the present " Tombs." He shipped a crew to go to Madagascar in
pursuit of pirates, and on the voyage attacked the Mocha fleet but
was repulsed. He plundered the coast. Taking one of the vessels
of the Mocha fleet he returned to New York in 1698, and was reported to have buried his treasure on Gardner's Island, off Long
Island. Kidd was seized in Boston by Bellamont, and the British
man-of-war " Rochester " was sent out to carry him to England,
but being driven back by stress of weather, it was reported that the
Government did not dare to take him. Kidd and nine of his men
were found guilty of murder and piracy in May, 1701, and were
accordingly hanged.

Dunlap's History of New York chronicles the hanging of one
John Wry, on the charge of being a Roman Catholic, in 1683.

LIST OF EXECUTIONS IN THE CITY AND COUNTY OF NEW YORK.

1784.—Francis Higgins....................Highway Robbery.
  "   Daniel Moore......................   "   "
  "   William Buckley...................   "   "
  "   Henry Blake.......................Housebreaking.
  "   Tunis Casey.............................Murder.

1784.—Barbara Stillwell..............................Murder.
"   William Flanegan.........................Burglary.
1785.—Jacob Pickings.............................   "
"   Dennis Kearney.............................   "
"   John Benson...............................   "
"   Benjamin Lewis ....Forgery.
"   John Heinbrow..............................   "
"   Stephen Grimes.....................Highway Robbery.
1786.—James Carr...............................Burglary.
"   Thomas Lee......... ....   "
"   William Wright....................Highway Robbery.
1787.—Isaac (mulatto).....................Theft from Prison.
"   James Wilson......................Highway Robbery.
"   William Stewart....................   "   "
"   Frederick O'Brien..........................Burglary.
"   Henry Heyleman............................   "
"   Richard Roach.............................   "
1789.—John Thomas..............................Robbery.
"   John Lucas...............................   "
"   Israel Young.................Complicity in Forgery.
"   Samuel Waters.................   "   "   "
"   Abraham Morehouse........................Forgery.
"   Henry Hombeck.....................Forgery of Bond.
"   John Lupton.......................Highway Robbery.
"   William Kenny...................   "   "
"   William Perin.....................   "   "
"   Michael Gaines....................   "   "
"   Joseph Butler..... ....Burglary.
"   Charles Barry.............................Forgery.
1790.—Thomas Knight....................Highway Robbery.
"   William Glover....................   "   "
1793.—Joel S. White.............................Forgery.
"   John Wm. Hartenbeck......................   "
"   George Blossing............................   "
"   John George Hobbold.......................   "
1794.—Jessie Hart...............................   "
"   Leonine Romanie...........................   "
"   Thomas Creman.............................   "

1795.—Peter Connor.....................Highway Robbery.
"   Martin McNeil.....................   "   "
"   John Murray......................   "   "
"   Joshua L. Remsen.................   "   "
1796.—Noah Gardner.............................Forgery.
1797.—John Young..............................   "
1799.—John Partland...........................Murder.
1806.—Francisco Low...........................   "
"   John Banks..............................   "
1810.—John Sinclair...........................   "
"   James Johnson...........................   "
1811.—George Hart.............................   "
1815.—Thomas Burk............................   "
1816.—Diana Silleck...........................   "
"   Ishmael Freeman...........................Arson.
1820.—Rose Butler.............................   "
"   John Johnson............................Murder.
1825.—James Reynolds..........................   "
1829.—Richard Johnson.........................   "
"   Catharine Coshear.......................   "
1832.—Daniel Ransom...........................   "
1835.—Richard G. Jackson......................   "
1837.—Samuel Ackley...........................   "
1838.—Edward Coleman..........................   "
1841.—Patrick Russell.........................   "
1845.—Thomas Eager............................   "
1846.—Charles Thomas..........................   "
July   20, 1849.—Matthew Ward.................   "
July   25, 1851.— —— Benson ....   "
"   "   "   —— —— Douglass................   "
Sept. 19, " —Aaron Stokey..................   "
Feb.   27, 1852.—Otto Grunzig.................   "
April 19, " —Patrick Fitzgerald............   "
Jan.   28, 1853.—Nicholas Howlett.............   "
"   "   " —William Saul..................   "
Feb.   11, " —Joseph Clark.................   "
Jan.   27, 1854.—James L. Hoar................   "
July   17, 1857.—John Dorsay..................   "

Nov. 12, 1858.—James Rogers....................... Murder.
Feb.   3, 1860.—John Stephens......................   "
March 30,   "   —John Crimmons...................   "
July 13,   "   —Albert Hicks...................... Piracy.
Feb. 21, 1862.—Nathaniel Gordon........ Slaver. (U. S. case.)
June 27,   "   —Wm. Henry Hawkins.... Murder on High Seas.
Aug. 17, 1866.—Bernard Friery..................... Murder.
Oct. 19,   "   —F. Ferris............................   "
March 1, 1867.—George Wagner....................   "
Aug.   9,   "   —Jerry O'Brien.....................   "
April 8, 1870.—John Reynolds.....................   "
March 5,   "   —John Real...........................   "
March 10, 1871.—John Thomas.......................   "
March 21, 1873.—William Foster....................   "
May 16,   "   —Michael Nixon.....................   "

LIST OF PRISONERS SENTENCED TO DEATH, BUT NOT EXECUTED.

George Vanderpoel.... Arson....... 1816.			Commuted.
William Miller........ Murder...... 1827.			Imprisonment for life.
Ezra White.......... " ...... 1840.			New trial; convicted of manslaughter.
John Swack .... " ...... "			Commuted.
Thomas Tappan....... " ...... 1842.			"
John C. Colt........ " Nov. 18, 1842.			Committed suicide in the Tombs.
William Harper....... " ...... 1847.			Commuted.
Calvin Rees........... " ...... "			"
Thomas Hayes........ " ...... "			"
Alexander Jones....... Arson........ 1849.			"
Joseph Wall........ Murder ...... 1851.			"
Michael Mulvay....... " ...... "			"
James Sullivan....... " ...... "			"
Antonio Lopez....... " ... .. 1852.			Pardoned.
James Doyle......... " ...... 1853.			Commuted.
William Johnson..... " ...... "			"
Thomas Nearey...... " ...... "			"
William Scharffenburg " ...... 1855.			"

CHAPTER XIII.

THE BOND STREET TRAGEDY.—THE MURDER OF DR. HARVEY
BURDELL.—STABBED TO DEATH IN HIS OWN OFFICE.—WHO
DID IT?—WAS IT A LEFT HANDED WOMAN?—ARREST AND
TRIAL OF MRS. CUNNINGHAM.—NOT GUILTY.—THAT WONDER-
FUL BABY.

"So, by the same rule, if a woman's a party to a secret that might hang or trans-
port her, I'm not afraid of her telling it to anybody, not I."—DICKENS, *in Oliver
Twist.*

THE night of Friday, January 30, 1857, was a dark, disagreeable one. A thick mucky fog rested on everything, and
blurred the light of the street lamps. The rain beat wildly against
the windows of the houses, and trickled, like tears, down the panes
of glass. The wind came sobbing and moaning up the bay from
its wild carnival at sea, as if it were telling of fearful shipwrecks,
and the ghastly skeletons gleaming white along the muddy bed of
ocean.

At 5 o'clock in the afternoon of that day a gentleman opened
the door of the house No. 31 Bond street and stood a moment on
the stoop. He was a fine, portly looking man, of middle age. It
was Dr. Harvey Burdell, and the house No. 31 was his residence
and property. In it he conducted the business of dentistry. By
his ability and industry he had amassed a moderate fortune. After
a glance at the angry sky, and a pulling up of his muffler around
his throat, he started for the Metropolitan Hotel to get his dinner.
That was the last seen of him alive.

MRS. CUNNINGHAM.

The landlady of the house was Mrs. Cunningham—Dr. Burdell
having leased all of the rooms to her except his reception parlors
and his operating room on the second story. Mrs. Cunningham
was a fine, matronly looking lady, of full habit. Rumor has it that
she loved the doctor, and, as it subsequently transpired, was very
jealous of him, and objected, quite naturally, to his paying atten-

tion to other ladies, which, it would seem, the doctor was in the habit of doing. On the 28th day of October, 1856, the Rev. Dr. Marvine married Mrs. Cunningham to somebody. Who was it? The certificate says it was Dr. Burdell; but, was he personated? Once his lawful wife, she would be in a condition, should the doctor die suddenly, to stand in for her share of the property. But the doctor does not appear to have been a marrying man, and the consequence was that the perfumed flame of love between the two died out, and in its stead the fiercer glow of hatred sprung up in the gentle heart of Mrs. Cunningham-Burdell. Her character does not appear to have been any of the best, according to testimony given at the Coroner's inquest.

There lived, also, in the house at No. 31, Mr. John J. Eckel, a rather good looking man, who played the part of a lover to Mrs. Cunningham, and sought to supplant Dr. Burdell in that lady's affections. A Mr. Snodgrass, aged 18, also lived there. He played the banjo. Then there were two sons of Mrs. Cunningham's, aged eight and ten years; two daughters (Helen and Augusta), a Mr. Daniel Ulman, and Hannah Conlan, the cook. These were the inhabitants of the famous house in Bond street on that day when Dr. Burdell walked out to get his dinner.

" MURDER !"

About half past ten o'clock that night a gentleman, living at No. 36 Bond street, was about retiring for the night. The street was silent, and there was no sound save the distant rattling of a coach in Broadway, and the rain beating against the windows. Suddenly the cry of " MURDER !" rang out on the night—one distinct, blood-curdling shriek, and then all was silent. The gentleman could not tell exactly from whence the sound came, but thought it was from the direction of Broadway.

Later in the night some one saw a light in an attic room at No. 31; it was not the light of a lamp but the light of a fire—of a fire in which something was being burned. The smell of consumed clothing and leather was noticeable.

WHAT WAS FOUND IN THE MORNING.

About eight o'clock the next morning (Saturday) a small boy, who took charge of the doctor's room, came to the house for the purpose of making a fire, as was his usual custom. He went into the basement, got a scuttle of coal, and carried it up to the door of the room on the second story, whistling blithely as he went. The morning was a beautiful one—no traces of the last night's storm remained. The boy opened the door—it was unlocked—and pushed it back. It struck something. In an instant he stood frozen with horror. The something it struck was the head of a man—of a man lying upon the floor, in a pool of blood. There was blood everywhere—upon the chairs, upon the door, upon the wall. Murder had smeared the whole apartment with its crimson fingers. The life-fluid of the man lying there, and staring up at the ceiling, had spurted five feet high against the door. There was blood in the hall, on the stairs, in the lower hall, on the front door. There was blood on the stairs going up towards the roof, and blood on the floor of the attic room. In the room where the dead man lay the gas was burning at full head. The dead man had not been to bed, but lay here just as he had come in from the street. It was the corpse of Dr. Harvey Burdell.

The boy staggered back and alarmed the house. Then there was great commotion, and much running to and fro. Mrs. Cunningham and her family were composedly eating breakfast—all unconscious, apparently, of that horrid scene up stairs. When told that Dr. Burdell was murdered she gave way to wild grief and would not be comforted. Eckel did not appear particularly disconcerted.

An examination of the body of the dead doctor showed fifteen distinct stab wounds, any one of which was enough to have killed him. They were made, as it appeared, with a long, keen, narrow dagger. Around his neck was the mark of a cord, as if he had been strangled. The appearance of the room made it evident that the death struggle had been terrific. The furniture was upset and knocked about in a chaotic manner.

WHAT OCCURRED THE NIGHT PREVIOUS.

During the evening previous, and while Dr. Burdell was out at dinner, Mrs. Cunningham came down to the kitchen. No one was there save Hannah Conlan, the cook. The following conversation occurred :

" Who was that woman, Hannah, you were showing through the house to-day?"

" That was the lady who is going to take the house."

" Then the doctor is going to leave it, is he?"

" Yes, ma'am."

" And when does she take possession?"

"The first of May."

" He better be careful; he may not live to sign the papers!"

THE EXCITEMENT IN THE CITY.

Immediately after the discovery of the body the news spread as rapidly as does a prairie fire. The city became lashed up to the white heat of excitement. All day long a curious, morbid crowd surged through Bond street, so terrible was the fascination surrounding the house No. 31. There they stood and gazed up at the windows, as if even that idle occupation had some pleasure about it. The police guarded the door, and allowed no one to pass in but a favored few and the reporters of the press. The Coroner's inquest was held in the house, and lasted for some days. The evidence submitted was full and explicit, but no ray of light was thrown upon the mystery, and when it was over the conundrum, " Who killed Dr. Burdell?" was as unanswerable as ever. The finger of suspicion, however, pointed at Mrs. Cunningham and Eckel. Medical experts gave it as their opinion that the dagger was wielded by a left handed person. *Mrs. Cunningham was left handed!* When the inquest was over, therefore, the jury brought in a verdict implicating Mrs. Cunningham and Eckel, and they were accordingly locked up in the Tombs.

MRS. CUNNINGHAM'S TRIAL.

The trial of Mrs. Cunningham (Eckel was not tried) began on May 6th, 1857, and lasted three days. She was defended by Henry L. Clinton, Esq. John Graham was retained for Eckel. District Attorney Hall conducted the prosecution. The existence of a motive was clearly established, but that was all, and at the end of the trial the jury, after being out an hour and a half, returned a verdict of " Not guilty." Mrs. Cunningham was immediately discharged, and returned to her home in Bond street. She is now in lower California, cultivating a vineyard. Eckel died at the Albany Penitentiary, where he had been sent for complicity in some whiskey frauds in Brooklyn, and Snodgrass died quite recently.

SKETCHES OF THE PARTIES CONCERNED.

During the progress of the trial the *Herald* published the following sketches of the parties concerned in the mystery:

MRS. CUNNINGHAM, *alias* BURDELL.

Emma Augusta Hempstead was the daughter of Cristopher and Sarah Hempstead, of Brooklyn. Her father was a rope maker by profession, and moved from New York to Brooklyn about thirty-five years ago. He was a very religious man, a member of the Methodist church, and died reputed rich. Mrs. Cunningham was born in the City of New York, on the east side of the town. She became acquainted with George Cunningham, and had her first child in her father's house in Classon avenue, Brooklyn, previous to his death, which took place in 1836 or 1837. Afterwards she lived in New York in splendid style until her husband failed in business, when she again moved to Brooklyn. Mr. Cunningham went to California with the intention, if possible, of getting into business there, and sending for his family. He, however, was unsuccessful, returned, did not do much of anything afterwards, and finally died in Flatbush, Long Island, at or near the residence of the brother of Mrs. C. There was an insurance on his life at the time of his death of $10,000, which Mrs. Cunningham received, and on which she lived after the death of her husband.

It has been stated that Mrs. Cunningham was the mother of the Miss Van Winkle who, with her lover, Mr. Caldwell, committed suicide some years since in Troy. It was not so. They were cousins; the father of Miss Van Winkle was the brother of the mother of Mrs. Cunningham.

We have a letter in relation to Mrs. Cunningham but it is not fit for publication. It gives her a very bad character, and states that she was not the lawful wife of Cunningham. It will be noticed that this point is touched upon in the evidence. The evidence of Mr. Stephens and the servant girl Mary go to show a very bad state of feeling between Mrs. Cunningham and Dr. Burdell, but whether their quarrels formed a sufficient motive for the commission of a capital crime has yet to be seen. It is stated that Mrs. Cunningham had been the mistress of Eckel for four years, during which time she has passed by several names. It seems quite probable that the difficulties in the household were caused by Mrs. Cunningham's reputed intrigues with Dr. Burdell and Mr. Eckel at the same time. It appears by the evidence that this bitterness of feeling had latterly widened to an entire separation, so that Dr. Burdell's house was made a pandemonium to him. Mrs. Cunningham is described by those who know her as a well bred person of agreeable manners. It appears that she has lately been somewhat straitened for money. On the 14th January last we hear that she gave a large party. Everybody that she knew or had even met (watering place acquaintances, etc., etc.) was invited, and there was a great crowd. There was plenty of champagne, music and dancing. Peteler, the confectioner, furnished the supper—everything being sent in. In a few days Peteler sent in his bill, amounting to about $200, which she did not pay. A short time afterwards Peteler had a personal interview with Mrs. Cunningham, when she stated that she could not pay the bill, but would give him a note of hand for the amount, to fall due about the 9th of February, at which time she stated she would have "plenty of money." It is a curious fact, and as it may have a bearing on the case, Mr. Peteler has been summoned to give evidence in the case.

JOHN J. ECKEL.

Everything, so far, bears against this person. It appears that he was on the most intimate terms with Mrs. Cunningham. At the party above mentioned he was *major domo*. He is a man of powerful frame and of middle height. It is stated that when he left the house on the morning after the murder he was followed by Mrs. Cunningham, and was seen near his factory giving her money. Eckel has frequently stated that he had a very expensive mistress. Whether or not he was concerned in the murder, his position in Mrs. Cunningham's house was an unenviable one.

GEORGE V. SNODGRASS.

This young man seems to have been a sort of *cavalier sereinte* to the Demoiselles Cunningham. He has been pretty well known about the saloons in the Fifteenth Ward, and has generally borne the reputation of a harmless, good natured, gentlemanly young man. In his room—the northeast room of the attic—his clothes were hanging upon the wall, and a couple of bronze statuettes stood on the drawers. There was no wash bowl. The bed was in a very topsy-turvy state—bolster and pillows being mixed up with feminine under clothes in the greatest confusion. The drawers—all but one—were filled with all sorts of knick knacks—articles of feminine wearing apparel. A dozen or so of replies to invitations to the party given on the 14th were mixed up with the rest. On a piece of paper were these lines, traced in a delicate hand:

> " What would the rose, with all her pride be worth,
> Were there no sun to call her brightness forth ?
> Maidens unloved, like flowers in darkness thrown,
> Want but that light which comes from love alone."

A little lulu book, entitled " The Boat Builder," published in 1852, was found this morning on the piano in the front parlor. " Miss Georgena A. Cunningham, 10 years old and 3,900 days," was written on the fly leaf, in a child's hand. The leaf containing the 79th and 80th pages was cut out ; blood was visible on the edges of the leaves not cut out ; the two leaves containing the 91st to 94th pages were torn out; the 95th was smeared with blood. These three leaves were the only ones missing.

A SKETCH OF THE LIFE AND CHARACTER OF DR. HARVEY BURDELL.

To write the life of a good and great man is one of the most agreeable duties that devolves upon the chronicler of public events, but to perform the same service to a man of bad moral or doubtful character, is an unenviable task.

Dr. Harvey Burdell is now a historical character, and if there is a moral in his life or death, it is sufficiently pointed to drive home the barb of conviction without any comment from us. We therefore merely give the following well authenticated and but too notorious facts in his history and character :

The late Dr. Harvey Burdell was born in Herkimer County, in or near Herkimer village, New York, in 1811. His father died before he knew him ; while he was yet a child his mother moved to Sackett's Harbor, New York ; with her he resided till he was thirteen years old ; his mother then turned him into the street, and forbade him ever to return to the house. The boy thus turned forth upon the world at so early an age felt the throb of ambition, and was determined, according to his own words, to raise—to become great—to gain gold. Without a profession, education or means, he looked around him to see what course he should take—what path pursue—to achieve his desired success. The press held out the tempting bait. He determined to begin on the lowest round and mount the ladder, and consequently went to a neighboring country town and engaged himself as a compositor. He remained there for some years, and either did not like the business or had better inducements held out to him in this city, for before his seventeenth year we find him here studying dentistry in his brother John's office, which was then located on the corner of Chambers street and Broadway, where Stewart's store now stands; he was of studious habits and made good use of his time. Forming a taste for the medical profession, he went to Philadelphia when about twenty-one years old, and pursued a regular course of study in the Pennsylvania Medical College. He partly supported himself during his studies by the practice of dentistry, and was partially maintained by his brother, John Burdell, of this city. Having graduated in the college at Philadelphia he returned to this city and entered his brother's office, learning and practicing dentistry during the day and practicing medicine at night. He expressed himself ready to do anything or practice any profession to make money. John Burdell soon after marrying, Harvey lived in the house with him as a member of his family. Their dwelling house was in the same building, directly over the dental office. John Burdell owned two or three houses on the corner of Chambers street and Broadway at that time.

Harvey Burdell, after being in his brother's office a short time, opened an office for himself in the house of his brother, and the next door to his office. They kept their offices there a number of years, doing a fair business—Harvey living all or most of the time with his brother. Harvey Burdell was a man of strong feelings and passions, and he frequently quarrelled with his brother; he was very penurious in his transactions and economical in his dress and habits. With these traits strongly marked, he began to manifest a very licentious and loose character, and had a great many difficulties in consequence of it; his name is found on the books at the Tombs, in the law courts, and he has been known to the head of the police for many years.   While living in Chambers street he was sued by a disreputable woman for non-payment of money. alleged to be due to her.

In 1835, or thereabout, Harvey Burdell was engaged to be married to a respectable young lady, but her father peremptorily refused to permit the marriage, at which Burdell got angry, struck the father and gave him a black eye.   Subsequently he was engaged to be married to another young lady, an adopted daughter of a worthy lady and gentleman; the day and hour was set for the wedding, the wedding party assembled, the bridesmaids and the bridegroom were present, the clergyman was ready to perform the ceremony, when Dr. Harvey Burdell entered the room of the old man and told him that before he married the girl he wanted a check for $20,000.   The old gentleman told him that if he was marrying his daughter for her money he should have neither, so the wedding was broken up.   Subsequently the young lady married the person who was to be groomsman on the former occasion—he received the check for $20,000.   The check on the previous occasion was made out for Burdell, and would have been given him immediately after the marriage ceremony was performed; and, when he heard about it, he is said to have become greatly excited, and declared that he would never get married.

Dr. Burdell had a very curious servant girl, called Biddy, who was with him five years at 362 Broadway and two years at 31 Bond street, during the whole of which time she never went to bed.   He never furnished her with a bed, or anything to sleep upon.   She was poorly clad, and hardly ever had anything to wear on her feet.   He never provided her with anything to eat, but gave her a small weekly salary, upon which she supported herself, buying her food at the groceries.   This is an example of the doctor's penuriousness.   The girl could speak four languages fluently— namely, the English, French, German and Spanish.   She had a great passion for studying and learning languages.   She was an Irish girl, and a most faithful servant.   She frequently saved the doctor from being beaten, for if a fight occurred she would run between him and his assailant and stand there till she stopped the fighting.   She slept sitting on a stool in the kitchen below the hall door, so if any person rang the bell or entered the house at any time of night she would know it and attend to them.   Yet, for all these services, she barely received enough pay from the doctor for her subsistence· Dr. Burdell, as before mentioned, was a loose character, and consequently was surrounded by such.   He generally let his house to persons of bad character.   Mrs. Totten occupied his house in Broadway for some time, and he, as usual, had trouble with her and a lawsuit.

About three years ago Mr. Bulin, whose wife is half sister to Dr. Burdell, took the house No. 31 Bond street; they quarrelled, the parties moved from the house, and have never spoken to Burdell since.

A little over a year ago Harvey Burdell employed his brother James to build some houses for him in Herkimer County, N. Y., and agreed to give him a certain interest in them or remunerate him for building them, but a quarrel and lawsuit followed between them.   Dr. Burdell also has a lawsuit with Benjamin F. Maguire, a relative, to whom he sold the office tools, etc., of John Burdell, at Union place.

There was a wealthy widow lady of this city who used to visit Dr. Burdell almost every day for two years.   On one occasion she called on him in the afternoon to go to the theatre with him in the evening.   On the way to the theatre she said she would like something to eat, and entered Thompson's saloon and called for what she wanted.   Burdell refused to call for anything for himself, saying he had been to tea.   She told him to order something and be decent.   He refused, when she ordered for him.   He would not eat; and, on coming back for her, would neither pay for himself nor her. The doctor is represented by those intimately acquainted with him to have been a very peculiar man.   He hated children; and never had any pets in his life except some Guinea pigs.   He was a member of the New York Historical and Statistical Society, and a director in the Artizans' Bank of New York; he was one of the principal parties engaged in getting up that bank; he took $25,000 worth of its stock; he had about $10,000 in it at the time of his death, and money in the Broadway Bank; he owned the house and lot No. 31 Bond street, worth $25,000; the house and lot No. 2 Bond street, worth $30,000, property in Shrewsbury, N. J., and real estate in Herkimer County, N. Y., and other property, so that he was worth at least $100,000. There were five brothers in the Burdell family—Harvey and John, both dentists of this city, are deceased ; there is one brother living in Ohio; another, who formerly lived in Michigan, is now in Indiana; the fifth, formerly of Valparaiso, was not long since in this city, and is now in the Lunatic Asylum on Blackwell's Island.

When Dr. Burdell bought the house No. 31 Bond street he occupied the first floor and other rooms ; the rest of the house was let. Mrs. Conway first rented it in 1853; Mr. or Mrs. Bulin next; Mrs. Cunningham then took it for a year ; after which a Mrs. Jones occupied it a few months, when Mrs. Cunningham again took charge of it on the 1st of May last and still occupies it.

THAT WONDERFUL BABY.

The story of Dr. Burdell's murder would be incomplete without some allusion to the phantom baby which Mrs. Cunningham did not have. As wife of the dead man she would get one third of his estate, or, as the mother of his child, she would get it all—it therefore became necessary to have a baby. It was a remarkable idea, and was skilfully managed ; but owing to her indiscretion in confiding the plan to Dr. Uhl—an indiscretion which could hardly be avoided, however—the bubble was burst, and this infantry move of Mrs. Cunningham on the Burdell estate came to nought.

It was while in the Tombs that Mrs. Cunningham conceived this idea—that it was now policy for her to prove to the world, by the presence of an heir, her relation to the deceased doctor. She informed Mrs. Foster, matron of the prison, of her interesting condition, and completely deceived that estimable lady. Once back in Bond street she continued her deception. She went about it systematically, and in her "make-up" showed she was a true artist. Her form became daily more rotund, and more in accordance with Hogarth's line of beauty. Of Dr. Uhl she made a confidant, and he in turn confided in District Attorney Hall. The latter scented a huge joke, and eagerly went into the game. The plan was for Dr. Uhl to pretend to aid Mrs. Cunningham in procuring the heir, she promising to pay him $1,000, and at the proper time the District Attorney was to arrest the operation and the woman.

The first thing was to get a baby—this Mr. Hall undertook to do for Dr. Uhl. The perfected plan agreed upon was as follows: Hall was to obtain a baby when it was needed from the Bellevue Hospital, and Mrs. Cunningham was to send for it. Apartments were hired at No. 190 Elm street, and Mrs. Cunningham was told by Dr. Uhl that there lived there a California lady, who, wishing to return to her husband in California, it became necessary that a child soon to be born should be spirited away,—she being as anxious to get rid of a baby as Mrs. Cunningham was to have one. This was told Mrs. Cunningham, and she was delighted to find everything going on so smoothly. She kept up a stout heart and a stouter form, and anxiously awaited the confinement of the charming Californian. This was certainly the first instance in which two women went on shares in having the same baby.

Mrs. Cunningham-Burdell's heir was expected about the 28th of July. The eventful day finally arrived. A baby was borrowed from the Bellevue Hospital, and Mrs. C. was told the infant not wanted in California was at her disposal. Disguised as a Sister of Charity she went to Elm street with a market basket, and returned to Bond street with the baby inside the basket—just as if it was a pound of soap. Then she became very sick, and Dr. Uhl was sent for. After suffering intensely! the baby was announced—born all over again—had a second deal in the game of life—and the mother and child were pronounced as doing as well as could be expected. Just then Mr. Hall and the policemen appeared upon the scene, and Mrs. Cunningham became truly confined—in jail.

Nothing came of the case, however, and Mrs. Burdell was once again at liberty, with permission to have just as many babies as she chose. The little girl used in carrying out the deception was called Justitia Anderson, and both she and her genuine mother were secured by Mr. Barnum, and exhibited at the Museum at "25 cents a head, children half price." She was a pretty, blue-eyed little girl, and seemed to enjoy her notoriety very much.

CHAPTER XIV.

THE STORY OF THE FRENCHMAN WHO DID NOT WITNESS THE EXECUTION, AND HOW IT HAPPENED.

"Every window was now choked up with heads; the house-tops teemed with people clinging to chimneys, peering over gable-ends, and holding on where the sudden loosening of any brick or stone would dash them down into the street."—DICKENS, *in Barnaby Rudge.*

SOME years ago, when the late Judge Stewart was on the bench, a prisoner was to suffer the death penalty, and the impending execution caused rather more than the usual excitement.

The demand for tickets of admission to the prison yard to witness the execution was very great, and hundreds had to be refused. Among the number was a Frenchman, who had resorted to every conceivable means to obtain the coveted pass. He had approached every one connected with the Sheriff's office, and had even offered to pay a good price for a ticket, but all to no purpose.

Presuming on a slight acquaintance with the Judge, he rushed up into the court room on the day of execution and begged him to contrive some means by which he might gain admission to the yard and witness the execution.

"I have no power," replied the Judge; "the Sheriff of the county only can let you in."

"But, *Mons. le Juge,*" said the Frenchman, "I have see ze Shereeff —he tell me he have no more *etiquettes.* I have try every one connected wiz ze office; I have offer to pay ze money, but I cannot get in. I beg of you, on ze ground of fransheep, if it ees at all posseeble, to let me witness zese execution—I have a *grande passion* to zee eet."

"I can commit you to prison," replied the Judge.

"Ah, *grande idée!* How can I zank you for zese kindness. By gar! but you have ze—vat you call? ze *longer* head to think of zuch a thing. 'Tis *un grand coup d'invention,* by gar!" and the Frenchman fairly danced with delight.

"Make out a commitment for lunacy," said the Judge to the

clerk, who, with a broad grin on his face, proceeded to fill up the necessary papers.

An officer was called, the Frenchman given in charge, and he was taken down to the prison, where he was handed over to the keeper at the desk, by whom he was assigned to a cell.

When the Frenchman perceived what was being done to him, " By gar! sare," he exclaimed," " What you will do wiz me?   I am no lunatic; ze *Juge* and me, we understand one anozer—he do zese for me for fransheep, so I can see zese execution."

The keeper looked at the prisoner, examined the commitment, which he carefully read over again, saw that it was regularly made out, and, turning on his heel, remarked to the man in attendance, " Lock him up!" And the poor Frenchman, in spite of his protestations that the commitment was but a trick of the Judge to enable him to witness the execution, was locked up.

At length the execution was over; the yard was cleared of the crowd, and night coming on, the Judge was preparing to leave for his home, when the clerk called his attention to the man who had been locked up.

" Oh, yes; by the by," said the Judge, " I must discharge him. It may prove a good lesson to the Frenchman, and in future, perhaps, he will not be so anxious to see a fellow creature hanged."

The discharge was accordingly made out; and, when the prison officers learned the circumstances of the case, a hearty laugh was enjoyed. When the prisoner was let out he gesticulated violently, and gave utterance to expressions in his native tongue, which was accompanied by an expression of the eyes and a demeanor which is generally assumed by persons when cursing and swearing in English.

He declared that he would " get even wiz ze *Juge* if he should stay long enough in ze country." As he had not up to the Judge's death got even with him, the author concludes that either the Frenchman must have left the country or that his idea of the time requisite for getting even must be very vague.

CHAPTER XV.

JOHN MAHONY, THE AMERICAN JACK SHEPPARD.—AN ACCOUNT OF
HIS ADVENTUROUS LIFE, WRITTEN BY HIMSELF.—HIS CAREER
OF CRIME AND HIS REMARKABLE ESCAPES.

"But to give it to you short and handy I'll put it at once into a mouthful of English.
In jail and out of jail, in jail and out of jail, in jail and out of jail. There, you've got
it."—DICKENS, *in "Great Expectations."*

THIS chapter is certainly one of the most interesting in the book.
It is the life of a noted criminal, written by himself, and
reads like a romance of Ainsworth. It will be noticed that this
young man was possessed of an intelligent mind, and was not
devoid of the graces of composition. He handles the pen quite as
well as he did the "jimmy," and has given a vivid picture of his
checkered career. It was written expressly for the author of this
work, at his request.

LIFE OF JOHN MAHONY,

as written by himself in the Massachusetts State Prison, Christmas
night, 1870:

I was born in the City of New York, in the year 1844. Of my
early childhood my recollections are imperfect, but I still remember
that I was very wild, and ran into every sort of danger. One day,
while playing on the ice, I broke through, and would have been
instantly drowned, had not my sister, at the risk of her life, saved
mine.

I was the only son of a family of four children. While quite
young my father was taken sick and confined to his bed for a long
period. I remember, every afternoon my mother would take me
up to my father's room, when he would give me some little luxury,
and fondle me on his bed.

My recollections of my father's death are vivid and distinct,
although at the time I had no correct idea what death was. I and
my sisters and a few friends were standing at his bed side, and my
mother was kneeling at the head of the bed.

While my father lay dead in the house I recollect looking into his coffin, but did not feel bad, for I thought my father would come home again.

After a few days I began to miss my father, and would ask my mother when father was coming home. My mother used to take me into her lap and tell me that father was in Heaven with the angels, and that if I would be a good boy the angels would come and take me there too.

A few weeks after my father's death my sister was born. We then moved into the heart of the city. After a short period my mother fulfilled a promise, made to my father on his death bed, to send me to a boarding school. She accordingly sent me to a school in B——, N. J. I recollect very well my first appearance at the boarding school. As my mother was leaving the school she put some pennies into my lap and kissed me, and then walked out of the house without looking back. I rushed after her, but was stopped by the teacher. When I saw her get into the carriage I gave way to my grief and was flogged !

While I remained at school I was constantly in all sorts of boyish mischief, and got so used to whippings that they seemed quite natural. I remember a trick that was once played, when three other boys and myself were made to kneel down, and fifteen minutes were given us to confess the deed, or all of us would be punished. I was as innocent as the child unborn. One of the boys promised me a tin box and six cents if I would say I did the deed. After a great deal of coaxing I got up and told the teacher that I did it, took the punishment, but got cheated in the bargain.

Even at this day I recollect how often I would lay awake at night thinking of home and of my father. Time has erased his features from my memory.

I did not remain long at this school, for I ran away so often that my mother thought it best to take me home. I was then sent to a French boarding school in J——, Long Island, N. Y., and in this school I learned a great deal of wickedness and nothing good. The teacher's son, a young man of twenty-two years of age, used to take delight in frequently setting me to fighting, and even did his best to get me to chew tobacco, but I never became accustomed to it. I ran away from school so often that they were obliged to keep me without pants, and I was permitted to wear nothing but a long apron, resembling the dress of a young girl.

I remember one day I got out and caught the gutter of the roof, and, while hanging to it, I moved along until I got opposite the room that contained my clothes, and then swung myself into the room and got back the same way. Had I fallen I would have been dashed to pieces. I went home, and, as usual, my mother took me back.

While at this school they undertook to teach me French, and at the table they had a rule that each pupil should ask for whatever he wished in the French language. I could learn French very quickly in the dining room, but in the school room I made little or no progress.

I recollect how I used to write the multiplication table on a slate with chalk, and place it behind the teacher's desk, and then run over my lesson with one eye at the slate and the other on the teacher.

"Well, Jack, you have done well; you can go and play, but look out and don't get to fighting."

While at this school one day I stole some powder and put it into an inkstand. I then went into the yard, thinking I was going to have a grand Fourth of July celebration. I introduced a small piece of paper into the neck of the bottle, expecting to see it burn like those blue lights on the Fourth of July. The bottle exploded, and, as I was standing directly over it, a large piece of glass flew into my leg, of which I carry the mark to this day.

On another occasion I came near killing the servant girl. While school was out I went to the teacher's closet and took a rifle, and held it over my head. Bang! I found myself lying on the floor from the recoil of the rusty charge. The slug went through the ceiling and floor overhead, and passed very near to a point where the servant girl was making up the beds. Being of such a wild disposition my mother was obliged to take me home.

I was then sent to a "pay school," one block from my home, but the school room was a cage to me, and I took every opportunity of escaping from it when forced to go. Mother was then advised to send me to the "House of Refuge," which, at that time, was situated on Twenty-third street, in the City of New York.

One morning I was put into a carriage with my mother, and I thought we were going to visit my father's grave. This was a *ruse* to keep me quiet. However, as we rode through the gate of the House of Refuge I gave way to a fit of grief, because I had often heard of the place before.

My mother did not think it was a bad place, otherwise she would not have put me there. I went to the House of Refuge a wild but innocent boy, and left it initiated into all sorts of wickedness.

There was only one man who threw sunshine around the institution, and the little fellows called him " Poppy Ringlin." He was indeed a kind, humane and excellent man, and the boys loved him with a feeling as affectionate and true as if he had been their father; in fact, he was a father to many of the little fellows. He shared his dinner with one of the boys every day. His pet boy was poor Jerry O'Brien, who was subsequently executed in New York in 1866.

I distinctly recollect the first morning I spent in the yard of this institution. The good old man, " Poppy Ringlin," told me a story about his birds, and remarked that they would come to see him every morning and sing to him. I believed every word this good old man said. I mention this little incident to show you *how innocent I was* when I entered this NEST OF CRIME.

Within the House of Refuge boys were confined from the age of eight to twenty years, and the greater portion of them were from the lowest streets in New York city, such as the " Five Points," Water street, etc. There is, therefore, little surprise that the younger boys should have been corrupted and ruined by those older in crime than themselves.

The authorities in charge of the House of Refuge were cruel and unfeeling men. I have seen boys of tender years tied up and whipped (whilst they were in a naked condition) until the blood ran down their backs.

There is no exaggeration about this statement, for the act frequently took place. I have also seen the tender backs of poor little fellows all covered with running sores, so that they were scarcely able to move around from the effects of those cruel and inhuman whippings.

WHIPPING BOYS AT THE HOUSE OF REFUGE.

We worked all day in the shops, and if we did not have our tasks done at night we were punished. I worked in the chair shop, and still remember how the boss used to fling things at our heads and curse us. We nicknamed him "Gunner."

When the cold season began we were kept without shoes until the weather became intensely cold, and the poor boys found it necessary to put their feet into their caps to keep them warm. They had no under clothing, and consequently suffered much from this circumstance.

Sometimes they used to whip us on our bare feet, which is one of the most cruel punishments that can be inflicted on a human being. I understand this punishment is inflicted on criminals in the East. Those who cannot realize how painful it is, had better have some one tap them a few times on the soles of their feet some cold winter's morning, and I promise you they will soon change their opinion.

The cells of the House of Refuge were narrow, confined and unhealthy. The doors were of stout plank, studded with rivets, and had small wickets to admit the light and air.

The beds were of straw and the cells were filled with vermin—so much so was this the case that the boys could not sleep unless almost dead for the want of it. I remember they used to burn brimstone in the cells—hence I take it that no better proof could be given that the cells were filled with vermin. The food was coarse and repulsive, consequently the poor boys were frequently hungry.

After remaining nine months at the "Refuge" my mother took me home again, but in a few weeks was obliged to send me to the Juvenile Asylum. At this institution my mother paid my board and I wore my own clothes. Dr. Russ, the Superintendent, was a very kind man, and his wife was an excellent and kind-hearted lady. In fact, all the boys who were under the charge of Dr. Russ could not have been used better at their own homes than they were at this institution.

We had good food and plenty of it, and attended school every day. But, as I had been in the "Refuge," it was impossible to expect that I would be a good boy in this institution. I ran away, every chance I got, until they had to put shackles on my legs, and many a pair I spoiled for them by sawing them off with table knives that I would nick like a saw.

They at last made a dress out of bed ticking (a girl's dress) and made me wear that, also with shackles on my legs, and then chained me to another little rascal like myself.

One night I made my escape and started for the city, but was recaptured and brought back. Dr. Russ then put a chain around my waist and then attached it to another boy who had shackles on his legs. One day I took the boy on my back and started for the city, but was retaken a second time before I got far from the institution.

The boys in this institution were treated with great kindness; Dr. Russ and his wife acted the part of a father and mother to all under their charge. I look back to the days I spent with Dr. Russ as the happiest in my life. Had I been sent to this institution when first sent to the House of Refuge, I cannot doubt my whole life would have had a different tendency.

After leaving the Asylum, through the advice of some gentlemen, mother sent me to the House of Refuge again. Had I been sent on a whaling voyage it would have been much better for my future life, for then it was that my education for a thief began in earnest. I got acquainted with quite a number of boys who were brought in from the Five Points, and every Sunday, while in the yard, all the boys would sit together and tell stories. I used to listen to stories of burglaries and murders that took place at the Five Points. The boys went so far as to instruct each other in the science of stealing pocket-books, and some of them were quite proficient at the business. I would sit for hours listening to such stories, and took great delight in them.

MY FIRST PROMPTINGS TOWARDS CRIME

originated in the House of Refuge. Every species of petty rascality was daily practiced by some of the boys. We used to break into the shop and alter the boss's account book, that we might not be found short of work.

We boys would sometimes make our fingers sore to keep from being punished, for then we would not have to work. We would stick a needle under the nails, and then insert copperas into the wound. This substance we got from the copper pipes. Some of the boys lost their fingers from the effect of this poison.

One time I tried to break my arm; I made a boy jump on it whilst I held it in a slanting position, and would have ultimately succeeded only the whistle blew to form into companies. In fact, the the poor boys were

SO SHAMEFULLY TREATED

and cruelly punished that we would do almost anything to escape it. I frequently saw poor little fellows forced to go into cold water during the winter season. The water was very cold, so that it would make a stout man suffer, and, because we did not get into the tanks quick enough, the assistant superintendent would jump among us with a large rattan and strike right and left.

I was frequently so hungry on going to bed that I could hardly sleep. Such luxuries as tea, coffee and milk I never saw whilst in the institution. I have often been kept on bread and water, and on one occasion for eleven weeks. When my mother came to visit me I never complained, although at the time my body would be a complete mass of sores, from the effects of the whippings I received. I could not bear to make my mother feel bad, so I kept silent and suffered all without a murmur.

The House of Refuge was a perfect *Pandemonium*, and I cannot doubt that many turned out to be thieves from the effects of habits and acquaintances formed there, who otherwise might have adorned society. I could at this day, if I were in New York, muster up a company of Refuge boys who are now thieves and gamblers.

One little playmate of mine, who was in the Refuge with me, was executed in New York city in 1866, for murder.

POOR JERRY O'BRIEN!

I often think of him, for he was a good boy, and only twenty-three years old when executed. Another playmate was sentenced to this prison twenty years for murder, but was pardoned after serving six years. He was only out three months, when, under the influence of liquor, he committed another crime and was sent to Sing Sing.

I could mention scores of young men, who are now confined in Sing Sing, who were initiated into every species of wickedness in the House of Refuge.

I have been a prisoner in Sing Sing State Prison when it was at its worst, but, in many respects, I would rather he confined in Sing Sing than the House of Refuge, as the "Refuge" was conducted when I was there.

THE PRESENT HOUSE OF REFUGE

is situated on Randall's Island, and the building is large and commodious. I have no means of knowing what course of treatment is adopted in the new institution, except from report. The food of the institution, when I was a prisoner, was insufficient in quantity and poor in quality. Every morning we used to get one large tablespoonful of molasses with a small piece of bread, and some cold water was given us instead of tea or coffee. For dinner we got a dish of poor soup and a piece of bread, and for supper we got a bowl of mush and molasses. This was our food from the begining to the end of the year, except on Fridays, when we got codfish, and Sundays bean soup and pork. Sunday was the only day in the week that we got enough to eat. I have been informed, by boys who were in the Reform School of Massachusetts, that they fared much better—having milk, tea, coffee, fruit, cake, etc.—good treatment generally, with the opportunity of receiving a good education.

What a difference exists between those two institutions! One makes honest men, while the other makes thieves and murderers!

There are five "Refuge" boys in this prison to-day, and they can be counted by scores in the Sing Sing State Prison, Blackwell's Island, and other prisons of the State of New York.

I might say a great deal more about this New York *Pandemonium*, where thieves and murderers are prepared for their professions, but would be thought to be exaggerating its cruelties.

I frequently was hungry, and sometimes with the other boys we used to steal the horses' corn and eat it, after breaking into the barn and committing a burglary to get it. Very often in the shoe shop the boys would steal dirty flour, and make little cakes and eat them to stay their hunger.

A few weeks after leaving the "Refuge" I sought out some of the old "Refuge" boys, who then loitered around the Five Points, and began stealing for a living, and became a constant visitor of

THE OLD BOWERY THEATRE.

The delight I received from visiting this place of amusement, and the temptation to return to it, was such as to render it impossible to stay away. The corrupting influence was very great, and I used frequently to resort to every species of thieving and dishonesty to obtain the little means requisite to gratify the passion which the nightly scenes there witnessed inflamed. Crowds of small boys resorted to the same expedients as myself to obtain little sums of money to spend at the theatre.

BOWERY THEATRE.

After leaving the theatre, late at night, I usually went with a few boys to their "bunk" for lodgings. This "bunk" lodging establishment consisted of the steps of a printing office, where the heat would come from the boiler and printing office to the steps below.

Sometimes we would sleep in hay barges, wagons, and, in fact, any hole into which we could crawl, and very often would wake up and find ourselves painted with cart grease—an operation that some of the other boys would perform while we were asleep.

We then would steal all day to raise "pit money" for the theatre. In this way I lived for months, while my poor mother would be hunting the streets night and day for me.

ONE NIGHT

I crawled into a shutter box in Greenwich street, and my sister, while hunting for me, stood by the box to rest herself, and, hearing some one snoring, she looked into the box, but did not recognize me until she held me close to a street lamp. There was Jack, dirty, ragged and hungry! I was brought home, and as soon as my mother saw me she took me up in her arms and began to cry over me for a long time. I promised my mother that I would be a good boy for the future, so, on the following day she took me out and bought me a new suit of clothes. Things went on quite well for a short time, but the temptation to visit the theatre was so great that I could not resist it, so I ran away from home and went to the Five Points. Being well dressed, and smart looking for a boy of my age, I was picked up by a notorious thief and villain called

ITALIAN DAVE.

I was then called his "kid." Every morning Dave and his "pal" would go down town and rob the large stores that would be just opening. While they would "button-hole" the porter, as they called it, I would sneak into the store and look for valuable goods, such as silks, etc. During the afternoon we would go up town and rob dwelling houses. Sometimes I would be taken to the Battery, which, being a very dark park, we would frequently waylay gentlemen as they were wending their way to the Brooklyn Ferry boat. It seemed very cruel to me thus to knock men down senseless; however, my job was to go through their pockets and take all valuables from their persons. I used to feel deeply for those poor men while engaged in robbing them. I was made to return to my superiors in crime all the valuables I could find, and out of the plunder they would usually give me a few shillings. One night, after robbing a gentleman, Dave's "pal" made me drunk and left

me sleeping on an old canal boat on the North River. Had I
rolled in my sleep but three feet I should have been drowned. In
this way I lived for some time with this infamous scoundrel, Italian
Dave. One night Dave armed himself with a large knife and then
started across the street to a "den" to kill another thief, who, it
seemed, had done Dave some great personal injury. Dave was
drunk, and, while reeling across the street, a party fell upon him
and beat him with clubs until he was almost dead.

Next night I went to the National Theatre, and, while there, was
arrested by

A DETECTIVE

whom mother had hired to hunt me up. He promised my mother
that he would bring me home if he found me. I was sick of the
life I was leading, and would have been only too glad to go home,
but was afraid. The detective frightened me so that he made me
tell him all I had been doing, under the promise that if I did he
would let me go. He said if I did not he would take me back to
the "Refuge," and have them keep me until I was twenty-one years
of age. Like a fool I told him everything I had been doing, and
then, of course, he made me tell where all the plunder was sold.

I was thus lodged in the Station House, and afterwards taken
with three officers to the Five Points. One officer held me, and I
led them up through an old building, with their revolvers in
hand. The house was searched, and a great deal of jewelry, such
as watches, pins, rings, etc., were found. The receiver of the goods
was arrested, and I was put into the House of Detention, to appear
as a witness against him. I did not wish to appear against the
man that bought the goods, so I made my escape from the House
of Detention three or four different times. The last time several
other boys and myself set fire to our beds, and, through the excitement, escaped. I then

WENT TO NEWARK, N. J.,

and while there I robbed a jewelry shop and escaped with six gold
watches; these I sold to a Jew for fifteen dollars. After a few
weeks I was arrested and confined in the Tombs (City Prison). I
was put into a cell with ten other boys, the most of them older
than myself. During the day we were taken out and confined in a

cell, in a different part of the prison from the men, and during the
night we were again taken back to the men's prison. We had
nothing except a large wooden bunk to sleep on, and not half
enough covering to keep us warm, for sometimes it was very cold.

THE RATS

used to eat through our pockets to get at the waste crumbs of bread.
Sometimes we would place large pans of mush on the floor to keep
the rats from us. Notwithstanding all this they would still come,
and in the morning all the food in the pans would be gone. To
keep them from the bread that we would be saving we had to
hang it to nails on the walls. I used to watch the rats sometimes,
and they were *big fellows.* Occasionally the keeper would put a
poor fellow into our cell that had *delirium tremens.* I have seen
some very bad cases of this dreadful disease. I have seen them
thrown into a cell with no one to look after them, and the next
morning found them dead. We were half starved. My mother
used to come and see me, and bring large baskets full of good
things, which, of course, did not last long among the hungry boys.
I never made any complaint to mother, but told her I was well and
happy.

One day I became quite sick while looking at a dead young girl
who had poisoned herself. It was such a dreadful sight to see them
cut the poor girl's body that it made me very sick, and I could not
stand up for a week after.

ESCAPED.

One day I picked the lock on my cell door, and all the boys in my
cell got out into the hall, and, being very small, we crawled through
the bars of the window facing Franklin street. I had very hard
work to get through, and had a very sore breast for months afterwards from the crushing that I gave myself in crawling through
the bars. I went home and dressed myself up in my sister's
clothes, and mother sent me to a relative in the country who resided
on Long Island. I remained a few months, but could not behave
myself. Being sent on an errand one day, I broke into a house
and stole the silverware; I was caught with the plunder but managed to escape. After escaping from being sent to jail for my misconduct on Long Island, I went to

JERSEY CITY.

While there I was arrested and committed to jail. Italian Dave was arrested and sent there on a charge of burglary. After being confined in jail a short time I made my escape and went to New York, where, after committing a series of crimes, extending through two years, I was finally arrested. I was sentenced for two years to Sing Sing on an old charge which had been on file against me. Italian Dave was sentenced to the New Jersey State Prison, at

ESCAPING OVER THE CRADLE.

Trenton, where he subsequently died. A few days before his arrest he had abused his girl in such a shameful and brutal manner that she lost one of her eyes from the effects of it. The poor unfortunate girl, although she had little cause to love him, stood by the miserable wretch to the last, when all his own relations deserted him and refused to go near him, at a time when he was confined to his bed by sickness and on the point of death. After Dave's death the unhappy girl reformed.

Poor Dave was more to be pitied than to be blamed. Brought

up in the Five Points, among the filth and pollution of society, it
is little wonder he turned out the consummate villain he afterwards
became. When I reached

SING SING,

it contained twelve hundred prisoners, three hundred of whom were
doubled in small cells that were scarcely large enough for one man.
I was put in with a notorious old criminal, who soon initiated me
into the mysteries of a " cross life."

MAHONY'S CELL.

In consequence of close confinement I was taken sick and removed to the hospital, where I was confined three weeks. After
recovering I was put to work with a gang of convicts building
docks. Being young and small I had a good time of it, and was
well treated both by officers and convicts.

I soon became acquainted with some of the worst characters in
the prison, and listened with great wonder and astonishment to the
stories and crimes they had committed, and was perfectly thunder-
struck at the exploits they intended to perform as soon as they

should be set at liberty. When I entered the condition of the prisoners was wretched and degrading beyond expression. The food was unfit for human beings, and scores of men were afflicted with scurvy. The men were constantly being murdered by the brutal punishment inflicted. The shower bath, crucifix, bucking machine, cages, horns, were all in daily use. It was not a strange sight to see twenty-five men march into the chapel with their heads shaved and clipped in every conceivable style and fashion—some with both sides off, some with one side off, others with nothing but a small bunch of hair on the top of their heads. Scattered through the chapel might also be seen a number of men with

CAGES AND HORNS ON THEIR HEADS.

These cages and horns weighed about eight or nine pounds, and were kept on the prisoners night and day—for weeks sometimes.

Now, if to all this artistic exhibition we add the natural music generated by the clanking of chains worn by a still greater number of prisoners, we shall not be surprised that Rev. John Luckey's congregation was the most interesting in the world. I remember having one of those cages and horns on my head that weighed eight or nine pounds; when it was taken off I thought it weighed a ton. Men were put into

A SHOWER BATH

in the dead of winter, and showered until they were senseless. I know it to be a fearful punishment by experience. One time they showered a man to death. He died shortly after being taken out. This murder created a great excitement in New York. The murder, and the different systems of punishments then practiced at Sing Sing Prison, were illustrated in *Harper's Weekly* at the time. Through the articles published in the New York press the Warden and principal keeper were discharged. What seems strange, they both died on the same week shortly after—the Warden fell from his horse and broke his neck, and the principal keeper died from heart disease.

PUNISHMENTS.

The shower bath is a box about four feet wide and eight high, with a large water tank on top. The victim is made to sit in a seat placed inside the box; his feet are then fastened in stocks, and his hands are strapped on each side of the bath. A tub is then placed around his neck and secured with wooden pins. This tub is to catch the water, so as to keep the victim's mouth under water. When these infernal demons wished to "sweeten" a poor fellow, as they termed it, the operation was usually performed in this way; They tied a cloth around the victim's neck, in order to make the tub fit tight; this would prevent the water from running off quickly. After this was done they would then put questions to the wretched object of their cruelty, and as the victim would be in the act of answering their questions the water would be instantly thrown upon his head with such violence as almost to produce strangulation.

This experiment was repeated until, very frequently, the poor convict was almost dead before removed. While the operation was going on several of the ignorant, brutal keepers—men who were as mean and cruel to all those over whom they had any authority as they were cowardly and cringing to those above them—stood by and seemed to enjoy with great satisfaction the horrid tortures they inflicted. Nothing is a surer indication of an utterly depraved, as well as corrupt and cowardly nature, than indifference to human suffering, real or assumed, and can only be explained on the principle that it was possible for those wretches to be as far beneath every instinct of humanity as for many of their victims to be superior to themselves.

Another refined and exquisite method of punishment was the crucifix. This consists of a straight, heavy bar of wrought iron, which was placed on the shoulders of the victim and then fastened around his neck; his hands were then stretched out and fastened on each end. The crucifix is very heavy, and is considered a severe punishment. While a convict was undergoing punishment in this way the kind and humane keepers would be sitting by and taunting the poor victim in his agony.

A still more inhuman system of punishment was practiced by the bucking machine. In this case the poor convict's hands were handcuffed, and then a pole run through between the elbows and the knees, and thus secured the victim was hung on a wooden frame. This latter is a severe punishment.

The punishment of placing horns on the prisoner's head was not so cruel as those above mentioned. The horns consist of a round iron cage, fastened to the head by a padlock, and on the top has three iron prongs on each side. The cage is the same without horns.

In the principal keeper's office (which was the punishment room) they had a worthless, brutal Irishman ("stool pigeon") named Sheenas. This mean and cowardly rascal was used as an instrument of torture in the hands of the miserable prison authorities. Whenever an especial act of cruelty was to be performed, and the dastardly officers were too cowardly to perform it, this unmitigated villain was brought in for the purpose. The man Sheenas then signalized his petty authority by knocking the convict down and afterwards compelling him to enter the bath box.

Another noted scoundrel, who was used as a "tool" by the keepers, named Ben Luke, seemed, if possible, to rival Sheenas in his brutality and villany.

To get a smile from a dirty ruffian of a keeper (no better than themselves) paid both Sheenas and Luke well for all the important service they rendered to the prison authorities. It would be useless to enumerate all the acts of individual cruelty and brutality perpetrated by those depraved vagabonds, Sheenas and Luke, for these affairs were of daily occurrence.

On one occasion a man refused to strip for the bath, as it was winter, and very cold. The poor convict ran to the river. He was fired upon and wounded in the leg; then the keepers rushed upon him and dragged him to a solitary cell. His leg was dressed, and afterwards he was kept in a solitary cell. One day the poor fellow in his misery rushed out of this cell (hopping on one leg) and went to his own proper cell. Three keepers followed him, but the miserable wretches were afraid to go in and bring out their victim. They called to their assistance the noted "stool pigeon," Ben Luke. "Do you want me to take him out?" exclaimed this depraved and incorrigible wretch. "Yes, Ben, go in and haul him out," responded these brave and humane officers of the law! Luke went in and dragged the poor fellow out, and in doing so struck him. The wretched and suffering man cried out, "Oh, my leg, my leg!" "Never mind his leg, Ben, haul him out," replied these worthy State officials. I will mention a few cases of

BRUTAL PUNISHMENT

that I know to be true, one of which I witnessed. On one occasion a colored man, who had a life sentence, was very sick in his cell. The Warden came to his cell and said, "Well, what game are you up to now?" "I am very sick, Mr. B——." "Well," said Warden B——, "I will give you *some medicine.*" Turning to one of the officers, he ordered him to lay the hose and pass it through one of the windows, so that he could get it. B——, the Warden, then played the hose on the poor sick man until he was quite exhausted. While this exploit was being performed several of the keepers, ignorant, vulgar cowards, stood by laughing, with a view to get a smile of approbation from the Warden—a sufficient compensation for their brutal conduct.

Another man, named Jesse A——, was ordered to strip for the bath. He refused. A number of keepers got around him and showed their accustomed bravery by knocking down an unarmed man with clubs. With all this they could not get poor Jesse into the bath box. The principal keeper then ordered one of the keepers to heat an iron poker red hot. When poor Jesse saw this he fell in a fit. The principal keeper then got the hose and played it right into Jesse's face until he had satisfied his mean and cowardly nature.

A man named Hughes was shamefully abused and kicked by his officer. He turned upon his officer and stabbed him. Hughes was then set upon by a whole crew of cowardly keepers, who treated him in a brutal manner and then threw him into a solitary cell. For a long time he was kept in solitary confinement and had his head shaved in the most disgraceful manner; he also underwent the usual number of baths, duckings, etc. In consequence of the inhuman treatment he underwent Hughes lost the use of his lower extremities, so that he could not stand on his legs at all; they then put him into the hospital. The poor fellow had been confined to his bed nearly three years, and was obliged to be lifted out of his bed and again lifted into it, so helpless was he.

The kind, humane Warden B——, not believing the man had lost the use of his limbs, ordered Hughes to be put into the chapel, in his bed. His food was then placed on the other side of the chapel, near the wall, so that Hughes could see it, with a view to find out whether Hughes would not get up and walk to it. The poor suffering man was kept in this condition for three days with-out food, after which he was taken back to the hospital. After the sentence of Hughes expired the Sisters of Mercy took charge of him. There were some

FAVORITE CHARACTERS IN SING SING

whilst I was there, and among them Charles B. Huntington, the celebrated Wall street banker and forger. Every indulgence was shown him. He wore a white shirt, side whiskers, and was per-mitted to walk all over the prison grounds with a spaniel following him; he was also permitted to lodge in the hospital and take his meals there.

Warden B——'s son, with Huntington and his friends, would sip their wines and smoke their Havanas in the hospital dispensary as if they were in Delmonico's, on Fifth avenue, New York.

The Warden's son had a salary of fifty dollars per month as night watchman in the hospital. Did he do his duty? He went to bed every night precisely at ten o'clock, with his fancy pet black and tan terrier, and in the morning everything was all right, for he had a few unprincipled rascals who acted as "stool pigeons" for the sake of a few favors.

Warden B—— had his fast yachts, boats, horses and dogs, and had his pet convicts to look after them. Of course it was a *model* institution.

THE REV. JOHN LUCKEY,

the venerable and respected Chaplain of the Sing Sing State Prison, was a gentleman highly esteemed and greatly beloved by all the prisoners, as a man of devoted and unfeigned piety. He secured the confidence of all by his unremitting efforts to better their con-dition.

He fought hard against the authorities of the prison, and strug-gled against popular prejudice in regard to the disgraceful and cruel manner in which these unfortunate men were abused. Nor were his noble efforts confined to the prison. Outside it was his habit to visit the friends and relatives of prisoners, to carry messages to them, and not unfrequently to devise means to relieve their wants and mitigate their sufferings. During his long and protracted charge of eighteen years he was incessantly employed in kind offices, and many pardons were granted through his agency and solely on his recommendation.

When this good man first came to Sing Sing convicts were not even permitted to have books, to write, or receive visits from their friends, but through his exertions all these privileges were secured. On one occasion a poor unfortunate convict was dying in the hospital, and in his delirium he kept crying for his wife and children. Mr. Luckey promptly went and brought the inspectors to the dying man's bedside. They were indeed deeply touched by his misery and distress. His wife was sent for, but before she arrived he had died.

Mr. Beal (of the New York Prison Association), a worthy co-operator of Mr. Luckey's, came to Sing Sing, and from the pulpit shamed the prison authorities for their want of sensibility to the condition of those whom the laws of the State had intrusted to their care. He related the fact that on one occasion, in the heat of summer, a poor discharged convict called at his office in New York, direct from Sing Sing, on the expiration of a five years' sentence. He was dressed in a worn out suit of clothing, and while in Mr. Beal's office he looked into a glass, and starting back exclaimed, " Good God ! is that me?" He had not seen his own face for five years.

After Warden B—— left, Mr. Hubbel, of Sing Sing village, was appointed Warden, and he at once began a work of reformation. He ordered all the barrels of " salt horse " to be thrown into the Hudson river as soon as he took charge of the institution. He made many important changes in the prison. He had a bath house built—a luxury that Sing Sing never had until Mr. Hubbel came there. He did everything in his power to promote the comfort of the prisoners, and abolished much of the cruel system of punishment in use by his predecessors.

For all the privileges the prisoners now enjoy in Sing Sing Prison they are principally indebted to Mr. Hubbel, who succeeded B—— as Warden. Mr. Hubbel was a most excellent and sincere Christian gentleman. There was no deceit in his character. He was a resident of Sing Sing, and a gentleman of wealth and high social position. He has represented his county in the Legislature of the State of New York, and was the Speaker of the House of Representatives at Albany.

He took the position of Warden reluctantly, and distrusting his own qualifications. His only object was to do good, and to raise and elevate, if possible, the condition and mitigate the sufferings of those unhappy victims of crime and misfortune. He was a gentleman of a warm heart, unselfish in all his feelings and pure in all his motives. He is remembered with love and gratitude by many whose misery he alleviated; by many who entered Sing Sing State Prison when it was a perfect Pandemonium—who left it after it had been made, through Mr. Hubbel's exertions, comparatively a Paradise.

ESCAPE OF MAHONY.

After leaving Sing Sing I sought out and found some of the "boys" with whom I became acquainted whilst there, and was arrested again for robbing a gentleman in a Grand street stage, but got off with six months to the Penitentiary on Blackwell's Island. Here I met with another misfortune, for one night, while attempting an escape, I fell on an iron picket fence. One of the pickets

went through my right wrist, and I also broke my left arm and
sprained my ankles in the fall. After this misfortune I ran as
rapidly as possible to the hospital on the other side of the island
and gave the alarm, for I was bleeding very fast. I was taken in
and examined. I asked them to cut my arm off whilst I had
strength to undergo the operation, for I thought it would have to
come off anyhow, and thinking mortification would set in, I judged
it best to have the arm amputated as soon as possible. My arm
was bandaged up, and in a few weeks I was almost well. As soon
as I recovered I escaped and went to

NEW ORLEANS.

I remained in New Orleans about three weeks and then returned
to New York, where I became acquainted with a lovely English
girl, of about sixteen years of age. She had been seduced, a few
weeks previous to my acquaintance with her, by a young man who
lived in the neighborhood of Newark, N. J. I have lived with this
unfortunate girl ever since, except when in prison.

After tasting the pleasures of a fast life I was again arrested, on
a charge of

STEALING A CASE OF SILK.

We were betrayed to the police by a little thief who belonged to
the tribe of Israel. The name of this young Iscariot was Morris.
It subsequently appeared that he had some resentful feelings
against the man who was to have bought the goods, who also was
a Jew. The little Shylock informed Capt. Jourdan, of the Sixth
Ward, and a watch was set on the house in which the goods were
concealed. At ten o'clock, whilst we were in the act of examining
the goods, the detectives came in and arrested us, but the party
who was with me worked the case so skillfuly that we all got
clear. We had to pay for our freedom on this occasion; at least
I had, for I was

OBLIGED TO ENLIST,

and give my bounty, $300, besides everything else that was of
value which they could squeeze out of me. I was sent to camp
on Riker's Island, and from there I escaped, but was recaptured
and sent to Castle William, on Governor's Island. While confined
in Castle William a party of us tried to escape. We succeeded in

bribing two of the guards, and when the bribed guards came on duty we cut through the floor of our room into the casemate below. We got into the yard, but were detected by the other sentinels, and came near being fired on, just as we were in the act of prying off a lock attached to one of the casemate doors.

We were then tied up by the thumbs—not a very pleasant operation. Next day we were ordered to the blacksmiths' shop, to be measured for shackles, ball and chain, but an order came for a squad of prisoners, and we were shipped to Alexandria, Va., and from thence to the front. We stopped at Brandy Station, about seventy miles south of Alexandria.

This was my first appearance on the rampage as a soldier. After taking an observation of the state of the army, and not being very favorably impressed with the condition of things, I began to look around with a view to give them the slip. An opportunity soon presented itself, and taking advantage of the circumstances, I

MANAGED TO ELUDE THE GUARDS

and escaped. I came back to the depot at night, and hid myself away in a car containing embalmed bodies of soldiers, who were being sent to their friends.

I arrived at Alexandria safe about two o'clock on the following morning. While the guards were searching the train I managed to elude them and got into a graveyard opposite the railroad. It was not a very pleasant neighborhood in which to locate, and I must confess I felt a curious sensation creeping over me while I laid behind a large tombstone, disturbed by every little noise I heard, causing me to peep in all directions, and expecting every moment to have some ghostly visitor tap me on the shoulder. After remaining in this unpleasant predicament for an hour I made an effort to get out of Alexandria, but was picked up at last by the night patrol, and, not giving a good account of myself, I was sent to the Alexandria Jail, then used as

A MILITARY PRISON.

When I entered the prison I was accosted by one of the boys and asked to pay a "society fee" or be pitched up in a blanket. I knew from experience there was no fun in being pitched up ten or twelve feet against the ceiling, so I talked to the President of this gymnastic association, who ordered me to be initiated into the mysteries of the "Toss-up Society" without being tossed up myself.

I must mention about a young man, named

WILLIAM THOMPSON,

who had been in the jail five months, and expected every day to be sent to his regiment, from which he deserted. One night, as we were all playing "blind man's buff," the guard called for Thompson. Thompson felt very happy, and began to shake hands with the boys, for he thought he was going to his regiment. He observed to me on leaving, "Good-bye, Jack, I hope you will soon get clear." He went down stairs with the guards, but, instead of being set at liberty, the sentence of death was read to him, and he was confined in a cell to await his execution. He was to be executed on the following Friday. Every evening I used to watch him as he walked by the window, under guard, taking exercise. Poor fellow, he used to look up and smile as he passed by the window. On the morning of his execution he shook hands with all the prisoners in jail; he then took his seat in an ambulance and was followed by another containing his coffin. He was shot upon his coffin, with his hands tied behind him, and one of the guards brought me a small piece of white paper that was stained with his blood. Poor Thompson's death made a deep impression on me at the time, but I soon forgot it.

A RUSE.

One day another fellow and myself took a notion to shave our heads, having no idea at the time that we were soon to be set at liberty. It happened that the day after I had my head shaved I was discharged. I tied a black silk handkerchief around my head and started for New York. It had been reported in the city that I had been executed. On finding this to be the case I resolved to turn my shaved head to account and make it pay. Never at a loss for an expedient I encouraged the report, and caused it to be circulated that I had been under sentence of death and was reprieved, had my head shaved and was drummed out of camp. Everybody believed it, and by this means I was saved from being rearrested for desertion.

After leading a life of crime and dissipation for a long time I was again arrested and convicted for crime, and on this occasion was sentenced four years and six months to Sing Sing Prison. I had been there only a few weeks when another fellow and myself made our escape through the roof. We were arrested the same morning on the Harlem Railroad, twelve miles from the prison, by four men. While they were taking us down to the city, with a view of remanding us to Sing Sing, I made up my mind I would run any risk to escape. As we were going through the Thirty-fourth street tunnel I brought my fist to bear on the constable's eye, then

MAHONY'S LEAP FROM A CAR.

jumped the train, and escaped through the excitement that I produced.

I then made the acquaintance of some "safe operators," and went with them for a few weeks, until one of the party was arrested, which took place as follows: While operating on a safe the store was surrounded and we were fired upon by the night watchman. One of the party was captured, tried and convicted, and sentenced three years at Sing Sing Prison. I then came on to Boston, and, after being a few weeks in that city, I sent six thousand dollars' worth of goods to New York with a view to dispose of the same, when I was detected and remanded to Sing Sing. The authorities then put a ball and chain on my leg, and kept me sitting in the prison hall, under the eye of a keeper.

Five months passed in this way, and I was getting tired out wearing the jewelry, so I asked Mr. J——, the Warden, to take it off and let me go to work in one of the shops. I told Mr. J—— that I had the ball and chain so fixed that I could remove it, and that if he would take it off I would not attempt to escape. He only laughed at me.

BALL AND CHAIN.

On the following day I managed to get an old coat and the keeper's spectacles. At twelve o'clock I played sick and did not go to the mess room with the rest of the convicts, but remained in my cell. While the prisoners were at dinner I took my ball and chain off and then walked to the end of the shoe shop, where the contractor had his horse in a stable. I harnessed the horse to a light wagon, and got through just as the convicts were leaving the mess room for their shops. I put on the spectacles, wrapped the horse blanket around my prison pants, jumped into the wagon and started.

I had to pass twenty muskets before I got outside the prison grounds, and was discovered before I got half way, for the guards gave the order, HALT, but I made up my mind that I should escape or be shot in the attempt. The horse being a fast one I put him to his full speed, and when passing the last guard post the guard told me to halt, but I only made the horse go faster, and paid little attention to the guard or his talk. I got clear without a scratch.

After riding about seven miles, with the whole village of Sing Sing after me, yelping at the top of their voices, "There goes a convict! there goes a convict! Fifty dollars reward! whoever catches him will get fifty dollars!" I thought it best to hide in some barn and let the horse go, which I did, and hid under the hay. About eight o'clock I heard the barn door open and a horse and sleigh come in. The driver came up in the hay loft and commenced to pitch hay down for the horse's feed. Every moment I expected to have the pitchfork run into me.

About ten o'clock I came down from the hay loft and gave the horse a good feed of oats, then harnessed him to the sleigh and started, as I supposed, for New York. After riding about two hours I found myself right back of the place from whence I started. I then started again for New York, and, after riding about seven miles, was chased by a double team ; after a long and exciting race I escaped, and reached New York city in the morning about seven o'clock. As soon as I arrived in New York I sent word to my girl, and she came where I was concealed.

ANOTHER ESCAPE.

We then left New York and came on to Boston. Being in Boston a few weeks, I started for the City of Philadelphia with a notorious character now dead. We committed a crime in Philadelphia, and the detectives got some clue of the place at which we were stopping, and came at night and surrounded the house. I was the first one arrested. While Nellie, my girl, was talking to one of the detectives, I jumped out of the second story window and escaped.

IN BOSTON AGAIN.

I then came back to Boston much poorer than when I started, for the detectives seized my trunks and I lost all. My poor Nellie lost her trunk, too, for it contained something that would have cost her trouble had she applied for it. We found ourselves in Boston without clothes and greatly in debt. In this state of things I got up and started out one day and confiscated thirty-five hundred dollars' worth of broadcloth. I took the cloth to a store which I had rented previous to my leaving Boston and there repacked the goods, after which I expressed them to New York and thence to Yonkers, on the Hudson river. The men I employed to put the goods on the wagon read a name that was on the wagon. Through this circumstance I was

TRACKED TO YONKERS.

As soon as I arrived in New York I hired a carriage, and, in company with the man to whom I had sold the goods, started for Yonkers. While on the way the thought flashed through my mind, while looking at the telegraph, that possibly at that moment an order for my arrest was being transmitted, and I made a remark to that effect to the man who was with me. On my arrival in Yonkers I was instantly arrested and brought on to Massachusetts by Detective Baker. At the time of my arrest no one knew me, and I would not have come on with Baker, only I felt sure I would get a chance to jump the train, as I had been successful in exploits of this kind before. I had no doubt that I would get an opportunity to escape between New York and Boston.

I was brought safely to Boston, tried and convicted, and sentenced for the *moderate term* of five years to the Charlestown Academy of Music, to be enrolled as a member of *Gideon's Band.* I could have stayed in New York if I had wished to, being an escaped convict, but having tasted of life in Sing Sing, I preferred to try Charlestown. After a few weeks' residence in this "water cure establishment" I made an

UNSUCCESSFUL ATTEMPT AT ESCAPE.

Having procured an old suit of clothes, one morning I asked permission to visit the hospital to see the doctor. After returning from the hospital I watched until a good opportunity presented itself, and then jumped through the window of the whip shop store room, and dressed myself as soon as possible. I then took an oil can in one hand and a can of varnish in the other and started for the gate.

The guard stationed at the gate opened it, but when on the trap (between the two gates) he inquired where I belonged. This question, being unexpected, nearly took the breath out of me. However, I replied that I belonged in the bronze house, outside the wall. The guard looked at me very sharply, and, still suspecting all was not right, inquired further, "How did you get into the prison?" "Why," replied I, "did you not see me when I came in this morning on the wagon, with three other men?" He cast another sharp and inquiring glance at me, and said, "When did you come in—was it before or after breakfast?"

Knowing the guard was not on duty before breakfast I replied, "Yes, certainly, before breakfast." He then said, "I was not on duty then; that is the reason I did not see you; you can pass."

As I opened the last gate I felt greatly relieved, and was congratulating myself that the "day of jubilee had come." This rejoicing, however, was premature, for I had only advanced a few steps when I was accidentally met by an officer who knew me well.

THE ALARM WAS GIVEN

and I was arrested. A large piece of jewelry, weighing about twenty-five pounds, was then attached to my leg. This ornament I nursed for the space of three months. I subsequently made another attempt to leave the institution without a ticket from the authorities. In this case I managed to obtain a good impression of a key, from which I made a duplicate that I had no doubt would do the execution required; but just as I was getting ready to take "French leave" I was betrayed by one of my fellow prisoners, and this scheme, also, was nipped in the bud.

A second time the ball and chain were brought into requisition and fastened to my leg; as these ornaments were old friends, they stuck to me closer than a brother. After wearing the jewelry for one month I made up my mind that I would not attempt to escape any more, as my partial success had frightened the authorities and awakened their suspicions. I knew that my every movement would be watched. The first attempt was well contrived, and but for an unforeseen event, which was purely accidental, it would have proved a complete success. My recapture outside the walls was rather an accident than otherwise, for it was impossible for me to foreknow that an officer would by chance be on the outside. I asked permission from the prison authorities to leave my jewelry at the blacksmith shop, which was granted, and thus ended any further attempt to escape from the Charlestown State Prison.

THIS SKETCH

has not been written for the sake of notoriety, but in the hope that the young and thoughtless may be induced to stop and reflect before they do wrong. It has been the writer's object to offer such facts, taken from his own life and experience, as he thought would serve as a warning to the young who are starting out in life, full of hope, without for a moment reflecting how easily their brightest prospects may be ruined and dashed to pieces. It is doubtful whether any who are in the State Prison for crime would ever have committed a crime in their lives if they had thought that they would be detected and sent to the State Prison for it. The prevailing idea, that deceives all men who commit crime, is that they will do it, for there is no danger—they can easily escape. A little experience soon undeceives them, though not until they have found themselves the inmates of felons' cells. It is only when thus reduced that they begin to see their folly and become painfully sensible of their degradation. Then, when it is too late to remedy the mistakes of the past, they realize what they might have been had they continued in the path of rectitude.

Young men, then, who are starting out on a career of carelessness and dishonesty, I would beg of you and caution you to stop where you are and retrace your steps, for you cannot travel far in that direction without bringing up in the State Prison. It has certainly been my experience, and, so far as my acquaintance with prisoners extends—and that has been very great—it is the history of nearly all with whom I ever conversed. As a general rule, the majority of prisoners who fill our State Prisons are men by no means so bad as people suppose. Among them are many young men of great intelligence and fine education, capable of adorning any circle of society; young men who have the same feelings, sympathies and associations as those outside, and very often have much better hearts, who know that if many young men outside had been tried by the same temptation that they too would be in State Prison.

I am now twenty-six years old, and my life has indeed been a stormy one, filled with events and full of experience learned in a rough school. When I reflect what I might have been, and then turn to what I am, I can without difficulty trace all my mistakes through life—the suffering and disgrace they brought upon me and those dear to me at my early home, and the associations that home calls up—to disobeying one of the kindest and best of mothers.

I have not spent one year under my mother's roof since I left the House of Refuge, many years ago, when I was yet a small boy, nor have I seen my mother for over five years. She has often wished to visit me, but I begged her not to do so. I could not bear to have her visit me in prison, for she is now getting old and is in feeble health, yet nothing can shake her love for her worthless Jack, for she remembers him in letters and packages of good things, which, through the kindness of the inspectors, iron bars cannot keep from Jack or any of the prisoners.

Thank God! my five years will soon expire, and, in a few weeks I shall again be thrown upon the world, with poor prospects indeed, but not without hope. I would not make any rash promises about reforming. I have not the least Christianity in me; yet I frequently have good thoughts, and, must confess, feel better while under their influence than otherwise, but they don't remain long, for the devil soon enters into my head and drives them out.

Long continued habits, and bad ones, and the influence of old associations take possession of me, and I find it very difficult to shake them off; but when I leave this prison I should like to become an honest, upright man. I have tried dishonesty and rascality long enough to convince me that it don't pay in the long run. I have never earned an honest dollar in my life. I have, however, resolved to make the effort to do so when I leave this prison. I know how much I shall have to contend against, if I depend on any encouragement where my history is known. It would be folly to talk of reforming, because nobody would think of trusting me or giving me employment.

This misfortune has no doubt prevented many young men from reforming and leading an honest life. Take a young man who has spent four or five years in Charlestown or Sing Sing; he is discharged by the Warden, after four or five years of labor, with three

or four dollars, a shake of the hand and a " God bless you," with a
" Don't get into prison again."

This is easy advice, but it is a dose of medicine that is pretty
hard to take. The poor fellow leaves the prison resolved to
reform; he seeks employment and can't get it; in a day or
so his money is spent; and now let him call upon one of those
who, for the five years while he was in prison, were preaching
religion and reform to him, for a small sum of money or
their aid to procure him employment, he is soon repulsed, with a
number of oily excuses, which it requires little judgment to understand. He is thrown upon the cold charity of the world without
money, friends or employment, and he is almost driven to steal.
He is brought before the Court for sentence, and his crime will not
justify a sentence of more than two years, but the Judge learns
that the villain has been in the State Prison before, so he gives him
five years—two for the crime, and three for having been there before. Society calls this justice, and so it is all right.

As soon as he gets back he is reminded by men who visit the
prison, with a view to reform prisoners, of the correctness of their
prophecy: " I told you if you did not go to work you would be
in the State Prison again," and for five years more the prisoner
is regaled with the same coldness and hypocrisy, and an occasional
tract now and then, which added to the comforts of his previous
five years. I shall, therefore, as soon as released, leave for a
Western city, a thousand miles away from old haunts, acquaintances and associations, and will do what I can to reduce the
promises to practice that I have made in the Massachusetts State
Prison."

STILL ANOTHER BOLD ESCAPE.

The following newspaper extract is from one of the New York
dailies of the 10th of April, 1872. It gives a vivid account of an
operation of Mahoney, and a bold escape of his, subsequent to his
discharge from the Charlestown Jail, where this history of his life
was written. Although he is called William Jones, he is none
other than our hero, Jack Sheppard. It will thus be seen that, in
spite of his promises to reform, he was no sooner at liberty than
he began his old career of crime :

JACK SHEPPARD'S ESCAPE.—THE ESCAPE OF A PHILADELPHIA
BURGLAR FROM THE NEW YORK CENTRAL OFFICE.—THE POLICE
ASTONISHED.—THE INVISIBLE THIEF.

On Monday afternoon Capt. James Irving received a telegram
from Detective Charles S. Smith, of Philadelphia, informing him
that a heavy burglary was committed in the store of H. M. Day,
325 Chesnut street, between Saturday night and Monday morning,
and that it was supposed the goods stolen, consisting of laces,
alpacas, Italian cloths, etc., had been shipped to this city.

Officers Macdougal and Walling were directed to take up the
case, and, believing that the goods would come by express, they
had a watch placed upon the general express offices, especially the
Adams. Subsequent events showed the soundness of their judgment, for while watching, yesterday forenoon, they saw a well
known burglar and sneak thief, known as William Jones, *alias*
Jack Sheppard, and one John Hathaway present a receipt for six
cases of goods to the clerk at the office of the Adams Express. The
officers waited until they saw Jones and his " pal " give directions to
the carman whom they had employed as to where he was to convey the articles, and they immediately secured both the men and
the property, which is valued at over $5,000. All were taken to the
Police Central Office, where their photographs were taken, and
they were locked up in a light, airy room on the first floor.

Officer Smith, of Philadelphia, arrived in the meantime, and
intimated his intention of taking the prisoners back in the 6 o'clock
train. Jones has obtained his *soubriquet* of " Jack Sheppard " from
the fact that no prison has yet been able to hold him. He has
been " wanted " since he broke out of Sing Sing for numerous
burglaries and robberies, among which were many trucks and carts
containing valuable goods, which he has driven away while left
without drivers in the street, or after inducing a driver to leave his
charge for a short time, on pretence of taking a case of goods from
him to be left at some place on the same route. About half past
4 o'clock last evening everything about the Police Central Office
was in confusion. Crowds were rushing to and fro, shouting
" Send out a general alarm," and others shouting some one thing
and some another. Mr. Manierre, being the only Commissioner in
the building, called on Captain Irving, who explained that the pri-

soner Jack Sheppard had escaped. A general alarm was sent out, but Jones had not been rearrested up to a late hour.

The man who locks up the prisoners is a good, honest, and altogether an excellent man, named Guerin. He is strictly temperate and all that, but probably too old for his position, as a prisoner could easily knock him down and get away before he could give the alarm. Whether Sheppard did use violence or not does not appear; at all events, when Guerin was questioned he was as white as a sheet, and could give but a very incoherent account. He said that while the prisoners were waiting to be taken to Philadelphia by the officers, dinner was ordered and a messenger from a neighboring restaurant was admitted into the passage leading to the cells by Guerin, who advanced to the end where the prisoners were locked up. On opening the door Guerin found but one prisoner instead of two, and gave the alarm; but it was useless, Jack Sheppard was gone. Officer Butts, of the Sanitary Squad, said he saw a man run out by the Mott street door, but did not dream that he was a prisoner.

The iron bars over the door of the cell had been forced out, and it is supposed that he mounted on the back of his "pal" and thrust his body through the vacant space, then dropped to the floor and secreted himself against the wall behind the passage door, and as soon as Guerin opened the latter and went to the cell door Jones slipped out and ran off by the Mott street side, as he could not well get out by the Mulberry street door, there being a sentinel always posted there. His escape, however, in broad daylight, from under the very noses of his guardians, through a corridor in which people are always standing or walking, right opposite and within about ten feet of the door of the Detective Office, and having to pass the station of the Sanitary Squad, one of whose men actually witnessed the escape from the building, is something to cause surprise.

I had not seen Mahony for a period of eight years previous to my meeting him by a mere chance, while on my way down town in one of the Bleecker street line of cars. Mahony was accompanied by another young man; they were dressed like a couple of spruce, tidy young mechanics, and wore striped flannel shirts.

The recognition was mutual, and, on my motioning to him,

Mahony seated himself at my side and a conversation ensued, in the course of which the subject of this book was broached, when Mahony volunteered what information and assistance he could give, offering to bring or send the above MS., with permission to use the whole or part of it as the author should see fit. He took the author's address, promising that in the course of a few days he should see or hear from him.

A few days thereafter Mahony called, bringing the manuscript with him. In the mean time a house up town had been entered by thieves, who, but for the timely interference of the police, would have got off with a good share of plunder. The entrance to the house was effected as follows :

Early one morning two young men carrying paint pots and brushes in their hands rang the bell of the house adjoining. They stated to the servant who answered the summons that they were come to do some painting next door ; they had forgotten the key, and as their going back to the shop, which was quite a ways off, would necessitate the loss of considerable time, asked to be allowed to ascend to the roof of that house, as they supposed they would be able to effect an entrance into the next house through either the skylight or scuttle. The servant, suspecting no wrong, allowed them to go up. When the family came down to breakfast she told what she had done. The gentleman of the house chid her for doing so, and despatched her in quest of an officer. The officer arrived just in the nick of time, as the thieves had got together a lot of the most valuable and portable things in the house, which they were about making off with. He drew his pistols and commanded the men to surrender. One of them secreted himself behind a door, and, while the officer was securing the other, succeeded in making his way to the kitchen, through the window of which he escaped, climbing over the fence and making his way through a neighboring house in the street. The captured thief was taken to headquarters, photographed, and then committed to the Tombs for trial.

On the author's mentioning to Mahony that the man who escaped was said to resemble him, he (M.) "Guessed he would not go to see his friend." His friend was tried, convicted, and sentenced to State Prison for a term of years. He never reached there, however, having met his death in attempting to escape from the officer who had him in charge, by jumping from the train which was bearing them to Sing Sing while it was in motion.

Shortly afterwards Mahony went to Cincinnati, where he was implicated in an extensive burglary, for which he was arrested and sent to prison. But it is a good prison that can hold our Jack Sheppard for any length of time. He soon found his way out, but had not gone far ere he discovered one of the attachés in pursuit. The chase was a hot one, only terminated by Mahony's plunging into a canal, swimming to the other side, and secreting himself in a dense wood, where he remained for the night. The next day he started on his travels, and, after having walked about fifty miles, foot-sore and weary, he stopped at a farm house, telling the occupants some plausible story or other in order to prevail on them to keep him until such time as he should hear from his friends in New York, to whom he at once despatched a telegram, notifying them of his plight. He received by mail twenty-five dollars, with which amount he bought his way to this his native city.

Living in New York is no easy matter when one has luxurious tastes that must be gratified and no money to gratify them. Gentlemen (?) of that cloth live well; and, though their friends are willing to " put up " for them occasionally, yet, if they manifest a disposition to be idle, they soon receive a gentle hint to be up and doing. Mahony was not long idle. He stole a cart load of valuable goods while in transit from the ship to the Government warehouse. He wrote to the cartman requesting him to meet him with $1,500 in an open field on Long Island, when the goods would be delivered up to him. Mahony failed to keep the appointment, and the cartman was a loser of about $4,000.

A bonded warehouse on the West side was entered and robbed of about $14,000 worth of silks, etc., belonging to H. B. Claflin & Co., who offered a reward of $5,000 for the apprehension of the thief or thieves. There is reason to believe that Mahony was concerned in the burglary, as all traces were lost of him in the city until his arrest at the express office, as described in the above article.

JOHN MAHONY AS A POET.

As an evidence rather of the love which John bore for his

mother, than of any particular poetical ability, I give the following piece of verse from his pen:

TO MY MOTHER.

BY JOHN MAHONY.

I long for my old seat, mother,
 With my head upon thy knee;
Many's the changing scene I've seen
 Since thus I sat by thee.
Oh! could I look into thine eyes,
Their meek, soft-looking look
Would fall like a gleam of happiness
Upon my heart to-night.

Years I've been away, dear mother—
Nearly four years have gone and passed
Since last the tear-drop on thy cheek
My lips in kisses met.
A score of years it seems at last;
 Oh! how very long it seems;
Though every night I come to thee,
 Dear mother, in my dreams.

I bear a happy heart, mother,
 But a happier one would beat
If my prison life had ended,
 And I had the dear old seat.
Oh! mother, darling! will the day ere come
 When from this prison free
I can direct my steps to my boyish home,
 And take my seat by thee?

MASSACHUSETTS PRISON, 1871.

I have not seen John Mahony for some time, but, at last accounts, he was in the State Prison at Joliet, Illinois, probably under an assumed name. That is the strongest jail in the country, and it will tax Jack Sheppard to his utmost to escape.

CARRYING MAHONY TO SING SING.

CHAPTER XVI.

MURDER MOST FOUL!—ENTRANCE TO THE CHAMBER OF HORRORS.
—HICKS, THE PIRATE.—HIS BLOODY DEEDS ON BOARD AN OYS-
TER SLOOP.—EXECUTION ON BEDLOE'S ISLAND.

" With what a rattling noise the drop went down, and how suddenly they changed
from strong and vigorous men to dangling heaps of clothes!"—DICKENS, *in Oliver
Twist.*

WHEN Bluebeard is leaving the lovely Fatima, he cautions
her, as told in that charming fantasy of W. W. Story, "Bluebeard's Cabinet," not to venture into a certain chamber, for there

> ——" Horrent dreams steal noiselessly about,
> And opiate shapes of sick delirium swarm,
> And nightmares wander. There the marids dwell,
> And ghouls, and ginns, and afrites huge and black,
> And forms so faint that they elude the eye ;
> These, as you look upon them, shift and change,
> Now mock, threaten and pursue your steps,
> As, wild with fear, you strive with leaden feet
> To flee their presence. There, in awe and dread,
> Vague horrors creep that have no name on earth,
> Found in the fevered dreams of wicked souls,
> And sent me from the East. There upward stretch,
> Leading to nowhere, monstrous galleries,
> Where slipping, sliding, goes the 'wildered thought
> Up endless convolutions, into height
> So vast we totter in a vague dismay,
> Or drop to blankness. There huge caverns gape,
> Dripping with terrors, into which we slip,
> Despite our death-like graspings for support.
> There whirl a million dizzy wheels of thought,
> And spin to madness."

And now, reader, we approach our cabinet of horrors. The
atmosphere will be found heavy and suffocating; iron chains will
clank on the cold stone floor of condemned cells; we will see the
fatal noose, the dismal black cap, and the ghastly coffin; the gallows will loom its horrid shape against the sky; hideous things,

which once were men, will dangle from black beams—for it is the Gallery of Death—the apartment in which the masked executioner holds his fearful court.

To reach this cabinet we must first go through the ante-room of Murder. Here the drapery is red—blood red. Crimson curtains shut out the light. Rivulets of blood crawl over the floor, like loathsome snakes, and end in stagnant pools. The walls are smeared with clotted gore, and brains dashed out by furious blows. Daggers, dripping with the life tide, lie around, and scattered here and there are smoking pistols, blood-besmirched axes, and bludgeons with tufts of human hair clinging to them. This is truly a rare sight! Ranged round the room are glass cases, in which we see many curious things. Here are any quantity of broken hearts, blasted lives and ruined hopes. A phantom panorama is continually gliding by. The first picture is Cain, with the brand upon his brow, gazing down at the dead Abel at his feet. And then we see men crawling upon their victims at dead of night, the stiletto point jewelled by the blood-red moon, which rises on the scene. There are pictures of mothers strangling their babes, of husbands shooting their wives, of footpads waiting in lonely lanes for the unsuspecting traveller, of jealousy urging men and women to fearful deeds, of yellow gold drawing, with its basilisk charm, men through seas incarnadine; of murder in all its shapes; and all the while there breathes fitfully through the room the mad melody of delirium, anon dying away into a wail of despair, and then rising to the clashing height of madness!

Murder will now be our theme for many pages to come. There will be no attempt made to give all the murder cases in which the perpetrators of the crime have been brought to the Tombs. It would take several volumes to do that. The prominent ones—those in which the story is interesting by reason either of its romance or its horror—will be selected. Neither is there any attempt at chronological order. Each crimson narrative will stand by itself, and the story will be told independent of what has gone before and what is to follow. We will begin with

HICKS, THE PIRATE.

On March 16, 1860, the oyster sloop E. A. Johnson left this port for Deep Creek, Va., to procure a cargo of oysters. The company on board consisted of Captain Burr, two boys, named Oliver and Smith Watts, and a man known as William Johnson. The captain had with him a considerable sum of money. At six o'clock on the morning of Wednesday, the 21st, this small sloop was picked up by the schooner Telegraph, of New London, Conn., and subsequently towed to Fulton Market slip by the steam tug Ceres. Everything on board denoted confusion and violence. Here she was boarded by Captain Weed, of the Second Precinct Police, and Coroner Schirmer, who at once proceeded to make an examination.

The sloop had evidently collided with some other vessel, as was indicated by the damaged condition of the bowsprit and cutwater. The sails were loose upon deck, and everything denoted confusion and violence. The floor, ceiling, benches and furniture in the cabin were stained with blood, as were also the clothing, bedding, papers, etc., which had been scattered on the floor. Marks of the dragging of some bloody substance from the cabin door to the sides and rails of the vessel were discernible, and the spectacle on board the sloop was altogether ghastly and horrible. The small boat at the stern was discovered to be missing.

John Burke and Andrew Kelly, two men residing at 129 Cedar street, appeared at the Second Police Precinct Station House, and stated that Johnson, one of the crew of the sloop, had arrived home the day previous with a considerable quantity of money in his possession, and had started East with his wife and child. Officer Nevins traced Johnson and his wife and child to a house near Providence, R. I., where he arrested them. He denied that his name was Johnson, or that he had ever been on the sloop; but the officers conveyed him to this city, where he was soon fully recognized as having belonged to the crew of the E. A. Johnson. A yawl was picked up off the coast of Staten Island and identified as belonging to the unfortunate vessel, and a deck hand on the seven o'clock boat from the island testified to having been accosted by a man answering the description of Johnson, whom he assisted to count a quantity of money into two small bags.

Captain Burr's watch, and a daguerreotype which a young lady had given to Oliver Watts before sailing, were found in the possession of the prisoner, and he was fully recognized by John Burke, who had lived in the same house with him at No. 129 Cedar street, as well as by several others.

He behaved all along with the utmost coolness, declared that his name was not Johnson but Albert E. Hicks; that he had never been on board the sloop.

He was transferred to the custody of United States Marshal Rynders, and committed for examination. His trial came off in the following May in the United States Circuit Court, and the jury, after a deliberation of only seven minutes, found him guilty of murder and piracy. He was sentenced to be hanged on one of the islands in the bay on Friday, July 13. While confined in the Tombs Hicks made a confession. He described the affair as having occurred at 9.30 or 10 o'clock at night, when Captain Burr and one of the Watts boys were asleep in the cabin. "I was steering at the time," said Hicks, "and the other Watts was on the lookout at the bows." Suddenly the devil took possession of him, and he determined to murder the captain and crew that very night. Creeping forward softly, he stole upon the boy at the bows, and with one blow knocked out his brains. The noise attracted the attention of the other Watts, who jumped out of bed and came up the companion way to see what was the matter. Just at that moment Hicks struck him a heavy blow on the head with an axe and left him weltering in his blood on the deck. He then went down in search of the captain, and upon entering the cabin they once came into conflict. The captain, who was a short, thick set, but very muscular man, grappled with his assailant and there was a long tussle, during which the stove was upset. The Captain was beginning to master the murderer, when a well directed blow of the axe felled him to the floor—another blow and he was dead. Hicks then went on deck, and taking up the bleeding and helpless man he had left there, threw him over the vessel's side. The man clutched at the taffrail, but Hicks chopped off his hands with the axe, and the poor fellow dropped into the sea. The other bodies were then thrown overboard, the captain's money bags were rifled, and Hicks headed the sloo for shore. He used the small boat to effect a landing.

When brought back to the Tombs, after sentence, a great many people came to see him—among them Mr. P. T. Barnum, of the museum, who asked for a private interview with the prisoner. When Hicks was informed of Mr. Barnum's wish, he asked to see the

Warden first. The Warden proceeded to his cell, when Hicks asked the object of Mr. Barnum's visit. He was informed that the great showman was desirous of obtaining a plaster cast of his head and bust, for exhibition with the other curiosities in the museum.

"Oh," said Hicks, "Barnum's on the make; but if he's a mind to pay for it he can have it. Let him come and I'll make my own bargain with him."

Mr. Barnum was accordingly admitted, and at the conclusion of the interview he stepped in the office to tell the Warden that he had effected an arrangement with the prisoner, agreeing to pay him twenty-five dollars and two boxes of cigars, after which he left, but returned the same day with an artist and the necessary appliances, and succeeded in getting as good a cast as could be desired.

On the day following Mr. Barnum again called to see the prisoner, and offered to give him a suit of new clothes in exchange for those he had on. Hicks was pleased with the offer and accepted it. The next day, however, he complained to the Warden that Mr. Barnum had got the best of him—the new clothes not being as good as his old ones.

At 6 o'clock on Thursday, July 12, the day preceding his execution, Mrs. Hicks took farewell of her husband, but neither of them exhibited the slightest emotion.

It was more like parting for a few days than forever. Father Duranquet then entered his cell and remained with him until 11 o'clock, at which hour he partook of a cup of tea and retired for the night. He was awakened at four o'clock the following morning and told to dress. He was perfectly unconcerned as to his fate, and manifested no signs of grief or penitence.

At nine o'clock Marshal Rynders, Sheriff Kelly and others entered, when he quietly arose and saluted them. The Marshal then read the death warrant, and told him to prepare himself for the approaching execution. He did so by arraying himself in a suit of blue cottonade, made expressly for the occasion.

He marched out of prison attended by Father Duranquet, Marshal Rynders, Deputy Marshal Thompson and Sheriff Kelly, all of whom got into the first carriage. In the second carriage were the Deputy Sheriffs, and in the others police and representatives of the press.

The procession then drove quietly to the foot of Canal street, there to embark on the Red Jacket for Bedloe's Island, where it was arranged the execution would take place. About 1,500 persons, consisting of gamblers, politicians, pugilists, reporters and medical men, were assembled on board the Red Jacket. The party arrived on board at 9 A. M. and immediately started for their destination.

The Marshal, finding that he had plenty of time to spare, and the Great Eastern, then lying at the foot of Hammond street, having but recently arrived on her first voyage to this country, concluded to give his guests a little excursion and a view of the monster ship. The steamboat was accordingly headed up the river, whither it proceeded as far as Hammond street, sailed round the Great Eastern, and then started for Bedloe's Island.

Immediately Hicks and the officers boarded the Red Jacket he entered the saloon and engaged in prayer with Father Duranquet. The Red Jacket started down the bay at 10:15. The party arrived at 11 o'clock, and at once formed themselves into procession. Hicks went first, between Father Duranquet and Deputy Marshal Isaacs, and was followed by the others in due order.

The pier was lined by a platoon of marines, under command of Captain John B. Hall, and on the passing of the procession, they, with the troops from Fort Hamilton and Governor's Island, formed themselves into a hollow square all the way to the scaffold.

The scene was altogether a very imposing one—hundreds of boats, large and small, being within easy distance of the shore. For eighty or one hundred feet out the boats formed one solid mass, and again on the outside of these were numerous excursion boats moving about.

The execution was witnessed by about 10,000 people. Hicks maintained his coolness and air of bravery to the last. He never quailed beneath the glance of the crowd. Immediately on landing on the island he knelt down and silently prayed for a few moments, and then proceeded to the scaffold, which was within fifteen or twenty feet of the shore.

The fatal signal having been given, Hicks was executed at precisely 10:45. For three minutes he struggled severely, but after that exhiblted no signs of pain. The body was allowed to remain suspended for half an hour, when it was cut down, placed in a coffin, and born back to the ship.

The remains were buried in Calvary Cemetery, but no stone has ever been erected to show the precise spot.

Should the family of the unfortunate man ever desire to remove to the place of his birth, the dust that the law left as a legacy to his posterity, we fear they would find the grave without a stone, also a grave without a body—snatched hence, as is so often the case of criminals hurried from the scenes of their bloody deeds by the decree of inexorable justice, to make another subject in the laboratory of the College of Physicians and Surgeons, where the students, with keen relish, would, with the body under the sharp knife, contrast their scientific skill with the horrid butchery committed on board the Oyster sloop.

CHAPTER XVII.

CHARLES WALTERS MURDERS HIS FAITHLESS WIFE WHILE MAD WITH RUM.—THE DEATH SENTENCE.—EFFORTS OF JUDGE STEWART.—COMMUTATION OF SENTENCE TO IMPRISONMENT FOR LIFE.

" Cant as we may and as we shall to the end of all things, it is very much harder for the poor to be virtuous than it is for the rich; and the good that is in them shines the brighter for it."—DICKENS, *in American Notes.*

PEOPLE who live in up town palaces, dress in purple and fine linen, and ride in coaches, have very little appreciation of the trouble it is to love and be loved when the affectionate couple are miserably poor. There may be such a thing as the " love in a cottage" that we have heard so much about, but there is very little of it in New York. It is very frequently the case that when " Poverty comes in at the door Love flies out of the window;" and, in view of that statement, there is a grim and satanic humor about the remark of the fashionable young lady, who, in a disquisition upon matrimony, said: " Oh, yes; I could live with any brave young man, no matter how poor we were, provided there was an elevator in the house, and hot and cold water, and a nice parlor, and I had a couple of servants, and the meals were brought in from a hotel. Yes, under these circumstances I think it would be quite jolly to be poor." And so do we.

This being so—if love in a cottage is a myth—what must love in an east side rookery be? Listen to the tragic tale of Charles Walters, and resolve, my fair readers, to marry, but to marry in no worse way than that suggested by the young lady we have quoted.

Charles Walters was a native of Ohio, where he worked at his trade of carpentering. He had a young and beautiful wife, whom he loved dearly.

It would have been well for Charles Walters had he staid in Ohio. There he was earning a decent living, and the twain were happy; but the fascinations of the gay metropolis took possession of the soul of Walters; he sighed for the "populous pave," the glitter and glare of city life.   In an evil hour he came to New York, bringing Amelia with him.   He arrived here in 1863.

Being a good workman, he naturally counted on success here. But times were dull, and there was no building going on.   His

NEW YORK TENEMENT HOUSES.

little purse was soon exhausted, and the growl of the grim wolf was heard about his door.   Starvation stared them in the face.

Finally, they commenced to drift adown that dismal tide, which washes up against the poor house.   From respectable boarding houses they passed on to shabby and obscure quarters, and finally

brought up in a tenement house of the most wretched kind.   There
they were in a dark, dirty room under the roof—no fire, no bread,
no anything.   We can see them on the night when Walters told
his companion that it was necessary for him to go somewhere in
quest of work.   He sat with his head buried in his hands.   Amelia,
shivering with the cold, drew her ragged shawl more closely about
her.   Even in this dismal plight she was pretty, and a certain air of
refinement about her spoke unmistakably of better days.   The
room was lit by a single candle, whose fitful gleam illuminated
dramatically her sad face.   A close inspection would have revealed
a something in the eye which should not have been there—a shadowy
recklessness, a determination to end this farce of a life in some way
or other.   She had come to the unfortuate conclusion that in the
game of existence hearts are not trumps, and that it is diamonds
which are the better hand.

"Amelia!"

"What is it, Charley?"   This in a careless sort of way.

"I am going to leave town to-morrow."

"Are you?"

"Yes."

"Am I to go along?"

"No, I shall leave you here."

"What, in this hole, to starve?"

"It is the best I can do—I must get work."

"Well, I suppose it will have to be so"—and the tears upon
her cheek glistened like jewels in the way of the candle light.
Would that they had been—would that some fairy had made these
tears sparkling gems, then the tragic end would never have come.

On the next morning Walters started down the bay to one of the
islands, where Government troops were quartered.   He was gone
two months.   How about Amelia in the meantime?   Did she
emulate Phyrne or Penelope?   Did she strive to earn money by
her needle, as her husband expected, or did she sell her body for
gold to whoever took a passing fancy to her comely face?

Let us come back to New York with the husband.   He has
been moderately successful, and his heart beats high within him at
the loving reception he had so long anticipated.   "Now," he no
doubt mused, "I can take Amelia from that wretched place, and

we can *live* once more. Poor little girl! I wonder how she has been getting along."

With such thoughts he reached his home, to find—what? To find his home deserted. Then he began to hear dreadful stories about Amelia. He was told that she had become an abandoned woman—had taken to drink, and had sunk to the lowest grade of fallen womanhood. This set his brain ablaze—he raved, swore, and acted like a madman. Rushing to the nearest groggery he drank himself into a frenzied condition, and then started out to find Amelia. He did find her at last—found her in a low cellar in Centre street, opposite the Tombs. There she lay asleep upon a bench, surrounded by drunken women and their worse male companions. With a cry of rage he sprang upon her, knife in hand, and, before her astonished companions in crime could interpose, he stabbed her seventeen times, almost cutting her body into pieces. Then he threw the knife away and walked into the street, surrendering himself to the first officer he met, and was locked up in the Tombs. In due time he was tried for the murder.

His counsel was Judge Stewart, who acted without fee or reward, and did all that could be done in his client's behalf; but he was found guilty of murder in the first degree, and sentenced to be hanged in the prison yard.

The case was carried to the Supreme Court, which confirmed the original decision. It was then taken to the Court of Appeals, where it lay for a long time—but at length came its decision, confirming that of the lower courts, and nothing remained for the prisoner but to prepare himself for eternity.

A short time after Judge Stewart's attention was again called to this case. He thought the matter over carefully, viewed the subject in every light, and saw the peculiar circumstance which prompted the deed. He determined on having an interview with the prisoner, and accordingly called for that purpose at the Tombs. The prisoner was sent for and the Judge had a long talk with him. He heard the man's history, and the story of his trials, saw that he was not at heart a bad man, and that there certainly were mitigating circumstances in his favor; and the Judge determined that, if it lay in his power to prevent it, the man should not be hanged.

Accordingly he set to work, procured the necessary letters in the prisoner's behalf, and defraying all expenses from his private purse, and losing his valuable time, for which he never expected to receive the first cent in payment, he proceeded to Albany and laid the case before the Governor. He obtained an interview, and, after remaining closeted with him for a long time, was asked to call again, though but little encouragement was given him. He returned to New York quite hopeless, and informed the prisoner of the result of his mission, advising him at the same time to make his peace with God and prepare to die.

But the good Judge persevered in his efforts, and the day preceding that set down for the execution to take place again visited the Governor, remaining with him until late in the day—not leaving him until he obtained a respite for two weeks. He at once repaired to the telegraph office and despatched a message to the Sheriff, directing him to delay the execution until the last moment, lest he should meet with any delay in reaching the city with the necessary papers.

When, on the next morning, the Judge arrived at the prison, he found that all the preparations for the execution had been made. A crowd of spectators were assembled, most of whom were pleased though some were disappointed. The gallows was taken down, the crowd dispersed by the Sheriff, and things resumed their usual course.

Judge Stewart discovered an uncle of the prisoner, who was doing business in this city, and whose aid he secured in endeavoring to obtain a commutation of the prisoner's sentence. Together they worked indefatigably—the one at least—out of the purest motives of humanity.

The time passed quickly, and the prisoner's last day was come. Judge Stewart had been for some days at Albany, constantly importuning the Governor. The Sheriff and the Warden had each received a message from the Judge, late the preceding night, informing them that he had succeeded in obtaining a commutation of sentence to imprisonment for life, and that he would be down with the boat that left Albany that night. It was seven o'clock, and the Sheriff (Kelly) was in a ferment. No Judge Stewart—no papers had yet arrived. He telegraphed to a friend at Albany to see the

Governor immediately, and report the result of the interview at once. The Warden telegraphed to the Governor direct.

Eight o'clock came—no reply, and yet no papers—and the Sheriff concluded to proceed with the preparations for the execution. After a while came a telegram to the Sheriff to delay the execution until the last possible moment. At length, at half past ten, breathless with haste and excitement, the Judge rushed into the prison yard, bearing the papers in his hand. A feeling of relief, as though an immense weight had been removed, was experienced by all.

The boat, it seems, after leaving Albany, got aground on what is called the overslaugh, and was delayed for a long time. Early in the morning Judge Stewart went to the captain and informed him of the importance of his mission—it was a case of life or death—and the necessity of his being at the Tombs at the earliest possible moment. The captain appreciated his position and promised to let him off at Canal street, that being the nearest point to the Tombs, instead of carrying him to Liberty street, the regular landing place. Arrived at Canal street the Judge got off; seeing no carriage, he hastened as fast as his legs would take him to Hudson street, where he got on an Eighth avenue car, and rode as far as Franklin street, where he got off, and with all possible haste proceeded to the Tombs, arriving as above mentioned.

The prisoner was notified of the arrival of Judge Stewart with a commutation of sentence. He clapped his hands over his head— he thought it would burst, so great was the pain he experienced there, caused by the reaction in his feelings. He felt grateful to God for his mercy, and thanked his counsel and friends for their untiring exertions in his behalf, and promised so to conduct himself while in prison that no fault should be found with him.

The prisoner, the author has lately heard, is still at Sing Sing Prison, where he bears a good character, works cheerfully at his trade, and enjoys the confidence and good will of all connected with the prison.

CHAPTER XVIII.

WIFE MURDER BY ARSENIC.—THE CASE OF JOHN STEPHENS.—
PERSECUTION OF HIS WIFE'S NIECE.—HER BROTHER ATTEMPTS
TO SHOOT HIM.—THE FINGER OF SUSPICION.—EXHUMING OF
THE BODY.—TRACES OF ARSENIC FOUND.—THE TRIAL, THE
CELL AND THE ROPE.

"To be hanged by the neck 'till he was dead—that was the end. To be hanged
by the neck 'till he was dead."—DICKENS, *in Oliver Twist.*

THE web of fate is curious in its warp and woof. We know
not to-day the black or golden letters upon to-morrow's page
of life, and, like driftwood in a mountain torrent, surge on to our
doom. The criminal, after the commission of his crime, skilfully
covers up, as he thinks, every evidence of his guilt; but how
seldom does he succeed, and how curiously does he drift into the
fatal meshes! The lariat noose of Justice is always circling in the
air, and seldom misses its deadly mark. Eugene Aram covered
up the body of his victim with leaves, but the wind and the rain
undid his work, and exposed to the eyes of men the horrid sight.

Little did John Stephens think, when he dropped the arsenic in
his wife's cup, that there was a piece of rope and an executioner
waiting for him in the dim future. The murder was quietly done,
there was no suspicion at the time, and all might have been well
for him but for one trivial act. Had not the nephew of Stephens'
wife attempted to assassinate him in the street the murder of Mrs.
Stephens would have been unavenged.

Stephens was a member of the church, punctual in his attendance, correct in his deportment, and apparently devout in his wor-
ship—enjoying the respect of his minister and the esteem of his
fellow members of the church.

He was employed in the car and coach manufactory of John
Stephenson, on Twenty-seventh street, near Fourth avenue. He
was a good workman, exemplary in his conduct, and had won the

confidence of his employer, who esteemed him highly, and who believed in his innocence to the last.

His family consisted of himself, wife and child, a little girl of about eleven years of age. He occupied apartments in a house on the same street with his shop.

Mrs. Stephens became ill—a physician was sent for to attend her. At that time there was living with the Stephens family a young woman, niece of Mrs. Stephens, who nursed her during her

JOHN STEPHENS.

illness and assisted in the management of the affairs of the house. Owing to the limited accommodations this young woman was obliged to sleep in the bed with Stephens and his wife.

Though, as above stated, the young woman nursed the patient, yet did her husband take it upon himself to administer the medicine; instructing the nurse to hang a cloth out of the window, which he could see from the shop, as a signal to him when the time arrived for his wife to take her draught.

Mrs. Stephens, instead of improving under the treatment, sank gradually—growing worse and worse from day to day. At length, after three weeks' illness, she died.

A burial certificate in proper form was duly obtained, the remains were given in charge of the undertaker, and the funeral ceremonies were properly conducted. Stephens made the customary outward demonstrations of a decorous grief, and had the sympathy of his employer and his friends in his affliction.

He went to his work and attended church as usual. His deceased wife's niece took charge of his house for him, and everything went on as though nothing out of the usual course of events had occurred. After a while, however, Stephens having conceived a passion for the young woman, made her an offer of marriage, but she declined his suit. At the time she was engaged to a young man doing business on the Bowery, and whom she expected shortly to wed.

Stephens, stung by his niece's refusal to marry him, determined on breaking up the match between her and her lover. Accordingly, he wrote a long letter, disparaging the young woman, but to which he omitted signing his name, and forwarded it to the address of the young man.

This letter evidently annoyed the young man, but he still continued his attentions to the girl. Another letter was written, which was followed by still others, in which the young woman's character was assailed—the writer stating that he had slept in the same bed with her on different occasions. These letters had the desired effect—the young man ceasing entirely his visits to the girl.

The young woman very naturally felt grieved at the strange, and, to her, unaccountable conduct of her lover; she could not rest until she ascertained the cause. She called on him for an explanation, and was shown the letters he had from time to time received.

She recognized the writing as her uncle's, and at once surmised that he had resorted to the writing of these anonymous letters in a spirit of revenge for her rejection of him. She explained to her lover the circumstances of her aunt's illness—the inadequacy of Stephens' means to engage a professional nurse, hence her undertaking that office, and, in consequence of the limited accommodation, the necessity of her sleeping in the bed with her aunt and uncle. But the young man refused to have anything further to do with her, and so the engagement was broken off.

Poor creature! Alone and friendless! None to consult with or to advise her in the hour of her trouble—none to avenge her wrongs. What should she do?

She had a brother, but an ocean rolled between them. Would he, or could he, even if he would, come to her and afford a brother's protection? She could at least write to him and ask his advice—perhaps that would comfort her.

The brother received his sister's letter. His spirit chafed within him when he thought of his sister's sad plight and her lonely condition. So far away! So truly alone! He whose protection she had a right to receive—whose interest in her welfare every claim of humanity and of relationship demanded, doing all he could to injure her—assailing her virtue—the jewel of her womanhood! O, was it not too much for human nature to bear!

He completed his arrangements and came over to this country to seek his sister, whom he found, and who told him more, very much more in the bitterness of her spirit than she could write. She told him of the domestic affairs of their uncle—of their deceased aunt's illness—how their uncle would allow no one but himself to administer the medicine. O, horrible suspicion! Could he have poisoned her?

The story so worked upon the feelings of the young Irishman that he determined to wreak vengeance on the sanctimonious hypocrite. He armed himself with a pistol and went in pursuit of Stephens. He met him on the street, deliberately shot at him, but missed his mark. He was arrested and taken before Judge Welch, who was then holding court in the basement of the City Hall.

Stephens made his statement, which was in effect as follows: He was quietly walking along the street, when this young man, without any cause or provocation that he was aware of, deliberately aimed his pistol and fired on him, but, fortunately for him, missed his mark.

The Judge ordered a commitment to be made out, intending to send the young man to the Tombs. The young man, who was very intelligent, asked permission to say a few words in defence of his conduct.

He then told the story of his sister's wrongs in such eloquent and feeling words that his auditors were visibly affected. He also narrated the circumstances of his aunt's death, and gave utterance to his suspicion, shared by his sister, that his aunt had been poisoned by her husband.

So plausible was the young man's story that the clerk was ordered to make out a commitment for Stephens, who was thereupon taken to the Tombs, while the former was removed to the House of Detention to await an investigation of the case.

The body of Mrs. Stephens was exhumed after having been buried for about a year, and found to be in a tolerable state of preservation. The contents of the stomach were examined by Prof. Doremus, who found arsenic enough to kill half a dozen men.

After remaining in the Tombs for several months Stephens was tried for the murder of his wife. His counsel was Mr. Ashmead, ex-District Attorney of Philadelphia. The prosecution was conducted by Mr. Nelson J. Waterbury, the District Attorney. The trial lasted seventeen days and was conducted before Judge Roosevelt.

One of the principal witnesses for the defence was the little daughter of the prisoner. When placed on the stand she was asked the usual questions as to her knowledge of the nature of an oath and the responsibility of her position as a witness, to all of which she gave satisfactory replies. She was accordingly admitted to the stand and her evidence taken.

She told a plausible story, and her replies to the lawyers' questions were straightforward and to the point. When Mr. Ashmead had got through with her, the leading question put to her by the District Attorney was the following: "My dear, who taught you to tell this story to the court?" to which she innocently replied "aunty"—meaning Stephens' sister.

At length the trial was ended. The case was given to the jury, who brought in a verdict of murder in the first degree, and Stephens was accordingly sentenced to be hanged on the 3d day of February, 1860.

During his incarceration Stephens proved a very troublesome customer, getting himself and other prisoners frequently into trouble. Before his trial he claimed to be a freemason, and appealed to the fraternity for assistance. In two instances was he visited by a committee of these brothers from different lodges, but on neither occasion was he able to prove himself a mason.

He sent many anonymous letters to Judge Roosevelt and others while awaiting his trial. Among the letters he wrote was one purporting to come from the wife of Felix Sanchey, who was in the

FELIX SANCHEY.

Tombs for the murder of his father-in-law. This letter was put in evidence. The authorities cited Sanchey's wife before them, when upon examination it was discovered that the letter was a forgery. Sanchey subsequently admitted the same, and stated that it had been written by Stephens.

Sanchey's cell adjoined Stephens', and the two prisoners were in the habit of conversing with each other through the soil pipe which runs along the wall through the cells.

Quite an intimacy sprang up between the two prisoners and

they decided, if possible, to effect their escape—at any rate they would make the attempt.

But the plot was discovered in time. One Sunday, about two weeks before Stephens was to be executed, while the Warden was sitting in his office engaged in conversation with Mr. Pinckney, one of the Governors of the Alms House, he was told that a gentleman, who had an important communication to make, desired to see him for a few moments. The Warden granted the man the desired interview.

When the man was brought before the Warden he stated that, as a good citizen, he felt in duty bound to inform him of what he had heard and seen. Stephens was an acquaintance of his, and he had been to visit him. The prisoner had informed him that he did not mean to be hanged; that he had contrived a plot to effect his escape. He also showed him two pistols with which he was armed. The man refused to say anything further concerning the plot, remarking that it had been told him in confidence, and that he thought he had done his duty in notifying the proper authorities, thus giving them a timely warning, and that it remained for them to ascertain the particulars and prevent its consummation.

On the following morning Stephens' cell was examined—the prisoner having been transferred to another. The keepers found that a large hole had been made in the wall directly over the head of the bed, which was concealed by a lot of empty cigar boxes, piled up on a shelf which was there. The *debris* was hidden under the bed. The soil pipe was next examined, and in it were found files, saws for sawing through iron, a powder flask filled with powder, and many other things.

The hole in the wall was repaired, and in the evening Stephens was put back in the cell, having, however, been previously searched for the pistols, but they were not found upon him.

On the Wednesday following the Warden, in passing through the Park, met the man who had given the information and told him that Stephens had been searched, but that no pistols had been found. The man reiterated what he had said on Sunday, stating that he had seen the pistols with his own eyes.

Nothing further transpired until the Monday following, about noon, when Sanchey sent word to the Warden that he desired to see him. The Warden repaired to Sanchey's cell, who, pulling a pistol from his pocket and giving it to him, showed him two holes which he had made in the wall to meet the hole which Stephens had made in his cell, and confessed the plot which had been formed to effect their escape from prison, but which had been thwarted by the timely interference of the prison officers.

During this interview of the Warden with Sanchey, Stephens, in his cell adjoining, was engaged in prayer and singing with a minister, named Knapp, and two ladies. At the conclusion of the religious exercises one of the ladies called on the Warden and asked permission to visit the prisoner, Stephens, daily until the day of his execution, which, however, was denied her. She was not allowed to see him again.

The Warden sent for Mr. John Kelly, the Sheriff, in whose care the prisoner nominally was—all prisoners under sentence of death being in charge of the Sheriff of the county. When Mr. Kelly arrived he was shown the pistol which had been given up by Sanchey, and informed of the plot that had been concocted between the two prisoners to effect their escape.

The Warden suggested that Stephens be searched. "I'll go with you," said the Sheriff, and together they proceeded to the prisoner's cell.

The Warden entered first, the Sheriff following immediately behind. Stephens on their entry retreated to the further end of his cell, drawing his chair with him. The Warden stepped up to the prisoner and laid his hand on his (the prisoner's) shoulder and Mr. Kelly got on the other side of him. Stephens was then informed of the object of their visit. He complained of this treatment, and said that other prisoners were not used thus. He was told that all prisoners were obliged to submit to being searched, and that if he were an honest man he would undergo the operation without any further ado. He then said that he would like to see a friend of his first. He was informed that the friend would be sent for, but that the search must be made then and there.

Stephens kicked over the chair on which the Warden had placed his foot and made an attempt to draw his pistol. Mr. Kelly then threw his arms around the prisoner's neck, while the Warden held down his arm to prevent his drawing the pistol, and called to a

WARDEN SUTTON'S STRUGGLE WITH STEPHENS.

keeper to come and take it from him and put it in his (the Warden's) coat pocket, which was done. The prisoner was then ironed and thrown on the bed, and the search proceeded with, after which he was removed to another cell.

On the following morning Stephens was visited by the Sheriff, to whom he complained of the irons, and asked to have them removed. The Sheriff, however, refused to order them off unless the Warden should give his consent thereto. The Warden was then appealed to, who, on Stephens promising to behave himself for the future, ordered the irons to be removed.

The prisoner was cast down and gloomy—his spirit was evidently broken—and he gave no further trouble. When asked how he came in possession of the pistol he told some story which was not credited.

Nothing unusual occurred until the afternoon preceding the day of execution, when he expressed the desire to be shaved. The barber was sent for, who soon after arrived and performed the desired operation, the prisoner in the meantime talking to the Sheriff, who had brought two deputies to aid the keepers in their care of the prisoner, and instructing him as to the final disposition of his body and effects. He requested to be buried in the same grave with his wife—that is, if there was any portion of her body left, he having understood that the doctors had used it all up in their search for the poison. This was promised him. He talked freely of his execution, and spent the night with his clergymen in devotional exercises.

Early the next morning the Sheriff arrived with his deputies to prepare the culprit for the gallows. At the appointed time the death warrant was read to him, the Coroner's jury appointed, and he was marched out of the prison to the gallows, with his minister, the Sheriff and his deputies, and citizens following in solemn procession.

He was executed in the yard of the prison, and everything connected with the execution was ably arranged and well conducted throughout.

Stephens was a native of Ireland, about 5 feet 11 inches in height, and rather well built. He was possessed of a great degree of cunning and deceit.

CHAPTER XIX.

THE beautiful Virginia Stewart was shot to death on the steps of the Brandreth House, in this city, by her lover, Robert C. MacDonald, on the 23d day of July, 1859, while he was frenzied with rum, rage and jealousy—grim triumvirate.

MacDonald was a North Carolinian, a man of elegant presence, liberal education, and respectable connections. By business he was a cotton broker, and frequently made large sums of money. Chance threw him in the way of Miss Stewart. They loved; and living in the sunny South, where the balmy air toys with the orange blossoms, and the cane, bending to the breeze, rolls over the valleys in waves of shimmering green; where the tum-tum of the darkey's banjo makes night melodious, and emulates dusky pickaninnies to terpsichorean marvels; where everything in nature served to fan the flame of love in the two young hearts, as they wandered together over the beautiful hills, rolling away to where they broke into purple mountain foam against the sky. Such was the South before the red sea of war came with a thunderous tidal wave to submerge it, leaving in its wake ruined fields, blackened cities and countless graves.

And Miss Stewart was well worthy of being loved. She trod the earth like a queen, and her entrance into a room was like the sudden presence of some faint, tantalizing, delicious perfume, such as came up from the garden beneath the lattice, where the lovely Queen of Egypt waited her faithless Antony. In figure she was tall and commanding, and her form was as delicately moulded as any which ever grew into wondrous beauty beneath the magic chisel of Pygmalion. Her head was perfect, and was crowned with sunshine, the blonde tresses sweeping back from a face of peculiar beauty and power, while in the alternate melting and flashing of the deep blue eyes could be seen the love and passion surging across the heart that lay beneath the heaving bosom of snow.

With such a woman one might think that life would be but a stroll through a garden, and that the only stones would be showers of rose leaves. But the demon Drink came to blight this picture, as it has in the past many a one as fair. Bacchus dethroned the love queen, and the wine cup proved more attractive to MacDonald than his beautiful mistress. It was but natural that she should become disgusted; it was but natural that she should shrink from the embraces of a man redolent of rum. Hers was a jealous heart —it must have all of the man she loved, and she could not brook a a rival. Therefore, finding that MacDonald gave no promise of reform, she left him and came to New York.

As soon as she had gone MacDonald determined to follow her. He did so, and put up at the Metropolitan Hotel; once here he began to drink desperately, and soon his brain was on fire. Like a maniac he roamed the streets in quest of his mistress. After a few days he saw her, in company with a lady friend, just as she was entering Taylor's saloon, corner of Broadway and Franklin streets. He followed them and took a seat at the table near theirs. Calling for a bottle of wine he drank it, all the time watching the ladies opposite. When they had finished their lunch he arose too, and followed them out—followed them to the corner of Broadway and Canal streets. They turned the corner to go into the Brandreth House, and just then MacDonald stepped up to Miss Stewart and importuned her for an interview. She refused, and told him to go away and not annoy her. He then said, excitedly:

"I am told you are living with another man—is that so?"

No reply, save a contemptuous glance, and Miss Stewart turned to go.

With that MacDonald put his hand in his breast and drew out a Colt's navy revolver. Divining his purpose Miss Stewart cried aloud for assistance, and ran towards the entrance of the hotel. MacDonald bounded like a panther after her, and, placing the pistol almost against her head, fired. She fell senseless upon the step, her beautiful hair all dabbled with blood.

A Mr. E. Van Ranst, who was standing there, immediately threw himself on MacDonald. A deadly combat now ensued for the possession of the pistol, it being evident that the murderer intended to take his own life. Assistance was finally procured, and MacDonald was overpowered and removed to the Tombs. Miss Stewart was carried to a coach and driven to the New York Hospital.

There she lingered for eight or ten days, most of the time in an insensible condition. At times there were conscious moments, and she could tell her name, but did not know where she was. She imagined herself to be in Richmond, Va. Her mother, then living in Boston, was sent for, and passed the days and nights by the bedside of her dying child. The flame of life flickered on in this manner and then went out, leaving the darkness of death. The beautiful world had closed forever on Virginia Stewart. Her body was taken to Boston and placed beneath the daisies.

MacDonald lived in a regal way at the Tombs. He had a colored waiter from the Metropolitan, and lived on the best the Lelands could furnish him. The following letter was found on his person:

" JOHN W. SMITH, *Mobile, Ala.*

DEAR JOHN: I am about to commit that which will astonish you and most of my friends in Mobile. I have left some instructions with Messrs. Simeon Leland & Co. in regard to my body, but have since drawn $300 of the amount I first wanted, leaving $1,500 in their hands, which, after deducting my expenses, I will remit to you. Affectionately yours forever, BOB.

My love to Harry and the boys. ROBT. C. MACDONALD.

P. S.—And to you who find my body, have my trunks opened, and you will see a letter addressed to Messrs. Simeon Leland & Co. in regard to the disposition of my remains. Buried with my beard on. ROBT. C. MACDONALD."

MacDonald engaged the most eminent counsel to defend him, and openly declared that he would never be hanged.

One day his attendant called on the Warden to tell him that he had been instructed by MacDonald to buy some strychnine.

He was directed to make the purchase, but on his return to the prison to leave the end of the paper in which it would be wrapped sticking out of his pocket, when the keeper at the gate would take it from him—which fact he could report to MacDonald. After that a very strict watch was kept on the prisoner.

Among the visitors to the Tombs was a lady who was in the habit of conversing with MacDonald through the grated door of his cell. She procured a letter of introduction to the Warden from one of the most prominent men in the country, and through this letter obtained an interview with the prisoner. It has since been supposed that it was she who gave him the poison—a bottle of Muir's Elixir of Opium—with which he committed suicide.

Though discovered but a few minutes after he had taken it, and Drs. Corell and Simmons did all that lay in their power, they nevertheless failed to extract the poison, and he died about seven hours after.

The body was embalmed by Dr. Holmes and sent to his friends South.

CHAPTER XX.

CONFIDENCE MEN.—ROMANTIC ADVENTURES OF EUGENE MICKI-
WEEZ, THE RUSSIAN COUNT.—THE DIAMOND RING.—COLONEL
MARMADUKE REEVES.—HOW HE CUT OFF A COSSACK'S HEAD.—
HIS ERRATIC CAREER.

"The frankness of the country gentleman, the refinement of the artist, the good
humored allowance of the man of the world; philanthropy, piety, forbearance, tol-
eration, all blended together in a flexible adaptability to anything and everything."—
DICKENS, *in Martin Chuzzlewit.*

SOME time during the year 1863 there figured quite conspicuously in New York society a stylish young man calling himself Eugene Mickiweez, and who claimed to belong to the notability
of Russia. He was, he said, a Count, and his father was one of the
wealthiest of the Czar's subjects.

He was stopping at the Fifth Avenue Hotel, and living in the
style becoming a young nobleman whose resources were unlimited.
He very naturally made the acquaintance of many of the young
bloods of the town, whom he entertained in princely fashion, and
he soon earned the reputation of giving the best *petite soupers* at
Delmonico's, on Fifth Avenue.

A live nobleman always was, and we no doubt always will be a
subject of interest to simple republicans like us Americans; and
so it is not at all to be wondered at that the young Count soon became quite a loadstone, whose magnetic influence was felt by all
who came near him.

At the hotel there seemed to be quite a rivalry among the ladies
stopping there as to who should obtain the greatest share of the
Count's attention; and so great was the desire of the fair creatures
to possess some memento of their acquaintance with this young
"sprig of nobility," that they even resorted to cutting off pieces of
the lining of his hat whenever an opportunity offered.

Among the innumerable fair acquaintances of the Count was a
charming young lady, who resided on Fifth Avenue, and who, evi-

dently, was the favorite (?) one. He was very lavish of his attentions to her, and almost invariably accompanied her on her drives and promenades.

On one occasion he placed the young lady's ring, a brilliant of of the first water, on his little finger, playfully remarking that he would wear it for a few days. Being at the time somewhat embarrassed pecuniarily, he conceived the idea of removing the gem and having inserted in lieu a bogus stone, which idea was carried out, thus replenishing the young man's purse.

After some days had elapsed, the young lady's friends, thinking the count had worn the ring quite long enough, asked its restoration. The ring was returned to its owner, but it was not many days ere it was discovered that the gem had been removed from its setting, and that in its place flashed only an imitation diamond.

A warrant for the Count's arrest was procured, and he was taken to the Tombs, where he remained for some time, but was finally let out on his agreeing to enlist for the war.

He was accordingly sent, along with some other recruits, to one of the islands in the harbor, where troops were stationed waiting to be forwarded to the front.

The regiment to which the Count was assigned was, in a few days, to proceed to Washington. He succeeded, by his superior address and assurance, in ingratiating himself in the favor of the colonel and officers, and, on the plea of having some business with the Russian Minister at Washington relative to his home affairs, succeeded in obtaining a furlough for a few days, with the understanding that he was to meet the regiment at Washington.

The business between the minister and the Count was never transacted; nor did he rejoin his regiment at Washington. Though a Russian, he was evidently familiar with and thoroughly posted in the art of taking French leave. A few weeks afterwards he was heard of in Canada.

Nothing further was heard of the Count, and, excepting by his victims, he was as completely forgotten as though such an individual had never existed. One day, a few winters ago, however, a paragraph appeared in one of the daily papers to the effect that the young Russian Count who had some years since victimized a young lady residing on Fifth Avenue, by borrowing her diamond ring and substituting a paste imitation therefor, had turned up again, and was pursuing a young lady of wealth somewhere down East. The facts of the case were as follows:

It seems that he had met the young lady and her mother at Paris, France, and the acquaintance between the young people ripening into intimacy, they became engaged to each other. The mother and daughter returned to this country and went to live with an uncle of the young lady, a professor in one of the Eastern colleges, who had been named as the young lady's guardian. It further appears that the professor had a son of suitable age, and as a match between his son and his ward was "a consummation devoutly to be wished," he left no means untried to bring the young folks frequently together. But the girl's heart had been given to her foreign lover. A regular correspondence had been kept up between them. When she saw how things were shaping she wrote to her lover, informing him of the exact position of affairs.

The Count, fearing that the prize would be snatched away from him, on receipt of the girl's letter determined to come over after her; accordingly he engaged his passage, and, in due season, arrived.

He proceeded to the village where dwelt his love, and engaging rooms at the hotel, despatched a note informing her of his arrival, etc., etc. Not getting a reply he sent another letter, with, however, no better result. He was so well assured of the girl's affection as to know that, had either of his missives reached its destination, he would have been favored with a response, and correctly surmised that the letters had been intercepted. He resolved to call in person, and accordingly one day sallied forth to see the lady of his love.

On nearing the house he saw her seated at the window. She instantly recognized him and signaled him not to come further—that she would meet him at the hotel. He returned to his hotel and patiently awaited her coming.

After some time she made her appearance at the hotel; but, following in close pursuit, came the uncle and mother. She threw herself in her lover's arms and declared that nothing but death should part them.

The elders, wishing to avoid scandal, invited the young couple to the house—which invitation was accepted. Seeing that the young lady had fully made up her mind, and that nothing would dissuade her, a compromise was finally effected. The Count was to return to Russia and bring back sufficient evidence of his genuineness, when the marriage should be duly solemnized.

This arrangement was perfectly satisfactory to the young lady, and as the gentleman could offer no reasonable excuse why this course should not be pursued, he, in a few days, took his departure ostensibly for the purpose proposed.

Up to the present writing his return has not been announced, and as the lady has not in the meantime heard anything satisfactory of him. it is presumable that she has arrived at the conclusion that he is a Count of little or no account.

COL. MARMADUKE REEVES.

Though some years have since elapsed, and the people of this country have in the meantime feasted on the horrors of the battle-field, experienced "the pomp and circumstance of glorious war," and learned its cost in blood and treasure, by having its scenes enacted, as it were, at their very doors, yet must the great Anglo-Franco-Russian war of the Crimea be yet fresh in the memory of the present generation. Excepting the Revolutionary troubles of 1848-49, and our own "little onpleasantess" with Santa Anna in Mexico, the peace of the civilized world has not been disturbed by any serious warlike events. It was the first war of the generation, and was welcomed as an agreeable relief—a change from the monotonous ways of peace—and folks set their minds on matters martial. Inventors turned their attention to the construction of weapons and missiles that should prove more destructive to human life than those at the time in use, and many were the productions, good, bad and indifferent.

Among the numerous inventors who turned up was a wealthy gentleman residing on the heights of Brooklyn, who had but recently returned from El Dorado, whither he had gone to seek, and where he found his fortune.

His invention was a gun—in his estimation the most *killing* thing that had yet been presented to the world, and bound to insure the ultimate success of that army which should be supplied therewith. Its range was unprecedented, its accuracy beyond question. All that was requisite was GOOD MARKSMEN. Get together an army of such, and the ranks of the enemy would be decimated ere it could get within the range of the old fashioned smooth bore.

The gun was the gentleman's hobby, and he sought every occasion to ride it. Every one whose acquaintance he made, who was or whom he thought to be at all interested in warlike movements, was called upon to witness his equestrian evolutions; and as the circle of his acquaintance was large and continually extending, and his time wholly his own, the exercise was oft repeated—so much so that the gun and its inventor achieved quite a notoriety.

About this time there appeared in New York a noble looking specimen of the *genus homo*, with a decidedly martial bearing, who styled himself Colonel Marmaduke Reeves, of the Royal Army of Great Britain, and who claimed to be commissioned to examine and make the necessary arrangements for the purchase of such arms and ammunition as his judgment should approve.

He sought the Brooklyn gentleman, and introducing himself as the agent of the British Government for the purchase of arms for the Crimean army, easily made his acquaintance. He stated that he was in quest of a superior gun, the merits of which he had heard extolled, and of which he understood the gentleman was the inventor.

The conversation, bearing and general deportment of the man was that of the commonly conceived notion of the British army officer, and he succeeded in ingratiating himself in the good graces of the inventor, who produced his gun and expatiated on its merits and its superiority to all other weapons of the kind.

The Colonel examined the gun with the critical eye of a *connoisseur;* suggested some slight alterations—among others that of shortening the barrel about an inch; but, upon the whole, he was favorably impressed, and did not doubt that it would quite come up to the gentleman's opinion of it, and engaged to see him again.

The gentleman was elated; visions of increased wealth and of fame danced before his eyes. Workshops would be built, hundreds of men would be employed in the manufacture of his gun, and his name would become famous throughout the world; possibly he would be the recipient of some token at the hands of Her Majesty the Queen, in honor of his great invention.   He was delighted, setting aside all thoughts of gain, even, to think that he had made the acquaintance of so distinguished a personage as the Colonel—a man who held so prominent a position in the army, and enjoyed the confidence of the Queen and Government of Great Britain.

He spoke of this Colonel to his wife, and it was agreed between them that such a *rara avis* must not be allowed to flutter about at large, to be finally pounced upon by one of the innumerable hawks that infest the American social sphere.

Accordingly, when he again saw the Colonel, he pressed him to accompany him home to dinner and make the acquaintance of his wife, who, the moment she saw him, was charmed with him, for he was a fine looking fellow, aged about forty, six feet one inch in height, elegantly attired, straight as an Indian, and in appearance every inch the soldier.   His bearing and address were those of the most finished gentleman, and his conversational powers were un-surpassed.

No wonder the giddy creature's head was turned.   It was more than the realization of the most brilliant of her girlish fancies.   A real English gentleman ; an officer of rank in the Royal Army ; the trusted friend and agent of the Queen and her counsellors : fresh from the *salons* of Her Majesty and of Britain's nobility— what a triumph !   How she would enjoy the ill concealed envy of her rivals in society !

A grand party in the Colonel's honor was given, and the *crème* of Brooklyn society was invited.   The Colonel was the lion of the evening.   The guests listened in admiration as he told his stories of court and camp, of battles, of dangers unheard of that he had gone through.

The hostess whispered to an intimate friend that the Colonel was one of the famous Six Hundred—the Light Brigade, which had covered itself with glory at Balaklava.   The report spread, and in a few minutes he was importuned for an account of the charge.

"But, my dear friends," said he, " I really don't like to disoblige you, but——"

"No, no, Colonel," broke in the silvery voices of the ladies present; "let no feeling of delicacy restrain you from mentioning what must certainly be familiar to many others. Let us have the particulars of that charge. Who could be better able to tell the story than an eye-witness, and one, too, who shared in its glory?"

·" Well, then, my friends, since you insist——"

·" Insist! why, yes, of course we insist."

" Ladies, loth as I am to recount my own exploits, yet must I in this case stifle my own feelings to oblige you. The soldier's heart, which beats as regularly on the bloody field of battle, amidst the thunder, lightning and hail of artillery and the smaller arms, as at the camp fire, yet quails and bounds to the throat when assailed by the ever conquering glances of your sex."

A dialogue of some such nature having occurred between the Colonel and the ladies present, he proceeded to tell the story of the Battle of Balaklava with an eloquence which was perfectly irresistible. It is impossible to convey the full effect of his narrative; to be thoroughly appreciated it should have been heard as it fell from his own lips. Having fully posted himself, and being perfectly familiar with military tactics, technical terms and expressions, he named and placed in position the different corps and divisions engaged—the Enniskillens, Scotch Grays, etc.—and by gesticulation and emphasis fairly carried the auditors with him through the fight. Lord Raglan, the Commander-in-Chief, through an *aide-de-camp*, ordered the Earl of Cardigan to take a redoubt. Cardigan replied that there must be some error, as a swallow could not pass where he was ordered to take his men and escape death; but, on the command being repeated, Cardigan called his officers together and formed the plan of attack (which the Colonel minutely and elaborately described). The Earl then, drawing his sword, exclaimed, " The first duty of a soldier is obedience to orders—Forward—this is the last of the Cardigans !" (the Earl was the last male of his line).

Here the Colonel was truly magnificent—the effect produced by his recital was such as would ensure the fame of any actor. The very beating of the heart was audible, and the eyes of the listeners seemed peering out of their sockets as they hung on his every word, as it dropped from the narrator's lips.

" The ground over which they had to charge had recently been ploughed, making it dangerous for men and horses. Their numbers were being continually thinned, but, as men and horses fell, others took their places. Success crowned their bravery, and their object was attained.

On their return the Colonel saw, far in the rear, a brother officer defending himself against three Cossacks. On the impulse of the moment, and without claiming any particular credit for bravery, on he started on the noble black charger, which bore him with the swiftness of the wind to the rescue ; and, bearing on his right stirrup, threw himself in position, and thrust two of them through the body with his sword, and striking with the force of a giant the neck of the third, clove his head from the body. The ground being declining the head rolled down the hill. Jumping from his horse he arrested its course, and picking it up, found to his horror the tongue vibrating, as though cursing him for the act! This made an impression on him which he had never forgotten, and the recital of it so completely unnerved and unmanned him that his friends could readily understand why he should be loth to repeat the story of that day's deeds.

With such stories did the Colonel entertain his hosts and their guests. In the meantime his intimacy with the gentleman and his wife was growing greater. He dined frequently with them—accompanied them on their drives to the opera, etc., etc.

The gun was approved by the Colonel, and all that remained to be done was to have the contracts signed, when the factories would be set to work, turning out these weapons by the thousand for John Bull, to the immense profit of the infatuated Brooklynites, who desired the Colonel to take $6,000 in hand to meet his incidental expenses and proceed to England to have the papers signed.

But the Colonel was playing for a larger stake. He asked to be introduced to the gentleman's lawyer, to whom he explained the advantage of his going over backed by the weight and influence of his old friend and school fellow, Governor McNab, of Canada.

The lawyer coincided with the Colonel. Of course, he must get the Governor's endorsement, as that would expedite matters, and probably enable him to return in the same steamer on her return voyage. The Colonel complimented the lawyer, at the same time remarking that " though the gentleman was perfectly qualified for the arrangement of a mere matter of business, yet it was but natural that he should not be versed in the ways of diplomacy," and it was understood that he should visit the Governor of Canada.

The day after the interview with the lawyer the Brooklyn gentleman called at the Colonel's hotel (the Clarendon) quite early in the morning. The Colonel was still abed, but desired the gentleman to be shown up to his room. He manifested his surprise that the Colonel should not yet have arisen, and desired to know if he was ill.

"O, no," replied the Colonel, in one of his grandiloquent moods. "You see I was to Mrs. So-and-So's party, on Madison avenue, last night, and didn't get home until four o'clock this morning. Your beautiful countrywomen—I'm afraid one of them will yet capture me ere I get away."

The gentleman then stated the object of his thus early calling on the Colonel was to secure his company to dinner at his residence that day, there to meet some gentlemen who were desirous of forming his acquaintance.

The Colonel positively declined, stating that he had important financial business to attend to, and that he allowed no one to make dinner or other engagements for him without being previously consulted.

Determined not to be put off, the gentleman, rather crest fallen, continued to inquire the nature of the business which would so disappoint him and his friends, when he was curtly informed that he (the Colonel) was to receive a thousand dollars down town, out of which he had some payments to make—among them his hotel bill.

The gentleman offered to advance the money, but the Colonel declined, with thanks ; the gentleman insisting, however, and assuring the Colonel that it would not in the least inconvenience him—in fact, that he should regard it as an especial favor—he was finally persuaded to accept the proffered check, and agreed to meet the party at dinner.

A day or two after a circumstance occurred which proved not wholly to the Colonel's liking. As he was walking up Broadway, dressed to perfection, gracefully twirling his gold headed cane, the admiration of the belles, the envy of the beaux, he was beset by a poor, miserable specimen of humanity, who manifested great joy at having found him, and addressed to him the most endearing epithets. He called an officer, who chanced to be passing, and requested him to take that woman off as she annoyed him. She persisted, saying that he was her husband and owed her support. The officer could not believe that such a miserable creature could be the wife of so fine a gentleman, so he ordered her to move on or he would take her in, and the Colonel breathed freer.

The Colonel hastened to his hotel, but had scarcely reached there when his wife, who had followed him, again presented herself and created quite a disturbance. The Colonel having paid his board with the money he had received from the Brooklyn gentleman, and there appearing to be nothing in common between him and the woman, she was regarded as some poor, demented creature, and accordingly turned away.

The affair created quite a commotion at the hotel, however, and it getting to the ears of the dweller on the heights, he for the first time instituted inquiries which led him to the conclusion that the Colonel was a *first class fraud*, who had most outrageously duped him; so he had him arrested for obtaining money under false pretences.

The Colonel was taken to the Tombs, when some one remarking that this business might send him to State Prison, "Not at all," he said, "you don't for a moment suppose the gentleman or his amiable lady would appear in a Police Court for a paltry thousand dollars." In a few days the Colonel was discharged for want of evidence.

About this time a number of respectable and intelligent gentlemen, representing the officials having charge of the prisons and public charities of Boston, visited this city, for the purpose of examining and getting information in relation to the management of similar institutions here. A committee was appointed by the Board of Governors of the Almshouse to receive them, and grant facilities for forwarding the object of their mission. Of course the Tombs was visited; and, as most prisons generally have some inmate worthy of note, the question was asked if they had not a CAGED LION?

In reply, the Colonel was described as an officer of the British army, one of the famous 600 of Balaklava notoriety, who on some trumped up charge, had been arrested, and although the British Consul and other highly respectable gentlemen had importuned him to allow them to bail him, he, from a mistaken sense of honor, refused their kind offers. Of course all were anxious for an introduction; but they were told, although a prisoner, he was a gentleman, and unless it was agreeable to him, his privacy could not be disturbed. To this they, of course, acceded. The offer was made to consult him on the subject and request an interview.

The whole matter was explained to the Colonel and he promised his best efforts in the cause—being very much amused at the idea that he was the *gentleman who refused to be bailed.*

After the usual courtesies in his cell, and receiving the sympathy of his visitors, together with their arguments to induce him to allow himself to be bailed, he replied, " that a British officer could alone decide what he considered a proper and honorable course to pursue," and begged them, with considerable hauteur, not to mention the subject again, as it was a *particularly painful one.* After much solicitation he—claiming that an actor in the scene would compromise himself by recounting his own deeds—favored the gentlemen with a description of the battle of Balaklava, the famous charge of the Light Brigade, and his own exploit with the three Cossacks.

The recital was rendered with the same dramatic effect and regard to minutiæ as at the party in Brooklyn, and the audience, as on that occasion, believing all he said, were wonderfully excited, and shrank with horror at the decapitation; and at the close there was hardly a gentleman present but would have willingly bailed the brave and gentlemanly officer. When informed afterwards that, at the time of this feat which he described, he was an inmate of a prison, they were still more astonished than at the recital, and acknowledged that the Colonel had sold them elegantly.

The Governors of the Almshouse happening to learn that a little deformed girl, then on the Island at the city's expense, was a daughter of the Colonel, had him brought before them, and exacted from him a pledge to pay $2 per week towards her support, which was faithfully performed for several years.

A few years after the Colonel made his appearance at the Tombs, and was introduced to the author, who had recently been appointed

Warden, by the physician connected with the institution. The author mentioned having heard of him before, and his famous story of the battle of Balaklava, and begged to be favored with a recital. The Colonel was at first loth to repeat it, but was finally prevailed on—the condition that he should not be laughed at having been laid—and the story was told as on former occasions.

The next day the Colonel was brought in by an officer of the Court, for having stolen the clothes, watch and chain, and diamond ring of a lady. The author expressed his surprise at finding him, so soon after having made his acquaintance, a boarder at his hotel, and intimated that he must have conceived a liking for the new landlord. He nonchalantly replied that his stay would in all probability be of short duration, as it was a charge trumped up by a bad woman. The facts of the case, however, were as follows:

He had inserted in one of the city papers an advertisement for a governess to take the entire charge of three children, on a plantation South. Among the replies was one from a lady residing in a large and fashionable boarding house opposite St. John's Park; when evening came he repaired thither, and asking to see the lady, was ushered in the parlor. The lady soon made her appearance, and he, handing her the note she had written in reply to the advertisement, introduced himself as the advertiser.

He suggested that they go somewhere where they would be free from intrusion—as dinner being about over, the boarders would naturally seek the parlor. She proposed that, as the evening was pleasant, and the house had a key to the park, they go there, where they might discuss the matter in perfect freedom.

The Colonel was well pleased with the proposition, and they left the house together. He expatiated on the loveliness of his home, the salubrity of the country, the good qualities of his children, etc., etc.; told her of the easy, comfortable life she should lead, with slaves at her command, carriages, horses, boats, society, etc., and at length succeeded in effecting an engagement—desiring her to get ready, if possible, to leave with him on the following day, as, having concluded his business, he was anxious to return home.

The lady, having nothing special to detain her, agreed to get ready; and it was arranged that an expressman be sent for the trunks, and that he should call for her with a carriage.

The expressman duly arrived the next day; but, as the day wore on and the carriage failed to make its appearance, the lady's suspicions were aroused, and she reported the case to the police authorities, giving a description of the impostor. After a few weeks' pursuit the Colonel was found and taken before Alderman Brady, who was on the bench in the absence of the Judge.

"Well, Colonel," he remarked, when the Colonel was brought before him, "here you are again. This time I think you stand a good chance for a trip up the river."

The Colonel became indignant at the remarks of the Alderman, and answered that, "If he alluded to the—aw—prison—he begged him to understand that the—aw—prison was not yet built that was to hold him—nor the Judge born who was to convict him."

The magistrate ordered him to be taken down.

When taken to court for trial he was handcuffed to a strapping negro. He asked a friend who was standing by to "call at the—aw—court and see the farce"—not for a moment entertaining a thought of his conviction. But his mind was soon set at rest (?) by a sentence of four years and a half to the State Prison at Sing Sing.

Among those present at court was the Colonel's wife, who, when she heard the sentence pronounced by the Court, manifested her appreciation thereof by such lively demonstrations that it was found necessary to remove her. When turned out of the court room she at once made for the Tombs, where she arrived before her husband, the Colonel, accompanied by a young woman, her daughter—who did not, however, acknowledge the relationship, the mother being in a beastly state of intoxication—and two boys, sons, with portable boot blacking shops slung over their shoulders.

In due time the Colonel was brought in by an officer of the court, and locked up in a cell assigned to him until he should be removed to Sing Sing. He did not countenance any of his family.

Two or three years later the author, in company with several other gentlemen, visited the Prison at Sing Sing. He found the Colonel seated at a desk in a large room, engaged in writing the annexed Report of the Prison, for which business he was well adapted, being an expert penman, and an easy, fluent and graceful writer. He at once recognized the author, and greeted him, saying:

"How glad I am to see you, Mr. Warden. How do you do—and how have you been? In a few days I think I shall have the —aw—pleasure of calling on you at your place. I had a long talk with Morgan (Hon. E. D. Morgan was at the time Governor), and satisfied him of my ability to command troops. He seemed to—aw —think favorably of it, and will, I have no doubt, pardon me and give me a commission—knowing as he must the wants of the country, and her need of first class military officers." The Colonel assured the gentlemen present that he could handle an army of 100,000 men with greater ease and better success than many an officer could a company of 100.

The Governor was evidently sceptical as to the military qualifications and capacities of the Colonel, as he allowed him to quietly serve out his full term; at the expiration of which he quit the State, and next turned up as a Bounty Agent "over in New Jersey," and engaged in other schemes of, to say the least, doubtful legality—no doubt making plenty of money.

As to the Colonel's present whereabouts the author is uninformed, though he does not doubt that he is serving some State in one of the establishments specially provided for the accommodation of its malefactors.

CHAPTER XXI.

BURGLARY.—A MERCANTILE TRANSACTION.—CHAUNCEY JOHNSON.

"'Stop thief! Stop thief!' There is a magic in the sound! The tradesman leaves his counter; the carman his wagon; the butcher throws down his tray; the baker his basket; the milkman his pail; the errand boy his parcels; the schoolboy his marbles; the child his battledore."—DICKENS, *in Oliver Twist.*

BURGLARY is an institution which will undoubtedly flourish so long as men keep money and valuables in their houses. At least it is so in this world; in the next we are promised better times, and the police will be of little use, for there the thieves do not break through and steal. Burglary is a dangerous operation, and no one but desperate characters engage in it. It is no murder to shoot the man who is getting away with your plate, and the house breakers have to run all such risks. The consequence is, that those thieves who are careful of their health generally take up some lighter branch of the business—such as picking pockets, for instance. It is also an unpleasant business to the man who is burglared. To be awakened in the dead of night, with a cold sensation at the end of your nose and to find it the barrel of a pistol, is not a very cheerful way of returning from the land of dreams. And then the sight of some masked villain, dark lantern in hand, going through your bureau drawers, is not calculated to restore your equanimity. To receive calls is always a pleasant task, but these midnight visitors, who come by the way of the bath room window, are seldom welcome.

Burglars, the same as the members of any other profession, are of different grades. Some are polite, and as polished as a Duke. These will say to your terrified wife:

"Not the slightest occasion for any alarm, my dear Madame," and will even go so far as to nurse the crying baby awhile, while the other operators are "bagging the swag." Others are brutal wretches, who would just as soon silence you with the butt of their pistols, as eat, and, perhaps, give the preference to murder. They are of all ages and all nationalites, and even of both sexes—there having been female house breakers. England produces the most finished cracksmen, and all the big jobs in the United States are generally put up by cockney experts. Dickens, in his Oliver Twist, has given us a pretty picture of these gentry. Who will ever forget the desperate Bill Sykes and his dog, or the "Flash Toby Crackit," whose nobby appearance made him a particular favorite with the "slavies."

A MERCANTILE TRANSACTION SOMEWHAT OUT OF THE USUAL COURSE.

Some years ago a man engaged in the wholesale straw goods business, whose establishment was located on the second floor of one of the large stores on Warren street, proved himself quite an adept at burglary.

It seems that trade had not been so good as it might have been, and the man's paper becoming due, and money being rather tight, he was considerably annoyed as to the proper course to pursue in order to meet his liabilities. In an evil moment the devil took possession of him, and suggested a way out of his difficulties.

The lower part of the building was occupied by a firm in the dry goods trade. Every one who is familiar with the construction of the large stores in the lower part of the city must have remarked the manner in which light is admitted to the middle of the store, by means of a skylight in the roof, and the large well-hole extending through the building to the lower floor, and in some cases even to the cellar.

In cases where the building is occupied by but one firm this well hole is usually left open, thus affording a good circulation of air through the building, as well as admitting the light. When, however, the building is occupied by more than one firm, it is customary to close this opening with glass the same as the skylight—thus making the different establishments wholly independent of each other, and yet affording sufficient light to the occupants of the lower floors.

The house occupying the lower floors of the building in question was extensively engaged in the silk trade, and had constantly on hand a choice line of goods.

One day, while thinking over the state of his affairs, the straw goods merchant was struck with an idea. The sight of his neighbor's goods, which were conspicuously arranged on the counters and shelves below, and which were plainly visible through the skylight, put the notion in his head.

The next Sunday morning he went to his place of business, and, locking himself in, set about making a rope ladder. When it was done, he carefully removed a pane of glass from the sash (skylight) and descended by means of his rope ladder to the premises below.

Arrived here, he selected his goods from different portions of the store, and in such a manner that they would not be easily missed. Having taken a sufficient quantity, he put them in a bag and hoisted them up to his own establishment, after ascending to which he replaced the pane of glass, leaving no trace of his neighbor's premises having been burglariously entered.

He at once removed all tags and marks from the goods, substituting others with which he had provided himself, and packed them in a case which he had marked for shipment to Philadelphia.

Early the next morning the case was regularly despatched, and the merchant leaving word with his clerk that he was obliged to leave town, took the first train for Philadelphia, in order to make the necessary arrangement for the disposal of the goods.

He called on an auction house there, informing them that he had consigned to them a case of silks, which he desired them to sell to the best advantage. He was, he stated, an importer, and occasionally disposed of a case or two in this manner. He had thought of trying Philadelphia as a market, with the expectation of realizing better prices than he got in New York. Should the venture prove successful, he would send on another lot on his return home.

The goods arrived all right, and the next day happening to be the regular day of sale, they were arranged in lots, and the merchant concluded to remain over and see how they would go off.

The sale was perfectly satisfactory. An account of sales was rendered, the customary charges and commissions deducted, and the merchant was given a check for the amount due him. He left well pleased, and engaged to send on another lot for the next sale, the following week.

The merchant was in the habit of calling on his neighbors in a sociable, neighborly way, to talk over business and discuss the current topics of the day. He discovered that they had not missed their goods, and so concluded to try it again on the following Sunday; and on the following Monday morning another case of silks was on its way to the Philadelphia "slaughter house" (a term sometimes applied by the trade to auction houses). In a few days a proper return was made, and the merchant was notified of the next sale and a consignment solicited.

It is of course unreasonable to suppose that the disappearance of their goods by the "wholesale" should go unnoticed by the owners; but as there was no evidence of the premises having been entered from without, suspicion naturally pointed to some employé as the depredator. The services of a detective were engaged, and the outgoings and incomings of the clerks carefully "piped," but all to no purpose.

It was by the merest chance that the thief was discovered. A customer of the house, from Philadelphia, having bought quite a "bill" of domestic goods, they were desirous of selling him some silks, also, to complete his assortment.

"It's of no use," he replied; "I can't trade with you in that line; I can buy these goods at a greatly reduced price, in Philadelphia."

The salesman was surprised; he could hardly believe it, as he had the best reason in the world to suppose that his was the only house in the trade that had those goods; and even did any other house have them, it could not afford to sell them at the prices named by the Philadelphian.

But the customer was positive; the same goods that had been shown him were being regularly offered at auction in Philadelphia, and if no other house in the trade had that line of goods, then they must be the consignors. Now he would like to trade with them; and if circumstances compelled them, at times, to sacrifice their goods in that manner, he would, for a reasonable consideration, be a ready customer, rather than see them "slaughtered."

The merchants were surprised at this speech, and assured their customer that he must be laboring under a delusion. They had never sent any of their goods to an auction house in Philadelphia or anywhere else.

The Philadelphian only reiterated that "they were the same identical goods;" and agreed to prove it to them on his return.

One of the firm at once got ready and started for Philadelphia. True enough, he found, when he reached there, that the goods had been regularly "slaughtered."

On making the proper inquiries at the auction room the consignor of the goods was found to be their neighbor, the straw goods merchant, who had been doing an extensive business, which was yielding ever so much per cent. profit, and which would, should it continue a little while longer, enable him to retire the possessor of a fortune. Unfortunately for him, however, that Philadelphian had to come to New York to buy his goods—his game was blocked, and he was locked up in the Tombs, there to ruminate and to cogitate over the vicissitudes of this life.

He was tried and ably defended by the Hon. Wm. M. Evarts, but was found guilty and sentenced. By some means or other he managed to get out of the scrape, however.

CHAUNCEY JOHNSON.

Chauncey Johnson, the name by which he is most familiarly known, a man of many *aliases*, and who is at present serving out a term of imprisonment at Sing Sing under the name of Jackson, has perhaps committed more bold burglaries, robbed more banks and money institutions, than any one person the criminal records of this country make mention of.

He is quite tall and good looking, has a bright, piercing eye in his head, a careless, easy carriage, and is modest and unassuming in his general demeanor. Not one in a thousand would suspect his real character. He is a great smoker, hardly ever being without a cigar in his mouth, which he is continually chewing on. He says that he never attempted the life of any one—not even in self-defence, nor has he ever taken a penny from one who could not easily afford to lose it. In his private transactions he is honesty personified, promptly paying his debts and taking a mean advantage of no one. His mother, of whom he thinks a great deal, and to whom he is greatly attached, is living in a handsome house which he bought and settled on her, having previously elegantly furnished it throughout. He has great confidence in himself. He does not steal for the purpose of hoarding up his money and amassing great wealth, nor has he extravagant tastes to be gratified. To a friend in need he would give his last penny. He operates with but few, his chief lieutenant being the notorious Dutch Heinrich.

The name of Chauncey Johnson appears on the Court Record on the 9th January, 1854, for having stolen $37,870, for which he was sent to State Prison for three years, which term he served out. On his discharge from State Prison he resumed his operations. How often he was arrested and sent up under other names the author cannot state. He went up twice from this city as Chauncey Johnson.

Some time during the year 1858 he spotted a bank messenger with a large amount of money in Wall street. He followed the messenger, entering the bank immediately behind him, following him even within the enclosure behind the railing, when he nonchalantly took off his hat and set it down on the table. He picked up the bundle which the messenger had laid on the table and coolly walked off without attracting the notice of the clerks, who did not suspect anything wrong or out of the way.

Johnson has a great passion for the gaming table, his favorite pastime being faro playing. With the large amount of money he had taken from the bank his passion was easily fed, and for over a week he literally lived in the gambling saloons. Through the gamblers detective officer O'Keefe learned of his having a large amount of money, which the officer rightly conjectured was the money which a short time previous had been stolen from the bank. The officer arrested Johnson, charging him with the theft, which he did not deny, but offered to share with the officer on condition that he be not arrested. The officer accompanied him to his house, where was found in an old valise about $30,000 of the stolen money. Johnson was taken to the station house, and on the following morning removed to the Tombs. In a few days he was tried, convicted, and sentenced January 20, 1858, to four years and three months' imprisonment in Sing Sing State Prison, which term was also served out. The year after his discharge from Sing Sing prison he is said to have spent at faro $190,000!

It was during the summer of 1864, the author believes, that Johnson entered the Central National Bank, and got away with

$17,000. He threw his hat and coat carelessly down, walked be-hind the railing, picked up the package and coolly walked out. A boy standing on the sidewalk, looking through the bank window, saw the whole proceeding, but, when brought before the prisoner, could not identify him. The bank officers finally compromised the matter with him, declining to prosecute on his agreeing to give up the most of the money.

The Chemical Bank was also a victim of one of his raids, but he was caught on the same day and made to disgorge.

He is supposed to have been the man who entered the Adams Express office on Broadway, making his way to the Cashier's office, which he entered, seeing no one within. The safe was wide open— a good subject for the "cracksman." Hearing some one coming he coolly picked up a newspaper lying on the desk and commenced reading. The Cashier on entering his office was horrified at seeing a stranger there, and asked what he wished, to which he coolly re-plied that he was waiting to see a gentleman connected with the office. On being informed that that was not the place for him to wait, he left. After he was gone a package of bills amounting to $1,800 was found to be missing.

On the same or the following day the American Express Com-pany missed a package containing $7,000. Officer Gil. Hayes saw Johnson in the neighborhood, and mentioned his having seen him about there to one of the gentlemen connected with the office.

August Belmont & Co. lost $25,000 from their office. Chauncey Johnson was arrested for the theft; but at his trial proved an *alibi* by a friend, who swore that at the time the robbery was committed Johnson and he were playing at cards in a lager beer saloon on the Bowery.

Johnson and his friend, Dutch Heinrich, determined on a visit to Philadelphia; and, while there, happening to pass a bank building, Johnson remarked to his friend that he must do something to keep his hand in; but he was cautioned by the latter not to take any chances, as he had no friends in Philadelphia. With the remark that he would take care of that, he entered the bank. Seeing that the clerks were all busy, he stationed himself at the paying teller's desk—which opening, however, owing to the teller's ab-sence from his desk, was closed. Johnson had provided himself with a long piece of very thin wire, which he bent so as to go over the top of the railing and then down to the counter. The end of the wire was bent in the form of a hook, and provided with a bit of soft, gummy wax—the hook serving to pick up the packages of money which were done up, and the wax to pick up the single bills. There was a large amount of money laying on the counter, promising a good harvest to the bold operator. The teller's back was turned to the counter—directly in front of him was a mirror. Imagine his surprise, on looking at this mirror, at seeing the money, in packages and in single bills, jumping as it were of its own accord from the counter over a high railing into a man's pocket on the other side! He stopped a moment to view the operation in the glass, and without turning around, and as though wholly unconscious of what was going on, rose, stepped outside and caught Johnson in the act. For this attempt he was tried, convicted and sentenced to seven years' imprisonment in Moyamensing Prison. He served about ten months of the term when influences were brought to bear which resulted in his being pardoned.

He went to New Orleans, but returned ere a great while with plenty of money, which, as usual with him, was left with the keepers of faro banks.

His next exploit was at the Fifth Avenue Hotel. He was there one evening, rather short of funds, and waiting like Micawber for "something to turn up." Presently the Hon. Thomas Murphy, Collector of the Port, with several other gentlemen, entered the private office of the hotel with the proprietor, where was the safe, which was open. Johnson entered the office with the party of gentlemen, leading the clerks to suppose he was one of them. Seeing a package quite handy in the safe, he appropriated it, and, putting it in his pocket, started leisurely for the reading room, no doubt purposing to leave by the Twenty-third street door. The movement had been observed by one of the porters, who followed him and had him arrested. He was tried, giving his name as Jackson, convicted, and sentenced to one year's imprisonment in Sing Sing State Prison. His time was up in February, 1872.

He is now back again at Sing Sing, serving a sentence of ten years for the robbery of a store up town.

CHAPTER XXII.

COUNTERFEITING. — FORGERY. — SPENCER PETTIS. — MONROE ED-
WARDS.—CANTER.—REDMAN.—THE WEBB-MARSHALL DUEL.

"He had come to look upon felony as a kind of disorder, like the scarlet fever or ery
sipelas; some people had it—some hadn't—just as it might be."—DICKENS, *in the Old
Curiosity Shop.*

IN this chapter we shall speak of counterfeiting and forgery—two
branches of nefarious business which are extensively practiced
on this continent, and from whose votaries the Tombs obtains many
an inmate. The desire to obtain wealth by counterfeiting, whether
it be the imitation of the coin of the realm, by means of a die, or
the signature of a banker, by means of a pen, is a strong one among
those individuals who are averse to earning their bread by the
sweat of their brow. We generally find that it is the intelligent
and intellectual members of the swell mob who drift into this
branch of crime. The rough customers become highway robbers,
bank operators or cracksmen, but the gentility and refinement of
the profession prefer the more dexterous and high toned groove of
forgery. We shall have several stories to tell in this connection.

JOHN CANTER.

This is one of those jail birds that, somehow or other, manage
never to keep out of prison for any length of time. In fact, to
judge from the answer he once gave, when asked why he could not
keep out of prison, one would naturally think that he made it a
point to get back as soon as possible after having served out his
time—having said that "it was not so terrible a thing as many
people supposed, particularly when situated as he always had been,
i. e., employed in the office." He is but forty-two years of age,
twenty-two of which have been spent in prison!

He is an expert counterfeiter and a most proficient penman,
nothing that was at all possible with pen and ink being beyond his
capacity. He could produce a *fac simile* of the most difficult signature at the first trial by seeing it once written.

He had been sentenced to fifteen years at hard labor in State Prison, but his proficiency as a penman and his knowledge of book-keeping procured for him a position in the office of the prison —hence his punishment was not quite so hard to bear as that of the poor devils put at hard manual labor.

It was but a short time after his discharge from prison that he was arrested for having been concerned with another man in committing a burglary. He was tried, convicted and sentenced to ten years' imprisonment at Sing Sing. He served but two years of the term, however, when his counsel, the late Judge Stewart, succeeded in getting him out.

He married, and it was supposed that he would settle down and become a useful member of the community. Not a great while thereafter, however, he was arrested at his home—there being found in his possession quite an assortment of counterfeiters' tools, and dies, and plates of fractional currency. He was locked up in the City Prison (Tombs), where he remained for some time, but was finally discharged.

While in the Tombs he executed, with pen and ink, a *fac simile* of an engraving representing the Collect Pond, and drawings of an experimental steamboat (the invention of a Mr. Fitch) which is said to have sailed thereon, and which is reported to have been the first attempt at steam navigation made in this country. The specimen is at present in the author's possession, and a copy of the map will be found in this book.

Since his discharge from the Tombs he contrived to find his way back to State Prison, where, as usual, he was assigned to work at the desk in the office. He was detected in altering the time of some of the prisoners—changing nine years to seven years, five to three, etc., thus virtually giving them two years of their time, for which he was of course paid—and remanded to the prison, his services being no longer required in that capacity.

Canter is a native of this country, small of stature, and of about 110 pounds weight. He is very smart and apt. His accomplishments ought certainly to have secured for him a position that would insure him a good and comfortable living; but, somehow or other, the prison occupies to him the same relative position that the lighted taper does to the moth which, continually fluttering about the flame, at length falls a victim to the fascination and is consumed.

During the author's connection with the public institutions he saw many such instances. Cases in which no earthly cause could be traced or reason assigned for the commission of crime were but too frequent. Instances of prisoners whose wealth, whose culture, whose position in society—everything in fact—would naturally lead one to suppose them the least likely occupants of prison cells, came so often under his observation, that not unfrequently there arose in his mind the question whether it were not better to treat such as invalids rather than as malefactors—as fitter subjects for the physician than the jailor.

SPENCER PETTIS—COUNTERFEITER, FORGER.

About 1863–4 there figured rather conspicuously in the Eighth Ward a young man, who always made his appearance clad in the most costly and stylish garments, and with the manners and address of a gentleman accustomed to the usages of the best society.

His habits were those of a gentleman of leisure, always having plenty of money and living on the fat of the land. Though taking no particular part in the local politics, he associated with the leading politicians of the district and their friends, and almost every morning could be seen on Broadway in company of the Alderman or some other dignitary of the town belonging to the Ward. In the evening he could be seen in the bar room of the St. Nicholas Hotel, or at that popular resort of sporting men and gentlemen about town, on the corner of Prince and Wooster streets, kept by William Mitchel. He was a *connoisseur* of wines, his favorite being champagne, of which he consumed not a small quantity. Few of the many gentlemen he nightly met at either of the above named places, and with whom he seemed to be on intimate terms, knew anything about him, or what he did for a living.

This fine young gentleman was none other than the counterfeiter, Spencer Pettis. He had been implicated in a number of forgeries and was ultimately arrested, with a friend of his, for having forged the signature of Messrs. Lathrop, Ludington & Co. for $25,000, and was lodged in the Tombs to await his trial.

The friend was sent to State Prison. Application for Pettis' release, under bail, was made. The amount of bail fixed was very large, but his friends succeeded in having it reduced, and in a short time thereafter Pettis was at large.

Pettis after that changed his headquarters, and located himself in the more aristocratic part of the city, near the Hoffman House, where he figured as a speculator in stocks and bonds, dealing extensively in United States bonds. But few of the *habitues* of that quarter knew him.

Quite recently Pettis was detected in a $10,000 bond operation in Boston, for which he was arrested and sent on there for trial. It is quite likely that he will find it no easy matter to hoodwink the Boston authorities, and no doubt will, ere long, be doing that State some service in one of the prison shops.

MONROE EDWARDS, THE FORGER.

On the list of forgers the name of Monroe Edwards, *alias* John S. Cauldwell and Hugh S. Hill, must ever occupy a conspicuous place as one of the boldest and most expert this country has ever produced.

One of the earliest efforts was his going to England, bearing what purported to be letters of introduction from Daniel Webster to some of his friends there—among others to an earl, who was a great personal friend of the distinguished statesman. His mission to the other side, he claimed, was for the purpose of working with the English Abolitionists in their crusade against slavery.

He represented himself as a Southerner, owning a large plantation and many negroes, whose manumission he desired to effect. He was anxious to consult with the leading British philanthropists as to the best course to pursue in so laudable an undertaking.

Being a man of good education, pleasing address, and having the finish and polish of one used to the ways of good society, he easily won his way into favor, and was an ever welcome guest at the house of the gentry, particularly as he was endorsed (?) by so eminent a personage as Daniel Webster, who had many warm personal friends and admirers in England, and none more so than this earl, who at once conceived a strong personal regard for the impostor, not dreaming that such he really was, and invited him to make his house his home during his stay in England.

Some six weeks passed, when, Edwards' money giving out, he applied to the earl for a loan of one thousand pounds, alleging as a reason some irregularity in his remittances from America, and as he had received advices from home, which rendered his return at his earliest possible convenience necessary, he was obliged to raise the money in order to settle up some business matters ere he left. On his arrival at New York he promised to forward a draft for the amount.

The money was cheerfully loaned, the earl being only too happy to do a service to a friend of his esteemed friend, Mr. Webster. At the proper time the earl received a draft for the amount, which was duly honored. Edwards evidently commenced to forge to raise the money to pay off his debts.

He next turned up as a forger of the signature of a prominent cotton broker of New Orleans, having forged a draft on Messrs. Brown Brothers, bankers, of this city (New York), for the sum of $25,000, getting the money in Virginia funds, he having represented himself as a planter on his way to Richmond, to buy negroes for his plantation—and, furthermore, that that currency was as well adapted to the purpose as city funds.

He then went to Baltimore, when he again forged a draft on Messrs. Brown Bros. for a large amount, and thence proceeded to South Carolina, when he again drew on the house for some $4,000 —the amount being this time paid in gold put up in marked bags. These bags figured quite conspicuously in the evidence at the trial, and contributed greatly to Edwards' conviction.

He was traced to Philadelphia, where he was arrested for the perpetration of three forgeries, amounting in the aggregate to over $60,000. His money was taken from him and deposited in the "Girard Bank" of that city. His lawyer resorted to all the contrivances of the law to obtain possession of the money, but without success.

Edwards was brought to New York and locked up in the Tombs to await his trial. His wardrobe was extensive, and of the finest material. He furnished his cell elegantly, making it look more like a little parlor than a prisoner's quarters.

His trial commenced on June 7, 1842. Edwards had a magnificent array of counsel, consisting of Hon. J. J. Crittenden, of Kentucky, Thomas F. Marshall, of Kentucky, W. M. Evarts, J. Prescott Hall, Wm. M. Price and Robert Emmett.

James R. Whiting, District Attorney, conducted the prosecution, assisted by Ogden Hoffman, United States District Attorney.

Edwards was the great attraction every day, and the court room was always crowded by those anxious to have a glimpse at him. He was a man of middle height, rather slender, with dark hair and whiskers, and, singular as it may seem, light blue eyes. He was elegantly dressed, his linen in particular being faultless. He wore no ornament save a gold watch chain.

On the day set down for his trial there appeared in the columns of the *Courier and Enquirer* newspaper, edited and published by Major Noah and Gen. James Watson Webb, a very bitter article about Edwards. Mr. Marshall took occasion to allude to the article in open court and abused Gen. Webb therefor. A duel was the result, in which Gen. Webb was shot. Gen. Webb and his second, on their return to the city, were arrested for violating the laws of the State by engaging in a duel. They were tried and convicted, and would have been sent to State Prison but for the pardon of the Governor (Wm. H. Seward)—a monster petition, which appeared to bear the signature of everybody in New York, asking their pardon, having been presented.

The trial of Edwards was conducted before Judge Kent, son of Chancellor Kent, and one of the ablest judges at that time on the bench. The trial was ably conducted—the District Attorney and the prisoner's counsel bringing their full powers in play.

The defence tried to prove an *alibi*, endeavoring to show by the hotel register that at the time he was alleged to be in New York he was actually in New Orleans; but the District Attorney had got possession of some letters which showed that he would be in this city at the time he tried to prove that he was in New Orleans. Among them was one to a friend in this city, in which he stated that he would be on, with a pocket full of *rocks*, the very day he claimed to have been at New Orleans.

The Court desired the prisoner to show where he had got the large amount of money which had been taken from him in Philadelphia. He claimed that it was furnished by his partner for the purpose of buying lands in Texas, and stocking it with negroes and

other necessities of an extensive plantation.   In the meantime he
had received a letter from the alleged partner, in which he (the
partner) expressed his regret at his inability to go on and serve his
friend—business of the utmost importance demanding his presence
on one of the West India islands—which letter was presented and
read in evidence.

At length the trial was concluded and the case given to the jury,
who deliberated long, but finally brought in a verdict of guilty.
The Court, however, suspended sentence until news should be received from the island whither the prisoner's partner had gone.
The American Consul at that place had been instructed to cite the
supposed partner before him, and ascertain, if possible, the nature
of the business between him and the prisoner.   The man appeared
before the Consul and told a very plausible story concerning his
connection and money transactions with Edwards.   As he was
leaving the Consul's office he was met by a gentleman (a sea captain), who was coming to transact some business with the Consul,
who addressed him somewhat in this strain:

"Hello Bill! what brings you here?   How long have you been
here, and how long do you intend to stay?"

After he was gone the Consul inquired of the captain if he
knew the gentleman whom he had just left.

"Know him," he replied. "Why, of course I know him. That's
Edwards, and he's got a brother who's in a bad scrape in the
States."

The Consul forwarded a report of the examination, and mentioned the meeting of the two men at his office, and what had been
told him by the captain.   Edwards was sentenced to ten years at
hard labor in State Prison.

Edwards was not only a man of fine appearance, he was also a
man of culture, as the following speech he made in court will
testify:

"My position, if it please the Court, is the most agonizing one
conceivable.   I have been hunted to the death, persecuted with a
malignity unparalleled in the history of man; but, unequal as has
been the contest, and sanguinary as will be the end, yet all will not
prevent me from preserving the dignity of a man.   Like an old
oak that has stood the blast of a hundred years, I gather new ener-

gies from the opposition that calls them forth. I was forced into the last trial unprepared—had no means to compel the attendance of witnesses, and two important ones were prevented from being here by ill health. I, therefore, consider that the benefits of the constitution, which secure a fair and impartial trial, have been denied to me. During the last trial some of my most trivial actions, some that would have been considered virtuous in other men, have been tortured into acts of crime. The press, too, that mighty engine, has lent its aid to crush me by every species of misrepresentation. From Maine to Louisiana they have presented in regard to me one of the most diabolical pictures, and the dominions of his Satanic majesty have been ransacked to show this monster in human shape to be everything bad and terrible. I have had money, and power, and prejudice arrayed against me, and it would be strange indeed if under all this a man who is separated from his friends, from his home, from everything which could aid or support him, should not be overwhelmed. The result of the last trial did not surprise me. One of my persecutors said he was determined I should be convicted, and that he would expend $100,000, if it was necessary, for that purpose. I am to be offered up a sacrifice on the altar of avarice, to satisfy the designs of a set of brokers, and consequently have been set upon by a lot of brokers and of brokers' boys, whose trade it is to swindle, who are generally dishonest, and whose profession is regarded in this light. Some of these, I perceive, are now present, and I can read in their looks the savage joy that possesses them in observing the position in which I am placed; they have manacled my limbs, persecuted me to the uttermost, and they rejoice at the idea that I am now to be consigned to a living tomb. But their triumph will be brief; they can dispose of my body, but the soul, that immortal part, they cannot reach nor control. In relation to my case, your honors appear to be in haste to consign me to a living tomb, in which the man who once crosses its threshold is doomed to perpetual disgrace—to bear the damps and dews of its walls, to suffer the loss of every happy privilege, and where almost hope itself is dead. This is the doom to which I am to be consigned by a conspiracy of the darkest kind; but who so powerful as to escape the demon eye of malice, or, by representations of innocence, escape its venom. Through its influence even your Honor might be hurled from the high place you occupy; by the misrepresentations of the basest wretch your best motives might be assailed, and a wound given which could not be remedied. Think not, because I am threatened, that I shall for one moment degrade myself by asking suppliant favors. I am well aware what the law imposes. I wish, however, it compelled you to consign me at once to total annihilation. I am made the victim in this charge, yet I am innocent—innocent as the Saviour of the world or as the child unborn. Still I ask no favor. I would disdain to ask mitigation as to my fate; that man has yet to be born before whom I would bend a suppliant knee. I recognize but one judgment seat, that of the Eternal, to which you and I are equally amenable, and where, only, I expect to have an impartial hearing. As to my sentence, I care not if it is for an hour or a thousand years. When I enter that prison to me it will be forever—never more to come into the world—and it is to be hoped that those who have hunted me to my present position will leave the ashes of the man whom they have destroyed to remain undisturbed. My only fault has been that they knew I had money, which they wished to have. As to myself, I care not; death has no terror for me; on a hundred occasions I have fearlessly faced it; but I think of others—of those connected with me. In conclusion, I have but one request to make. Your Honor has already expressed an opinion on the trial —any remarks added in relation to me, as a guilty man, may have a counter effect from that intended. No man thinks me a fool. If there was in your Honor all the concentred wisdom of the world I could not be more sensible, from observations you might make, than I already am of the offence imputed to me, even if I deserved them. My situation is extremely painful, and any addition would be unnecessary. I would ask your Honor to spare me further remark. That is all I have to say, sir."

Among the incidents of this trial was the alleged robbery of the prisoner in the court room and while the court was in session. It seems that he had promised his counsel some money one day, claiming to have received some from his partner. When the court adjourned for a recess he excitedly rose up, and thrusting aside his coat tails, cried out that he had been robbed, while in court that day, of a large sum of money, showing how the lining of his coat had been cut out. The affair created quite a commotion, and many sympathized with the prisoner, though the District Attorney was rather inclined to be sceptical, and doubted his ever having had the money.

While at the Tombs, Monroe Edwards was favored with the visits of many lady friends and admirers, who brought him bouquets and other nick-nacks and trinkets. Among the gifts he received from them were fine, highly tempered saws, for sawing through iron, a pistol, and rope ladder made of silk, with grappling irons attached, to enable him to effect his escape from prison.

The Warden, learning that he had these articles in his trunk, went to the prisoner's cell and demanded that he produce them, which, however, he refused to do; but being threatened with punishment, and the forcible opening of his trunk by the prison authorities, he at length complied. The articles were found concealed in a false till at the bottom of the trunk.

A day or two subsequent Edwards was taken to State Prison, but he no sooner arrived there than he set his wits to work devising some means to effect his escape.

He conceived a system of telegraphy with some of his fellow prisoners, by means of grains of corn so disposed as to appear the result of pure accident, but perfectly intelligible to those in the secret. One of the grains getting accidentally displaced one day, by being blown away, the "communication was interrupted," and the attempt to repair the accident led to its discovery by the prison authorities.

On another occasion he got into a large drawer in the workshop, which was pushed to by one of the convicts. When evening came, and the convicts were taken to their cells, it was discovered that one of them was missing. The alarm was sounded and search instituted, but without result. At daybreak the search was resumed with no better success. The keepers were puzzled, but did not relax their efforts, and extra guards were put out. Edwards' position in the drawer was necessarily a very uncomfortable one, and, beginning to experience the pangs of hunger and thirst, he could stand it no longer, and so he gave himself up. The Warden ordered him to be whipped, and henceforth to work with ball and chain attached to his leg, which, in addition to being very painful, was extremely degrading to a man of his nature, and for a time it quite broke his spirit.

But he rallied after awhile, and determined to make one more effort to regain his liberty. He wrote a letter, signing it with the name of the foreman of the shoe shop of the prison to the contractor, making a report of the progress of the work, and asking that a fresh stock of leather be forwarded, making the requisition in true business style—so many uppers of such a grade, so many of another, etc. etc. At the bottom of the letter he affixed a P. S. requesting him (the contractor) to forward an enclosed letter to its destination. The enclosure was a letter addressed to his Excellency Silas Wright, Governor of New York.

The letter addressed to the contractor was dropped in the passage way of the prison on visiting day, in the hope that it would be picked up by one of the visitors and placed in the post-office box, and thus reach the contractor at New York, who in his turn would forward the enclosed letter to its destination.

True enough the letter was picked up by a lady who was visiting the prison; but, instead of placing it in the post-office box, she left it in the office of the prison. The Warden, thinking he recognized the writing as that of Edwards, imparted his suspicion to the State Prison Inspectors, who at the time were visiting the prison on a tour of inspection.

They had the prisoner brought before them, and handing him the letter in question, requested him to open it, which he, however, declined to do, saying that as he was then paying the penalty of one crime, he did not care to commit another by opening a letter which was not directed to him.

The inspectors however insisted—telling him that they knew that he had written the letter. It was accordingly opened and read; and Edwards, finding himself foiled in this attempt, also, acknowledged the authorship of the letter and its enclosure. The enclosed letter was then opened, and found to run about as follows:

"Silas Wright, *Gov.*

Dear Sir—You have confined, in one of the prisons of your State, a man named Monroe Edwards. If you can, consistently with your sense of duty, pardon and send him on to me, I will see to it that he never again troubles your State.   His father and I have been on the most intimate terms for years.

Yours truly,

ANDREW JACKSON."

Had this letter reached its destination, Edwards would, in all probability, have got out and been up to his old tricks. He begged of the inspectors not to have him punished with the whip or the irons, and promised, for the future, to so conduct himself that no fault should be found.

He died in prison a year or two after.

THE WEBB-MARSHALL DUEL.

A few pages back I alluded to the duel between Mr. Webb and Mr. Marshall, which grew out of this celebrated trial. This book would be incomplete without a more extended mention of that *affair d'honneur*.

While the trial was in progress the following article appeared in the *Courier and Enquirer*, of which James Watson Webb was editor and propietor:

" We learn from the *Tribune* that the Hon. T. F. Marshall, after wandering about the country for some thirty days lecturing on temperance, and giving his experience as a devotee of the bottle, has returned to this city to defend the notorious Monroe Edwards. When he gets back to Washington he will have been absent about forty days, for which he will doubtless draw from the Treasury, with the sanction of his brother members, three hundred and twenty dollars!   Now, while the editor of the *Tribune* was advocating the reduction of the Army and Navy, why did he not gently hint to Congress the necessity of reducing their own pay, and of not paying themselves anything from the public purse while making mountebanks of themselves or devoting their time to advocating the cause of notorious swindlers ?"

When the Hon. Mr. Marshall was making his celebrated speech towards the close of the trial he alluded to this attack upon him, and said :

" Now, I would venture to assert that, under all the circum-stances of the case, so far as the public are acquainted with them, that the parallel of that paragraph cannot be found in the whole history of the press of this country. And from the fact of my being an entire stranger to almost every human being in the City of New York, and by being under the apprehension that this thing might operate against my client, I beg leave to explain the relations between him and me. The prisoner at the bar, gentlemen, is a Kentuckian by birth, and although I never laid eyes on him till I saw him in the Tombs here, I am acquainted and intimately acquainted with a variety of his relations in the State from which we both came, and of which we are both natives. I was applied to in the City of Washington by two of his near relations—one of them a member of Congress, and the other a young man with whom I was acquainted and associated as a member of the Legislature of Kentucky for years, and for whose character as a gentleman, if such would be of service here, I would gauge my oath. I was informed by these gentlemen of his desolate situation, and they requested me, as a personal favor, that I would defend him if I was applied to. I came on here and I was applied to. And to me it appeared the most natural thing in the world that, situated as he was, so completely desolate and friendless, and in his situation, had he been in any other part of the world, it was the most natural thing in the world that his eye should turn to his native State—to the land of his birth—and that he should invoke the aid of one born where he was, in the dread crisis that was approaching, and the hour of his calamity. I say it was the most natural thing in the world. And if I had not been applied to by those whom I have mentioned—one of whom is above challenge, whose name ranks high in the annals of his country—if in his forlorn and desolate condition he had applied to me, as a Kentuckian by birth, to aid him in a strange country, I would have undertaken it, and braved all the slanders that could have been heaped upon my head for months, surrounded as he was by such extreme peril and calamity, rather than to have deserted him under such circumstances.

But I feel less difficulty now than I did before ; for he has found another countryman to be his counsel who holds before him a shield and an escutcheon against which the utmost malice of slander itself can cast no blot. So far, then, as the character of his countrymen is concerned, he stands no risk of being lowered in the estimation of any. But as to this attack itself, gentlemen, let me explain the nature and cause of it; it is, let me tell you, a mere personal matter; it is intended for me alone, and for the sole gratification of wreaking private revenge, in certainly *the most manly, the most honorable, the most dignified manner, and under the most humane circumstances.* In short, I did not believe that human revenge on one individual could be conceived in so lofty, so exalted a manner; but I do believe I was alone the motive, the sole victim sought. But so elevated were the feelings of this writer, so intent was he of gratifying his revenge on me, that he entirely forgot the cruel and unmanly manner in which he was wreaking it upon the unfortunate prisoner, who had never done him the slightest injury or ill will. I regret exceedingly that this thing is so, and I regret that it occurred, and that this explanation is necessary. I feel the awkwardness of it; and I am aware, if the counsel on the opposite side choose to make an ungenerous use of it, it may be made a subject of attack on me. But I felt compelled to make this statement, and it has happened to be my misfortune—my most unpleasant situation—to have had to notice this same disreputable source of attack twice recently, and both times in the discharge of my public duties, and I will explain to you the circumstances that drew forth this *noble* mode of revenge—this precious morsel against myself. Last winter this same writer made a charge against Congress—I state the substance of the charge—that a quantity of British coin had been brought to this country for the purpose of bribing the members of Congress, of which I was one, and that they had been bought to the tune of $100,000 apiece! I, in my place in Congress, instantly repelled the charge, and in very mild language for so gross an attack. This brought a letter from the writer of the article, asking me to retract what I said. Well, I reviewed the ground, and *I didn't retract it, and haven't retracted it, and I never would retract it on the face of the earth till I die!* This brought a second letter, but no retraction followed, *and there stuck the correspondence, and here is the revenge.* Well, I don't know that I am exactly the thing represented in this corrupt paper, but I believe that I can lay some claim to the character of a gentleman—that I am a tolerably good judge of what pertains to the character of a gentleman—at least as well as the man who wrote that article, and who *pretends* to be a gentleman. But I will simply remark that in Congress, at the bar, before the people, in all these various characters—all of which I consider are merged in the character of a gentleman—*that I stand ready to answer at any time and at all times for whatever I am responsible*, and for anything that may have occurred in this so *perfectly filthy a quarrel!* Under any circumstance I pledge my honor that I shall plead no privilege that pertains to my position as a member of Congress; and I do hope that such gentlemen as have any personal revenge to gratify against me will seek *some other mode and place*, if they can—and not by means of the public prints gratify their malice against me by attacking my client—*such time and place as gentlemen can seek, and they will always find me ready to meet them.*"

This being a direct challenge it is not strange that it resulted in a duel—a little affair in the gray of the morning at ten paces. It came off in Delaware, on the 20th day of June, 1842. At the first fire Webb was wounded slightly and the matter terminated.

On the return of Webb and his second to New York they were arrested, as has been previously stated, for a violation of one of the statutes of the State. Webb was tried and became one of the sensations of the day. He was found guilty, and it would have fared hard with him but for the influence of his friends and the clemency of the Governor.

CHAPTER XXIII.

THE HAUNTED CELL.

"I have heard it said that as we keep our birthdays when we are alive, so the ghosts of dead people who are not easy in their graves keep the day they died upon."— DICKENS, *in Barnaby Rudge.*

YES, the Tombs has had its haunted cell—a ghost has made it its abiding place, and the blood of at least two mortals has been all but frozen in their veins. The strong frames of two men, hardened by a life of danger and of daring—frames that were never known to quail before anything on earth or in the heavens, on land or on sea—quivered and trembled like the aspen before this unseen though not unheard—what? The courage that had faced every danger, that had looked the grim monster full in the face time and again, was wanting—gone entirely when assailed by this strange and unaccountable voice.

And why should not the Tombs as well as other buildings have its ghostly legends? Simply because a modern, a prosaic age scouts the very idea of visits from dwellers on the other side of the dread Styx. The building is a creation of this age, built by hands, many of which still toil from morn till night in order to procure the food necessary for the sustenance of that body of which they are members.

'Tis distance, we are told, that lends enchantment to the view; 'tis time, we know, gives interest to the tale. Tell us of the past, if you desire our attention—the present, what is it? How true the proverb that "Familiarity breeds contempt."

Were the Tombs some relic of antiquity—a production of times long, long gone by, bearing on its cold, gray walls the impress of the heavy hand of Time, how many a strange, wild, weird story would be told of it! Who would not have heard of its subterranean passages, leading none knew whither? Its damp dark cells, placed away down under ground, far from the noise and hum of the busy street, excluding the faintest ray of the glorious sun. In such a cell would have lingered and pined away some noble prisoner of state, seeing no human face save that of the cruel, heartless jailor, who from time to time came to bring him his coarse, unpalatable fare, and to heap fresh indignities upon him. To such an one would have been consigned the fair form of some beautiful maiden, a martyr, who, in defence of her virtue, repelled the advances of some notorious but all powerful libertine. Such a cell, we would be told, had been last opened nobody knew when; the key thereto was nowhere to be found; and at times strange noises were heard to proceed from it—clanking of chains, stifled groans, and all the stereotyped attendants of ghostly visitants.

Even those portions of the building receiving the full benefit of light and air would have their stories; not an old stain on the floors or walls but would be the mark of something terrible. Here would be the chamber of horrors, now used as a sort of store and lumber room, filled with the rubbish that had been accumulating through a long series of years, and which, we would be told, was the nightly meeting place of the spirits of malefactors who had ended their days within the prison walls. There would be the cell which, for some cause or other, no one could tell why, had long been unused, and which was looked upon with a feeling of dread. Its very contiguity would be shunned, and prisoners would beg, as though for their lives, not to be assigned to a cell in its vicinity.

But no, the Tombs belong to us; it is the offspring of our brain, the result of our handiwork. The Present—the practical, the sceptical Present—can tolerate no such nonsense. We know all about it. We knew the locality where it stands, and all about it, long before it was even thought of. We can name the very quarries whence came the huge granite blocks which compose the massive structure.

"And yet it moves," the great astronomer, Galileo, is reported to have said, even after the Inquisition had extorted a denial of the earth's motion around the sun. And yet, too, the Tombs has had its ghost, in spite of the incredulous Present. Why, the very name is suggestive of death and its abode! Tombs! O horror! It makes the very blood run cold in the veins as 'tis uttered.

'Twas night, and the cold silvery moon, not yet at the full, was quietly, as is her wont, pursuing her steady onward course through the skies. The street was unusually quiet, and the massive structure, that cold, forbidding specimen of Egyptian architecture, cast a deep black shadow, like the pall of death, over it. The great granite pillars at the portal, extending in solemn rows far back into the enclosure, stood like grim sentinels at their posts, silent and motionless.

Within the quiet was horribly oppressive. At other times the voices of prisoners occupying adjoining cells might be heard as they engaged in conversation—or some other circumstance might occur to relieve the stillness of the night. But on this night Silence reigned in all her supremacy. Not a sound but the steady tick, tick, tick of the great clock in the hall, measuring the flight of time, and the keeper's footsteps, as he made his customary tours of inspection—seeming to fall with unusual distinctness on the ear of the sleepless prisoner, who sought to while away the weary hours by reading—awakening echoes that had not before been heard.

Reader, do you know the misery of a sleepless night? Have you ever retired in perfect health, thinking to enjoy the boon of a good night's rest, and the moment you have summoned the presence of Morpheus, chanced to think of some trifling incident in your life which led to a chain of thought that set the brain at work thinking, thinking how this might have been, how that ought not to have been, and so on interminably, until at length the whole nervous system was aroused, defiantly refusing the advances of " Nature's sweet restorer?"

Do you, reader, know the misery of such a night? If so, then you can appreciate the position of the wretched prisoner who, on the night in question, was sitting in his lonely cell, trying to divert his mind with a book which he was reading. He was one of Capt. Gordon's mates, who, with the captain and the other mate, were confined in the prison, having but a day or two previous been removed by the United States Marshal from Eldridge Street Jail, which was not considered sufficiently secure for their safe keeping. His crime was having engaged with Captain Gordon (who was subsequently hanged) in the slave trade.

For some cause or other this prisoner could not sleep that night —he had been up and down repeatedly, and at length, giving up all idea of trying to sleep, he decided to spend the night in reading.

The keeper had just passed on his round, and as the rays of his dark lantern flashed into the cell the prisoner started up. What ailed him on this night? What made him so nervous? He was no coward, and yet every little noise startled him; but what was *that?* A groan—a deep, horrible groan, half suppressed and preceded by a long drawn sigh—seemed to fill the cell. Whence came it? Surely there was no one in the cell. He looked in his bed—he looked under it. The cell was not very spacious—it certainly afforded no hiding place for any one, even had it been possible for any one to have gotten in. He peered through the grating of the door into the long corridor; no sign of any one there— all was silent as death itself—no sound audible save that steady tick, tick, tick of the clock; and how loud it did tick on this night. Could he have been the victim of an illusion? He had heard of such things. Possibly after all there was nothing unnatural, and only the peculiar nervous condition he was in tortured some distant creaking hinge into a sigh and groan—but, great Heaven! there it goes again. Surely there is no mistaking that—a distinct, perfectly audible sigh, followed by the same deep, unearthly groan. "Help! Murder!" rang the prisoner's voice through the prison. "Come here, some one, quick—take me out of this!" he shouted at the top of his voice, his hair on end and his eyes bursting almost out of their sockets.

In an instant all was commotion. The ticking of the clock was no longer audible. Prisoners jumped out of bed and sprang to their cell doors, and the employés hastened to ascertain the cause of this untimely outcry—his screech as of one in the last agonies of distress.

"Take me out of this," gasped the affrighted prisoner, when the keepers made their appearance at his cell. "Put me anywhere—I don't care where—only don't let me remain in this cell. It's haunted, and I couldn't live in it until morning. Do with me what you like, but, for God's sake, take me out of this.

Was the man crazy? He had shown no symptoms of derangement—he had hitherto seemed perfectly rational.

He was taken out of the cell, and after being allowed the time to collect himself, was asked the cause of his thus alarming the prison. He then told that how, not being able to get asleep, he had concluded to sit up and read, when all at once he was startled by a terrible sigh or groan, which, on being repeated, worked him up to such a pitch that he could not contain himself.

The preceding night's adventure, as was perfectly natural, was the universal topic of conversation among the inmates of the prison on the following morning. Various were the opinions expressed, and innumerable the stories of ghosts and goblins, and haunted houses and rooms, that were told. Many there were who put full faith in the man's story, and corroborated it by the narration of similar adventures that had befallen others whom they named. Others again thought that the man had perpetrated a good practical joke, but those who had seen him as he came out of the cell knew better than that, for a more perfect impersonation of fright could not be conceived. Still others, and they were in the majority, thought that the man had fallen asleep over his reading and had been dreaming. Among those who were of this opinion was one, a prisoner also, in for being engaged in the slave trade, who rated him for his cowardice.

The man stoutly denied having been asleep at all, and said that he had never in all his life been more wide awake than on the preceding night. Quite an animated discussion ensued between the two slavers, which was only ended by the acceptance of a wager that the other dared not pass a night in the cell.

Though the attachés of the prison were inclined to believe that the man had only been dreaming, yet his emphatic denial seemed somewhat to shake their faith in that theory. At any rate, it was a subject that demanded investigation, and a thorough examination of the cell, as well as those adjoining, and their occupants, was begun.

The cells in the prison are arranged in four tiers, one above the other. The ceilings of the cells are formed by two large, heavy stone slabs, which also form the floors of the cells immediately above.

The cell in question was on the second tier, and a thorough examination revealed nothing remarkable. The cell above was occupied by a prisoner whose name the author prefers not to mention, who had been arrested for shooting a man during a quarrel in a restaurant in Grand street. On extinguishing his lamp on the night previous he noticed a streak of light coming through a crevice, formed by the stones which made the floor of his cell not being well joined. He applied his eye to the opening, and seated at the table reading he saw the occupant of the cell underneath.

Being something of a practical joker, he thought the opportunity for a little sport too good to let pass—and so, applying his mouth to the crack, he filled the cell below with the sighs and groans which had so alarmed the slaver.

The mystery was solved; the joke was thoroughly appreciated and highly relished by the employés of the prison. The perpetrator was informed of the wager between the two slavers, and asked to repeat it, but to be sure to "do it up brown."

The investigators did not let it become generally known that they had discovered the cause of the last night's excitement; they simply reported that they could discover nothing wrong or out of the way about the cell, and the other slaver was transferred thereto.

He was at the time engaged in writing a book of his life and adventures, and would often sit up late in the night. About ten o'clock, and when all was still as on the night previous, the man who was hard at work writing heard the half suppressed sigh and deep groan which had so alarmed the other. Perhaps his cheek blanched; at any rate he was not to be easily frightened; but simply raising his eyes to look about him, he cried out, "Go it again, old fellow." After waiting in vain for some time for a repetition of the sound he resumed his writing.

After he had been writing a considerable while again that awful sigh and that terrible groan, more frightful than before, filled the cell. Then he was annoyed. He got up, looked under the bed, in the bed, under the table, on the shelf over the bed. He went to the soil pipe running along the wall, through which prisoners in adjoining cells frequently converse. He called to the occupant of the next cell: "Hello, Jim!"

Jim, who had been asleep, rose to learn what was wanted of him.

"Do you ever groan in your sleep?" he was asked.

"Not that I know," was the reply.

"It's darned strange," muttered the slaver, as he resumed his writing; and Jim, who was but half awake, tumbled back into bed.

But the terrible groan again came; this time followed by a hollow, sepulchral voice, which spoke as follows:

"My name is McDonald; I was murdered, foully murdered in this cell."

Fright now took complete possession of the man. He threw himself on the bed; and, as he did so a tin cup, which, either by accident or design, had been placed on the very edge of the shelf over the head of the bed, so that the least jar would cause it to topple off, fell and struck him on the head.

He sprang up and yelled, in a perfect frenzy of terror, to the night watchman, "For God's sake come and take me out of this." "He was," he said, "no believer in ghosts; he would follow where any man led, or essay what any man had done. He had faced danger in every form. He was no coward; but there was such a mysterious something about that cell that all the wealth of the world would not induce him to spend a night in it."

The next day the trick became pretty generally known; the ghost was embodied, and a good laugh at the expense of the victims enjoyed.

CHAPTER XXIV.

"Ho! ho! It is a grand thing to be mad! to be peeped at like a wild lion through the iron bars—to gnash one's teeth and howl through the long, still night, to the merry ring of a heavy chain, and to roll and twine among the straw, transported with such brave music. Hurrah for the Mad-house."—DICKENS, *in Hard Times.*

THE Tombs has, at different times, been the temporary abiding place of many singular and remarkable personages.

Among the many interesting characters who have been lodged there was a young man named Burdett, a lunatic. At the time he was brought there he was employed as clerk in a large establishment in New York. His particular mania was the formation of ragged schools for boys, on the plan of the ragged schools of England. He had received a very good education and was possessed of a remarkable memory. He had read a great deal, and was a first rate biblical scholar, and in a discussion might bring the blush of shame and defeat to the cheek of many a divine. Quotations from the Scriptures were literally at his tongue's end and always apposite.

He had been brought up on a charge of lunacy, and was sent to the Asylum, where he remained for some time, but was finally discharged, as supposed, cured.

All traces of the young man were lost, and it was generally supposed that he was getting along in much the same manner as the great mass of his fellow creatures—conducting himself as became a staid, sober citizen, quietly attending to his business, etc., etc.

One winter the steady burghers of the ancient town of Albany, on the Hudson, were in quite a flutter of excitement and expectation over a grand charity concert shortly to be given, in aid of a very laudable purpose, which appealed directly to the sympathies of the good people of the place.

The entertainment had been euphoniously styled "The Bouquet Concert," and arrangements had been made to present each and every one of the audience with a handsome bouquet on his or her entrance to the hall.

The moving spirit in this enterprise was a young man with a fluent tongue, good presence, and easy, gentlemanly address. The charity in aid of which the entertainment was to be given was the establishment of a ragged school, for the benefit of the ragged urchins running about the streets of Albany.

The young gentleman waited on the ladies of the leading families of the place, and enlisted their sympathies in behalf of the scheme; and many a conservatory was despoiled of its choicest floral gems for the purpose of making the necessary bouquets to be given away at the entertainment.

The voice of the Press was eloquent in its laudation of the young gentleman, the noble charity and the entertainment—which, the public was assured, was to be the most fashionable and popular of the season.

One of the largest and most fashionable halls had been engaged for the occasion; several first class pianos, with the makers' names conspicuously displayed over the key board, had been kindly sent by their respective agents, to be used at the concert; the services of some of the most eminent professionals and amateurs had been volunteered and accepted, and everything betokened a complete success of the undertaking.

The young gentleman was the hero of the day—*fêted* by the ladies and respected by the gentlemen. He ingratiated himself in the favor of the clergy by his scriptural knowledge; and they, too, loaned their influence in furtherance of the project.

Elaborate handbills and posters, setting forth the nature of the entertainment, the laudable charity in the behalf of which it was to be given, and bearing the names of the wives of leading citizens of the place as patrons thereof, were freely distributed and conspicuously posted about town.

At length the evening of the entertainment arrived. Elaborate toilets for the occasion had been prepared by the belles, and the beaux were gotten up regardless of expense, in full evening dress— for the affair was to be *first class*.

They came singly, in pairs and in companies—on foot and in carriages—and at the appointed hour a large concourse had assembled at the hall, which had not yet been lighted up, and the doors of which were found to be closed.

Gentlemen consulted their watches and muttered, "Strange"— ladies impatiently waited for something to be done—and after a while, when inquiries for the young gentleman were made, and he was found to be *non est*, the idea flashed upon them that they had been sold—that they were the victims of a practical joker—and they dispersed to their homes anything but highly pleased with their evening's entertainment, while Burdett, for he was the nice young man, was at the very time entertaining a number of friends at Delmonico's, on the corner of Broadway and Chambers street, with an account of the concert which was *not* taking place, and exhibiting specimens of the handbills and posters he had gotten up.

The next morning the finely written articles and criticisms on the preceding evening's entertainment, which had without doubt been carefully prepared beforehand, did not appear in the local papers, but instead a simple announcement that the concert did not take place, and that the nice young gentleman had left for parts unknown.

It was but a few days after the above occurrence that Burdett was again committed for lunacy, and sent to the Lunatic Asylum on Blackwell's Island, where he afforded great amusement to the patients by his numerous jokes and pranks.

The doctor in charge of the asylum (Ranney), who was a most estimable gentleman, and well qualified for the position which he had long and ably filled, was in the habit, on public holidays, of getting up entertainments for the amusement of the inmates.

One Fourth of July, being desirous of celebrating the day in a becoming manner, and at the same time affording entertainment to his patients, he determined on a patriotic celebration according to the most approved fashion of the country. A procession was form- ed, a meeting organized, and an orator for the occasion determined upon, who was to deliver the customary patriotic oration. The lu- natics had all been properly instructed how to conduct themselves on the occasion, and a more orderly meeting or attentive audience could certainly not have been found anywhere on the continent.

The orator chosen was Burdett, who acquitted himself ably. His speech was a master effort, and would have reflected credit on any one. Among the audience were five of the Governors of the Almshouse, who were on a visit to the island on that day. The heat was oppressive, but in spite of that these gentlemen, used as they were to festive gatherings and the oratory of the most accomplished speakers of the land, and who could scarcely find the time and patience to sit out any entertainment, remained for over one hour fairly entranced by the vivid flashes of imagination and the eloquent patriotism of this poor inmate of the Lunatic Asylum. They pronounced the day's entertainment one of the most remarkable and enjoyable they had ever had, and the orator one of the most wonderful of men.

Burdett was finally perfectly cured and discharged from the asylum. The last heard of him by the author was to the effect that his services had been reëngaged by his old employer, and that he had been sent somewhere up the river to take the charge of an establishment there.

AN INCIDENT OF BUMMERS' HALL.

Connected with the Tombs, on Franklin street, there is an old stone building known as the Station House—for which purpose, in fact, it had been built and formerly used. After the completion of the Tombs the cells and partitions were taken out of this building, and it was thus converted into a large room or hall, and benches were placed along the walls. In this shape it was used as a sort of House of Detention for vagrants and others who were brought in for the purpose of being sent to the island, and it has, in consequence, been called Bummers' Hall.

The floor and walls are of stone, and in the middle of the room is a large stove with the pipe running through the roof of the building.

In this hall were put, as they came in during the day, all such as were arrested for vagrancy, drunkenness and minor offences, there to remain until the next morning, when they would be placed in the " Black Maria " and forwarded to Blackwell's Island.

One day there was brought in a soldier just returned from the army, who had been found wandering about the streets. The doctor pronounced him demented, but perfectly harmless. He was put in Bummers' Hall to spend the night with its motley crowd of occupants.

About two o'clock A. M. a terrible racket was heard, the noise proceeding from Bummers' Hall, whither the keepers at once repaired, and where they found, to their consternation, that the soldier had wrenched an iron bar from the stairway and commenced an indiscriminate attack upon the occupants of the room as they sat or lay sleeping on the benches and the floor. He was not secured until after he had killed one or two, more or less injured several others, and overturned the stove and scattered the fire over the floor.

The next morning, when asked what he had done and why he had done so, he replied that he had been dreaming that he was attacked by the enemy, that he seized his musket by the barrel and fought his way through.

He was sent to the Lunatic Asylum on Blackwell's Island. He was a native of Ireland, about twenty-eight years of age, and was quite small.

CHAPTER XXV.

PIRACY AND PRIVATEERING.—BAKER AND HIS CONFEDERATE CREW.
—BABE, THE PIRATE.—THE DOOMED UNKNOWN.—ANECDOTE OF
THE ELDER BOOTH.—WHAT MRS. ANN S. STEPHENS DID.

"No man should have more than two attachments—the first to number one and the
second to the ladies."—DICKENS, *in Pickwick.*

CAPT. BAKER with his entire crew were the first privateers-
men captured during the late War of the Rebellion, and as
the Government had but recently subscribed to the Treaty of Paris,
one of the articles of which declared privateering abolished, and
that henceforth all privateers should be considered as pirates, it
was generally supposed that they would be treated as such, and
punished accordingly.

They were brought to this city in irons and locked up in the
Tombs. The mate, a Mr. Hartshorn, on entering the prison yard,
remarked to his captain, "This looks like a pretty strong fortifica-
tion."

They were there some time awaiting their trial. Jeff. Davis, on
learning the capture of these men, and that they were not to be
held as prisoners of war, but, on the contrary, treated as pirates,
and, in consequence, liable to suffer death, threatened retaliation on
some prisoners in his hands—among whom were a member of
Congress from this State, a general, and other officers. He had
them removed to other quarters, there to await the action of our
Government in the case of Capt. Baker and crew. He wrote to
the authorities at Washington notifying them of the course he had
pursued, and threatening to retaliate in kind, man for man, according to rank, on the prisoners whom he had set apart, if the extreme
penalty was inflicted on Baker and his men.

The privateers' trial never came on, and they were finally removed to Fort Lafayette, there to remain as prisoners of war until
exchanged, which was shortly after effected.

BABE, THE PIRATE.

The eccentricities of the elder Booth, the famous tragedian, are familiar to all, and innumerable are the stories which are told of him. The following incident, however, the author believes, is not generally known, and may be of interest to the many friends and admirers of the great actor.

At the time when Mr. Fallon was the Warden of the Tombs there was confined in one of the cells a young man called Babe, who had been brought in for piracy and murder on the high seas. He was then under sentence of death. This young man and his crimes caused at the time considerable excitement—particularly as it was generally supposed that the name he was known by was fictitious, and that out of consideration for his family he had declined to give his real name. A prominent bishop of the Episcopal Church had a very wild son, who had been the cause of much sorrow and trouble to his worthy father and family, who at the time was missing from home. Many pretended to recognize in the prisoner the missing son of the bishop, and scandal had a theme for her busy wicked tongue.

The author had occasion one afternoon, while Babe was in confinement, to visit the Tombs, and while there Mr. Booth called and asked to see the prisoner. With Mr. Booth was a young man who invariably accompanied him and acted as a sort of secretary and companion—reminded him of his engagements, etc.

Booth had been drinking pretty freely that day, and was quite unmanageable. The author's curiosity being aroused, he made up his mind to witness the interview between the tragedian and the pirate.

At that time prisoners under sentence of death were chained to the floor by the ankles. Booth, when admitted to the prisoner's cell, was moved at the sight of the young man thus ironed. He threw himself on the prisoner's bed and asked that the irons be taken off Babe and put on him, remarking that he (the prisoner) was too young to die by the halter. He asked Babe if he wanted for anything, and offered him money, which was refused, the prisoner saying that he was in want of nothing, and that Mr. Fallon was very kind to him, doing what he could to make him as comfortable as circumstances would permit. Seeing that his wants were all supplied, Booth then asked the prisoner to smoke, and, removing his hat from his head, took out his handkerchief (which at that time it was the fashion for gentlemen to carry in the hat) and emptied the contents, twenty-five or thirty segars, on the bed.

After remaining a little while longer in the cell Booth became restive and asked to see some other prisoners. He was taken to the cell of a negro, with whom he had a long talk, and to whom, when he left, he gave a twenty dollar bank note. Mr. Fallon hearing of it went to the negro's cell for the purpose of getting him to return it. The negro refused to give up the note; and, when an attempt was made to take it away from him, he put it in his mouth and would have swallowed it had not Mr. Fallon almost choked him in his efforts to take it from him.

Mr. Booth's attendant then informed Mr. Fallon that he (Mr. Booth) was under an engagement to play that night at the Park Theatre for Mr. Simpson's benefit, and, as he appeared to be wholly unmanageable, he requested Mr. Fallon to keep Mr. Booth in prison until he could notify Mr. Simpson of his whereabouts.

Booth was accordingly taken to an empty cell, to see, as he was told, some one else. As soon as he entered the cell the door was closed, the key turned in the lock, and Booth was a prisoner, although certainly not " committed according to due process of the law."

The author concluded to remain and see the farce out. After awhile Mr. Simpson came with a carriage, and was taken to the cell in which Booth was locked.

The illegally detained prisoner was found fast asleep, and snoring furiously, wholly unconscious of his position. He was awakened, and rubbing his eyes, and seeing Mr. Simpson before him, " Come," said he, " let's go take a drink;" and together they left the prison.

The play selected for the evening's entertainment was Richard the Third, and the author, having no other engagement on hand, decided to go and see for himself how the leading character would be sustained after the day's adventure. A seat at the side and near the stage was secured, and the actor could be plainly seen before he appeared before the audience. He hesitated, as though undecided whether to go on or turn back, when another actor stepped up, and giving him a push, he landed on the middle of the stage. Once behind the footlights the man was lost in the actor. That night he excelled himself; the audience was fairly wild with enthusiasm; and on the following morning the papers were filled with glowing accounts of the performance, and proclaimed Booth one of the greatest, if not the greatest of tragedians.

To return to Babe. The day appointed for his execution was drawing nigh. Speculation as to who the prisoner was, and as to where he belonged was still rife. Few knew, but among those few was Mrs. Ann S. Stephens, the authoress, who took great interest in him, and called frequently, in her quiet, unassuming manner, at the Tombs, to talk with and cheer up the unhappy prisoner. She exerted all her energies and talents in his behalf, and went to Washington a number of times to see the President about his pardon.

At length her unceasing efforts were rewarded; the desired pardon came, and the prisoner was set at liberty. To this day but few are aware of the influence which was brought to bear on the Executive in behalf of the unknown prisoner.

Babe remained here but a short time after his release from prison. He shipped for a cruise to the Mediterranean entered, the naval service of some foreign power, and, in course of time, attained a position of rank and importance in the service.

He was a fine looking young man, well formed, and of about twenty-eight years of age. He had a good education and was very well informed. His identity was never revealed to the public, and has ever remained a profound secret with those few who knew him. His father was a man of some prominence in the Methodist Church.

CHAPTER XXVI.

"Change begets change. If a man habituated to a narrow circle, out of which he seldom travels, steps beyond it, though it be never so brief, his departure from the monotonous scene on which he has been an actor of importance would seem to be the signal for instant confusion."—DICKENS, *in Martin Chuzzlewit.*

ONCE in jail, the desire to get out again is strong. Iron bars and stone walls are not pleasant surroundings, and no one likes to tarry near them. It is not surprising, then, that the inmates of those massive hotels, maintained at the expense of the State and of the City, should occasionally make a break for. freedom. Considerable ingenuity has been displayed by these imitators of the famous Baron Trenck, and the various devices resorted to for effecting escapes are almost as numerous as the escapes themselves.

It is impossible to furnish an accurate list of all the prisoners who have escaped from the Tombs. In the earlier years of the prison's existence the records were kept in a very loose and careless manner. " Sufficient unto the day is the evil thereof " evidently was the rule under which the officials of that period worked. Such records as were kept were not preserved with that care that should have been exercised, and the consequence was that many interesting, not to say important events connected with the Tombs and its history are lost trace of and forgotten.

It is only within the last quarter of a century that a due regard has been paid to the proper keeping of the books and records of the prison—hence the author's inability to go back of that time in making up his criminal records.

The first escape that he finds mentioned is that of Henry A. Clark, who escaped at night, December 1st, 1851. He was retaken, however, and sent to State Prison for two years.

Aug. 2, 1854.—James Hampton escaped through the window of the court room in the day time.

Nov. 6, 1854.—Robert Green, who was imprisoned for grand larceny, escaped from the second tier in the day
time. He had been visited by a friend, from
whom he obtained a visitor's ticket, which he
counterfeited, and by means of which he effected his escaped. Watching his opportunity he
slipped out of his cell, passed the keepers on
the corridors and in the yard, presented his
ticket to the keeper at the gate, and thus got
out. By referring to the sketch of Sheppard
(Mahony), elsewhere given, it will be seen that he
thought to effect his escape in a similar manner.
His scheme was killed in the germ—though its
fruition, owing to the adoption of the colored
ticket, was next to an impossibility.

Nov. 17, 1855.—Daniel H. Johnson escaped from the prison yard
in the day time.

Oct. 16, 1856.—Patrick McCanna, in for grand larceny, and under
sentence of five years' imprisonment, escaped
from the fourth tier at night; was recaptured
Nov. 7, 1856, and sentenced to State Prison.

April 11, 1859.—Bartholomew Upton, Edw. Upton, Peter McCann,
Frederick Lowe, Thomas Flynn, John Mahony,
all boys, in for minor offences, excepting the latter, effected their escape through the window on
Franklin street, in broad daylight, at about four
o'clock P. M. The escape was witnessed by
some men standing on the opposite side of the
street, who, however, neglected to inform the
officers. The escape was planned by Mahony,
who is to-day, perhaps, the most successful jail
breaker in the country. A sketch of his life,
from his infancy up, giving an account of his
various exploits and escapes from prison, will
be found in another part of this book.

July 6, 1860.—Henry Hawk, committed for burglary, made his
escape by answering to the name of another prisoner, who was called to receive his discharge.

Sept. 19, 1863.—Conrad Smith, *alias* Schrader, escaped from cell No. 50 on the second tier. In this cell were two other prisoners—one of whom was committed for murder. By the aid of the other prisoners Smith managed to turn the bedstead up endwise against the bottom of the cell. He next removed the iron lintel under the window, making an aperture in the wall 29 inches long and $6\frac{1}{4}$ inches high. He then soaped himself thoroughly from head to foot, in order to facilitate his slipping through the opening he had effected in the wall. He slipped his head through first, and bracing himself with one hand against the inner side of the wall, by twisting and contorting his body, succeeded, after great effort, in forcing his way through the aperture, and let himself drop to the ground below. He then made his way to the top of the cook house in the rear of the prison, and from there to the top of the wall, from which he leaped (a distance of thirty feet) to the street below, and was free. In consideration of the services rendered by his fellow prisoners, he was to have assisted them in making their escape also, but once free himself he was wholly unconcerned as to what befell them.

When the officers learned of his escape they immediately started on his track; but a month elapsed ere he was recaptured—being taken after a desperate struggle, in a lager bier saloon on the Bowery, on the night of the 21st October following. He was sent to State Prison at Sing Sing for four years.

While on this subject it may not be out of place to mention the case of James Foster, whose proper name is James Dunn. He had been convicted of burglary in the first degree, and sentenced to ten years' imprisonment at Sing Sing. While in prison he procured, or made out of a block of wood, a decoy duck, such as is used by gunners, to which he attached an India rubber tube, with a sort of mask at the end. Watching his opportunity he went to the river, where, divesting himself of his clothing, he got into the water and swam beneath the surface, breathing through the tube, which was so fastened to the decoy as to permit a sufficient supply of air necessary for carrying on the process of respiration. The decoy was no doubt seen floating on the water by many, but as the duck's partiality for that element is familiar to everybody, it attracted no particular attention, no one for a moment supposing *that there was a convict making his escape.* He was afterwards again sent up for ten years, and again he effected his escape. He was next sent up for life, having been convicted of manslaughter, but was pardoned by the Governor. He was again sent up for burglary for ten years. Again he resorted to his duck and tube, but was this time caught by an officer attached to the prison, as he was coming out of the water.

The following is a list of prisoners who escaped from officers and from the court:

Sept. 16, 1853.—Arthur Graham, Wm. Early, Jeremiah Totten, Thomas Thompson, Frederick Winslow. } Burglars, escaped from the court room.

Nov. 5, 1853.—Theodore Beach, from an officer of the court.

"   15,   "   David Ford, charged with forgery, from an officer of the court.

Nov. 24, 1854.—John Simpson, charged with grand larceny, and sentenced to five years' imprisonment, escaped from an officer, was retaken April 28th, 1855, and sent to Sing Sing Prison for five years, whence he escaped, and nothing has since been heard of him.

July 31, 1855.—Morris Regan escaped from court.

Sept. 12,   "   Andrew McFall escaped from an officer.

Nov. 13, 1856.—Barnard Ford escaped from court.

Aug. 4, 1857.—Charles Lewis escaped from court.

March 9, 1858.—John Hawkins, sentenced to imprisonment for four years and seven months, for having committed a burglary, escaped from an officer.

April 13, 1858.—John Henry, bigamy, from court.

Nov. 20, 1858.—Theodore Gallaudet escaped from an officer.

This is the Dr. Gallaudet who in that year assaulted Mr. Cranston, the proprietor of the New York Hotel. It seems that a case of small pox had occurred in the hotel, and the doctor, who also boarded there, was called in to attend the patient. The doctor did not report the case to Mr. Cranston, who was greatly incensed thereat, and who, at the dinner table one evening, took the doctor to task. Some words ensued between Mr. Cranston and the doctor, when the latter, getting very angry, seized a water decanter, which he threw at the proprietor's head, knocking him down and inflicting a dangerous wound.

The doctor was arrested, tried by the Court of General Sessions, convicted, and sentenced to the Penitentiary for one year.

When taken from the court room he suggested to the officers who had him in charge, and who were to take him to the Tombs, there to await the regular trip of the "Black Maria" for the Penitentiary, that, inasmuch as he was to be shut off from the world and its enjoyments for so long a time, they accompany him to a fashionable restaurant up town to dine with him and a few friends. The officers were not at all averse to having a good dinner, no doubt to be washed down with choice wines, at the doctor's expense, and acceded to his proposition, feeling perfectly easy as to the security of their prisoner. They met the doctor's friends and had a good time generally. Wine was poured out like water, and the officers, drinking freely, became exhilarated, and entertained the doctor and his friends with stories and adventures incidental to their calling. They were having a first rate time, when the doctor was obliged to leave the room for a few moments. As he left his hat behind him the officers did not suspect anything wrong. But the doctor never called for his hat, leaving it as a trophy to the officers, who were on the next day informed by Judge Hoffman that their services as officers of his court would be no longer required.

The doctor was next heard from at Havana, where he was joined by his family, and, shortly afterwards, returned to France, his native land.

Sept. 23, 1859.—John F. Snooks, sentenced to five years and six
                 months' imprisonment for forgery, escaped from
                 an officer.

Jan. 12, 1860.—Thos. McIntyre escaped from an officer.

Nov. 11, 1863.—Wm. Duffy, larceny, escaped from an officer; retaken Nov. 16 and sent to State Prison for four years and six months.

Nov. 23, 1873.—William J. Sharkey, indicted for murder, escaped from the Tombs. Disguised in woman's clothes he walked past two keepers out of the door, and, jumping on a street car, was out of reach of the officers of justice.

Dec. 28, 1873.—Henry W. Genet, better known as "Prince Harry," a member of the Legislature of the State, and prominent member of the Ring, was committed to the Tombs by Judge Daniels, but was suffered by Sheriff Brennan to visit his house in Harlem, in charge of two deputy Sheriffs, from whom he escaped and fled, it is supposed, to Canada.

CHAPTER XXVII.

"It was terrible to see—if any one, in that distraction of excitement, could have seen the world of eager eyes, all strained upon the scaffold and the beam."—DICKENS, *in Barnaby Rudge.*

THE case of Capt. Nathaniel Gordon was, the author believes, the first and only one in this country in which capital punishment was inflicted for the crime of engaging in the slave trade.

Nathaniel Gordon followed the profession of the sea from early life. Beginning, as most persons of that predilection do, as a cabin boy, he rose by degrees to the position of captain. It is said that on one occasion, when he was leaving the coast of Africa with a cargo of slaves, he was pursued by a British man-of-war, his vessel was captured, and Gordon escaped in female attire. He was a pale faced, dark eyed little man, and with an appearance which would negative the idea of being engaged in so nefarious a traffic. He was about twenty-eight years of age, was five feet seven inches in height, and weighed 140 pounds. He was born at Portland, Me.

Captain Gordon was arrested, with two of his mates, by Isaiah Rynders, the Marshal of the district, and lodged in Eldridge Street Jail.

On the change of administration, by the succession of Abraham Lincoln to the presidency, Rynders was removed and Robert Murray was appointed in his stead. The prisoners, who had been enjoying many privileges—Captain Gordon occasionally having been allowed to spend a night at home with his family.—were placed under stricter surveillance.

On an inspection of their quarters the newly made Marshal arrived at the conclusion that Eldridge Street Jail was not sufficiently secure for such important prisoners, and accordingly he ordered their removal.

They were transferred to the Tombs, there to await their trial. They had hitherto felt but little concern at their arrest and imprisonment—there never having been as yet any one hanged for their offence. When they found that the new administration was disposed to view the case in all its enormity, and to treat the criminals accordingly, they became greatly alarmed at their position.

The wife of Captain Gordon visited him daily, and did all in her power to cheer him, asserting that the authorities would never hang him.

The circumstances of his life and crimes, as elicited upon his trials (for he was tried twice) were as follows : His father was a captain in the American merchant marine service, and frequently took his wife with him. One of the points insisted upon in the defence of the unfortunate Nathaniel was that his nativity was not proved to be American, as he was born at sea, and in British waters, under the British flag.

On the first trial, before Judge Shipman and a jury, there was no conviction. On the second trial, before Judges Nelson and Shipman, which occupied the court three days—the 6th, 7th and 8th of November, 1861—he was convicted. Testimony was adduced by Mr. E. Delafield Smith, even from the West Indies, and that indefatigable official used every exertion to follow out the extreme penalty and sentence of the law. Yet the counsel of the unfortunate man were not remiss. Ex-Judges Beebe and Bean were tireless in their efforts to prevent what they conscientiously believed to be the immolation of an unfortunate and innocent man on the altar of fanaticism.

They failed alike before the Court and the President. On the 30th November the following order was made by the Judges in the United States Circuit Court :

"Motions for an arrest of judgment and a new trial having been argued by the counsel for the government and the prisoner, and mature deliberation having been had, it is now ordered that said motions be denied." Whereupon the United States District Attorney moved for judgment upon the prisoner.

The Court then proceeded to pass judgment as follows, as pronounced by Judge Shipman :

"It appears from the evidence in this case that in the summer of 1860 you sailed in the ship Erie from Havana, in the island of Cuba, bound to the coast of Africa. You were master of the ves-

sel, and had on board a competent crew and a large amount of
provisions, of a kind and quantity appropriate for food for a large
number of persons, and such as is usually carried out in vessels
which are intended for the slave trade.   The ship also had on
board a large number of water casks as well as a quantity of liquor,
which latter was to be left in Africa, probably exchanged for the
freight which you undertook to bring back to Cuba.   In command
of this ship, thus equipped and provided, you proceeded to the
Congo river, on the west coast of Africa, and there, after landing
your cargo, and subsequently reshipping all, or nearly all, but the
liquor, and filling your water casks with fresh water, you dropped
your vessel down the river to a point a few miles from its mouth,
and in a few hours, on the afternoon of the 7th of August, you
took on board 897 of the inhabitants of that country, thrust them,
densely packed and crowded, between the decks of the ship, and
immediately set sail for Cuba.   On the morning of the 8th, in the
Atlantic Ocean, about 50 miles from coast, you were captured by
the United States war vessel Michigan, your ship taken to Monrovia, where all the unfortunate victims of your crime then living
were put on shore, and you were brought in your ship to this port.
Upon these facts you have been accused, brought to trial before a
jury of your countrymen, and found guilty of a crime for which
the laws of your country adjudge you a pirate, and inflict upon you
the punishment of death.   In the verdict of the jury it is my duty
to say that the Court fully concurred.   The evidence of your guilt
was so full and complete as to exclude from the minds of your
triers all doubt.   You are soon to be confronted with the terrible
consequences of your crime, and it is proper that I should call to
your mind the duty of preparing for that event which will soon
terminate your mortal existence, and usher you into the presence of
the Supreme Judge.   Let me implore you to seek the spiritual
guidance of the ministers of religion, and let your repentance be
as thorough and humble as your crime was great.   Do not attempt
to hide its enormity from yourself; think of the cruelty and wickedness of seizing nearly a thousand human beings, who never did
you any harm, and thrusting them between the decks of a small
ship, beneath a burning tropical sun, to die of disease or suffocation, or be transported to distant lands, and consigned, they and

their posterity, to a fate far more cruel than death. Think of the sufferings of the unhappy beings whom you crowded on the Erie; of their helpless agony and terror as you took them from their native land, and especially think of those who perished under the weight of their miseries on the passage from the place of your capture to Monrovia. Remember that you showed mercy to none—carrying off, as you did, not only those of your own sex, but women and helpless children. Do not flatter yourself that, because they belonged to a different race from yourself, that your guilt is therefore lessened—rather fear that it is increased. In the just and generous heart the humble and the weak inspire compassion and call for pity and forbearance, and as you are soon to pass into the presence of that God of the black man as well as the white man, who is no respecter of persons, do not indulge for a moment the thought that He hears with indifference the cry of the humblest of his children. Do not imagine that, because others shared in the guilt of this enterprise, yours is thereby diminished, but remember the awful admonition of your Bible, 'Though hand join in hand the wicked shall not go unpunished.' Turn your thoughts toward Him who alone can pardon—who is not deaf to the supplications of those who seek His mercy. It remains only to pronounce the sentence which the law affixes to your crime, which is, that you be taken back to the City Prison, from whence you were brought and remain there until Friday, the 7th day of February next, and then and there, the place of execution, between the hours of twelve o'clock at noon and three o'clock in the afternoon on that day, you be hanged by the neck until you are dead, and may the Lord have mercy on your soul."

The death warrant was then signed, and the convict handed over to the Marshal.

Strenuous exertions were made by the mother and wife of the unfortunate man to save him. Together they repaired to Washington, hoping that the clemency of the President might be secured. They arrived in Washington on the same morning that the President's little son died, and therefore could not obtain the desired interview. Had they seen the President it is quite likely that they would have succeeded in getting, if not a pardon, at least a commutation of sentence.

A respite of two weeks had been granted.

The wife and mother of the prisoner returned from their fruitless journey to Washington on a dark and rainy night, quite heart broken. The poor old mother seemed to realize fully the awful position of her unhappy son. On their arrival they at once went to the Tombs, but it being midnight when they arrived, they did not succeed in gaining admission, and they accordingly went to a hotel, where they remained until morning, when they returned to the prison to impart the sad news of the failure of their mission. Mrs. Gordon remained with her husband the whole of the morning, leaving him at noon, but returning again towards evening.

From the *New York Herald* of Saturday, Feb. 22d, 1862, we take the following account of the execution, and the sad scenes which preceded it, together with Gordon's attempt at suicide:

"The last meeting between Gordon and his family took place on Thursday evening, and the interview between the culprit and his wife is described as being very affecting. Mrs. Gordon, together with the prisoner's aged mother, called at the prison about six o'clock in the evening, and remained with the condemned about an hour. He received them in a most affectionate manner, and talked most tenderly of his little son, who was absent. He seemed to care little about his own fate, but for the well being of his wife and child he appeared very solicitous. Even the jailors were moved to compassion, and the sobs of the broken hearted wife found an echo in every heart. The final separation took place about seven o'clock, and was a most painful scene to all present.

Soon after Mrs. Gordon retired from the prison Marshal Murray called upon the prisoner and conversed with him upon the subject of the approaching execution. It was arranged that the execution should take place about two o'clock the following afternoon. The prisoner then bade the Marshal good night. The remainder of the evening was spent by Gordon in writing letters to his relatives and friends. He wrote no less than a dozen letters, one of which was directed to his mate on board the Erie and another to his son, to be opened when he arrived at the age of discretion. Having despatched these letters the prisoner commenced to smoke, and continued in the enjoyment of his segars until a late hour. At half past one o'clock he went to bed.

Nothing worthy of note occured until about three o'clock A. M., when the keepers were alarmed by the prisoner being suddenly seized with convulsions. At first it was supposed that he was trying to strangle himself; but on a close examination it was evident that he was suffering from the effects of poison. Dr. Simmons, the prison physician, was immediately sent for and stimulants were freely administered, for the purpose of producing a reaction. For the first half hour or so the efforts of the physician appeared to have but little effect. The patient became quite rigid under the influence of the poison, his pulse could scarcely be felt, and it was thought that, after all, the gallows would be cheated of its victim Drs. James R. Wood and Hedgman, who were also in attendance on the prisoner, labored hard to resuscitate the dying man, and finally, by means of the stomach pump and the use of brandy, the patient was sufficiently recovered to be able to articulate. It was not until eight o'clock, however, that the physicians had any hope of saving Gordon's life. From that hour, however, the prisoner gradually recovered, although he was subject to fainting fits for hours afterwards. When sensible, he begged of the doctors to let him alone—preferring, he said, to die by his own hand rather than suffer the ignominy of a public execution.

It has not been satisfactorily explained how or in what manner the unfortunate man procured the poison with which he contemplated self-destruction. The symptoms were evidently those of strychnine; and the only way in which the keepers could account for the presence of the poison was its introduction in the segars which Gordon had smoked so freely the night before. On Thursday the prisoner was compelled to undergo a rigid search, his clothes were changed entirely, and he was placed in a new cell, so that it would seem impossible almost for him to have procured the poison in any other way than that suggested by his keepers. The last request Gordon made was to have a lock of his hair taken from his head and given to his wife.

Owing to the attempt at suicide the hour of execution was fixed at twelve o'clock, noon, instead of two o'clock. In the meantime Gordon was plied with brandy, so that he should not falter at the last moment. At eleven o'clock a company of marines, under command of Captain Cohen, entered the prison and took their position around the scaffold. The marines were accompanied by a band of music, and were armed with loaded muskets with fixed bayonets.

The scaffold—the old one used in the execution of Saul, Howlet, Stephens, and a host of other criminals—was erected in the yard fronting the main prison. Outside of the police and marines there was not more than 100 spectators.

As the fatal moment drew nigh the excitement of the spectators was only equalled by their sympathy for the condemned. At half past eleven o'clock Judge Dean, one of Gordon's counsel, gained admittance to the prison, and, seeking Marshal Murray, informed the latter that Governor Morgan had interceded for the prisoner, and had telegraphed to the President asking for a respite. Judge Dean begged that the execution might not come off until the last moment, with the hope of a reprieve being granted, but the Marshal was inexorable, and said the sentence of the Court should be carried into execution at noon. Judge Dean argued that a reprieve might be on its way from the President, and cautioned the official not to exercise too much haste, but in vain.

Precisely at twelve o'clock Marshal Murray, in company with his deputies, entered the cell of the unhappy culprit and bade him prepare for death. The prisoner, who was weak, and trembling like a leaf, arose from his bed and asked for something to drink. He was handed brandy and allowed to drink some three or four glasses before the work of pinioning was begun. The death warrant was read, and then the Rev. Mr. Camp administered spiritual consolation to the doomed man.

At twenty minutes past twelve o'clock a procession was formed in the corridor of the prison, and, the word being given, the *cortege* moved in solemn silence to the gallows in the following order:

Deputy Marshals.

Marshal Murray.

The culprit, supported on each side by the Marshal's deputies.

Deputy Marshals.

Physicians.

Jury.

Members of the press.

As the procession moved through the yard all eyes were fixed upon the condemned, who tottered to the scaffold like a man half dead with fear, or stupefied with liquor, it is hard to say which. The feebleness of the culprit, the agony with which he viewed the preparations which had been made for his execution, the solemn and careworn appearance of the Marshal and his deputies, the presence of the military drawn up in line, all contributed to render the scene a most impressive and painful one. When the culprit reached the gallows he took his position immediately under the fatal noose. There was a pause of a few seconds, but all was as still as death. The work of adjusting the rope was quickly performed, but it was evident that Gordon could not stand long; hardly had the task been completed when he showed evident signs of fainting. The cap was quickly drawn over the culprit's face, and the Marshal was about to give the signal to the executioner, when Gordon staggered and would have fallen to the ground had he not been caught by one of the deputies. In another moment, however, he was straightened up, the signal was given, the axe fell, and the body of Gordon was dangling in the air.

CHAPTER XXVIII.

"'Damn you,' cried the desperate ruffian, throwing up the sash and menacing the crowd, 'do your worst! I'll cheat you yet!'"—DICKENS, *in Oliver Twist.*

ON the evening of the 29th of January, 1870, William Townsend was sitting in his basement at No. 192 Hudson street. He was a tailor by trade, but kept a grocery store. With him at that time were his wife and his three little children. It was Sunday evening, and that peaceful calm which comes in with the church chimes pervaded that little household.

Right next door was the shop of a shoemaker. There was one man in it, busy at work. He used a long, keen bladed knife to cut his leather, and occasionally laid it down on his bench. It was just six o'clock.

Before the clock had finished the striking of the hour Jack Reynolds, a vagrant, came down the steps and entered the shop.

"Can you give me any work?"

"What kind of work can you do?"

"Pegging."

"No; we have none for you."

"Good night."

"Good night."

Reynolds walked up into the street, and as he did so something glistened in his hand as he concealed it in his sleeve. It was the long, keen knife. *He had stolen it!*

All unconscious of danger William Townsend sat with his wife and babes.

Suddenly there was a rap at the door.

One of the little girls opened it, and Jack Reynolds walked into the humble apartment. There was silence for a moment, and then he said to Townsend, who was looking inquiringly at him:

"You are my brother, and l want to stay here to-night."

"I am not your brother," said Mr. Townsend, "and you cannot stay here; I have no room except for my family."

Reynolds sat down doggedly.

Mr. Townsend approached him and said, "Won't you please go out," and laid his hand gently on his shoulder.

No answer from Reynolds. "Come, my good fellow, please go out."

With that Reynolds seized Townsend and dragged him out on the steps. There was a short, sharp struggle; a knife gleamed in the light of the gas lamp, and in another moment was buried in the heart of Townsend. He fell to the pavement, carrying Reynolds with him.

"My God! I am stabbed! This man stabbed me!" rang out on the night.

Citizens came flocking to the bloody scene. One man seized Reynolds and threw him on his back. He struggled like a mad bull and shouted, "If you will give me a sight I can lick two like you!"

Then a couple of stars flashed on the scene, and the murderer found himself in the strong grasp of two patrolmen.

Townsend was carried back into his store, where in twenty minutes he died.

On the way to the police station the crowd following the officers and their prisoner swelled into a mob. They surged up against the trio in angry waves. First there were low mutterings and muffled threats. It was the rumbling of the thunder; the storm broke at last.

"Hang him! hang him!" This bawled forth from a hundred throats.

Reynolds turned round and uttered his celebrated epigram, "*Hanging is played out in New York.*"

At the police station he gave his birthplace as the United States and his occupation that of a thief!

The trial commenced on February 21st, 1870, at half past ten o'clock. There was a tremendous desire to see the prisoner, and the court room of the Oyer and Terminer was crowded to suffocaton. Among the miscellanous audience were many handsomely dressed ladies. Reynolds came in between two deputy sheriffs. The audience rose *en masse* to catch a glimpse of the prisoner. It was seen at once that he was a brute. His appearance was dogged and sullen, and his head seemed unnaturally formed. The widow and children of the murdered man occupied seats in the court room, and remained throughout the trial.

JACK REYNOLDS.

Mr. William F. Howe was assigned as counsel for Reynolds. He made an elaborate defence, striving to prove that his client was insane; but it was of no avail. The trial lasted three days, and Reynolds was found guilty of murder in the first degree. He was sentenced to be hanged on the 8th day of April.

At the close of the testimony on both sides Mr. Howe proceeded to address the jury as follows:

"*May it please the Court, and you, gentlemen of the Jury:* To say that I feel acutely the responsibility of this case, is but to convey feebly to you the impression and workings of my heart at this

moment; for I cannot divest myself, gentlemen, of the solemn
knowledge that, to me, to some extent, is confided the life of a
human being. But, thank God, not to me alone is that responsibility confided ; it is a common one, in which we all participate,
and, for some good reason, known only to Him 'through whom
we live and move and have our being.' It is left to-day to you, by
your verdict, to say whether this poor, wretched, animated piece of
'ruined nature'—one, certainly, of the poorest of God's creatures, is,
upon testimony such as has been introduced, to be strangled by
the cord of the hangman, when a powerful indication of insanity is
there, defying science—fallible as it has proven itself in many instances—defying doctors, defying district attorneys, and, in the
monitory voice of God, telling you, in a portion of God's own
image, that you *should not hang an insane man.*

"Gentlemen, that a most revolting crime—murder, if you please—
was perpetrated ; that the sympathies of all of us must be extended
to the utmost to the widow and the orphans, I admit; that the
horrid circumstances—the details of which made us all shudder, in
sympathy with the living, sorrow for the dead, and, perhaps, at
first, indignation against the accused—are true, there is no doubt ;
but in proportion to the horror of the crime, in proportion to the
atrocity of the revolting details, so do I positively and with confidence urge, that the greater the enormity the more extravagant
the horror, so here, gentlemen, is that man's proportionate insanity
evidenced. Ask yourselves this question : Would any sane man—
shall I say, would less than fiend—without revenge, without malice,
without gain, without notice, have committed so horrible a crime?
"and in, entering upon the consideration of this case, start with
that point. The weakest of us never act without motive. The
hand is never lifted to the head without design or motive. It is
motive which actuates each action in our daily lives ; and I start
the consideration of this case by asking 'What was the motive of
this man, if sane, for the commission of so heinous and cruel a
murder ?'

"But I am prepared in the discharge of my duty—and it is one
from which I will not shrink, notwithstanding public indignation
and prejudice—to demonstrate to you as men of common sense, as
men who have in your hands this man's life, that the testimony,

from beginning to end, even to the last scene upon that stand, proclaims in mighty voice, that permeates your understanding, and never will be eradicated from your minds, when you retire for deliberation, that 'Jack Reynolds,' as they call him, who, without cause, and as the District Attorney properly said, with no provocation, plunged a knife, which he had stolen, into the heart of a man *whom he believed to be his own brother*, IS AN INSANE MAN. To detail the testimony would be almost unnecessary, for it is fresh in your minds. You heard from the lips of those poor little orphans the circumstances of the deed. You heard the testimony of Kline, who caught the prisoner on the step, on the top of his victim, and you will remember he stated that he found the knife in Reynold's grasp long after the perpetration of the fatal deed ; held by the prisoner with a tenacity of purpose which speaks volumes that he was insane ; for the District Attorney must tell you that those who murder do not retain the evidence of their guilt. The first impulse of the SANE assassin is to destroy the evidence of his crime, and not cling to it, as did this imbecile, when outside the scene of blood, and long after the perpetration of the deed.

"Stepping from the scene of the strife and walking along the street, he resists. Would a sane man, without a friend near, act thus ? Take the case of a murder committed in this court room by a stranger here, without a friend, surrounded by the police, would he attempt an impossible escape ? That was resisting insurmountable power. He resists upon the street, and as one witness described it, ' *this frenzied man*,' and *he* used the word, but with subtlety which may be excusable, thinking it was his duty to say all he could against this wretched man, he said it was not exactly 'frenzy,' but he was wild and rough.

" Oh, but gentlemen, in going along he uttered not a word about the deed ; but he said, ' I can lick any two of you,' resisted and struggled, hopeless maniac as he then was. He was taken to the station house. He stands in front of the desk, and in reply to the interrogation of the sergeant, says his name is ' Reynolds,' that he was born in the ' United States,' after ten minutes before telling one of the witnesses (the shoemaker, if I am correct) that he was a Scotchman ! And there was no necessity for these discrepancies ; they only go to *evidence his wandering mind*, if mind he had.

" ' Your occupation ?'   ' Thief !'

" Do sane people degrade themselves ?   Has my friend, the learned prosecutor, than whom a more zealous or faithful official never existed, in the course of his long experience, ever yet have arraigned at his bar, or known a person accused of crime to say, ' *I am a thief ?*'   Oh, no !   They cloak, they shroud, they conceal their occupation ; and they urge, and sometimes with good effect, their extreme respectability   But why did this man enter the shoemaker's shop ? why steal that knife, of no value except for the interpretation which I shall give by and by, supported by medical authority ?   You may remember, gentlemen, the question I put to Dr. Hammond, as to the sight of deadly weapons engendering the desire to kill.   And I do believe that wretched being, as he was then, and is now, if he can feel remorse or sorrow—if he has mind yet left to feel that, which I doubt—maniac as he was then, the sight of that knife created the desire to kill, and he stole that knife to take the life of some one—whom he cared not.   For whether it was epilepsy, whether it was mania, whether it was impulsive insanity, let it have assumed what form it might, let science designate it with her fancied appellations, and all the learning with which to dignify disease, disease was there ! *A diseased mind, which prompted the taking the knife ! A diseased mind, which prompted the taking also of the life of Townsend !*   But there is a conversation at the shoemaker's.   See if this is not important. You are told by one of the policemen, Sergeant Tuck, that this man ' *appeared* ' to have been drinking, and that he smelled his breath, and that there was some smell of whiskey ; but the conversation in the shoemaker's forbids that construction.   I say that the prisoner was sober at the time, and he had a sober conversation with the shoemaker, and I asked how many steps he ascended, and he said ' three or four.'   He watched him walking soberly up them, then he came to the scene of this homicide.

" The first words he uttered to the deceased were, ' *You are my brother.*'   Was that a delusion ?   To that my friend, Dr. Nealis, has told you to-day that this man had no delusion ; but I say the evidence contradicts the doctor beyond the shadow of a doubt, because it is sworn here to-day that he said, ' *You are my brother.*' What reply will be made to that ?   It was unquestionably a delusion !

"Pray, gentlemen, what purpose could he have in telling a stranger—a man fifty years of age—a hale, hearty, stout, corpulent man, unlike this lunatic prisoner in features, unlike him in physical development, unlike him in every aspect—for what purpose, I repeat, would a poor, miserable, dirty, filthy, half savage, half idiotic wretch go into that house and tell the deceased that he was his brother? If sane, gentlemen, could that operate upon one of you to admit relationship which never existed? Could it have been for the purpose of extortion, which may be suggested? But that idea must be at once repelled, because it is absurd upon the face of it, for there is no evidence, or even suspicion of attempted extortion; so that with the delusion, I say, that this man was his brother, he entered that store; he sits down upon a milk can, and, I suppose, gentlemen, you can picture the scene. This wretched being there, moody, dejected; his brain diseased from one of the causes to which I shall call your attention. You remember Dr. Hammond spoke of the quality and poverty of the blood generating disorders. You remember my asking one of the witnesses if this man's appearance had not improved since his entrance to the Tombs. Even prison fare, and prison treatment have improved his wretched looks, his blood, and his *physique;* and when I tell you that, and you look on him to-day, you can form a pretty accurate picture of him at the time he was sitting on that milk can in the store. Poor Townsend asks him to leave; and then—*without a word, without a blow*—he takes this knife and plunges it into Townsend's heart. Now, if I rest there, without another observation, ask your own hearts, resting on that spot, what motive could any sane man have for such deliberate, for such revolting, murder? I am content to rest the issue of the case upon that simple state of facts alone, for what answer can you give as to his motive to stab, with this deadly weapon, an inoffensive, unoffending stranger?

"The killing of a human being is not murder. It is the killing with a bloodthirsty intent, and with a wicked heart. Did that intent exist here?

"But let us now look at the medical testimony, and see what bearing it has upon this case.

"The learned District Attorney, with the power of this great

county at his control, can send forth his edict and bring before
you the most eminent physicians, and the greatest ornaments to
science in the community. How different with that poor, I had
almost said friendless man—but if I had it would be an insult to
your intelligence, for I believe now, as surely as I am here, that
you *are* his friends to this extent, that you will not permit him to
be hung unless you have no lingering doubt of his sanity. You
won't let his poverty condemn him; you won't place the outcast on
the gallows tree, when, in our Tombs to-day, are numbers of powerful assassins—men of influence, men of means, men of friends,
men of great resources—who have been immured there for months
and months, and have, so history tells us, committed *murders ten
thousand times more fearful than this*, because done in deliberation
and surrounded with intelligence. *They* have not been brought to
trial within twenty days of the commission of their deeds. They
are fed and pampered, and have luxurious cells, and able counsel
employed! This poor victim is friendless and alone, and it is
only through the mercy of the Court that my feeble humble services are now tendered to present my views to you. But for that
intervention this man to-day could not speak, for, as I before
stated, he is without a friend; is here, '*not himself*,' for he has *no
mind*, but I, as his counsel, believe and say for him that he is here
to-day for a fair and impartial investigation. Now, gentlemen, for
the poor outcast, the '*motiveless murderer*,' the man with the 'unsymmetrical cranium,' as Dr. Hammond called it, in the words of
science, but which, to my humble interpretation, means a faulty
skull; on behalf of him let me show you what science says of
people in this country, in France and England, who have committed worse crimes, under circumstances analogous to the state
of this man's mind. The Court gave me permission to read from
these authorities as a matter of justice, and I think that an apology for detaining you would be out of place, for no time can be
too long, nor can any of us make too great a sacrifice to ascertain
whether we should contribute to the taking away lightly of the
life of a human being. And I am sure that, by medical science, I
shall be able to demonstrate that the prisoner was irresponsible for
the act for which he is now being tried. The vulgar notion of
insanity is, that it consists in an entire deprivation of reason and

consciousness, but the slightest acquaintance with the insane proves that they are not only perfectly conscious of their actions, but that they reason on their feelings and their impressions.

" The medical testimony discloses that monomania generally assumes one of two forms: either the thoughts are lively and gay, or they are oppressed with gloomy melancholy, as was poor Reynolds' when seated dejected in the store. In the first state the persons will fancy themselves to be kings and queens. In the second (as in Reynolds') we find silence, seclusion, sorrow, dejection. The latter condition is called ' *melancholia*,' and is by no means an uncommon thing. Melancholia frequently leads to acts of suicide or murder. In the lighter form of the disease there is no sign of mental aberration, and the patient will go through his usual routine of duty, but always with some desponding air. In other cases the delusion is well concealed UNTIL THE ACT IS COMMITTED (AS IN THIS CASE) LEADS TO THE INQUIRY AS TO THE SANITY.

" My learned friend, the District Attorney, asked Dr. Hammond as to homicidal mania, and Dr. Hammond agrees with Dr. Taylor. ' Homicidal mania is a state,' says Taylor, ' of partial insanity, accompanied by an *impulse to the perpetration of murder*, and is called ' *impulsive mania*.'

" There may or may not be evidence of intellectual aberration, but the destructive impulse, like a delusion, cannot be controlled by the patient. *It dominates over all other feelings, and leads a person to destroy those to whom he is most* FONDLY ATTACHED.

" Now, please do not forget, in this application, the opening words of this poor fellow to the deceased: 'You ARE MY BROTHER.'

" Sometimes the impulse is long felt, but concealed and restrained; there may be mental signs of depression, loss of appetite, and then only for the first time, when the act is committed, to appear. Then, we are led to conclude, certain peculiarities of language and conduct, scarcely noticed beforehand, which must have been the symptoms of insanity, and an act of murder is perpetrated *with great deliberation, and apparently with all the signs of sanity.*

" These cases are rendered so difficult by the fact that there

may be no distinct proof of any disorder of the mind, so that the
chief evidence of the mental disorder is *in the act itself.* Is not,
then, the act of Reynolds stabbing the man whom he mistook for
his brother the special, demonstrative, positive evidence of Reynolds' insanity at that time ?

"Now, gentlemen, an erroneous notion may prevail, that a homicidal mania is easily to be distinguished from a sane crime by certain infallible signs and characters, which it is the duty of the
medical witness to display in evidence ; but a perusal of the evidence given at a few trials will satisfy those who hold to this
opinion that each case must stand by itself. Here it is. Dr.
Hammond says, '*Each case must stand by itself.*' Each act must
have its own signification to the jury—and that you may draw the
distinction between the burglar who breaks into your house at
night and intends to rob, and, when detected in the act, turns
round and fires the pistol or strikes you with a dagger ; there the
motive of escape to avoid detection and punishment is the answer
to the commission of the offence, because that is the motive. So,
the man who finds that the partner of his bosom has committed
adulterous intercourse with a friend, buys a pistol and shoots the
adulterer, who has deprived him of that which is dearer than life,
invaded his domestic home, and made that which is happy forever
miserable. There the motive was both jealousy and revenge.
'But,' says Taylor, 'Each act must judge for itself,' for Reynolds
had no motive to murder Townsend. He had taken nothing
there ! He had stolen nothing there ! He was not going to be
arrested ! He had not even been hurt ! Townsend, instead of
offering him an indignity, spoke in terms of kindness, and mildly
expostulated as to the delusion which actuated him. 'You are
mistaken,' said poor Townsend. 'You must leave my house;' and
then he killed him. Is the motive there ? Ask that question
again and again to yourselves. At each point of your deliberations, when you come to consider, let that intrude. Do not fail in
this, but ask, 'What motive ?' But I had previously said, gentlemen, that, in words of mild forbearance, the poor deceased said,
'*Please go out;*' and for that kindness of expression he caused the
blow of death, without any earthly attributable reason ; and yet
you are to be asked to find that he had a motive, because three

doctors, subpœnaed by the prosecution at this trial, and this alone, and *whom the prosecution did not dare to call*, and who have been taken by me from the enemy's camp, say they did not find the prisoner actually insane at the times they examined him.   I do feel justly and honestly defiant on this point, and I beard science in its own den; and the authorities I now produce, and which I shall refer to hereafter, the facts of the case, and the inspection of that wretched man himself, all now potently unite and compel you to admit that this wretched, demented prisoner had no motive for the assassination of Townsend.

"Gentlemen, look around this vast assemblage ; scan each vis age in this court room with care and with deliberate scrutiny, and I tell you, without fear of contradiction, and I will hazard this verdict upon the position I advance, that there is none here to-day (and if I am not complimentary to some at the extreme end of this spacious court room I may be pardoned) amongst one of the not most select audiences in the world, upon whose face, upon whose '*unsymmetrically formed cranium*,' as Dr. Hammond has called it, can you find the delineation of insanity, as is plainly visible in this little miserable maniac, Jack Reynolds !   You cannot, amongst this great concourse, find one who can descend to him in appearance or intellect.   He is abjectly poor.   He is abjectly friendless. He is abjectly demented.   He was placed upon the stand.   Why did I do that?   The District Attorney, than whom, as I before told you, none abler, preceded him—an experienced criminal lawyer long before he became our public prosecutor—could have cross-examined that man—could have gone back to his history from his cradle; and with his skill, and (pardon me I know he will for using the word '*subtlety*' in the sense I mean) with his *subtlety*, if that man had been sane, why, gentlemen, none so able as Judge Garvin, in putting a dozen pertinent questions, to have demonstrated that beyond a doubt.   I threw down the challenge, and why?   Because I was satisfied that, idiot as he is, one of you, or the District Attorney, would have discovered, in a few questions, of his sanity—if sane he were—and that from his own lips you should learn whether he committed this murder knowing that he was doing wrong.

"And, believe me, gentlemen of the jury, in the course of a

somewhat lengthened experience at the bar, I have never known a man accused of murder submitted to the examination of the jury and of the District Attorney. This poor imbecile, oblivious to-day of the enormity of the crime he has committed—in fact, entirely forgetful of the perpetration of the horrid crime at all—has been by me submitted to the prosecuting officer for examination; and I can well understand why my learned friend, the District Attorney, refused to avail himself of the opportunity. He was afraid; afraid of an imbecile! But I was immeasurably gratified when, in honest sympathy and in integrity of purpose, one of you gentlemen questioned this poor maniac as to the circumstances; and, my auricular faculties being pretty good, I heard one gentleman of the jury suggest to another, 'See if he remembers going to the shoemaker's.' And, indeed, a pertinent question that was. I might almost say that, to an extent, did his life hang on the answer. But God had perhaps ordained that the idiot should not give an apparently sane answer to that question; and he told you, in reply to the interrogatory, '*I don't remember being there at all.*' I cannot imitate him, for he is 'NATURE's MADMAN,' and he has told his story. It is God who is speaking in him, in volumes of powerful eloquence and dictatorial language, to spare the madman, and the Divine interposition will be proclaimed by your verdict, that a lunatic shall not be hanged!"

Here the counsel enlarged on the testimony of the medical experts, and in severe terms denounced the apparent inconsistency of their evidence, as given in this case, when compared with that in previous cases, where the criminal *happened to be rich* or popular. Citing the case of Senator Cole, he continued: "He was tried at Albany before the learned Judge who now presides. Cole had a pistol, or procured one somewhere, before the commission of the deed, when he had time to reflect, and went the next day with deliberation to the hotel where Hiscock was, and shot him dead!

"Oh, but *then*, gentlemen, Professor Hammond was a witness for an '*ex-senator*,' I believe. Professor Hammond, at all events, was a witness for a man of vast property—of high standing in the community—who commanded the highest intellect the bar of the country afforded—who was surrounded by professional skill; but who, *nevertheless, committed that act with premeditation and delibera-*

tion! He deliberately shot a human being, and in that case HE WAS PRONOUNCED INSANE!!! Sane a moment before, and insane at the commission of the offence, and sane a moment afterward!!!

"*Judge Ingraham* (interrupting). Sane before the commission of the offence and sane after; but the jury were in doubt as to his sanity at the time of the perpetration of the murder.

"*Mr. Howe* (continuing). Very well; I accept the amendment. All the better for my comparision. This rich man, this rising man, this intellectual man *with a finely formed head—he* hadn't ' *an* UNSYMMETRICAL SKULL', was pronounced by the jury, as the learned Judge told you, to be not guilty, for the reason the Judge gave you!!! And shall it be said that in Albany they let go the rich and powerful, whilst in New York, where they don't bring to justice with speed, at all events, the powerful and the influential assassin, that you twelve men, singled out from this great community, will hang this idiot for his poverty? That you, in opposition to all precedent, will say, we have no doubt of his insanity; will say, by your oaths, that he was sane at the time he committed this deed—a poor, forsaken, friendless man, with the malformed skull— the vacant dejected imbecile. Oh, yes! Hang him, and let the ex-senator go!!! And then,

> 'Over the stones rattle his bones,
> He's only a pauper, whom nobody owns.'

"But I am greatly mistaken in you if in this case that result ever happens.

" Gentlemen, I have, to the best of my ability, reviewed the testimony. I have cited medical authorities, showing cases where conversations and acts of peculiar and extraordinary nature, and even homicide, have been committed, when people have been unconscious and temporarily insane. I have brought cases right to this man's door, and I have gone, as I before said, into the camp of the enemy. I am alone, unaided, save by the patent fact, which they cannot deny, permit me to reiterate, of this man's idiocy. I have placed him upon the stand! You have heard the circumstances of horror under which this deed was perpetrated. It now becomes your duty to consider this momentous question— was he, BEYOND ALL DOUBT, a sane man when he committed that motiveless deed? And inasmuch as you cannot answer in the affirmative, you must not, you dare not convict this prisoner!

"The learned District Attorney may, and probably will, with his power and his eloquence, appeal to you as I could—nay, not as I could, but as they *do* themselves—those dear little children and that poor widow. They are here to-day to tell you, gentlemen, of their father's murder, and I am not in error when I say, with the District Attorney, that no eloquence can depict the sad reality before you. They are entitled to and they must have your sympathies and mine.

"But you should not convict this idiot, because your sympathies are, as mine are, with those orphan children and their widowed mother. I warn you and I implore you, and whilst I feel it is, indeed, a hard task to ask you, as fathers, for the time to disregard their sufferings, the same humanity, gentlemen, the same propriety of feeling, the same humanity which prompts that undeniable sympathy for these little ones, asks this, also, for him who made them orphans! and I tell you why: because it is not a cold blooded assassination of premeditation, of malice, of revenge, of purpose, or of motive; and because it was a horrid deed, perpetrated by a lunatic, and one *who knew not the effect of his act; who knew not the suffering he was entailing upon them;* and I verily believe, now, that the ordeal through which we all have passed, has had no more effect upon that piece of vitalized clay (here counsel pointed to the prisoner) than upon this chair which is beside me. He seems to have no terror for the consequences of the deed he committed; but his entire demeanor, gentlemen, endorses the question put by the juror; that after the commission of that deed, as Hamlet says,

'The rest was silence.'

"Oh, how much there is in that! No knowledge of the wrong, but unconscious of everything—knowing nothing of the past, and alone in the world! Let me ask you what will society gain by strangling an insane and lunatic human being? I acquiesce with the District Attorney, most cordially, that when murder has been committed, let juries be prompt to render their verdict; let the assassin be taken from the court room, and, if you please, within a few brief weeks, let the law vindicate justice; let the executioner perform retributive justice for society, but be sure, gentlemen, oh, be terribly sure, that you have a *culprit* and not a *victim ! ! !   Be sure, I say, about it, and no doubt,* for your conscience sake, and for your everlasting peace ! ! !

" Oh, gentlemen! your position is, indeed, an awful and responsible one. It is the most painful, the most trying that has ever happened; and I say, without fear of contradiction, it is the most painful ordeal through which you will ever pass. This case now rests with you. I have discharged my duty to the best of my ability, and according to the dictates of my conscience. This poor outcast has no paid advocate to defend him. I am speaking for him for charity, for humanity, and for justice.

" Oh, gentlemen! do not deem me rude or offensive when I tell you to discard the doctors; discard the language of the District Attorney, and, with all deference, even the dictates of the learned Judge. Consider the common sense facts of this case, and take with you to your room the picture of that idiotic, imbecile man; and if, amongst you twelve, one or two suggest, " Oh, convict him; hang him !" then let his picture, photographed upon your minds, obtrude itself, and you will silence the man who asks for a conviction. Oh, do not mistake, lest you may think that I urge that you should let loose upon society one who may be dangerous to us, as has been proven. Let me call your attention to the words of the statute on the subject :

" ' Upon any indictment of any offence consisting of different degrees, the jury may find the accused not guilty of the offence in the degree charged, but may find the prisoner guilty on any degree of such offence inferior to that charged in the indictment.'

" Now, gentlemen, in this case, with all its bearings, you may find that poor wretch, if you please, if you can reconcile it to the evidence and to your consciences, guilty of murder in the first degree; and murder means the killing of a human being with premeditation and malice—*knowing that he was killing*—knowing that he was doing wrong. I am sure I may safely discard that in this case.

" You have the power and the privilege to find him guilty of murder in the second degree. For that this poor pitiful object may be immured within the dungeon walls for the term of his natural life ; and in that event, I predict that, when within his coffined tomb of stone Death claims its victim, and when after death an examination of the brain proclaims insanity, you will remember the scene in this court room ; you will remember my feeble voice proclaiming disease within that malformed skull, and then how great : oh ! how happy will be your congratulations that you did not hang the poor lunatic outcast—that you did not hang, as a victim for all the refined and cultured criminals of great New York, the poor beggar who is " *out in the streets.*"

" Oh, gentlemen ! to violate the living temple which the Lord hath made, to quench the human flame within a human being's breast, is an awful and a terrible responsibility ! And I tell you, that if you improperly condemn this wretched man, and consign him to an ignominious death, and a *post mortem* examination shall hereafter reveal his brain diseased ; then, gentlemen, the recollection of this day *will never die within you.* Your crime, for so it will be, will pursue you with remorse, like a shadow, through your crowded walks. It will hover beside you on your pillow ; it will sit at your table ; it will ever be present through the remainder of your lives ; and at the "*Great Last,*" taking the form of this man's spirit, it will rise to sink and condemn you before the judgment seat of God ! ! !"

As counsellor Howe concluded, the District Attorney, Honorable S. B. GARVIN, addressed the jury as follows :

May it please the Court, gentlemen of the Jury.

" I have, through the period of a quarter of a century, tried a great many cases of great importance, not only civil but criminal, and in all such cases I have found that sensible men always sympathize with the prisoner. They consider his position and his condition more than that of any other person, for the reason that he himself is present, a living man, to answer for himself. But in all these cases, gentlemen, you must remember that there is one who is absent. He is gone. He never appears on the stand. He cannot testify. His mouth is ' *sealed in death.*' He is away from his own family, and his children who were around him are with him no more.

" You must remember that when he sat at his fireside he sat as you and I sit in our own houses, under our own vine and fig tree, with the right of no man to invade it. And, gentleman, it is protection that we want for your wife and mine, your children and my children, when we come forth every day to prosecute the ordinary business of life. We do not know whether we shall be safe when we sit at our own table with our children, after a hard day's work, to enjoy a season of rest.

" Now, gentlemen, I make these observations, that you may be called back to consider this terrible deed—an awful deed—because the prisoner's counsel does not stand up here for one moment to say that this prisoner did not inflict the blow that sent Townsend to his long home without a moment of preparation. He went unanointed into the presence of his Maker by the hands of this prisoner, whose face he never saw before. And he knew it when he went into the house, just as well as he did when he went into the shoemaker's shop and stole the knife with which he committed that deed of blood.

" In considering this case, I trust you will do it yourselves alone, without any aid from me, after hearing such observations as shall strike me as pertinent to the case. It is not for me alone to say that this man shall be convicted or acquitted; but you, yourselves, every man on his conscience, shall say whether or not the case is made out against him. You are responsible. You are responsible to yourselves; you are responsible to the community; you are responsible to this great people; you are responsible to Him before whom you must soon appear, be it longer or shorter. The time will come when you must give an account of your conduct here to-day, whether it be for good or evil.

" Now, gentlemen, as I said before, in considering this case, the Court will say to you, I have no doubt, what the rule of law is in regard to cases of this description. I walk up to my friend and take his life with a knife, or a ball, or dagger, or by any physical force, and who is going to punish me? Not the District Attorney, nor anybody but a jury of twelve men; they are to say whether or not crimes of this kind are to be tolerated. We come down to the jury of twelve men in all the great transactions of life, civil as well as criminal. Men hang by the jury's verdict; men hold their property by the verdict of a jury. Society is protected by the verdicts of juries. You are protected, by night and by day, by the verdicts of juries.

"Why is it, then, that the law has said that when a man takes the life of another he shall forfeit his own life?

"It is just to inflict the highest penalty known to the law, which is life for life. If you take life you shall be executed. If you take your neighbor's life you shall be executed. If you take the life of any human being, no matter who he is, whether the highest or the humblest man in the community, you shall forfeit your life for his. My life is as dear to me as is yours. It is God's honest rule; it was ordained by Heaven. It should be observed by all men, and no sickly sentimentality should deter you, when satisfied that murder, foul murder, has been committed, from doing your duty.

"Is there any doubt about this case? The case is clear on the part of the people. What is the plea the defence set up? It is that this prisoner is insane, therefore, not responsible. Have they given us a single fact as to his former history? Have they given us a single fact as to where he has been? what he has been doing? or what has been the course of his life? No foundation has been laid by the witnesses for the prosecution, or the prisoner, upon which to found such an opinion. Nothing on that subject; and that is the reason that, when I rested the case for the prosecution, I had not a single doubt as to his mental condition, character, state of sanity, or otherwise; and the Court will charge you that sanity is always to be presumed unless there is some evidence to the contrary. That is the rule of law. All men are presumed sane until there is some evidence to the contrary. Thus we stand.

"Prisoner's counsel says there is no motive for what he did. Motive! Why, some of the very cases that he reads here to-day arose from personal inconvenience. It may be from a sudden miff. It may arise from laying a hand on a man's shoulder—this depraved condition of the human mind bursts forth, resulting in violence. What did this prisoner go in there for? He did not say, 'You are my brother;' the evidence is, 'I am your brother.' Was there anything strange about that? The great Lord Chatham said to a colored man, 'You are a man and brother.' How often is it that men say to each other, 'My brother?' Is there any delusion about it? Is that one of the things upon which a man can stand defended in a court of justice? That won't do.

"Did this prisoner talk like an insane man? Did he act like an irresponsible being? Was any portion of his conduct like that of a man who did not know what he was about—the difference between right and wrong? He went down into the basement, five steps, and walked right through into the store, seated himself on a chair and said, 'I am your brother. I wish to stay all night.' And Townsend told him, 'You cannot stay here; I haven't room enough for my own family. I can't keep you; you must go. Please go.' In the mildest possible manner, 'Please go out.' Prisoner went into the front part of the store and sat down on a milk can.

"Mr. Townsend, seeing that he was not going out, walked up to him again, and said, 'Please go out,' and put his hand gently upon his collar or shoulder. Is there anything, even the slightest evidence of insanity, thus far? Then the prisoner turned round and stabbed him to the heart in a moment; but by reason of the great strength and vigor of Townsend, a man of fifty years of age, he carries this prisoner, by main strength, to the steps, and he there falls down from the loss of blood from the wound which this prisoner had perpetrated. He killed him because he would not keep him all night—because he would not recognize him as a brother or as a man. Motive!

"Take the case of Rodgers. What did he do? Rodgers was walking with two of his comrades in the street, in this city. He met a gentleman walking with his wife, and ran against them, and the gentleman asked him why he did so, and Rodgers turned around and stabbed him to the heart. He died instantly on the spot, and went to the God who made him, without a struggle or a groan, on the streets of New York. I ask you what possible motive could Rodgers have for such a murder? He was tried, convicted and executed. The motive he had in committing crime was malicious, and the law says it is malice. The jurors say it is malice. All the civilized world says, if a man takes the life of another, he does it through malice, unless he can show to the contrary.

"Again, take the case of Friery, who was tried in this city. He went into Lazarus' place and said, ' You are a good fellow,' and he put his arm round his neck, and plunging a knife into his back, killed him. What was the motive ? Friery was tried, convicted and executed.

" Now, again, gentlemen, was he (Reynolds) insane ? Was going into the shoemaker's shop any evidence of it ? What does he say when there ?

" ' Have you got any work ?'

" ' Where have you been at work ?' and he says I haven't had any work for so many months.

" ' What kind of work do you do ?' ' Pegged work.' The man says, ' I have no work for you.' A little consultation takes place between the parties and he goes away. Before he goes he steals a knife and puts it in his pocket. The next place he goes into he sees if he cannot get something else, and he says so in so many words. When he goes into Townsend's he has the knife in his pocket, and is told, ' I cannot lodge you.'

" You must recollect that he had been stealing. Perhaps he did the same thing in several different places during the day; and he comes along after six o'clock, when darkness had come over the earth, and he says to Townsend, in the basement, ' I am your brother,' and ' I want to stay all night;' and he was told that he could not stay there, and he leaves the back room, and Townsend follows him, and puts his hand gently on him, and says, ' You must go,' or ' Please go'—or whatever was the form of expression ; but I think it was the latter—and he stabbed him.

" What else does he do ? He resists with all his strength. The officer is unable to take the knife out of his hand. Does the counsel know any reason why ? Do you know any reason why ? Has any sane man any doubt as to the reason why ? He expected to get away, and he did not mean to leave that evidence of his guilt behind him.

" One of the witnesses swears that he lay perfectly still for a few moments, and then, suddenly jumping up, tried to run away. On his way to the station house some one said, ' Hang him,' and he said, ' Hanging is played out !' Did he not understand what he was doing ? Perfectly. Did he not know what the penalty for his crime was ? Perfectly. What did he have on his mind when he said 'Hanging is played out?' The crime he had committed; the murder he had done.

"Again, gentlemen, when he goes to the station house, what does he do? Is it very remarkable that a man, when he stands up before a captain of police, and is charged with some offence, and is asked what his business is, should say he is a thief? The counsel thinks so; I do not. I have heard hundreds say the same thing in court.

"Bring a man up on an indictment. Are you guilty or not guilty? 'Guilty.' He takes the chances of going to the State Prison, and hundreds of them admit every day they are thieves and burglars, in our courts of justice, and this man only said, 'I am a thief.' That is his business—a thief; and yet it is said, 'Acquit him.'

"Again, what is the medical evidence on this subject? Now, the counsel on the other side says I did not call the medical witnesses.

" Why should I call them? I have proved that Townsend was alive and well, and on the 29th of January he died, and this prisoner killed him. I made out my case. But why should I have the doctors subpœnaed? because the counsel, when the prisoner was arraigned in this court a few weeks ago, said that his defence would be insanity. What could I do, as the prosecuting officer, but subpœna medical men to attend, and have this prisoner examined, and to converse with him? and if Dr. Hammond had reported to me that this man was insane, I would have said, let him go. The medical testimony is certainly entitled to some weight. I did not call it out. I haven't called these witnesses. I should not have called a witness at all on that subject, but when they were on the stand I examined them.

" Dr. Hammond says : 'I have had two conversations with this prisoner of an hour each.' The result of those examinations you have heard. Had he been insane before that? Had he had any disease of any description? You have the declaration of the prisoner that he had not. The doctor now says he would not take his word for it. 'We went on to examine him, and we found everything in a natural condition.'

" Dr. Nealis says that he has examined him every day since he has been in the Tombs, and talked with him every day, and saw no signs of insanity whatever. He has attended 700 or 800 to 1,000 cases, and he has not found one single indication of insanity in this prisoner at all.

"Now, gentlemen, all the facts in the case go to show that the prisoner is sane. The law is, that if a man shall murder another he shall forfeit his life for so doing. What have you got to say about this case? I do not propose to talk to twelve men about it for any length of time. I propose to discharge my duty and then let you do yours.

"Gentlemen, the facts are against this prisoner; the medical testimony is against him; common sense is against him; but the counsel stands up here to-day, and asks you to find him insane. He is guilty of murder in the first degree or else he is not guilty of anything, and must be acquitted.

"Let me say to you, you give this man his liberty, and let him go, and you give license to every scoundrel and cut-throat in the City of New York to butcher anybody they see fit to, and all they have to do is to go into a court of justice, and plead insanity, and then be discharged.

"I say, again, that when crime is as rife as it is at present in Philadelphia, in Boston, in Brooklyn, and all other large cities in this country, and seems to be spreading and permeating the whole country from one end to the other, and a case is clearly and fairly made out, is it right that the prisoner should be acquitted? Such a course is fatal to the safety of this metropolis. I can stand it, perhaps, and you can, but when you do it, remember that every time you walk out after dark the assassin may be upon your heels for the purpose of taking your life. When you leave your wife and children in the morning, to attend to your daily avocations, you do not know but when you return you will find them all dead. It may be with you as it was in the case of Townsend. When you go up to your bed at night, it may be to find a burglar within your room, and if you resist him your life will be taken.

I tell you, gentlemen, there is blood in the air, and unless you put a stop to this carnival of crime by your verdict, there is no knowing where it may end. This is not the first time that I have addressed a jury in this city in important cases. A year ago to-day

I stood here before a jury in the case of John Real. That case has been pressed by the utmost efforts of the District Attorney, and he lies in the Tombs to-day on an appeal to the Court of Appeals.

It is not my fault, or the fault of the public, but it is the *law's delay*, and we cannot help it. He has a right to all the forms and delays the law gives him. Other cases, which have been of long standing, are in the Tombs. In one case a commission has gone to Liverpool, and another somewhere else. One witness is being examined on the island of Cuba in another case.

It is not for me to tell you why men are not tried. All cases will be tried when they are ready, and not before. When prisoners are ready for trial we bring them before a jury; and I ask you, as sensible men, not to be led away by this sort of nonsense.

"When a man plunges a knife into the bosom of another, and kills, he must have some other evidence of insanity besides this theory of astute counsel, read from books, without any facts to sustain it, before the prisoner can be acquitted. You have this case. I have done my duty, and I ask you to do yours; and I ask you to do it courageously, and as high minded, common sense men, and give us such a verdict as will satisfy your own consciences when you shall stand in that awful presence where the secrets of every soul shall be revealed, and a light like that of ten thousand suns shall illuminate the inmost recesses of every heart."

Judge Ingraham then delivered his charge to the jury.

The jury then retired, and returned again at 4:55 P. M., and the clerk called their names. They were then requested to arise, and asked to look upon the prisoner, and the prisoner upon the jurors. They declared that they had found the prisoner guilty of murder in the first degree.

The jury was then polled, and declared that the above verdict was theirs individually.

Assistant District Attorney Fellows, who was present, arose and spoke as follows:

"May it please your Honor, I move that the judgment of the law, which this sentence carries with it, be imposed upon the prisoner, John Reynolds."

Mr. Howe said: "May it please your Honor, having now discharged my duty, so far as this tribunal is concerned, for this friendless man, I ask your Honor, as is usual, that you will defer the passing of the sentence until I may resolve in my mind what course I shall adopt in reference to this man, and as to what motion I will have to make in arrest of judgment. I only ask until to-morrow morning."

Judge Ingraham.—"Let the prisoner be remanded till to-morrow morning."

The court then adjourned at 5 o'clock P. M.

The court reassembled at 10:30 next morning, and the prisoner, having been placed at the bar of the court, and duly interrogated by the Clerk of the court as to what he had to say why sentence of death should not be passed upon him according to law; and, making no reply,

Judge Ingraham said: "You are to be sentenced, Reynolds, for killing Townsend, a man with whom you had no difficulty, and for whose killing there was no excuse. Before doing it you went into another place, and there took a knife and concealed it, keeping it concealed until you found an opportunity of stabbing him, in his own house, among his own children, with none others present. What your motive for doing it was we do not know, but there is some suspicion that it was for the purpose of doing other wrong and improper acts. You have been tried by a jury of very intelligent men, who have given your case a very thorough examination; listened attentively to the testimony, and have agreed that you are guilty. With that verdict the Court does not at all differ. The murder was a cruel one on your part, entirely unprovoked; and there is nothing to excuse or justify it. You don't now offer any excuse?"

Prisoner.—"I don't know anything about it."

Court.—"Your conduct shows you did know."

Prisoner.—"I don't know only what they told me."

Judge Ingraham.—"You may have been excited by liquor, but that don't excuse you. If a man is allowed to indulge in drinking and then kills his fellow man, he is not excused on account of drinking. The law does not excuse you—it holds you responsible; and I have no other duty left for me now but to pronounce upon you the sentence of the law. It is not the sentence of the Court but the sentence of the law, and the law makes your life forfeit to the country for taking the life of another. And now I advise you, before pronouncing that sentence, to lay aside any hope that you may have that this decision may be altered or extended.

"The character of your offence, as well as the great number of offences of a similar kind that have been perperated continually in this city, calls for the execution of the law, not only in your case but in that of others, when they shall have been convicted, and instead of looking for hope here, I urge you to prepare yourself for the event that is before you. When the time comes which will be fixed for the execution of your sentence you will be executed, and you will pass from this world into another. In the meantime you have the opportunity afforded you to prepare for that event. It is not too late for you to make that preparation, and I advise you, therefore, to lay aside the hope of getting pardoned, and seek for that preparation which is necessary for you before the time comes which is fixed for your execution.

"The sentence of the Court is that you be carried hence to the prison from which you have been brought, there to be confined in close custody until the 8th day of April, and that on that day, between the hours of eight o'clock in the morning and two in the afternoon, you be hanged by the neck until you are dead, and may God have mercy on you."

The Clerk of the court, Mr. Vandervoort, then read the death warrant, and delivered it to Deputy Sheriff Isaiah Rynders, who had charge of the condemned.

At this announcement the doors of the court were ordered to be barred, to prevent the egress of the vast audience, and the condemned man, who seemed in no perceptible manner affected by the sentence, was conveyed to an adjoining room and from thence to the street, but before gaining the Tombs the crowd again flocked around him, and, amidst the hootings and yelling of the *gamins*, he was lodged in his dark cell on the lower tier of the prison, moody and dejected, to receive such spiritual comfort as would prepare him for the next world.

CHAPTER XXIX.

TEN DAYS IN THE TOMBS.—A BONA FIDE PERSONAL SKETCH.—A VIEW FROM THE INSIDE.—HOW THE TEN DAY FOLKS ARE TREATED.—THE MANIAC.—POOR KATE GOLDEN.—THE " BLACK MARIA.—OFF FOR THE ISLAND.

"The sanctuary was not a permanent abiding place, but a kind of criminal Pickford's. The lower passions and vices were regularly ticketed off in the books, warehoused in the cells, carted away as per accompanying invoice, and left little mark upon it."—DICKENS, in *Our Mutual Friend*.

A YOUNG journalist of this city, anxious to emulate the enterprise of James Greenwood, the London "Casual," who voluntarily went through a Workhouse course of sprouts, suggested, during the preparation of this book, that it would be a good idea for him to get locked up in the Tombs—and he did it. Proceeding to get drunk—which required considerable effort and no little cash—he started out one summer evening not long ago. Now let him tell his marvellous story :

"Half an hour later a miserable, dilapidated, drunken specimen of humanity might have been seen staggering along Water street He was perfectly oblivious to everything in the nature of a bee line. Two or three police were met, who looked suspiciously and savagely at him, but let him pass until he had taken a second round through Baxter street, when he stove right into the arms of one, who said, 'Here, my boy, I want you; come along.' Expostulations were useless, and I (for it was I) was collared, and forthwith found myself ushered into the Police Court at the Tombs, and shoved unceremoniously into the prisoner's dock, where sat two other forlorn looking individuals—a man and woman. The officer whispered to the Judge, the Judge winked mysteriously, the officer smiled satanically, the Judge nodded—my trial was over. I was convicted, sentenced. *Veni, vidi*—I came, I saw—that was all, for I was immediately rushed out of the court room, out of the building, across an open area into another building, and thrust into a small grated cell, in which I found only one other occupant, seated on his haunches, with his head buried in his hands and snoring like a high pressure steamer. After the lapse of a few minutes the cell door opened with a clang, and a gruff voice said to me, 'Come out here!' I walked out as meekly as a lamb led to the shambles, and was taken before a high desk, behind which sat a man who asked: 'What's your name?' 'Teddy Flynn, plaze your Honor.' 'How old are you?' 'Sweet sixteen.' 'None of your lip; where were you born?' 'On the old sod.' 'Ireland?' 'Yes.' 'What's your occupation?' "Taxidermist.' 'What the devil's that?' 'Bird stuffer, plaze.' 'Ha! you look more like a whiskey bloat and ballot box stuffer. Take him out!' when I was again shown into the open area, and the man who accompanied me sang out, 'Smith, ten day house.' Here was my first introduction to Smith. The man (!) called Smith eagerly approached me. Great God! language palls for a description; simply, he was disgustingly horrid—and drunk—and an involuntary shudder shivered through me as he came up and growled out, 'Come along, get down there,' pointing with his bony, skinny hand to a large grated door in another building, a little below and across the paved court. I went down there, closely followed by Smith, clanging a bunch of keys; the large, iron barred door was opened, and as I passed in it was banged and locked. I was now in what is known in Tombs parlance as 'the ten day house.' In this house are confined all those committed for being drunk, violation of city ordinances, simple cases of assault and battery, and all that grade of evil doings that does not amount to crime. The ten day house is about two stories and a half in height, forty feet long by twenty feet wide, with a bench running the full length each side, a stone paved floor, and open to the roof. A deathly, sickening heat and stench welled out from it as I entered. It contained some thirty occupants, representing the very lowest *habitues* of the dens and slums of Water and kindred streets, to the merchant, mechanic, sailor and soldier; the floor reeking with tobacco spit, vomit and filth. All here were on a par; the bloated, blear eyed, ragged, filthy old bummer, and the tidier appareled merchant and artisan. There was but little sociability in that mongrel crowd. Each seemed to have his own sombre thoughts and cares. Some threw themselves with an air of utter indifference upon the benches, and stretched out at full length; some walkel nervously and rapidly backward and forward through the rooms; some smiled grimly; others stared vacantly, maniacally, idiotically. All looked careworn, besotted and haggard; their debauch was over; the unnatural excitement of the vile poison that had brought them there was dying out; reaction was taking place. In this stage vitality is weakened, the whole system exhausted, the nerves unstrung, the brain on fire, the tongue parched and feverish, the eyes inflamed and aching; chills, fever and sweats shiver, burn and drench you in rapid succession; you tremble, gasp for breath, your heart stops, then leaps and rushes madly like a wild horse, and the brain whirls in fear, agony and frenzy. Of all feelings this dying out of alcoholic poison is the most horrible.

Here we remained (receiving every little while additions to our number) until about seven o'clock in the evening, when we were taken out and marched to the *sleeping* cells in another building. They are on the ground floor. You enter a wide, arched, gloomy hall, on one side of which are three large cells, about fifteen feet square, with open barred grates the whole front of them, and open grates as partitions between them; there are eight bunks in each cell—the yard workmen, the tier men and other prisoners doing work occupy these bunks, the other prisoners accommodate themselves as best they can upon the floor. Into these three cells are crowded nightly all the ten day house class of prisoners. Now Smith is in his glory—the keepers have gone—only the night watchman is on; Smith is monarch; he feels his power, and now his mean, cruel spirit creeps out; his cold, leaden gray eyes emit a fiendish glare; his hyena nature gloats, purs and grunts out its inward satisfaction. He reels about; he is drunk; he clangs his keys exultingly. He yells, 'get in there!' but it is full. 'Get in there, I tell you!' He packs one cell full, the other two only comparatively; he locks the doors, rattles the bars and chuckles aloud. Now commences a perfect pandemonium—the prisoners rave—they ask to be put into the less crowded cells; the more they growl the louder he chuckles; they abuse him, curse him, and call him all the bad names known to obscenity and profanity. Smith retorts in the same vile language; they yell and hoot at him. He yells and hoots back. For hours it is a miniature hell—there is no such thing as sleep—vermin of every kind crawl over you and *eat* you. You are on fire, you tear your flesh with your nails; huge rats rush between your legs or over your body; vulgarity, obscenity, profanity of every description reigns supreme.

Smith brings out an old straw mattress into the hall opposite the middle cell and throws his loathsome carcase on it, undivested of his filthy vermin infested clothes, and is soon snoring away in his drunken sleep. But what is that which strikes the ear ever and anon, sending a shuddering thrill through your heart; loud and strong as the roar of the lion it reaches to every crevice, even to the outer walls of the prison, and in bitterness, in agony, in passion it resembles the commingled yells of a hundred infuriated demons. It is the maniac, confined in a cell of the main prison. Great heavens what power of lungs, what physical strength he must be endowed with; the live long night his horrid shrieks resound. Oh, there is a terrible tragedy connected with him; cold chills creep over me now as I write and think of it. It never can be effaced from my memory.

At about half past six o'clock in the morning we were let out of the *sleeping* cells and returned to the ten day house. Smith then asked if there were any mens to work. This was my opportunity. I stepped forward and said 'Here, I'm one.' 'You? You's too small!' No I ain't, I replied. 'You no carry coffee on the tier.' 'Yes I can,' I said; 'then come along,' 'take a broom and you an' de oder man dere take a broom and sweep the yard.' Shortly eight men were called for to carry breakfast to the prisoners in the main building, and I was luckily one of them. The prisoners have for breakfast coffee (burnt rye), bread, a small piece of meat and potatoes. The main '*male prison*' consists of a four story stone building about 200 feet in length by about forty feet in width; inside an open skylight extends the whole length, from the ground floor to the roof; the narrow cells are on each side, and open on a narrow portico or corridor extending all around the skylight in each floor; each floor is called a tier. No. 1 tier is the ground floor, and the cells in this tier are used only for sentenced prisoners, lunatics and *delirium tremens* cases. Tier No. 2 is used only for murderers, burglars, garroters, highway robbers and other heinous felonies. The cells of tier No. 3 is for grand larceny and similar

crimės, and the 4th tier for petty larcenies and petty crimes. As
soon as any one is convicted and sentenced they are immediately
transferred to tier No. 1, and placed in a small cell in solitary confinement, and do not come out from it until sent to their destination—the Penitentiary, State Prison or gallows.   Cell No. 4 on tier
No. 1 is known as the murderers' cell, and is now occupied by Murphy, under sentence of death, to take place second of August next.
There is a very erroneous impression existing in many minds in
regard to the fare of a person sentenced to capital punishment.
Some claim they are allowed only bread and water, while others
contend that the moment sentence of death is passed upon them
that they are supplied with anything they desire—the best of food
the market affords, and even liquors and segars.   The facts are, they
are only entitled to prison fare the same as other prisoners—besides,
there is a rule of the prison denying them to have other food,
though brought by their friends or purchased with their own
money.   I do not think this rule is strictly carried out, however.
Murphy is a young, hearty and rather pleasant looking man.   He
spoke cheerfully, smiled and laughed.   I thought the laugh grated
with harshness upon my ear, as if forced and not natural—it could
hardly be otherwise, immured in that narrow cell, solitary and
alone, with the thought ever uppermost, as it ever must be in his
mind, that he can never again leave that cell except when the gallows is reared and awaits him.   Further down on this tier are two
cells padded and stuffed, the floors covered with straw matresses;
they are for cases of *delirium tremens* and raving maniacs.   Could
these cells speak they would unfold tales to harrow up your very
soul.

On the tier above No. 2 are confined Stokes, Foster, Vogt (the
alleged Belgian murderer) and several others charged with this
capital crime.   These prisoners, as well as all the others, excepting
those confined on tier No. 1, at a stated time each day are allowed
out of their cells for half an hour, and walk around and talk in the
corridors of their respective floors.   Stokes has greater privileges
than the other prisoners, and is for the greater part of the day out
of his cell.   He wears a serious and careworn expression, and is
quite gray; he dresses neatly, and is affable and gentlemanly in
his manners; there is nothing of the coxcomb, the rough, the brute

in his actions, expressions, or appearance. He has a servant to wait upon him, whom he pays; his food is brought to him from a restaurant. He eagerly watches for the arrival of the morning papers, and each morning he may be seen sitting in the corridor, alongside one of the keepers, perusing them. He is now on his trial. He goes from the prison to the court and back in a carriage, which he pays for, usually in charge of deputy sheriff Shields—the other prisoners for court go in the van, shackled together in couples. Every afternoon about half past five he goes over to the reception room, which is in the front building, to see friends or his counsel. No lawyers are now allowed within the prison, on account of the shystering business done heretofore. Now, the lawyers go to the reception room and the prisoners are brought there to see them.

The multifarious duties of the day over—each succeeding day but a repetition of the previous one—we are again locked up in the three *sleeping* cells. Each night the same drunken Smith is there; the same yelling, the same hooting, quarrelling, profanity, obscenity and blasphemy are there; the same stench, the same vermin, the same rats, only more of each and all of them; and, as your term of imprisonment drags its weary length along, you find the *sleeping* cells only progressively accumulating horror and misery, and each night there crawls out from under the cadaverous hide of Smith some hideous trait of tyranny, cruelty or beastliness not seen the night before.

Each day Smith may be seen staggering along from the main entrance of the male prison to the ten day house, with some prisoner just committed, often more sober than his jailer. Near the door of the ten day house is the hydrant, and it is quite a custom of Smith's, after locking any one up, to slip off his shoes and let the hydrant play on his feet—the keepers say it's to draw the whiskey out of his head.

Day succeeded day with its same monotonous rounds. The maniac still made night more hideous with his yells and ravings. In the meantime an important addition had been made to the number of the ten day men in the shape of a man named Duffy. Now, 'twas said, Smith will have to abdicate—Duffy will fill his place. When Smith heard of it he changed to all the colors of the chameleon, but finally settled down to a grayish blue and remained so.

MURDERERS' ROW

I thought, is it possible such men as these are put in authority over any human being, however fallen or degraded? Yet it is so. It seems strange that this is a part of *Charities and Correction*—does it not rather belong to something else the opposite? Such a state of things, it appears to me, ought not to exist in such an institution. Such an example, in its very nature, is of the most pernicious character. Ought there not to be a decently dressed, sober, firm man to exercise such authority as is now solely and uncontrolled in the hands of Smith? All the keepers in the male prison appeared strictly attentive to their duties, courteous and gentlemanly, and such I found the two night watchmen. Several times they came in in the night and changed those from the crowded cell into those less so, and rectified several of the petty tyrannies imposed by Smith.

Once a day at least, sometimes twice, the vans, or Black Marias, arrived to take prisoners to Blackwell's Island. They are close vehicles with narrow lattice work or a few auger holes near their tops for ventilation. Into these vans are crowded and packed, almost to the verge of suffocation, men and women indescriminately—the decent and the indecent, the tidy and the unclean, the blazoned, hardened old criminal, and the timid shrinking novitiate. The door closes upon them, shutting them up as it were in a living oven. The papers say strong men and women were dropping dead in the open air from the intenseness of the heat; what must have been the sufferings endured in those vans?

To this pitiless indifference and reckless disregard of the feelings or sufferings of their fellow beings I attribute the following terrible occurrence, which happened on Saturday forenoon, June 29th. The Black Maria as usual came into the prison yard to convey the prisoners to the island. Some fourteen or fifteen women and girls were put into it, and two weakly, sickly old men; it was now already full. 'Hold on, driver, there is one more,' some one cried out. I involuntarily said, as I saw what was coming, 'In Heaven's name are they going to put that maniac into the van among those women?' but they were. His hands were loosely tied; his countenance writhed in horrid contortions as they brought him along; his clothes were nearly torn off him; three or four stout men bundled him into the van, slammed the door and fastened it. The van

moved slowly down the paved court ; the maniac yelled with the
ferocity of an enraged tiger, the women screamed, shrieked, implored, but far above their commingled cries was heard the demoniac
yells of the maniac ; no heed was paid by the keepers; slowly the
van turned the corner of the main building towards the gate and
stopped. From the inside of the van came yells and shrieks, screams
and groans; minutes elapsed—how many I have no idea. I was
terror stricken.   The yells of the maniac increased, the screams of
the women died away into hysterical yelps or agonizing groans—
finally the keepers arrived—the maniac was hauled ruthlessly out,
the women next; one was insensible ; she was brought and laid on
the stone pavement of the kitchen yard and a cup of water dashed
in her face. She did not revive.   The doctor was hurriedly sent
for. He came and ordered a pail of water, which was brought and
dashed upon her. She remained unconscious—the poor girl was
dead. To her life's fitful dream was over. I learned she had been
committed for intoxication, and had got up that morning saying
she felt so well, and as she going to the island she would tidy herself up. She was plainly but cleanly dressed—a fine, hearty looking young woman, of about twenty-five years. Strong men, with
sad hearts, carried her gently to the *female prison*. A few hours
afterwards a pine corporation coffin was brought. She was placed
in it, a handful of shavings placed under her head, the cover nailed
down, and Kate Golden had gone forever from the world as if by
the touch of the wand of magic—not by the wand of the fairy but
by that of bloodless Moloch—pitiless, merciless and uncaring.

Imprinted in my mind, seared into my memory, I ever see the
words '*Charities and Correction.*'   At dusk the coffin was brought
into the hall of the *sleeping* cells and placed upon two empty barrels—a dingy oil lamp was lighted and set upon it. All that long
night, though there was the presence of the majesty of death, ribaldry, profanity and obscenity reigned unabashed. Smith and Duffy
slept a drunken sleep alongside of it. Sunday afternoon the dead
wagon came and took the corpse away—where ? to an humble grave
in Potter's field, or to the knife of the dissecting table ? 'Echo answers—where ?' When the maniac was hauled out of the van he
was reconveyed to his prison cell. The other women were repacked into the van and taken to the island. How many of them died

on the way, or were permanently shattered for life, is not as yet known.   An hour after another van came, twelve *men* were put into it, the maniac brought out, securely bound hand and foot, and thrust into it, and the van was driven off.   Scene first in the act of tragedies was closed.

KNIFE OF THE DISSECTING TABLE.

That night one of the prisoners in the cell I was in, I noticed, was making queer grimaces and acting very strangely.   After watching him intently for some time I became convinced he was deranged— was in a state of *delirium tremens*.   I called the night watchman and he took him out of the cell over to the main prison.   Tuesday morning he was brought back in a blanket, a coffin got, a bundle of straw for his pillow; the dead wagon came and the coffin went away—where? and scene second in the act of tragedies was closed.

The morning of our glorious Fourth arrived.   Smith had had a heavier than usual carousal (if possible) the night before, and he woke up late.   The night watchman came to rouse him up; Smith grunted out, 'I no git up till seven o'clock—it's Sunday.'   However, after a little he got up, something less cross and cruel than ordinarily, and said: 'Boys, it's Sunday; you'll have no work, only just to clean up the yard, and you'll have good time to-day.' This piece of news was hailed with expressions of pleasure, and to show their gratitude to Smith, and a *warm* appreciation of his kindness, some of them procured a pint bottle, filled it about a quarter full of kerosene and the balance with whiskey, and made Smith a present of it. *Such* a present, and one he prized so highly as this, had probably never before been offered to Smith. He was profuse in his thanks, and hastily hurried away into the dingy caverns at the rear of the sleeping hall to hide his precious treasure; but he did not return until he had copiously imbibed of the delicious elixir. He came back smacking his lips, muttering, ' 'Tish goot—very goot.' A grim smile passed from one to the other as Smith went off to look after some minor details of duty. In about half an hour he arrived back, staggering and roaring like a mad bull—'Git out of here, you lazy loafers; you no tink you work.' And all day long his fertile brain for ingenious devices for human torture, now doubly active under the influence of the elixir, left us no peace, no rest. But to every tether there is an end, and night came finally to our relief, when we were all securely locked in the *sleeping* cells.

Smith carefully tried the doors, and finding them securely fastened, he brought out from its hiding place the remains of the morning's present, and at one long gulp drained it to the bottom. For a little space he raved, stormed and cursed, and then sank helpless on the floor, rolled over on his back, and lay to all appearance dead as an Egyptian mummy, which, from his now mahogany complexion and withered, sunken features, he very much resembled. The night watchman came, rolled him, punched him, but to no purpose, so he took the keys away from him and left. In a little while Duffy came in, hauled out his pallet of straw and lay down. Completely exhausted I sat down on the floor, rested my head on my knees, and for an hour or two dozed away in an unquiet sleep. I finally awoke, roused myself up and looked through the bars. Smith lay there still. Duffy was sitting up on his pallet, muttering incoherently to himself, and vainly trying to get his head through his shirt sleeve. I felt that Duffy was certainly very ill, and as I sat there in that foul place, gloomy and sepulchral, an undefined awe crept over me. Ah! Duffy, you will soon join the other two. Too true! In the morning papers appeared the following notice:

'James Duffy, a man of education, formerly a school teacher, but without home or permanent means of support, yesterday morning died in the Tombs, where of late he had spent much of his time. Deceased was a single man, fifty years of age, and a native of Ireland. Some acquaintances of deceased about the Tombs will give the remains a decent burial.' And scene third of the act of tragedies was closed.

Morning came. Smith arose feeble and weak—almost a shadow of his former self. He was very much frightened. 'Oh, I'm very sick! Mine Got, I got the cholera one hundred times last night! Oh! Oh!' A gallon of castor beans and jalap would not have been near as effectual as this precious elixir, and it is now recognized by all apothecaries as 'Smith's Fourth of July Cordial;' for sale in every groggery, distillery, bucket shop and rum hole in the land, and is a most potent agent in inducing so many to seek the comforts, the kindnesses, and the Christian, ameliorating influences of that goodly institution, Charities and Correction."

CHAPTER XXX:

THE ASTOR PLACE RIOT.—EDWIN FORREST.—CHARLOTTE CUSH-
MAN.—MACREADY, THE ENGLISH TRAGEDIAN.—CHEVALIER WI-
KOFF.—"WORKINGMEN, SHALL AMERICANS OR ENGLISH RULE
IN THIS CITY?"—THE RIOT AND ITS INSTIGATORS.—ARREST OF
E. Z. C. JUDSON ("NED BUNTLINE").—HIS INDICTMENT, TRIAL,
CONVICTION AND SENTENCE.

"A mob is usually a creature of very mysterious existence, particularly in a large city. Where it comes from or whither it goes few men can tell. * * * * It was not an easy task to draw off such a throng. If Bedlam gates had been flung open wide there would not have issued forth such maniacs as the frenzy of that night had made.—DICKENS, in *Barnaby Rudge*.

EDWIN FORREST, the great American tragedian, and Charlotte Cushman, the American queen of tragedy, both of them young and comparatively unfriended, were compelled to seek, in a foreign land, the fame and fortune denied them in their own country. It was on the stage of Drury Lane Theatre, in London, that Edwin Forrest achieved his first success. He was kindly treated and made many friends, and, with his British endorsement, returned to his own country with an increased reputation and additional professional experience. He made his first appearance at the Old Park Theatre, then standing opposite the City Hall Park. His reception was a perfect ovation, and he speedily attained that prominence in the dramatic firmament which he held among his friends and admirers to the day of his death.

In 1827—one year after the successful commencement of Mr. Forrest's career as a star of the first magnitude—Mr. William C. Macready, an English actor of great eminence, visited the United States. In a fit of petulance, in which such actors are too apt to indulge, Mr. Macready came near fomenting a disturbance in Baltimore, which, but for his adroit management, might have caused him then to have been driven from the American stage. In playing "William Tell," the property man had forgotten to furnish the arrow to be broken, and Macready was obliged to break one of his shooting arrows. In his anger at the offending party he said, "I can't get such an arrow in your country, sir!" or, as was reported, "I can't get wood to make such an arrow in your country" This was construed into an insult to the country. Anonymous letters were sent to the newspapers ; but, as these were sent to Mr. Macready, he had an opportunity to make an explanation and avoid a row.

EDWIN FORREST.

Macready and Forrest were starring through the country, playing alternate engagements—but not, so far as we know, developing any very decided feelings of rivalry. Their *roles* of characters and spheres of action were quite apart; and when they met each other their intercourse—as it was many years after—was of the most gentlemanly character.

About the year 1835 Mr. Forrest went to Europe, and spent time in travelling on the continent; after which he returned to America for a short time, and then went back to England to fulfil professional engagements—in which he was so highly successful

that, on his return, he was honored with a public dinner in Philadelphia; and about this time he was tendered a nomination to
Congress by the Democracy of New York, before whom he delivered a Fourth of July oration.

In 1844 Mr. Macready again visited the United States. Mr.
Forrest tendered him the courtesies due to so distinguished a professional brother; but it so happened that, in most of the cities
where Macready was engaged, there were more theatres than one—
and, of consequence, rival managers. When one of these had secured Mr. Macready the other was anxious to get the best talent
to be found to run against him, and there was no one so available
as Mr. Forrest—who was not the man to refuse a profitable engagement, nor did any rules of courtesy require that he should do so.

The result was that the constant rivalry of Forrest, though carried on in the most friendly manner, could not fail to injure
the success of Macready. A certain degree of partizanship was
everywhere excited—for Forrest was everywhere placarded as the
" *American* Tragedian "—and the tour of Macready was comparatively a failure.

The applause that the American actor had received in Europe
made him long to visit again the scenes of his first triumph, and
he journeyed to the British metropolis, but not to meet with that
hearty greeting so warmly extended to him but a short time before.
Charles Dickens, who had been petted and *feted* by the American
people on the occasion of his first visit to this country, had returned home previous to Forrest's second visit, and by his caustic
and ludicrous criticisms on American customs and manners there,
had been instilled into the hearts of John Bull an antipathy for
everything American. Just at this moment, while the literary associates of Dickens and his friends of the London press were at fever
heat against everything in this country, Forrest made his second
bow before a London audience.

The opposition to him was, from the first, marked and fatal;
and, so far as the metropolis was concerned, his tour was a failure.
It was only in the provinces—away from London influence—that
he met with any degree of success.

There was no need of Mr. Macready taking any active part in
this matter, and there is no proof that he did so, but much to the

contrary; still, Mr. Forrest hastily and indignantly, and, we doubt not, sincerely, charged it upon Mr. Macready ; and one night, when the latter was playing in " Hamlet," at the theatre in Edinburgh, Mr. Forrest, who was seated in a private box, had the bad taste as well as bad feeling to hiss a portion of his performance in the most marked and offensive manner.

Then appeared the unfriendly notices, and then were made the attempts to hiss him off the stage. This undoubtedly was the cause of Forrest's unkind and ungenerous treatment, and the demon entered his heart. Forrest returned home embittered against the London *litterateurs* and actors. He made no exceptions in his sweeping denunciations ; nothing could convince him that he was anything but the unfortunate victim of circumstances over which he had no control.

The welcome that awaited him on his return to New York more than compensated for his abuse abroad. He was now the American tragedian *par excellence.* Nightly he appeared to crowded houses, and the yells of the " b'hoys " that greeted him from the third tier and the pit were manna to his heart. While in the zenith of his popularity, playing a long engagement at the Old Broadway, Macready again arrived in this country.

His reception at any other time would have been most cordial. Previous to his coming Chevalier Wikoff, a then notorious journalistic *diplomat,* who had recently been abroad, instilled into Mr. Forrest's ear poisonous insinuations against Macready. It was claimed by Macready's friends that he had made every effort to stop the unkind criticisms of the London press, but without success, as a bitter feeling had been raised against him, which found its first public expression in the *Boston Mail* on the morning of Mr. Macready's appearance at the Howard Athenæum, Boston, Monday, Oct. 30th, 1848, as follows:

" Mr. Macready has at length arrived, and, next to the grand water celebration, will create such excitement as will emphatically mark the present epoch in time's calendar. He plays this evening at the Howard Athenæum, and refuses to show himself for less than one dollar a ticket. This was his price in New York, and, with the exception of the first night, resulted in a 'beggarly account of empty boxes.' We repeat what we said in a former

article, that Mr. Pelby, the enterprising manager of the National
Theatre, deserves immortal honors for not acceding to the dictatorial terms of this actor autocrat.   Although Macready saw fit, on
his opening night in New York, on being called out by some
friends, to slur a *'certain penny paper,'* that had *'dared'* to express an opinion regarding his talents and conduct, we shall not by
any means give him the retort churlish ; we only pity his ignorance
of the institutions of this country, and hope, for his own credit's
sake, that he will not, when he gets home, write a black book about
American manners, etc., *a la* Trollope and others, but if he does,
that he will spare us in the production of his brain.   The reader
will no doubt ask what fault we find with Mr. Macready.   Has he
not the same right as other men have to do as he pleases ?   We
answer yes.   He has a right to come to this country in the exercise
of his profession ; he has a right to demand a dollar from every
person who witnesses his acting, and if managers of theatres are
willing to accede to his arbitrary proposals, he certainly has a right
to make them.   We complain not of any of these.   Our charges
against Macready are based upon more important grounds.   It is
his conduct in his own country, in relation to Mr. Forrest, that we
are about investigating ; *his inhospitality, his crushing influence, his
vindictive opposition, and his steadfast determination to ruin the prospects of that gentleman in England,* that we bring to his door.   Let
him deny them if he can.   Every true American takes a pride in
that which represents his country's interests, industry and enterprise, and from the smallest commodity gathered from his soil to
the loftiest labors of his genius, his ambition goes with it, and the
strong arm of his power will protect it in every clime.   Mr. Edwin
Forrest is titled the American Tragedian; he is justly entitled to
that honor ; he has acquired it by his own labors ; from a poor boy
in a circus he has risen to be a man of fame and wealth, all of
which he has lastingly gained by enterprise and talent, and secured both by economy and TEMPERANCE.

Every American born man is willing that Mr. Forrest should
wear this title, and when he visited England they were anxiously
interested in his success.   Macready had previously been in this
country, and played engagements in every city, and made a fortune.
He was extolled by the press, and treated as a gentleman by the

citizens of every place he visited; but instead of returning this kindness he acted openly towards Mr. Forrest as his determined foe. We speak by card, and write upon the very best information, viz., the highest authority. In Paris Mr. Macready and Mr. Forrest met. The latter was anxious to appear on the French boards, but Macready threw obstacles in the way, and this was the first time that the two players were enemies. Mr. Mitchell, the enterprising lessee of St. James' Theatre in London, took an English company of actors to the French capital, with Mr. Macready at the head of the list. Macready was to be the hero—the great attraction of Paris. He failed, however, to draw money to the treasury, and Mr. Mitchell lost a large sum by the speculation, or rather would have lost it if Louis Philippe had not made him most liberal presents. Mr. Forrest had letters of introduction to Mr. Mitchell from his friends in London, but Macready was jealous lest Forrest should prove to be *the* great star, and he cautioned Mitchell not to allow Forrest to appear. The result was that Mr. Mitchell refused to see Mr. Forrest.

The parties returned to London. The hypocrisy of Macready is apparent in his note of invitation to Mr. Forrest to dine with him. The latter, knowing the intrigue that had been carried on in Paris between Macready and Mitchell, refused, as every high minded man should, to dine with him. This is a very different version to that recently given by some of Macready's friends—if friends he have —that Forrest was offended because he was not invited to dine; as if such a man as Mr. Forrest could take offence at such a trifle, when, at the same time, he was invited to dine with many of the leading nobility of England, but especially of Scotland, where he passed several months as their guest.

The next mean act towards Forrest, brought about through the influence of Macready, was when Mr. F. appeared at the Princess' Theatre in London. Mac had been endeavoring for a long time to effect an engagement with some London manager, but was unsuccessful. The success of Forrest stung him and he resolved to ' put him down.' It was said, at the same time, that he or his friends actually hired men to visit the theatre and hiss Forrest off the stage, and Forrest was consequently received with a shower of hisses before he was heard. This mean conduct was followed up by the press, by which Forrest was most outrageously assailed, and not Forrest alone but his country, which is proud to own him as one of her sons.

Forrest and Macready next met in Edinburgh, and from this city were sent forth the grossest calumnies against Forrest. Macready was playing at the Theatre Royal in *Hamlet*—Forrest was present. During the beginning of the piece Mr. Forrest applauded several times, and, as we are informed by an eye witness, he started the applause when some brilliant effect had been given to a passage, so that the whole house followed him. But now comes Forrest's great sin—that giant sin which Mac will never forgive—the sin of hissing Macready for throwing up his handkerchief and dancing across the stage in the *pas de mouchoir*.

Mr. F. not only hissed but the whole house hissed, and yet Macready dared to write to London that Forrest had singly and alone attempted to hiss him from the stage.

To show that Mr. Forrest was not alone in this matter, we are able to state that two weeks afterwards *Hamlet* was repeated, when the whole house again hissed Macready's dance across the stage.

Out of this simple incident Macready contrived to create a great deal of sympathy for himself. He is or was part proprietor of the *London Examiner ;* or, if not sole owner, he possesses the body and soul of its theatrical critic, Foster, who does all kinds of dirty work for his master. Macready gave the cue to Foster, and Forrest was denounced by the *Examiner* and other papers in which Foster or Mac had any influence. A false coloring was put on this affair, and Mac appeared to the world as a persecuted man, whereas Forrest was the one who met with persecution at every corner—in Paris, in London, in Edinburgh, and in London a second time.

But Macready's persecution did not stop here. Forrest wished to appear in London, in Bulwer's *Lady of Lyons* and *Richelieu.* To do this permission must be obtained of the author. Forrest addressed a note to Bulwer, asking his terms for the plays. After a long delay Bulwer replied that he should charge Forrest £2 per night for the use of them, and he must play forty nights ! Such terms, for plays that had in a great measure lost their interest, compelled Forrest to reject them. It was ascertained that Macready and Bulwer had been much together, and that the former had pre-

vaile 1 on the latter not to allow Forrest the use of his composi-
tions.

Forrest could not entertain any jealous feelings towards Mac,
for he drew crowded houses during his engagements at the Princess' Theatre, whereas Macready had very slim audiences ; and, on
one occasion, we know that our own charming actress, Mrs. Barrett,
on one of the off nights at the time Mac was playing, actually drew
more money to the treasury than Macready.

We have now given a plain statement of facts, and such as cannot be controverted. It proves that actors like Macready, Anderson and others, find it very hard scratching in their own country,
and much better pickings here. It is to be hoped, however, that
we Americans will finally become awakened to the mercenary motives of such artists, and when we have any surplus of dollars to
spend, that we will be generous and just to our own home genius."

Here is displayed the feeling of the friends of Mr. Forrest, and,
to a great extent, of Forrest himself, for the writer of this article
asserts that its statements are made on the " very highest authority." On his part Mr. Macready unwisely alluded to this article
in one of his before-the-curtain speeches, speaking contemptuously of the attacks of a certain penny paper. But the Bostonians
are a quiet people, and Macready and Forrest played through their
engagements without any popular demonstration. At New York
Macready played at the Opera House and Forrest at the Broadway
Theatre. There were rumors of a disturbance, but they amounted
to nothing. Both engagements were finished in peace, and both
actors went to fulfil engagements at the rival theatres in Philadelphia, and then Macready went south.

On his return from the south Messrs. Niblo and Hackett, who
had taken the Opera House for that purpose, announced that Mr.
Macready would open an engagement on Monday night, May 7th.
Mr. Forrest was playing at the Broadway Theatre. Previous to
the commencement of this engagement Mr. Macready gave a reading of a play of Shakspeare before the teachers of the public
schools of New York and Brooklyn.

The announcement of this engagement was the signal for an out-
break of long smothered indignation. It was determined that Mr.
Forrest should be avenged, and that Macready should not be per-

mitted to play before a New York audience. There was a combination of exciting causes—the feeling against England and Eng-
lishmen, handed down to us from the Revolution, and kept fresh
by the insults and abuse of British writers on American manners;
the injury committed against Forrest, with Macready as its presumed cause, and this was increased by the fact of Macready play
ing at the aristocratic kid glove Opera House.

The public and magistrates have been accustomed to look upon
theatrical disturbances, rows and riots, as different in their character
from all others. The stage is presumed to be a correction of the
manners and morals of the public, and on the other hand the public
has been left to correct, in its own energetic way, the manners and
morals of the stage; and magistrates, looking upon it as a matter
between the actors and the audience, have generally refused to interfere, unless there was a prospect of a violent breach of the
peace, when they have usually ordered the house to be closed. In
these theatrical disturbances performances were hissed, plays cried
down, and actors and actresses driven from the stage with whatever degree of force has been necessary for their rejection. This
has been the practice in the United States as well as in Europe,
and no actor, in any free country, has thought of acting with a
posse of police at his back, much less a file of soldiers or a piece of
artillery to defend his rights.

On the announcement of Mr. Macready's engagement at the
Opera House, it was determined that there should be a pretty forcible expression of opinion on the part of those who were indignant
at the treatment of Mr. Forrest in England, and were willing, for
any reason, to revenge it on Mr. Macready. There was, doubtless,
some organization of forces to bring about this result, and one person, the well known Capt. Rynders, admits that he purchased and
distributed among his friends fifty tickets, with the understanding
that those who used them were to assist in hissing Macready from
the stage.

Macready was not daunted at the unpleasant situation of affairs,
and was announced to appear in the character of Macbeth, supported
by a talented and favorite company, which, it was thought, would
ensure him a peaceable if not an enthusiastic reception. Whether
by accident or design Forrest appeared the same evening in the

same character, and it was hoped that Forrest's admirers would be attracted by his presence, but subsequent events proved the contrary.   The audience that greeted Forrest was composed of the *elite* of the city, and the fact that his hated rival was playing in the same character at another theatre put him on his mettle.   While Forrest was receiving the plaudits of his friends at the Broadway Theatre, scenes of a very different character were being enacted in a central square of the most aristocratic quarter of New York, where thou-sands of citizens were gathered around one of the most conspic-uous and magnificent edifices, the Astor Place Opera House.

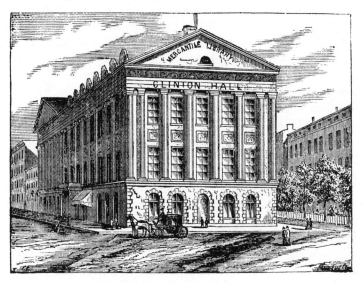

MERCANTILE LIBRARY, FORMERLY OPERA HOUSE.

This Opera House was built expressly for the performance of the Italian Opera, but had been used at intervals for the legitimate drama, vaudevilles, and for balls and concerts.   It was fitted up and decorated with taste and magnificence, and in the opera sea-sons was patronized by the most wealthy and fashionable people, who made extravagant displays of luxurious adornment.   While the private boxes were taken for the season by those who wished to enjoy the music and could afford the expenditure, the other seats were let at a dollar admission, and the upper tier or amphitheatre was reserved for people of humbler means or more modest pretensions, at twenty-five cents a ticket.

Long before the opening of the doors the portals and sidewalks and streets surrounding the theatre were filled with people. There was no noise nor any demonstration, but it required very little penetration on the part of the theatrical *habitue* to discover that there was a probability of there being a portentous upheaving among the crowd on the opening of the doors. The house was quickly filled, and then there was an ominous silence. There was a small sprinkling of ladies in the dress circle, whose presence it was believed would deter the rowdy element, which had taken possession of the galleries, from any breach of the peace. It now began to be whispered about that the reception of Mr. Macready would not be favorable on the part of a large portion of the auditory, and the appearance of Mr. Matsell, the Chief of Police, with a very strong body of the force under his orders, seemed to strengthen the rumors which were circulating throughout the theatre. The house was, however, perfectly quiet until the curtain rose upon the first scene, when the appearance of Malcolm elicited loud and enthusiastic cheers from the parquette and galleries. The appearance of Macready in the third scene was the signal for the most deafening outburst of groans, hisses and cat calls that ever greeted an actor, accompanied by a deluge of asafœtida, which filled the entire house with its unfragrant odor. The actor, however, was not disconcerted. The play went on amid a shower of stale eggs, old shoes and other objectionable missiles. Macready appeared at the call boy's signal, evidently determined to play his character to the end. At last chairs were hurled on the stage, and when it became apparent that violence was intended, the curtain was rung down. The confusion was now intense. The ladies started from their seats and retreated to the lobbies, while the angry mob were surging back and forth. The crowd outside were thundering at the doors, threatening to break them down. The Chief of Police with a strong party had barricaded the entrances. The ladies were hurried out by one of the doors on Eighth street, and in a few minutes afterwards Mr. Macready, in a close carriage, was driven rapidly and safely away.

That night the roughs were triumphant, having succeeded in

driving Mr. Macready from the stage ; but he was determined to appear again, and accordingly was announced for the following Thursday evening. The outrage on Macready was the topic of the week, and was denounced by all the respectable papers of the day. His calm demeanor challenged the admiration of many of his enemies, and they flocked to him by hundreds, and tendered him substantial support and aid. Among those who invited him to appear again were Washington Irving, Ogden Hoffman, Moses H. Grinnell, Henry J. Raymond, Simeon Draper, Richard Grant White, James Brooks and David Graham. In the same edition of the New York *Herald* which announced his intended appearance was a voluminous correspondence, submitted by Mr. Macready to prove that he had in no way been inimical to Mr. Forrest while he was in London. In the meantime the " b'hoys," as the roughs were then termed, were determined to prevent the final appearance of Mr. Macready. They issued a pronunciamento, which was posted in various parts of the city, that read as follows :

"WORKING MEN!
SHALL
AMERICANS
OR
ENGLISH
RULE IN THIS CITY?
The crew of the British steamer have threatened all Americans who
shall dare to express their opinions to-night at the English Aris-
tocratic Opera House! We advocate no violence, but
a free expression of opinion to all public men.
Workingmen! Freemen! Stand by
your lawful rights!
AMERICAN COMMITTEE."

This was certainly a bold and daring step on the part of the rioters, and it was the question of the day whether the authorities would be equal to the emergency. There was every evidence that there was to be an attempt by an organized mob to again prevent Mr. Macready appearing at the opera house. The respectable portion of the city were determined that he should appear, and that the honor of the city should be vindicated. The municipal authorities were prepared to prevent any disorder, and the militia were ordered to be in readiness at their armories. At an early hour in the evening persons began to assemble around the theatre, and at about seven o'clock crowds were seen wending their way to the theatre from all parts of the city. By half past seven there were several hundreds in the street in front of the opera house, and the rush to get admittance was tremendous. Tickets for a sufficient number to fill the house were soon sold, and the announcement was made on a placard that no more could be had. Meantime the crowd outside was increasing every minute.

Every avenue to the theatre soon became densely crowded. Astor place was occupied by an immense assemblage, almost all of whom had apparently been attracted by curiosity. The portion of the Bowery adjoining the theatre was also crowded, and in Broadway, which had at that point been opened for the purpose of constructing a sewer, hundreds of persons were seen crowded together on the top of the mound of earth thrown up from the centre of the street. The house itself was filled to the dome. A great portion of the assemblage in the theatre consisted of policemen, who had been distributed all over the house in detached parties. There was not any appearance of an organized party of rioters in the house. When the curtain rose there was an outburst of hisses, groans, cheers and miscellaneous sounds, similar to those which interrupted Mr. Macready's first appearance. The opening scenes, however, were got through with after a fashion—several persons who hissed and hooted having been seized by the police and immediately conveyed to an apartment underneath the boxes, where they were placed in confinement under the charge of a posse of police officers.

Macready's appearance was the signal for a great explosion of feeling. Hisses, groans, shouts of derision assailed him, intermingled with loud cries of "Out with him! out with him!" Large numbers of the auditory started to their feet, and called on the police to eject the individuals who had expressed their disapprobation, and several arrests were made in the manner before described, each arrest being followed by loud cheers and applause all over the house. It was speedily apparent that those unfriendly to Mr. Macready were in the minority. Thus the play proceeded through the first two acts. There had been a great deal of trepidation behind the scenes, but the heroism with which the actors and actresses sustained themselves on the stage was worthy of all praise. Mr. Macready repeatedly expressed to Mr. Hackett his wish to desist, and his desire to avoid any further collision with those who were opposed to his appearance, but amid the groans and hisses the play went on.

The first persons who were arrested in the parquette were some fashionably attired young men, who were locked up in a room in the basement. In this apartment there was a gas light burning, and the prisoners, pulling up some shavings and pieces of wood, set fire to them. When the policemen opened the door the place was full of smoke, but the officers speedily extinguished the fire.

NED BUNTLINE.

These desperate incendiaries were immediately placed in irons At this moment a shower of stones assailed the windows of the theatre, and the cries of the furious mob could be distinctly heard inside the house. It was now ascertained that Edward Z. C. Judson, *alias* Ned Buntline, was heading the mob outside and calling on them to stone the building. He was immediately dragged from the crowd by the police and taken to the nearest police station. Volley after volley of heavy paving stones were discharged against the windows until at last they were smashed to atoms. The windows having been barricaded they resisted the further progress of the rioters, but the missiles fell among the frightened audience and they became terror stricken. The scene in the house was most exciting. The faces of strong men were blanched with fear, hedged in as they were on all sides by an infuriated mob, bent on destroying the building. The police displayed the most undaunted courage as they rushed in amidst the crowd, seizing the most conspicuous rioters and bringing them off prisoners.

When it was announced that the militia were coming to the scene of the riot the mob became still more demonstrative. As the first company wheeled into Astor place from Broadway they were met by groans and menaces. The crowd did not give way an inch, and the company by a flank movement gained the sidewalk. Marching in single file, they forced a passage by means of the bayonet until they gained a position before the doors of the Opera House. Unfortunately for the militia the rioters were masters of the situation, as they were yet in possession of the pile of paving stones at the intersection of Broadway and Astor place. The militia remained on the defensive until they were assailed by a volley of stones. The mob, and those people who had been drawn to the scene by curiosity, believed that the militia were supplied with blank cartridges only, hence they were emboldened to continue their assaults. One by one the unfortunate militiamen dropped from the ranks—in some cases sustaining serious injuries. The captain of the company was loth to undeceive the angry rioters, and did not give the command to fire until above the din of the tumult he heard the suppliant voices of his men entreating him to give the word. It was a fatal moment when the order was whispered along the line to fire high. Innocent persons, far from the tumultuous scene, fell to the ground fatally wounded, while the rioters at the front only became more incensed against the militia, who, as yet, were maintaining their position alone—the other companies not having reached the ground. The scene was now one of the wildest excitement. The fury of the mob became uncontrollable, and it was apparent that unless the militia were permitted to act in a sharp and decisive manner they would be overwhelmed and driven from their position. Company after company of the brave citizen soldiers were now ordered to the scene of the riot; Generals Sandford and Hall had also arrived, and, there being no alternative, the order was given to load. All this time the rioters, led on by desperate men who had nothing at stake but their worthless lives, were urged on to attack the troops. They made one final charge, hurling the heavy stones right into the ranks of their opponents. In the rear of the rioters the people pushed on, crowding the street from building to building. The decisive moment had

THE ASTOR PLACE RIOT.

arrived and the command to fire was given. There was a flash, followed by a deadly fire of musketry, and the sharp cries of the wounded pierced the night air as they fell in the agonies of death. Terror stricken the cowardly rioters turned to the right and left, and rushing frantically through the intersecting streets, they trampled over the prostrate forms of those who had fallen while quietly waiting for the *denouement* which terminated so fatally. The militia now had little difficulty in clearing the streets surrounding the opera house. Howitzers, loaded with grape and canister, were placed at the head of the streets, and at midnight they were deserted by all but the troops. All night long groups of men were seen carrying the dead and wounded away. The drug stores in the neighborhood and the City Hospital were surrounded by an anxious crowd of persons inquiring for their missing friends. On wagons and litters the wounded were conveyed to their homes, where many of them lingered for weeks in pain and distress.

On the following day Mayor Woodhull, finding the "b'hoys" were preparing to renew the riot, issued a proclamation requesting the people to remain away from the Astor Place Opera House, and at the same time ordering the militia to remain on duty, to prevent any further demonstration on the part of the rioters.

It was reported that twenty-seven persons had been killed and thirty wounded. But the exact number of the wounded could not be ascertained, from the fact that in many instances they were taken to their homes. The respectable portion of the public, while they deplored the slaughter of so many innocent people, were grateful to the authorities and the militia for their prompt action, but the brawling "b'hoys" were anxious for war, notwithstanding the object of their wrath had left the city. Posters were placarded throughout the city calling for an indignation meeting, which was held in the City Hall Park on the evening of the 11th. The meeting was addressed by Isaiah Rynders and Mike Walsh, prominent leaders of the democratic party. The speeches were of an incendiary character, and it was recommended that the Mayor, Recorder and Sheriff be indicted. However, the Coroner's jury, a few days afterwards, by their verdict justified the authorities in giving the instructions to the military to fire on the mob.

The opera house was temporarily closed—Mr. Macready refusing to remain in the city. The more desperate of the riotous crowd lingered for days around the New York Hotel, expecting to find Macready, but it was finally ascertained that he left the hotel from a rear door on the morning after the riot. When, after the play had been finally interrupted, Mr. Macready ascertained that there had been bloodshed on account of his second appearance, he was horrified, and was very much distressed. His friends, solicitous for his safety, decided that he should leave the city disguised as an officer of the militia, and accordingly he mounted a horse provided for him, and, escorted by several officers, he left the New York Hotel before dawn, and proceeded to New Rochelle, where he was taken up by the express train and carried to Boston.

The authorities gave instructions for the prosecution of all the ringleaders of the riot.   More than sixty persons had been arrested on the evening of the riot, and ten of them were indicted by the

JOHN M'KEON.

Grand Jury.   The chief instigator was E. Z. C. Judson, generally known as Ned Buntline, who at that time edited a weekly paper called "Ned Buntline's Own."

The trial of the rioters began on the 12th of September, 1849, before Judge Daly, in the Court of General Sessions.   The prosecution was conducted by District Attorney John McKeon.   The trial occupied a fortnight, resulting in the conviction of the indicted parties.   Judson was a great agitator, and the verdict gave universal satisfaction to all lovers of law and order. On the 29th of September he was brought up for sentence. The Judge's charge was withering. After characterizing the enormity of the crime of which the prisoner had been found guilty, he concluded by saying, "We feel it our duty to go, in your case, to the utmost limit of the law. We deem even that punishment inadequate, and, in imposing it," said Judge Daly, "I never felt so forcibly the want of power to make respected the laws of my country, whose minister I am."

Ned Buntline was, therefore, sentenced to one year's imprisonment in the Penitentiary on Blackwell's Island, and a fine of $250, and to be imprisoned until paid. The prisoner was in no way discomfited at the prospect that was presented to him. He served out his term of imprisonment without undergoing much if any privation. Shortly after his commitment to the island the Warden was prostrated by an apoplectic fit, and Ned became a very kind and attentive nurse. While there he distinguished himself by erecting a small library for the prisoners. Since then he has led an adventurous life, and at the present writing he is an earnest exponent of total abstinence. In his palmy days he was a great favorite with the "b'hoys."

CHAPTER XXXI.

ABORTIONISTS.—MADAME RESTELL.—HER CRIME, ARREST, TRIAL,
CONVICTION, IMPRISONMENT IN THE TOMBS AND ON BLACK-
WELL'S ISLAND.—HER FIFTH AVENUE PALACE.—ROSENZSWEIG.
—THE TRUNK HORROR.—ALICE BOWLSBY'S MELANCHOLY FATE.
—QUACK DOCTORS AND DOCTRESSES.—THEIR PATRONS AND PA-
TIENTS.—ESCAPE OF ROSENZSWEIG.

"Even her propriety could not dispute that there was impropriety in the world;
but Mrs. General's way of getting rid of it was to put it out of sight, and make believe
there was no such thing."—DICKENS, *in Little Dorrit.*

BORN of the atheistic and communistic atmosphere that surrounds fast Parisian life, and, spreading thence, permeates
with its blighting influence a considerable portion of what we are
pleased to call the civilized world, the crime of abortion is undoubtedly one of the most heinous in all the gloomy catalogue of
man's and woman's lapses from virtue. The glamour of an exotic
existence beneath the golden rain of chandeliers that ornament
regal drawing rooms; the rout, the ball, the party, and all the other
necessities of a fashionable career, are so potent with Madame of
the period that she has but little time, and less inclination to fulfil
the *role* of maternity destined for her by her God. It is sad to
think that such is the fact; but there is no disguising that the
Malthusian doctrines find eager votaries in the upper circles of
society. It is no longer the *mode* to bear children—they are out
of style, like last season's bonnet. At least it is getting to be so
among the butterfly people of the world—those who prefer to look
at life as if it were an immense carnival—one tremendous masked
ball, with the crash of the band never silenced, and the dizzy waltz
kept up unceasingly. Madame, who is having her hair arranged
in her *boudoir* previous to the opera, thinks children are a nuisance.
If she has none she thanks her lucky stars; if she is a mother, the
children are left the most of the time to themselves, or the French
bonne who airs them daily in the Park. Their place is the nursery
—the mamma's the parlor. It is, therefore, in the lower classes of

society that we will oftener see the cradle and oftener hear the sweet lullaby sung.   The woman in moderate circumstances, who is a stranger to silk slippers, and does not base all her happiness upon the genteel appearance of her waist, is not ashamed of maternity.   Unlike the dreamer Rousseau, who wrote rapturously of the delicious delights of domesticity and sent all his own bairns to the foundling asylum, she takes a pride and a joy in hearing the name of mother lisped by baby lips.   Would that it were so in every instance, for then this secret, cankerous vice, of which we are forced, in the completion of our task, to write, would not exist. But so long as babies are not fashionable, the abortionist, lurking in the shadow of a great metropolis like New York, will ply his nefarious calling and reap his golden harvest.   He is a murderer, pure and simple, and should be treated as such.   But, alas! only when the victim of his butchery dies does the law notice the case.

There are in New York, to-day, hundreds upon hundreds of these surgical assassins.   Two classes of people support them—the fashionable Madame and the unfortunate girl.   And they will continue to be supported in their illicit calling so long as society brands maternity without marriage as an unpardonable sin, and so long as the married lady prefers the whirl and excitement of an outside life to the seclusion of her home.

Abortionists are of two kinds, male and female, aristocratic and democratic.   We will give a portrait of each, and to one of them will append a tale of murder that is yet fresh in the memory of New York society.   We allude to the Alice Bowlsby case—otherwise known as the trunk horror.   But let us start at the other end of the line, and take a look first at the aristocratic and elegant phase of child murder.

On the northeast corner of Fifty-second street and Fifth avenue, in this city, stands a superb double house, stamped with all the peculiarities of the lordly mansions of that swell neighborhood.   To the pedestrian loitering along the pave, and to the more fortunate individual who rolls by in a clarence or landau it would appear, did they not know its history, to be the residence of some opulent merchant.   It is the home of opulence, but no merchant dwells there. The house on the northeast corner of Fifty-second street and Fifth avenue is the palace of Madame Restell.

Perhaps it would be no exaggeration to state that Madame Restell's house is the most handsomely furnished of any in the city. All that money could do, guided by a delicately feminine and yet voluptuous taste, has been done, and the result is apparent on every hand. Seen at night the interior is peculiarly striking. From tinted globes the soft light streams over furniture as elaborate as any that ever graced the *salons* of the *Tuileries*, over magnificent velvet carpets from the famed looms of the Old World tapestry from Gobelin's; pictures that a prince might envy, and a thousand costly articles of *vertu* and *bagatelle* from bric-a-brac Paris. Scarcely a sound is heard. The attendants move softly to and fro; and, save the closing of a door up stairs now and then, there is naught to break the silence that broods over the scene. In the house are those who have come to buy with money the skilful assistance of the Madame. On many a pillow rests a pale, fair face, the pathetic expression of which attests the agony that is being endured. Nurses are constantly in attendance, and every want is gratified as soon as it is expressed. Everything is done on a scale of magnificent splendor. In the superb grounds that surround the palace the convalescents stroll when the sun shines brightly; and could you look over the high fence that jealously guards the scene from the vulgar gaze, you might see, any warm spring morning, one, perhaps two, perhaps more of the patients who have passed the crisis of their treatment and are now recovering from the shock. When tired of the open air they wander through the house, read a book, look at the pictures, or, may be, sit down at the piano and strive to stifle the voice of conscience with the melody of the keys.

Those who come to Madame Restell live royally while in her palace. Never did duchess or empress have her palate coaxed by daintier dishes than those prepared in her *cuisine*. True, the price is exorbitant, but what is money when honor is at stake? What is a handful of gold to the magdalen whose betrayer can afford to spend it, or to the married lady who is willing to pay for her folly?

The convictions for the crime of abortion have been few and far between, and there is no crime on the calendar that has caused so much misery and suffering. Notwithstanding the risks incurred by these inhuman butchers and their victims, certain papers daily insert advertisements directing unfortunates where they may be relieved of their difficulties. The people principally engaged in this nefarious, odious business, are a sordid, cruel horde of wretches of both sexes, who have become so hardened that they are as destitute of pity as so many wolves.

MADAME RESTELL.

The first important conviction in New York for performing an abortion was in the case of Mrs. Ann Lohman, *alias* Madame Restell, who has to-day a world wide notoriety.

Madame Restell began life as a dressmaker in Greenwich street. She was very clever with her needle, which enabled her to earn a

respectable livelihood.   Being handsome, and of more than ordinary intelligence, she eagerly sought any opportunity that offered
which would enable her to travel abroad.   Accompanying a family
to Paris as governess, she became intoxicated with the gaieties of
the French capital and was loth to return to America.   While
there she became acquainted with a woman who was quite successful in the sale of certain nostrums, of which she alone possessed
the secret of their ingredients.   Restell induced her to come to this
city, and they soon reaped a harvest.   Madame Restell married one
Lohman, a journeyman printer, and one day she informed him that
he need never work again.   This state of affairs was not at all
pleasing to her newly married husband, but he gradually accepted
the situation and became her consort.   Her French partner died in
a few years, bequeathing to her the recipe for the golden pills which
have reaped so many golden dollars.   Madame Restell experienced
no difficulties in carrying on her business.   She soon became a
skilful anatomist, and her services were constantly in demand.

Prior to the year 1847 she had her office in the lower part of
the city, below Cortlandt, in Greenwich street, where she dispensed
her medicines and "assisted ladies in trouble."   The feelings of the
community were greatly outraged by the boldness with which she
prosecuted her nefarious calling, and when at length it was discovered that one of her unfortunate victims lay at the point of death,
in consequence of the treatment experienced at her hands, the indignation of the people could not be restained, and the clamor for
her arrest and punishment was irresistible.

The subject of her malpractice was a young girl, Maria Bodine,
who had been employed in a factory in Orange County, and had
been seduced by her employer, Joseph P. Cook, who, to save himself from any unpleasant consequences, as well as to hide the girl's
shame, sent her to Mme. Restell for treatment.   The desired operation was performed and the girl returned to her country home,
where she was taken seriously ill.   The doctor who was called in
to attend her discovered the cause of her trouble, and on the
patient being told that the chances of her life being spared were
nearly hopeless, she confessed all.

Word was at once despatched to this city, a complaint of malpractice having been entered by the girl's friends, and after a little

while the abortionist was arrested at her residence and remanded to the Tombs, there to await her trial.

Being possessed of considerable means, it was feared by the citizens that she would escape a just punishment for her crimes. Ogden Hoffman, who at that time enjoyed considerable celebrity as a criminal lawyer was engaged to assist in the prosecution.

DAVID GRAHAM.

At the trial, which lasted for eighteen days, and occasioned no little excitement, Mme. Restell was ably defended by the late James T. Brady and David Graham, who spared no pains or exertions to secure her acquittal. The case was opened by Jonas B. Phillips, Esq., Assistant District Attorney; after having briefly presented the main facts in the case, he ended by saying: "The heart sickens at such a narrative, Nature is appalled that woman, the last and fairest of her works, could so unsex herself as to perpetrate such fiend-like enormities. The gardener watches with jealous care the seed he casts into the fertile earth until it germs, and buds, and blooms in the consummated perfections of Nature's loveliness. But this defendant destroys the germ—she kills the unborn infant; endangers, if she does not destroy the mother's life, ruins her health, and all for the sake of the base lucre which she allures the frail or wicked who have fallen to pay her, in the vain hope that she can aid them to conceal their shame. It is for you, as jurors, husbands, fathers and brothers, to say whether these monstrous crimes are to continue; whether God's laws, and those enacted for your safety and protection, are to be violated with impunity. The community look to you for a fearless, firm and faithful discharge of your duty. In their behalf the progress of this cause will be watched with intense and anxious interest by your fellow citizens. A sacred and important responsibility has devolved upon you, the sworn conservators of their peace and their security."

The main witness for the prosecution was the young girl herself, who, owing to the tender nursing and skilled medical advice she had received, was spared to convict the abortionist. She came into court rescued, as it were, out of the very jaws of death, a wreck of a once beautiful, robust young woman. It was apparent that she was not a willing witness, for she appeared sorely distressed and seemed to keenly feel her disgrace and shame. From her tottering, feeble steps, as she approached the witness chair, it could be seen she was in a rapid decline of health. The agony pictured in the face of the unfortunate woman pierced the hearts of all present, eliciting the utmost sympathy, which went far towards convicting the prisoner. She told the story of her woes in a plain, straightforward manner, which moved the audience, in some cases, even to tears. It was the old, old story over again, of man's perfidy and woman's disgrace. Reluctantly she gave a history of her life down to the hour of her fall. Then followed a description of her trials and sufferings at the den of the abortionist. It was a tale of horror and agony, the terrible phases of which were graphically depicted; but the details cannot here be given, as they are sickening in the extreme. During the direct examination the witness was so overcome that she was compelled to leave the court room. Again and again she appeared to continue her testimony. Trying

as was this ordeal, it was nothing when compared with the treatment she received from the counsel for the defence. They pronounced her a prostitute from the beginning, and David Graham
attributed her present feeble condition to a long course of intemperance, a constant career of prostitution—which was the natural
consequence, not of any act of Madame Restell but of the manner of her life. The counsel spared neither the feelings of the
witness or the sensibilities of the crowded audience in denouncing
the character of Maria Bodine. In the midst of counsel's argument the witness again became overpowered by sickness, and was
obliged to be withdrawn from the stand by the attending officer.
It was with difficulty she was prevented from sinking to the floor.
The counsel for the defence never relented, so persistent were they
in their efforts to break down her testimony. The police officer
who had been detailed to watch Madame Restell's house testified
that he had followed the last witness from the house and ascertained her name and residence. The most eminent medical prac-
titioners testified to the fatal effects caused by abortions, and in
turn were rigidly cross-examined. The only witnesses for the defence were a half dozen village gossips, who attempted to prove
Madame Restell's victim an improper character from childhood.

Never was there a trial in this country in which there were such
revolting facts elicited as in this case, and it was a relief to all concerned when the last witness had finished. On the fifteenth day
James T. Brady, by previous agreement among all the counsel,
proceeded to address the court and jury on the part of the defence.

Mr. Brady was followed by District Attorney John McKeon on
behalf of the prosecution, after which David Graham, Jr., of counsel for the defence, followed for the prisoner. His argument consisted principally of points of law quoted from and supported by a
number of authorities in England and the United States. When,
on the seventeenth day of the trial, Ogden Hoffman arose to begin
his summing up argument for the prosecution, the court room
was crowded. The magnetism of this celebrated jurist reached
every person within the sound of his voice.

When Mr. Hoffman had concluded his address to the jury—one
of his grandest speeches—the conviction of the abortionist was a
foregone conclusion.

The deafening applause that greeted Mr. Hoffman struck terror 'to the prisoner.

The Recorder then charged the jury, who remained out but a short time, and returned with a verdict of guilty, whereat the audience manifested their approval. Her counsel made a motion for arrest of judgment, and proposed to argue it at once, but it was fixed for the following day—pending which the prisoner was committed to the Tombs, she having previously been out on bail. The following day the court room was again crowded to hear the sentence. About twelve o'clock Madame Restell was brought from the Tombs, and, accompanied by her husband, entered the court and took her usual seat at the table. She was elegantly dressed in a rich black silk gown, handsomely trimmed black velvet mantilla, white satin bonnet, and wore a large, heavy lace veil. She looked extremely pale, however, and was evidently anxious as to the result of the day's proceedings.

Mr. Graham then presented a bill of exceptions, which he was desirous the Court should sign. The District Attorney again moved for judgment, which was again opposed by Mr. Graham, but at the same time he intimated that he would withdraw his motion if the Court would direct the Sheriff to defer sending the accused to the island for twenty-four hours.

The Recorder answered, " I do not see why any difference should be made in this case. Every day some poor devil is brought up here and sent off to State Prison without ceremony, probably because he has no counsel. This woman is the same as any other woman convicted of a similar crime, and we can make no distinction. Mr. Clerk arraign the prisoner. She was sentenced to one year at hard labor at the Penitentiary on Blackwell's Island.

The author had the satisfaction of seeing her clad in the prison garb, when accompanying the Grand Jury on a tour of inspection of the prisons. One of the jurors, seeing that she wore a silk apron over her tow cloth frock, remarked (facetiously) to the Warden, Mr. Jacob Acker, " that he must be rather partial to her in allowing her thus to array herself in silks."

On her release from the island she resumed her business without let or hindrance. In 1850 she bought what was then a palatial mansion in Chambers street. It was furnished sumptuously and contained every convenience and accommodation for patients. Possessed of a matchless team of Cuban horses—one snow-white and the other coal black, with a comely six foot mulatto in gorgeous livery, she could be seen any fair day riding, with her husband at her side. Her removal to her magnificent dwelling on Fifth avenue, near Central Park, created great consternation among her neighbors. In the entire City of New York there is but one dwelling more stately than Madame Restell's, and that is the marble palace of A. T. Stewart. Her residence, which is nothing else than a private hospital, is furnished throughout in the most magnificent style. Here none but those who can pay for their accommodations find a refuge. Her prices are so exorbitant that none but the very wealthy seek her aid. Everything about the house and grounds is as quiet as the grave. Her patients, when approaching convalescence, walk in the high fenced grounds adjoining the house. She is never molested now. She is wealthy—and riches in Gotham, as elsewhere, covers a multitude of sins. Her advertisements appear every day, and patients come and go as they do to a water cure. Whether it is an unnatural mother or some rich man's darling, the world never hears of it. The law which prohibits procuring abortions is still on the statute book, but this woman has an immunity for her crimes vouchsafed to none other. It cannot be denied but that Madame Restell is very skilful in the trade which she has so long practiced. In fact, with her it has become an art, but the crime is just as much a crime.

By far the greatest evil is the innumerable quacks who infest every portion of the city. Thousands of human beings are murdered before they have seen the light of this world, and thousands upon thousands more of adults are irremediably ruined in constitution, health and happiness. So secretly are these crimes committed, and so craftily do the perpetrators inveigle their victims, that it is next to impossible to obtain evidence and witnesses. There are many facts known to the police authorities that cannot be given in this book—but could even the meagre outlines be given it would almost freeze the blood, if all the hideous facts were known. It is one of those subjects that the pulpit and the press are loth to discuss, hence there is little to deter the unscrupulous horde from carrying on their inhuman butchery. Those who are engaged in the business seldom if ever possess genuine medical diplomas. In most part they are persons who have been employed as nurses in hospitals, and, picking up here and there some fragments of knowledge, they undertake operations which are rarely successful in their results. Their offices are scantily and shabbily furnished, the only article of furniture being in most cases a dilapidated lounge and a sideboard containing bottles covered with mysterious labels. Very rarely do these people use their true names. Nearly all have one or more *aliases*. One fellow, who appends M. D. to his circulars, was recently a shoemaker. Suddenly he closed his shop, moved to another part of the town, and was metamorphosed into a "doctor." One was a barber, another was a blacksmith. Undoubtedly a large number of quacks in the country, as well as in the city, practice the same method, and thus the fools and their money are parted. There are others, however, who pursue a widely different course. They compound and prescribe the most dangerous drugs with reckless disregard of human suffering and life, and venture upon operations that are always hazardous. It is stated that $60,000 is paid annually in New York city for advertising the business of these murderers. There are papers that would not insert this class of advertisements at any price, but there are those who daily publish them without hindrance from any quarter.

It is only at long intervals that the public are startled by any revelations regarding the crimes of abortionists. Perhaps no case excited such a horrible sensation as that of the unfortunate girl, Alice Augusta Bowlsby, whose mutilated and disfigured remains were discovered cramped into a trunk which had been left by a truck driver at the Hudson River Railroad depot on the afternoon of August 26th, 1871. The truck bearing the trunk was followed by a *coupe* containing a woman, who, on alighting, procured a ticket for Chicago, and requested that the trunk be checked for that place. As there was no train until evening, the woman loitered around the depot, after having seen the trunk checked as she had requested. It was a fortunate coincidence for the ends of justice that the woman happened to have asked some questions of a bright little urchin, who was well known about the depot as a light "baggage smasher." Some time after the woman had left the depot, to which place she had no intention of returning, the baggage master turned over the trunk in the reckless way common to that class of officials. There was nothing about it to invite attention except that from it there came an intolerable stench. It required no effort to force open the trunk, as the lock was of the flimsiest quality. The first thing that met the baggage master's view was an ordinary quilt; removing this there was an old army blanket. Lifting up this the cause of the stench was discovered. Doubled up in the bottom of this small frail trunk was the body of a full grown woman, and a sadder sight has seldom been presented, even in the darkest phases of metropolitan life. It was a most revolting picture. This young woman, full five feet in height, had been crammed into a trunk two feet six inches long and eighteen inches deep. She had been put in on her right side, the legs doubled up, and the head bent forward so that the face and knees almost met. Seen even in this position, and rigid in death, the young woman had a face of singular loveliness. But her chief beauty was her great profusion of golden hair, that hung in heavy folds over her shoulders, partly shrouded the face, and lay in heavy masses upon her bosom. She was quite slender, and the hands gave evidence that she had toiled. There was no mark of violence upon the body, although there was some discoloration and decomposition about the pelvic region. It was apparent that this was "one more unfortunate," who had risked death rather than exposure.

Had it not been that the boy before alluded to had happened to notice the name of the driver of the truck, there would undoubtedly never have been any clue by which the guilty parties could have been detected. The boy gave the name of the driver as Tripp. It turned out that he was wrong in the name, but nevertheless he was taken around the city in a hack under the surveillance of an Inspector of Police. The search proved fruitless, as every driver by the name of Tripp or Trapp established his innocence of any participation in the affair. While the search was being continued the driver, named Pickett, gave himself up to the police and furnished all the information which led to the arrest of the perpetrator. It turned out that the driver was entirely innocent of the business in which he had unwittingly engaged. His

ROSENZSWEIG.

story was that about noon a woman came to his stand and engaged him to take a trunk from 687 Second avenue—that he
performed the service and received his pay. The house was
immediately "shadowed" by a police official in citizen's attire,
accompanied by the driver. While waiting across the street the
miscreant that was wanted was seen to enter a liquor store near his
house, and it was then that he was seized. It was well for the
prisoner that his captor was reinforced, for, had it been otherwise,
he would have been killed by the infuriated crowd that surrounded
him. The officers, to resist the fury of the citizens, were compelled
to draw their revolvers. The prisoner was identified by the police
as " Dr. Ascher, *alias* Rosenzsweig," who for several years had carried on his nefarious business without molestation ; a coarse, fat,
and sensual looking fellow, without any traces of refinement in
person or manners, his very appearance was against him. One by
one his victims appeared at the District Attorney's office to give
information against the wretch. In the meantime the police were
making the most untiring efforts to discover the identity of his
latest victim. The house was searched from cellar to garret, but
the only clue to the mystery was the discovery in a corner of the
cellar of a pile of rubbish, under which was concealed some bloody
rags, portions of an old petticoat and the half of a chemise. This
last was seized as a valuable atom of evidence. It was of fine
quality, and a determined effort had been made to destroy both its
identity and the blood stains upon it. The latter had been attempted by partial washing, with the usual result of spreading the
stains evenly through the fabric, and the destruction of the identity
had been sought by tearing the chemise into parts, only one of
which had been left in this spot. This portion had been torn from
the yoke and one of the arm-holes, but the sleeve had been
wrenched out, as the ragged edges plainly showed, with sudden
violence. With the bloody rags and petticoat the chemise was
wrapped up and taken to the Station House—nor did this bundle
contain all the evidence carried away from the house. Among the
papers in the drawer was a scrap on which was written, " Ladies
cured, with or without medicine, by Dr. Ascher, Amity place,"
thus conclusively proving the identity of Rosenzsweig with Ascher.
Link after link was furnished in the chain of evidence until,

on the 30th of August, a physician and a dentist from Paterson,
N. J., went to the Morgue and there identified the remains as those
of Miss Alice Augusta Bowlsby.   Finally the chain of evidence was
made complete by the finding in a wash tub, at the house of
Rosenzsweig on Second avenue, a linen hem stitched handkerchief, on the corner of which, by the aid of a magnifying glass, the
initials A. A. B. were discovered.

ALICE AUGUSTA BOWLSBY.

In the city of Paterson, where the unfortunate woman was well
known, there was great excitement occasioned by the suicide of
Walter F. Conklin, which occurred but a few days after the remains were identified as being those of Miss Bowlsby. It appears
that Conklin had been keeping company with Miss Bowlsby for
some time.   He was employed in a mill, and finding that his connection with Miss Bowlsby was the only topic of conversation, he

shot himself in the head with a revolver, and his remains were found near the desk of his office. The following lines, written on a piece of paper, were taken from the pocket of his vest:

" I have long had a morbid idea of the worthlessness of life, and now, to be obliged to testify in this affair, and cause unpleasantness in my family, is more than life is worth. Good-bye, dear father, mother, brother and sister. (Signed), WALT."

Rosenzsweig was tried in the General Sessions, before Recorder Hackett, in October, 1871, for causing the death of Alice Augusta Bowlsby by medical malpractice. The evidence against him was conclusive and he was found guilty. He winced considerably under the indignant denunciation contained in the Recorder's sentence, which was that he should be confined in the State Prison at hard labor for the period of seven years. The prosecution was conducted by District Attorney Garvin, the prisoner being defended by Counsellor W. F. Howe. Rosenzsweig was sent to Sing Sing, but was afterwards transferred to Auburn Prison. Through a technicality in his trial Rosenzsweig was subsequently brought to New York for another trial, pending which he was discharged on account of a flaw in the new indictment.

CHAPTER XXXII.

MURDER IN THE TRIBUNE OFFICE—THE RICHARDSON–McFARLAND
TRAGEDY—ABBY SAGE RICHARDSON'S SAD HISTORY—THE WEDDING
AT THE ASTOR HOUSE—HENRY WARD BEECHER—MARRIAGE CERE-
MONY—"SO LONG AS YOU TWO BOTH DO LIVE"—DEATH AS A
DIVORCE LAWYER—TRIAL OF McFARLAND—"NOT GUILTY."

"Ill-assorted couple, unhappy in themselves and in each other, bound together
by no tie but the manacle that bound their fettered hands, and straining that so
harshly, in their shrinking asunder, that it wore and chafed to the bone."

DICKENS, *Dombey & Son.*

THE flash of McFarland's pistol lit up luridly the surface of the
social sea, and showed the public whither they were drifting.
The marriage at the Astor House between the dying Richardson
and Abby Sage McFarland was the second act in the drama of the
period; the trial and acquittal of McFarland, the last. And from
the time the report of the revolver rang through the *Tribune*
office until the moment the court-room was hushed to hear the
"not guilty" of the foreman of the jury, all of society watched
the affair eagerly, for all of society knew that there was more
than the life of a man at stake; that the murder and trial were
not accidental events that were likely to have occurred at any
time, but that they were outgrowing incidents of this progressive
modern age. Men, with handsome wives who had a taste for
literature and literary society not shared by their husbands,
thought and said that McFarland did right. The wives of these
men, remembering their own unhappy condition, and with their
heart yearning for an affinity, hoped he would be hanged. In
fact, all of the world that reads the newspapers made the McFarland trial a subject of endless argument. Every tea-table was a
battle-ground.

There is to this day, and we are glad that there is, a veil of
doubt and mystery over the love-life of Abby Sage and the
murdered journalist. Into such matters no one has a right to
pry save the injured party. But we recognize, nevertheless,

viewing the subject simply from a platonic stand-point, that theirs was a friendship typical of the tendency of the day. It is quite as typical as the shyster divorce lawyer of Chicago. It shows us that the matrimonial map has changed since our grand-mammas were wed ; that what was then a solemn life-drama is now too frequently a French comedy; that the wedding-ring differs but little from other jewelry; and that the marriage-certificate is too often vaulted through after the style of the young lady in pink tights who does the balloon business in the circus.

It would be well if the terms husband and wife were always synonymous with sweetheart. In times past they were either more so, or the scandal that arose from any disturbance of matri-monial felicity did not attain the blatant voice it now possesses. We recognize, in looking down the centuries, it is true, the fact that people of high degree—kings, queens, dukes, and duchesses —were not over-properly behaved. But then they are always privileged people. " A king can do no wrong " is an axiom, and the Prince of Wales has extensively demonstrated it already. Nowadays, however, lapses from virtue are not confined to royal circles. Common people eat plentifully of the forbidden fruit, and are turned out of their Edens.

Some said there was an excuse for Mrs. McFarland, acting as she did. Having an uncongenial husband, one whom she con-sidered cruel and overbearing, her womanhood cried aloud for sympathy. Chance threw her in the way of Richardson, whose nature had the fine chivalric tone of a Sidney. He saw a chance to befriend a woman in distress, and he did so. The rest was a natural gradation of events up to the time that Death acted as his groomsman, and then blew out the candle of his life.

THE MURDER.

On the afternoon of the 25th of November, 1869, Daniel McFar-land, then occupying the position of Assistant Assessor in the city of New York, walked into the counting-room of the New York *Tribune*, situated at the corner of Spruce and Nassau streets. It was fifteen minutes past 5 o'clock. Walking to the end of the counter, he passed behind it and took a seat upon a stool that happened to be there. Mr. Geo. M. King, a clerk in the employ of the *Tribune*, was present in the room, and was occupied in writing within a few feet of McFarland. There were several others engaged in their various duties, but none were prepared for the terrible tragedy so soon to be enacted within the usually quiet counting-room, and nothing in the action of McFarland betrayed a design on his part to lie in wait for his victim; at least no such

TRIBUNE OFFICE TRAGEDY.

purpose was apparent to those present. Everything was moving on as usual; one gentleman called to look over the newspaper-file, another to purchase the morning issue, and the clerks were busily assorting the mail.

About ten minutes after McFarland entered the office the Spruce-street door opened, and Albert D. Richardson, journalist, came into the room. He went straight across the office to the desk at the other end of the counter, and inquired for his letters. On the instant McFarland rose, pistol in hand, leaned half across King, and fired at Richardson. The latter turned just in time to recognize his assassin, and then staggered up against the counter from the effects of the shot. McFarland either ran around the counter or jumped over it, and disappeared. Richardson walked out of the door, up the stairs to the editorial rooms on the fourth floor, and lay down upon a lounge. Dr. Swan, of the Astor House, was sent for. He probed for the ball, and then directed that the wounded man be taken over to the hotel. It was done, Richardson being taken to the Astor House upon a litter. He was placed in room No. 115.

McFarland was arrested at 10 o'clock that evening in room No. 31, Westmoreland Hotel, corner Seventeenth street and Fourth avenue. When told of the shooting he displayed great agitation, denied it, and then said, " It must have been me." Capt. Anthony J. Allaire, of the Fourth Police Precinct, the officer who arrested him, took his prisoner to room No. 115 at the Astor House, and asked Richardson if this was the man who shot him. Richardson looked at him a second, and said : " That is the man."

The shooting, as will appear in our account of the trial, and as we have already intimated in our introductory remarks, grew out of the unpleasantness which is always produced by two men battling for the same woman. Abby Sage McFarland was the lawful wife of Daniel McFarland. Becoming acquainted with Richardson, she fell in love with him, her love growing more fervid in that direction in the direct proportion of its cooling in the other. Eventually she left her husband and went to live in the same house with Richardson. Then it was that she made up her mind to procure a divorce, which she did in Indiana. So that it happened that when Richardson lay dying at the Astor House, Mrs. McFarland was in a legal condition to marry. It was resolved by herself and by her friends, and in accordance with the request of the wounded man, that the marriage should take place. On November 30, 1869, five days after the shooting, it did take place. The Rev. Henry Ward Beecher and the Rev. O. B. Frothingham together tied the nuptial knot, while Death stood by as a witness.

The Hon. Horace Greeley and several of Mrs. McFarland's lady friends and advisers were also witnesses to the strange and solemn ceremony.

On the night of the 2d of December, 1869, the witness—Death —claimed his own. There were present Colonel T. H. Knox, Mr. Junius Henri Browne, Mrs. Sage (mother of the bride), Dr. Carter, and Dr. Swan.

Such is a plain matter-of-fact narrative of the shooting, the arrest, the marriage, and the death. What led to this tragedy cannot be told in a few words, but can be gathered from the facts brought out on the trial, which was certainly one of the most remarkable that ever took place in this country. We shall give a full and interesting synopsis further on. But as a simple act of justice, prompted by a chivalric spirit which dictates that a lady should be heard first in any case that concerns her honor, we produce here the sworn statement of Mrs. Abby Sage Richardson. Let it be read carefully, for it is the cry from the heart of a woman who was either one of the most erring of her sex, or the most unjustly injured :—

MRS. RICHARDSON'S STATEMENT.

I feel that I cannot break the silence which heretofore I have rigidly maintained without saying a word as to the cause which leads me to make a public statement. I fully believe that any one of any degree of pride or delicacy will bear reproach and contumely, and even the vilest slanders, in silence, rather than drag out to public comment the most sacred details of his inner life, and that only the meanest soul will babble of that which concerns itself most deeply. But during the last six months, and not a little during the last three years, I have been exposed to such a storm of public opinion, that all others I ever knew sink into insignificance beside it. And now, after I have waited in patience the verdict of newspapers, of the public, and of a New York court and jury, I have decided that I will speak the first and last word I shall ever speak for myself.

Not for any attempt at my own vindication do I write this explanation. But for the sake of the noble men and women who have stood by me through all revilings, often without any explanation from me, and always in the full faith that I was most cruelly wronged; for their sakes, and for his who lost his life in my behalf, I wish to tell the whole story of my life. When I was once advised to do so and hesitated, a good woman said to me, "Do not be afraid to tell your story once to all the world. Tell it once exactly as you would tell it to your Maker, and then keep silence forever after."

And this is what I mean to do ; to write as exactly as I can the whole and simple truth to the minutest details, reserving nothing and extenuating nothing. In doing this, I neither ask nor expect sympathy or justice from the press or public. I do not hope to convince any who are not already convinced that I have been most ungenerously traduced. Once I should have believed of the public press of America that it would be only necessary for it to *know* the truth to speak it, especially where a woman was involved. Now bitter experience has taught me

A. D. RICHARDSON.

that political prejudice, personal malice, and private vengeance are motives before which chivalry and pity and generosity, or a desire to be true, go to the wall.

So it is to my friends I write this. To but very few of them have I ever told my story. To a very sacred few have my lips been unsealed. And to the host of generous men and women, known and unknown, who have upborne me when the way was very dark and hard for a woman's feet to tread—above all, to the women, brave and noble beyond expression, whose sympathy has forever refuted the slander that women are not generous to one of their own sex—to them I lay bare my heart. Of all my women friends from earliest girlhood, I know of not one who has fallen off from me in my great trouble—not a single one. If it had not been for their unswerving trust and love and sympathy ; for the readiness they have shown to help me bear up my heavy burdens ; for the bravery with which they have defended me, where it was a reproach to do so— if it had not been for them I believe I should have been utterly crushed. I have accepted their loving sympathy as the one compensation for all the unspeakable misery of my lot. Having said thus much, which was in my heart and could not be kept back, I begin my story.

I married Daniel McFarland in 1857. I was a girl of 19, born in Massachusetts, and educated in New England schools. I had been a teacher, and was just beginning to write a little for the press. Daniel McFarland was an Irishman of 37 or 38, who had received a partial course at Dartmouth College, and had, seven years before I knew him, been admitted to the Massachusetts bar. When I married him, he represented himself to be a member of the bar in Madison, Wisconsin, with a flourishing law practice, brilliant political prospects, and possessed of property to the amount of $20,000 to $30,000. He also professed to be a man of temperate habits, of the purest morals, and, previous to my marriage, appeared neither intemperate, nor brutal, nor profane.

Immediately after our marriage we made some visits and then went to Madison, as I supposed, to reside permanently. I remember we were detained in New York during our very bridal-tour while he borrowed the money to get back to the West. After we had been in Madison a few weeks, Mr. McFarland informed me that he was going to remove to New York ; that all his property consisted of Wisconsin State lands to the amount of a good many thousand acres, on which only a small amount per acre was paid. He told me that there were large opportunities for trading these lands in New York City, and that he was going to reside there while he disposed of them for real estate or personal property. He told me at the same time that he had no money except just sufficient to pay our fares to the East, and that he never had any law practice of consequence, having devoted himself solely to land speculations in the West.

We came to New York, consequently, in February, 1858. I was taken ill on the way with a violent cold and fever, and we were detained in Rochester ten days. On leaving Rochester he had to leave his watch and chain in pawn with the hotel-keeper for our board-bill. In New York City he kept me three or four weeks, and then, taking all the jewelry I had to the pawnbroker's, to pay the board-bill, he sent me home to my father's in New Hampshire. I simply tell these things to give some idea of how they must have affected a young girl fresh from a comfortable New England country home, to whom a pawnbroker's shop was almost an unheard-of institution, and not to convey the idea that it was his poverty which shocked or estranged me.

I went home then in less than three months after marriage. He gave me no directions where to write him, and for fourteen days I never heard from him.

Nearly beside myself from anxiety, I went to New Haven, and from thence telegraphed to a friend of his in New York for news of him. He appeared in two or three days in answer to the telegram. Then, for the first time, I had a vague suspicion that he might be intemperate. But I knew nothing about intemperance. I had never in all my life seen a man drunk, except some accidental drunkard in the street, and I tried to dismiss the suspicion. In a week or two I again went back to my father's, and remained through the summer of 1858. During this time he came once or twice to visit me, and seemed to be attached to me. But during the short time I had lived with him, I discovered that he was not temperate (although I had not then seen him *grossly* intoxicated); that he was terribly profane in my presence, and that his temper was very fitful and passionate; and that for some slight or fanciful causes he would become sullen and morose, not speaking to me for a day or two. I did not leave my father's roof in the fall of 1858 without many misgivings; but I was very young and very cheerful in disposition, and hoped for the best.

On returning to New York Mr. McFarland hired a cottage in Brooklyn, and furnished two or three rooms. For a few weeks I kept a servant, but otherwise I lived all alone, almost without acquaintances, and entirely at this man's mercy. Some of the time—perhaps half of the time—he was good to me, and professed for me the most extravagant and passionate devotion. But he here first began to come home intoxicated. He would also come home sober, bringing with him bottles called " Schiedam Schnapps," containing a quart or so of vile liquor, and would put them by his bedside, and drink sometimes the whole before morning. When I begged him not do this, he said " his brain was on fire," and this made him sleep. This is the first time he began to tell me about his " brain being on fire," which was a favorite expression with him after he had been drinking, and to which so many people have testified to his using, on the recent trial for his life. As this was only two or three months before my first child was born, and all my senses were nervously acute, and as I was also, as I believe, a woman of refined taste and feeling, his breath and whole body steaming with the vile liquor which he drank during these nights while I lay awake beside him, made him very odious to me, so that before I had been married to him a year my affection for him was very much chilled, I might say nearly destroyed. During this fall of 1858 he had made two or three trades of his Wisconsin lands for real estate, and had made what he called excellent bargains. But during all the time I was oppressed always by want of money, and with great difficulty got a scanty wardrobe for my baby, which was born in December, 1858.

In November my sister came to visit me, and then I sent away my servant, and we did the housework. During her visit Mr. McFarland took her to a *matinée* at the theatre; left her and returned at the close of the *matinée* grossly intoxicated; made love to her in his drunken foolishness, and frightened her exceedingly. When I reproached him with this conduct he swore he would never drink again, and drew up a written pledge to that effect, which he kept apparently several months. At Christmas-time my baby was born, my mother coming on to nurse me, and early in the spring I went home again. My baby died at my father's, and was buried in our family burial-place, my father bearing the funeral expenses. In July of 1859 I returned again to Mr. McFarland.

I remained with him this time about three months. My heart was sorely bruised by the death of my baby, and I was less able to bear up under the brutality and violence of Mr. McFarland's temper. I will not enter into the details of his treatment of me during these three months; but it was so bad that I went back to my father's in October, 1859, and remained almost a year, till August, 1860. At this time, in October, 1859, when I returned home, if I had had courage to have told my mother and father of my troubled life, I should probably never have returned to this man. But I could not speak. It was so hard a thing to tell. My idea of a wife's duty was most conservative. I believed she should suffer almost unto death rather than resist the laws of marriage. I had a conscience sensitive to any appeal against itself, and I tried hard to love my husband and convince myself I was in the wrong. Besides, I was expecting, in a few months, the birth of another child. No one shall say I mean this narrative as an appeal to sympathy; but those who believe in my truth must see my case was hard, and realize somewhat the suffering I endured.

In April, 1860, my second child, Percy, was born. While at home during these ten months Mr. McFarland had represented to me that he was doing exceedingly well in business, and had made large trades for real estate to the amount of many thousand dollars. One of these pieces of property was in Greenwich street, and was mortgaged to Trinity Church for $10,000, and afterward sold to recover judgment against him for $10,800. The other property was in East Fourteenth street, near the river, a block of tenement-houses, which I am inclined to believe were mortgaged pretty nearly up to their whole value. At all events, I lived at my father's during this year, which he describes as the "year of his prosperity," and did not share in it. Part of this time, for the first and only time in my married life, I paid a very small sum for my board, which was all I ever paid in my long and repeated visits to my father's house. I mention this because Mr. McFarland claims to have supported me while at my home. Two of my children were born at home, and the expenses came principally on my father, although at the birth of my youngest child I paid my physician's bill myself with the results of a public reading which I gave for that purpose.

In 1860, after I returned to Mr. McFarland, a suit was brought against him by some one in Wisconsin for money, which was, as I believe, the borrowed capital with which his Western lands had been purchased. This suit was decided against him by Judge Leonard, of New York City. While it was pending Mr. McFarland ordered me to pack up my trunks and be ready to leave the city, as he might at any time be arrested and prevented from leaving the State. So again in December, 1860, I was sent back to my father's with my baby now six months old. Mr. McFarland soon followed me there, and he stayed till February, when he told me again to get ready and go away with him. He had at this time $1,200, which was the largest amount of money I ever knew him to have at any time, and which he said he had got from the sale of a piece of property, put out of his hands at the time judgment was obtained against him. With this he started with myself and Percy for Philadelphia, where he left me, saying he was going on to Washington to seek office under Lincoln's incoming administration. In a few weeks he returned and told me he was going West again, as he was disappointed in his political expectation. So we went West in the spring of 1861, just as the

Southern guns were opened on Fort Sumter. We went back to Madison, where we had lived previously, took a small house, and went to housekeeping. We lived here a year and two months, and this was the happiest time of my life with him, although I did my own housework most of the time and took care of my baby. But I was so thoroughly weary of the terrible vagabondish life I had always lived with this man, that under almost any condition a home I could call *mine* seemed delightful to me. Mr. McFarland never did any work while in Madison, or earned any money. I lived with extreme economy, and he had $800 or $900 left when he reached Madison, which, with the addition of $200 or $300 more which he received from the sale of a tract of land which he owned somewhere, bought the furniture for our little house and supported us for the fourteen months we lived there. At the expiration of this time Mr. McFarland began to grow more and more morose and ill-tempered, and told me finally he was getting out of money and had no way of getting any. He endeavored to get a public office of some kind in Madison, but was not supported even by those on whom he counted as his friends. I had attracted some attention in private circles by my reading, and had given a public reading for the benefit of a soldier's hospital. On this Mr. McFarland proposed to me that he should take me to New York and have me fitted for the stage in the profession of an actress. He also announced that he should himself adopt the profession of an actor in case my success became assured. He had been at some time a teacher of elocution in a military school in Maryland, and he began training me in the reading of stage parts.

In June, 1861, he sold all our little furniture in Madison, and brought me East, first going to father's, in New Hampshire, to leave my little Percy, so that I could devote all my time to the stage. He made no secret of this to my parents, who did not approve of this step on his part, but did not interpose, on the conservative Puritan ground that even the parents have no right to interfere in the affairs of husband and wife. We went to New York, boarding first on Beach street, and afterward with Mrs. Oliver, at 58 Varick street, in the same vicinity. As soon as we were settled in the first of the places, Mr. McFarland began drilling me for the stage, which, I may say here, was the first and only instruction of any kind whatsoever he ever gave me; and he also sent me to take lessons of Mr. and Mrs. Geo. Vandenhoff, to be fitted for the stage. I also began to give readings this fall, and paid our board during the fall and winter with my own earnings. At Christmas of 1862, I was so anxious to have Percy with me, and I felt so hopeful of doing well during the winter with the dramatic readings which I had begun, that I sent Mr. McFarland on to New Hampshire to get Percy, who had been all this time at my father's. On this occasion Mr. McFarland took with him all the little stock of jewels I possessed—my rings, brooches, watch and chain (which had by this time been so frequently pawned and repawned that I did not care for them)—and sold them all in Boston. These were the last jewels I ever possessed, except a plain gold ring, which is the wedding-ring placed on my hand by my dead husband.

Mr. McFarland was unspeakably cruel to me this fall and winter of 1862 and 1863, while we boarded at No. 58 Varick street. We occupied the only sleeping apartment on the parlor floor, and he could give full scope to his furies without fear of being overheard. I was all the time working hard to study for the profession for which he had designed me, and to make a success in dramatic readings, by which I was supporting both him and myself. I was still very young and very proud and reticent. I had a most unusual cheerfulness and elasticity of temper, or I never should have lived through so heavy trials. He would lock himself into the room with me, and give way to such terrible furies that only the extremest pride and self-control prevented me from making my misery known. He brought home what he professed was prussic acid, and threatened to take it and to force me to take it. He would snatch my scissors from my work-basket, and, tearing open his breast, he would brandish them about, swearing he would "let out his heart's blood" before me. He told me (then a shrinking girl) that he kept loaded pistols, with which he would at any moment shoot me. He left me one evening, declaring he should shoot a gentleman because he had invited me to join himself and wife and another lady in a party to some public picture-gallery, although I had the most general acquaintance with the party and refused the invitation as soon as made. He rarely professed to be jealous of me, however. My conduct gave him no shadow of a cause. I owe it to myself to say that, in my long and painful life, I have seen many happy women, shielded by home, by loving and good husbands, and all that protects and guards a woman's honor, and that never have I seen one thus guarded and cherished who was more faithful to her wedded vows than I was to the unhappy marriage relation in which I lived, under the protection of a drunken and brutal master, and obliged again and again to leave the boarding-houses I called homes to earn the means to pay for their shelter. So much I shall say, even at the risk of seeming over-bold in saying so. And in all my journeys away from Mr. McFarland, when I went alone to read in public, my prudence protected me even from gallantry or compliment, and I made my success among the best and most conservative audiences.

One morning during this winter which I am now describing, after Mr. McFarland had been out nearly all night in a drunken orgie and had risen from bed in one of his worst tempers, I approached him as he stood by the mirror finishing his toilet, and began to say something soothing to prevent the outburst of ill-temper which I feared was soon coming. He turned round and struck me a blow across my face which made me reel backward. Although he had often pinched and bit me in some of his fits of drunkenness, he had never before struck me so cruel and cold-blooded a blow. I felt as I shall never forget it. I think an American woman does not easily forgive a blow like that. At all events, I remember I said to him, without raising my voice, "I shall never be able to forgive you such an outrage," and I think I never could forgive it. From that time I took an entirely different course with him when in one of these furies. I had shed a great many tears under his cruelty, had tried to reason with him, had tried entreaties and persuasions. After this, whenever he was in one of his paroxysms—as he himself called them—I never moved or spoke, but, keeping perfectly self-controlled as far as I could, I sat quiet, always keeping my eye on him, because I always fancied as long as I looked steadily at him he would not do me any mortal violence. And I believe now, as I believed then, that my life has been saved by this silence and self-control. He has sometimes approached me with his hands extended, the fingers bent like claws, as if he were about to clutch my throat, and cried, "How I should like—*like* to strangle you." Or, "Your life is bound some time to end in tragedy." Or, "Your blood will be on your own head," and has, as I think, been restrained because I simply looked at him without saying a word.

In these furies he would often seize and break anything which was at hand —lamps, glasses, mirrors, and sometimes the heavier furniture of the 100m. Often he would rise from bed in these uncontrollable attacks of passion, tearing away all the bed-clothing, tearing in shreds his own night-clothing, throwing anything he could find which was breakable crashing about the unlighted room, till it had seemed to me as if there could be no Pandemonium worse than that in which I lived. And all this he would do without explanation, or even a pretext for complaint against me, and when I knew no more what excited his frenzy than a babe unborn.

He would sometimes keep up this conduct and this abuse for hours, without a syllable or a motion being made on my part, and would then burst into tears, beg my pardon, say I was the best woman who ever lived, and then go to sleep exhausted. I never told him after this winter that I could forgive or could love him, although he sometimes implored me to do so, because I could not say so with truth. Generally I told him I pitied him, which was true. Sometimes he said, "Your d—d silence irritates me more than if you talked;" but I was sure my course was the best.

At the time he struck me this severe blow, in 1862, I told Mrs. John F. Cleveland (a sister of Mr. Greeley, who had been very kind to me in my dramatic readings) about the blow, and something of Mr. McFarland's conduct to me. I did not tell her all, nor the worst, but I told her how he had struck me, principally because I was engaged to read at the house of some friends of hers an evening or two after, and I feared she would notice the mark on my face. She was the only person to whom I ever spoke of Mr. McFarland (otherwise than in a manner becoming for a wife to speak of a husband) till the winter of 1867. And I devoted all my woman's skill and tact in hiding his conduct from casual observers at our boarding-houses or elsewhere.

In the spring of 1863, Mr. McFarland got appointed to a position in the office of one of the Provost-Marshals, under the Enrollment act. I went to see Mr. Greeley in company with his sister, Mrs. Cleveland, and also to see several other persons, to get influence for Mr. McFarland. In doing so, I acted under Mr. McFarland's orders, and against my own feelings, which always revolted at the idea of seeking office for him, though he never scrupled to use my efforts. As soon as he got this office I ceased my reading in public and my preparations for the stage, and in the spring after he was appointed went home to my father's and remained a short time. Then McFarland summoned me to New York with Percy, who was ill at the time and hardly able to travel. I objected to leaving home, when he sent peremptorily, saying "he would burn my father's house over my head" if I did not come. I arrived in New York in August, and was there a few weeks when the physician said Percy would die if he were not sent back to the country, and I again returned to my father, and stayed until November. In November, 1863, I came back to New York. We took rooms for a

few weeks on Varick street, but soon removed, early in January, to No. 16 Lamartine Place, West Twenty-ninth street.

During the winter of 1862 and 1863 I had met Mrs. Sinclair often at her
cousin's, Mrs. Cleveland's, and she had shown me many and great kindnesses.
She had given me her parlors for one of my readings, and had sold the tickets
among my friends. At the time Mr. McFarland received his appointment in the
Provost-Marshal's office she used her influence and her husband's influence to
get him appointed. No person living has a stronger claim on the gratitude of
this unhappy man than the noble woman whose charity he has so abused. In
this winter of 1863 and 1864, while we lived in Lamartine Place, we were Mr. Sinclair's neighbors. One night while there, Mr. McFarland came home so bruised
and bleeding from some street broil—a not uncommon occurrence on his part—
that I was obliged to call on Mr. Sinclair for aid in getting him in bed. It was
only three or four weeks before the birth of my youngest child, or I should
not have done so. Then I kept Mr. McFarland in his room for more than a week,
carrying his meals to him myself, that his disgrace might not be seen and commented on by the household where we boarded.

From the time he got his place in the Enrollment Office in '63 until the fall of
'64, Mr. McFarland sent me home three times, and moved me to *eight* different
boarding-houses. If, for one moment, I was peaceful in the possession of a
shelter, his habits or his dissatisfied temper drove him to change. At last, in
the fall of 1864, Mr. Sinclair offered us, rent free, his unoccupied farm-house on
the Hudson River, and we moved there for the winter of 1864. During this
year my youngest boy, Danny, had been born on one of my visits to my father's
house. I stayed at Croton, in Mr. Sinclair's house, all winter, and during the summer, in a small tenement which we rented there, and which I furnished very cheaply
with $200, borrowed by Mr. McFarland from my father. Here Mr. McFarland's
conduct was more endurable, for he was away nearly all day, and the quiet and
pleasantness of the country, when he came there, I fancied had a good effect
on him. In the summer of '65, however, he lost his place under Government,
and seemed to make no further attempt to do anything. He informed me one
day that he was out of a place, and had no money. Then I told him I supposed
I should have to give public readings again. As usual, when I made such suggestions, he swore at me in his terrible way, but made no other answer. I went
on and made my arrangements to give dramatic readings ; gave several before
leaving Croton ; and then, with some of the money I had raised, I went to my
father's, who had now moved to Massachusetts, and from his house went away to
give several other readings in New England, leaving the children with mother.
At this time I paid the bill to the physician who attended me at Danny's birth,
now eighteen months old, which had been all this time unpaid. I also arranged
with Messrs. Hurd & Houghton, this fall, to print a little book for children,
called "Percy's Year of Rhymes," which I had written during the summer.
From Boston I went back to New York, to occupy some small rooms over a stable
in Thirty-sixth street, which Mr. McFarland had hired. This winter I made a
desperate struggle for life. I had my two babies—the youngest just weaned ; I
had this man, half of the time coming home intoxicated, and I had nothing but
my woman's heart and hands to look to for support. I gave all the readings I

could. I did all my own housework when at home. I took faithful care of my children, but I often sank into such utter despondency of heart as only God knows and can pity, when he sees the poor human soul sinking under it.

On one of these days Mrs. Sinclair came in. I had never said a word to her about my troubles, and she had been too delicate to broach the subject to me. When she went away she put a little paper in my hand, and after she had gone I found it was a $50 bank-note. Next morning came a letter from her enclosing another $50 note, which she said was a present from some other friends of mine. I confess I could not endure such a wound to my pride. I had been reared in comfort and plenty, and in my veins ran some of the proudest blood in Massachusetts. I knew not one of my kin had ever taken alms. I had to use some of the money sent me, for we were absolutely pinched with want at that moment; but the next week I sold all our furniture, which was bought with money borrowed of my father, and parted with many articles of comfort which had been sent to me from my home, and with the proceeds of the sales I was able to send back the money to Mrs. Sinclair, telling her I could not yet receive alms from my friends. But her indefatigable friendship did not cease here, and she sent me back much of it in clothes and other necessaries. Then in April, 1866, she and some other friends arranged a reading at Steinway's Rooms, on Fourteenth street, of which the proceeds were more than $150.

Mr. McFarland abused me in his usual violent way for giving this public reading at Steinway's. He argued that if I wanted to read I had better go out of town to do so; that it disgraced him as a gentleman in the eyes of the public for his wife to read in a city where he had acquaintances. He made this an excuse for getting grossly intoxicated on the evening of the reading, and collected the whole receipts of the evening, and gave me $25 out of the whole amount to pay my fare and the children's to my father's house in Massachusetts, reserving the rest for his own uses.

In May, 1866, Mr. McFarland came to my father's, bringing with him $1,000 in money. He had got this money from a wealthy owner of oil-lands in Pennsylvania, residing in New York City (whose name I do not like to mention), by threatening to expose him for some irregularity in paying his income-tax, and Mr. McFarland told me this man had given him the money if he "would not trouble him further." He also told me he had "several other men under his thumb in the same way." The manner of getting this money was inexpressibly shocking to me, and I told him so; and then I told him that I should try and make arrangements to go on the stage in the fall, that I could not try another winter of public reading, a profession so precarious and so wearing, and advised him, since he had some money—which I thought dishonorably obtained—he should go into business at once before he spent it. He answered in his usual brutal manner, and I said no more about it. It was agreed, however, that I should go to a small farm-house in the White Mountains, where I knew Mrs. Oliver Johnson was going to spend the summer, and that he should pay my board there—which was to be very cheap indeed—for myself and the children. In June, 1866, I went from my father's with the children to Shelburne, N. H., among the mountains. I remained there till September. During this summer he sent me $160 in a check signed by Mr. Sinclair, and I had $50 on arriving, which he had given me, making in all $210, with which I paid my board and washing bills for myself and the children, during my four months' stay in Shelburne. In September, Mr. McFarland came up to Shelburne himself, instead of waiting for me at my father's, as I had proposed. He told me little or nothing of his financial condition or prospects during the summer, and I had written advising him of various plans for earning his living. In the fall he told me that he had got out of money, and was going into some kind of patent-gas company, which I did not understand fully, and was going to make his fortune. He paid my fare to Boston, and then told me he was out of money, and asked me to go to H. O. Houghton & Co.'s, whom he knew were going to print my little book that fall, and see if I could get some money. I did do this, and got $50 while in Boston, where I stayed nearly a week. Mr. McFarland's niece, a daughter of his brother Owen, had been at the White Mountains with me, and was with me in Boston. After getting the money from Mr. Houghton, I gave McFarland half of it, and with $25 I went with Miss Mary McFarland to Newark, where her father lived. Owen McFarland was worse, if possible, in his fits of intemperance than his brother Daniel. I stayed there three weeks in scenes which would baffle description, often in daily or nightly fear of my life from this terrible madman, all of whose family held him in most supreme fear.

While here, in the winter of 1866, I had met Mrs. L. G. Calhoun, and during this summer at Shelburne I had corresponded with her. I have been most fortunate in my friendships; but I never knew any woman more loyal to affection, more overflowing with tenderness, more ready with healthful sympathy than she. My whole nature, usually reticent, went out to her in confidence and friendship, and I had written from the Mountains asking her aid in getting an engagement on the stage. She had succeeded in arranging an engagement at Winter Garden, the theatre which Mr. Edwin Booth controlled, and a place which we both considered particularly fortunate for a lady to be connected with, on account of Mr. Booth's position as a gentleman in private life, as well as his eminence in his profession.

This fall of 1866, while at Newark, I saw the manager of Winter Garden, and my engagement was made certain at a salary of $20 per week. I wrote this to Mr. McFarland, who still remained behind in Massachusetts and New Hampshire, and also wrote him that I could not and should not stay longer at his brother's. He came down to New York shortly after this, borrowing money in small sums of my father to pay his expenses back, and took me from his brother's and to a wretched boarding-house in Amity street, near Sixth Avenue. Here he borrowed some money of Mr. Sinclair, and gave me $25, which was the last money I ever received from him. This was in October, 1866. He left me at this house, informing me that he should probably not be back very much of the time during this winter.

Then I was so worn out by the anxieties and the terrible weeks I had spent at Newark that I broke down and was ill at this strange boarding-house, alone with my two babies. While here, Mrs. Calhoun called and found me in this condition, and, going home, she wrote a note in which she told me in the most delicate manner that whenever I wanted money her purse was at my service. The same day Mrs. Sinclair called, and, shocked at the wretched and desolate condition in which she saw me, took me and both my children to her house. As soon as I was there and had begun to recover, Mr. McFarland came back and made his preparations to come there also. As gently as I could I told him Mr. Sinclair's house was over-full, and if he were coming back to town I must get a place somewhere for all of us. It was then about two weeks before my engagement began at Winter Garden. Mr. McFarland instructed me that I might get board for myself and the children, but only occasional board for himself, as he should be absent about the gas-business most of the time. I then engaged board in Macdougal street, in a very respectable house, where I had a small attic room for all my family. As soon as I got here my health again gave way, and I was ill in bed nearly two weeks. It was only by sheer force of will that I got up from bed and dragged myself to the theatre to begin my engagement. During these two weeks' illness, Mrs. Sinclair and Mrs. Calhoun visited and ministered to me. Both of them sent me nourishing food from their own table, by their own servants. They sent me money, and gave me the lovingest sympathy that woman ever gave to woman. I had already got an engagement to write for *The Riverside Magazine,* and one day during this illness, when Mrs. Calhoun found me sitting up in bed, weak and exhausted, finishing a child story, with my two noisy little children playing at my bedside, she took it away, and interested the managing editor of *The Independent* in my work, so that he sent me word he would take some of my stories for his paper.

As soon as I went on the stage (this was the 28th of November, 1866) I told the woman in whose house I had been boarding about three weeks, of my new profession. She immediately told me that she could not possibly have an actress in her house, and I must get a new place as soon as convenient. As quickly as I could I found a new place at No. 86 Amity street, I went to No. 86 Amity street about the 16th or 17th of December, 1866. On the 20th of December I had an engagement to read at Salem, Mass., before the Lyceum Lecture Course. My mother had written us that if I would bring on one of the children she would take him and take care of him for an indefinite period, because she feared I had too much to do with the two children and all my other duties. So I concluded to take the youngest child, Danny, to my own home on this journey to Salem. I played at the theatre the night before starting for Massachusetts, and was obliged to sit up nearly all night to get myself and child ready. About 1 o'clock in the night McFarland came home in a state of beastly intoxication. He was past talking then; but toward daylight, while I was getting ready to take the morning train for Boston, I roused him, and told him I had been intending to take Danny home, but now I thought I would take both the children and leave them with mother till I could do something better, and come back and separate myself from him entirely; that I could not possibly work as I was doing and bear his habits any longer. On this he professed great penitence; begged me to try him once more; said he would do better if I would give him this one trial, etc., etc. I did not believe him, but I hardly knew what to do, and I finally went off with Danny to my mother's. This was the morning of the 19th. Read in Salem the 20th, returning to New York the 21st, and going to the theatre the same evening. At New Year's time I foolishly allowed McFarland to draw two weeks' salary from the theatre, which had been lying over because the money I had earned at

Salem paid the necessary board-bill, and he went again and got drunk, and remained so for two or three days. At this time I made up my mind I would do something. On the afternoon of January 2d, I wrote a long letter to Mrs. Calhoun, to whom, in all of my acquaintance, I had never spoken of McFarland except incidentally, telling her some of my troubles.

In this letter, which it cost me terrible pain and humiliation to write, because my habits of concealment were so natural and difficult to overcome, I glozed over some of the worst facts. I concealed the fact of his hopeless intemperance, and I tried, with all the humanity and justice which was in my nature, to speak most gently and impartially of the unfortunate man. The following is the exact copy of the first confidence I ever made to this loyal friend, of my anxieties and struggles :—

JAN. 2, 1867.

MY DARLING AND COMFORTER : I have seated myself with the intention of writing you a long, long letter; of telling you some things which I have never before told any one; but which, kept secret and brooded over, seem to eat out my heart and consume my life day by day. I was miserably unhappy yesterday, all the latter part of the day. Yesterday morning, after I had got all ready to go to Mrs. Sinclair's, after I had kissed Percy "good-by," and had my parcels in my arms ready to take them over, some little impatient words I said irritated Mr. McFarland, who is very sensitive and quick-tempered. It arose from my asking him to help me carry some of my bundles, and his resenting it, and our both getting a little bit angry. I did not say half as much as I hear women every day say to their husbands, without its being remembered on either side. I should not have remembered it one instant, but he does, and I went away without smoothing out the snarl. It was perhaps a little perverse, but I got *so* tired of constantly smoothing and coaxing. But all day I was nervous, when he did not call with Percy as he had promised, and I was very anxious. I could not get away in the evening without showing how uneasy I was, so I stayed. When I got home, I found Percy in bed, hugging up a book with which he had got himself asleep —alone. After an hour or two of agonizing waiting, waiting—listening for footsteps, and dreading to hear them—which are only a few of the *hundreds* of hours I have spent so—he came in, two-thirds intoxicated and very morose. I asked him why he could so spoil my day, and cause me so much unhappiness, and he answered that " I had treated him outrageously, and he should spend the New Year's as he chose."

Two weeks ago—the morning of the Tuesday before I went to Salem to read, you remember—I got utterly discouraged, and I said something, not reproachful, to Mr. McFarland about my feelings. One *cannot* always keep up, you know. There was no unkindness between us, only when I sink a little in hope he sinks in despair. That night he did not come home to dinner, and I was obliged to leave my babies when I went to the theatre, awake and alone. All the evening I was burning with anxiety to get home. He did not come for me, and I went home alone after I got through the play. I found him in a beastly slumber, from which I could not rouse him ; he had been drinking all day. I was to start that next morning for Massachusetts, and it made me almost crazy. Next morning he was in sackcloth and ashes for his conduct. He wept, and begged me to forgive him —not to tell my father and mother, and swore he would vindicate himself before me by a different life this year.

Dear, I try to write these things coldly and mechanically. I *want* to do so, so as not to be unjust, but I *must* write you. I feel I must let you know something of my inner life, and of the struggles that no one can see, or I shall die.

You know, my darling, when I was married I had not much experience of life, or judgment of character. When Mr. McFarland asked me to marry him, I said "yes," without proper deliberation. I was not in love with any one else; *everybody* got married, I thought, and I never questioned whether I was sufficiently in love or not. I *thought* I was, and did not reason. After I was married and began to know Mr. McFarland, I found him radical to the extreme in all ideas. He seemed to have many heartfelt schemes of philanthropy and lovely traits of character. He had beautiful theories, and he believed he acted on them, when he did not, and was often cruelly unjust to me and my motives. He was madly jealous of me from the first—a jealousy which seemed to me to have its root in a radical want of confidence in woman's virtue. A bachelor's experience had made him believe women were not always chaste, I think; but to me, who was chaste as ice and pure as snow, if ever woman were chaste, these things were *horrible* outrages. They struck the first blow at the tenderness I felt for him, which might have ripened into a real affection, I have no doubt.

This was the first shock; the second was the discovery that if anything annoyed him, if I was impatient or a little cross (as I think all women are at times, and I know my temper is naturally sunny), or if business cares oppressed him, or a hundred other annoyances which might trouble one, then, as a refuge from any of these, he would drink liquor, and come home under its influence.

I was bred in the New England idea of temperance, and this was to me a vice more odious than I can speak. I had for it little compassion. When Mr. McFarland came home thus, I loathed him with unspeakable loathing and disgust. I was living, when this first happened, in Brooklyn. I had not a single intimate friend in either city. I had no one to speak with from morning till night, and I was pregnant with my first baby, which made me very nervous and easily affected. What I suffered that first year, God only knows; what I suffered many hundred times since, He only knows; but it is enough to tell you that in a year the possibility of ever loving him was utterly extinguished.

This is an awful thing to say, dearest. To drag out for eight or ten years an existence with a man whose whole nature overflowed with passion, who by turn adored and abused you, and who wanted to absorb both body and soul, and to feel nothing but a feeling of pity. . . . .

I *want* to do Mr. McFarland justice, and I pity him more than I pity myself. His condition and his suffering are worse, perhaps. He had noble theories, and not strength enough to realize them. The mistakes that he made embittered and still embitter him. He meant his life to be noble, and it *is* a failure. I am glad and proud to say that for the last years he has ceased to be jealous of me or of my feeling toward any man. I should never be anything but a chaste woman in my relations with men; but his feeling has made me more than prudent, and I have been always *most* reserved. I have never had any sentiments so warm as friendship for other men, and my actions would bear the most jealous scrutiny.

After his affairs—his business affairs—had become hopelessly entangled (this was in the third year of our marriage), he insisted on returning West, where he had formerly lived. We stayed there for a time, and came back here again. The first year after our return home from the West, before he took the position in the Provost-Marshal's office, his habits were again dreadfully bad, and he drank in a way in which none of my friends mistrusted it. He would go out evenings and spend them in low bar-rooms, and come home at 2 or 3 o'clock in the morning reeking with liquor. Three times he has come home beaten and bruised. When he is drunk, all the good in him is turned to evil; he is simply and truly a fiend. Undisciplined in his temper in his best moments, he has then been dreadful.

My darling, I have spent hours and nights in scenes before which tragedy grows pale. I have no words to speak of them.

I have tried and do try to do my duty. I have the most sincere pity for this unfortunate man; my heart bleeds for him. I try, Heaven knows, to be as patient as I can. With all my troubles, my life is not as unhappy as his. My heart and soul are my own; he cannot touch them. I pity him, but I do not love him enough to let him wound me to the quick.

I don't know what to do—what course to take. I want to be advised. I have written these wild words, incoherently I know, since writing is not my natural method of expression—to get some of this weight off me, and I have tried to write justly. I know I must, in some way, protect myself from Mr. McFarland's mode of revenging any careless word upon me. I have half made up my mind to-day to tell the Sinclairs that I fear the encroachments of his habits. I dread my future so much, and I have my babies to think of besides.

Yesterday he drew two weeks of my salary at the theatre and paid the week's board-bill, and I fear will spend a good deal of the money, which we need *so* much, in liquor.

Don't come to me after reading this ; I fear I shall repent writing it. Yours *always,* ABBY.

P.S.—I just went down to breakfast and left him in bed. When I came up he was gone ! I shall be so anxious till night.

The evening after I thus wrote her, Mr. McFarland not coming home, I went to Mrs. Sinclair's, before going to the theatre, and told her what great distress I was in. She then told me she had been herself to Mr. McElrath, who was a friend of Mr. Sinclair's, and had asked him for a place for Mr. McFarland in the Custom-House, and he had promised to give him one. "But," she added, "if he gets drunk habitually, I can't ask Mr. Sinclair to recommend him, because Mr. McElrath will not give a man of such habits a place." I then implored her to say nothing about it, because he *must* get the place, else I should not know what to do with him ; and she promised to say nothing of it, unless something more was done on Mr. McFarland's part.

Within a few days after the 1st of January, 1867, I found the boarding-house at No. 86 Amity street intolerable, for various reasons, and removed to No. 72 Amity street, taking the back parlor and extension-room for my rooms, and preparing our meals for myself, Percy, and Mr. McFarland. The rooms were very comfortable, and I rented them from a Mrs. Mason, who herself rented half of the house. I took these rooms somewhere in the first or second week in January. I had not money to move from the other boarding-place, and, on informing Mr. McFarland of the fact, he told me he "should think I would borrow it from Mrs. Calhoun, as she had loaned me money before ; " and I went to her and borrowed $25, in addition to other sums received from her before going to this house, at No. 72 Amity street. At this new place, besides going nightly to perform my part at the Winter Garden, I wrote during all of spare moments, being then engaged to write regularly for *The Riverside* and the children's column of *The Independent*, and endeavoring to do work for other papers ; and I also did all the cooking for three persons, a large part of the washing and ironing for three, and all the sewing, mending, etc., for my family. Consequently I had little time for anything but work.

Somewhere about the last of January or first of February, Mr. Richardson came to lodge at this house. He came there because there was a good room vacant there, and he was obliged to move his lodgings, which were in the vicinity, and he told me that he did not wish to move very far, as he expected to leave the city altogether very soon. He called on me when he came to the house to see the room, which was the first time he ever called on me, or that I ever saw him in any house where I was boarding, although I had before met him occasionally at Mrs. Sinclair's, where he was a frequent visitor, and at Mrs. Calhoun's, where he had been an inmate of her mother's family.

On the 4th of February Mrs. Sinclair and Mrs. Calhoun were going to Washington. Just before going, Mr. McFarland had a terrible and unusually danger-ous attack of rage, of which I told Mrs. Calhoun. She said she was afraid to go away and leave me with that man, for fear he would kill me, and asked if she might tell some of our friends about his conduct, so that we could have some advice in the matter before she went away; but I felt as if I could not consent to this, and told her so. Mr. Oliver Johnson told me afterward that she did speak to himself and his wife of her great anxiety for me, and her fear that Mr. McFarland would murder me in some of his paroxysms.

After Mrs. Calhoun and Mrs. Sinclair were gone, I devoted myself more closely than ever to my work. Mr. Richardson was there in the same house. He had been there a few days, perhaps a week, when they went away. On the evening of the 19th of February, when McFarland came in from the Custom-House, where he had been employed since the 1st of February as clerk in the office, procured for him through the influence of the Sinclairs, I was standing at Mr. Richardson's door in the front hall, and he was just handing me some manu-scripts which he had offered to lend me to make use of, if I could, in some liter-ary work. Mr. Richardson's room was used as his working-room; and at this time, as at all parts of the day, he had with him a stenographer, a messenger-boy, and an artist, who were engaged in his literary works. When Mr. McFar-land came in he objected to my going to Mr. Richardson's room, to which I replied that "I had not been in, was not in the habit of going there, and even if I had been in there, it was not a private room, but an office, in the day-time." With this the matter dropped, and I supposed this was all of it; but in a few moments Mr. McFarland commenced to say something again on the same sub-ject. I saw he was in ill-humor, and I supposed he wished to make anything the pretext for one of his passions, and I said little or nothing. From this he worked himself up into a great fury, in which I left him, to go to my necessary work at the theatre. He continued in this rage through the night, and I spent a terrible night with him. All through the next day (the 20th) he remained at home abusing and tormenting me. He used to me expressions which I never could forgive or endure; and, still harping on the fact of my being at Mr. Richardson's room, asked me before Percy, who was all the time present: "Did Mr. Richardson ever kiss you?" "Have you ever been in his room alone with him?" and others which I considered insulting and unpardonable.

He was under the influence of liquor all day, remaining at home, and going out every little while to the nearest bar-room to drink, and then coming in still more furious. At last he declared he was willing to be separated from me, and that I might go home to my father's and leave him. When I assented to this, he wanted to bring in some of my friends to talk the matter over before them, but I refused to take counsel from any one till my father could be sent for. And I only prevented him from rushing out and calling in some of my friends by representing to him that he was then so intoxicated that his cause would be prejudiced by that fact.

On the evening of the 20th, before going to the theatre, I secreted his razors, his pocket-knife, my scissors, and all articles I considered dangerous—as I fre-quently did on such occasions—and left him. When I came home he was still raging. He frequently had made threats of committing suicide, often going out of doors with that avowed purpose. On this occasion, about midnight, he bade me an unusually solemn "eternal farewell," and told me that this time he was certainly going out to destroy himself. He had done this so many times that I said nothing, and made no effort to detain him. At the door he hesitated, and asked if I had nothing to say "in this last parting." I said, "I can only say that I am hopelessly sorry for you." He went out, and in a few minutes returned, as I knew he would, cooled and sobered by the cold night-air, and then, it being nearly morning, as mildly and firmly as I possibly could, I began to talk with him ; I told him decidedly that I should leave him forever ; that I had borne with patience for many years great outrages from him ; that he had made my life miserable, and had often put me in great dread of my life ; that I could not endure it any longer; that by his outrageous conduct for the two days past, and by the language he had used when he found me at Mr. Richardson's door, he had added the last drop to my cup of endurance, and I should go away from him at once. On this he grovelled at my feet in the most abject penitence. He wept and sobbed, and begged me to forgive him. He confessed that he had wronged me, that no woman would have borne with him as I had done, and about daylight went to sleep exhausted.

The next morning I did not allude to my purpose, but after seeing him leave the house for Mr. McElrath's office, I went to Mr. Sinclair's and placed myself under the protection of his roof, and never afterward saw Mr. McFarland except once or twice in the presence of others.

Up to the time of his coming to room at the same house in Amity street, my acquaintance with Mr. Richardson had been very slight and formal. He was a frequent visitor at the house of two of my most intimate friends—Mrs. Sinclair and Mrs. Calhoun—in whose mother's family he had been an inmate after his return from prison, and where he was like a son and a brother. I met him there quite often, but on very formal terms. At the time, on the 1st of December, when I was obliged to leave the place in Macdougal street, because the boarding-house keeper refused to keep any one of the profession of an actress in her house, I spoke of this circumstance to the family at Mrs. Calhoun's when we were all at the lunch-table, and Mr. Richardson was present. They were all indignant, and Mr. Richardson, with the friendliness and sympathy which were his chief characteristics, proposed that I advertise for a boarding-place. He also said that at the house where he lodged were some vacant rooms, and that if I were to look at them and like them, he would himself speak to the landlady of my profession, and he thought she would not object to it. On this I called next day at the house where Mr. Richardson lodged, looked at the vacant rooms, and saw him at the time for a moment in the front hall. The rooms were too expensive for me, and I took lodgings at that time at No. 86 Amity street. Shortly after this, about the last of December, Mr. McFarland, who fancied Mr. Richardson had some influence in the Pacific Railroad, sent me to call on him to ask for his aid in getting a place as clerk or something of that kind on that railroad. He had not then received the place promised for him in Mr. McElrath's department at the Custom-House. These were the two occasions on which I was at the house where Mr. Richardson lived. In the course of these matters he sent me several notes, one of them inclosing a letter of introduction for Mr. McFarland to Mr. George F. Train, asking some favor of him on the Pacific Railroad, which I believe Mr. McFarland presented without result. These notes were all written by Mr. Richardson's stenographer, all of them unsealed. They related to the favor I had asked of Mr. Richardson at Mr. McFarland's suggestion, and this was the extent of my acquaintance with Mr. Richardson up to January 20th, 1867.

After I removed to No. 72 Amity street, Mr. Richardson being obliged suddenly to change his lodgings, and knowing I was living nearly opposite in the same street with himself, came to see if he could get rooms there. I introduced him to Mrs. Mason, the lodging-house woman, but beyond that had no interest or influence in getting him installed there. Mrs. Mason, who is an Irishwoman, and in full sympathy with Mr. McFarland, has in this case made many erroneous statements. If I had any feeling about Mr. Richardson's coming to take a room so near Mr. McFarland and myself, it was one of aversion, from the fact that he could not be there without knowing something of my unhappy life, and I felt keenly that such a knowledge would pain and humiliate me. But I could not control the event, and about a month before I finally left Mr. McFarland, Mr. Richardson had come there to lodge. I saw him often, and he did me many kindnesses. I knew very well he pitied me, because he thought I was overworked and not very happy. His treatment of me was always most respectful and reserved. There was never, prior to my leaving Mr. McFarland, a word or even a look passed between us which I should not be glad now if all the world had seen and heard. He called sometimes at my room, which was next his, but from its situation, and the fact that it was my sleeping-room, parlor, and dining-room in one, it was in no sense a private room. My boy, who was then seven years old, was always with me, and Mr. Richardson's calls were made usually in the afternoon about the time he got through work, and oftener after Mr. McFarland had got home from down town. This is the exact and careful statement of my acquaintance with Mr. Richardson up to the time of my separation from Mr. McFarland.

The afternoon or night of the 20th of February, while Mr. McFarland was in the worst rage, I wrote in my dressing-room at the theatre, a letter to Mrs. Sinclair and Mrs. Calhoun, then in Washington, telling them that I was suffering, and my fears for my safety. I felt that if Mr. McFarland should murder me in some of his outbursts, it was right that they should know the very worst, and I was frank to the utmost. They answered that letter on the instant, with the two noble and womanly letters which have already been produced in print as evidence of "their conspiracy to take a devoted wife from a loving and chivalrous husband."

On the last night of my life with Mr. McFarland, the night of the 20th of February, it happened, as was not usual, that Mr. Richardson was in his room the whole evening. He almost always spent his evenings at Mrs. Gilbert's, which was his home in New York, and where he was loved like a son. He has since told me that he heard the greater part of what had passed that night, as was unavoidable from the position of his room, and that he feared he might be obliged to call help, or himself interfere in my behalf, against Mr. McFarland's violence. The next day, when I left my rooms to go to Mrs. Sinclair's, I found

Mr. Richardson there when I entered. No one else was present but Miss Perry, Mrs. Sinclair's oldest sister. Under ordinary circumstances I should have controlled myself until I could see Miss Perry alone; but worn out as I was by the misery and excitements of the last two days, and the fact that I had still been obliged to keep at work at home and at the theatre, I broke down and burst into tears as soon as I entered the room. As soon as I could speak I began to talk to them both. Mr. Richardson said very little. I remember he said, "This is a matter in which I cannot advise you, but whatever you make up your mind to do, I shall be glad to help you in."

He *did* help me in ten thousand ways in which I never should have permitted him to take part if I had had the slightest knowledge of the feeling which was to grow up between us. He helped me make arrangements to send Percy home, which was the first thing I was anxious to do. He telegraphed for me to one or two friends, and wrote to Mrs. Calhoun and Mrs. Sinclair of the step I had taken, which I asked him to do at once. All these things, which common prudence would have prevented him from doing if there had been any guilty secret between us or any relation except the simple one on his part of sympathy toward a very wretched woman, he did openly and unreservedly. He saw Mr. McFarland and told him he was my friend in this, and that he had telegraphed to my father to come on.

On the 23d my father came, and on the 24th, in the presence of Mr. and Mrs. Oliver Johnson, Mr. Sinclair, and my father and Mr. McFarland, I announced to him my absolute determination to leave him. I told him he knew he had lost my affections years before, and that what I now did would be final. I said very little except this, for any allusion to his conduct Mr. McFarland interrupted immediately. But he was unusually calm for him, and said several times that he accepted my decision as final, and added, "I bow to it and submit to it." I treated him with a great deal of pity, as I always had, and urged my father to go home and remain all night with him to see that he did nothing desperate. Of course, his constant threat that he would commit suicide, and that in such a case "his blood would be on my head," had always caused me some anxiety, which I am now convinced I might have spared myself.

The evening after this separation took place, Mr. Richardson called at Mr. Sinclair's and stayed an hour or two with the family. He told us all that in a few days he was going to Hartford to finish his book. I was going to Massachusetts the 7th of April, when my engagement expired at the theatre, and I thought if he went away in a day or two I might not see him again, so when he arose to leave that evening, I went to the door to say—what I could not say before the others— that he had been *very*, VERY good to me, that I never could repay him, but that God would surely bless him for it. I could not say this without strong emotion, and while I spoke he said: "How do you feel about facing the world with two babies?" I answered: "It looks hard for a woman, but then I am sure I can get on better without that man than with him." At this, Mr. Richardson, still holding my hand, which I had given him to say "good-by," stooped down, and speaking in a lower tone so that he could not be heard through the door opening into the parlor where the others were sitting, said these words: "I wish you to remember, my child, that any responsibility you choose to give me in any possible future, I shall be very glad to take." I think those were his exact words. And with this, he went away without a single word more being spoken by either of us. I turned and went up-stairs and said nothing to any one that night. It may have been two days later Mr. Richardson called again. It happened I was in the parlor alone when he came in. In the talk which took place then, he told me that during the storms of the last few days of my life he had become interested in me and very fond of me, that I was the woman of all the world whom he had seen to whom he would gladly intrust the care of his motherless children ; that my prudence and reserve during all our acquaintance, when he knew I was unhappy, had won on him greatly ; that he *loved* me, and that if in any future, however far off, I could be free to marry, he wanted me to know fully this feeling. What could I say ? Mr. Richardson had all my respect for his chivalry and generosity to me before he had spoken thus. When he spoke, all my heart went out to him as freely as the river flows toward the sea. The formal separation from Mr. McFarland, in which he seemed to release me from the bondage in which he held me, had had to me the moral effect of a divorce. I had a feeling which perhaps no one can understand. It was as if a millstone had been cut off from my neck, and left me as free and unbound as I ever felt in girlhood. Mr. Richardson seemed to me in every respect the opposite of the miserable man who had so long tormented me. His goodness to me, his unusual strength of character, united with his tenderness and sympathy, made it absolutely impossible not to love him. While he waited for me to say something to answer what he said, I did not think of the imprudence of it at all. I only asked him earnestly if his chivalry and a generous impulse to assist a woman in trouble had not led him to mistake this for a warmer feeling. He laughed at this, and then I began to think of my family and Mr. Richardson, and of my whole unhappy position. Mr. Richardson blamed himself afterward, and our friends all blamed us for this declaration on his part and my acceptance of it, as an act most rash and imprudent, but I know we neither of us meant to do anything either immoral or even improper. He counselled me to tell my friends all he said and take their counsel. Our talk at most was not a very long one, and within a few days he went to Hartford, and I did not expect to see him again for an indefinite time.

After his departure I went back to my old room in Amity street, where my trunks and wardrobe still remained. It was convenient to do this, and some one of my lady friends went to spend the nights with me. Two nights after I went there, Mr. Richardson unexpectedly came from Hartford, intending to go to Washington for a day or two. He had written me several letters during his stay at Hartford, which I had received and answered. He arrived in New York on the 12th of March, and on the evening of the 13th, when I went out of the theatre, I found him there waiting for me. He was asked to call for me by the friends who usually took me home, and who, on that night, were gone to the opera. After walking a few yards from the theatre, Mr. McFarland came up behind us and shot Mr. Richardson, inflicting a severe but not dangerous wound in the thigh. As soon as he had done this, he fired two shots in quick succession at me, but without wounding me, as Mr. Richardson had told me to run as soon as he felt himself hurt. On this evening, after he had been at the Station-House with the policeman who arrested Mr. McFarland, Mr. Richardson went with me to the house of our friends, and remained in New York till he was out of danger, and then returned to my father's in Massachusetts.

At this time I heard first of the intercepted letter from Mr. Richardson to me, which he had written from Hartford after the conversation which had taken place between us. I never saw the letter or knew its contents till it appeared in print. The letter was a mixture of jest and of sentiment, which any one who knew Mr. Richardson would readily understand. I shall not go on to explain it point by point, but the allusion to his love for me being the "growth of years" was simply a sentimental expression, as in point of fact I had known him only a few months, and had been acquainted with him not more than four months.

Just after the shooting, while I was in the great distress of mind following such a horrible occurrence, Mr. McFarland went to my rooms in Amity street, and gaining access to my rooms by such representations as poisoned the minds of the landlady and the servants against me (to whom, of course, I had said nothing about my affairs), he broke open my trunks, took out all the private correspondence I had preserved during my whole life, rifled my writing-desk and portfolio, and even searched the pockets of my dresses. He took not only my letters, but all my accounts and receipts by which I could show what money I had earned, the notices and advertisements which I had preserved of my dramatic readings, and even robbed me of all the MSS., and odds and ends of literary labors, some of which I had a long time had on hand, and from that day to this I have never seen any of my private papers of all kinds. He also succeeded in intercepting two or three more letters from friends out of town. This is the history of the private letters he has been able to introduce into the case ; and I feel compelled to add, as was proved in a measure at the trial, that all these letters, except those two intercepted from Mrs. Sinclair and Mrs. Calhoun, he had previously read ; that the letters from Mrs. Calhoun to me about the stage had been read by him months before I left him, and that all her efforts to get me an engagement were as well known to him as to me. While I lived with Mr. McFarland I never had a letter which in any sense could be called private. He never, that I remember, brought me a letter of which he had not first broken the seal and gone over the contents. And I am glad to feel that few people's private letters (things so susceptible of being misunderstood or put under false construction) could have borne so well the test of publicity, and the most malicious attempt at misrepresentation, as the letters of which I was robbed in the manner I have described.

After I went back to Massachusetts, terribly hurt by scandal which had been caused by the shooting of Mr. Richardson in the open street, I wrote to Mr. Richardson, telling him that I had feared—and that the thought grieved me inexpressibly—that in a moment of romantic generosity he had offered me his love, and that the events had proved that such an offer on his part becoming known, had made an enemy of McFarland, who had proved a more dangerous man than I should ever have believed him, and that I released him from any allegiance or fancied allegiance to me in my misfortune, which at best would only be sacrifice on his part. To this letter of mine, of which I can only remember the substance, not the words, Mr. Richardson wrote me in answer the following letter, which shows so well the chivalrous nature of the man, and the rare traits which won me to love him so deeply as I do, that I print it without reserve, because I believe it will bear to a candid mind his vindication, as well as corroborate my story :—

MARCH 31, 1867.

MY LOVE: If Heaven shall ever grant me the last blessing of calling you mine by the most sacred name of wife, it will compensate me for all waiting and sorrow. And, precious, should one of us go hence by unalterable destiny before that blessed hour come, it would still be blessed and full compensation to know that you had loved me; that you had found in my poor nature somewhere hidden any worth that deserved *that*.

And, precious, about our immediate situation. There isn't a bit of any sacrifice or generosity about it on my part. *Once for all*, remember that. Partly from my own rashness, partly from things neither of us could control, you and I are in a little boat on a high and somewhat perilous sea. If I had had any sense, you would not have been there. But I believe devoutly in the proverb that a man who isn't a fool part of the time is one all the time. It was foolish, imprudent, *cruel* in me to let you be on such a craft with me, when patience could have avoided it. But I loved you and took no counsel of reason.

Well, darling, here we are in the little boat, waves high, some sharks, some pirates. For me it is nothing. I have faced all perils in life and death before, and their familiar faces don't disturb me. ,And I am not a bit afraid to die; so I am not afraid of anything in life. But, precious, for you my heart reproaches me. I am so sorry when I should have been your helper and comforter and shield, to have brought you into such a storm. But, darling, *if I live*, I am going to see you safely out of it. If I should not live to get into harbor with you, the Father will take care of your sunny head.

But, precious, let us take our chances. I have been in rougher waves before, and ridden them safely. Let us exercise the best seamanship we can, provide for all contingencies as far as possible, and then keep the serene mind which defies fate and fears nothing but guilt, and knows how infinitesimal all these pretty things of life are, and feels sure that infinite love and absolute justice rule the world.

My darling, in all that I am or do, or have or hope for, in life or death, you are irrevocably interwoven. I regret nothing that I have done, save just to the extent that it has affected or marred your happiness. My whole heart, my whole life, go out to you. I think I see a happy future, sunny days, loves of children, loves of home, good to others. I *know* I see a loyalty nothing can shake, a trust that is absolute, a love that is utter and vital.

This letter is the key-note of the absolute love and trust in which Mr. Richardson held me for the three years which passed until his death. For the feeling with which I tried to repay his loyalty to me, and the gratitude I felt for the chivalry with which he tried to avert, as far as possible, all the misfortunes which seemed destined to fall on my helpless head, I have no word to speak. I saw him rarely, and our meetings were always guarded by the strictest regard for propriety, and were either under my father's roof or in the presence of friends. But the last sentences of the letter I have just quoted were in my heart always. If I do not expect my story to be understood or to be believed by a public which seeks its appropriate food in the vile garbage of *The Police Gazette*, how can I hope that it will understand *him?* To such a public he does not belong. The age of Sidney or of Bayard should claim him as its own.

After my return to Massachusetts, in March, 1867, Mr. McFarland commenced proceedings to get possession of my children in a suit of *habeas corpus*. Not satisfied with these proceedings, he assailed me in every way possible to harass a woman. I hardly have one friend in New York or New England into whose house he did not enter to force them to listen to his story. He assailed my character with vile epithets, which I should blush to repeat, and which he knew, in his own consciousness, I would die ten thousand deaths rather than deserve. I am glad and proud to say that none of my friends fell off from me, and that among all my friends and acquaintances, only one door has been shut against me, in spite of all the heavy slanders which I have had to bear. At last, weary and worn out with more contests than I can describe here, pursued by his revenge, in the form of anonymous letters, by spies set to watch my footsteps, by all that can wear out a woman's courage and heart, I made a compromise with Mr. McFarland. It was agreed that all proceedings should be stopped by a division of the children, and that he should take Percy and I should keep Danny in my charge. Hitherto I might have been imprudent in allowing myself to love a good man, and to allow him to confess that he loved me, when we had no legal right to admit it to each other, but I had never felt any sense of guilt about it, for I knew I meant to do the best I could. But now I confessed my baseness, my want of courage, in giving up my boy, nursed at my breast, and dearer to me than my life, to compromise with my sworn foe. My remorse for letting the child go without letting the legal proceedings take their course has been terrible. But I was very weak. I was in Boston, where I had no friends except my own family. In the midst of all these proceedings, Governor John A. Andrew, who was my lawyer, died suddenly. I was instructed that, by the common law, the children belong to the father, and that it is in the discretion of the court whether the mother shall have her children or no. Last of all, Mr. McFarland came to my mother and promised, with a solemnity which seemed like truth, that he would put my child in school; that he would only consult my wishes in choosing a place for him, and that there should be no bar between me and the little boy. So I let him go in November, 1867. It was only a little while before I heard the child was not in school, was not going to be there, and that he was dragged from one lodging-house to another, till I became so anxious I came to New York to see him. Then, accompanied by my lawyer in New York City, Mr. Runkle, I went to the lodgings where Percy lived. I was met by Mr. McFarland with such a storm of outrage and abuse as I will not try to describe.

It was in the spring of 1868 that I attempted to see Percy. After the outrageous scene, which nearly broke my heart, my friends all said one thing—that I must at once take legal steps to get free from Mr. McFarland. I decided very soon to go to Indiana. The laws there, as I found on consultation, permit a divorce for drunkenness, extreme cruelty, and failure to support a wife. I knew beyond a doubt that Mr. McFarland had committed adultery while I lived with him as his wife. I had been offered proof that he had committed that crime against marriage since I had ceased to live with him. I was told that adultery was the only ground on which a divorce in New York was obtainable. But I repeat now what I said then, with all my soul upon my lips, that I considered his treatment of me, his personal abuses, his terrible profanity, his outrages of all kinds, an infinitely greater sin against me and my womanhood than if he had committed again and again, unknown to me, the crime against the marriage relation which is the only cause the New York courts hold just grounds for divorce. My opinion in this remains unchanged even while I write.   So I went to Indiana, and remained there sixteen months, only once coming home for a little visit in Massachusetts at Christmas.   On the 31st of October, 1869, I returned to my mother's house, legally set free from my first marriage bond by the decision of one of the States under the Constitution, which affirms that full faith and credit shall be given in each State to the public acts, records, and judicial proceedings of every other State.

During the long time, almost three years, that ensued between my former separation from Mr. McFarland and my legal divorce, my acquaintance with Mr. Richardson had been most carefully guarded.   We agreed, and all our friends agreed, that we had been rash and foolish.   After I returned to my father's in March, after Mr. Richardson was wounded, I did not see him for months.   Then he came to my father's house in this wise: Mr. John F. Cleveland, of New York, an old friend of Mr. McFarland's, came to Mr. Richardson and told him that Mr. McFarland desired that he should go on to see me and see if some settlement could not be made.   Mr. Richardson, supposing this a trap, at first refused to go, but finally, after consulting his own lawyer, Mr. John Sedgwick, and on Mr. Cleveland giving his pledge as a gentleman that no mischief was meant, Mr. Richardson came on to see me at my father's.   This was his first visit to me, and these were the beginning of the offers on McFarland's part which led to the division of my children.   After Percy went away, when I was most sorely grieved and troubled, Mr. Richardson visited me again at my father's, in the fall of 1867. When I went to New York, in the spring of 1868, before I left for Indiana, I saw him occasionally in the presence of friends of his and mine.   During all my stay in Indiana, and in all his frequent journeyings West, I never saw him once, and he carefully avoided passing through the city where I stopped, to give no shadow of a cause for scandal.   But on the 31st of October, 1869, I came home *free*.   On November 17th, 1869, Mr. Richardson came on to his mother's house in Medway, to Thanksgiving.   On Thanksgiving evening I met him at the railroad station, as he came from his aged mother's, whose youngest son he was. For the first time since he was shot in 1867 I walked with him in the street.   In all that time we had entered no place of amusement together, and had only once met accidentally at an evening party at the house of a mutual friend.   It seemed as if, for the first time, I had a right to talk freely and unreservedly to him, so carefully had our acquaintance with each other been protected.

On the day after Thanksgiving, Mr. Richardson went back to New York. Nothing definite was planned about our future.   We could still afford to wait till events shaped themselves.   Just a week after he left, a despatch came that he was mortally hurt, and I came to New York to nurse him till he died.   When I came he asked me, if there should seem at any time to be no hope of his recovery, if I would marry him at once, and I said I would.   Otherwise we decided to wait till he recovered.   I supposed he wished to be married, that I might have a firmer legal right to take the charge and rearing of his three orphaned children; and also because he could die more peacefully, having made me his wife.   As for myself, if I had ten thousand lives, I should have been more than glad to have given them up for him who was dying for the crime of having loved me; and his lightest wish in the matter would have weighed with me against all other motives in the world. So, when it became plain that he must go away from all the hearts that yearned to hold him here, we were married.

This is the whole true story of all that has happened to me. I said when I wrote it I should tell the whole. If it were guiltier I should have told it just the same. I think the same thing might have happened to any man or woman who lives, without bringing to them either remorse or shame, and often without bringing any reproach.

As to Mr. McFarland himself, I believe now, as I have believed for years, that he was a man born to do a murder. The fact that he was always uttering threats of bloodshed does not so much convince me of this as the fact of his temperament, which, partly from hereditary causes, partly from his nationality, and partly from bad education, had become one of uncontrollable violence. I believe he feared this himself. Often during our early married life, when I told him, in his reasonable moments, that he would kill me in some of his fits of passion, he asserted with vehemence that he " should never harm a hair of my head." Towards the last of my life with him, however, he said several times, in answer to expressed fears, " I shall never harm you, if I *know* you," which convinced me that he did not feel sure of himself. And I believe simply and truly, that if I had stayed with him, sooner or later I should have been the victim of his blind fury.

I have written all without malice or hard feeling against him. Mr. McFarland married me, a girl in years, a child in experience. In every way he abused his claim in me, he turned my love to bitterness, he took all the bloom and sweetness from my life. When I went away, and he found I had begun, perhaps, to feel a hope of happiness, his wounded vanity and desire for revenge turned his naturally mad temper into blackest madness. He swore to my friends, by all the fiends, that he " would rob me of my reputation, my children, all I held dear." He has done so, and I pity him from my soul.

When the trial of his life commenced I commiserated him deeply. I knew that death, which seemed so infinitely sweet and peaceful and blessed, when I turned from Mr. Richardson's death-bed, was to this unhappy man the most terrible of horrors. I hoped with all my heart that he would escape the barbarous penalty of a barbarous law. And when I heard that Judge Davis was engaged in the case, I went to him and said: "You understand fully that in this case I have one interest. The man on trial is on trial for his life, but I am no less on trial than he, and for something infinitely dearer to any woman than life could be. The best friends I have are assailed with me, good people who have befriended both the prisoner and myself. If you can only let in a little light of truth in all this cloud of abuse and calumny, I beg that you will do it. For the rest, I hope this man will not be convicted, and no one is more willing to believe him insane than I am." Judge Davis promised that all he could do to the end I asked him, should be done. That if possible, Mr. Richardson's memory, my own honor, and the reputation of my best friends, should be vindicated. What stumbling-blocks were placed in his way I will not try to disclose. It is enough to say, that at the last moment a change was made in the summing-up, contrary to the expectation of every person concerned.

There is but one word more to say, and I will say it briefly. It is well known that I have been on trial before a New York court as much as Daniel McFarland, and for a crime more heinous and more bitterly punished in a woman than murder committed by a man. And it is clearly seen, by all who see dispassionately, that wherever a loop-hole was opened for any truth about my conduct or Mr. Richardson's, it was immediately stopped. I have tasted to its dregs the cup of justice, which, in the nineteenth century, men born of women mete out to one whose worst crime was the mistake of marrying a man who was half madman from natural inheritance, half brute from natural proclivity. Of the justice I have received, let those who read my story be witnesses.

City and County of New York, ss. : Abby S. Richardson, being duly sworn, deposes and says that the above statement is true, according to her knowledge and belief.

ABBY SAGE RICHARDSON.

Sworn to before me, this 9th day of May, 1870.

WILLIAM BARKER, *Notary Public, N. Y. Co.*

THE TRIAL.

The trial began April 4th, 1870, before Recorder Hackett. District Attorney Garvin, Assistant District Attorney Fellows, and private counsel Judge Noah Davis represented the commonwealth. John Graham, Charles Spencer, and Elbridge T. Gerry appeared for McFarland.

Four days were spent in procuring a jury. District Attorney Garvin opened for the prosecution. The clerks of the *Tribune* office who witnessed the shooting were then examined. Their evidence merely went to show the manner of the act, and particularly the rapidity with which the deed was accomplished. When Captain Allaire came upon the stand, and recounted the taking of McFarland to the Astor House and his identification by Richardson, Mr. Graham brought out his forensic batteries and poured hot shot into the too-zealous policeman, claiming that what he did and saw, and what the prisoner said while in his custody, should not be taken as evidence.

Dr. Swan testified to his probing the wound, and to the death of Richardson. He was assisted in his medical attendance by Dr. Sayre. In alluding to the marriage ceremony, Mr. Graham took occasion to remark as follows:

" I propose to show that this man was responsible for the death to which they sent him. They cannot rest their case unless they satisfy this jury of the cause of which on the night of the 2d of December this man died. I will show that they called in the aid of the most terrible and disgraceful ceremonies merely to get the property of this man. They could have married these parties by mere form of contract. It did not need the performance of

HON. JOHN GRAHAM.

any religious ceremony. They might have simply agreed to become man and wife, and it was not necessary to bring in this blasphemy to give an appearance of decency to what was then going on. If I show that the deceased came to his death by the unlaw-

ful act of another person, and that those who were called around
him hastened his death, let the prisoner have the benefit of it.
Suppose I show that they strangled him. I have a right to show
that. Suppose I show that they put his mind under a much
more vexatious torture, that this was all planned nearly three
years ago, and then ripened into this murder, from the acts of those
who witnessed the Astor House iniquity ; those who witnessed the
planting of the tree, and who were also those to witness the full
growth, from the time it was first planted."

On the second day Mr. Spencer opened for the defence in his
usual flowery manner. From his very able address we extract that
portion which may be called the

STORY OF MCFARLAND'S LIFE.

I ask you, gentlemen of the jury, to listen to me while 1 tell
you the story of this defendant. Daniel McFarland was born in
Ireland, and at an early age came to this country. When he was
but eight years of age his mother died. When he was but twelve
years of age his father died ; and he was then left in this, the
land of his adoption, to fight his way through the world, without
fortune and without friends, as well as he could. He became a
mechanic. He would work all day long, and at night he would
study ; and during many years he worked as a harness-maker.
But all the time he thirsted for knowledge, and eventually managed to save enough to enable him to go to College ; and he went
and he studied hard ; and the Professor of Chemistry in that College—old Dartmouth—was so pleased with him that he made him
an assistant; and although he could not serve out his entire term,
he was honored with the degree of Bachelor of Arts. His health
was delicate, and the strain upon his mind was too great for the
health of his body. He was a sensitive man, with a mind cultivated, with mercurial impulses, easily excited, of an extremely
nervous, delicate mental organization, and far more liable to diseases of the mind than those who live but for the body. So tender and sensitive was his mental organization, that he was in
truth incapable of grappling with and bearing the deep sorrows
and misfortunes which awaited him. Ardent and impulsive, his

was the very nature which would make the woman he loved his very idol; and no man loved wife and children more unselfishly and idolatrously than did he, and woe to that man who shall rob him of either or all. Though before so great a storm the delicate

COL. CHARLES S. SPENCER.

structure of his mind must surely have fallen, yet that indestructible, mysterious instinct will survive to point out the wrongs, and subject him to, perhaps, fatal punishment. Gentlemen of the jury, the wild beast of the jungle, having no reason, revenges a wrong. After he had finished his studies at Dartmouth College, he struggled on, and finally succeeded in getting a competency, and went to Europe, and there he studied and listened to the lectures of Chevalier, Michelet, and Jules Simon. Then he returned to his adopted country and was admitted to the Massachusetts bar, and is a member to-day; giving him an additional claim upon us of the high and honorable profession to which the court, the able counsel for the prosecution, and his own defenders belong. After that, he was appointed Professor of Logic, Belles-Lettres, and Elocution in Brandywine College, Delaware, and remained there until that College was burned down. I have directed your attention, gentlemen of the jury, to this little history and these facts, as I believe they will all legitimately be called to bear upon the questions in this case. A man of intellectual development, ripe education, delicate, sensitive mental organization; a man of high, honorable, gentlemanly instincts is more apt to be driven to insanity by wrongs of this nature than a man who only lives to gratify the physical wants of the body.

In 1852, while passing through Manchester, in the State of New Hampshire, the defendant casually became acquainted with the woman who has figured so conspicuously in this case. We derive from woman, I might say, most of the happiness we enjoy in this life; and yet from the fall of Adam, tempted by Eve, and from the siege of Troy, brought on by the seduction and adultery of Helen, down to the present day, woman has often been the cause of the downfall of individuals and nations. This girl was then but fifteen years of age. She was a poor factory girl at that time, without education, and this mind which she possesses to-day, as you will hear by and by, has been the fruit of the careful, affectionate, and assiduous attentions of my client. Her father was a poor weaver. He remembered him, and five years afterwards, on the 14th of December, 1857, he married her. She was then young and beautiful. Little, upon that wedding-day, did the happy bride dream that the day would come when unholy love for her should place her seducer in his grave and the wrecked victim, her husband, should be on trial for his life. After this marriage, gentlemen of the jury, they lived for years happily together. The first child was born to them, and they named that child Jessie. A kind, merciful Providence removed that first-born from this to a better world, and spared it from the misery of to-day— far more fortunate than those who are living—and it may be that Jessie to-day, before the Throne of the merciful God, is pleading for the fallen and ruined mother that has wrought out all this misery. They had two other children. This bright boy, the eldest, Percy, who stands by his father—the only one of the family who appears here. I am not at all certain but that he appears here the best counsel this defendant has. The next child is a golden-haired boy, whom this woman has spoken of in poetry, named after his father, upon whose face that father has not been permitted to look for many a weary, miserable year.

. . . .

He became unfortunate; his speculations were disastrous; he lost his property, and then it was that the seeds of dissatisfaction first began to be sown. On one occasion this woman said, " All I need to make me an elegant lady and popular with the *élite* of New York, is money." Yet he was content. Upon his marriage he gained nothing but his wife. She had neither property nor influential connections. He was ever kind to her and to her family, and provided a comparatively lucrative employment for her father. He took a sick uncle from the hospital, paid his expenses home and cared for him, and that uncle of this woman died with blessings of this defendant upon his lips. He was, as I have said, an ardent, impulsive man, worshipped his wife and loved his children. She brought him beauty and virtue, and he asked for nothing more. If she shall fall, if this his idol shall be shattered, the same felon blow that strikes his idol down shall break his heart; grief will sap the foundation of subtle reason, and finally it shall fall to ruin.

. . . .

In the summer of 1866, a year prior to this homicide, at great expense he sent his wife to the White Mountains, and every dollar he could save he sent to her there. At this time, gentlemen of the jury, this woman became acquainted with the people who are to be so instrumental in effecting her ruin. In an evil hour she fell into the society of these Fourierites, agrarians, Mormons, spiritualists, free-lovers, amidst whom every Jack has some other person to Gill. She went to parties where she met with people of supposed prominence and distinction, and her husband stayed at home, taking care of the children. I can best elucidate that love of a kind, good father for his children, as it existed in the breast of this defendant, by reading to you a quotation from " Jeremy Taylor," which I have extracted.

"Does law, so jealous in the cause of Man,
    Denounce no doom on the delinquent?

                                    None!
He lives, and o'er his brimming beaker boasts th' inglorious feat—
But many a crime deemed innocent on earth
Is registered in Heaven, and these no doubt
Have each their record, with a curse annexed.
Man may dismiss compassion from his heart,
But God will never."

.   .   .   .

In the year 1833, beneath an evil star and in an unfortunate hour for this man's family and for his peace, Albert D. Richardson was born. He grew up to manhood, and became an educated man. He became a literary man, and in the time of the war, as a correspondent of the *Tribune*, he was taken prisoner by the enemy. He remained a prisoner some considerable time. He finally escaped, and published several very able works. He was a man of very fine mind, and well calculated by his fascination to charm the very woman for whom his machinations were presently laid. He was introduced to her by one of the parties of whom I have spoken, and some time after, on an isolated evening, when this defendant went out with her, he was introduced to Richardson. The first indication of the approaching storm was the fact that notes were sent by this man from day to day to Mrs. McFarland. He pretends to be her friend, and with cool and diabolical deliberation he proceeds to accomplish his purpose.

In connection with this woman Calhoun and one or two others, he lays out his plans. The first stage is, if possible, to alienate this woman from her husband. This woman's vanity was the medium. He has taught her to recite, she becomes inflated with the idea of becoming an actress or a reader. She becomes a passable good reader; and it occurs to Richardson and Mrs. Calhoun that if an engagement could be procured for her it would

make her independent of her husband. So, through the instru-
mentality of Richardson, an engagement is procured for her at
the Winter Garden Theatre, and she makes her *début* as "Ne-
rissa," in the "Merchant of Venice." She afterwards played in
other parts, and rehearsed that part which, in another capacity,
she had been playing already—the part of Marion de L'Orme,
the mistress of the Duke of Richelieu. This man Richardson
used to go for her at night to the theatre, and get her. At first
Mrs. Calhoun went. Her husband opposed all this, but she had
her own way. At first, I say, Mrs. Calhoun used to go for her,
but by and by it is discovered that it is Richardson now that
comes for her—in a carriage or on foot, as the weather permits—
and between the leaving of the theatre and the arrival home
much time elapses.

I do not believe that the people connected with the management of the theatre dreamed of what was going on. Richardson
was very careful not to show himself inside the theatre, but
crawled along on the sidewalk outside till she came out. But
during the time this man was away this woman went out in the
day-time on various pretences. They would go out to lunch and
to dinner together. They would send this little boy (pointing to
Percy) on some specious errand away, and lock themselves for
long hours in the room together. We have no more doubt that
we will satisfy you of the truth of this, than you have of your
own existence.

The next step ; Richardson did not intend to rest content with
sacrificing upon the unholy altar of his lust the virtue of this
woman. He intended to pile Ossa upon the Pelion of this man's
wrongs and take his children from him besides. They sent away
little Danny at first, to visit his relatives. And, gentlemen, permit me to call your attention to the precise situation of the
various actors in this drama. Mr. Richardson was boarding and
had a room with a person by the name of Benedict, at 61 Amity
street. Mr. and Mrs. McFarland were living at 72. The facilities for intercourse were not great enough, so Mrs. McFarland
(as we shall be able to show) goes to Mrs. Benedict one day and
demands to engage rooms from her for her husband, children,
servants, and herself, and this without the knowledge of her hus-

band ; and it is Mr. Richardson himself that introduces Mrs. Mc-
Farland to the Benedicts. There were no rooms, and that application failed. But that application failing, what is the next step ?
Why, Richardson goes to Mason's at 72 Amity street, and makes
application for rooms. He wants two. They can give him but
one. He says ladies often visit him, and it would be indelicate
to receive them in a room where there is a bed—imagine a
butcher ashamed of the sight of blood ! However, this application succeeds. The attempt has been made to bring the mountain to Mahomet. It failed. Then the attempt was made to
bring Mahomet to the mountain, and it succeeded.

And now we have them all under the same roof. Mr. and
Mrs. McFarland in one room. Mr. Richardson in another.
The time when Richardson came to Mason's was in January,
1867 ; and after he came there this intimacy was continued of
which I have spoken. They continued to lunch and dine together. On the Monday before she absconded, McFarland
accidentally learned she had been out for some time with this
man, and asked for an explanation, and she said she had been
out to Carpenter's studio. On Tuesday, this absconding being
about to take place (it took place on the 21st February, 1867),
McFarland came home unexpectedly at three o'clock, and met
her as she came out of Richardson's room. Then, for the first
time, this long-suffering man expostulated with her in reference
to her intimacy with Richardson. She replied in a careless and
flippant manner, and he resolved to stay home next day and
guard his home. He did so, and while he was sitting there with
his wife, Richardson opened the door, but upon seeing her husband, hurriedly retreated. Now, gentlemen, the pear is fully
ripe. This woman has become thoroughly corrupted. She
dreams of triumphs upon the stage and in society, and the world
inside of her family circle is not sufficient for her. She moves
in circles now to which this Richardson introduced her, among
people of prominence, with men like Colfax, Greeley, Johnson,
and Newton. She has placed before her as temptations the
honors of the stage and its wealth—the honors of the society of
great men. She dreams of fame, and pants for more refinement
—a higher intelligence. She is now too elegant, too refined, too

intellectual, too popular for her humble lot, and, gentlemen, the demon that placed before her all these temptations, for which she has to pay the price of her soul, is Richardson. He points out the way, and leads her on; and yet with a careful, with a rare dissimulation, he conceals it. This defendant finds a change in her manners and appreciates it.

The Sunday before she went away her nephew happened to be there, and McFarland seemed to be very much troubled, and spoke about woman's ingratitude to a poor man, and advised him never to marry till he was very rich. Mrs. McFarland replied that was a morbid state of mind for a man to get into, and advised the nephew when he did get married to get a wife like her. On the morning of the 21st day of this month of February, 1867, Daniel McFarland arose as usual, little dreaming of what the day was to bring forth; and when he went out she kissed him and said to him, "Darling, good-by!" He returned that afternoon to find his idol shattered and the altar of his home destroyed. She had absconded, and she went to No. 8 Washington Place, taking with her the remaining boy—this bright boy, Percy. Richardson met her there, and sent the boy away into Massachusetts. Before the sun had set he makes inquiry for his wife, seeks to find where she is, makes offers to arrange these difficulties, and finally he removes from 72 Amity street. No sooner had this husband moved away from his late home, which was to him then, indeed, desolate, than this man Richardson goes back to that very place.

> " O, woman! woman!
> One corner of a passing gallant's fancy
> Pleaseth thee well; the whole devoted heart
> Of man matured is to thee a yoke
> Of cumbrous weight from which thou wouldst escape,
> And friendship, filial duty—every tie—
> Defrauds thy husband of his dear earned rights."
> *Joanna Baillie.*

.   .   .   .

Now, gentlemen of the jury, I am informed and believe that this prosecution, as I have once before said, will pretend that there was something in this man's conduct to justify this action on the part of his wife. I shall show there was not. But if there had been, it would have been no excuse. Woman never better fulfils her office as a guardian angel than when she is watching over an erring and failing husband. It is in that hour, when he first begins to totter, that her influence should be exerted to the uttermost, and her arms be wound round him in a tighter and more affectionate embrace to win him back. Gentlemen of the jury, many thousands of husbands have thus in the past been saved, and by the neglect of this, many thousands have in the past been lost. Well, these people remained, as I have said to you, at No. 72 Amity street; but by and by business calls Richardson to Boston. McFarland, now having no home, no child, no life, no hope, no joy, occasionally at this time goes into the *Tribune* office to see a man that pretended to be his friend— Samuel Sinclair. He is there when a boy comes in and tosses a letter down, "Here is a letter for you, Mac." He takes the letter. It was meant for his wife. He finds it in the handwriting of Richardson, and it bears Richardson's seal. In the position in which he was placed he felt he had the right to read that letter, and he did; and that letter told the whole story—that letter from this adulterer to this adulteress, at this point, discovered in this manner by this unfortunate man—that letter in which he takes occasion to ridicule the strait-laced Puritans, and gives utterance to sentiments that will shock the sense of honor of every gentleman upon that jury.

The following is the letter which was intercepted :—

MARCH 9, 4.50 P.M.

I received two hours ago, darling, yours of yesterday.

At noon I mailed you the *Atlantic* for March to No. 72. This I send in care of Mr. S., hoping that you may get it to-morrow.

Don't be disturbed about your family, little girl. Families always respect accomplished facts (my hobby, you know). I once outraged mine a great deal worse than you ever can yours, and they are the straightest sect of Puritans— but Time made it all correct.

So you couldn't go to Mrs. M.'s till Monday, and couldn't have my room. Be patient, little girl, and *you* shall have to give, not take, orders about my room.

Funny about Lillie and the young lady I am engaged to. It only confirms my theory that you and Molly are first-class intriguers.

Will order your scrap-book on Monday.

Learn all you can about the material and contents of the new book within the next few weeks; for we may want to announce it in my book. Please remember that it *ought to have* plenty of humor, and that it *must* have some horrors. If you recoil from them you shall not do them.

Darling, I smiled at my being " pining and hurt." Why, I am like a man who has got rid of his elephant, I weigh 258, and am lighter-hearted than I have been for years; indeed, I felt as if a weight had been lifted from me, even before your sweet love came to sweeten and bless my life.

All the trouble was that she thought she could not let me go. Long ago, when she and I first came together, I said to her, we will make no vows to love each other always—of that we cannot tell—I will only exact that you tell me the *perfect* truth, whether it keeps us together or separates us, and she replied, God helping me, I will. She tried to, but the leopard could not change its spots, and she did her best, and was very tender and loving, and I have nothing in the world to complain of. If you had not come to me, little girl, it would have made no difference there, *that* scene was ended long ago.

It will rather startle Mrs. S., won't it, darling; I think she will like it in the end. Rose's letter is very graceful and kind, and I am very glad you go, for it will do you much good. It is a great breezy, restful place.

What a goosie it is about my coming home. *Of course* I shall come, whenever my business compels or will let me. What judgment shall you fear, doing no wrong ? The circumstances make it right and unnoticeable, and I will not stay away for 40,000 Mrs. Grundies. I will not neglect work to come; but it is quite possible I may have to come next week. I have not been waiting for you, darling, all these long years to wear haircloth and serve seven years now; I want you always. A hundred times a day my arms seem to stretch out toward you. I never seek my pillow without wanting to fold you to my heart, for a good-night kiss and blessing, and the few months before you can openly be mine will be long enough at best. No grass shall grow under my feet, but I never let public opinion bully me a bit, and never mean to ; so, sunbeam, I shall come whenever I can, and stay as long as business will permit. I will decide about the summer just as soon as I can, darling; can probably surmise by Monday or Tuesday.

Darling, I should be *afraid* if you had fascinated me in a day or a week. The trees which grow in an hour have no deep root. Ours I believe to be no love of a noonday hour, but for all time. Only *one* love ever grew so slowly into my heart as yours has, and that was so tender and blessed that heaven needed and took it. My darling, you are all I would have you, *exactly* what I would have you, in mind, body, and estate, and my tired heart finds in you infinite rest, and riches, and sweetness. Good-night, my love, my own, my wife.

Burn this--will you not ?

Soon after this letter was discovered, this man Richardson returns to New York, and returns to 72 Amity street. Mark, in the mean time, McFarland had left, and before McFarland had left she had absconded ; and when Richardson returns to 72 he finds no one there. But hardly had he returned before she makes her appearance there, accompanied by a lady; and now she wishes board there again, in order that they may again be together, and sacrifice upon the altar of unholy lust at their full convenience. Mrs. McFarland brings this other woman with her as a cover, and she actually tells Mrs. Mason that this lady she has brought with her is engaged to be married to Richardson, and under cover of that lie she gets back into that house, and the amours of that couple are resumed. Soon after this, Richardson leaves 72 Amity street, and goes back again to Washington Place, to the house of Samuel Sinclair; and night no more surely and steadily follows day than again this woman follows Richardson. She leaves 72 Amity street, and goes to No. 8 Washington Place; and there, beyond the shadow of doubt, they occupy for weeks the same apartments, night and day, without a door between them; and so shameless were they that the very servant who came into the room found them on the same bed, hugging and kissing; and all this, this man learned before the homicide took place.

He went to 72 Amity street and opened her trunk, and out of that trunk tumbled the photograph of the accursed Richardson. Here, too, he finds letters from this man, this woman Calhoun, Mrs. Sinclair, and others, showing their participation in accomplishing the ruin of his wife. What is his condition now?

> "In extremes
> Of this condition can it be in man
> To use a moderation? I am thrown
> From a steep rock, headlong into a gulf
> Of misery and find myself past hope,
> In the same moment that I apprehend
> That I am falling! And this the figure
> Of my idol few hours since, while she continued
> In her perfection, that was late a mirror
> In which I saw miraculous shapes of beauty,
> Staid manners, with all excellence a husband
> Could wish in a chaste wife, is on a sudden
> Turned to a magical glass, and does present
> Nothing but horns and horror."

. . . .

By and by again Providence, for its mysterious purposes, restores him. He struggles up and begins the fight again. In the mean time this man Richardson has openly proclaimed his intention, if he can obtain her a divorce, to marry this woman; and he is guilty of the infamy of publishing a card under his own name in the *Tribune* advertising the world of that fact. He had seduced this man's wife, had robbed him of his children, thrust on him a load of debt, and yet wished to add to that the pleasure of advertising him as a cuckold before the world, and he did it.

. . . .

And now it is the 25th of November, 1869. Half an hour before the homicide, an old friend, a member of the bar, meets him in the street, takes hold of him and asks: "What is the matter with you, Mac; you look doubled up and queer—go home." In the air before him he still sees the semblance of Richardson, and his wife, and his little boy. They are beckoning him on; fate directs his steps into the *Tribune* office; scratches at a desk upon a piece of paper lying there, "I saw suddenly two eyes closed upon me like those of a demon, I saw a flash, heard a report—I recollect nothing more." By and by he is arrested, and he is told Richardson is shot, and exclaims: "My God, it must have been me—No!—It was not—Yes! it must have been me!"

There was but one thing left needed to crown this infamy; and we shall claim, gentlemen of the jury, that we have a right to prove it as corroborating the story of this man's life and the evidences of the truth of that story that I have told you. It was a fitting close to this fearful tragedy. It agreed in its violation of all laws, human and divine, with all that preceded it. A woman covered by the flimsy veil of an illegal divorce, unmindful of her husband's happiness, of her husband's reason, and of her own honor— angels weep and devils laugh at the consummation, as benedictions were pronounced upon that union by a man of the name of Frothingham: "We thank thee, O God, for what these two have been to each other." That they have lived in lust and adultery? Why, when that divine made that invocation, he did not remember how, amidst the thunder and lightnings of Sinai, the finger had written upon the table of stone for the guidance of the ages while time shall last, "Thou shalt not commit adultery." "We thank thee, O God, for what these two have been to each other!"

Gentlemen, the divines that officiated on that occasion made a fearful mistake.

The evidence produced by the defence tended mainly to prove the insanity under which McFarland was laboring at the time of the murder, a condition of mind superinduced by the agony he endured at the thought of his separation from his wife. One of the witnesses testified to having had a conversation with the prisoner, and illustrated his manner in the following words : " He came in— Mac did—in an extreme state of excitement; in a perfect frenzy. He placed his hands to his head, exclaiming, ' Oh, my God! my God! What do you think?' I said, ' What is the matter?' he replied, ' I have heard Richardson has obtained a divorce for my wife, and they, with my children, are living over in Jersey City; I will go home and kill myself! my God! my God!' As he walked up and down the room I tried to advise him; I told him to appeal to the law; he said he knew no one in Jersey, and had no money; I told him I would give him letters of introduction, and a letter to an eminent lawyer there; that it would require no money; ' No! no!' he said; I might as well have talked to a rock; he would go home and kill himself, and so he went out of my office like a madman."

During the trial there were a number of letters produced and read, which light up tolerably clearly the progress of this remarkable amour and its grim wind-up. We reproduce them:—

I.—THE CALHOUN LETTERS.

77 CLINTON PLACE, NEW YORK,
Sunday Evening, June 24, 1866.

MY DEAR MRS. MCFARLAND:

It was a good inspiration which led you to write me, and to believe that I wanted to hear from you. A dozen times since you went away I have sat down with the express and absolute purpose of writing you, and then some dreary manuscript interposed, and my interesting pen labored until it was so tired that it had no power of purpose left. My work is of that discouraging order that consumes time and patience, and exhausts the forces, without building any monuments of progress. Revising, correcting, and mending—comparing, rejecting. Eminently useful, greatly easier than writing, of which I am not fond, but rather dreary. I have been so very busy that I have not written much since you went away. Besides my work for the *Tribune*, I do a certain class of book reviews for *The Independent*, and go about with hands so very full, that I have seldom opportunity to take up private letters. For, as I dare say you know already—but as

it is the central fact of the universe, it will bear repetition—I am housekeeping!
I attained that blissful condition, to my extreme surprise, on the first of May.
We heard of the house but two days before; took it, and bought one tea-kettle at
once. For myself, I am most pleased. I enjoy the freedom and largeness and
hospitality of home. And as we must live in shells through all this mortal pil-
grimage, it is so much more comfortable to have them of the largest and pleas-
antest. Our house is very pleasant, as you shall see when you come back. But
for this ignorant present, I could wish myself with you, in the smallest farm-
house that ever took root in a cleft of the hill. For know, O mountain nymph,
that the weather is terrific. Doors and windows swing wide, the generous palm-
leaf is plied, but we carried over the ghostliest breeze from Northern peak, or
Western lake, or Eastern ocean. June in the country, with a wreath of roses and
white hands scattering dews, and June in town, in the brassy helmet of August,
witr sunburned fingers shading blinded eyes, are no kin together. Last week,
the *Tribune* sent me on a flying visit to Saratoga, Lake George, and Lake Cham-
plain, the fruits whereof you shall have when they become immortal in Tuesday's
issue. Saratoga is dreadful, but the lakes and far-away hills filled me with delight. You know I am a cockney of cockneys—know nothing of the heart and
wonder of country life. Never have seen the mountains in my life, save a scattered peak or two, and yet, to me, they are wonderful—things not to talk about
unless the dweller be very fine; constant companionship with nature belittles
him. I think men grow blind and deaf to the glory that is above their heads
and beneath their feet. *Don't they?* I walk in the dark, but it seems to me
that meadow and mountain, roses and river, are more to me than to the man of
whose estate they are part. And, as art and culture must teach me the wonderful secrets and charms of nature, so I fancy must city life train me into country
uses. I have no taste for wigwams; but, all through the soft spring and passionate summer, an eagerness for woods and waters possesses me. Just now, I am
imprisoned in the loop of the editorial scissors, and am so base that I shall doubtless continue to be a bondsman all the season, save when the *Tribune* lets me out
to do its journalistic warbling, keeping a string about me, that I may not fly too
far. If it should believe its vital element of the success of the paper to have two
or three letters from the White Mountains, I am the person to sacrifice my ease in
its interests, and I shall find some practicable route through Shelburne, that I
may take a peep at you.

Everybody is out of town. Mrs. Ward has gone, and the Sinclairs went last
week, and everybody else whom I know, except Mr. Richardson, who has a room
here, and is so delightfully agreeable and good-natured, that not even this dreadful weather makes him cross, which is saying a great deal for his Christian
discipline. Mr. Greeley has almost finished his book, and then he is going away
—probably to Saratoga, to trip the light fantastic toe. Mrs. Greeley has had a
hemorrhage, and is very feeble. For myself, I am very well, rather tired, having
made my jaunt in three days and written three letters, and very anxious of the
dryads and hema-dryads.

I hope you will study *toward* the stage, if not *for* the stage, this summer.
That goal seems to me so inevitable, and so desirable, if you cultivate your very
great gift at all, that whenever I think of you, I wish you were in your rightful

place. The drama is the beautiful art, and you are worthy to be its prophet. My own dreams of serving it will never be hopes now; but, whenever I see brave young feet set toward it, and thoughtful brows bent thitherward, I cry "god-speed" from my inmost soul. I am so weary to-night, and so warm and uncomfortable, that I have written a most stupid letter; but I would not longer let your dear note go unanswered. I love you, and want to know you better. I have no doubt that we met in this great high-road because each had something for the other, and we will know what it is. Write me at the office or here, and be assured of answers as speedy as my tired pen can write. Ever and always, believe me, affectionately yours,

Lu G. Calhoun.

II.

77 Clinton Place, Aug. 26, '66.
Sunday afternoon.

My Beloved Friend:

It is after dinner, and I am bilious, so expect a soporific. Your last two letters were forwarded me at Long Branch, but I had no time to answer them there, and I came home only last night. You have been very good to take so much trouble for me, and I want to see you, and thank you with lips and eyes, and yet it is quite miserably possible that I may not be able to come at all. I am going to tell you all my private affairs, so you will see that this letter is only for your dear self.

You know we are housekeeping for the first time in three years, and expenses are terrifying; but I knew Mr. Calhoun wanted to do it, so I thought we could manage; and when I began to receive a regular salary, I resolved not to ask him for anything for my personal wants. Therefore, I have taken care of myself entirely for the last six months. But I have been away for the *Tribune* three times; though the paper pays my travelling expenses and my board-bill, still I had to dress more than I should at home, and I am forced to buy many things which I should not otherwise. Moreover, I was obliged to put out all my sewing, because I have not had time to do it, and my clothes, and dressmaker's and seamstresses' bills this summer have been over two hundred dollars. Then I took one of my sisters, who is not well, to Saratoga, and that cost me almost fifty dollars, and I pay the school bills of the other, which are ninety dollars a quarter, and altogether I have exactly no money now. Of course, if I were to ask Mr. Calhoun, who is the best man in the world, he would tell me to go, but I know he can't well afford to let me just now, and I don't want to break my resolve.

So I shall have to wait till I can hoard a little, and I fear that will be too late to find you. I shall not go to Shelburne if you are not there, of course. I have not much cared to go at all, except to see you—only that. I wanted to take mother, who has never seen the White Mountains; whose health is delicate, and who is of course growing old. It will be a bitter disappointment to me, on her account, if I can not go. *You* will soon be at home, so that I shall see you in any event. But one thing I will not do, is to "rustle in unpaid-for silk." I had the spectacle of new dresses, and don't mean to have another for a year. I have been trying all summer to save money for some books, for I which am famishing, and some other delightful things, but I suppose I never shall. Do you know I have almost decided to lecture this winter, if I can persuade anybody to hear me, which is problematical. I am going to work at my lectures at all events, and shall resume my elocution lessons to strengthen my voice. I *know* there is as much in me as in Anna Dickinson, and I mean to coin my heart for drachmas, if it be possible. If I can arrange to earn seventy-five dollars by doing extra work these next two weeks, look for me. You know I shall have just double bills to pay, but I want mother to have a nice time, and be able to go just where she likes. Father used to be rich, and now they are. poor; but mother has never been reconciled, and I want to give her all the pleasure within my very narrow grasp. So, my darling, I have told you all my disappointments. When I thought I should be able to go by this time, my bills had not come in, and I did not know how difficult it would be for me to manage them. And I have so many persons besides myself to consider. My heart has gone to you ever so many times, and I shall follow in my body if possible.

And now to leave this miserable ledger business for something better. For myself, I have avowed my immediate future. All this fall and winter I shall do my speedy utmost to make money. It is the one potent servant, the comforter, and consoler, and helper. In its uses I mean, of course, not in itself. And you —I hope your desire and purpose for the stage has not faded nor been trampled out by hard hoofs of necessity. Have you had any encouragement? I am very useless in that way, having no direct theatrical influence, but I'll try to obtain some. I *know* that you would succeed, and I fully believe it to be your best and noblest work. Nothing so much as the stage needs good lives and good heads. I know I could help you in the direction of your wardrobe, but I feel there isn't much else I can do.

However, my dear child, the helpers will come. Of course, I know that the life is by no means an easy one. I know that I counsel you to discouragement and toil, and contact with coarse people and slights. But if I had half the confidence in *my* powers that I have in yours I should have been on the stage months ago, and I know that I should not have failed. I think you have so many gifts; your beautiful voice, your changing color, your varying, soulful face, your earnestness and freshness of nature, your love for your art—and in your love for your art and your love for your children you have also the highest incentive. Dear child, I wish I could make your path straight and smooth to the highest success ; but only that success is highest to which we make our way with pain and toil. When you come back we will have long talks about this matter, and see if we cannot make our eager ambition give place to excellent doing.

I believe Stuart might be induced to place you on the staff. They have absolutely no lady at Winter Garden. That Miss Johnson is a chambermaid of the most hopeless order, and how Edwin Booth can play with her passes my understanding. Now, if ever, women of power are needed on the stage, and I believe way can be made. You know Stuart loves the *Tribune*. I'll write to Mr. Gay and persuade him to use his influence if it will do any good. A Mr. Long would help me. Write me anything—all your hopes and fears and troubles. I have seldom in my life been so frank with *old* friends as in this morning of our love with you. I hope you will be moved to let me help you with your burdens, if that be possible, or at least to tell me what they are.

Meanwhile, I shall indulge a lovely dream of seeing a fitting Desdemona, and Juliet, and Ophelia, and Maritana, to an Othello long unmatched, though often dreadfully wedded ; a doting but imcomprehensible Richelieu ; a Hamlet, who must have been mad to love such a maiden as the stage has long cursed him with ; and a Don Cæsar, whose one unpardonable crime was his admiration of the abominable Gipsy he is compelled to make love to. If you do succeed in making an engagement, I shall not have one shadowy fear of your histrionic success, and I shall really feel that I have done some good in the world—a condition of feeling which I have often felt to be unattainable. One has no business not to do his peculiar work. I shall always feel that it was mine, and that I wronged myself in not doing it. But I was helpless. I swam strong seas, and was wrecked in peaceful waters at last. But take care, my darling, that you do not make the same mistake. I know that you will be a happier woman, and therefore a better one, if you *can* do the work which is in you.

When are you coming home ? We must see much of each other this winter. We cannot afford to miss that, I think. I need you, and I am sure you want me. My dear, I don't quite suppose we shall be able to set the world right, but we may do something toward keeping each other right. I get dreadfully tired and discouraged, and the mistakes of my life well-nigh overwhelm me at times ; and if I can catch somebody to preach to, I always find myself wonderfully improved in temper and cheerfulness. I perceive that you have a beautiful patience, which fits you to be a victim, and I dare say I shall make you one. On the other hand, when other people are worn out, I possess the most indomitable patience and hope, so I may help you.

I hope you will bring back health and strength from those far hills, and a whole harvest of freshness, to be used all winter as need calls. With the spirit of prophecy strong upon me, I foretell that this winter will be a crisis to us both, and I hope a long season of good work in the right direction. Let us weave our hopes about the coming months, and cover them with garlands of peace. I need that, O, so much.

I must stop for the charming interruption of correcting an endless proof. This worthless letter must go, because I shall not have time to write another. Let me hear very soon from you, please ; and remember that, whether I am so happy as to come or remain here and await you,

I am ever freely yours,

Lu G. C——.

Did you ask me what was my name ? It is the pretty Italian name, Lu-ci-a ; but everybody mispronounces it, so I like the diminutive better. Please use it.

III.

77 Clinton Place,
Saturday, 1st.

My Dearest Child :

Do you know what is my panacea for all my woes ? Mr. Richardson. Nobody is half so kind or unselfish as he, and when I am "*stuck*," as the newsboys say, I just tell him, and his clear common sense and kind heart always finds a way into smooth paths again. Therefore, if I and he were here, I should just trust him with the whole story, and send him to see Stuart, whom he knows very well. Alas! he left for Kansas on Wednesday, and my right hand is wanting. So I must e'en do the next best thing. I can not at this moment tell what, but my inspiration will come in the course of the day. It always does. I never met Stuart but once, when he was very courteous. He would not remember me now, but if it is the best thing for me to go and see him, I shall go. I shall just find out all his ways from one or two Bohemians who know him intimately, and then visit him and ask him to come and take luncheon with me, as will most propitiate his lordship. My dear, this thing is going to be done. I *know* it *can* be, and I *mean* it shall. I shall set about it to-day, and have progress to report when you come back. Mrs. Mowatt is a shining exception to Mr. Stuart's theory. Mr. Vandenhoff is another. Charlotte Cushman went on the stage to sing, not to play. Madeline Henriques, to her admirers, and Mrs. Jennings, are two more. But it is for us to establish precedents, not to follow them. What did our fathers die for else!

Actresses are born, not made, and if most of our actors were trained for the stage, it is quite time we had some who were not. We may hope for decency, if not for genius. Think of that dreadful Johnson, at Winter Garden, as one of the trained school! Or indeed, of all Booth's support, for that matter. I know that we can do this thing, and we must. Of course, you can take a feigned name for your country engagement, and when you are announced here, they can say "her first appearance at this theatre." I should do it, by all means. Of course, it is no *previous reputation* that Stuart wants, but only the assurance that on the stage you will know your right hand from your left. It vexes me when he has such materials in use that he should interpose objections to better, but I suppose it is necessary.

Well, my darling, there is more glory in plucking bright honor from the pale-faced moon than in being petted with sugar-plums of ease, isn't there? The very effort will make the fruit better worth. We'll see; but don't have one doubt of the end. It is perseverance and will that win in the end, and you have talent for *fifty* actresses as at present rated. Your letter has but just come, and I dashed off this sheet that you might not be kept waiting. I'll write again when I have news to tell. I want to come to you more than I can tell you. *I want you*, and I am starving for the living bread of rocks and hills and rivers, but I must e'en feed myself with paving stones, I fear. I don't suppose it will be possible for you to come. If any kind fate should bequeath me a lottery ticket of value in the brief interim, I will be with you on that good Friday. I am the scribbling Sisyphea whose rock rolls down faster than she can bring it up again. I fear I don't sing at the endless task like my antetype. Ah! well, life is nothing but the use we make of it, and it is better to get false teeth for people who need them than to gather apples of Olympus for one's self. What will be your Salem address? Come to me as soon as you are back, and let me know the New York number. We must gather what gold we can in town, if the mulleins and Aaron's rods did have to fall into melancholy graves without the benediction of my smile. You will be very good indeed to let me read with you.

I shall enjoy it and profit by it immensely. My voice is penetrating when in best condition, but strong only in low notes, and they are rusty now. What I want is fulness of tone, and I think I can gain that by diligent work. I must stop. I hope you can read this crooked scrawl.

Ever and always, my beloved, yours fully,

Write often.   Lu.

IV.

77 Clinton Place,
Thursday, April 27.

Hurrah, my darling! All my wheels are turning the right way, and the world moves. Mr. Stuart has just gone. He *did* answer your second letter at length. Booth was with him when it reached him, and he read it to that divine man, "who feels interested in" you. I quote the words of the Potentate. And if you will play such parts as Queen, in Hamlet, and others at first, you can have an engagement with the miracle! here!! this winter!!! under an assumed name!!!! Or if you don't want to do that, Mr. Stuart will give you an engagement in the country; but I advise here *first*, by all means. My darling, I could not be happier if I had discovered a gold mine. Maybe we have. Think of playing with Booth. I believe I should die of that rose in aromatic pain if such a privilege were mine. My dear, this is such a good omen. Youth, and hope, and beauty, as poor Miss Flite used to say; but there is no sad moral in this case. I hope this will reach you in Boston, it will comfort you so much; but if it does not, it will be only because you will be here, where I can tell you of all the wire-pulling I have done. I am really good for something, I believe, after all; and when you succeed I shall felicitate myself as none other. I pray you pardon this incoherent scrawl. I am so delighted I know not how to be consecutive. In all my prayers hereafter, I shall name W. Stuart by name. Nobody could be kinder than he, and he wants you to come and see him as soon as you are here. "Such larks, Pip!" And Booth! he has talked about you, and himself proposed to bring you out! See Naples, and then die!

I must stop to catch the mail. My darling, I put two loving arms about you, and gave you the heartiest and hopefulest blessing you ever had in your life. Come at once. If you should come on Saturday, and don't have time to come and see me, go to church, Mr. Frothingham's, Fortieth street, near Sixth avenue, on Sunday morning, and sit with me, pew 89, and we'll talk it all over afterward.

Ever devotedly,

Lu.

V.

My Darling:

I suppose you must be snow-bound, as I am, and I send a good-morning. Lillie and Junius pronounced your "Lucy Capulet" better than Madame St. Juliet. There is *incense* for *genius*. I shall work all day, and be ready to help you to-morrow. Sacrifice yourself by going to Hennessey's, or in any other way!

My fate cries out, and informs me that I wish to know him. Really to get *at* him.

I am quite sure there is something behind his gray eyes and mobile face. I don't like knowing people indifferently. Husks are such dry fare. But people with cores and fruit within draw me so; there are just three persons who are much to me in the flesh—you—and you can guess the other two.

But my dream-friends are numerous. Booth is one of them. Spiritually, he is my intimate. He would be amazed to see with what I have endowed him, and how confidential he is with me. Do *you* have such whims? My novel will be a study of psychology, I fancy. A strange story. The boy waits. I begin to say that I love you dearly—always shall—always must. That you are heroic and high, and a gospel to me who need one. Some day, or rather some night, I shall tell you such a story of my turbulent existence. I would rather write it, but I shall never have time. Suppose I write my novel in letters to you? How much we have to say to each other, that we never shall utter till the leisure of the New Jerusalem offers opportunity.

Ever, my darling, yours,

Lu.

———

VI.

FRIDAY MORNING, Feb. 22.

MY DARLING CHILD:

What *can* I say to comfort thee? My heart bleeds over thee. Would I could enfold thee for evermore. My darling, if it were not for Percy, I should take thee away and keep thee as soon as I go home. I do not suppose Mr. C. would let me keep him. My precious, you *must* make your decision. It is profanation for you to stay with that man—you *shall* not. No woman ought to put her womanhood to shame as you have been forced to do for years. It is most cruel, most devilish. You cannot work, you cannot advance, you can make certain of no future for yourself and the children while you stay. There is no justice, no reason, no hope, in your doing it. My darling, you will leave him scatheless; the world is more generous than we think about those things. Every thoughtful man or woman will justify you, and you can shake off the shackles and work with free hands. It is dreadful to have you fight against such odds. I think you could live, yourself and Percy, for what you earn now; and if you can only be free so that you can improve, your salary will be increased. It is wonderful that you have been able to do anything with your disabilities, and I do think that now you may do so much. Oh, *do* leave him, my darling. It is so wrong that you should stay with him.

FRIDAY EVENING.

MY DARLING:

We have just received Mr. R——'s letter. I am *so* glad that you have left M.; do not, I *beseech* you, return. Do not let any weakness of mercy possess you. It is happy that the stroke has fallen, no matter what heart-break come with it. I could be glad that you suffer, if your suffering would keep you away from him. My darling for whom I would die, *do* not so wrong your womanhood as to go back. You *must* not; *shall not.* When I come back, you shall come straight to me and *stay.* I will have it so. I will come to-morrow, if you need me. *Write* me, my darling—all things. Even if you are distracted, write. It will calm you, and help you. All my heart flows to you. I would help you, guard you, heal you, if I could. My darling, you cannot be misunderstood. I, a proud woman, tell you that only by leaving him can you justify yourself to yourself, and to the world of *noble* people. My darling, my money and purse and grief are yours forever. You will not hesitate to come to me, for you love me. *This* is a poor note, I have had to scrawl in pencil what I have not had time to say in ink; to-morrow, if you are better, I shall write you a better letter. All my heart is yours. Let Mr. R—— help you. He is good and strong. Stay where you are till I come. Then come to me. My darling, I love you and sorrow for you.

Thine ever,

Lu.

VII.

MRS. SAMUEL SINCLAIR TO MRS. M'FARLAND.

WASHINGTON, Feb. 21.

MY DEAREST FRIEND:

Mrs. C. read your letter to me this morning, and I am almost heart-broken for you. My dear, what are you going to do? Whatever you decide upon, of course, your friends—your *true* friends—will accept. But I do hope you will act with firmness and decision. It seems to me that one great effort is only a question of time, and the sooner it is made the better for you and your children. Do not for one moment longer entertain that morbid idea that you are responsible for the life of one who is sure to break you down completely, and ruin, perhaps, your children, if they continue to live with him. It will kill you to live this way, and you must not do it. Those dear little boys must be taken care of, and who can do it but their own dear mother?

My dear Abby, I love you like a sister, or I should not write this. Anything that I can do for you, I will cheerfully. Do not despair. You have health, youth, and good friends, and all your friends, without exception, will support you. I have no doubt of your success on the stage, but should you find that too trying for your health, you can do equally well by writing. I think you are very modest in your own estimation. I think you *write* better than almost any one I know; and should you give your time to it, I have no doubt of your exceeding any American female writer in a short time.

I must suggest one thing, and that is to get Percy away from his father as soon as possible. You know Percy now believes in him, and the longer he remains with him the more intensified will this feeling become, and, of course, the longer it will take to erase it.

It seems a long time since I left you, and I am quite ashamed of not having written before; but our time has been wonderfully filled with Washington gayety, and I am very apt, as you know, to neglect writing to my friends when I feel certain all is well. I have not been jealous, although you have written to Mrs. C. several times. I love her too much not to be willing to give her more than half of what I would receive. Is she not good and charming? How is dear little Danny? I wish he could come to Mary's birthday—the 9th of March. You must come, and bring Percy. We may not be home before the 8th, but I don't dare write that home. Remember, that *Fear* is your friend. I hope you will not neglect her in my absence. Now, my darling, do write soon. I shall hope for something definite.

Your devoted friend,

C. A. S.

A great number of witnesses were examined for the defence, and among them were men and women of considerable prominence in the social and literary world. Horace Greeley, founder of the *Tribune;* Fitz-Hugh Ludlow, journalist, author of the "Hasheesh Eater," and since dead at Geneva; Junius Henri Browne, magazinist; Amos J. Cummings, of the *Sun;* Lucia Gilbert Calhoun Runkle; Whitelaw Reid, of the *Tribune;* William Stuart, formerly manager of the Winter Garden Theatre; F. B. Carpenter, the artist; Samuel Sinclair, then publisher of the *Tribune;* Oliver Johnson, journalist, of the *Christian Union.*

It would, of course, be a useless task to attempt, in a book of this description, to keep to the line of the testimony adduced from these people, and the scores of others who were brought upon the stand for the purpose of throwing what light they could upon the murder and its antecedents. The purpose of the prosecution was to prove that the shooting in the *Tribune* office was a wilful murder; that of the defence to sustain the insanity plea they had advanced. Over this line the skirmishing took place, and it was hot work most of the time. John Graham was particularly pugnacious and on the offensive—the word being taken in its dual and duel meaning—most of the time. He found a foeman worthy of his steel in Judge Davis, the private counsel for the commonwealth. When the argumentative rapiers of these doughty knights crossed, and the sparks of repartee flashed forth, the audience applauded with delight. Most of the time the Court presented the appearance of a cock-pit, rather than a hall of justice, and any one who dropped in casually might well be excused for not knowing that a man was on trial for his life. Never before, perhaps, at a sitting of a court was there so much cheap wit gotten off, so much nasty *badinage* indulged in, so great a quantity of mud spattered about.

Summed up in as few words as is possible, the trial may be said to have presented in nauseous extenso the rather unsavory story which we have given in decent detail. It all hinged on the intimacy of Mrs. McFarland with Richardson, the various places she and he had boarded, the supposed cruelty with which Mr. McFarland treated her, the going upon the stage, how many pieces she had in the wash at such a time and what they were, her leaving her husband, the visit to Indiana, the divorce, McFarland's insanity and drunkenness—rage and ruin! Dash all this spicy *potpourri*, with a good deal of Free Love, and a strong flavor of Bohemianism; add some very remarkable revelations concerning intellectual life in New York, which we do not choose to give, and we have a kaleidoscopic picture of an amour which began in a gilt-edged and spiritualistic exhibition of platonic love, passed—perhaps—into a more passionate state, and ended in the death of the man who had undertaken the rather dangerous experiment of stealing another man's wife.

Knowing then the story of the crime and what led to it, it is unnecessary to dwell further upon the statements of the witnesses, and we will pass at once to the last act, only pausing to remark that the fight the defence made was a gallant one, and the plea of insanity was ably sustained, being illuminated by a perfect coruscation of medical lime-lights.

Mr. John Graham summed up for the defence. In the course of his address, in which he spared neither the witnesses for the prosecution nor the opposing counsel, in his efforts to find in the conduct of Mrs. Richardson or the action of her champions some excuse for the deed of his client, and outside of the plea of insanity he sought to make the acts of the wife justify the means employed to remove the cause. He continues:

Now, let me ask your attention to the cause of this woman leaving her husband. They were living at No. 72 Amity street, whence the absconding took place on the 21st of February, 1867. Dr. McFarland tells you that he visited them on the Monday before she absconded, at No. 72 Amity street, and that then he first noticed any disagreement between them, and how foolishly fond they were of each other, so much so that he thought it silly. It is true he had found her coming from Richardson's room, and had reproved her for it. That, however, had passed, and they were reconciled; how he bid her "good-by" in the morning, and how she kissed him, and how, when he returned at 4 o'clock in the afternoon, he found her gone. She had gone to No. 8 Washington Place, and the boy Percy had gone on his way to Boston. And you will remember where she went at 2 o'clock in the afternoon. Richardson engineered the whole matter, furnishing the money to carry it out. You will recollect how she gave as a reason for her conduct that defendant had commenced to drink, and how she said " he did not go on sprees, but would get drunk about once in four months," and how she said she was too proud a woman to go back. And you will recollect that in an interview before leaving her husband she told the witness that all she needed to make her an elegant lady, and gather around her the literary people and the *élite* of New York, was money. That was the way the poor foolish being was intoxicated by Richardson ; she was to live no longer with mortals, but with gods. " I will have you," he said to her, " with Greeley and Colfax." She was to be fed on ambrosia and nectar, and the sustenance of mortals was to be laid aside altogether.

When they commenced boarding at 72 Amity street, Richardson was living at No. 61. McFarland and his wife occupied the back room and extension on the first floor. Now, in a few days, Mrs. McFarland applies for a room for a friend of hers, who had to leave the room he was in on the opposite side of the way. Mrs. McFarland negotiates the matter, and Richardson gets into the house and occupies the front room on first floor, and Richardson places his bed against the thin partition separating the two rooms, where he could hear that married couple breathe, and there the libertine lay night after night, till at last even his conscience could allow him to stand it no longer, and he forced this woman to leave her husband.

McFarland is away during the whole day, and they have full access to one another. The adulterous intercourse between them had been prepared, and there was nothing in the way of its consummation and gratification. On one occasion McFarland discovers her coming from Richardson's room, and reproves her, but they make it up and he goes to his work, and, as I said before, returns at 4 o'clock to find his wife at Sinclair's and his son kidnapped and on his way to Boston. Now, why was it that this woman left

her husband in this way, unless it was that Richardson wished
her? Does not Richardson say that all the world needs is only
accomplished facts? Failure is vice, success is virtue—that is Richardson's doctrine. He knew the intimacy between him and Mc-
Farland's wife was getting to be a little too marked, and, for fear
McFarland should discover them, he wanted her away from the
house, and so pressed her away in the barbarous and cruel manner in which he did.

Percy was sent away because little pitchers have long ears, and
because he might tell what he saw, and as it is, that boy could tell
much now, and therefore he had to be got out of the way. She
reasoned that this heart-broken husband, if he did not drown himself, would naturally seek an asylum away from that room
and house, and they wait till he leaves it, and he does leave it;
but Richardson holds on to his room, for the programme is that
she is to come back there under pretence of staying till her engagement at the theatre is concluded, and in that way these two
are together again, in that house, where they can "bill and coo"
to their hearts' content. Is not that the case?

Now, if your Honor pleases, I will call your attention to a fact
that ought to startle any person with human feeling in his heart.
It was not enough for this woman to drag her husband in the
gutter of her infamy, but she coolly seeks to drag him to the house
in which Richardson lived to gratify herself with him. She
would actually drag her very children to the home of her paramour. Can this man ever have any peace of mind as long as that
occurs to him? She goes to Mrs. Benedict's and tries to get in
there; that was to go to Richardson; and when she could not get
there, Richardson comes to her.

Now, I repeat, what must be this man's feelings to think that
she could be so base as not only to bring her paramour to the
house in which she lived, but that she was base enough to drag
her husband and children across the street and make them companions of herself in her unnatural degradation. In reference to
the house in Amity street, the evidence shows that it was a comfortable house. We have had the owner on the stand who lived
there. It is true that Mrs. McFarland had no servant there; $5
per day would not permit that; she had to do her own housework;

that she was not rustling in silks, nor living with the gods, and she was discontented. I admit that it was not a life that would please her; but if this man could have done better he would have given her more ease and luxury. You will remember the testimony of Mrs. Mason, that her servant did all the principal part of the work; and you will remember how, on the morning after his return, Mrs. McFarland went down and cooked his breakfast. She did not complain of that, though she felt it a labor to cook her husband's. She returned to that house of her own good will when her husband was out of it, for to her, with Richardson in it, it was a palace, but with her husband it was a tenement-house. Another important matter to which I call your attention is this, for it puts a ball through two witnesses of the prosecution. I have shown you that they meant to drive McFarland away from 72 Amity street by her absconding, and then the wife is to return and take sole possession of the rooms which before were not good enough for her when her husband was with her, and Richardson, who has been in Hartford and kept his room, is also to return to the same house. She receives a telegram informing her when he will return at night, and she lets him in. Miss Gilbert and Mr. Browne were brought here to prove that Richardson got in with a night-key, and Miss Gilbert says she slept there; but Mrs. Mason says she did not sleep there at all; and Mr. Mason tells you that the idea of a night-key was a fabrication, because before that he compelled Browne, with whom Richardson had left his key, to surrender it, for though he did not take it, he says, from his hand, Browne threw it angrily on the mantel-piece in the room, and Mr. Mason took possession of it.

Why do they want to show that Richardson had a night-key? Simply because they knew that if Mrs. McFarland was willing to let Richardson in under these circumstances, there must have been adulterous intercourse existing between them; hence Browne and Lillie Gilbert are brought in to prove that Richardson had a night-key, and that no improper intercourse could have taken place, because there was a young lady sleeping with Mrs. McFarland both the nights in question. The testimony for the defence is entitled to credit just as much as the evidence for the prosecution. If Mrs. Mason is to be believed, no young lady slept with

Mrs. McFarland either night, and that Mrs. McFarland cooked Richardson's breakfast the next morning. If Mr. and Mrs. Mason are to be believed, Richardson had no night-key, for Richardson applied next morning for a night-key, and Mr. Mason tells you he forced Browne to surrender the one he had. Now I will call your attention to another fact; Mrs. McFarland comes with Percy after absconding to No. 8 Washington Place; Richardson is there to receive her, goes to get a carriage; he gave the money to pay the expenses of Eliza Wilson to Boston and back; he oversees the whole business; he sees them embark in a carriage; he is there when Eliza Wilson returns, and hears what it is that she told to the Sages about Percy going there, how it was the fear of the small-pox that induced them to send him away. This man had taken the prisoner's wife, and, with a view to make her perfectly free, supplies the money to take this man's child from him beyond the jurisdiction of the State. The child is removed, and the wife is to remain, with a view to make her cohabitation with him more certain, and this I assert is a villany that has hardly been paralleled in the annals of infamy or vice.

Now, gentlemen, we wanted to show a little instance in connection with the circumstances under which Percy was sent to Boston, but the prosecution objected. We wanted to show that, with a view to put a plaster over Eliza Wilson's mouth, Sinclair gave her $50 as a present. If Sinclair had been so very tender of his honor when he took the stand as a witness upon this trial, he should have said: "An insinuation has been made that I tried to purchase the silence of a witness for $50, as to the use made of my house by Richardson and Mrs. McFarland. But I, upon my oath as a witness and my honor as a man, pronounce that it is destitute of foundation." Why did not Mr. Sinclair do this? You will also remember the fact that after the return of Eliza Wilson she is questioned by Richardson as to whether she made safe delivery of the boy; that after that Mrs. McFarland and Richardson are known to be two hours together in a room in Sinclair's house, where they could have carried out the disreputable intercourse that existed between them before they came there. Mrs. Calhoun became acquainted with Mrs. McFarland in January, 1866, at an evening entertainment. In less than fourteen months from that time this man and wife are apart. It is for you to say who separated them, and who had a hand in bringing about this separation.

The first letter Mrs. Calhoun writes is dated 24th of January, 1866, from 77 Clinton Place, and refers to a letter from Mrs. McFarland, which she assumes to answer. The first sentence reads, " My dear Mrs. McFarland " (after a while it is " My Darling," and she is ready to eat her up pretty soon). " It was a good inspiration that led you to write to me and to believe I wanted to hear from you." In another place she says, " But for this ignorant present I could wish myself with you in the smallest farm-house that ever took root in the cleft of the hills." Why did she wish to be with her in seclusion ? Why this inordinate love of a person she had scarcely known six months ? Then she goes on, and in another place says (speaking of the *Tribune*): " If it should believe it a vital element of the success of the paper to have two or three letters from the White Mountains, I am the person to sacrifice every ease in its interest, and I shall find some practicable route through Shelburne that I may take a peep at you." This was to impress a weak and probably unsuspecting woman at the time with the idea of her disinterested love for her. Next we hear her writing: " Everybody is out of town ; Mrs. Ward has gone, and the Sinclairs went last week, and everybody else whom I knew had gone before, except Mr. Richardson, who has a room here, and is so delightfully agreeable and good-natured that not even this dreadful weather makes him cross, which is saying a great deal for his Christian discipline." [Laughter through the Court.] Richardson, you see, looms up at last ; but let us see a little further down as to who pushed this foolish woman on the stage. In the very next paragraph Mrs. Calhoun writes : " I hope you will study toward the stage, if not for the stage, this summer." Now, Mrs. McFarland had said nothing about the stage—how comes it that Mrs. Calhoun suggested it ? She goes on : " That goal seems to me so inevitable and so desirable, if you cultivate your very great gift at all, that whenever I think of you I wish you were in your rightful place." Does this read like persuasion ? Does this read like advising her to go upon the stage ? Then she concludes this first letter thus: " I love you, and want to know you better. I have no doubt we met in this great high road because each had something for the other, and we will know what it is." Now let us look at her next letter, which, you will perceive, is dated 16th of August, 1866. In this she calls her— " My Beloved Friend." This is quite a leap from the " Mrs. McFarland " of the first letter. She goes on, after telling her she is making her a confidante, and comes to this : " My heart has gone to you ever so many times, and I shall follow in the body if it be possible. And now to leave this ledger business for some-thing better. All this fall and winter I shall do my exceeding utmost to make money. It is the one potent servant, the com-forter and consoler and helper—in its uses, I mean ; of course not in itself. And I hope your desire and purpose for the stage has not faded "—[Mrs. McFarland had evidently written nothing about the stage]—" nor been trampled out by the hard hoofs of neces-sity. Have you not had any encouragement ? I am very useless in that way, having no direct theatrical influence ; but I will try to obtain some." [Is this not trying to get her on the stage ?] " I know that you would succeed, and I fully believe it to be your best and noblest work." It is said by some friends of this lady that these letters were not written for the public eye. No, they were not ; and that is what makes them more potently significant. They are written for the eye and mind of one person, and their publicity was not reckoned on. Well, she goes on : " Nothing so much as the stage needs good lives and good heads."

This is not complimentary to the stage, nor is it true in point of fact. I have the honor of being acquainted with many noble men and women on the stage, and I have their testimony that the stage is as high, morally and in every other way, as any other avocation pursued on this continent. Then she says : " I know I could help you in the direction of your wardrobe, but I feel there is not much else that I can do." Now, the woman was an abor-tion as an actress—never could and never was meant to succeed, yet she says : " I think you have so many gifts, your beautiful voice, your changing color, your varying, soulful voice, your ear-nestness and freshness of nature, your love for your art, and in your love for your children—you have also the highest incentive. Dear child, I wish I could make your path straight and smooth to the highest success; but only that success is highest to which we make our way with pain and toil." This list of gifts for the stage is a list that was not true in Mrs. McFarland's case : she had none of the talents or the requirements for the stage—it is simply a statement that was meant to work upon her weakness, and it did. Then she tells her: "If you do succeed in making an engagement, I shall not have one shadowy fear of your histrionic success, and I shall really feel that I have done some good in the world—a condition of feeling which I have often felt to be unattainable." Then she goes on to say: "We must see much of each other this winter; I need you, and I am sure you want me. My dear, I don't quite suppose we shall be able to set the world right." After this she tells her: "With the spirit of prophecy strong upon me, I foretell that this will be a crisis to us both, and I hope a long season of good work in the right direction." It was a crisis in the affairs of Mrs. McFarland—a crisis which this woman had worked to bring about. I will now read from her letter of the 1st of September, 1866: "My dearest child, do you know what is my panacea for all my woes? Mr. Richardson. Nobody is half so kind or unselfish as he; and when I am 'stuck,' as the newsboys say, I just tell him, and his clear common sense and kind heart always find a way into smooth paths again." Why should she compliment this man to another woman? This is for the jury to explain. She then goes on to say: "If I and he were here I should just trust him with the whole story, and send him to see Stuart, whom he knows very well." And after referring to Stuart, she says: "My dear, this thing is going to be done. I know it can be, and I mean it shall. I shall set about it to-day." Now, is it an unfounded charge to say that Mrs. Calhoun did put Mrs. McFarland upon the stage? She adds: "I know that we can do this thing, and we must; of course you can take a foreign name for your country engagement." Then she tells her: "It is perseverance that will tell in the end, and you have talent for fifty actresses;" and she ends by saying, "I hope you can read this crooked scrawl. Ever and always my beloved. Yours fully, Lu." And now we come to a letter written on the 27th of September, 1866. "Hurrah, my darling! all my wheels are turning the right way, and the world moves. Mr. Stuart is just gone. He did answer your second letter at length. Booth was with him, and he read it to that divine man, who feels interested in you." Then she says: "My dear, this is such a good omen: 'youth, and hope, and beauty,' as poor Miss Flight used to say, but there is no such moral in this case. I hope this will reach you in Boston—it will comfort you so much; but if it does not, it will be only because you will be here, where I can tell you all the wire-pulling I have done. I am really good for something, I believe, after all, and when you succeed I shall felicitate myself as none other." We have it here from the first idea of the stage in these letters to the time the writer gets Mrs. McFarland upon it.

An attempt has been made to bully the counsel in this defence, one of the most impudent and audacious I have ever known. We have said nothing in reference to this lady but what she has written herself, and I ask you if the counsel for this defence have taken any other stand than they have in claiming that Mrs. Calhoun was chiefly instrumental in placing Mrs. McFarland upon the stage, they would not have been guilty of perjury to the unfortunate man they represent. I have read to you the connection of Mrs. Calhoun with this matter, but it is for you to say why she was so particular in some of these letters to press upon the consideration of Mrs. McFarland her estimate of Richardson's virtues.

As soon as she gets upon the stage, who do we find going for her? Richardson is the man that goes, McFarland does not go—he never was seen there. Richardson is the man who goes in at the back door. Yet all this time so confident is Mrs. McFarland of the goodness of her husband and of his kindness—so much shame does she feel, that she tells Mrs. Burdock that she has a husband who is good and kind, but that there was a great disparity in their years. If Mrs. Burdock is to be believed, in January or December, 1866 or 1867, was not this man a dutiful husband to that woman, on her own showing?

Now permit me to call your attention to some extracts from Mrs. Sinclair's letters. As a lawyer I stand here, and am bound under oath. To read these things it is no pleasure to me. I have toiled in this case, night and day, till I could scarcely stand it. My health has become affected, but I ask no higher death than to die with my harness on. However much my professional brethren may find fault in me, there is no lawyer at this bar but will tell you I stick to my client as close as his own skin.

Let me read you a few extracts from Mrs. Sinclair's letter of the 21st of February, in which she says: "My dearest friend— Mrs. C. read your letter to me this morning, and I am almost heart-broken for you. My dear, what are you going to do? Whatever course you decide upon of course your friends, your true friends, will accept, but I do hope you will act with firmness and decision. It seems to me that one great effort is only a question of time, and the sooner it is made the better for you and your children."

Just see how cruel this is: "Do not for one moment longer entertain that morbid idea that you are responsible for the life of one who is sure to break you down completely, and ruin perhaps your children if they continue to live with him. It will kill you to live this way, and you must not do it." Then she proceeds to say: "I must suggest one thing, and that is to get Percy away from his father as soon as possible; you know Percy now believes in him, and the longer he remains with him the more intensified will this feeling become, and, of course, the longer it will take to erase it."

When she wrote that sentence, I ask what cause had she to write the inhuman words to this erring woman? All she testified to against this man was, that she found her in a house she thought it scarcely safe to enter; and that she had been instrumental in getting up an entertainment for her benefit. What consideration, I ask your Honor, in that knowledge to induce the penning of a sentence that would do disgrace to a savage? Let no considerations of sex cause us to mince any truth; tell me, what did she know that justified her in writing this inhuman language to this wicked woman?

Now, let me ask your attention to what Mrs. Calhoun knew when she wrote the letter of the 22d of February, to which I shall presently refer. What did she know, I ask? A more inhuman letter, unless it had facts to build it upon, could never have been written. She knew nothing against this man except that in January, '67, while she was sitting at No. 72 Amity street, reading some manuscript, McFarland came in under the influence of liquor and insisted that Mrs. Calhoun was reading a letter from a lover to his wife, and objected to her being in his house at all. To no other fact did she testify concerning this man. It is true he did object to her being in his house, and well has she revenged herself for it.

Is there another fact in this case that caused that woman to hate this man? He did object to Mrs. Calhoun being there with his wife. If he was poor—grant that he was poor, what consideration was that for the letter to which I shall presently call your attention? But I ask you as men who have heard this evidence, does she specify any other instance of brutality against this man, but that he insulted her because he found her in the society of his wife? Go over this evidence and let my learned adversary do it and cull from it—if you please to call it so—another flower to make up the bouquet of this prosecution, if he can.

What did Mrs. Calhoun not know when she wrote this letter of the 22d of February, to which I shall presently call your attention? She did not know what Mrs. Mason and Mr. Suarr swore to, as to the indecent conduct of Mr. Richardson and Mrs. McFarland. She tells you that, and it is to her credit to say it, she never heard of that until this trial—giving us to understand that if she had known of the adultery that had been going on, as to the circumstances under which Richardson entered that house, and as to the illicit intimacy that there existed, she would not have written that letter at all. She stated further that she never read this intercepted letter until after this trial commenced; so that she didn't know the contents of that letter until the time she wrote this letter of the 22d of February. Now you will perceive how this prosecution felt themselves pinched by this part of the case. [A handcart full of manuscript was brought in here about this time, and it was as much as the strong arms of the private counsel could do almost to lift it and exhibit it.] He wanted to prove that this letter of the 22d of February had been influenced by a written statement of Mrs. McFarland to Mrs. Calhoun of her wrongs, so that Mrs. Calhoun could fall easy upon the ground, that if she had written strongly in this letter of the 22d of February it was because she had been deceived and deluded by the

statements of Mrs. McFarland. The Court very properly excluded that in obedience to the doctrine of the Court of Appeals
to which I have referred: " You can extend the hand of humanity to either husband or wife, but you must not actively get in
between them." That was a correct ruling, and would be upheld
by every lawyer in the land.

Now this letter reads thus:

MY DARLING CHILD: What can I say to comfort you ? My heart bleeds over
thee. Would I could enfold thee for evermore !

My darling, if it were not for Percy, I should take thee away and keep thee as
soon as I go home. I don't suppose Mr. C. would let me keep *him*.

My precious, you must make your decision. It is profanation for you to stay
with that man. You shall not !

All he had done was to insult Mrs. Calhoun by objecting to her
presence with his wife; but had he not a right to ? He did not
order her from the room, but he showed by his conduct that he
didn't want her there, and so conscious was she of it that she left
the room. All that this man ever did to Mrs. Calhoun in the
world has been to show that he didn't wish her to be in company
with his wife. It is enough for me to show that as a husband he
had a right to speak in reference to the associates of his wife.

She then goes on to say.

"It is profanation for you to stay with that man. You shall
not ! No woman ought to put her womanhood to open shame as
you have been forced to do for years." Now she never knew her
until January, 1866. " It is most cruel, most devilish. You cannot work, you cannot advance. You can make certain of no
future for yourself and the children while you stay." Then she
goes on to say:

MY DARLING: You will leave him scatheless ; the world is more generous
than you think about those things. Every thoughtful man or woman will justify
you—and you can shake off the shackles, and work with free hands.

It is dreadful for you to strive against such odds. I think you could live—
yourself and Percy—for what you earn now, and if you can only be free so that
you can improve, your salary will be increased. It is wonderful that you have
been able to do anything with your disabilities, and I do think that now you may
do so much.

She has been upon the stand. Her mouth has been open.
She has been asked to tell against Daniel McFarland all she

knew, and I ask where is the heart that does not shudder and recoil with horror at the reading of *this* letter?

FRIDAY EVENING.

MY DARLING : We have just received Richardson's letter. [The wretch was so exultant over his victory that the first thing he did was to write to those who would be most gratified in knowing the fact] I am so glad you have left him. Don't I beseech of you—[Here is prayer all the time]—Don't, I beseech of you, return. Don't let any weakness of mercy possess you.

What is it that makes a woman angelic? It is the tenderness of her heart. It is the readiness with which her eye suffuses and drops the tear of pity and sympathy at human suffering. Here she exorcises from her own bosom that celestial element of woman's character, and asks this wretched, erring woman also to expel it from the limits of her own breast.

" Don't let any weakness of mercy possess you. Don't forgive your husband." What a remark that is to make. She wrote to a woman that she knew was likely to forgive him. But she says, " Don't forgive him, don't extend to him any mercy. It is happy that the stroke has fallen, whatever heart-break may come."

He (pointing to the prisoner) sits here to-day as the result of that heart-break. That broken heart has placed him where you now see him.

I could be glad that you suffer, for your sufferings would keep you away from him. My darling, for whom I would die, don't so wrong your womanhood as to go back. You *must* not ! *Shall* not ! When I come back you shall come straight home and stay. I will have it so ! I will come to-morrow if you need me. Write me, my darling, all things, even if you are distracted—write.

She knew that the woman then had not given up all love for this man, but she had determined she should if it was in the power of her persuasion to accomplish that result. I do not mean to read more of this letter than the final portion of it; it is this :

All my heart is yours. Let Mr. R.—
[She turns her then over to Mr. Richardson]—
Let Mr. R. help you. He is good and strong. Stay where you are until I come ; then come to me, my darling.

Read these letters for yourselves, and put your own construction upon it.

One more letter, and I have done, and then I shall pass very briefly, and I hope your Honor will allow me to finish ere the adjournment. I am not afraid, for I am emboldened by my oath to do it, to read these letters, and let them carry their own comments.

This letter is not dated, but it was written in February, 1867.

MY DARLING : I suppose you must be snow-bound as I am, and send a good morning. Lillie and Junius pronounced your "Lady Capulet" better than Madame S.'s "Juliet." There is incense for genius. I shall work all day and be ready to help you to morrow.

[Now, gentlemen, tell me the meaning of what I am now going to read to you, and I ask the Court to attend it while I read it.]

Sacrifice yourself by going to Hennessey's, or in any other way. My fate cries out and informs me that I wish to know him. Really, to get at him. I am quite sure there is something behind his gray eyes and mobile face. I don't like knowing people indifferently.

Now, gentlemen, does not that mean this ? " You go to Hennessey's, make his acquaintance and then introduce me." Is that a false construction of it ? If it is, I desire to stand corrected. I have always regarded this as a note which should never be presented to the public eye, and I have only consented that it be presented under a sense of duty that satisfied me ; otherwise I would be traitorous to this man. Let me read it over again, for there is a possibility of mistake about it.

" Sacrifice yourself by going to Hennessey's or in any other way. My fate cries out and informs me that I wish to know him. Really to get at him. I am quite sure there is something behind his gray eyes and mobile face. I don't like knowing people indifferently."

Now, gentlemen, a word upon this intercepted letter. You have heard this letter read over and over again. It would be a waste of time, therefore, to read it to you. My construction of this letter is this, that it refers to a perfect system of philosophy that was professed in and practised upon by this man Richardson. You will perceive—and almost the outset of the letter shows it, and the sooner Richardson went to his grave, if this was his doctrine, the better for society—" Don't be disturbed about your family, little girl ; families always respect accomplished facts— my hobby, you know—I once outraged mine." Here he implies that she has outraged hers. She had no excuse to leave this man, nothing of the kind. He continues : " I once outraged mine a great deal worse than ever you can yours, and they are the straightest sect of Puritans, but time made it all correct." Now, I ask you this—Doesn't he here concede that in leaving her husband she outraged her husband ? But he tells her that the iniquity of the outrage is really to be its success, that the world don't look to how ends are brought about, so long as those ends are brought about. " Accomplished facts " are all the world wants.

Mr. Graham closed the able argument as follows :—The position you undertake, Gentlemen of the Jury, is a broad one. Little did you think when this event first happened that you would be called upon to assume the responsibilities of such an occasion. Meet them like husbands, fathers, men. The highest interests of society are involved in this proceeding. Beware how you announce that the desecration of the marriage relation creates no other emotion in a manly bosom than that of mere manly passion or revenge. By all the considerations which hallow it in your eyes, do not thus lightly esteem it. A home in ruins, how distressing the desolation. All sublunary happiness is short-lived at best. That of the family circle is not exempt. One by one its members may be summoned to other spheres, to take part in other cares, to put on other relations. Death may enter its portals and receive from its number its victims. In all this there is pain ; but grief is endurable in any form but that of dishonor.

Domus amica pro Domus optima. Home is home though ever so lonely. The best home for us is that which receives us with the warmest heart and welcomes us with the most cordial hand. *Inter paternons parietes.* Within the walls of the family mansion how happy, how joyous those words. At their mention does the memory revert voluntarily to the abode of our earlier days, where gathered around the family fireside, in which a correspondence of love and affection—father, mother, brothers, and sisters— constituted a little community in themselves. Who, if we could, would not be a child again? To you were committed those social interests; upon you are rivetted the eyes of an anxious public. You are to reflect in your action the value you place upon your own hearths and the affection with which you regard your own firesides.

When you release them from this place, remember to bear the gladdening news that cannot be desecrated with impunity by the trade of the adulterer. Let these helpless innocents who look upon you feel that they are still safe, that they still enjoy security. The purity of woman is not to be questioned; her virtue is a tower of strength, it has proved itself able to withstand the strongest and most persistent assaults, still are we not taught daily to pray that we may not be led in a tempter's plot? In her appropriate and exclusive department may she ever illustrate her scriptural portraiture, and may it be the highest ambition of every wife and mother to have it said of her that "she perceiveth that her merchandise is good—her candle goeth not out by night; that she openeth her mouth with wisdom, and in her tongue is the love of kindness; that she looketh well to the ways of her household and eateth not the bread of idleness; that her children rise up and call her blessed; her husband, also, and he praiseth her; and her husband is known in the gates where he sitteth among the elders in the lane." Let those who dare dishonor the husband and the father, who wickedly presume to sap the foundations of his happiness, be admonished in good season of the perilousness of the work in which they are engaged. As a result of your deliberation, may they realize and acknowledge the never-failing justice of the Divine edict that jealousy is the rage of a man, and that he will not, cannot, must not spare in the day of his vengeance.

District Attorney Garvin then summed up for the people in an able and effective argument, occupying nearly two and one-half hours, in which he disclaimed the insanity plea, and enlarged on the brutality and dissipation of McFarland and his premeditated design on the life of Richardson. At the close of his argument Recorder Hackett charged the jury, cautioning them to remember that there were no persons besides the accused on trial before them, and that the testimony of the witnesses must be taken or their credibility as witnesses impeached. He then gave the points of law as governing the subject of insanity, and touching the social relations, added :

The counsel for the defence has stated in your hearing that several times in kindred cases, he has been called upon to vindicate the sanctity of the marriage tie, or of upholding and defending the marriage relation. I charge you, gentlemen, that no such ideas as those should find entrance into the jury-box. You are not to uphold nor to prostrate the marriage relation by your verdict. Fourierism, free-love, or sentimentalism on the one hand, and moral reflections upon the conduct of the deceased man or living woman upon the other hand, are not legitimately to affect your verdict. Some of you might arrive at the conclusion upon some of the extraneous matters that have been foisted into this case, that Richardson was the demon whom counsel for the defence describe him to have been, and others of you might arrive at a conclusion that the fact of Richardson and Mrs. McFarland both desiring a divorce and a marriage was proof that no criminality existed between them down to the time of the homicide. Yet, either conclusion would be foreign to your duty—your sworn and solemn duty—your duty to the public and respect for due course of law and order, as well as your duty to the accused. Unsworn men, not clothed with the solemnity of jurors' oaths, and interpreting a worldly code, may say that he who seduces the wife of another ought to be killed, or that he who does so upholds the marriage relation. But judges and jurors must interpret the strict legal code—a code that to swerve even a hair's breadth from is often as fatal to human society as the slighest variation of the mariner's compass is sometimes fatal to the ship and her passengers, whose safety depends on the unswerving integrity of the magnetic needle. And in interpreting that code the inflexible rule of jurors should be, that the aggrieved husband, or father, or relative, who takes the correction of wrongs into his own hands with pistol or knife, and is not in a state of insanity when he did the correction, is not to be acquitted because it is the duty of any man to uphold the sanctity of the marriage tie unassisted by legal procedure. When the prisoner brought his suit against Richardson he was within law. When he became executioner, he took the law into his own hands. If he took this law into his own hands in a state of sanity, and with malice, however sentiment for the living prisoner may applaud the act, he is guilty of felonious killing. If in a state of insanity, however much sentiment in favor of the dead might reprehend the act, or all persons reprehend the wrong done the State by killing its citizen in unauthorized mode, he is not guilty.

The idea of maintaining the law strictly is that jurors shall not speculate on provocation. Wrongs occasioned by a swindler, by a betrayal of political friendship, by the numerous variety of social insults, could be just as logically estimated by jurors in other cases outside of law, as the wrongs occasioned by a seducer. All wrongs may extenuate homicide from the degree of murder to one of manslaughter when the violent vindicator of them is in a state of sanity, and under a passion which does not permit a design to take life. But laws against homicide are enacted and enforced because society is full of wrongs and of temptations thereby to commit violence at the instigation of malice or passion. Under any wrongs the sane person whom they may have impressed is not at liberty, after his passions have had time to cool, and after the tempest of excited feeling has subsided, to stalk abroad, seek out the unconscious and unprepared victim of his resentment, and without the intervention of forms of law or the judgment of his peers, become the self-appointed avenger of his own wrongs, or vindicator of the violated majesty of the law.

The law must be left to maintain its own dignity, and to enforce its own decrees through the constituted tribunals of its own creation, and has not in any just or legal sense commissioned the accused to the discharge of the duties of this high office. We must carry into effect the law of the land ; we must enforce its solemn mandates, and not nullify or relax its positive commands by misplaced sympathy or morbid clemency. If our duty is clear, we forswear ourselves if we do not perform it. This duty we must discharge at whatever hazard, whether painful or disagreeable. Neither manhood nor honor, the restraints of conscience nor the solemn mandates of the law, allow us to decline its performance, or to hesitate at its execution.

Let us content ourselves with administering the law as we find it in our own appointed sphere of duty. Then we shall have consciences void of offence toward all men, and the happy consciousness that in the spirit of our oaths, and in conformity with the obligations which rest upon us, we have, as faithful and law-abiding citizens, executed the laws of the land.

The Recorder closed his charge at about five minutes before 6, and the jury retired.

The jury were out one hour and fifty-five minutes. While they were absent the usual court-room scenes were enacted. Men gathered together in knots of two and three and discussed the situation. Ladies chatted gayly, the reporters engaged in a game of chaff, and no one seemed particularly oppressed save the counsel on either side. Mr. Graham appeared to have broken down after his immense strain. He would rest his head wearily on his hands, and then, starting to his feet, pace the floor nervously. Gerry's face was white as a sheet. The Recorder left the room.

The prisoner sat like a statue. His little boy Percy climbed upon his knee and tried to caress him, but as the father took no notice of the act the child got down to romp with another boy.

Suddenly the voice of the court crier was heard—"Make a passage there!—make a passage there for the jury!" and the twelve solemn men filed in. The hum of conversation died instantly. There was absolutely no sound to be heard, but on everything rested that painful hush experienced nowhere else than in a court-room when the decision is being given that affects a man's life.

Gerry's face was as pale as the leaf of a white camelia, and down the broad cheeks of the burly Graham tears coursed one another in rapid succession. No face unmoved, unchanged, but McFarland's; even the Recorder's lips twitched, and his fingers moved restlessly. One by one the jurymen took their seats; and, as the last head was lowered, the Clerk of the Court, with a paper in his hand, rose. As he did so, a rustle of paper proceeded from the reporter's table; they were getting ready to write.

"Gentlemen of the jury, please answer to your names." Each name he called answered with its "Here," the silence between each continuing as oppressive as ever.

"Have you agreed upon your verdict?"

"We have," answers the foreman. Here again a murmur rises from the crowd so faint as to be more *felt* than heard.

"How say you, gentlemen, do you find the prisoner at the bar guilty or not guilty?"

HON. NOAH DAVIS.

Another pause of a second in time that seems a year in duration, and the foreman clearly and loudly answers, "Not Guilty."

As the thunderous sea, breaking through the dykes of Holland, roars with its giant voice, so did the audience. There arose one long, spontaneous shout, that shook the building. Then the people began to cheer spasmodically, to throw up their hats, and indulge in the most fantastic demonstrations of delight. The ladies caught the enthusiasm and whitened the air with their waving cambric.

ELBRIDGE T. GERRY.

It was soon over, for the excitement was too intense to last. The usual formalities were gone through, the usual questions asked, and, making his way through the turbulent throng, Daniel McFarland walked out into the Park a free man.

CHAPTER XXXIII.

THE CASE OF CHARLES JEFFARDS—HE KILLS HIS STEP-FATHER—HOW
THE CRIME WAS TRACED TO HIM—HIS DEATH IN PRISON—HENRY
CARNELL—HE MURDERS HIS LANDLORD—THE UNLUCKY JUMP
INTO THE AREA—FOUR YEARS IN THE TOMBS.

"Verily, verily, travellers have seen many monstrous idols in many countries;
but no human eyes have ever seen more daring, gross, and shocking images of
the Divine Nature, than we creatures of the dust make in our own likeness of
our own bad passions."—DICKENS, *in Little Dorrit.*

ON January 5th, 1862, the Sunday morning thoughts of the
adult portion of the community of New York City were
turned from their usual course of devotion or of pleasure, to the
horrible double-murder which had been committed the preceding
night. A citizen, who was quite extensively known, had been
shot down on his way from his place of business; and another
citizen, while in pursuit of the murderer, met a similar fate at
the assassin's hand.

Suspicion was instantly directed to Charles Jeffards as the perpetrator of the two murders, he being known to have cherished
an intense hatred for one of his victims, John Walton, who was
his step-father, and to have uttered threats to kill him.

Mr. Walton was not at the time living with his wife, the mother
of young Jeffards; and if the writer's memory serves him, proceedings for divorce were then pending.

The domestic relations of the unfortunate man were very un-
satisfactory—due, in a great measure, it is thought, to the course
of his stepson, who at times manifested a most ungovernable
temper, and would not submit to the correction or listen to the
advice of his step-father. He was the cause of many quarrels
between his mother and her husband—she invariably taking her
son's part.

On the night of the murder young Jeffards was stopping at a
hotel in Brooklyn, near the ferry, and it was there he conceived

the idea of killing his step-father. He accordingly armed himself with a revolver, and set out to put his thoughts in execution.

It being Saturday night, he knew that his father would not leave his place of business until late—about midnight. He posted himself behind a tree on 18th street, near Third avenue, and calmly awaited his victim, who, he knew, would in all probability pass that way on leaving his office. He had waited but a little while when Mr. Walton came along. Stepping from his lurking-place, he deliberately shot him through the head, killing him instantly. The murderer then fled.

A Mr. Matthews, who chanced to be passing, on his way home from his work in the market, hearing the shot fired, and seeing a man running at the top of his speed, started in pursuit.

Jeffards, finding that his pursuer was rapidly gaining on him, turned around, and with a well-aimed shot from his pistol killed him also.

By this time quite a mob had collected, who gave chase to the murderer, but he succeeded in eluding his pursuers by jumping over a fence into an area, and hiding behind the stoop. No one saw this movement but a servant girl on the opposite side of the street; but she, at the trial, could not swear positively to the prisoner's identity.

When the crowd had passed, Jeffards. left his hiding-place, and, running towards Fourth avenue, got on a car which was on its way up town. Meeting a car going down town, he got on that and rode to the terminus of the route opposite the Astor House; thence he ran down Broadway, through Whitehall street to South Ferry, and caught the boat just as it was leaving the slip.

When he reached his hotel, he asked to know the time, and being told by the landlord, retired to his room.

The excitement throughout the city on the day succeeding the murders, and for several days, was intense. Jeffards, seeing that popular suspicion pointed towards him as the murderer, and knowing that in all probability he would be arrested, concluded to give himself up, thinking that he had too well arranged and executed his plans to be convicted—relying greatly on his ability to prove an *alibi*—as it would naturally seem improbable, if not quite impossible, that he should be at his hotel in Brooklyn within so short a time after the murders were committed.

He was accordingly locked up in the Tombs to await the action of the Grand Jury, which soon after indicted him for the murder of his step-father, John Walton, on which indictment, after waiting a long time, he was tried.

The Prosecuting Attorney was Nelson J. Waterbury; and the late James T. Brady was retained for the defence.

At the trial, Mr. Waterbury proved the possibility of his having committed the murder, and his being at his hotel at the time mentioned, by having a man accomplish the feat of going from the corner of Third Avenue and 18th street, *via* 4th Avenue cars and South Ferry, to the hotel in Brooklyn within the specified time.

The trial lasted for many days, and was ably conducted; but as sufficient evidence could not be adduced to convict the prisoner of the murder, he was acquitted and accordingly discharged. He went with his mother to spend the summer at a quiet country place on Long Island.

The District Attorney, however, felt satisfied that Jeffards was guilty of the crime, and that a murderer had gone out on the world unpunished. Although the murder of John Walton was unavenged, it might still lay in his power to convict the assassin of Matthews.

In the course of his walks about town, the District Attorney came across a man from the 8th Ward, who, having nothing to do, and being by nature specially adapted to the business, agreed to aid him in working up the case.

As above intimated, the District Attorney's suspicions were directed towards one man alone—and that man was Jeffards. He accordingly directed the detective to proceed to the place where Jeffards was stopping with his mother—make his acquaintance, and learn all he could about him.

The detective equipped himself in the style of a man off for a few weeks' vacation in the country, and went to the place indicated.

The first man he met, from the description which had been given him, he concluded to be the game of which he was in quest. He accordingly accosted him in an off-handed manner, asking,

"What kind of a place it was for a gentleman of leisure to stop at?"

Jeffards, for he it really was, replied that it was "a first-rate place," and that there was a great deal of rare sport to be enjoyed. The two became friends at once, and Jeffards introduced the detective to the hotel at which he was stopping.

This ceremony attended to, they repaired to the bar-room for a drink and a chat.

Quite an intimacy sprang up between Jeffards and the detective. They planned little fishing and gunning excursions—smoked—drank and played at cards together—in fact, got along like boon companions and warm personal friends. Jeffards introduced the man to his mother, and made him spend considerable of his time in her society.

When in his cups, Jeffards was very much given to boasting of his prowess—his bold deeds—the numerous scrapes he'd been in—and how nicely he had always managed to get out of them. He told the detective of his having killed the two men—how he had pre-arranged everything—where he had bought the pistol—where he concealed it—and where at that time it was. In fact, he gave a complete history of the tragedies to his new-found friend (?).

The detective wrote to the District Attorney informing him of all that he had learned. The District Attorney wrote to him, in reply, telling him to come on to New York, and, if possible, to bring Jeffards with him.

The detective, having obtained all the information he desired, informed Jeffards that as his time was up, and his business demanded his attention, he must return to the city; and in consideration of the good time he had had with him in the country, was very pressing in his invitation to Jeffards to accompany him, and spend a few days in town.

Jeffards was nothing loath, and accordingly accompanied his supposed friend to New York.

Having made up his mind to have a good time while in New York, and a good time, in his opinion, being impossible without a bountiful supply of drink, they immediately, on their arrival, began a liberal patronage of the various bar-rooms.

Going up Centre street, and coming in sight of the Tombs,

Jeffards proposed to his friend (?) that they take a look in at his old quarters. He accordingly took his friend (?) in, and introducing him to the warden, asked permission to show him over the prison, which was granted.

They remained for some time, and when they left resumed their drinking, stopping at every convenient place to take a glass.

About 9 o'clock in the evening, Jeffards being greatly under the influence of liquor, and being in the vicinity of a bar-room which was kept by his late step-father's brother, they entered and asked for something to drink, which was refused them, Mr. Walton saying that he (Jeffards) should not drink at that place.

This greatly exasperated the young man, who drawing a loaded pistol from his pocket, exclaimed:

"Damn you, I killed your brother, and have a good mind to kill you too," at the same time pointing his pistol at Mr. Walton's head.

The detective took the pistol away from Jeffards, remarking that he (Jeffards) must not get him in trouble, and drawing the charge, restored the weapon.

The following day was Sunday, and according to a plan which had been pre-arranged by the detective, they went to a place in Bleecker street, between Mercer and Greene, called "The Store," —a public-house—to partake of some refreshments.

On their leaving the place, they were accosted by an officer, who, presenting a warrant for the arrest of Jeffards, took him in charge, and led him to the Tombs. When they reached the prison, the warden, who was sitting at the gate, passed in the officer with his prisoner, but refused to allow the friend to enter. Jeffards pleaded hard for his friend's company, and the warden at length accorded the permission.

The prisoner seemed to realize his position, and told the detective that they would, no doubt, now try to hang him, and begged of him never to mention what had, in confidence, been told him. He also desired the detective to go to his mother, notify her of his arrest and incarceration, and she would, in all probability, supply him with money for his immediate wants. But, above all things, he again cautioned him to say nothing of what had occurred between them that might hurt his case.

The District Attorney laid the case before the Grand Jury, which indicted him for the murder of Mr. Matthews, and in a few weeks his trial took place. He was ably defended by his counsel, Mr. James, but after a long and tedious trial, was found guilty of murder in the first degree, and sentenced to be hanged.

His counsel carried the case to the Supreme Court, which confirmed the decision. The case was then taken to the Court of Appeals, which, in its turn, sustained the other courts.

In the mean time, the law relative to capital punishment had been altered. The culprit, under the new law, was to be sent to State prison, there to remain for one year, then to be taken out by the sheriff on a requisition signed by the Governor, and executed.

Jeffards remained for several years in prison, and was finally killed in an altercation with a fellow prisoner by a blow on the head with an adze.

The perpetrator of the deed was taken to White Plains and tried for the murder, but acquitted—when he was remanded to prison to serve out the remainder of his term.

Jeffards was a young man of fair education, and was respectably connected. At the time of his arrest for the murder of Walton, he was a member of one of the prominent military organizations of this city.

HENRY CARNELL.

This man was arrested for the murder of an old man named Louis Rousseau, who kept a bar-room and lodging-house in Dey street. The circumstances, as elicited at the trial, were as follows:—

It seems that Carnell and a friend called at the house one night for lodgings. After agreeing on the terms, the old man showed them to their room, bade them good-night, and then went to shut up.

After a while the two lodgers, feeling that some refreshment would be welcome to their stomachs, repaired to the bar, where they helped themselves pretty freely to the contents of the various decanters and bottles displayed on the shelves.

The demon of drink getting complete control of them, it was but natural that some mischief should be done. They repaired to the sleeping apartment of the old man, which was just off the bar-room, and cut his throat as he lay asleep in his bed. After robbing the place of what money they could find, they left precipitately.

All this occurred while two young men, sons of the proprietor, were sleeping in the place. The first intimation they had of the ghastly crime that had been committed was that, when coming down in the morning, and finding that the house had not been opened, they discovered their father's corpse all covered with blood lying on the bed, in his room.

They gave the alarm, and a search for the murderers was instituted, which resulted in finding Carnell, with a broken leg, lying in an area of the house adjoining. It seems that in trying to effect his escape Carnell jumped over the fence and fell down this area, not knowing of its existence. His companion in crime had succeeded in making good his escape.

Carnell was locked up in the Tombs, and in due time tried for the murder. The prosecution was conducted by Nathaniel Blunt, the District Attorney, and Henry L. Clinton was retained for the defence. The trial resulted in the conviction of the prisoner, and he was accordingly sentenced to be hanged.

Mr. Clinton was very active in his endeavors to obtain a stay of proceedings, but met with no success in this city. He went to Albany to see the Governor, but found that he had gone to Buffalo. Mr. Clinton not having the time to proceed to Buffalo, laid his case before one of the Judges of the Supreme Court, whom he met at Albany, who granted the desired stay of proceedings. Mr. Clinton took the boat for New York that night, and arrived on the following morning, the day set down for the execution to take place.

There was another man to be executed at the same time. The sheriff, Thomas Carnley, knowing that the murder of the old man in Dey street was most foul and unprovoked, had declared that he would carry out the sentence of the court and execute Carnell. Mr. Clinton showed him the order, signed by the Supreme Court Judge, granting the stay of proceedings, and threatened, did he (the sheriff) not heed it, to have him indicted for murder. The sheriff concluded to let Carnell alone, and proceeded with the execution of the other man.

Carnell remained in prison some four years, and then got a new trial. Pleading guilty of manslaughter in the third degree, he was sentenced, April 25, 1855, to four years' imprisonment. At the expiration of his term he returned to New York.

He is now living, his counsel says, on his own farm in Pennsylvania, and is doing well.

CHAPTER XXXIV.

MURDERS IN HOT BLOOD—THE CAR-HOOK MURDER—FOSTER'S CRIME, TRIAL AND FATE—EFFORTS TO SECURE EXECUTIVE CLEMENCY— IS A MAN CRAZED WITH RUM RESPONSIBLE FOR HIS ACTS?— FELIX SANCHEZ STABS HIS FATHER-IN-LAW—MURDERED WITH A BAYONET—STABBED TO DEATH WITH A SWORD-CANE.

"The game was up. The race was at an end, the rope was woven for his neck. . . . He sank down in a heap and never hoped again."

DICKENS, *in Martin Chuzzlewit.*

GOING up? Yes! The gentleman who thus answered the usual query of the car-driver entered a Broadway car on the evening of the 26th of April, 1871, accompanied by two ladies. The gentleman was Avery D. Putnam; the ladies were Madame Duval and her daughter. Mr. Putnam had sauntered out for a stroll, and passing the residence of Madame Duval, dropped in for a short call. The ladies were about leaving home to proceed up town, and Mr. Putnam offered to accompany them. As the car approached the Gilsey House, corner of Broadway and 29th street, Mr. Putnam called the attention of the ladies to the illuminated clock which surmounts the Gilsey House, remarking that it would require a glass to tell the time in cloudy weather. The younger of the two ladies stooped down and peered through the glass in the door to observe the clock. This motion attracted the attention of the driver, who, giving her an insulting glance, nudged the arm of a drunken man who was standing beside him.

The fellow turned, and pressing his face against the glass in proximity to Miss Duval, who had just sat down, smirked in an insulting manner. This was William Foster, conductor on the Broadway line. He had been drinking and carousing for several days, and was on his way to the terminus of the road. Not being noticed, he opened the door, and continued to grin at the ladies in a vulgar manner. After he had stepped back on the platform Madame Duval got up from her seat and closed the door. This only exasperated Foster, and he violently opened the door again. Mr. Putnam becoming indignant, left his seat and passed out on the platform, closing the door behind him. Here Mr. Putnam expostulated with the ruffian, and actually begged him, as Madame Duval was suffering from nervous prostration, to desist. This remonstrance enraged Foster, and as Mr. Putnam entered the car, he was quickly followed by Foster.

Foster made a feint to sit close beside Miss Jennie. Seeing this, Madame Duval clasped her daughter and placed her on the left side, away from Foster, whereupon he said:

"What is it your business?"

To this Madame Duval replied: "She is my daughter, sir."

Foster then turned around, sat down by Mr. Putnam, chuckling and jeering to provoke anger. Finding that Mr. Putnam took no notice of this, he then commenced to talk, but without any response from Mr. Putnam. At last, nettled by the silent contempt of his poor victim, he burst forth in saucy tones:

"Say? How far are you going up?"

Repeating this question twice, and receiving no reply, he brutishly said:

"Well, I'm going as far as you, and before you get out I'll give you hell."

With this Foster rose and passed to the front of the car. Nothing further transpired until the car stopped at Forty-sixth street, upon the request of Madame Duval, and Miss Jennie had already alighted. Mr Putnam was still standing with his right foot on the platform, and his hand in that of Madame Duval, when the glare of the car-lamp flashed upon a piece of upraised iron, and a moment more a crushing sound was heard. The blow descended on the head of Mr. Putnam, and he tumbled backward on the down track. Madame Duval shrieked for help, and shouted for the conductor to stay the car, but he violently jerked the bell, and the driver whipping up the horses, the car started at a break-neck speed up town, the assassin the meanwhile throwing the murderous instrument on the front of the car and running away in the darkness. Here the crushed skull of the murdered man lay bleeding with no assistance near, and no officer in sight. After some time spent in persuasion, Madame Duval finally took the body, and, with the aid of her daughter, dragged it to the sidewalk.

The police arrested the conductor and driver of the car before midnight, and by 3 o'clock the murderer was also in custody.

The great thoroughfare of the metropolis has been the scene of many an act of violence, but never before was there such a ferocious and unprovoked murder as the killing of Mr. Putnam. There was no sympathy for the murderer, notwithstanding he had a wife and children, and was respectably connected. He was born in New York, and had received a passable education at the public schools. His people were dissatisfied with his marriage, and it appears from statements made in the papers that his demoralization began at this stage of his life. He roamed around the world, seeking employment in San Francisco and Australia. He tried many vocations, to finally become a car conductor.

He was speedily brought to trial on the 22d of May, a month not having elapsed since the enactment of the terrible deed. The press denounced the crime in unmeasured terms, and demanded a speedy settlement. There were no palliating circumstances, and it was evident that Foster was a doomed man at the opening of the trial. On the 24th of May, the testimony for and against the prisoner was all in, and counsel for the defence having closed on behalf of the accused, District Attorney Garvin proceeded to address the jury for the prosecution. After a lengthy exordium, replying to certain strictures made by Mr. Bartlett (Foster's counsel) upon the conduct of the case for the people, Mr. Garvin said: No capital case on the records of this Court had been presented with equal promptitude. The prisoner's counsel had admitted that a great crime had been committed—a view in which the whole community had concurred. It was therefore the Court's duty to afford protection to the people of this vast metropolis, over which crime was now riding almost unchecked. It was true that the prisoner had a wife and children. So had Mr. Putnam, who had been slain by the accused. What was law? What was it worth if it did not furnish a security for life, and a condign punishment for criminals? Order and the best interests of society were in peril if such an act as Avery Putnam's murder was allowed to go unrequited.

The jury found him guilty of murder in the first degree, with a recommendation to mercy. The verdict was rendered on the 25th of May. The sentence was passed on the 26th, and the 14th of July was fixed for Foster's execution. Early in July an application was made for a commutation of sentence, and a Writ of Error was granted on the 6th of July. On the 21st of February, 1872, the former judgment was affirmed at the General Term in the city of New York, and the 21st of March, 1872, was again fixed for the execution of the sentence. The application for commutation was renewed, and denied by Governor Hoffman on the 4th of March, 1872. On the 11th of the same month, another Writ of Error to the Court of Appeals, with a Stay of Proceedings, was granted, and on the 21st of January, 1873, the previous judgment was again affirmed at the last-named tribunal.

The most earnest appeals were now made to Governor Dix to commute Foster's sentence to imprisonment for life. Rev. Dr. Tyng, with seven of the jurors, petitioned the Governor in Foster's behalf. Some of the principal papers were clamorous for Foster's life, and insisted that no man's life was certain while ruffians like Foster should be permitted to escape the gallows. Governor Dix finally reprieved Foster, allowing him a fortnight to better prepare himself to meet his fate.

As soon as the action of Governor Dix—in reprieving the condemned man—became known, the entrance to the Tombs was thronged with representatives of the press and a curious crowd. Foster for some days previous had been steadily declining in health, and was unusually subdued and melancholy, scarcely speaking to any one, and seeming to be resigned to his fate. The night before, feeling cold, he requested permission to leave his cell and warm himself before the great stove. He sat alone before the fire, buried in deep thought. When he saw the officers approaching he glanced at them with the stolid indifference which of late had become habitual to him, but suddenly catching sight of the document in the hand of Deputy Sheriff Dunphy, and quickly divining that it contained tidings of vital importance to him, he arose and advanced to meet the officers, his countenance betraying his terrible anxiety, though he did not speak.

Before the silence was broken on either side, Foster had

learned that his case, but a few moments before so desperate, was not altogether so hopeless now. Yet, when the Deputy Sheriff seized his hand in a congratulatory grasp, and joyfully told him that a reprieve had been granted, for a moment the fortitude which had upheld the prisoner through the latest and darkest hour of his imprisonment forsook him, and placing his hand upon his heart, he staggered back as though he had received a blow. For some seconds he was unable to reply to the congratulations showered upon him, and stood with his eye fixed upon the Governor's despatch. His first words, when he had sufficiently recovered himself to speak, were: "Is it possible? You don't say so?"

But a few days had passed before Foster saw that there was no hope for him, and when the hour approached for the condemned man to part with his wife, he wept bitterly.

On the morning of the 21st of March, 1873, Sheriff Brennan entered the Tombs and proceeded directly to Foster's cell. The police were drawn up in a hollow square in the yard, and in front of the scaffold were standing about three hundred spectators. Shortly after 9 o'clock, Foster passed from his cell to the scaffold, and in five minutes thereafter he was hanging by the neck.

He showed no fear, and died easily, after which his remains were given to his relatives.

FELIX SANCHEZ, THE MULATTO.

Felix Sanchez was a good-looking young mulatto, of twenty-five years of age, a native of Cuba.

He had been committed to the Tombs for the murder of his father-in-law, a peaceable old man, who at the time of his death was in the employ of Messrs. Haughwout & Co., on the corner of Broadway and Broome street, in the capacity of porter, and very much thought of by them.

The murder of the old man was not premeditated, but was committed on the impulse of the moment in a frenzy of rage. Sanchez was jealous of his wife, with whom he frequently quarrelled, and it was during one of these quarrels that the old man was stabbed, he being at the time in Sanchez' way.

Sanchez was arrested and committed to the Tombs, where he remained for a long time before his trial, when he was convicted of the murder and sentenced to be hanged.

His case was carried to the Supreme Court, which confirmed the decision of the lower court. It was then taken to the Court of Appeals, where it lay for a long time.

In the mean time Sanchez and the prisoner who occupied the adjoining cell—Stephens, who was under sentence for the murder of his wife, and shortly to be executed—concerted a plot to escape from the prison, which, however, was discovered. By referring to the story of Stephens, the reader will get particulars of the plot and the circumstances which led to its discovery.

While Sanchez' case was pending in the Court of Appeals, the people were greatly excited over the trial of the beautiful Mrs. Hartung for the murder of her husband in the upper part of the State. The Legislature altered the law relating to the punishment for capital offences, abolishing the death penalty and substituting imprisonment for life. It has been intimated that this was done for the purpose of saving Mrs. Hartung, the feeling against hanging a woman being very strong. At the next session of the Legislature, the law was again altered—the culprit to be sentenced to State Prison for one year and then hanged. Since then the law has been again changed, and the one previously in force virtually re-enacted.

In the mean time Sanchez was lying in the City Prison awaiting the issue of his case before the Court of Appeals, which at length decided against him; but owing to some defect in the law the Court concluded that the death penalty could not in this case be inflicted, and the prisoner was to be taken down to court for the purpose of getting his discharge.

A few days previous, Sanchez stabbed a man in the prison, who was taking his food to him. The warden made a charge against him, and he was accordingly tried, convicted, and sentenced to five years' imprisonment in State Prison.

While in State Prison, Sanchez became insane, and was transferred to the State Lunatic Asylum, where he remained for the balance of his term, at the expiration of which he was sent to the Lunatic Asylum on Blackwell's Island, where he now is.

JOHN CRIMMONS, EXECUTED MARCH 30, 1860.

John Crimmons was a young man not over twenty-five years of age when he was executed.

He kept a bar-room in the Fourth Ward, and his business or pleasure demanding his absence from home one day, he left the place in charge of his wife. He returned home towards evening tired and out of humor, and found in his place several loafers of the neighborhood who were importuning his wife for drinks, which she refused, however, to serve them with. They, thereupon, became abusive and used offensive language towards her which exasperated Crimmons, who ordered them out of the place, for which they revenged themselves by throwing stones at the windows.

In a corner behind the bar stood an old musket with bayonet affixed. Crimmons seized this weapon and started in pursuit of the loafers, one of whom, in running away, tripped over the shaft of a cart standing in the street.

Crimmons struck at the prostrate man, and in his passion repeated the blow, running him through the body and killing him.

Crimmons was at once arrested and taken to the Tombs. Some time elapsed before his trial came on, when he was convicted of the crime and sentenced to be hanged.

Strenuous efforts were made to save the prisoner's life. Men standing high in the community, socially and politically, and representing millions of dollars, exerted themselves in his behalf. They waited on the Governor and urged a pardon or commutation of sentence, but without avail. The Governor was firm, and declared that the law should take its course. The man had committed the crime of murder, and he must pay the penalty.

The day of execution came; and at the appointed time Crimmons was taken out and executed in the prison yard. At the awful moment he was the most self-possessed of all there assembled, to whom he made a short address from the gallows.

MOSES LEWINBURG.

Moses Lewinburg, a German, was professor of languages, and a man of great erudition. He was very passionate, and when his temper was once fairly aroused, was wholly beside himself. It was while in one of his fits of ungovernable rage, that he committed the murder for which he was arrested.

He dwelt on the East side of the city, occupying with his family the part of a house—the other portion being tenanted by another family. The apartments were so divided that each of the families had one of the basement rooms, the front room being tenanted by the professor's family.

One morning the man residing in the rear saw fit to open the hall door, which not proving to the professor's liking, he left his apartment and closed it. When the other discovered that the door was closed, he went out and reopened it, whereupon the professor stepped out of his room and remonstrated with him for opening the door.

Some words ensued between the two men, when, something being said that exasperated the professor, he re-entered his room, but returned in a few moments with a sword-cane in his hand, and drawing the weapon, stabbed the man, inflicting a wound from the effects of which he died the same day.

The professor was arrested and taken to the Tombs, and in time tried for the murder. He was found guilty and sentenced to be hanged. His case was appealed to the Supreme Court, then to the Court of Appeals, both courts sustaining the lower court.

While the case was pending in the Court of Appeals, the law relating to capital punishment was changed. No requisition was ever made for this prisoner, and he is still confined at Sing Sing.

There are several prisoners at Sing Sing whose status is the same as that of Lewinburg, and it has been a question with the legal fraternity whether or no they are legally detained, some of the most learned members of the bar having privately expressed the opinion that they are illegally held by the State.

CHAPTER XXXV.

RIVER-THIEVES—THE BIRDS OF PREY WHO PROWL NIGHTLY ALONG
THE RIVER-FRONT OF NEW YORK—HOW THEY OPERATE—THE
SHADOWY SKIFF PROPELLED BY MUFFLED OARS—THE DARK LAN-
TERN OF THE RIVER POLICE—REVOLVER PRACTICE—"MY GOD! I'M
SHOT"—THE HOWLETT AND SAUL CASE—THE DOUBLE EXECUTION—
HAUNTS AND HABITS OF THE RIVER-GANG—THEIR DEEDS—TRAGIC
END OF "SOCCO, THE BRACER."

"Many of them are not early risers at the brightest of times, being birds of
the night who roost when the sun is high and are wide awake and keen for
prey when the stars are out."   DICKENS, in *Bleak House.*

TO those who nightly cross and recross the rivers on either side
of the metropolis, the singularities which strike others so forcibly are of no effect. Familiarity has bred contempt; and where a
visitor to the great city would naturally and necessarily be stricken
with awe and wonder, the *habitué* is nonchalant and unmoved. In
the gloaming, when the variegated lights of the ferry-boats flash
like a kaleidoscope of precious stones, more brilliant in their relief against the inky darkness of the river and adjacent shores,
the boat of the river-thief shoots out from its concealment like an
evil spirit on the night. The shadowy ghostliness of the ships'
rigging nor the sad sobbing of the waves has any romantic interest for the thief. To him it is as much a matter of practicality
and convenience as is the honest merchant's broad daylight. With
all the risk he knows he must encounter, the river-thief is com-
plaisant, and as happy as a criminal can be, when darkness and
storm combine to aid him in his nefarious excursions. Shrouded
by the murkiness of the night, the boat shoots out into mid-stream,
and the muffled oars are plied by strong and skilful arms. There
are three men in the boat, and from their unwavering course it is
evident that their business has been well planned. No haphazard seeking after stray trifles: the river-thief is too thoroughly
a professional. He has previously been instructed by the cap-

tain of the gang of the work expected of him. His only is it to find the means, and his long experience renders this an easy matter. The occupants of the boat in mid-stream have made a survey, and seeing no hindrances, they pull rapidly in-shore and listen for the sound of the spy on the dock to tell them whether or not the police boat is in waiting for them. 'The signal is favorable, and, under the shadows of the docks and ferry-houses, the light skiff is impelled swiftly and silently to its destination. A brig lies in the river, and alongside her the boat pulls and is made fast to her chains. Stealthily one of the crew of the boat climbs to the deck of the vessel, and carefully appropriates whatever loose pieces of chain and rope lie about, but while doing this he does not neglect to note the presence or absence, drowsiness or watchfulness of the guard, for it may be that the booty is rich, and lies in the cabin. If this be the case, four men have been sent, and they are desperate, resolute pugilists, who, if death be necessary to the success of the venture, will not hesitate to take life or sacrifice their own. The men who are lying in the Tombs at this writing, under a sentence of twenty years' imprisonment, were of the character described. Boarding a ship lying in the bay, one knocked the mate on the head, another shot the captain, and the twain then kept the crew at a safe distance while the cabin was ransacked for the plunder they knew to be concealed there; and not content to have secured this, the wife of the captain was held down while a pair of valuable ornaments were taken from her ears. They escaped, but were captured, and are paying the penalty of their misdeeds.

It sometimes happens that as the river-thieves are seeking a haven of safety after a robbery, and as their boat glides quietly along in the dark, that another is seen, and shooting out from behind some wharf or from the shade of some vessel, she makes rapidly for the thieves. They see their enemy and know it for the police-boat. Now comes the race. The police-boat has more men and gaining rapidly on her prey, the latter is called on to surrender. The answer is a laugh of derision as the men lay aside their oars and drawing weapons, prepare to defend themselves to the last. One shot fired at the police-boat brings a dozen in return, and the fusilade is fast and furious for a minute. A cry. "My God, I'm shot," comes from the boat of the thieves, and when the police pull alongside, they find all the men wounded and faint, but one, and he has passed over the river to the Thither Shore.

The tales which these men, criminal as they are, could tell of life at the water-side, would form a page which might be read for the edification of those who seek to know the dark side of life. For as the river-thief, like Rogue Riderhood, pulls up and down in search of plunder, or, in the thieves' vernacular, "swag," he not infrequently hears the splash in the water that tells him of "Another Unfortunate" who has ended a world of trouble and sorrow in that one leap from life to death. He has seen them when they first stood gazing moodily into the water below, and knew from his own experience of life that they, contemplating in bitter agony the past of sorrow and wondering how in the future they may escape the judgment they have been taught to believe is in store for them; he has seen the last leap that told of the first embrace of death; he has noted the rising bubbles that tell of the spirit departed, and the prow of his boat has pushed aside from its course the floating body. And yet none of these things have moved him to reflection, or to such reflection as brings repentance and reformation. And when his trip is performed and he has come safely away with his plunder, he resorts to the vilest drinking saloons of the river-side, and there in the company of his "pals" he forgets the dangers he has passed and sinks deeper and deeper into crime in the exchange of ideas and experiences to be put into practice at the first opportunity.

THE DOUBLE EXECUTION.—HOWLETT AND SAUL.

Twenty years ago, river-thieves were more numerous, if not more daring, than they are to-day. The execution together of Howlett and Saul, which took place in the Tombs on the 28th of January, 1853, struck terror to the hearts of the entire fraternity, and for a brief period their depredations almost ceased.

One murky night in the fall of 1852, a trio of river pirates quietly pulled alongside of the ship *William Watson*, then lying between James slip and Oliver street. They stealthily climbed over the ship's side to her deck. Entering the cabin, they were detected in the act by private watchman Charles Baxter. But one shot was fired, and the watchman fell to the deck dead, the ball having passed through his neck, but the report of the pistol had been heard by a vigilant policeman, and the result was that the murderers were arrested. They proved to be Nicholas Howlett, William Saul, and one Johnson, well-known river-thieves. The three were tried and found guilty of murder in the first degree, and sentenced to be hanged January 28th, 1853. The night previous to the execution, the condemned men appeared in excellent spirits, and laughed and conversed as if their hours on earth were not numbered. They retired about midnight, and both dreamt of being hung. Early on the day of execution, they expressed a desire to see the gallows. When Howlett ascertained that there was a weight to be used, he remarked, "We will go up, instead of going down." Saul answered, "If the spirit went up, it did not matter as to the body." Howlett accompanied the priests to the chapel, where mass was celebrated, while Saul, who was a Protestant, was visited by several eminent clergymen. In the yard surrounding the gallows were about three hundred persons, many of whom had known the condemned men from boyhood. Johnson, whose sentence had been commuted, the day previous, to imprisonment for life, took an affectionate farewell of the men who were to soon suffer the extreme penalty. Sheriff Orser appeared and notified the doomed men that the hour had arrived for their execution, and with little ceremony they were prepared for the gallows. On reaching the foot of the scaffold, Saul expressed a desire to meet several persons, and a number came forward and shook hands with him; among whom were Tom Hyer and Bill Poole, the noted pugilists. Saul uttered a heartfelt prayer for Howlett and himself, and committed his soul to God. The Sheriff, who was much affected, kissed each of the men, and then gave the signal. The axe fell, the rope was severed, and they were jerked six feet from the ground and into eternity.

A BACKWARD GLIMPSE AT THE RIVER PIRATES.

Not having the inclination, nor the opportunity, in the preparation of this work, to delve into the " flash " memoirs of the

river-thieves of New York and Brooklyn, for the purpose of producing a panoramic history of their *personnel* and operations, we
gladly avail ourselves of the subjoined article from the *Brooklyn
Eagle*. It has evidently been collected by a careful hand, and is
a miniature painting of the daring exploits, for years back, of
these reckless men. It scarcely needs any comment, as it adorns
its own tale and points its own moral.

"Ever since the days of Saul and Howlett, organized bands of
pirates and river-thieves have infested both shores of the East
River. This fact has been long and well known to the police of
New York and Brooklyn, who have not alone become familiar
with the members of the different gangs, but have learned their
resorts, their 'molls,' their 'pals' and their 'fences,' and yet
have failed to make any organized attempt to break up river
piracy. The Harbor Police of New York freely admit their inability to suppress stealing on the river, and claim that too much
duty is required of too few men, while the Brooklyn Police urge
as an excuse the fact that they have no Harbor Police. That
there is some truth in these explanations none can deny, for with
the many miles of water front possessed by both cities and the
inducements held out by the junkmen, the wonder is that more
depredations are not committed.

"River-thieves as a class are more reckless of human life than
either burglars or highwaymen. They believe in the doctrine
that 'dead men tell no tales,' they always go well armed, and
never hesitate to sacrifice life rather than jeopardize their own
liberty. They are like wharf-rats, as much at home in the
water as on shore, and when once they have committed a robbery
or a murder, if too closely chased, they are prepared to jump
overboard, dive under a pier, and thus escape arrest or even detection, as has often been done. Probably within a day or two
afterward the vessel they have robbed and the friends of the man
they have murdered will have gone to sea. Thus the circumstances will soon die out of the recollection of the detectives,
who, not stimulated by the hope of a reward, will, of course, fail
to make any efforts to discover the perpetrators of what the newspapers will style, 'Another River Outrage.'

"The river-thieves of New York and Brooklyn are divided

into two classes, namely, those who steal from the docks in the day-time, and those who board and rob vessels by night. In this city the former class abound. Though troublesome, they are not considered dangerous. New York is the haven of the more desperate class; men born on the river who have graduated in crime, and who, after serving several terms in reformatories, jails, and penitentiaries, come forth full-fledged pirates, ready to scuttle a ship, rob a cabin, cut a throat, or throw a watchman overboard. This class belongs to the peculiar institutions of New York city, while our own dock thieves, less known, cruise from Hudson avenue to the Atlantic Dock, paying occasional visits to the Wallabout, back of the Navy Yard Dock, and sometimes inside the Cob Dock of the Navy Yard, thence to that still sparsely-settled region between the built-up portion of Williamsburgh and Brooklyn proper. If closely pressed they leave their boats and their 'swag,' and soon find refuge in the classic regions of Irishtown.

"Twenty years ago river pirates were more numerous, if not more daring, than they are to-day. There were 'Sow' Madden, 'Slobbery Jim,' 'Bill Lowrie,' and 'One-armed Charley,' the pals of Saul and Howlett. As they met their fate, younger men took their places. 'Old Tom Flaherty,' 'Tommy Shay,' 'Bum' Mahoney, 'Cow-legged Sam,' 'Socco,' 'Denny' Brady, and others then became the chief of the river-thieves, and more recently there has been 'Scotchy Lavelle,' 'Tom the Mick,' 'Larry Nevins,' Martin Broderick, Dougan, Carroll, Preslin, Coffee, Merricks, the Commodore, and the gangs so well known about the Hook, the Navy Yard, and the shores of Brooklyn, New York, Jersey City, Hoboken, and Staten Island.

" The exploits of these river-thieves make a perfect romance of crime. Devoid of sensationalism, it is a chapter in the criminal history of New York and Brooklyn as thrilling and interesting as it is true.

" Many old citizens will recollect the excitement caused by the murder of a watchman on board the ship William Watson, lying between James slip and Oliver street, nearly twenty-one years ago. Three river-thieves boarded the vessel at night for the purpose of committing a robbery. They were discovered by the watchman while in the act of rifling the cabin, and thinking to escape detection by murder a shot was fired. The watchman fell dead, shot through the neck, but the pistol-shot had been heard by a vigilant policeman, and the result was that the murderers were arrested. They proved to be Saul, Howlett, and one Johnson, all well-known river-thieves. Justice was then more swift than it is now. Johnson turned State's evidence, and Saul and Howlett expiated their crime on the gallows. What became of Johnson is a mystery to the present day, but it has been hinted that he was killed by 'Bill' Lowrie and others of the Saul and Howlett gang for having 'given them away.' At any rate, Lowrie and 'Slobbery Jim' became the leaders of the gang, with their headquarters at Slaughter-House Point, a low gin-mill at the corner of Water street and James slip, kept by Pete Williams, formerly of New Orleans. After seven murders had been committed there, the place was closed by Captain (now Inspector) Thorne, of the Fourth Ward Police. Then 'Bill' Lowrie and his reputed wife, 'Moll' Maher, opened a grogshop in Water street, near Oliver, next door to 'Bilker's Hall.' It was called 'The Rising States,' and for many years was the headquarters of the river-thieves. About this time Charley Monnell, *alias* 'One-armed Charley,' became a recognized power among the thieves and murderers in the Fourth Ward. He opened a place in Dover street, which he called the 'Hole in the Wall,' and with Kate Flannery and 'Gallus Mag' as Lieutenants, soon made his den attractive to his kindred spirits. It was there that 'Slobbery Jim' stabbed and killed 'Patsey the Barber;' it was there that thieves and junkmen would meet to 'put up jobs;' it was there that men were drugged and robbed and women beaten under 'One-armed Charley's' directions; it was there that young thieves became graduates in crime.

"In 1858 the pirates were stronger, more numerous and better organized than they had been since Saul and Howlett were hanged. The police of the Fourth Ward had nightly encounters with the river-thieves, and Roundsman Blair and Officers Spratt and Gilbert were making themselves notorious by shooting a round dozen of the pirates within a year. 'Slobbery Jim' had meanwhile made his escape, and never more was heard of until he turned up as captain of a company of rebels during the late war; Bill Lowrie had been sent to State Prison for fifteen years; Sam McCarthy, alias 'Cow-legged Sam,' had given up the river and become a burglar, and the rest of the mob had moved up town toward the Hook, or to the neighborhood of the Brooklyn Navy Yard. And thus the old Saul and Howlett gang dropped out of existence, and to a great extent out of the recollection of almost everybody. About this time business began to increase in the Seventh Ward, New York. Junkmen, who, as a class, are not inquisitive and buy anything from anybody without asking any questions about where it came from, began moving from the Fourth to the Seventh Ward. They seemed to do a thriving business, thanks to such thieves as Bill Murray, George Williams, John Watson, Socco, Jim Coffee, Valentine, Billy Woods, Tom the Mick, Larry Nevins, Scotchy Lavelle, Martin Broderick, Abe Cokeley, Denny Brady, George *alias* Pat *alias* Sow Madden, Piggy, Beeny, Nigger and a score of others. This mob did their work very quietly for several years, and were really being forgotten except by the junkmen, when Perry, the junkman, shot and killed ex-Police Officer Thomas Hayes at the Harbeck Stores, Furman street. Perry, the junkman, was one of the New York mob, and Hayes was employed as a private detective at Harbeck Stores. It was found necessary to kill Hayes in order to commit a particular robbery, and his life was sacrificed. With a bullet in his breast, his life's blood flowing out in torrents, poor Hayes jumped on a passing horse-car, and as he fell into a seat, he said to the astonished passengers, 'My name is Thomas Hayes. I am a private watchman at Harbeck Stores. Ned Perry shot me'— and died. The murderer escaped hanging and is now serving out a life sentence in State Prison.

"Four years of comparative quiet again elapsed and the scenes of these midnight murders and robberies had again been transferred, this time to the neighborhood of the Battery. Vigilance on the part of the police soon drove them away, however, and the old ground was visited again. The old river-thieves had all been 'settled,' and the young ones were ambitious. This was the condition of affairs when on the night of May 29, 1873, Joseph Gayles, *alias* 'Socco the Bracer,' 'Bum' Mahoney, a first-class river-thief, and 'Billy' Woods, formerly a stone-cutter but now a murderer and expert river-thief, stole a boat from the foot of Jackson street, and with muffled oars pulled down stream to Pier 27, East River. They boarded the Brig Margaret, of New Orleans, and while ransacking the captain's trunk awakened the captain and mate. A scuffle ensued which resulted in the thieves leaving the brig and taking to their boat. An alarm brought officers Musgrave and Kelly to the scene of the attempted robbery. It was three o'clock in the morning, the sky was overcast, and not a star was to be seen. As Musgrave flashed his dark lantern under the pier, he saw a boat starting out. Throwing the rays of his lantern full upon it, three men stood up, revolvers in hand, and the firing began. Musgrave's first shot gave ' Socco ' his death wound.

" The officers continued firing until they had emptied their pistols, but the thieves escaped in the darkness, and pulled over toward the Long Island shore. 'Socco the Bracer' fainted from loss of blood, and his companions, thinking he was dead, threw him overboard to lighten the boat. The water revived him and he begged piteously to be taken in the boat again. This was done, after much trouble, but as soon as he touched the thwart he gasped and died. The boat was again stopped mid-stream and the lifeless body of ' Socco the Bracer,' with the tell-tale bullet hole through the breast, was thrown to the waters, but four days afterward it came to the surface at the foot of Stanton street, within sight from the residence of the dead river-thief. Secrecy was no longer possible, and now the thieves themselves admit that their pal was killed by Officer Musgrave, of the Fourth Precinct Police.

" Socco's just fate did not prevent the commission of other robberies.

" Less than three months ago the brig Mattano, Captain Connington, was boarded off the Battery by a gang of masked and armed men. The captain and his wife were subjected to many indignities and then robbed of everything of value they had on board the vessel. For this crime two well-known river-thieves, Dougan and Carroll, were arrested, tried, convicted, and sentenced to twenty years' imprisonment in State Prison. They confessed they had been river-thieves all their lives, but denied all knowledge of the crime with which they were charged. Despite their prayers, protestations and oaths, they were convicted, but it has recently been made known to the authorities that the robbery was committed by 'Denny' Brady, 'Larry' Griffin and 'Patsy' Conroy. These three men belong to the gang of masked burglars who have lately been committing such terrible depredations in the suburban villages. Brady is now confined in jail at Catskill, charged with the robbery of Mr. Post's house, and Griffin and Conroy are in the White Plains jail, awaiting trial for the robbery of Mr. Emmett's residence. Brady is a man well known to sports who travel down the Coney Island road; a medium-sized man, with broad shoulders and powerful build. A sentence of, at least, twenty years in State Prison awaits each of them, and the probabilities are that Dougan and Carroll will be pardoned— and arrested again at some not distant day, for a crime they will actually commit. In quick succession several other daring robberies were perpetrated, during the month of December. First came the robbery of the bark 'Zouma,' at Pier 22, East River. Louis Engleman, a Fourth Ward river-thief, who lived at No. 57 Rose street, New York, is the convicted thief. He was captured by Sergeant Blair, of the Second Precinct, after a chase of three hours, during which he jumped overboard and while hanging on to the rudder of a three-masted schooner, at Pier 27, was thrown a rope by a policeman. 'Go to h—l with your rope,' he exclaimed, rejecting it. 'You shan't take me alive.'

"He dove under vessels and docks, and for a long time defied half a dozen officers in boats, but he was at length captured, and is now doing the State some service. The following night an attempt was made to steal some bales of cotton-duck from Pier 8, North River. The watchman gave the alarm, which brought Officer Mulrooney and Captain Lowrie to the scene. The thieves, as they pulled away in their boat, opened fire upon the officers, which the latter returned, apparently with good effect, as one man was heard to exclaim: 'Oh, I'm shot,' but no trace of a dead or wounded river-thief has since been found.

"The 'Hook Gang' of river-thieves is probably composed of the remnant of the successors of Saul and Howlett. Its chief spirits are Merricks, a desperate and bold thief, capable of committing any crime, James Coffee, who has served one term in State Prison, and has his likeness in the Rogues' Album, Le Strange and Lewis, highwaymen, burglars, river-thieves, or pick-pockets, as occasion may require ; Preslin, a daring thief, Riley, who has just been sent to Sing Sing, and his three pals, Mc-Cracken, Gallagher and Bonner, who 'fell' on another racket. This choice crowd holds forth at the foot of Stanton street, across the ferry, and operates anywhere between Fourteenth street and the Battery. The week before Christmas they planned the robbery of a vessel lying at the Atlantic Dock, but for some unknown reason the job failed, and they had to look about for smaller game nearer home. The canal-boat Thomas H. Brick was lying off the foot of Fourteenth street, and shortly after midnight, on the morning of December 20, she was boarded by Sam McCracken, John Gallagher and Tommy Bonner. With pistols in their hands they confronted the captain, who succeeded in giving the alarm before he was bound and gagged. The battle was short and decisive. Officer Booz and Captain M. J. Murphy arrested them, and they are now doing three and a half 'stretches,' each, in Auburn State Prison. They are all very desperate characters, though Bonner, 21 years of age, is probably the most dangerous. Gallagher is only 19, and has served several times in the Penitentiary, and McCracken, 20 years of age, has been an inmate of Crow Hill Castle. Beyond a few petty dock-thieves who infest the First Ward, New York, and are kept in subjection by Captain Van Dusen and his officers, and the scoundrels who prowl along the Brooklyn piers, and whose histories are not different from those of other sneak-thieves, there is no other regular organized mob worthy of extended notice, except the Seventh Ward gang of New York, of which each man has his individual history. Of course, originally, the 'mob' was composed of more expert and daring thieves than it is at present. 'Bum' Mahoney is now the acknowledged leader, but as he is well known to the Brooklyn and New York detectives, his career on the river is gradually drawing to an end. When he and Big Dennis Brady 'worked' together, they were a powerful and dangerous combination.

" Brady, though only thirty-one years of age, has been connected with nearly every daring, prominent robbery in this country. It

was Brady who organized the gang of masked robbers.   He is one
of the three men who, about two years ago, went into the Kensing-
ton Bank, of Philadelphia, tied up the two watchmen and robbed
the safe of $100,000.   Brady, on that occasion, was dressed in the
uniform of a police officer, and for his share in the robbery received $12,000.   Shortly afterward he gave out that he had
‘ squared it,’ married a respectable young woman and opened a
lager-beer saloon in Bayard street, but before six weeks had expired the money was all gone.   Brady was ejected for non-payment of rent, and the reformed burglar became a greater thief
than ever.

   “‘ Bum,’ or Denny Mahoney, is about twenty-four years of age,
very dark complexioned, about five feet five in height, and weighs
140 pounds.   He is smart, brave as a lion, and as daring a little
fellow as ever lived.   No river-thief is better known than ‘ Bum ’
Mahoney.   Every policeman in the Seventh Ward and every detective in New York and Brooklyn knows him as a river-thief,
and yet he has never been to State Prison.   He has served two
terms in the Penitentiary for dock-stealing, has his photograph in
the Rogues’ Album, and claims an intimate acquaintance with the
notorious Jack Perry of Water street.   Perry, from being a notorious thief, has become a notorious liquor-dealer.   His saloon is
the resort for nearly all the Water street thieves and prostitutes,
to whom he likes to tell the story of his stealing Josh Ward’s
champion rowing belt, how he was captured by Sergeant Slater,
convicted, sentenced to State Prison for fourteen years and six
months, and escaped serving a full term on account of his political friends and his good looks.   ‘ Bum ’ Mahoney may be found
there often, particularly when about to ‘ operate ’ on the Long
Island or North River shore.   That is to protect himself in case
of arrest, by proving an alibi.   Nearly two years ago, ‘ Bum ’ was
caught one night by Detectives Jarboe and Shalvey in the act of
robbing a schooner at Pier 50, East River.   Jarboe threw himself
on his prisoner to pinion his hands, when Mahoney tried to throw
him overboard.   In the scuffle Mahoney made his escape, jumped
into a small boat, and then he and the officers exchanged several
shots from their revolvers.   Two days afterward Mahoney was arrested at his home in Water street, by the same detectives, but

meanwhile the schooner had gone to sea, and ' Bum ' was thereupon released, as there was no complaint against him.

" The true leader of the Seventh Ward gang of river-thieves is
not ' Bum ' Mahoney, but ' Tommy ' Shay or Shea. He is a
notorious villain. His likeness adorns the Rogues' Gallery, and
his pedigree is well known to the State Prison authorities. Shay
is 36 years of age, 5 feet 9 inches in height, weight 150 pounds,
is dark complexioned, and of a sullen temper. Ten years ago,
as now, he was a notorious river-thief, and was implicated in killing the mate of a vessel off Riker's Island, with ' Patsy ' Conroy
and ' Larry ' Griffin. He has served one term in Sing Sing, and
is looked upon by young thieves as their beau-ideal of a murderous river-thief.

" Probably the most remarkable man of the Seventh Ward gang
is ' Jimmy ' Whalen. He is 28 years of age, 5 feet 8 inches high,
dark complexioned, and weighs 160 pounds. Mr. Whalen is well
known to the Brooklyn Police, and when he finds business dull
in New York, may easily be found within a short distance of the
Navy Yard gate. He returned from a twelve months' sojourn in
the Penitentiary only a few weeks ago, having served a term
for a most remarkable crime. In company with ' Charley '
Davis, he stole a ship's cable, weighing eight thousand pounds.
Unaided, these two men piled that immense weight of iron in a
boat, and brought it from Pier 50, East River, on the New York
side, to a vacant lot in Van Brunt Street, Brooklyn, near Red
Hook Point. The men were arrested by detectives Shalvey and
Jarboe, and the chain was recovered, and although it could not be
taken to court as evidence against them, Whalen pleaded guilty
and was sent to the Penitentiary for one year, which he served.
Davis pleaded not guilty, was tried, convicted, and sentenced to
State Prison for five years. Whalen wields a large amount of
political influence, and although he had been arrested a score of
times, it had always been found impossible to convict him until
he stole the ship's cable. That was found to be too heavy a load
for his friends to carry, and now he knows how it is himself.

" Bob Taylor, *alias* ' Shipsey,' is properly one of the Seventh
Ward gang, although he is now hiding in this city of churches,
when he could and ought to be arrested, as well as his pal, John

Kane, *alias* 'Beeny,' who is with him. 'Shipsey' was sentenced to five years in State Prison for river piracy at the foot of Pike street, New York, where he robbed a schooner and shot at the captain. He made his escape at Sing Sing, nearly three months ago, since which time he has made his headquarters near the Navy Yard. 'Beeny,' his pal, is also wanted nearer home, and well he knows it. He is a smooth-looking scoundrel, light complexioned, about 5 feet 6½ inches in height, and weighs nearly 160 pounds. He has a round, full, rather good-looking face, and is continually preaching about his honesty. He has served in the Penitentiary, and having been unfortunate in a wheat speculation, he bids fair to reach that institution again within a very few days.

"James Wallace, *alias* 'Nigger,' is another one of this select crowd. He is about five feet ten inches, weighs 175 pounds, and is called 'Nigger' on account of his dark, swarthy complexion. He is a fresh arrival from Sing Sing, where he did the State five years' good work for a very clever river job. He sticks closely to the pier at the foot of Jackson street, New York, where he can be found with 'Johnny' Kirby, a young river-thief, twenty-four years of age, five feet eight inches in height, very light complexioned, and weighs about 130 pounds. Occasionally these two gentlemen, representing the blonde and brunette styles of beauty, make a tour of the watering places, as they call them. No. 275 Water street, kept by George Christopher and 'Long Mary,' is their Saratoga, 'Ann Sank's' dance house is their Newport, 'Kate Carroll's' is their Long Branch, 'Gallus Mag's' is their Coney Island, and the 'Flag of our Union' and 'Liverpool Mary Ann's' are respectively Jerome Park and Fleetwood. They are first-class beats when not in funds, and take great delight in being considered lady-killers and cheek-charmers.

"Excepting 'Tony' Gillespie, who is 'wanted' for a job, the rest of the gang are where they can do but little harm. Tony is a lively young fellow, who has served one term in State Prison and two in the Penitentiary. His particular pal was Michael Noles, *alias* 'Piggy.'

"'Piggy' is now in the Penitentiary for stealing a boat and its contents. Though a nice young man, 'Piggy' has visited the

Penitentiary four times in all, and his 'Moll' thinks it's 'a great shame, and he such a pivoter.'

"One of the 'best men' of the gang is one of the most unfortunate. Edward Sullivan, an accomplished river-thief and burglar, the bosom friend of 'Bum' Mahoney and 'Tommy' Shay, has again been torn away from the family circle. Sullivan is 26 years of age. Six years ago he was a terror, but one night he fell into the hands of a 'flatty cop' and was given 'five stretches' for a very badly executed river job. He served every day of his time, and returned to his old associates a short time ago, determined hereafter to do his work ashore and not afloat. In other words, he changed from a river-thief to a burglar. While practising he again fell, and last week he was sentenced to two years at his old quarters.

"Kings County Penitentiary contains only two of these choice spirits from the Seventh Ward of New York. They are 'Old Tom' Flaherty and James Smith. Smith is an ordinary river-thief and sneak, but 'Old' Flaherty belongs to a fine family. The old man has lived half a century, while Smith has yet to celebrate his twenty-second birthday. They would steal a boat from the New York side and then make for South Brooklyn; then they would work up stream, robbing farm-houses, hen-roosts, canal-boats, or anything else that came in their way.

"At length they fell into the hands of the Brooklyn Police, and were sentenced to the Penitentiary for five years. Flaherty's family has recently become somewhat divided. His wife, a notorious thief and shop-lifter, has been in the State Prison, and is now in the Penitentiary, Blackwell's Island. Their eldest son is serving a ten years' sentence in the Illinois State Prison for burglary, and their youngest son is in Sing Sing, where he was sent for highway robbery and garroting. He will be fifteen years older when he next visits his friends."

CHAPTER XXXVI.

SHARKEY'S CRIME, TRIAL, AND ESCAPE—"STONE WALLS DO NOT A
PRISON MAKE, NOR IRON BARS A CAGE"—THE LOVE OF MAGGIE
JOURDAN—THAT FAMOUS RED TICKET—THE VEILED LADY WHO
PASSED OUT OF THE GATE—MAGGIE'S TRIAL AND DEVOTION.

*" Is she his sister, who, of all the world, went over to him in his shame and
put her hands in his, and with a sweet composure and determination led him
hopefully upon his barren way ? "* DICKENS, in *Dombey & Son.*

IT was Sunday afternoon, September 1st, 1872, and the scene
was the liquor saloon of one Charles Harvey, known as the
" Place," situated at No. 288 Hudson street, this city.

A group of men were drinking at the bar. Their drink was
rye-whiskey. The men were William J. Sharkey, a stylish-dressed
young man, who lived at 119 Varick street ; Robert S. Dunn,
alias Bob Isaacs, of No. 102 Amity street ; William Welsh, Jacob
Phillips, and Will Betts. With the exception of Sharkey, these men
had been in the " Place " some time, engaged in the cheerful pastime of " passing the rosy " and " fanning the fire of conviviality
with the wing of friendship." There had been a funeral that
afternoon, the burial of Mr. James Reilly, a member of the
Michael Norton Association, which Mr. Dunn had attended. Mr.
Sharkey was also a prominent mourner on the occasion. When
the cortege reached the ferry, both Dunn and Sharkey left the
ranks and wended their way back to the liquor saloon in question,
but separately—Dunn arriving first, as we have stated. Dunn
was engaged in imbibition when Sharkey came in.

Now it so happened that Dunn owed Sharkey $600, and the
latter gentleman being in that financially depressed condition
known as " dead-broke," asked Dunn for the loan. Dunn did
not have it, and said so, whereupon Sharkey backed to the door,
drew a single-barrelled, hair-triggered Derringer, and levelled it
at his creditor.

There was a pause for a moment, and then Dunn said : "Don't

shoot, Billy." In the next instant the Derringer "barked," and the slender lance-like flame shot from the muzzle. When the fleecy smoke lifted, Dunn lay dead upon the floor, with a bullet in his right breast. Sharkey walked over to the prostrate form, and said: "Bob, I did not mean to shoot you," and then, turning quickly, ran out of the door and escaped.

SHARKEY.

The deceased was a corpulent, healthy man, and had, until within a short time of the killing, been employed as a dealer in a gambling-saloon, located at No. 149 Fulton street, and was also holding a position in the Comptroller's office, at a salary of $1,500 per annum. The assassin was a well-known Eighth Ward politician, having an association named after him, and he also belonged to all the influential clubs in the Fifth Congressional District.

Dunn was regarded as a harmless man, though he had been connected with faro banks in this city for fifteen years, and he had many friends in "sporting" circles.

On receipt of the news of the murder, Captain Garland and

MAGGIE JOURDAN.

the detectives under his command at once instituted a diligent search for the murderer, and succeeded in tracing Sharkey to a house in Washington street, near Perry, where the fugitive from justice was arrested. Sharkey declared the shooting was quite accidental; but the witnesses of the affair declared it was deliberate, evidently premeditated and intentional. At half-past two o'clock Monday afternoon Drs. Marsh and Houton, both of whom were attached to the Board of Health, held a post-mortem examination upon the body of the deceased, and the verdict that he received his fatal wound at the hands of William J. Sharkey was recorded.

In the Court of General Sessions, Recorder Hackett presiding, the Dunn-Sharkey homicide was first brought up. District Attorney Phelps appeared for the people, and Mr. Charles Brooke represented the prisoner. The witnesses examined were Dr. Stephen W. Root, William Welsh, William Helley, Jacob Phillips, Louis Schlam, and Captain Garland.

Sharkey was found guilty of murder in the first degree, with a recommendation to mercy, the jury being polled, at the request of the prisoner's counsel. The Recorder deferred sentence until the following Monday, and afterwards postponed it until Saturday, June 28; and then again, after hearing certain points and objections by the prisoner's counsel, until the following Wednesday. On that day the Recorder deferred the sentencing of the culprit until July 3, and on that day Sharkey was sentenced to be hanged on August 15, Mr. Brooke giving notice that he would apply, on behalf of the prisoner, for a writ of error and stay of proceedings.

On August 7, application was made in the Supreme Court, Chambers, before Judge Pratt, by Mr. Brooke, for a writ of error. The application was granted, and it operated also as a stay of proceedings. The prisoner, having been tried in the Court of General Sessions, there was no other alternative for the Judge than to grant the writ, and, consequently, no opposition was offered by the District Attorney. If the Supreme Court, General Term, had refused to grant a new trial, the case could have been carried to the Court of Appeals.

Now comes the most melodramatic portion of the story, for we shall have to tell of one of the most remarkable escapes from jail that has ever happened in this country. In broad daylight Mr. Sharkey, dressed as a female, walked out of the Tombs into Franklin street and liberty. The escape was planned and mainly executed by a young woman named Maggie Jourdan, a rather pretty female who rejoiced in being the sweetheart or wife of the con-

THE ESCAPE OF SHARKEY.

demned man. She was assisted in her plan by Mrs. "Wes" Allen, the handsome wife of the *gentleman* by that name who is now sojourning in the picturesque village of Sing Sing upon the Hudson, a guest of the State.

In writing of anything so startling as the escape of a murderer, the most careful rhetoric cannot surpass the realistic merits of a reportorial article that was stricken out red-hot at the time. For that reason—and before proceeding to a pen-picture of Sharkey and his "true-love"—we insert a local screed upon the subject taken from the *New York Herald* of Nov. 20th, 1873. It gives a graphic account of the *modus operandi* of the escape.

"About half-past one o'clock yesterday afternoon William J. Sharkey, the condemned murderer of Robert S. Dunn, made his escape from the Tombs in the disguise of a woman.

"William J. Sharkey had been confined in the Tombs Prison since September, 1872, and had been subjected to the regular prison discipline. He was allowed, some six months ago, a great many privileges, such as walking in the yard, on the tiers, etc. Notwithstanding all the leniency that was shown him, he was continually insolent and abusive to his keepers, and about four months since he became so violent in his demonstrations, that Warden Johnson ordered that he be locked up and put in close confinement. Since the middle of July last Sharkey has not been allowed to even walk on the tier, and all communications have been addressed to him through the grating of the cell door. Much, therefore, was the surprise of all the persons connected with the Tombs Prison, either officially or otherwise, when the news went forth that Sharkey had escaped—Sharkey, who had defied keepers, wardens, commissioners, and every official with whom he came in contact, and who was in durance vile and dire disgrace, had yet outwitted all, and in spite of the utmost surveillance had walked out through the army of his guardsmen in the broad light of day.

"The story of his escape is as follows: At ten o'clock in the morning Miss Maggie Jourdan, who has visited Sharkey every day since his incarceration, made her appearance at the Franklin street entrance, and was, as usual, admitted to see her friend the escaped prisoner. She went to his cell, which is on the second tier, No. 40, and talked with him through the grating for about two hours.

At half-past twelve Mrs. Wesley Allen, wife of Wesley Allen, who was lately sent to Sing Sing for six years on a charge of burglary, made her appearance at the Franklin street entrance. She asked to see Warden Johnson, and begged permission to be allowed to visit a friend of hers named Flood. Mrs. Allen had not visited the Tombs before since her husband's conviction. Warden Johnson, however, granted the required permission, and Mrs. Allen received the usual ticket which each visitor has to show to the several keepers on coming out of the prison. Mrs. Allen was seen to go as far as Sharkey's cell, have a somewhat protracted conversation with Sharkey and Miss Maggie Jourdan, and then proceed to the third tier cell 95, where the man Flood was confined. She remained there till two o'clock, when the gong sounds for the withdrawal of all visitors. Miss Maggie Jourdan, however, left the prison yesterday at one o'clock, though she had never been known before by any of the keepers to leave her friend's cell until the last moment. At half-past one o'clock a peculiar looking female passed down the corridor, through the two lower gates, and out the main entrance, passing three men, whose acuteness is presumed to be almost wonderful from their long and varied experience. This peculiar looking female was dressed in a heavy black dress, of woollen material; wore a black cloak across a pair of very broad shoulders, and had on her head an Alpine hat covered by a thick green barége veil. This veil, all the keepers allege, was kept close over her face. Keeper Falkner let this female pass, though he says he was somewhat suspicious, and sent keeper Jones to look after her. Officer Doran, who patrols Franklin street, from Elm to Centre, also noticed this peculiar female, and thought there was something suspicious. Keeper Jones went back to Keeper Falkner and said it was all right. Officer Doran watched the suspicious female, saw her run for a Bleecker street car and jump on board. The officer said that this peculiar looking female had on a new pair of gaiters with French high heels, and he was somewhat surprised to see the nimble way in which she alighted on a car which was going at the time at considerable speed.

"At five minutes after two o'clock in the afternoon, Mrs. Wesley Allen came to the main entrance of the Tombs Prison, and was passing out with the utmost nonchalance, when she was stopped by Keeper Kennedy and asked for her ticket. She fumbled in her dress for some time, and then suddenly exclaimed, " I must have lost it; I can't think how either; I put it in this pocket," pointing to the fob-pocket of her cloth sacque. Warden Johnson was then called by the keeper. He subjected Mrs. Wesley Allen to a severe cross-examination as to how and where she lost the ticket.

"The alarm was sent through the prison to examine all the cells, and in a few moments word came back to Warden Johnson that cell No. 40, lately occupied by William J. Sharkey, was empty. Mrs. Allen was then put under arrest by the Warden, and placed in charge of the Matron, Miss Foster. She was quite defiant, denied all knowledge of Sharkey's escape, and told the Warden in very plain language that she did not care what he did, he could not prove anything against her. Sharkey's cell was then visited and found in a state of general confusion. His clothes were thrown heedlessly around the room, and on a little shelf was found his black mustache still wet with the lather. It was evident, therefore, that he had shaved himself but a few moments before his departure from his late residence. The excitement in the Tombs was intense when the news went forth that Sharkey had actually made his escape. The prisoners confined there were many of them very much elated at the idea, and though the keepers thought to keep the thing quiet, still the rumor went round through the different cells, and Sharkey, who some time ago was looked upon with hatred, was now looked up to as a hero by his fellow prisoners. Warden Johnson was occupied during the whole of yesterday afternoon in examining all the keepers connected with the jail. Even the women who were in the habit of bringing Sharkey his meals were examined, but nothing was elicited to positively prove any collusion on the part of the officials, though Warden Johnson strongly suspects at least two of his keepers with being in some way connected with the escape. The Warden himself was summoned to appear before District Attorney Allen at three o'clock. He made substantially the same statements that he had already made to the reporter, and when the District Attorney endeavored to remind the Warden that he had warned him some months to keep a sharp lookout for Sharkey, as he would certainly endeavor to escape, the Warden denied Mr. Allen's statement *in toto*, and said he never remembered receiving any such communication from him. Later in the afternoon the Commissioner made his appearance at the Tombs, and he also made a personal investigation of the case. There will be a public examination before the Warden and all the Commissioners.

"Roundsman Dean, of the Sixth Precinct, jumped on board car 21 of the Bleecker street line about half-past three o'clock, and asked the conductor if that was not the car that passed the corner of Franklin and Elm streets at half-past one. The conductor answered that it was.

"'Do you remember a tall woman, dressed in black, getting on here?' said the roundsman. 'I do remember somebody dressed in black,' said the conductor; 'but that woman was a man, and he got off at Walker street.' This is the last trace of Sharkey.

"As soon as the discovery of the escape was made, information of the event was telegraphed to Superintendent Matsell at Police Headquarters. He promptly ordered a general alarm to be sent out to all the police stations in the city, that every effort should be made to recapture the criminal. Detectives were sent to watch the European steamers, and all ferries and outlets from the city were similarly guarded. Captain Irving and Detective Farley undertook the searching of the Eighth Ward, as it is supposed Sharkey will conceal himself there for at least some time. The police were ordered to make thorough examinations of every suspicious place in their precincts, and it is confidently expected the escaped prisoner will be brought into the Central Office to-night. Superintendent Matsell, after giving the above instructions, went to the District Attorney's office to learn the facts of the escape. Warden Johnson, the keeper who had charge of the door at the time Sharkey is supposed to have gone out, and the policeman who noticed him as he passed along the street, were sent for and examined. Superintendent Matsell, on his return to Headquarters, seemed very dissatisfied with the conduct of affairs at the Tombs. The warden admitted, he said, in his replies to the District Attorney, that the same tickets were used for men and women visiting the prison, and it also leaked out that while Stokes was confined there, he went in and out of the prison just as he pleased. Mr. Matsell thinks the plan of escape has been arranged for some time, and was not a thing of a moment's decision, as the prison authorities would pretend. The cells are

SUPERINTENDENT MATSELL.

supposed to be searched every week, but Mr. Matsell says he has no doubt the clothes Sharkey wore out of the place were in his cell, if not more than a week, at least that time. On two or three occasions since his return to the chair of Superintendent of Police, Mr. Matsell has discovered that efforts were being made to get prisoners out of the Tombs, and he has immediately laid the facts before Commissioner Sterne, and precautions were taken that prevented escapes. It is to be regretted that some of Mr. Matsell's spies were not able to find out something of this matter before it was brought to a successful issue. Charges of the grossest negligence and corruption are brought against the keepers in the Tombs on all hands ; but the investigation is to be made at once, and will, no doubt, bring out the truth of these assertions."

Maggie Jourdan was arrested at her mother's residence, No. 167 9th av., that evening. She appeared in good spirits and said she was "the happiest little woman in the world," and there is no doubt but that she was. She was taken to the Tombs and handed over to the care of Mrs. Foster. An investigation was going on in the meantime, but nothing came of it. Two thousand dollars reward was immediately offered for the body of the escaped felon.

In due time Miss Jourdan's trial came off before Recorder Hackett. She was defended by Ex-Judge Beach, Messrs. Wm. F. Howe and John O. Mott. On the last day of the trial, the only one to which we will refer, the court-room was crowded to suffocation. Ex-Judge Beach summed up for the defence, and, in a speech occupying two hours, addressed every consideration which his legal ability and eloquence could suggest in favor of his fair client. He felt it, he said, to be a relief and pleasure to defend one against whom no calumny could be breathed. This woman was not a dangerous element, presenting to society a dissolute example that should be confined within the walls of a State Prison. It was foolish, he thought, to claim that the law demands punishment in a case like this. He asked the jury to scrutinize carefully the proofs before arriving at a judgment. The liberality of the jury-box is necessary to the impartial administration of justice. The jury is not " cribbed, cabined, and confined " by the necessities which hedge around the District Attorney.

Mr. Beach then read from the statute applying to this offence, and held that there was no ground of conviction, as it could not be proved that the prisoner had performed any actual act of assistance to Sharkey. She might have been actuated by kindness in her contact with him, and might have desired that his escape should be accomplished, but these circumstances did not make her guilty. He thought the District Attorney had confounded the law applicable to aiding and abetting as an accessory before the offence with the express statute applicable to the offence. He then showed the equal complicity of the keepers with the prisoner, if

WM. F. HOWE.

any of them were guilty, and reviewed the testimony of Kessler, showing its weakness. He concluded with the history of the condemnation of the Count Lavalette after the fall of Napoleon and the restoration of the monarchy under Louis XVIII., and his subsequent escape, disguised in the garments of his wife. He hoped that, though his client might not be perpetuated in history, her conviction would not go down upon the records of the Court to its shame and disgrace.

Assistant District Attorney Russell followed for the prosecution, and in an able argument sought to demolish the structure of logic and sympathy which the opposing counsel had reared for his client's protection. He relied mainly on the second count of the indictment—that of aiding and assisting the escape—the Court having suggested, during Mr. Beach's address, that there was no proof of garments or other materials having been furnished to Sharkey by the prisoner. During his address he confined himself simply to statements of fact and reviewing the testimony.

Recorder Hackett then proceeded to charge the jury as follows:—

It is shown that the prisoner seemed to have intimate friendly relations with Sharkey, evidenced by her constant and unremitting visits to him while confined at the City Prison charged with the murder of Dunn, and after his conviction of the crime up to the day of his escape, with an intermission of six or seven weeks, when she was confined to her house from illness. She came the earliest in the morning and was the last to leave. So thoroughly were the keepers and doormen accustomed to her visits that she was permitted to ingress and egress without the aid of a ticket by order of Mr. Phillips, one of the keepers. On the day in question she came there between ten and eleven in the morning; she was at the door of Sharkey's cell when Warden Johnson went away at half-past twelve P.M. Mrs. Broderick, in her testimony, says she saw the prisoner there in front of the cell of Sharkey and another female there, and saw the woman dressed in black come out of Sharkey's cell, and the prisoner remained in front of the cell door. Do you believe that Sharkey, having intended to escape, did not communicate such intention to the prisoner? Do you believe that her affection for him induced her to help in his escape? Why did she remain in front of his cell after Sharkey had left, if it was he who left? The distinguished counsel for the accused has made a most earnest and impassioned appeal, not only to the exercise of your sober judgments, under your oath as jurors, but also to your sympathies as men. It is my duty to warn you against the influence of your sympathetic feelings, so profoundly moved by the eloquence of counsel, and to remind you that your duty upon your oaths requires that your verdict should be in accordance with the evidence that has been given, tending to show her confederation in the escape of Sharkey, and not to be led or guided by mere sympathy for the unfortunate prisoner. The penalty which has been read in your hearing makes the extent of the punishment 10 years; but its extent is committed to the discretion of the Judge. There are others charged in this indictment with participation in the crime, who, upon the proof substantiating the charge, would to my mind be a thousand times more culpable than the prisoner, if guilty of complicity. Phillips would seem to have been the keeper, the sworn paid officer. The prisoner is tried for an offence the character of which has formed an element of popular discussion, and it is your duty to carefully search your minds to detect if you have been at all impressed extraneous to the evidence. Since this trial was set down the public mind has become excited with the escape of another prisoner from the Sheriff, and the press has teemed with comments upon the duties of jailors. If the prisoner be in fact innocent of the charge made against her, it is an unfortunate time in which to try her. Jurors are human, and there is often an unconscious magnetism in the air to affect their prejudices or sympathies. I feel it incumbent, therefore, to ask you to carefully lay aside any semblance or impression of prejudice. History furnishes no sublimer spectacle than that of a jury, whether in old times or modern days, rising superior to popular clamor, and determining an issue upon the facts against such clamor, if the facts require their oaths so to pronounce. If the evidence shall have convinced you, free from reasonable doubt, that, on the 19th November last, the prisoner did aid and assist Wm. J. Sharkey, then held in legal custody within the City Prison of the city of New York, upon a conviction for the felony of murder had in the Court of General Sessions of the city and county of New York, to escape therefrom, then it will become your duty to find her guilty of the charge in the indictment named, of having aided and assisted said Sharkey in his escape, while confined in the City Prison for the felony of murder. If the evidence has satisfied you that the prisoner did any act, however slight, which contributed to and did aid and assist Sharkey in his escape, the prisoner having the intent to aid and assist Sharkey to escape, then it will become your duty to convict her of the charge, as I have stated to you.

The complications and legal technicalities of the case were too much for the average New York jury, and they conveniently disagreed and were discharged.

We will now give slight sketches of the murderer Sharkey, and his sweetheart Maggie Jourdan.

There was no particular reason why William J. Sharkey should have adopted the flash life he did. His family are old residents of the Ninth Ward of this city, and rate high in the social scale. But he fell at an early age into the companionship of thieves, and seems to have become fascinated with the irregular life of the " swell mob." It was not long before he began himself to act " off color," and while he was still a very young man he had achieved the unenviable notoriety of being a very expert pickpocket. Naturally enough his light-fingered talents led him eventually into the hands of the police, and on one fine morning he was forced to have his picture taken by the municipal photographer.

But Sharkey had a store of the shrewdest kind of talent, which he used in procuring his liberation. Then he graduated into the stolen-bond business, and into becoming star manager of " cracksmen's " jobs. Shortly after he was connected in some disreputable way with the notorious Louisa Jourdan, afterward known as Mrs. Derrigan, and at the same time organized the Sharkey Guard, a gang of young gentlemen of questionable habits, whose headquarters was at the corner of Wooster and Houston streets.

It was quite lucky for Sharkey then that the " Ring " came in power. The leaders of that brilliant political combination recognized in the young man an agent after their own liking. The consequence was they picked him up and made him one of their pets. This may be called the period of his political and influential life.

He was well adapted to be a leader in the nefarious transactions which grew out of the growth of the " Ring," and its giant struggle for supremacy and continued existence. The men who were robbing the city, putting their hands in the pockets of the municipal breeches, saw in the young pickpocket an able assistant so far as the management of minor rascalities was concerned.

He dressed well, and that alone was a recommendation. There was no better-dressed man in the city, after a certain style, than Sharkey, and his diamonds were of the true Tammany brilliancy. So successful was he as a wire-puller and leader that he received the nomination for Assistant-Alderman, and only lost the election owing to some row in the big wigwam. His defeat disgusted him with political life, and he returned to his first love—gambling and stealing. And now we come to the first link in the murder chain.

Not finding New York congenial, Sharkey determined to try a change of air. He proceeded to Buffalo and there opened a faro bank. In five days he had lost $4,000. Then he returned to New York and met Robert S. Dunn, *alias* Bob Isaacs, who was also a gambler, and something of an Eighth Ward sport. Between them they agreed that Dunn should go to Buffalo and take charge of the game, Sharkey advancing $600 to back it. That was the fatal debt. Dunn did no better in Buffalo than Sharkey did, and came back to New York utterly ruined. The $600 advanced was the money Sharkey asked for on that Sunday afternoon after they had returned from Mr. Reilly's funeral. Dunn didn't have it, and Sharkey, drawing his pistol, shot him down.

Maggie Jourdan is also descended from respectable parents who were residents of the Ninth Ward. When she first came within the flash of the police lantern it was as the companion of Thomas Murphy, the well-known pickpocket. Her sister Josephine seemed to have a like *penchant* for associating with men of stained characters. The disease spread also to the brother of the two, who was arrested by operator Sullivan, of the secret service force, and taken to Connecticut to answer a charge of bond robbery. About this period of her life Maggie met with Sharkey and immediately fell desperately in love with him. Her love became a perfect infatuation, fully equal to the adoration showered upon Abelard by Heloise.

Frequently while in conversation with Sharkey, she said that if he died for his crime she would not live after him, and even not later than Sharkey's conviction, said to him, " Willie, I can never let you suffer." She kept her promise faithfully. Her diamonds and dresses—even her gold watch—were sold by her and the proceeds given to Sharkey, to be used in his defence. Day after day she came to the prison, and sat at the cell door with her lover until the last moment allowed by the prison rules, and, while ill at home, sent to him baskets of fruit and flowers and books and cigars, to make his prison-life more pleasant. Her conduct in the prison during this time was most exemplary, and was favorably commented on by the officials. She never visited any other prisoner, and was always quiet in her demeanor. Sharkey's ruffianism was, to a great extent, quelled by her presence, and while sober he behaved very well.

And thus ends this strange, eventful tale. It combines at once the blackest and the most noble traits implanted in the human breast. We can conjure up no character more repulsive than that of the murderer of Dunn, and none more devoted than that of his sweetheart and liberator, Maggie Jourdan.

CHAPTER XXXVII.

"I think it must be somewhere written that the virtues of the mother shall,
occasionally, be visited upon the children as well as the sins of the father."
DICKENS, in *Bleak House.*

THOUGH the crime of infanticide is, among capital offences,
the one most common to civilization, that of parricide is most
infrequent.

The Fifth Commandment—the commandment of promise—
seems, to be better observed than any other of the decalogue.

It was, therefore, an occasion of unusual excitement when, on
June 3, 1873, the report spread through the city of New York
that a youth of gentle birth had deliberately slain his own father.
The circumstances, as subsequently developed, were briefly these:

On the afternoon of Monday, June 2, Frank H. Walworth arrived in the city from Saratoga, and upon registering at the Sturtevant House, an eminently respectable hotel on Broadway, was
assigned to room 267. Shortly afterward he left the hotel and
proceeded to the residence of his father, Mansfield Tracy Walworth, on Fourth avenue, near 54th street. Not finding his
father at home, he left the following note, which was found in
the pocket of the senior Walworth after the tragedy:

3 O'CLOCK.
I want to try to settle some family matters. Call at the Sturtevant House
after an hour or two. If I am not there, I will leave word at the office.
F. H. WALWORTH.

The following morning, at a quarter past six o'clock, Mansfield
Tracy Walworth called at the Sturtevant House, and upon inquiring for Frank Walworth, was, by direction of the latter,
shown to room 267. He knocked, the answer "Come in!" was

returned, the porter saw him enter; and father and son stood face to face.

A few moments later the occupant of the adjoining room heard several pistol reports, the cries of " Help," " Murder! " " My son! "

Immediately thereafter Frank Walworth descended the stairs to the office, and, approaching the clerk, said, without excitement, " I have shot my father," and, calling for a blank, sent a telegraphic despatch, to that simple effect, to his maternal uncle, in Chicago. He then asked that an officer be summoned, that he might deliver himself up.

A surgeon was called, but the victim expired in less than a minute after his arrival. An examination of the body disclosed four bullet-holes: one in each breast, one in the right side of the face, terminating in the brain, and one in the right arm, breaking it.

Upon surrendering himself, young Walworth made the following statement, and it was substantially the same as that subsequently made by him at the Coroner's inquest:

" I reside with my mother in Saratoga, my father having parted from her some years ago.

" My father is an author, and I have been studying law. I think my father is about forty-one years old, but do not know where he was born. My father has not lived with my mother since we left here three years ago, but he has repeatedly sent us threatening and insulting letters.

" It is only a short time ago since he threatened to shoot my mother and myself. I shot him because of this. Not long ago I met him on the street at Saratoga, and I then told him that if he did not keep away from us, or insulted my mother any more, I would shoot him.

" I also told him that there were bounds which I would not allow any man to go beyond with impunity, especially when my mother was being insulted.

" I went to his house yesterday and left a note for him to call on me, which he did this morning.

" When he came in the room I drew out a revolver, and told him to promise me that he would not threaten or insult us any more, which he promised. Shortly afterward we began speaking on family matters, and he used some very insulting language, and put his hand in his pocket as though to draw out a pistol, when I shot him. He then came toward me, and I fired three other shots at him. When I fired the last shot at him he had me by the collar. I only regret this on account of the effect it will have on my family. I would like Judge Barbour to know this, as he was interested in the case before."

Young Walworth was taken to the Tombs. On the way he composedly smoked a cigar, and indifferently asked questions about the changes in the appearance of the streets.

MANSFIELD TRACY WALWORTH.

Mansfield Tracy Walworth was born in Albany, Dec. 3d, 1830, and was the son of Chancellor Walworth—for twenty years the Chief Judge of the Court of Chancery in this State. He entered Union College at the age of 16, and graduated two years later. He spent three years at the Harvard Law School, and was there admitted to the bar. But his tastes lay nearer to the Arabian Nights than Coke upon Littleton. He became an aspirant for literary fame ; and succeeded to the extent of winning applause from fashionable Saratoga belles, if he failed in securing an echo from the coteries of critics and literati. "Lulu," "Hotspur," and "Stormcliff" successively appeared ; then came, in 1869, "Warwick," which was considered his best effort. These were followed by "Beverly" and "Delaplaine" —which was supposed to record his domestic experiences. At the time of his death he was occupied upon a graver subject —entitled "The Lives of the Six Chancellors of New York," and the first volume only was completed. He was also engaged in writing a serial for the *New York Weekly*—which, by some, has been regarded as prophetic.

Mansfield Tracy Walworth was a fair type of a certain class. The unattainable seemed ever within sight, but always eluded his grasp. He was a morbid egotist, and addicted to parading family and financial difficulties before the searching or indifferent gaze of personal or casual friends. In his marital relations he was unhappy. Such men are liable to be so. This fact was fully brought out on the trial of the son for the murder of the father.

Contrary to expectation, and in violation of modern precedent, the trial was called within three weeks of the homicide. The counsel for the defence might easily have interposed hindrances, but delay was deemed inexpedient. The case came up before the Court of Oyer and Terminer, Judge Davis presiding, on Tuesday, June 24, 1873; and twelve jurors were drawn without difficulty or delay—a most unusual occurrence in a capital case.

The State was represented by District Attorney Phelps, and Rollins, his assistant. For the defence appeared Hon. Charles O'Conor and Messrs. Beach and Garvin.

The testimony in behalf of the State was clear and conclusive as to the matter and manner of the killing.

On the part of the defence many witnesses were called with a view to justification and mitigation.

Mrs. Mansfield Tracy Walworth testified that she was married to the deceased in Saratoga, July 29, 1852; that eight children were born unto them; that she went to Kentucky in 1861, and lived there three years without seeing her husband; saw him at various places, and from time to time, until their final separation in New York, January 26, 1871; decree of separation April 8, 1871.

As a part of the defence, the venerable and distinguished Charles O'Conor—who had not appeared in a criminal case for the space of a generation—read to the court, with impressive voice and mien, a series of letters from Mansfield Tracy Walworth to his wife, then separated from him by her own choice and official decree.

In May, 1873, he wrote: " Prepare yourself for the inevitable." Then, after pleading to see his children—one of them born after the separation—he says, in case of refusal, " two pistol shots will ring about your house—one slaying you, the other, myself." In other letters, he complains of having been robbed under the terms of his father's will, and through the hard conditions of the agreement of separation. He wrote, "My precious money!" " Starvation begins to stare me in the face. . . I will murder you for depriving me of my sweet, darling money." " Sweet, darling money . . the hope of life: for industrious poverty there is no home, no hope, no success in life! "

These letters were written when the author was suffering under the burden of real or imaginary wrongs, and when he was gaining but a scanty subsistence from the exercise of his pen. Whilst the language which he used was constantly threatening, and frequently indecent, it was, evidently, the expression of a diseased imagination and a disjointed mind.

Charles O'Conor's argument for the defence was an able one; but stripped of its appeal to the passions, it presented but two points to be seriously considered by the jury, as named in the charge of the judge:

1st. The prisoner was outside of the law, because insane.

2d. The shooting was prompted by self-defence.

The jury retired at half-past four on Thursday, July 3, and in less than four hours returned with the following verdict:

" Guilty of murder in the 2d degree."

On the following Saturday Judge Davis passed the sentence of the law—that " You, Frank H. Walworth, be imprisoned in the State Prison at Sing Sing, at hard labor, for the full term of your natural life."

This case presents several peculiar features.   The criminal was a mere youth, scarcely nineteen years of age, had been well educated and carefully reared, was quiet in demeanor and of amiable disposition, and his crime was a most unusual violation

FRANK H. WALWORTH.

of natural and written law.   With a devotion scarcely paralleled, his accomplished mother clung to him through the fearful ordeal of trial for life, and by her presence and sympathy comforted him from day to day, and even up to the moment when the prison bars separated them.   Other relatives and many friends also stood by him.   The ablest legal ability of the country volunteered to defend him.   Immediately after the commission of the deed, during imprisonment at the Tombs, at the trial, pending the sentence, and at the instant of final incarceration " for life," the parricide bore himself with the utmost coolness and composure—seeming to feel that he had done but a simple act of duty.

The victim of the tragedy was a man of culture, well known, and, by those who knew him intimately, highly esteemed.

After remaining at Sing Sing for a few months, young Walworth was transferred to the strongly-walled and cheerless State Prison at Auburn, where he is now confined.

WALWORTH AS A CONVICT.

CHAPTER XXXVIII.

THE ADVENTUROUS CAREER OF MRS. VICTORIA C. WOODHULL AND MISS
TENNIE C. CLAFLIN—HOW THEY DID THE CLAIRVOYANT DODGE IN
THE WEST—" EASTWARD THE STAR OF WOODHULL TAKES ITS WAY "
—THEIR APPEARANCE IN NEW YORK—THE OFFICE IN BROAD STREET
AND THE UP-TOWN RESIDENCE—ESTABLISHMENT OF " WOODHULL &
CLAFLIN'S WEEKLY "—FREE-LOVE—GATHERING OF THE STORM—
VICKY'S LIGHTNING FLASHES—THE GREAT BEECHER SCANDAL " IN
THE TOMBS "—LUDLOW-STREET JAIL.

" All their cares, hopes, joys, affections, virtues, and associations seemed to
be melted down into dollars ; whatever the chance contributions that fell into the
slow cauldron of their talk, they made the gruel thick and slab with dollars."—
DICKENS, in Martin Chuzzlewit.

IT was about five years ago that New York woke up one morning to a new sensation. This time it was not a murder nor an
elopement, a defalcation nor a suicide—quite ordinary events, it
is true, in this metropolis—but on the contrary, the sensationalism
of the event resided entirely in its novelty. Two women, from
the Prairies of the West, had pitched their tents in Gotham, and
openly announced themselves as being engaged in the buying and
selling of stocks and gold—in a word, as female bankers.

Who are they ? Such the question young New York asked itself almost immediately. So far as their personal appearance
went, it only piqued the rising curiosity. The elder was a woman
of some thirty years, with clear-cut features, short hair brushed
carelessly back from an expressive and handsome face, gray eyes,
with the flash in them of burnished steel when the sunlight plays
upon it, a form elegantly refined, and a manner as *suave* and engaging as could be desired.

Such was Victoria C. Woodhull.

The other ! Stouter in person than her sister, the anatomical
curves of her body approaching more nearly Hogarth's famous
definition of the line of beauty, saucy and *piquante* where Mrs.

Woodhull was grave and reserved, having all the *chic* and dash of animal youth, possessed of a peculiarly seductive and persuasive power when talking to the opposite sex, dressing in rare taste and yet with a studied *abandon* and disregard for the sacred laws of Fashion.

Such was Tennie C. Claflin.

From the time they first burst upon the New York horizon as a sort of financial and female *Gemini*, their history is pretty well known. Be it our duty then to simply introduce them, tell plainly the story of their life in our midst, and leave them where they stand to-day.

VICTORIA C. WOODHULL.

Chicago was the earliest stamping ground of " Vicky and Tennie," *i.e.*, it was there that they first struck out for notoriety and cash. They belong to the West, and early selected the city of the lake as the field of their operations. Victoria launched out in the clairvoyant business, and did a lively trade with the assistance of an Athenian gentleman, sometime deceased, named Demosthenes. During life he was engaged in the business of making political stump speeches. " Vicky " was wont to meet his shade upon the housetop and in other unhallowed places, and between them Chicago went to the wall. " Tennie" was an admirable " left bower " in the game, and in Chicago and Cincinnati established quite a reputation for herself.

At an early age Victoria married a man named Woodhull. To them was born an idiotic son, whose birth seems to have cast a blight over all her life. At any rate she soon began to evolve peculiar ideas relative to the marital relation, and struck out into that erratic groove in which she now is.

Tiring of Chicago, Mrs. W. went to St. Louis. There she met Colonel James Blood, who had served gallantly in the war with a Missouri regiment. They fell in love with each other, and " Vicky," rising above the petty encumbrance of another husband, eloped with him—taking Mr. Woodhull along with the rest of her baggage.

The party came to New York. First they tried the clairvoyant card, but she met with less encouragement than she had received in Chicago. Nothing if not sensational, she next made her début on " 'Change " in the business of general broker. It was always believed that the female brokers, as she and her sister were then termed, were assisted in their first financial adventure by a prominent capitalist. Their offices were sumptuously furnished, but it was never supposed that the firm of Woodhull & Claflin was much concerned regarding the transactions of the gold market or the Stock Exchange. Nevertheless, they always appeared busy. They talked glibly of Central, Pacific Mail, and Western Union, and discussed the news of the street with their visitors, but made few if any investments. It was evident, from the start, that the banking business was a " blind," and finally they came out as advocates of social freedom, which they termed the " New Dispensation." They publicly proclaimed their intention to revolutionize society generally, and through the columns of their journal— " Woodhull & Claflin's Weekly "—they taught doctrines that were at least questionable in their tendencies. It is not to be wondered that they succeeded in drawing around them a coterie of choice spirits, every one of whom looked upon " The Woodhull " as the coming woman. Victoria's success exceeded her wildest dreams. Week after week she became more radical in her views regarding the relations of the sexes, until she finally capped the climax by denouncing modern marriage as a species of human slavery. Nothing pleased her more than to be interviewed by a journalist. Then she was in her element. She made a boast of her personal magnetism, and undoubtedly possesses a great deal of that mysterious power, which she sometimes exerts in a very fascinating manner. To build up her constituency was her mission in New York. That she might the better operate in a gilt-edged community she rented a handsomely furnished brown-stone mansion on 38th street. There nightly might have been seen congressmen, journalists, brokers, and in fact persons in almost every walk of life, who dropped in from pure curiosity to chat with the sisters and hear them " enthuse " on their pet theories. Their language was invariably unmistakably plain.

It is doubtful if " The Woodhull " has ever given the social problem much consideration. She had two husbands, and they were both under one roof. Neither was she worried particularly about the rights of women. As she expressed it, " I am breaking the way for future generations," and while she advanced, her second husband ran the paper. It was not long before the sisters of the free-love and women's-right persuasion began to draw towards " The Woodhull." They petted and caressed her, recited their grievances, and told her many a tale of domestic scandal. In fact, this woman became the sister-confessor of many a wife whose marital bonds were but galling chains. Such infelicities were manna to her soul, and it was rarely long before they were in correspondence, the foolish wives pouring out upon pen and paper the inmost secrets of their hearts. Day by day the written testimony of moral rottenness accumulated, and it was deposited in her safe. There were daily and nightly sessions of the " School for Scandal," and when her magnetic charm was not sufficiently potent to draw out the tale of woe, then would she pounce upon her victims and bring them captive to her feet. A consummate actress, she could, while expatiating on woman's wrongs, work her hearers into a state of frenzy. Grave senators and eminent clergymen, as well as brilliant *littérateurs* and crafty interviewers have been outwitted by this female agitator. If she has not blackmailed purses, she certainly has brains when she can call forth such gushing effusions as the following, which is a panegyric from the pen of one of her followers, which was published in a well-known paper :—

" Victoria C. Woodhull is a younger heroine than most of the foregoing, having come into the cause after some of her elders had already become veterans. But her advocacy of woman's right to the ballot, as logically deduced from the fourteenth and fifteenth amendments, has given her a national notoriety. If the woman's-movement has a Joan of Arc, it is this gentle but fiery genius. She is one of the most remarkable women of her time. Little understood by the public, she is denounced in the most outrageous manner by people who do not appreciate her moral worth. But her sincerity, her truthfulness, her uprightness, her true nobility of character, are so well known to those who know her well, that she ranks, in the estimation of these, somewhat as St. Theresa does in the admiring thoughts of pious Catholics. She is a devotee—a religious enthusiast—a seer of visions—a devout communionist with the other world. She acts under spiritual influence, and, like St. Paul, is ' not disobedient to the heavenly vision.' Her bold social theories have startled many good souls, but anybody who, on this account, imagines her to stand below the whitest and purest of her sex, will misplace a woman who in her moral integrity rises to the full height of the highest."

Vic. soon perceived that there was a scarcity of the long-haired element, and she began looking around for an apostle for the new dispensation, as she termed it. When she found that she had builded better than she knew, that in fact she was recognized as the champion agitator, she mounted the rostrum and gave utterance to the most radical ideas. Rarely did she appear in public without creating more or less disturbance. She was never dismayed or unnerved by the jeers of the mob, notwithstanding she was invariably alone on the platform. Vic. had plenty of admirers, but there was scarcely one who had the temerity to appear with her in public. She had announced that she would lecture on the "Naked Truth," at Steinway Hall, Nov. 21, 1871, and she determined that she would not go before the audience without being introduced.

The person she had decided on as her apostle of the new social order was the Rev. Henry Ward Beecher. To have a private meeting with him, where she could uninterruptedly discuss the situation of affairs, would be to her the consummation of her most sanguine hopes, and she set about it with the pertinacity and adroitness of a diplomat. Some time previously she had gained an entrance into a certain set in the City of Churches, where Mr. Beecher was a frequent visitor. She manœuvred for an interview with Mr. Beecher and obtained it. At the meeting she did, with the most unblushing effrontery, request him to come with her to New York and introduce her to an audience of scoffers and unbelievers. This to her was the golden opportunity, and it was here that she was terrible in her wrath, when she found that the great preacher was about to fail her, and she left the house after Mr. Beecher had declined to accede to her request, vowing that if she went alone before the crowded audience then waiting to greet her, she would introduce some startling topics in her lecture not down in the bills. An admirer performed the service required of Mr. Beecher, and she bottled her wrath to be exploded at a future day. So pronounced did she now become in her social views that the most prominent freethinkers deserted her standard and openly denounced her in the press. Her affinity deserted her, and she soon perceived that her charm was no longer potent. The women who had used such endearing expressions towards her were now lukewarm in their regard. She saw that she was excluded on every side, and she determined to be revenged.

It was on the 1st of November, 1872, that the number of *Woodhull & Claflin's Weekly* appeared which created so great a sensation. The publication of the paper had been suspended for several months, and its reappearance was, of itself, enough to awaken curiosity; but when the additional fact was developed that the reissue opened with a bold attack upon the character of that popular preacher who has occupied so prominent a place in the minds and affections of a vast multitude, curiosity rose to the dignity of intense interest. The demand for the "Weekly" was such that the price rose rapidly from ten cents to one dollar a copy.

The only evening paper which gave an account of the so-called "Beecher Scandal" was the *Evening Telegram*, wherein the eight columns of the *Woodhull & Claflin Weekly* were condensed to half that space.

For some days the press of the metropolis was silent in regard to this new sensation, but presently the country press, and noticeably the *Chicago Times*, began to discuss the question.

The day following the publication of the sensational article Mrs. Victoria C. Woodhull and Miss Tennie C. Claflin were arrested at their office, 48 Broad street, as they returned in a carriage from lunch, on a warrant issued at the instance of Mr. Anthony Comstock. Recognizing the situation at a glance, they raised their Alpine hats to the official representative of the U. S. Government, and, without display, went quietly to their quarters in Ludlow-street jail.

To the grave accusations Rev. Henry Ward Beecher made no public response. He is reported to have said that, "In passing along the way any one is liable to have a bucket of slops thrown upon him. It is disagreeable, but it does no material harm."

The Assistant United States District Attorney declared that it was the business of the Government to protect the reputation of its revered citizens, and the social pests were hurried off to jail without even a preliminary examination. Here they were visited by a number of persons of both sexes, every one of whom were at war with society, and all followers of the New Dispensation. The public were terribly incensed and the women and their followers were denounced on all sides. For some time no person could be found with sufficient temerity to go their bail, and in a cell at Ludlow-street jail they were obliged to stay for several weeks. Among those who visited them was George Francis Train. Every day he called and urged the women to bide their time, promising them his support and counsel. Reporters interviewed them and published their grievances, but the press generally insisted that these women should be speedily tried and disposed of. But it was evident from the start that the United States authorities, in their zeal to prosecute these vixens, had usurped the law.

The arrest should have been made on no such charge as that preferred in the beginning. It is doubtful if the objectionable publication contained matter that could be properly called obscene, any more than very much matter printed in the newspapers every day can be mentioned in the same light; the publication was grossly libellous, and that fact should have been the foundation of all the proceedings. We can hardly blame the libelled parties for not wishing to appear in court against the libellers; but perhaps it was their duty to do so, that there might be no further outrages of the kind and that the one in question might be properly punished.

The prolonged imprisonment of these women was a worse blunder than their original commitment. By a certain class they were regarded as martyrs, and each day brought them more visitors, principally women. In the meantime the Attorney-General of the United States decided that the post-office authorities had no legal right to seize and stop the transmission of any matter through the mails, and yet, in consequence of the administration of justice being in the hands of United States Commissioners, little experienced in either equity or law, the women were still detained in custody.

The scandal that "The Woodhull" had uttered through her vile sheet covered the land like a mist, and the irrepressible, invincible Train visited her daily to inaugurate a revolution, that, he said, would shake the very bulwarks of society. The parties most concerned in Brooklyn had sent messengers of peace to "The Woodhull," denying any complicity in her prosecution. She expressed no regret for what she had done, but, on the contrary, justified her actions, giving as a reason that the parties she had exposed had long since accepted her creed and had lived up to it, and now, just as she was about to grasp the sceptre of dominion, she was deserted by those who had communed and consorted with her. Train struck hands with Vic. and stiffened her backbone by daily depicting to her in glowing colors the radiance of the New Dispensation, in which she would figure as the central light. Train's clarion voice resounded through the corridors and drew to the cell-door the crafty debtors,* that, like Micawber, were daily waiting for something to turn up. Train was in earnest. He dashed off his epigrams and squibs against society

---

* Ludlow-street jail is the debtor's prison of New York.

THE AGITATORS IN LUDLOW-STREET JAIL.

and mankind generally, and finally declared that he would issue the "*Train Ligue.*" It became intensely dramatic when he drew his revolver and, raising it on high, vehemently declared that he would blow into eternity the first man that should forcibly lay a hand upon his shoulder. Train kept his word. He did issue a sheet that was filled with impiety and blasphemy. Prison walls had no terrors for him, and he said, as did Fitz-James to Roderick Dhu:

> "Come one, come all; this rock shall fly
> From its firm base as soon as I."

After the publication of the second number, Comstock, of obscene literature notoriety, went before the Grand Jury and complained of George Francis Train for editing what he styled an obscene journal, known as the *Train Ligue*. The Grand Jury found an indictment against Mr. Train, and Judge Ingraham ordered his arrest. On Thursday afternoon Mr. Comstock called on Captain Byrnes, of the Mercer-street police station, and placed the warrant in his hands. The Captain was informed that Train could be found at 735 Broadway. At that number John Wesley Nichols, the ostensible publisher of the *Ligue*, has a photograph gallery, and it was from his place and by him that the paper was supplied to newsdealers and others. Captain Byrnes went to the place, but Mr. Train was not there. Leaving officers Henderson and Young to watch the house, the Captain started on another clue in search of Train.

As he left the house a cart drove up. The Captain saw it and returned. In the meantime an indictment had been found against Nichols, and the warrant for his arrest had also been placed in the hands of Captain Byrnes. After the cart drove up to 735 Broadway it was loaded with about 1,500 copies of the *Ligue*, and then driven off. Nichols followed the cart. Captain Byrnes sent officer Carr with instructions to arrest Nichols and seize the papers. The driver turned down Fourth street, and thence drove down Mercer street, past the very door of the police station. Just there Nichols was arrested and the papers were seized. Captain Byrnes and officers Henderson and Young remained at 735 Broadway.

After the arrest Captain Byrnes saw a small boy hurriedly

leave Nichols's apartments with a letter. Shrewdly surmising that this boy was the bearer of a letter to Mr. Train from Nichols's wife, informing Mr. Train of the arrest of her husband, the Captain sent officer Henderson to follow the boy. The messenger went direct to 313 West Twenty-second street, and entered the house. The officer, who was in civilian's clothes, followed. In the front parlor he found Mr. Train and arrested him. Mr. Train was at first indignant, but finally became calm, proclaimed himself a martyr, and wildly extending his arms, shouted, "Take me to the Bastile!"

Train was now in his element and equal to any emergency. He was never silent. He said to us, as we grasped his hand, "On the 2d of November I addressed 10,000 people in Broad street. A few days after that Woodhull and Claflin were arrested. I became satisfied that these innocent women were to be punished to satisfy the morbid sentiments of a cowardly community. I wrote two letters to the press in connection with their arrest. These letters created a furore, and the press, afraid of the public, refused to publish any more of my letters. I volunteered not only to become bail for these persecuted women, but started this paper to show the community that I had the courage to face public opinion, the same as I faced and defied 2,500 infuriated Californians, when I advocated in San Francisco the introduction of greenbacks. I issued two numbers of the *Ligue*. They claim that it is an obscene publication. This I do not deny; but if it is obscene the obscenity is culled from the Bible, for there is in the last number three columns of extracts from the Bible. I have been in thirteen prisons, but this is the only one that I have been in where there is nothing to cover myself with. Besides, sir, the indignity that has been thrust upon me. I am a gentleman of means and education, and they have placed me in the very cell in which a woman made three attempts to hang herself, and in which Bleakley, the murderer of poor Maud Merrill, over whose body six of your moral Christian ministers refused to perform Christian devotions, were confined."

The officials tried the freezing process, but Train laughed at them. His hot blood was more than a match for the cold devices of his keepers. Wrapped in his travelling rug, he paced his

noisome cell like an angry tiger waiting for his rations. That
winter was a season of uproar in Murderers' Row.

He made the Tombs his home despite the authorities. They
consigned him to Murderers' Row in that prison, in the vain hope
that the rigors of the place might terrify him into a flight from
the city—for the Grand Jury which indicted him had made itself
a butt of ridicule, and his case threatened to give the Courts a
deal of trouble. But Train, on crossing the threshold of the
Tombs, said, " I'll raise hell in this Egyptian Sepulchre," and he
stuck to his cell, persistently rejecting the Warden's invitations to
a seat at his private tea-table, and absolutely refusing to go out
occasionally and spend a night with his family in their palace on
Murray Hill, saying: " If you once get me out you will lock me
out, and I intend to stay here until I fulfil my mission." What
his notion of that mission was passes human understanding; but
to ordinary mortals it seemed only to be to keep his name before
the public. This he contrived to do by organizing the Murderers'
Club, with himself as President. The business of that Club, which
was transacted in the hours set apart for the common herd of
prisoners to spend in exercise in the corridors, was to make the
place so much of a hell on earth as to invite the attention of the
newspapers, and thus keep Train's name before the people. Train,
however, did something for his fellow-prisoners in creating a
fraternity in Murderers' Row, and there is little doubt that, under
the fraternal feeling which he created, some of the money which
paved the way for Wm. J. Sharkey's escape from the prison was
paid in checks signed within the prison cells.

Finally his case came before the Courts, and never before was
such a ludicrous farce enacted in a Court of Justice. Dignity,
amid the scenes that daily occurred there, could not even be assumed by either Judge, Jury, or Counsel. It was one continual
roar of laughter. Train outwitted counsel, and even the experts on
insanity felt the keen shafts of his satire. On returning to the
Tombs, after the adjournment of the Court on the first day, Train
managed to elude the vigilance of the Deputy Sheriff, and actually
walked to the jail, where to his astonishment he found that the
Warden had, during his absence, removed all his traps to another
part of the building, where the accommodations were much more

cheerful. This Train denounced as tyranny, to be denied access to his cell. He struck an attitude, and said to the Warden :

" ' Stone walls do not a prison make, nor iron bars a cage.' Away! away with me to the Bastile ! "

Solitude, Train was not prepared for. The Warden found the weak joint in his mental armor, and he was forced to remain isolated from the Murderers' Club. After deciding in his own

GEORGE FRANCIS TRAIN.

mind that the American people were a nation of dogs, he shook the American soil from his soles, mounted the poop-deck of an English steamer, and left the country in disgust. But since then he has crossed and recrossed the broad Atlantic, and now is with us again, ready to become Dictator of an Empire, and thereby fulfil his destiny.

" The Woodhull " was released from Ludlow-street jail, some Brooklyn sympathizers becoming her surety, only to be rearrested and cast into the Tombs. Here she and Tennie remained two nights, when they were again released on bail. Her trial in the United States Court terminated in her acquittal, and the Challis prosecution will probably never be settled. She travelled about the country lecturing on objectionable subjects, and finally announced her appearance at Cooper Institute, where she would lecture on the "Naked Truth." Here the officers were waiting to arrest her, but she passed them dressed as a Quakeress, and while her absence was being discovered she threw off her disguise, came to the front and delivered a volley of invectives on society and the minions of the law. Her lecture was, as the character of all previous addresses, a mixture of personalities and strange philosophy, with a great deal that was piquant and prurient. At the conclusion of her lecture she was again arrested and taken to Ludlow-street jail, and afterwards released, when she again started on the war-path. Since then she and her retinue have rambled about the country the subjects of ridicule, contumely, and scorn, yet finding in almost every hamlet a small clique of unhealthy or epicene humans, most of whom, married, but not mated, found in her a champion of immorality and lewdness. When she designedly sought an interview with the most eminent clergyman in the land, she undermined his pulpit. When he declined to take her hand and go before the world an advocate of her peculiar doctrines, she jostled him upon the ground which he has long occupied in public estimation, and the contest which she began, but in which her voice is now scarcely heard, has been carried on by his former co-laborers in the Congregational vineyard in the City of Churches.

CHAPTER XXXIX.

MANSFIELD, THE MODERN CLEOPATRA—HER LIFE WITH THE PRINCE
OF ERIE — STOKES ON THE SCENE — SPECULATION, SIN AND
LAW — SCENE AT THE GRAND CENTRAL HOTEL—TRAGEDY ON
THE STAIRCASE—"THERE'S A MAN SHOT AT THE LADIES' EN-
TRANCE"— THE FUNERAL — TRIAL—CONVICTION—DEATH—SEN-
TENCE—NEW TRIAL—LUXURY IN THE TOMBS—SING SING—STOKES'
STATEMENT.

> "All people knew (or thought they knew) that he had made himself im-
> mensely rich; and, for that reason alone, prostrated themselves before him, more
> degradedly, and less excusably than the darkest savage creeps out of his hole in
> the ground, to propitiate on some log or reptile the Deity of his benighted soul."
> —DICKENS, in *Little Dorrit*.

ON Saturday afternoon, January 6th, 1872, Broadway, always
thronged on Saturday afternoons, was unusually crowded.
The air was clear and bracing, the sky wore its purest blue, and
nature—as much of it as can be seen in the city—was verdant with
a genial smile. Every one seemed happy, as if dull care, being put
aside until the Monday, life resolved itself into a delicious promenade. The ladies were out in force, rustling by in their coquettish
costumes, and saturating the winter breeze with the intoxicating
perfume that exhales when the amorous zephyrs of the south toy
with the maiden blossoms of an orange grove.

All around was the hum and roar of the great city. The stages,
rolling up and down Broadway, kept up that unceasing monotone
so dear to the ears of a Metropolitan. All was activity, life and
merriment. It had just struck four o'clock. The doors of the
various theatres had been flung open and the matinee audiences
came streaming out into the street, a kaleidoscopic flood of fashion and frivolity. The spectacular-loving people from Niblo's
swarmed up Broadway and met the staider folk of Wallack's,
while the "swell-mob" fraternity from the concert halls mingled
promiscuously. It was certainly an animated scene, and it could
not be otherwise—for it was Saturday afternoon on Broadway.

COL. JAMES FISK, JR.

Who would have thought at that moment that the virgin garments of the beautiful day were about to be stained with blood? No one. But it was so, and even then the cloud of a darksome tragedy was gathering. At 4.15 o'clock came the lightning flash.

Away down Broadway the silver voice of Trinity's bells had just struck the quarter hour, when a carriage drove up to the ladies' entrance of the Grand Central Hotel, and a stout gentleman, elegantly dressed, a heavy military cloak over his massive shoulders, his blonde moustache elaborately waxed, alighted. It was Colonel James Fisk, Jr., Comptroller of the Erie Railway, Colonel of the Ninth Regiment, N. G. S. N. Y., Admiral of the

EDWARD S. STOKES.

Narraganset Steamship Line, speculator in everything with money in it, from a paper of pins to a Grand Opera House.

At that same moment a handsome young man, attired as faultlessly as the Parisian swell who floats along the *Boulevard des Italiens*, at the absinthe hour—a young man with clear complexion, and glossy black moustache, was walking in a careless

THE POSITION ON THE STAIRS.

and listless manner along the hotel corridors towards the head
of the staircase.   That gentleman was Mr. Edward S. Stokes,
Fisk's former friend, but now his bitter enemy—a man of fashion,
and shrewd business operator generally.

Colonel Fisk walked across the pavement, opened the door, and
asked John T. Redmond, the porter on duty, whether Mrs. Morse
was in.   The boy replied that she was not, but that her daughter
was in her mother's room.

Fisk started up the staircase.   Seven steps from the street is a
platform.   When Fisk reached the platform he glanced upward
and saw Stokes, who was coming down.   Their eyes met.   What
the silent language was that passed between them none can ever
tell.   As it undoubtedly appeared afterwards, Stokes was in the
act of descending the stairs in order to reach the street.   Just for
a moment the men who hated each other stood irresolute.   Then
there was a mutual movement.   Stokes leaped swiftly to one
side, *as if to avoid something*, ran his gloved hand into the pocket
of his riding coat, produced a four-barrelled revolver, and fired
quick as thought at Fisk.   The ball struck the Colonel in the
abdomen, two inches to the right of the navel, and three above it.
As soon as he felt the perforation he staggered up against the wall
and made the single exclamation, "Oh !"   Another flash, another
report, and his left arm fell useless at his side.   He turned to
run down the stairs, staggered and fell to the bottom.   Redmond,
and others, who rushed in from the street, carried the wounded
man to room No. 213, just at the head of the stairs.   Stokes
in his bewilderment dropped his pistol, and walked leisurely past
the ladies' parlor, down the main staircase.   To the first man he
met he said, "There's a man shot—send quick for a doctor."
The alarm that was at once sounded startled the entire hotel, and
Stokes quietly surrendered himself to Mr. Powers, the proprietor,
who delivered him into the custody of the police, who took him
into Fisk's presence, in order to be identified by the latter as the
person who had done the shooting.   When Stokes entered the
room, they were undressing the Colonel, removing his diamonds
from his shirt-front, and his diamond sleeve-buttons from his cuffs.
His velvet coat had to be cut from him.   When Fisk was asked
the usual question, he looked up and said, " Yes—that is the man

who shot me." Stokes was then taken to the Mercer street Station House. The next morning he was driven to the Tombs.

In room No. 213 Fisk lay upon the bed, receiving the attentions of Drs. Fisher, Tripler, White, and Professor James R. Wood. They probed for the ball in the abdomen, but could not find it. Then it was that they came to the conclusion that the wounded man's condition was most critical. Coroner Young was sent for, and came in attended by Captain Byrnes of the Police District Station, where Stokes was even then incarcerated. A jury, consisting of Isaac W. England, of No. 141 East Thirty-ninth street; Charles F. Moore, of No. 143 West Twentieth street; William O. Chapin, of No. 273 Eighth avenue; John L. Hall, of No. 178 Jay street, Brooklyn; Edward C. Morse, of Grand Central Hotel, and Dr. E. T. T. Marsh, of No. 41 West Ninth street, was impanelled in due form, and the solemn act of obtaining the deposition was then proceeded with. At this time there were gathered at the bedside of the dying man the jury mentioned above, while in the outer room could be discerned "Boss" Tweed, Jay Gould, and other Erie magnates in close consultation. At the bedside stood Professor James R. Wood and Dr. Fisher, closely examining the features of their patient, while at the foot of the bed loomed up the tall and sombre figure of David Dudley Field, the eminent counsel retained by Fisk in the Erie suits. Seated at a table, which had been drawn up near to the bed, were Coroner Young and Dr. Marsh. The patient was lying on the bed, extended on his back; his left arm, through the fleshy part of which a bullet had passed, was lying outside the covers and propped up on a pillow.

All the preparations being in readiness, Coroner Young arose and asked Mr. Fisk if he was ready to make his statement. The patient answered in the affirmative. Coroner Young then proceeded with the usual questions, as follows:

Q. What is your name?

A. James Fisk, Jr.

Q. Where do you live?

A. No. 313 West Twenty-third street.

Q. Do you believe that you are about to die from the injuries you have received?

A. I feel that I am in a very critical condition.

Q. Have you any hopes of recovery?

A. I hope so.

Q. Are you willing to make a true statement of the manner in which you received the injuries?

A. I am.

Fisk was thereupon sworn, and made the following statement:

"This afternoon at about 4 o'clock I rode up to the Grand Central Hotel. I entered by the private entrance; and, when I entered the first door, I met the boy, of whom I inquired if Mrs. Morse was in. He told me that Mrs. Morse and her youngest daughter had gone out, but he thought the other daughter was in her grandmother's room. I asked him to go up and tell the daughter that I was there. I came through the other door, and was going up-stairs, and had gone up about two steps, and on looking up I saw Edward S. Stokes at the head of the stairs. As soon as I saw him I noticed that he had something in his hand, and a second after I saw the flash, heard the report, and felt the ball enter my abdomen on the right side. A second after I heard another shot, and the bullet entered my left arm. When I received the first shot I staggered and ran towards the door, but noticing a crowd gathering in front, I ran back on the stairs again. I was then brought up-stairs in the hotel. I saw nothing more of Stokes until he was brought before me by an officer for identification. I fully identified Edward S. Stokes as the person who shot me.   JAMES FISK, JR."

After Fisk had appended his signature to the statement he became very faint, and the attending surgeons were obliged to give him stimulants.

The jury having heard the deposition of Mr. Fisk, rendered a verdict:

"That James Fisk, Jr., came to his injuries by pistol-shot wounds, at the hands of Edward S. Stokes, at the Grand Central Hotel, January 6th, 1872."

The dying man had to be kept constantly under the influence of morphine, so intense was the pain that he would have suffered otherwise.

About 10 P.M. he became conscious, and said to Dr. Fisher,

who was at his side, "Doctor, is there an even chance of my getting well?" The doctor responded hopefully.

At 4 A.M., on being asked, he said he was doing nicely.

At 7 A.M. a carriage halted at the door of the hotel, the foam with which the horses were covered attesting the fearful rapidity with which they had been driven. It contained Mrs. Fisk, who came in response to a telegram sent to Boston. Fisk was then unconscious, and did not, consequently, recognize her.

At 9 o'clock a consultation was held. The result was the posting of a bulletin in the lobby of the hotel: "9 A.M—Col. Fisk is sinking."

At 10.45 o'clock, Sunday morning, James Fisk, Jr., was dead.

The body was placed in a coffin, carried out of the hotel by the way of the kitchen, and driven to his late residence, No. 313 West Twenty-third street.

His last will and testament, made just before his death, reads as follows :—

I, James Fisk, Jr., of the City of New York, being of sound mind and memory, do make, publish and declare this my last will and testament, hereby revoking all former wills by me made.

1. I give, devise and bequeath all my estate and property, real and personal, except the special legacies, hereinafter mentioned, to my beloved wife, Lucy D. Fisk, subject, however, to a trust to pay to my dear father and mother jointly, or to the survivor of them, $3,000 a year for their support during the life of them or either of them ; and further, to pay to Minnie F. Morse and Rosie C. Morse, each, $2,000 a year during their lives, respectively until marriage, when the annuity of the one marrying shall cease ; the property and estate aforesaid to rest absolutely in the said Lucy and her heirs forever, subject only as aforesaid ; and the said trust shall not affect her right freely to dispose of and transfer any such property.

2. I give and bequeath to my sister, Mrs. Mary G. Hooker, stock in the Narraganset Steamship Company of the par value of $100,000, for her sole and separate use forever.

3. I appoint my said wife and my friend, Eben D. Jordan, of Boston, executors of this my last will and testament.

In witness whereof I have hereunto set my hand and seal this 6th day of January, 1872.

[L. S.]   JAMES FISK, Jr.

Signed, sealed, published, and declared by the testator to be his last will and testament, in the presence of us, who have hereto subscribed our names as witnesses, at his request, and in the presence of each other.

THOMAS G. SHEARMAN,

No. 316 West Twenty-second street, New York.

JAY GOULD,

No. 578 Fifth avenue, New York.

F. WILLIS FISHER, M.D.,

Grand Central Hotel.

Leaving the dead James Fisk, Jr., in his 23d street house, we will go back to Saturday morning, and tell briefly the events that immediately led to the tragedy. The whole of his history is a romantic and complicated one, and will be detailed further on.

On Saturday morning, January 6th, 1872, before Justice Bixby of the Yorkville Police Court, was heard the continuation of a suit brought by Helen Josephine Mansfield against James Fisk, Jr., the charge being that of libel.

Mansfield had enjoyed the confidence and protection of Fisk, and had been the recipient of letters of a tender and confidential nature from him.

Stokes had been his friend, and his partner in certain business transactions, the prominent speculation being the management of an oil company at Hunter's Point.

He invited Stokes to Mansfield's house, where all three frequently dined together.

A rupture occurred between the two men, growing out of the marked attention Stokes paid to the woman. Then they fell out in a business way. Fisk had Stokes arrested on a charge of embezzlement. Then Stokes had Fisk arrested on a charge of false imprisonment. Mansfield sided with Stokes. She claimed that Fisk owed her $40,000, and threatened to sue him if he did not pay it. She held Fisk's notes. The following is an exact copy of one of the originals :—

Treasurer's Office,
Erie Railway Co.

Borrowed and received from Miss Josie Mansfield, fifteen thousand seven hundred and fifty dollars.

$15,750. JAMES FISK, Jr.

Fisk sought to prove a black-mail operation instigated by Mansfield, who immediately brought suit for libel against Fisk. That was what was going on at Yorkville that pleasant winter morning.

The testimony of that particular day is not of any special importance, being at the best but the public washing of some very soiled linen, and so—this being a moral book—we will skip it.

Fisk was not present at the court during the entire day. At the close of the hearing, Stokes, accompanied by John McKeon and Assistant District Attorney Fellows—his counsel—stepped into a coach and drove to Delmonico's, at the corner of Chambers street and Broadway.

On that same floor, some thirty years before, John C. Colt killed Samuel Adams.

After partaking of some lunch, Stokes visited the offices of several prominent lawyers, and took a carriage to the Hoffman House. He was next seen on Broadway, in the vicinity of the Grand Central Hotel.

Almost precisely at four o'clock, Col. Fisk got into his carriage that was standing in front of the Grand Opera House, and drove to his death.

On the morning of January 9th, Superintendent Kelso detailed a large body of police to act as guard around the Opera House, where, in a short while, the remains of Fisk were to be placed in state.

At half-past ten o'clock the crowd was tremendous. So great was the crush that five ladies fainted, and had to be conveyed to neighboring drug-stores.

The interior of the Opera House was the picturesque of gloom

Festoons of black and white crêpe were suspended from the dome and attached to the beams which support the galleries. A life-size picture of Fisk faced the entrance to the vestibule.

The body of Col. Fisk was lying in his residence, 313 West Twenty-third street. At half-past ten o'clock the casket which was to contain the remains of the Colonel was carried past the Opera House and into his residence. It was of solid rosewood, highly polished. On its sides were heavy gold bars. The inside was trimmed with heavy folds of white satin. On a silver plate, fastened on the inside of the lid, was the following inscription:

JAMES FISK, Jr.,

Died January 7th, 1872,

In the Thirty-seventh Year of His Age.

At eleven o'clock Coroner Young, with the jury which he had impanelled, called at the house and viewed the remains.

At half-past eleven o'clock, the casket containing the body was borne from the residence and up the grand stairway to the magnificent vestibule of the Erie Railway offices, where it was deposited on a catafalque.

Soon afterward the lid was raised, and the face was exposed to view. Not the slightest change was discernible in the features. The body was dressed in the complete suit of the Colonel of the Ninth. His sword lay by his side, and his military hat rested on the casket. His arms were folded across his breast, and his hands were encased in white kid gloves. Across his shoulders was a delicate wreath of tuberoses. A table at the head and one at the foot of the casket bore wreaths, crowns, and immense bouquets, composed of camelias, white roses, tuberoses and immortelles.

Lieut. Montgomery and Sergeant Aspel, of the Ninth Regiment, stood at the head of the casket. Capt. Fuller directed the ceremonies.

At twelve o'clock the lower doors were thrown open, and immense numbers of sympathizers began to move up the stairs and through the vestibule in single file.

For two hours the long line of mourners was unbroken, and when Capt. Fuller announced to Mr. Merritt, the undertaker, that there was scarcely time to reach the depot, and the doors were closed, there was no perceptible diminution in the numbers in front of the Opera House.

The members of the Ninth Regiment and the band, who, with the Aschenbroedel Verein, of which Col. Fisk was an honorary member, had been waiting in the lower hall. They next filed past the body. The arms of the soldiers were reversed. Many of the members wept freely.

Chaplain Flagg then read the funeral service in a deeply impressive tone of voice.

Just as the prayer for the dead commenced, Mrs. Fisk and Mrs. Hooker, Col. Fisk's sister, walked up the vestibule, leaning on the arm of Mr. Moore, a brother-in-law of the Colonel. They were attired in the deepest mourning. Their features were completely concealed by heavy black crape veils. They remained seated until the conclusion of the prayer. They then went to the side of the corpse. Mrs. Fisk raised her veil, and, bending over the body, kissed her dead husband's lips. She was then led away by Mr. Moore, sobbing bitterly. Mrs. Hooker's grief was apparently more intense than that of Mrs. Fisk.

The lid of the casket was then closed, and the well-worn battle-flag of the Veteran Corps of the Ninth Regiment was spread over the top. Assistant District-Attorney Fellows, who up to this time had remained in the directors' room with Jay Gould, entered the vestibule, and asked permission to look once more on the features of his friend.

The casket was then closed for the last time. It was taken down-stairs and placed in the hearse. Among the distinguished persons in the vestibule were Drs. Pollard and Eldridge, H. Ramsey, Henry Hurley, H. C. Rathbun, John Hilton, Jay Gould, H. Thompson, F. A. Lane, E. A. Buck, of Buffalo, H. N. Smith, Mr. Belden, James B. Bache, C. McIntosh, C. S. Spencer, Marshal Joseph H. Tooker, H. Sherwood, O. H. P. Archer, Mr. Simons, J. H. Bacon, D. D. Field, W. A. Beach, D. Field, T. G. Shearman, Mr. Drake, of Corning, Homer Ramsdell, B. W. Blanchard, J. W. Guppy, E. K. Willard, Charles Orcutt, Samuel Pike, L. D. Rucker, Henry Thompson, C. D. Earle, J. N. Abbott, Wm. R. Barr, W. Q. Chapin, T. B. Bunting, A. C. Radcliffe, C.

S. Brown, Geo. Fowler, E. B. Hill, E. O. Hill, J. K. Frothingham, H. L. Gatchell, H. W. Moore, A. L. Hall, C. A. Peck, W. H. Johnson, W. Drake, of London, Colonel Conklin of the Eighty-fourth Regiment, Gen. Varian and staff, and Richard Tweed.

The following-named gentlemen constituted the guard of honor: Adj. Allen, Lieuts. Wood, Montgomery, Bowland, Hussey, Bacon, and Palfrey. Messrs. Henry Thompson, John Hilton, and Dr. Edwin Eldridge were appointed by the Erie Railway directors as a committee to accompany the body to Brattleboro'.

The appearance of the pall-bearers was the signal for a movement in the band. A ruffle from muffled drums, followed by a plaintive dirge, broke upon the wintry air. Four hundred rifles came to a present as the remains of the dead Colonel were borne to the hearse. This done, the escort broke into column and moved off in the following order of procession:

Battalion of police under command of Capts. Copeland and Burden.
Ninth Regiment Band.
Drum Corps.
Aschenbroedel Society.
Officers of the Narraganset Steamship Company in uniform.
Ninth Regiment in column of companies, left in front.
Erie Railway Employees.
Carriage of Chief Mourners.

Col. Sterry,	HEARSE	Lt.-Col. Webster,
Col. Allen,		Col. Scott,
Gen. Funk,		Col. Clark.

Col. Fisk's horse led by groom in livery.
Two platoons non-commissioned officers and privates, National Guard.
Six platoons commissioned officers.
National Guard marching in single rank.
Gen. Varian and Staff.

Ninth Regiment Veteran Association, Gen. Hendrickson
commanding.
Platoon of Police.
Carriages.

From the New Haven depot the special funeral party that accompanied the body proceeded to Brattleboro', Vermont, where the remains were interred in a cemetery, situated upon a high bluff that overlooks the river.

James Fisk, Jr., was born in the hamlet of Pownal, Vermont, in September of the year 1835.

Before he had fairly gotten out of his teens he left his home and entered the employ of Van Amburgh, the famous circus and menagerie man, acting as a tent-hand and assistant door-keeper. He followed the circus business for seven or eight years, during which time he saw a great deal of humanity, and considerable of the country. Tiring, at last, of the profession, he returned to Vermont and took up his father's business, that of peddling. Fortune smiled upon him, and where the coy jade only scatters sparse coppers in the pathway of others, she showered golden ducats upon Fisk. He made money, and made it rapidly. As soon as he could afford it, he expanded into the proprietorship of a four-horse team, splendid in plated harness, and a natty wagon that was the marvel of all the country round. In this style Fisk flashed through the New England States, a brilliant dry-goods meteor. Eventually his exclusive custom became so great, that the then young Boston firm, Jordan, Marsh & Co., deemed it advisable to purchase his entire business and employ him as a salesman. Fisk accepted the offer. When the tocsin of civil war was sounded, Fisk heard in its thrilling notes the chink of gold. For him to see an opportunity was for him to embrace it. He did so. Wandering through the store of his employer one day, he saw a lot of old blankets. Quick as thought his brain chalked up the profit that might be made out of them. Going to Washington, he kept open house a few days, wined and dined the powers that were, and ended by selling his blankets at a handsome figure, and securing a contract for an immense quantity of the same kind.

So pleased were the firm with this stroke, that they made him a partner. One of the first things he did in that capacity, was to purchase an entire mill at Gaysville, Vermont—a mill which happened to be the only one of its kind in the country. Shortly after, the goods of that mill were in demand. A "corner" was inevitable, and Jordan, Marsh & Co. cleared over $200,000 in two years.

In 1865, this firm came to the conclusion that Fisk was not only smart, but entirely too smart, and so gave him nearly a quarter of a million to withdraw. He took it.

Boston was the next scene, where he started business at the corner of Summer and Chauncey streets. In that prudish city fortune scowled upon him, and it took but a few months to waste away his capital. Then he turned his eyes toward Gotham, and opened an office for the brokerage business in Broad street.

But he was unsuccessful, and it was not until he made the acquaintance of Daniel Drew, that any change in his fortunes was perceptible. Drew gave the sale of the Bristol line of steamers into Fisk's hands, and the firm of Fisk, Belden & Co. was established in Wall street, their operations being so successful that Fisk possessed a $1,000,000 bank account. The Erie directors quarrelled with Drew, and both Fisk and J. Gould became members of the board. From the start these two men determined to gain possession of the road, and their schemes ultimately proved successful. In February, 1868, the famous over-issue of Erie stock was completed, by which the capital of the road was nominally increased from $19,000,000 to $34,000,000. This operation led Fisk and Gould to imagine that they could secure colossal fortunes by operating in the stock. Commodore Vanderbilt held $10,000,000 of the stock, and they persuaded the Board to purchase $5,000,000 of Vanderbilt's stock at seventy per cent., at the same time making a private arrangement with the Commodore to have the "call" of the remaining $5,000,000 for six months, they paying him $1,000,000 cash for the privilege. Fisk and Gould then sold the $10,000,000 "short" and so manœuvred that the stock fell from 72½ to 35. They then "watered" the Company's stock from $34,000,000 to $57,000,000, and purchased Vanderbilt's stock with the proceeds of the sale, at forty per cent. Fisk is believed to have cleared by this transaction over $1,125,000. In July, 1868, the brokerage firm of Fisk, Belden & Co. was dissolved, and the two conspirators at once set about securing control of the Erie road. To effect this, Fisk and Gould prosecuted Mr. Eldridge, the president, for fraudulently using $5,000,000 of the Company's money to secure the passage of the bill which had enabled them to increase the stock. Eldridge resigned at last, and Jay Gould became president.

But Fisk became more notorious for his " Black Friday " operations than any one of the innumerable schemes he set on foot. A ring was formed by which absolute control was obtained of all the salable gold in the market, and the consequence was a " corner" in gold on Friday, September 24, 1869. The result was a panic in Wall street, gold suddenly sprang from 142 to 160, Fisk and Gould's agents forcing the rate by bids, until it was found that the Ring possessed all of the available gold, and intended to hold it for a further advance. Everything seemed in favor of the conspirators, as it was believed that the Government sales of gold would not relieve the market. The scenes in the gold-room were extraordinary, for a continuation of the crisis for twenty-four hours meant absolute ruin for all of the small operators, as well as many of the leading firms. While the panic was at its height President Grant ordered the sale of $5,000,000 of gold coin, and the rate dropped down to its old figure. Fisk and his confederates repudiated the majority of the engagements made by their agents, and several failures were the result.

When the over-issue of Erie stock gave him control of an immense amount of the shares, he purchased Pike's Opera House for $820,000 in the name of the Erie Company, but they, not liking the bargain, he assumed the purchase, reimbursing the Company with some of his watered stock. Subsequently the Company leased the upper part of the building at an enormous rent, and Fisk also dabbled in other property, among which is the Fifth Avenue Theatre and Central Park Garden.

Such is the way Fisk obtained his foothold in New York.

Edward S. Stokes was born in Philadelphia, but came to New York about twelve years previous to the scene upon the staircase of the Grand Central Hotel.

In writing the life of Ed. S. Stokes, owing to the fact that many trashy accounts have been written, entirely misrepresenting everything in relation to him, we have taken great pains to give our readers a correct and truthful history of his antecedents.

His grandparents, Thomas and Eliza Ann Stokes, left England to seek a home in New York in 1793, and soon after purchased a farm at Sing Sing, in the immediate vicinity of where the prison now stands.

JOSEPH DOWLING.

And it is a strange and noteworthy fact that the prison is built of the stone taken from their property, known as the "Stokes Quarry."

The old adjacent dock property for the last fifty years has been known as the "Stokes Dock."

Some of the old settlers of Sing Sing remember old Thomas Stokes, and speak of him in high terms. He was a strict member of the Baptist Church, and devoted a large portion of his time and money to the advancement of religion.

Thomas Stokes had five children—Edward, James, Henry, Sarah, and Mary.

In 1810 Thomas Stokes entered into the importing trade, and continued in business with his sons until his death, in 1833, dissolved the business.

Soon after James Stokes married Miss Phelps, the daughter of Anson G. Phelps, and at once entered as a partner in the house of Phelps, Dodge & Co.

Sarah married Mr. Charles Colgate, the well-known soap and candle manufacturer, now deceased.

Mary married Mr. Clinton Gilbert, a descendant of the old Knickerbocker Gilbert family, and now the President of the Greenwich Savings Bank.

Henry Stokes is the President of the Manhattan Life Insurance Company.

Edward H. Stokes, the father of E. S. Stokes, married Miss Nancy Stiles, of Philadelphia, and then retired permanently from business.

The Stiles family were one of the oldest and most aristocratic in the State of Pennsylvania, and were in the enjoyment of every comfort that wealth could furnish.

Edward S. Stokes was born on the 27th day of April, 1841.

Stokes was brought up with every possible advantage; every wish gratified, and schooled in the best academies in the State. He was always fond of out-door sports, was quite an expert cricket player, a member of the Athletic Club, a fair gymnast, and a pupil of Barrett's Gymnasium, which is still in operation at the corner of Eighth and Market streets.

From childhood he was passionately fond of horses, and in later years became quite a patron of the turf.

He left college in 1860, and next year came to New York, where he entered into the produce business, under the firm name of Budlong & Stokes, at No. 25 Water street.

He was known on Produce Exchange as a bold speculator, of quick conception and like execution.

The operations of this firm amounted to millions, and were

highly successful. In 1865, Stokes withdrew from the firm his entire capital—his partner, shortly after, met with financial embarrassment.

Stokes at once commenced the erection of the Brooklyn Oil Refinery, which was intended to be the largest of its kind in the State of New York.

It was completed at a cost of some $250,000, in the year 1865. His extended ideas in this undertaking led to serious disaster. Stokes invested largely in petroleum companies that were then organizing in Pennsylvania, just at the time the oil fever was at its height, and in less than one year the panic broke out, and when the bubble burst Stokes's fortune was lost.

Add to this, his refinery, which was heavily stocked with oil, took fire, and the buildings and machinery were destroyed, together with the entire stock of oil. His manner of doing business was, to say the least, loose; for instead of insuring his refinery, he took the risk of fire upon himself, and the consequence was it left him bankrupt.

Stokes had many friends, who have always clung to him in adversity, who willingly advanced him all necessary means to enable him to recover his fallen fortune. In 1867 his refinery was rebuilt and in successful operation. The profits of the business for the three following years were large, amounting to several hundred thousand dollars; and it is creditable to Stokes to say, that every dollar of his indebtedness in the Produce and Oil Exchange he paid up in full, notwithstanding he had been previously legally discharged; and, it is stated upon good authority, had it not been for the difficulty with Fisk, every single dollar would have long since been liquidated. It was at this particular time, when Stokes was in the height of prosperity—the sole owner of the "Brooklyn Oil Refinery"—that James Fisk, Jr., determined to get the control of the business, in the interest of the Erie Railroad. A copartnership was entered into. Stokes was made treasurer of the company, at a salary of $6,000 a year, and a rental of $27,000 being paid for the refinery, and also 30 per cent. of the net profits, which, had it continued any length of time (with the cheap freights Fisk gave the company) the profits would have been enormous. Eventually, however, the two men quarrelled, Fisk alleging that Stokes had embezzled $50,000 of the company's funds. He had Stokes arrested on Saturday, January 4, 1871, late at night, when he could give no bail, and of course he was kept in prison one Sunday.

On Monday he was brought before Judge Dowling, and held in $50,000 bail—the case was afterwards dismissed—it being proved that it was a malicious prosecution.

When Mansfield floated upon the scene, the two men were still fast friends. How they became mortal enemies, is a story told in few words. Stokes had met Mansfield in Philadelphia, but was reintroduced to her by Fisk. At the Twenty-third street house he was frequently a guest at dinner, and frequently the recipient of hospitality and favors from the fair hand of Josie when Fisk knew nothing about it. But the rumor of what was going on was bound to reach his ears, and it did. He became very jealous, and forbade Stokes the house. Finally the enraged colonel, seeing that his commands and remonstrances had no effect, wrote a farewell letter to Josie. It appears that Josie was much pleased at getting rid of Fisk, and took him at his word. Fisk repented having so written, and begged to be again replaced in her affections.

Several quarrels and reconciliations seem to have followed, until, finally, a positive enmity existed.

Law proceedings were instituted, and a threatened publication of letters, implicating Fisk and Gould in swindling the Erie stockholders, etc., caused Fisk to get an injunction from Judge Pratt forbidding their publication.

Then a proposition was submitted to Stokes for arbitration. Stokes accepted Mr. Clarence Seward as an arbitrator, the letters being placed in Mr. Peter B. Sweeny's hands for safe-keeping. Mr. Seward found against Stokes, on all points but one, but awarded him $10,000 for the malicious manner in which Fisk had persecuted him.

Then came crimination and recrimination, which led to the trial before Justice Bixby, at Yorkville.

Such is the way Edward S. Stokes obtained his first notoriety in New York.

Helen Josephine Mansfield was gracing the Pacific slope with her maiden beauty when Mr. Frank Lawlor, an actor, drifted into the blaze of her wonderful eyes, and felt the magic arrow from Cupid's bow strike his breast. She was at school there, and was probably imbued with all the romantic ideas which boarding-school girls are wont to be actuated by. She also fell in love. We cannot say that there was any rope-ladder, and a carriage waiting at the end of the lane, but there certainly was an elopement. Miss Josephine walked from her vestal boudoir, and out into the world as Mrs. Lawlor.

Being the wife of a gentleman connected with the stage, it was necessary that she should embrace his wandering life. Together they came East and stopped in Philadelphia, where it was that Stokes first saw the woman that was to be his fate.

The current of Mr. and Mrs. Lawlor's love did not flow on with that musical rhythm that is necessary to complete conjugal felicity, and it was not long after their return to this part of the world that the fickle Mrs. Lawlor concluded to get a divorce. After considerable opposition on the part of Mr. Lawlor, she finally procured the desired document.

It was on the very day she received her divorce that she was introduced to Col. Fisk, while visiting her friend, Miss Annie Wood, the actress. Fisk was perfectly infatuated, and soon established for her a home, in splendid style.

Left alone upon the surface of the social sea, Josie trimmed her silken sails and steered for the port of prosperity. In fighting the world she recognized that beauty was her most puissant weapon, and she used it skilfully. As the iron-filing flies to the magnet, so did Josie to New York. This metropolis is the Mecca for adventurers of every class. Her case was no exception.

Since the tragedy she has resided mostly abroad. When last heard from she was in Paris, driving in the *Bois de Boulogne* on week-days, and modestly saying her prayers in the church of the *Madeleine* on Sunday mornings.

Such is about the way in which Helen Josephine Mansfield obtained an unenviable reputation and momentary adulation in New York.

FISK'S LOVE-LIFE.

The love-life of Jim Fisk was fully as remarkable as any this country has witnessed. In many respects it was as remarkable as any that any century has witnessed. It was not very high-toned, however. We are forced, rather painful as is the thought, to confess that it was fully as immoral as it was romantic, and it was romantic, there is no doubt about that. From the evening that the Prince of Erie became fascinated with the lovely siren at Miss Wood's down to the time that the fire of hate was kindled upon their mutual altar of love, there was no lack of romance.

Josie was intended by nature to be admired. Tall and shapely, with just sufficient tendency to *embonpoint* to produce that generous curvature, claimed by more than one philosopher to be a necessary element of feminine beauty; having hair as dark as the darkest midnight; eyes always aglow with the light of the love-lamp; a dainty, coquettish manner that would seem to have been born of that fair city that lies glittering beneath the clear-cut sky of France; was it strange that such a creature should ensnare the susceptible colonel in the meshes of her beauty?

The change from her friend's quiet home in 34th street to the palatial house on 23d street, must have been a remarkable one for Josie. While she was thus situated life had scarcely a dash of rose-color in it. Her wardrobe was scanty, her bank account as slim as the chances of catching Sharkey, and her capital stock, which consisted of nothing but her beautiful self, was yielding no appreciable dividend. But when she became a power in the Erie Railroad, and gave up the quiet labors of an ordinary humdrum life for the more pleasurable task of quaffing "Mumm" with politicians and judges, her star began to hang dazzling in the zenith.

There is no question of the power she exerted in the affairs of the Erie Railroad, and the other schemes which were daily born in the busy brain of Fisk. She was the power behind the throne, the Princess of the road. In that elegant little house of hers in 23d street, she presided at the charming suppers given there with as much grace and tact as Marguerite Bellanger ever exhibited when she fondly stroked the waxed moustache of Napoleon III., and bought a diamond necklace with a kiss. Charming suppers they were, and a charming house it was. An exotic taste had arranged everything, from some trifling ornament worth a few thousand dollars upon the mantel-piece, to the lace and damask curtains that shrouded the bed of the Princess. Anything that money could buy was there, and Josie was the queen of the scene. Right royal nest it was for this bird of Paradise.

Perhaps in Pompeii there may have been suppers and dinners given resembling those spread in the 23d street house. Without a doubt, each age and city has had its "Jim and Josie." Not as regards the viands or their cost do we press the comparison, but solely with a view to the extraordinary spirit of the scene. It was a combination of beauty and business, of love and locomotives. Just above was the stately Opera House, wherein were transacted the affairs of a mighty corporation. The telegraph wire running from Josie's chamber to Fisk's private office was no more potent a connecting-link than that chain of roses which bound the Comptroller of the road to the modern Cleopatra. She presided at the feasts to which judges, bankers, politicians, and men of money generally, sat down. Amid the popping of champagne corks "jobs were put up," "corners made," and "mines constructed;" and the silvery laugh of Josie has been a musical indorsement of many a scheme of financial villainy. It was the greatest combination ever known of an amour and financial affairs. Cupid, seated at a mother-of-pearl desk, checked off the accounts of the Erie Railroad, with a feather plucked from his wing.

It was strange, also, that combination of theatre and trade in the Grand Opera House. The click of the telegraphic instrument telling its story of Wall street mixed with the voice of Montaland on the stage below, singing the rollicking music of "Les Brigands." The flash of the footlights penetrated even to the room where sat the Directors of the road in solemn consultation.

It was Montaland, the dashing Opera Bouffe singer, or rather the attentions paid to her by Prince Erie, that first ignited the fire of jealousy in Josie's breast. Fisk was undoubtedly captivated by the fair Parisienne, and nothing delighted him so much, during that time, as to be seen flashing through the Park by her side. Naturally Josie grew angry, and we do not blame her for not allowing his gum shoes to stand in her hall-way. Why should she? For the time being some one was occupying her gum shoes.

We have already alluded sufficiently to Stokes in connection with Josie, and the enmity between him and Fisk that grew out of it. He was a frequent visitor to the house, and was no doubt smiled upon by Mansfield, when she saw, or imagined, that Fisk was indulging in too many *liaisons*. But while she held a handful of trumps she took every trick. Whether it was in New York, or at Long Branch, Josie held the whip-hand.

The dead colonel was partial to Long Branch, and did much to make it what it is—the favorite watering-place of New Yorkers. While " on the sands "—free from the cares of the office—he shone with extraordinary brilliancy, and created quite a flutter among the butterflies of the Grand Stand at Monmouth Park, when he drove up in the regal style he was wont to assume, with Josie lolling upon the cushions as indolently as did her Egyptian prototype—Cleopatra—upon the cushions of her barge.

There is very little else that can be said about the love-life of Jim Fisk. Nearly all of its salient features either appear in our account of the tragedy or the trials. When he was forced to steal over to Jersey in an open boat, in order to avoid the impending arrest that grew out of the famous railroad fight between Vanderbilt and Drew, she followed him to Taylor's hotel, and solaced his exile with her company. That she really loved the man who robed her in silk and satin, and made her all ablaze with diamonds, we cannot say. The world seems to think she did not, and regard her as a sort of American Becky Sharp, who, in the faro game of the grand passion, knew how to " call the turn" properly. But it doesn't matter. " Jim " sleeps amid his native Vermont hills—" Josie " is adventuring in Paris. Their love-life is o'er.

The writer, being intimately acquainted with Stokes, after the tragedy at the Grand Central Hotel, through the courtesy of Police Justice Dowling, was passed through the iron gate that led to the room where Stokes was then conversing with his brother Horace.

His manner was calm and collected, and as he extended his hand he glanced furtively towards the door to see if there were any other visitors.   Being the bearer of news that, under most any circumstances, would strike terror to the heart of one in Stokes's situation, the writer's voice was tremulous with emotion, and when he said, "Ned, can you bear the worst?" he replied, "Yes.   I suppose Fisk is dead."   We were decidedly the most agitated, and intently gazed into Stokes's face as we communicated the sad news.   His young brother realized the terrible position in which Stokes was now placed, and his lips quivered as he asked if the report was true.   Stokes took from his pocket a neatly-bound diary, and as he tossed it up remarked, "As sure as you see this I am not Colonel Fisk's murderer."   On being asked for some particulars regarding the fatal encounter, he, in an entreating tone, answered: "Don't ask me any questions, my counsel have sealed my lips."   There was nothing in his demeanor that betokened remorse, nothing in his expression that resembled fear, and as he turned to go to his cell he bade us good-by as self-possessed as when we had parted with him on the street but a few days before.   His counsel, which had been retained the evening of the shooting, were the next to call.   To them Stokes gave a graphic description of his encounter with Fisk, which was never divulged until the day that Stokes told it from the witness-stand to rather an incredulous jury.   Besides his father and immediate relatives there were no other persons permitted to enter the Tombs on the first day of Stokes's incarceration.   The irrepressible interviewers besieged the portals like ravenous wolves, but their persistency was not rewarded.   Before noon a rumor reached police headquarters that the members of the Ninth Regiment, of which Fisk had been Colonel, were in council at their armory, and it was their intention to force an entrance to the Tombs, take Stokes from his cell and hang him from the corridor.   The Superintendent of police immediately ordered platoons of policemen from a majority of the precincts to proceed to the Tombs, and before dusk over 500 of them were marched into the halls ready for any demonstration that the angry militiamen might undertake.   But it proved to be a canard, and at midnight no sound was heard within those dismal walls but the cooing of the pigeons that nestled under the eaves of the granite pillars. Stokes lost no time in availing himself of those privileges, and indulging himself in the comforts that money will always purchase whether in a prison cell or a palace chamber. The sensation newspapers daily instructed their interviewers to ask him how he felt; how he had slept; what he had eaten; what he had dreamt during the night, and, day after day, they gazed at him like a wild beast, and then put words into his mouth that he had never uttered, thereby creating in the minds of the public a prejudice against him which he was powerless to dispel. Women of the town were passed into the corridors, by the officials with whom they were acquainted, in order that they might gaze at him, and the following day the daily *Sewer* would inform its readers that the dandy assassin was visited by several women of loose character. Stokes bore all this abuse with a contemptuous shrug, not a word of complaint passing his lips. Some of the papers clamored for an immediate trial, having already convicted him of the murder of Fisk. But John Graham had fought for Stokes like a lion since the day he had been driven to the fight of desperation at the coroner's investigation where he was surrounded by the minions of Fisk. There were friends of Fisk who were making every effort to secure Stokes's conviction, and it was this influence that Graham was combating. Not only the press was subsidized to convict Stokes, but the drama was used as an instrument whereby public opinion could be prejudiced. In the early part of May, 1872, "Black Friday," a sensation play, in three acts, was brought out at Niblo's, the author of which was Henry Harewood Leech, a Philadelphia stockbroker, who was ruined himself by the very sensation which he wove into a disreputable play. The curtain never rose on the sixth representation, for on the 4th day of May Niblo's was nothing but crumbling walls, smoke, cinders—a total wreck. Stokes, immured in his dungeon, read the criticisms of the play, and, driven to desperation, he recited his grievances to a newspaper reporter, and it was then that his principal counsel, John Graham, left him, giving as a reason that he had "given himself away," and that he could not undertake to defend him under such circumstances. This action on the part of Counsellor Graham occasioned considerable comment. There were those who said that there were other reasons that induced Mr. Graham to desert Stokes, but, be it as it may, Stokes now says that it was John Graham that snatched him from the gallows. Associated with Mr. Graham were John McKeon, Elbridge T. Gerry, Willard O. Bartlett, and Bartlett, Jr. Stokes was eager for a speedy trial, notwithstanding all the lawyers had withdrawn from the case except John McKeon. John D. Townsend and Henry Daily, Jr., were retained to prepare the case, and on the 19th of June, 1872, the long-anticipated trial began in the Court of Oyer and Terminer, Judge Ingraham presiding. The prosecution was conducted by District-Attorney Garvin; and William A. Beach and ex-Judge Fullerton, both of whom had been counsel for Stokes in his former difficulties with Fisk, were retained as private counsel to assist in the prosecution. Why they were retained was never positively known, nor was it ever known who paid them for their services. Several days were occupied in obtaining a jury. The principal witnesses for the prosecution were two hall-boys employed in the Grand Central Hotel, named Hart and Redmond, who had been confined in the House of Detention until the day of trial. They testified that they were in the hall when the encounter took place, and saw Stokes stealthily approach the staircase, lean over the balustrade and fire two shots. For the defence, George W. Bailey, a New York merchant, testified that he saw Stokes on the east side of Broadway, near Amity street, and got out of a stage to join him; they walked on down; he talked to Stokes about his brother and putting him in business; Stokes told him he was looking for Ferris, and asked him if he knew where he could be found; Stokes said he was going to Niblo's to get tickets; they walked on, and, passing the Grand Central, Stokes touched his hat and said " I think I know that lady at the parlor window." Then, Stokes inviting him to go in, they walked on to the corner, and then walked back till opposite the door, when Stokes took hold of his coat and again asked him to come over, saying he would not keep him more than a minute; Stokes ran over, and witness walked up, crossed over at Amity street, and a few minutes later met Horace Stokes and turned back with him, when they reached the hotel and discovered the shooting; they went to the station-house, where witness was denied access to Stokes; a few minutes later Redmond was brought in, looking very excited; Redmond told him he knew very little about the shooting; he thought there were three or four shots, but when the first shot was fired he was scared and jumped through the door; the boy appealed to him whether he wouldn't have done the same. Mr. Bailey was examined at some length as to the reason why, when his direct route home was by Twenty-third street, and he had gone up there, he returned down Broadway, but he had no special reason to give; he did not remember very clearly whether, when he met Stokes, the latter was standing or moving slowly on. To the last question he smilingly replied, however, that Stokes was no Broadway statue.

Jennie Turner, who had been a servant with the Morse family, testified she was in the hall-way of the Grand Central, near parlor 207, looking for a bracelet lost by Miss Minnie Morse, about four o'clock on the afternoon of January 6, 1872. She saw Stokes look into the parlors, go down the dining-room hall, return, and start towards the ladies' staircase. A few moments after she heard pistol-shooting. Stokes suddenly appeared again, and passed around by the elevator, saying, "Get a doctor." He looked excited. The witness afterwards saw a lady come up the ladies' stairs with a pistol in her hand, and give it to a gentleman, who led her into parlor 207. Two or three weeks after the homicide Mrs. Morse told Jennie that she was wanted for the trial, and had better go away.

The witness looked sickly, and gave way to tears during her examination. She said that her husband, William Chase, had deserted her at Middletown, in this State, and she was now residing with her mother at Lee, Mass.

On Saturday afternoon, July 13, 1872, after the arguments of the counsel had been heard and the judge had issued his charge, the jury retired to decide the fate of Edward S. Stokes. They came into court at five o'clock for instructions regarding premeditation, and again at seven o'clock, to say that they were unable to agree upon a verdict. The judge would not discharge the jury, and they were again sent out. On the morning of July 15th, after having deliberated forty hours, they were discharged, and Edward S. Stokes was again remanded to the Tombs. The jury stood seven for murder and five for acquittal.

The disagreement of the jury gave general dissatisfaction. With the masses there was very little sympathy expressed for Stokes. To them Fisk appeared in the light of a public benefactor, and they were clamorous for the death of the man who cut short his career of usefulness.

The prosecution and defence each redoubled their efforts, and it was soon made manifest that there were persons who were deterred from offering themselves as witnesses, for fear of being imprisoned for an indefinite time, and each day came some fresh and startling revelation, until on the 18th of December, 1872, the curtain rose a second time on this terribly agonizing tragedy. The second trial began in the Court of Oyer and Terminer, before Judge Douglas Boardman, who came from the western part of the State. The prosecution was conducted by Assistant District-Attorney Fellows, and Messrs. Fullerton and Beach were, as before, retained as private counsel. Lyman Tremain was the leading counsel for the defence, assisted by John D. Townsend and John R. Dos Passos, a rising young lawyer.

It was evident that public interest in the case had somewhat abated, yet there was much curiosity manifested regarding the new testimony that it was reported would be brought out during the trial. The characters and antecedents of many of the witnesses on both sides were thoroughly investigated, and it was supposed there would be more or less fluttering among them. During the second trial it came out that one Comer, who had been Fisk's private secretary, had applied for board at the house where Jennie Turner was then stopping. Contrary to general expectation, there was no additional material evidence elicited. The trial lasted fourteen days and terminated with a verdict of murder in the first degree. As before, the theory of the prosecution was, that Stokes went to the Grand Central Hotel, ascended to the private hall, and there laid in wait for his victim. The theory of the defence was, that there were two pistols, that Fisk made the first movement, and Stokes, believing his life in danger, jumped out of range, drew his pistol and fired two shots into the body of Fisk. The jury were out but three hours. On the first

ballot they stood ten for conviction and two for acquittal. The
trial was mainly characterized for the bitterness and rancor which
opposing counsel displayed towards one another. Mr. Beach
summed up for the prosecution, and Lyman Tremain replied for

"JAY GOULD'S MONEY HAS SECURED THIS CONVICTION."—STOKES.

the defence. The prisoner was unprepared for such a verdict, and
displayed considerable emotion. He was much excited, and remarked that Jay Gould's money had secured his conviction. The

STOKES RECEIVING THE DEATH-SENTENCE.

scene was rendered more impressive and solemn from the fact that it was nearly midnight. Stokes was returned to his cell, and on Monday, January 6th, just one year from the day of the fatal encounter, he was brought into court, and sentenced to be hanged February 28, 1873. Stokes received his sentence with meekness and resignation, and afterwards was condoled with by many of his friends. Stokes was again returned to the Tombs, but not to his old quarters. He was now placed in the condemned cell on the ground-floor, in which so many unfortunates had slept their last sleep. Here he was visited by his relatives, who never left him without displaying poignant grief at his melancholy situation. Stokes, however, was yet hopeful, always saying he would yet get a new trial. By January 12th, Mr. Dos Passos had ready his bill of exceptions, and on the 27th of January he appeared before Judge Noah Davis to set aside the verdict. Judge Davis remarked that it would be eminently proper that the motion to set aside the verdict, as well as the settlement of the bill of exceptions, should be argued before Judge Boardman. Lyman Tremain also made an argument before Judge Davis for a review of the case. On the 14th of February Judge Boardman, in an elaborate opinion, denied the prisoner a new trial. On the following day Judge Davis, in Supreme Court, Chambers, announced that since the decision of Judge Boardman he had given the subject careful attention, and had arrived at the conclusion that it was now his duty to grant the writ of error and stay of proceedings, pending the hearing of the appeal at the General Term.

Public opinion, in view of Judge Boardman's adverse ruling on the bill of exceptions, was that Judge Davis would not grant the application for the stay, but, luckily for the prisoner, that opinion was at fault, and the evil day—should it ever again appear on the calendar for Stokes in connection with his conviction and sentence—was at all events staved off for an indefinite period. The Supreme Court, Chambers, was crowded throughout the day, the crowd anxiously expectant of the result of Judge Davis's consideration of the application. It was after two o'clock when Judge Davis took his seat on the bench, and with his entrance followed a rush from the halls and corridors that instantly filled the room.

His attention was first called to a case of habeas corpus in which a young couple, claiming to be man and wife, sought the protection of the Court, the young woman having by illegal process been confined in the House of the Good Shepherd by Justice Bixby. The Court, learning from the lips of the young man himself that the lady in question was his wife, said he had nothing to do but accept the assurance, and thereupon good humor prevailed all around. The pair, once more united, left the judicial presence, at peace with themselves and all the world.

Judge Davis then proceeded to deliver his opinion, which, he said, was arrived at after a great deal of earnest examination of the points raised :—

The People vs. Edward S. Stokes.—Motion for allowance of writ of error in the stay of proceedings upon the judgment. Mr. Tremain, for the prisoner; Mr. Phelps, District Attorney, for the people. It was suggested by the respective counsel, when the motion was submitted, that its consideration should be delayed till the decision of the motion for a new trial then pending before Judge Boardman. That motion having been decided adversely to the prisoner, it becomes my duty to dispose of the present one. In doing so, I exclude from consideration the affidavits used on the motion for the new trial, and all the questions arising from them. They are not, in my opinion, property before me. I have not considered the questions made by the exceptions taken upon the preliminary trial of the pleas in abatement, but confine myself entirely to those which appear in the bill of exceptions made upon the trial of the indictment. The application to me is for a writ of error to bring the judgment record and the bill of exceptions before the General Term of the Supreme Court for review. Judgment having been pronounced in the case, no other mode of review is open to the prisoner, and it is apparent that to grant the writ without an order expressly staying his execution, would be an idle and cruel ceremony. The rule which should govern the Judge in determining a motion of this kind has long been clearly settled. It is well stated in The People vs. Hartung (17 How. Pr. Rep., 151) :—" When, on an examination of a bill of exceptions upon an application for a stay, the Judge has grave doubts of the correctness of the rulings of the Court at the trial, it is his duty, in the exercise of the discretion with which he is clothed, to allow the writ and stay the execution." In The People vs. Sullivan (1 Parker, 348), Judge Edmunds, in a case tried before himself, declared it to be his duty to allow the writ and stay the execution, where the question was one on which he felt no doubt, but upon which an appellant tribunal had passed; and in The People vs. Hendrickson (1 Parker, 396), the learned Judge said:—"In determining the question whether the prisoner shall have an opportunity for review by the Supreme Court of the exceptions taken, I am not necessarily called upon to arrive at a position conclusive that the Court erred as to the law. It is enough that there is an exception in the case which I deem not to be frivolous and which involves a gravely important question, respecting which there may be even a conflict of authority, but which remains unsettled by the Courts of the State." And in the very late case of Foster against the People, the Court of Appeals, while unanimously affirming the conviction, do not hesitate to say that the case was one eminently fit to be reviewed, and which properly called for the allowance of the writs and stays of execution that were granted by the several Judges below. The rule deducible from these cases is briefly this:—"That whenever the Judge to whom such an application is made in a capital case considers the questions raised upon the trial, and which may have affected the result adversely to the prisoner, to be of such grave moment and serious doubt, either from their not having been settled by the higher Courts, or because of conflicting authorities touching them, that in his judgment they are worthy of the solemn deliberations of an appellate tribunal, it is his duty to accord to the prisoner the opportunity to present them for review, and in such case, the duty should be discharged in view of the irremediable consequences that may follow his refusal." The exceptions taken upon the trial of this case are numerous. The great majority of them I deem to be either frivolous, or of such slight importance, that they cannot be regarded as having prejudiced the prisoner. But, in my opinion, they are not all of that description. Some of the exceptions to the rulings on receiving and excluding evidence will, I think, deserve attentive consideration upon argument. I cannot here consider them in detail. The exception upon which I have the gravest doubts arises upon a portion of the charge, which is a model of clearness and general correctness, laid down to the jury in the following rule of law :—" The fact of the killing in this case being substantially conceded, it becomes the duty of the prisoner here to satisfy you that it was not murder which the law would imply from the fact of the killing under the circumstances, in the absence of explanation that it was manslaughter in the third degree or justifiable homicide. Because, as I have said, the fact of killing being conceded, and the law implying malice from the circumstances of the case, the prosecution's case is fully and entirely made out ; and, therefore, you can have no reasonable doubt as to that, unless the prisoner shall give evidence sufficient to satisfy you that it was justifiable under the circumstances of the case." This was perhaps a clear and correct exposition of the common law rule in a case of homicide by violence, and with a deadly weapon ; but is not its correctness open to serious doubts under the statute of this State defining murder and its several degrees? The indictment was for murder in the first degree. The Court and the counsel for both sides concurred that the offence was either murder in the first degree or manslaughter in the third degree, or justifiable homicide. The killing by a fatal shot from a pistol fired by the prisoner was conceded ; and I understand the charge to have been, in substance, that from this conceded fact and the circumstances attending it, the law implies the malice, and makes out the case of the prosecution " fully and entirely," unless the prisoner gave evidence sufficient to satisfy the jury that the killing was manslaughter or justifiable homicide. In Wilson *vs.* People (4 Parker, 619), Judge Wright, an eminent and able jurist, in review at General Term, in a similar charge, says :—" The effect of our statute is to explode the whole common law doctrine of implied malice. Either of the cases put to the jury would at common law have been *prima facie* murder, for malice would have been implied from the act itself, and the burden of proof to explain or reduce the grade of the offence to manslaughter would have been shifted upon the accused ; but under our statute another ingredient was wanted to constitute the crime of murder—viz., an actual intention of the infliction of the blow to kill. It is true the jury would be at liberty to infer this intention in a proper case from the act itself, upon the salutary rule of the common law, that a man is held to intend that which in the ordinary course of things would be the natural result of his acts, but no legal implication of a felonious intention can now arise so as to throw upon the accused the burden of explaining the innocence of the transaction, or reducing the offence to manslaughter." To the same effect was the charge of Judge Edmunds in the case of The People *vs.* Austin (1 Parker, 154), and in The People *vs.* White (24 Wend., 520), and from the opinions had in the Court of Errors, the conclusion is reached that "express malice" must be proved, or the prisoner cannot be convicted under an indictment charging a premeditated design to affect death, understanding the charge of the learned Judge to have declared as a legal proposition, that the law implies the malice from the killing and the circumstances of the case, so that the charges of the indictment were fully and untruly made out, unless the prisoner proved by evidence sufficient to satisfy the jury that his act was a less crime, or no crime, and cannot but feel, in the light of the cases referred to, that there are such grave doubts, both as to the correctness of the charge, and its probable effect upon the deliberations of the jury, as to bring this application within the fair scope of the rule that should govern me in determining it.

It is neither necessary nor proper that I should form or express any positive opinions upon these questions. It is enough that I cannot say that my mind is free from grave and painful doubts. I reach my conclusion in this case with regret, but having it, I shall perform the duty that springs from it with no hesitation.

The writ of error is allowed, with stay of the execution of the sentence until the decision of the General Term.

The report of Judge Davis's action was not long in reaching the Tombs. The prisoners who heard of it were agreeably surprised.

It is almost needless to say that the condemned man himself was in an ecstasy of delight. For though all through he has manifested an utter indifference and a confident hope as to the final result, there was still an uncertainty which must have at times caused him a chill at the heart. But a matter so decisive as that of postponing any probability of a re-sentence for a year and a half, however stoical the demeanor of the prisoner, would naturally cause him great joy.

Soon after the decision was announced, the office of the Tombs prison was filled with friends of the accused, who clamored to be allowed to see Stokes. The request was denied by the new warden, Mr. Johnson, who took his place for the first time. He said that Mr. Joel Stevens had called on him in person during the morning, and had told him that the order relative to seeing Stokes by outsiders was still to remain strictly in force.

Stokes was soon transferred to his old cell, No. 73, in Murderers' Row, on the first corridor. Here he was more comfortable. At his own expense the walls had been hard-finished, and a walnut toilet-stand had been built across the head of the cell. He was daily interviewed regarding his prospects of a new trial, and in reply to a remark of ours, said:

"I feel myself profoundly obliged to Judge Boardman, that he only delayed his opinion about twenty days. He was very charitable. He might, you know, have kept it a few days longer; then I should not have had any chance at all.

"The majority of the jury were respectable men. There were a few of them that I believe went on the jury to hang me anyhow, if possible. They expressed themselves so, and carried out their intentions. Public feeling, at the time, was very high, and the excitement fearful against any one charged with murder, guilty or innocent; consequently their prejudice was so great that it was impossible for them to calmly deliberate and determine between perjured testimony and that which was honest. The former they believed and the latter they discarded. The consequence is, I am innocently convicted of a crime, not that I intentionally violated any of the laws, but because crimes are daily committed. I have no fault to find with the majority of the jury. They thought it was their duty, or at least forced themselves to think so. The future will reveal that I am wrongfully convicted, and that is a great comfort for me to know.

"Some newspapers take great delight in attacking me bitterly, and then wind up by moralizing in the hope that I am preparing for eternity. If the writers of these articles were devoting more of their time to their spiritual improvement and less to me, I think it would be better all around."

The application for a new trial was denied by the Supreme

STOKES DINES HIS FRIENDS.

Court, General Term, on May 7th, 1873, Judges Brady and Fancher giving their opinion, to which Judge Davis dissented.

Stokes's last chance for life now was the Appellate Court, and until June 10th, 1873, he underwent that mental torture, that to be known must be felt. It is undoubtedly the agony of a thousand deaths, but Stokes bore up under it. Those privileges—before referred to—that money can buy, he enjoyed to the fullest extent. He had a large room on the Centre-street side, where he was allowed to remain all day. Here he received his friends and visitors, ate choice cuts, drank champagne, and regaled himself with cigars. This state of affairs lasted several weeks, when suddenly it came to an end. Why we know not, but certain it is that there was never a more privileged character confined in the Tombs than Stokes. We might stop here to moralize, contrasting the situation of the petty thief on the top corridor with the blood-stained prisoner on the first floor; but we are writing history, and will keep to our task.

On the 10th of June, the Court of Appeals ordered a new trial, Justices Rapallo and Grover giving their opinion, in which all the judges concurred.

Stokes, almost snatched from under the black beam of the ghastly gallows, became still more hopeful. He realized the fact that public opinion was daily changing in his favor. His life had almost ebbed away in the swift torrent of an angered community, but now he could wait for that "tide which, if taken at its flood," might, at least, take him from his pestilential abode to some other place than eternity. To him, like many another, any fate was more acceptable than lingering for years in the cold, noisome cell, and in the language of one confined at the present writing, in the same cell that Stokes occupied, " If there is no other alternative, I would rather be jerked out from the end of a rope than stay here and die by inches."

On the 14th of October, 1873, the third act in the Fisk-Stokes tragedy began before Judge Noah Davis. The fact alone that Judge Davis was to preside was very comforting to the prisoner and his friends. Time, too, had worked many changes that were favorable to his case. The Tammany Ring, which the prisoner believed was a strong element against him, had been crushed and broken. The Supreme Court bench had tipped, upsetting a trio of its occupants, and Fisk's minions were scattered and demoralized. Those who were not, had formed new alliances, and in fresh schemes had forgot the misfortunes they had underwent through the death of their former employer. The public had become apathetic, and longed, like the boy in the theatre pit, for the moment when the legal foemen should again flash their steels.

On this occasion the prosecution was conducted by District Attorney Phelps, who did not avail himself of the services of private counsel. The prosecution did not offer any additional testimony, but the defence did. As the trial approached the close the public interest began to be again awakened. The police

BENJAMIN K. PHELPS.

found it difficult to keep the corridors leading to the court-room clear. It was quite evident, whether the result was to be in favor of or against the prisoner, it was the last time he was to be in jeopardy for the shooting of James Fisk. There was no more important testimony than that given by the prisoner. His state-ment did not materially differ from those made before. In man-ner he was energetic and nervous, and he told his story with candor and earnestness. He denounced the boy Thomas Hart as a perjurer, and denied that he had threatened to shoot Fisk. The jury listened with attention to the prisoner's story of the encounter, and it seemed to have a favorable impression.

To give the testimony of the various witnesses would occupy too much space, but summed up it was as follows :

That the prisoner believed that he had been sold out by certain lawyers who were formerly his counsel in various litigations with Fisk, and that they had conspired against him in the interest of Fisk. That he was afraid of Fisk's hired bullies, known as the Lynch gang.

John More, connected with the carriage department of the Grand Central, testified that he was standing at the large lamp in front of the hotel when Fisk's carriage drove up and he got out ; about ten seconds after Fisk had entered he heard a sort of dumb sound, and next Redmond came out in an excited state and shouted that Fisk was shot ; witness then went in and saw Fisk leaning on the banisters on the left-hand side. Witness explained his meaning on the diagram, after which he said he put his hand on his shoulder and asked if he was hurt ; Fisk did not reply at first, but upon being asked the second time, made the remark : " He was a little too quick for me this time." Witness helped him up and left him on the parlor floor ; subsequent to this, witness saw the boy Redmond and asked him what he saw of the occurrence, and he replied that he had seen nothing.

Robert S. Stobo, No. 53 Maiden Lane, testified that a few minutes before the shooting he was nearly in front of the Grand Central Hotel, at the west side, and saw the prisoner and Mr. Bailey walking together at the east side, and noticed the prisoner saluting some one at the hotel, and crossing the street immediately after ; Stokes then entered the hotel, and in about four minutes after, Fisk's carriage came down ; the street was very full of carriages, and Fisk's carriage came along slowly. In his opinion, Fisk's carriage must have been about five blocks off when Stokes entered the hotel.

Mr. Fisk's tailor testified that he made for Fisk the pants he wore on the morning of the homicide ; he also testified that he never made pistol pockets unless they were ordered ; that Fisk always personally ordered his clothes, and that the pants now produced have a pistol pocket.

On cross-examination witness said he identified the trousers as his work by his name on them and by certain peculiarities; not one in six of his customers order such pockets, and he does not have such pockets himself.

An entirely new witness, whose testimony did more, perhaps, than any other to save Stokes from the gallows, was that of Patrick Logan. This man had formerly been a policeman, but for interfering to save an old man's life, who was being clubbed by a brutal policeman at the Orange riot which occurred in the summer of 1871, was dismissed from the force.

He testified that he was a Court officer at the first trial of Stokes; the first day the two Harts and Redmond, the hotel servants, were taken to Court, but not examined; he took charge of Redmond on the way back to the House of Detention; Redmond said, "I'm glad I wasn't put on the stand to-day, or I would be puzzled." "How is that?" said witness. "Because," said Redmond, "I didn't study what I have to say; I didn't read it." Witness asked whether he meant that he had his testimony written down? and Redmond said "Yes." Witness asked him whether he wrote it himself, and he replied, "No, but it was written for them," and the two Harts also had copies, and that Thomas Hart was smarter than "Patchy" Hart, and had his copy so well committed to memory that if he repeated it a hundred times he would not miss a word; "I suppose," said witness to him, "you are well treated?" Redmond answered that at first they were treated badly, but Mr. Powers, proprietor of the hotel, ordered them a separate table, and they were well treated since; witness asked whether they were to be paid for their trouble, and Redmond said they were to get $1,000 each; "I then pondered," said witness, "whether I ought to pursue the conversation further."

"You what?" asked Mr. Phelps.

Witness—I pondered, but I concluded to get all the information I could.

The witness went on to relate, amid roars of laughter, how next day he was in charge of Redmond, going back to the House of

Detention, after Redmond had been sworn. Officer O'Donnell had charge of the Harts. It appeared that they called into numerous drinking saloons, at every one of which the witness objected, but they all insisted. The conversation during the drinks was very ludicrous. At last they came to one drinking place; drinks were proposed; "I objected," said witness, but it was no use; while all hands were drinking, Redmond asked, "How do you like my testimony?" Witness said he got on very well. "Oh," said Redmond, "I studied it well."

LUDLOW-STREET JAIL.

Mr. Tremain asked the witness whether he drank anything. To which he replied that he has been a temperance man for twenty years, and drinks nothing but soda-water and sarsaparilla.

The witness then related how on the way to the House of Detention Thomas Hart told him he expected, besides the $1,000 from Mr. Powers, Mrs. Fisk would pay him.

Cross-examined by District Attorney Phelps—Did you communicate this to any one? A. Yes, to John McKeon, but though he is one of the keenest lawyers in New York, he failed to take the hint.

Q. Any one else? A. Yes, to Mr. Desbrosses. (Roars of laughter—the witness meant Dos Passos.)

Q. When did you reduce it to writing? A. The 4th of this month.

Q. From what? A. From the tablets of my memory.

Q. From the tablets? Let us hear it again. A. Oh, I will look you straight in the face and answer. In January, 1872, I was an officer in the Court of Oyer and Terminer, and had charge of Connolly in Ludlow-street Jail.

"What Connolly?" asked Mr. Phelps.

"Richard B. Connolly, sir." (Laughter.)

"This was when you were a deputy sheriff?"

"Yes, sir."

"What were you before that?"

"A policeman."

"And you were discharged from the police, were you not?"

"Yes, I was; and I regard it as one of the proudest laurels of my life, for I saved an old and sick man's life from a brutal policeman."

"Were you not discharged because you refused to do your duty?"

"Mr. District Attorney, I want to explain it to you, sir."

"Never mind," said Mr. Phelps.

"You shall have a chance to explain by and by," interrupted Mr. Tremain.

"All right, sir," exclaimed the witness, and then, in answer to further interrogations put by the District Attorney, he went on to state how he told a Mr. Conroy what the Redmond boy had told him; how a gentleman called on him and asked him to go to the Coleman House and see Mr. Dos Passos, which he did, and at the same time saw Mr. Brainard; how he told them the story; how he afterwards met Mr. Conroy and rebuked him for telling him what he had told him.

"Why," asked the District Attorney in this connection, "did you not tell this at the other trial?"

"I did not want to be mixed up in the case," answered the witness, "but I should have made my conscience all right in the matter."

"How so?"

"Before I would have let Stokes be hung, I should have gone to Albany and called on Governor Dix and told him to swear me, and then I should have told the whole story."

"What is your business now?" asked the District Attorney.

"Selling boots and shoes."

"Why did you give up your place as court officer?"

"Because Comptroller Green wouldn't pay me anything; and I guess if the Comptroller did not pay you anything, you would give up your place too." (Laughter.)

Witness, having got the best, as he thought, of the District Attorney, was again taken in hand by Mr. Tremain. He explained all about his discharge from the police. It was on July 12, the day of the riots; he was no coward; he had his club in his hand and stood ready if he saw any one breaking the peace to break his club on his head, whether the peace-breaker was an Irishman, a German, a Frenchman or an Italian; he saw a drunken policeman beating an old man standing at the entrance of a dispensary, and he wrenched the club from the officer's hands; a sergeant who on that day never said, "Follow me," but kept in the van, preferred charges against him and he was discharged.

On Stokes taking the stand he gave his early history up to the time he went into the oil-refinery business, when he became acquainted with Fisk, which was in July, 1869. He then continued as follows:

I was spending the summer in Saratoga, and he telegraphed for me to come to the city. I came to the city to meet him, and at that interview agreed to go into the oil business with him, and continued in it with him until January 8, 1871.

I was arrested on a trumped-up charge, and simultaneously the refinery was seized by a lot of Fisk's men. I was removed as an officer and director—turned out.

My mother and myself went over to the refinery by the

advice of Mr. Beach, who was counsel for her, and took possession.

The conditions of the lease had not been complied with. I had
been her agent for several years. Previous to May, 1870, I had
one-half interest in this oil business, and Mr. Fisk desired me to
give up twenty per cent., retaining thirty per cent. In consideration of that, he agreed to double the capacity of the refinery. He
failed to carry out that condition.

I was a witness before Justice Bixby in the complaint against
Fisk for alleged libel in publishing the King affidavit, which
charged myself and Miss Mansfield with an attempt to extort
money.

Q.—How long before that day had you last seen Fisk?

A.—Two or three weeks before at Niblo's Garden.

Q.—Were you aware previous to meeting him at the Grand
Central that he had been sick? A.—I heard it rumored around
that he had been sick for a week or two.

Q.—You had not received any information prior to going to
the Grand Central Hotel about his going out of his house? A.—
None whatever. I knew nothing in regard to it. I left Bixby's
court a little after 2 o'clock in a carriage with Mr. McKeon and
Col. Fellows. Miss Mansfield must have left about the same
time, as I recollect we passed her coming down. We drove to
Delmonico's, corner of Broadway and Chambers street. I went
in and took some oysters and a glass of ale at the bar. Remained
about five minutes.

Q.—Give the Jury a narrative of your movements up to and
including the time of meeting Fisk at the Grand Central.

STOKES'S MOVEMENTS.

I conversed briefly with the Mayor of Utica, and then went
directly to Mr. R. F. Andrews's office, 51 Chambers street. I
asked Mr. Andrews if he thought it would be prudent for me to
go to Providence on Monday: told him I was afraid that if Fisk
knew I had left the city he might go before the Grand Jury and
say I had run away, and get a requisition to bring me back, so as
to disgrace me. Mr. Andrews said he did not think I need have
any apprehension. I don't know that he gave any special reasons.

He said that Fisk's indictment had been thrown out, and no proceedings were pending at all. I then went to see Mr. Francis
M. Bixby, who said to by all means go to Providence and have no
fears. The case in Providence was coming off on Tuesday, the
9th. I made up my mind that I would leave for Providence. I
got into a carriage at Broadway, near Chambers street, and
directed the coachman to drive to the Hoffman House. I went
directly there to prepare my case and get the papers ready. I
had boarded there since I left the Worth House on the 1st of
June the same year. I found there a telegraphic despatch that I
thought I had sent the day preceding. I had directed it to Mr.
Doty, Eatontown or Eatonville, anyhow the wrong end to Eaton,
and the operator had returned it marked, "No such station." Doty
was one of my most important witnesses in the appeal case. Mr.
Cottrell, the lawyer, told me the right address, and I sent the
despatch. Mr. McLaughlin was standing there, and intended to
accompany me on Monday. He directed me where to see Ferris
and David Smith. He said they would be found in the locality
of Broadway and Amity street. I had left the original agreement in this case at Miss Mansfield's, and took a coupé at the
Hoffman House and Twenty-fourth street, directing the man
to drive to 359 West Twenty-third street.

I drove there without making any stop. When I arrived there
I was about getting out of the coupé, when I noticed that the
house was all closed up, and I remembered she was ill, and I
concluded that I would not disturb her. I then ordered the
driver to drive to the corner of Broadway and Grand Central Hotel.

I would like to state in regard to that, that it was an invariable
custom of mine to direct a coachman to some particular landmark.

I say that because it might seem very singular to drive there,
or to direct the coachman to drive there, when there is really
nothing singular about it.

I directed the driver to change his course from Twenty-third
street to Seventh avenue, because I was reading some important
papers, and the pavement of Seventh avenue is smooth for
driving. When we approached Fourth street and Broadway, I
rapped with my cane, and the driver stopped and I got out.

Q.—Did you see Miss Mansfield at the window of the house

when you called there? A.—No one was at the window at all. I did not get out of the coupé.

Q.—Did you see Fisk's carriage anywhere from the time you left the Hoffman House until you reached the Grand Central? A.—I did not, and did not see it at the Grand Central either. I did not know that Fisk was going out that afternoon. I never saw the Morses, that I know of.

Q.—Had you any knowledge that Fisk was going to the Grand Central that afternoon? A.—No. I did not.

Q.—Did you know that Fisk was in the habit of going to the Grand Central Hotel? A.—I think I did. I had heard rumors of his visits there.

Q.—Had you ever been to the Grand Central? A.—Yes. Only on the first floor; never up-stairs; never on the second floor.

Q.—After you reached the corner of Fourth street, and got out of the coupé, what did you do? A.—I went to Dodge & Chamberlin's, which was a rendezvous for Smith and Ferris. I inquired for them as I went in. I found Smith, talked over this horse business with him, and remained there altogether ten or fifteen minutes, I think.

Q.—After you got through there, where did you go, and for what purpose? A.—I crossed to the east side of the street, either in order to avoid the obstructions on the west side or to see Ferris, who used to be on that corner three or four hours during the day. I walked to Amity or Great Jones street, met Bailey in that neighborhood and invited him to walk as far as the Metropolitan Hotel, as I wished to engage tickets for the Black Crook, and I promised that I would return with him. He consented, and we walked down. As we were passing the Grand Central, I noticed a lady looking out of parlor 207. She bowed to me, and I recognized her, as I supposed, and returned her salutation. At that time I had no idea of crossing over, but I thought it was a lady I had met at Saratoga and had not seen for three years, and so said to Bailey. I invited Bailey to go over. He refused. I then retraced my steps to about opposite the ladies' entrance of the Grand Central, finished my conversation with Bailey, and crossed. When I thought I recognized the lady, I took my hat off to her.

Here the witness took the iron rod, and indicated his meanderings through the hotel.

I went directly up the private staircase, into the hallway, and passed to parlor 207. When the lady saw me, she turned her head sideways and looked into the street. I saw she did not know me, or care to know me. I had never been up-stairs before, and I walked along the hall, went back, and along the dining-room hall, and as I came along there, the lady came out of the parlor and went up-stairs, up on to the third floor. I found I did not know her. I then walked directly to the private staircase.

I had on a light-colored overcoat, more of a gray, made for winter use, a pair of dog-skin gloves, lined with wool, and a cane in my hand. Had had the cane some months and generally carried it.

Stokes identified his gloves and overcoat.

Q.—Did you have any expectation to see Fisk? A.—No, I did not. None in the world.

Q.—Did you go into any room to see his carriage? A.—I went into no room at all. Had no suspicion that Fisk was coming in at that time.

I had a pistol which I had bought in June or July, on Broadway, next door to Delmonico's.

Q.—Relate the transaction which is the subject of this indictment. A.—I went down on the right-hand side of the private staircase. When I had gone down several steps, I saw Fisk coming. He came in with a rush—sprang through the doors on to the private staircase. I at the time was on the right side going down. We were then in a line. I jumped from the left to the right, and cried out, " Don't shoot!" and immediately pulled my pistol and fired two shots as quick as that. [Here Stokes struck his hands together twice with less than the interval of a second.]

I saw his pistol. He pulled his pistol up in this way in both hands. [Here Stokes acted as if drawing a pistol with the left hand, and holding it around the chambers with the left while cocking it with the right.] There was no light at all on the staircase.

It was all at once ; it was not a second.

Q.—You say you came down on the right-hand side? A.—I

called out before I fired. I jumped over to the left so as to get out of line of his pistol. My left arm was on the banister when the firing took place. Both my left and my right arms were extended. I jumped to the left in such a way as almost to lean over the banister.

Q.—Did you take any particular aim when you pulled out your pistol? A.—No, sir; I fired the pistol and cocked it with the same hand.

Q.—When you first found it was Fisk, what effect did it have on your mind? A.—It produced great excitement and fear when I saw him.

Q.—Had you any premeditated intention to kill him when you fired? A. (shaking his head)—I never wanted to kill him.

Q.—Never thought of it? A.—No, sir.

Q.—Did you believe your life in danger? A.—I most certainly did. I saw his pistol just as plain as anything could be seen.

I always carried my pistol in my overcoat pocket when wearing it; in warm weather, in my pistol pocket.

In reply to his counsel, Stokes said earnestly: "Hart's testimony is manufactured and concocted; false from beginning to end."

Q.—Did you crouch or bend going through the hall? A.—No.

Q.—How positive are you that that boy was not there? A.—Ridiculous. There was no one near. Charles G. Hill was the only man anywhere near the place.

Q.—Why did you not retreat when you saw Fisk? A.—There was no chance to retreat. He was right on top of me before I knew it.

The witness extended his right arm, saying, "My right arm was extended this way when the firing took place." After the firing my impression is that I ran to 220, thinking it a continuation of the hall. I dropped my pistol somewhere at the time of the shooting, because when I was down-stairs they searched me, and I had no pistol. The first person I met was Hill. I told him there was a man shot, and I went right on. I met a Frenchman, De Corley, who said, "My God, what is the matter?"

I have attempted to obtain De Corley for this trial, but he has mysteriously disappeared.

I did not go into parlor 207, or anywhere near it.

Q.—You did not throw away any pistol in that parlor? A.—No. As I went to the stairs I asked several persons to get a doctor, as a man was shot. I went through the office, and in the reading-room I think I heard a man say: "Here, they want you!"

No one put hands on me then. The man was several feet off, and I turned and met him. Then several came and put hands on me, and as they took me into the office I asked them to take their hands off, as I was not going to run away. I was taken to the second floor for identification, and taken into several rooms. Finally we went into a room at the extreme end of the hall, and in that room was Col. Fisk. He was sitting upright on a sofa by himself, with his coat off. He looked badly—pale. There were a great many people in the room, and they appeared to be around the sofa. The officer had to move them away in taking me through. He made some remark to Mr. Fisk.

Here Stokes bent his head down, saying Fisk bent his head the same way, and replied to the officer: " Mr. Stokes."

I was then taken away.

Stokes proceeded to state Fisk's threats. He said:

From a remark Fisk made, I judged that he procured and planned Mr. Eaton's assault.

Fisk was unscrupulous, vindictive, desperate and revengeful.

Q.—Did you arrange, before meeting Fisk, with Senator Sprague to meet him in Providence? A.—Not the Senator, but his brother Amasa. I arranged with him in December, about two weeks previous to January 9. I had engaged rooms at a Providence hotel through Horace Bloodgood. I never said that Fisk was a damned blackmailer, and I would shoot him.

When going on a side street I always rode in covered carriages, but would walk on Broadway or a prominent street. I did so from the same apprehensions that caused me to leave the Worth House.

Fisk was as hostile and vindictive toward me as he could be. We were reconciled on Oct. 26, 1870, but he commenced quar-

relling with me within a few weeks. There was another reconciliation after that.

Q.—When did this state of feeling first come up? A.—In
July, 1870.

On the occasion of our reconciliation on the evening of the
26th of October, 1870, we were sitting in Miss Mansfield's back
parlor, and Fisk said to me that he had put up a job in the District Attorney's office, that I was to be indicted, but that he
would send a friend to me and tell me not to attend to it, as he
would move in court to have it dismissed.

He said: "When you come into court, I would have you rail-
roaded to State's prison, and whenever I thought of you, my blood
jumped to fever heat." He also said: "Our touch is cold and
clammy. The men whom we touch don't prosper. I don't know
how it is, but it is the case." That was on Washington's birthday, 1870.

This closed the direct examination.

On being cross-examined by District Attorney Phelps, Stokes
said: I had a meeting with Fisk, when a reconciliation took
place, at Delmonico's. Subsequently we had another meeting
for the same purpose in the Directors' room of the Grand Opera
House. It was had at the suggestion of Fisk and others. I was
subpœnaed to appear at Judge Bixby's court as a witness in the
suit of Miss Mansfield against Fisk. I left in company with
Col. Fellows and Mr. John McKeon. They did not advise me
on the way down that the result of the proceedings would be that
Justice Bixby would dismiss the complaint.

Q.—Did you say on the way down in the carriage that if Fisk
got you indicted he would never live to see you tried? A.—No,
sir; nor did I say anything like it. After describing his movements on the day of the shooting, which he did substantially as
in his direct examination, witness said: When I saw a man
coming around the foot of the ladies' staircase in the Grand Central Hotel, I did not know at first that it was Fisk. He ran up
the first landing with a rush. He pulled the pistol out from
underneath his cloak. I had no idea it was Fisk until I saw him
jump on the platform and pull out the pistol. He had both
hands on the pistol, and I thought he was in the act of cocking.

I then drew my pistol out of my coat pocket and fired. He bent his body and exclaimed, "Oh!" After the second shot he said, "I am shot; don't shoot." The pistol was loaded when I bought it. It was the only one I had. When I retreated after firing the second shot, I was afraid of a return fire. When I met Mr. Hill I said, "There's a man shot." I did not say, "I've shot Fisk." There is not one word of truth in Tommy Hart's story from beginning to end. I did not say at any time before my arrest that I had shot any one. I was in such a state that I don't think I spoke a word to the officer who arrested me. Ferris called to see me at the Tombs before the first trial. I did not ask him to swear that he had an appointment with me on the 6th of January, near the Grand Central Hotel. I never followed a carriage in which there were two men whom I supposed to be Fisk and Gould, and afterward say that if Fisk had been one of the men I should have shot him. I am not a good shot. I made no effort to get Fisk indicted. He was all-powerful with the District Attorney, and there was no use in going against him.

Re-examined by Mr. Tremain. — Our reconciliations were broken up through Fisk's failing to carry out the terms. One of the conditions of the second reconciliation was that he was to give me $200,000—$50,000 in cash at once, and $50,000 in one, two, and three years, and that I was to give up property in Greenpoint. I bought this pistol (produced) to protect myself against Fisk and his men.

Previous to the last trial, Mrs. Minnie J. Benton, residing in her own house on Lexington avenue, was arrested and taken from her home to the House of Detention, at the instance of the District Attorney. The only cause for her arrest was, that at the time of the shooting she was stopping at the Grand Central Hotel. She stated that she did pick up a white-handled pistol. She did not appear at the trial. This was the lady that Jennie Turner saw ascend the stairs with the pistol in her hand. As at the former trials, there was nothing more important than the testimony of the hall-boys. Recorder Hackett appeared for the first time and testified that he saw Stokes standing on the stoop of the hotel. He expressed it "standing anticipating," and that he was so much absorbed that he did not notice him. This was supposed to go far toward proving premeditation.

Perhaps the most persistent witness was a man who, when Edward S. Stokes was sentenced to be hung, at the conclusion of his second trial, lost no time, waited not an hour, before he wrote and sent him a letter, which, for cold-blooded fiendishness, under the circumstances, could hardly be equalled. The letter, which we quote from recollection now, ran something like this:

ED: Forgive me. I did but my duty. *Remember me to the Colonel when you see him,* and tell him, that Gould affair is coming out all right. Yours, COMER.

This man, John H. Comer, who could write such a cold-blooded epistle as this to a man just doomed to be hung, was on the stand to-day, and faced, with all the brazenness of his nature, the man whom he had thus addressed when the scaffold stood waiting for him.

Never was there any scene so intensely dramatic as that presented in the court when Lyman Tremain arose to address the jury in behalf of Stokes.

The man's appearance and known character are in his favor to begin with. He is powerfully built, with a head of massive structure. When Homer spoke of "the ox-eyed Juno," he described Tremain. His eye—or rather, both his eyes are singularly magnetic; round, full, blue eyes that look down into one's boots with a glance. His few opening sentences caused every man and woman in court to feel the importance, the impressiveness of the task he had set before him. "This is," he said, "the third time it has been my professional duty to stand before a jury of my countrymen to assist Edward S. Stokes in his life and death struggle with the Commonwealth of New York." As he said it, his big frame trembled all over and the tears dropped from his eyes. His emotion for a moment or two was absolutely beyond his control, and even the Judge on the bench was affected by it. Everybody seemed instinctively to remember the dark hours of Stokes's imprisonment, after the second trial, with the shadow of the gallows hanging over his cell, and not illumined until the fervent telegram came from Tremain at Albany, "A new trial is granted. Thank God."

The emotion of Mr. Tremain commanded respect. It was not the tricky sorrow of the mere advocate; it was the genuine heartfelt grief and hope of a brave, true friend, whose entire sympathies were enlisted in the cause he espoused.

A sigh of relief escaped Stokes when the District Attorney had concluded his argument. The day before he had looked very ill indeed, and during all the morning kept his face buried in his

LYMAN TREMAIN.

handkerchief. Once or twice only did he show it, and then the traces of suffering and tears were plainly apparent. During Mr. Tremain's opening he had shed tears freely. When he did look up, he turned his agonized face to the jury, and when, at recess, he took the hand of Mr. Tremain, and bowed gracefully to kiss it, it was difficult to help a sympathetic thrill.

Judge Davis, at a quarter past one o'clock, commenced his

charge to the jury, occupying in its delivery over three hours. Stokes stood the whole ordeal with his accustomed firmness, although signs of unusual excitement were at times perceptible in him as the District Attorney treated and laid bare the harder points against him, and some of the points relied upon by the defence in his favor. Judge Davis was more than usually slow, cogent and analytical in his charge to the jury, explaining every point in the testimony upon which the law in the case more particularly applied. It was admitted that the charge was as fair and just as it was full and searching. But speculation ran high during the day, culminating after the retirement of the jury, as to the result, now that the most important issue of the trial was in their hands. The rumor that had gone abroad of the conduct of two jurors was, of course, severely commented upon, and there were none on either side of the question who ventured for a moment to commend, excuse, or palliate the acts attributed to them.

THE VERDICT.

At twenty minutes past eleven o'clock there was another emptying of the jurors' chairs, another return of the jury, judge, counsel and the prisoner; another keen scrutinizing by Stokes and the throng of spectators of the jurors' faces as they took their seats; another few moments of suspense.

"Have you agreed on your verdict?" was asked again of the jury by Mr. Sparks.

"We have," responded the foreman, Stokes meantime having been told to rise.

"Jury, look on the prisoner; prisoner, look on the jury," said Mr. Sparks, in his clear, ringing voice, and then came the unvarying but all-important question, "Do you find the prisoner guilty of murder in the first degree?"

"We find him guilty of manslaughter in the third degree," answered the foreman.

Upon the announcement of the verdict a burst of cheers rose from the crowd, which the officers with difficulty could suppress.

"You find the prisoner not guilty of murder in the first degree," continued Mr. Sparks, when the temporary tumult had subsided, " but of manslaughter in the third degree. Hearken to your verdict as recorded. So say you all."

The jurors signified by a nod that such was their verdict.

Assistant District Attorney Russell at once moved that judgment be passed upon the prisoner in accordance with the verdict as just rendered.

Mr. Tremain asked that he might have a few minutes in which to confer with his associate counsel and his client. This was readily consented to by Judge Davis, and thereupon the counsel of Stokes, accompanied by Stokes, withdrew from the room. In less than a minute they returned.

Mr. Tremain then said : May it please the Court, the counsel for the prisoner feel that they have done all that is in their power to do to save the life of the prisoner. They feel that they have had a full and fair trial, and in the name of the prisoner I desire to thank the Court and the jury, who I know to be perfectly conscientious, and say that we ask for no delay. We might present evidence in mitigation as to the character of the prisoner ; but I presume Your Honor has sufficient knowledge to act intelligently in that and other matters, controlling your discretion in meting out punishment following that verdict. I simply remind Your Honor that the prisoner has been confined in the Tombs two years ; that he has been sentenced to death, a punishment I think Your Honor will be inclined to take into consideration in determining the amount of punishment to be awarded him after a jury has finally determined, upon a full trial, that he is not guilty of murder in the first degree, but of manslaughter in the third degree. I submit that the punishment to which I have referred, the sentence he has received and the sacrifice he has necessarily been subjected to in defending the case, may be considered by Your Honor in determining the amount of punishment to be imposed upon him.

THE SENTENCE.

Mr. Stokes was now directed to rise, and asked what he had to say why judgment should not be pronounced against him according to law.

In an almost inaudible voice, and with bowed head, he replied, " I have nothing to say."

Judge Davis, in a deep, stern tone, then passed sentence, as follows :—

In rendering this verdict the jury have exceeded, and more than exceeded, all the mercy that should be extended. No appeal to this Court can diminish the sentences below the highest penalty fixed by statute to the degree in which you are convicted, and that is apparently slight when compared to the great crime you have committed. I do not desire to make any further remarks in this case, but shall impose upon you all the punishment that the law authorizes, only regretting that the sentence cannot be more adequate to the awful crime that rests upon your guilty head. The sentence of the Court is that you be imprisoned in the State Prison at Sing Sing at hard labor for the term of four years.

Stokes received the sentence with a fortitude that astonished nearly everybody. At first his head was bowed down, but at length he straightened up, and at the close showed no feeling.

Thus ended, on the 29th of October, 1873, the trial of Edward S. Stokes for the killing of James Fisk, Jr. The various trials ; the opinions of the judges and counsel who were successively engaged therein ; the deliberations of the juries and the verdicts they rendered, form a chapter in the history of the *causes célèbres* of criminal trials that will not soon be forgotten. The verdict gave general satisfaction to everybody except the friends of Fisk, and the prisoner himself. Stokes's counsel and friends considered him a fortunate man, but Stokes felt that he should have been acquitted. He alone knows the causes that led to the fatal encounter, and as a jury of his countrymen have decided his crime was manslaughter, he cannot longer stand accused as a murderer. Some scandal was provoked after the trial was ended by the conduct of one of the jurors.

By the kindness of the Court he had been allowed an opportunity to transact some private business. This privilege he abused, and he used it to declare his determination that he intended to save Stokes from the ignominy of capital punishment. The phraseology he used was not so refined as this, but that was

the meaning of what he said.   Deputy Sheriff French, who had
this juror in charge, stated that he and the juror visited Bryant's
Minstrels, the Fifth Avenue Hotel, and other notable places
where convivial parties congregate.   In the hearing of a miscellaneous company the juror declared that Stokes should never be
convicted.   This fact was substantiated on the testimony of more
than one witness, whose evidence was furnished to the proper
legal authorities.

THE SOCIAL GLASS AT DAILY'S.

A few days following the conviction of Stokes he was brought
before Judge Davis and committed to the Tombs for contempt of
court, where he was detained for sixty days and compelled to pay
a light fine.   He occupied the cell vacated by Stokes.   Warden
Johnson, between Stokes and whom there was not the most
amiable feeling, now that Stokes had been condemned, removed
him to a cell on the ground-floor, there to await his transfer to
the State Prison.

Early on the morning of Nov. 1st, three days after his conviction, Deputy Sheriffs Shields and Cahill called at the cell-door

of Stokes, and told him to prepare for his departure to Sing Sing.
Stokes was surprised, believing he would be allowed a longer
time to make his final arrangements, but he never murmured.
Stoical to the last, he hastily gathered together his papers bearing on his case, many of which were documents the world had
not yet heard of, and stepped out in the corridor. He lit a cigar

A CONVICT AT THE HOSPITAL WINDOW.

and stood with his back to the stove, coolly anticipating the first
act of degradation that was to remind him that he was now a felon.
The deputy, who had walked many a mile with him in the
Tombs yard, while taking his daily exercise, approached him
with the handcuffs, and as Stokes put out his arm and bared his
wrist, he looked up to the skylight to conceal his emotion. The

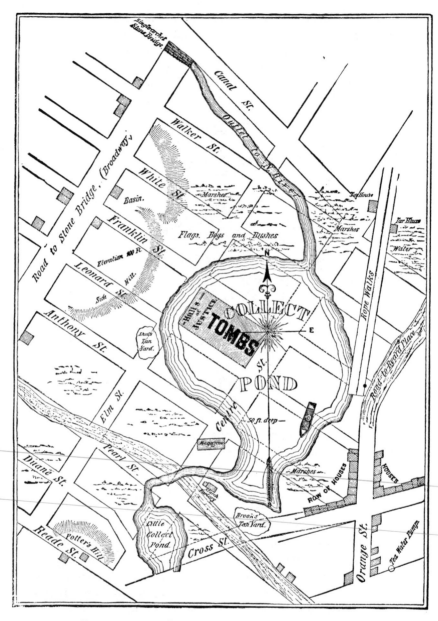

MAP OF "COLLECT POND," GIVING THE PRESENT SITE OF THE "TOMBS,"
AS DRAWN BY JOHN CANTER, THE COUNTERFEITER.—SEE PAGE 259.

glistening bracelet snapped with a sharp click, and a shock like that from an electric battery shook his frame. The steel that encircled his wrist had sent its cold embrace to his heart, and Stokes, for the first time since the fatal encounter with Fisk, realized that he was now an outlaw from society and the world. Stokes bade a hasty good-by to some of the prisoners who were standing on the corridor above, and crossed the yard that led to the prison entrance.

Arriving at the Sing Sing Prison he donned the repulsive costume that was handed to him, and was soon lost to view in a community of outlaws.

So much has been published regarding Stokes and his crime; we being acquainted with him previous to his troubles, and desirous of adding to this chapter something authentic regarding his intimacy with Fisk and Miss Mansfield, called on him at the Prison and requested an interview. He met us with his usual courtesy and discussed every event preceding the fatal tragedy. We found him on the top floor of the hospital, officiating as clerk of prison register. Here on an old-fashioned desk were a number of standard books which already showed signs of much handling. Stokes was in the prison garb and was already showing the effects of his imprisonment. His hair was quite gray, and, contrasted with his olive complexion and black eyes, gave him a decidedly *distingué* air; closely shaven, he needed but a cowl to give him the exact resemblance of a Franciscan monk. There was yet perceptible some of the hauteur that characterized him during his trial, but his imprisonment evidently wears on him. He cheerfully performs his duties, and has already gained the respect of the officials. Warden Hubbell has advanced ideas on the treatment of prisoners, which may yet be adopted in all prisons. There are those in Sing Sing who are not curbed and scourged. Stokes is one of them. The warden thinks that there should be gradation in punishment, and that different organizations require different treatment, and he acts accordingly. At our solicitation Stokes has written his own story, and we give it in the Appendix.

CHAPTER XL.

" That he should, for a term of years, reside in a spacious mansion where
several other gentlemen were lodged and boarded at the public charge . . . .
had their hair cut extremely short, and chiefly lived on gruel and light soup."

DICKENS, in *Old Curiosity Shop.*

PREVIOUS to 1828, the two prisons of the State were located,
one in the city of New York, the other in the village of Auburn. That in New York, popularly known as " Newgate," was
on the block bounded by Amos, Christopher, and Washington
streets on the north, east and south, and by the North River
(now West street) on the west. The old prison stands there to-day,
outwardly as it was then, except that workshops and tenement
houses, and eating-saloons and rum-shops have covered the vacant spaces that once spread away from three sides of it. It was
first opened as a prison on the 25th of November, 1797—convicts,
previous to that time, being confined in the county jails of the several counties where they were tried and convicted. It was of the
Doric order of architecture, and contained fifty rooms, twelve by
eighteen feet in the clear; besides cells for solitary confinement,
kitchens, offices, and workshops. Its capacity was the safe and
proper accommodation of not to exceed four hundred ; but the
records show that at times there were more than double that
number within its walls. It was surrounded by a high wall, and,
until it was finally abandoned, that wall, and what it enclosed,
with the cry of " Old Hays," had more terrors for the boys of those
days than fills the boys of to-day, with the Municipal Police
in full chase, and the Tombs, the State Prison, or the Gallows,
in the foreground.

At last the crowded condition of " Newgate " so forced itself
upon the public attention, that the Legislature, on the 7th of
March, 1824, passed an act providing for the appointment of
Commissioners to select a proper site for another penal institu-

tion, and to adopt a system and provide for the erection of suitable buildings. Under that act STEPHEN ALLEN, SAMUEL MILES HOPKINS, and GEORGE TIBBITS were appointed commissioners.

At that time there was much discussion, and consequent division of opinion, as to the relative merits of three systems of prison government. The first was the continuously isolated and non-laboring system of Pennsylvania; the second was the triple or quartette occupancy of large cells, with such labor as could be adapted to small rooms, as practised at "Newgate;" the third was what has since become known as the "Auburn" system, which is a combination of the two first, viz.: solitary confinement at night and through Sunday, and constant silent or non-intercourse labor in large shops.

The commissioners were thinking, deliberate men, and puzzled as only thinking and deliberate men can be by the facts and arguments of the contestants. The advocates of the solitary, non-laboring system professed little regard for either the moral condition or physical comfort of the felon. With them it was a naked proposition to kill or cure, and they came boldly to the front with a plan to locate the prison on Bedloe's Island, and to build and conduct it upon the system that a felon once within its walls should see no living being except his keeper until he had served out the period of his incarceration. He was to be turned inward upon himself—to be allowed to commune only with his own thoughts.

It is more than probable that these views would have eventually prevailed had not the advocates of what was claimed to be the more humane system linked with their other arguments the alluring theory that felons should and could be made to pay their way, and also contribute to the public treasury. They not only advanced the theory, but they professed to be able to point out the unquestioned road to success. About thirty-three miles from New York, on the east bank of the Hudson, was a partially developed strata of white marble that was known to be inexhaustible. The State should buy this—set its convicts to work drilling and blasting, and hammering and chiselling—and so the city would soon become one vast expanse of marble palaces, at a cost that would hardly exceed that of the adobe huts of the Aztecs, while the State treasury would grow so plethoric as to warrant the early discharge of the inevitable tax-gatherer. The friends of humanity computed the thousands of millions of billions of feet and yards and tons of the raw material that lay embedded in those everlasting hills ; they had the exact cost of maintaining a felon twenty-four hours ; they knew to a feather's weight just how much marble he could delve out ; it would by natural gravitation slide down the hillside to large barges that would be waiting to receive it, and thence go floating with the tide down to the growing white metropolis of the western world. Honest citizens would henceforth dwell in marble halls that knaves would shape from the great limestone formation which nature had so temptingly located on the very confines of the city.

The Commissioners might—and doubtless would—have turned a cold shoulder towards the humanitarian, but they could not resist the economist and his statistics. They negotiated with the owner of this marble El Dorado for the purchase of his farm, which they obtained at what then was a fair price for farming land. It contained about one hundred and fifty acres of rough, unimproved land, on which was a large dwelling, of most fantastic design and construction, since known as the State House, and which for several years was used as the residences of those connected with the prison.

Capt. ELAM LYNDS was then the Principal Keeper in charge of the discipline of the Auburn Prison. He was ordered to detail one hundred from the convicts in that institution, with the privilege of selecting such persons as he thought fit for keepers and guards, and with this force proceed to the new location at Sing Sing, and commence with the construction of a prison capable of accommodating six hundred inmates upon the plan of the Auburn system, viz., a separate cell for each convict.

Capt. Lynds had been a commissioned officer in the United States Army, and was thoroughly imbued with the views of discipline which at that time characterized the regular service. His will was a law of itself, which he never permitted to be violated by any subordinate—citizen or convict. Clothed with ample powers to purchase materials, and urged to prosecute with unceasing vigor the construction of the new buildings, he and his party landed at Sing Sing on the morning of the 14th of May,

1825, and proceeded at once to work. Before night barracks had been erected capable of sheltering men and provisions and implements, and in twenty-four hours he had commenced blasting out material for the proposed structure. From that day until May, 1828, when six hundred cells had been completed, officers and men continued in unpausing labor—held under their accustomed discipline by the vigilant eye and unrelaxing hand of the master spirit. The convicts moved from Auburn had been chosen for their physical power, regardless of their moral standing in the prison—there was no enclosure to restrain them —they were in the open fields, guarded by less than one-tenth of their own number, and yet from the day they left the cells at Auburn until they had finished the cells that were to entomb them at Sing Sing, there was not one attempt at escape, and no infraction of discipline that called from the master spirit a more harsh admonition than the single word " Beware ! " The moral energy of that one man was sufficient to awe into subjection the most turbulent, while the most desperate were hardly rash enough to provoke a contest which they well knew would be " short, sharp and decisive."

The original plan of the prison called for a building five hundred and forty feet long, forty feet wide, and three stories high, which gave six hundred cells. These were in blocks, divided by an arch or passage-way in the centre, and having stairs at each end of each block. The cells are back to back, and encased by a wall (pierced with a small opening in front of each cell), which supports the roof. Before the roof was finished it was ascertained that the accommodations were entirely inadequate, and therefore a fourth story was added. Subsequently two additional stories have been added, so that at this time there are twelve hundred cells—six hundred in each block. These cells are seven feet in depth, by seven in height, by three and a half in width in the clear. The dividing walls are eighteen inches thick, and the ceiling stones about a like thickness—the same stone forming the ceiling of one cell and the floor of the one above it. The cells are approached by galleries, now sustained by iron brackets let into the masonry. There is a clear space of seven feet between these galleries and the outer shell. The cells are closed with grated doors one-half their width. Those in the south block are each locked separately; those in the north block are locked in divisions of fifty each, by a lever working a bar, to which are attached fifty bolts, one of which fits into an eye on each door. If all the doors are not closed the lever will not work. The lever being down, is fastened in place by an intricate combination lock.

When the first six hundred cells were completed, and also suitable buildings for offices, kitchens, hospitals, guardhouse, storehouse, and a residence for the principal keeper, the convicts from "Newgate" were removed to the new quarters, and that prison abandoned and sold.

OFFICERS OF THE PRISON.

When the city prison was abandoned, and its inmates transferred to the Sing Sing prison, the management or general direction of the latter was nominally vested in a Board of Inspectors, composed of five persons appointed by the Governor and confirmed by the Senate. Three of these were required by law to be residents of the town in which the prison was located, and two could be chosen from the State at large. They were authorized to appoint an Agent, a Principal Keeper, Clerk, Chaplain, Architect, and such number of Keepers and Guards as they deemed requisite, not exceeding one of each to every twenty-five men. The highest salary paid was $1,000 per annum to the Principal Keeper, and the privilege of a house with lights and fuel. Medical attendance was provided by a physician resident in the adjacent village, who paid a daily visit, at the munificent compensation of $300 per year. For many years this daily service was rendered by Dr. ADRIAN K. HOFFMAN, father of the late governor. In practice, until 1843, the Inspectors had little to do with the internal affairs of the prison, beyond the appointment of the principal officers. The Agent purchased the supplies, and the Principal Keeper had an almost exclusive charge of the discipline. The Inspectors were generally men of respectability and worth, and that was all. In the list of names, until the period above named, there is hardly one that was ever heard of beyond the locality. In 1843, Governor BOUCK, by some strange departure from the regular custom, chose to nominate as the two non-resident Inspectors Hon. JOHN W. EDMONDS, of New York, and Gen. THORNTON M. NIVEN, of Orange. The latter was in a short time succeeded by Hon. JOHN BIGELOW, then just commencing public life.

From the advent of these men, the Inspectors have more and absolutely assumed control of the details of the management, and absorbed the powers and privileges of the subordinates. Judge EDMONDS came to the prison as the advocate and representative of the views of prison reform or system of discipline and treatment then being advanced by the Prison Association; and as he was a man not easily argued out of a position or swerved from a purpose, he succeeded in grasping full control and insuring the adoption of his views. During his administration the government became most thoroughly that of the Board, and so continued— though, with perhaps one or two exceptions, the members of the Board have never been marked for theoretical or executive capacity. As we have said, the location of the prison was determined by the settled purpose to employ the convicts in the working of the quarries. For a brief period this business appeared to be prosecuted with satisfactory results. Contracts were made with the State, and with the Corporation of the City of Albany, for the stone for the State House and the City Hall. The French church that was partially built in Canal street, near Elm, in the city of New York, Grace Church on Broadway, and several minor buildings, were also contracted for. The earnings from these sources being all carried to the credit of the convicts, and the expenses charged to the State under the head of Construction and Improvement, it did look for a few years as if the promises of self-support, so lavishly made, might be partially realized. But elements were at work that were soon to dispel these hopes. First, it was discovered that the quality of the stone was very inferior. Unless taken from the deepest strata, it would not bear the effects of the climate. Under the alternate operations of heat and cold, it would in a short time decompose and crumble away into sand. This was a serious drawback; yet the expenditure of labor and money in sinking shafts down to the more compact formation would doubtless have been rewarded with stone of the

best quality. But another element was busy that was not to be
overcome. The stone-cutters of the State became alarmed at the
prospect of having their trade monopolized by convicts. Through
the public journals, and by the voice of public men, determined
efforts were incessantly made before the Legislature to pass laws re-
straining such employment of convicts. The Legislature was not
slow to listen to a voice so potent; and accordingly, laws were
enacted forbidding the cutting of stone by convicts, except those
that had learned the trade previous to their incarceration. That
substantially ended the practical use of the quarries, and they have
since been a fruitful source of loss. Efforts have been made, on several occasions, to utilize them, but without any permanent success.
The last was particularly illustrative of the fortunes that appear
to follow all schemes looking to profit from the employment of
convicts by the State. Three or four persons had, in a small way,
been prosecuting the business of lime-making, with apparently
satisfactory results. They employed about fifty men, for whose
services they paid the State forty cents a day, on a contract for
five years. As they paid nothing for the raw material, and no
rent for yard, shop, or wharf room, gave the business their personal attention, and had an average credit of six months on their
labor account, they were readily supposed to be doing a paying business. The Inspectors conceived the project of buying
their fixtures and the unexpired term of their contract, and en-
larging the business so that the entire force of the prison should
eventually be employed in its prosecution. Listening to their
representations, the Legislature paid the contractors $125,000 for
their good-will and fixtures—have since expended about as much
more in enlargements—and very easily managed to lose from ten
to twenty cents a barrel on every barrel of lime shipped. After a
three years' trial, the use of the quarries was substantially abandoned. In 1873 and '74 the lime business revived—40,000 barrels being made in 1873; the quality being superior, it commands
a higher price than any other in market.

Since the prohibition of stone cutting, the authorities have been
constantly making efforts to obtain employment, but without any
settled success. Carpet-weaving, the making of shoes, saws,
files, chains, barrels, furniture, hats, toys, clothing, cutlery, har-

ness hardware, small castings, machinery, and almost every variety of mechanics, has been alternately tried and abandoned, or not prosecuted to the extent of the labor that is at command.   A few years ago an effort was made to establish a stereotype foundry, which promised to be very successful, but the Legislature promptly prohibited its prosecution.   The prices paid range from thirty to sixty cents per day, which does not include fuel.   The men generally have an allotted task which they can do in half a day, and are then paid for overwork.   There are many skilled workmen among them, but the work turned out, even of the coarsest kind, never compares favorably with outside labor.   It all has on it what experts call " the stripe," and can be readily distinguished by those in the least familiar with prison workshops.   Now about one-half the inmates are at work for contractors in the manufacture of furniture, boots and shoes, and harness hardware—the only three branches of industry that have been continuously prosecuted for any length of time.

At the present time the expenses of maintaining the prison exceed by about $175,000 per annum the earnings of the convicts.

SANITARY CONDITION.

Notwithstanding the admitted fact that the prison is badly ventilated, and unfit for the confinement of so large a number as 1,200, it is also a fact that the sanitary condition is far more satisfactory than that of the same number of adults in private life. The average of deaths is less, and the general health better. When it is borne in mind that nine out of ten of those sentenced come to the prison from a life of debauchery—that they are to a large extent diseased and broken down when they come there, the exemption from sickness and death is remarkable.   The average of hospital inmates is less than two per cent.—a result that speaks strongly in favor of regular habits, plain food, and restraint from excesses.   The pure, bracing air of the locality doubtless promotes this exemption from disease, but the primary cause must be due solely to the ample, but simple and regular diet so rigidly enforced.

It is a remarkable fact that but two men have ever attempted to commit suicide. One started out with the determination to starve himself to death. He resisted food for six days, when the doctor resorted to the stomach-pump and forced sustenance down him, until he finally gave up. The other attempted to cut his throat, but was very willing to have the wound dressed and readily seconded the efforts made to restore him.

PRISON-LIFE.

Prison-life is always monotonous. Convicts have their social classifications as well defined as the habitués of the Bowery and the Fifth avenue, and, whether in or out of prison, they naturally gravitate towards their respective classes. The forger may be called the representative of the highest type of criminal society— the sneak-thief as of the dregs; and these distinctions are as promptly recognized within the walls as they would be without. The pickpocket looks upon the cracksman with awe and admiration; the burglar ardently aspires to the higher level of the counterfeiter.

Few incidents occur to break up the regular routine. You might be connected with the prison for years, and beyond an occasional attempt to escape, or a rash and probably futile attempt to violate the rules, you will notice nothing to form the ground-work of a reminiscence that would linger in the memory more than a year or two. Ask the oldest of the officers for items of interest connected with his prison experience, and he will hardly recall a half-dozen.

That there are so few occurrences of note is due to the cowardice and the shrewdness of the criminals. The lower classes are in perpetual fear of the rules—the more intelligent, like Monroe Edwards, Huntingdon, Graham, Ketchum, Walworth, Stokes, and men of that type, know that they will best promote their own comfort and render their incarceration less burdensome by a careful observance of all the rules and customs of the prison. The men of the highest intelligence will do the most to screen themselves from the attention of the public, and generally ask no greater favor of their keepers than perfect isolation from the world during the period of their confinement.

DISCIPLINE AND MEANS OF ENFORCING IT.

As we have said, the Auburn system, adopted at Sing Sing, was very strict in its requirements. It gave no privileges to the convict. It required prompt, implicit obedience. Under it the man was a machine, wound up in the morning to work so many hours, and at night laid away to remain silent and motionless until the morning came again. He knew only his keeper in the prison— of his fellows he knew nothing or next to nothing. Of the outside world he knew only what might be told him by the one relative that at long intervals was permitted a brief visit.

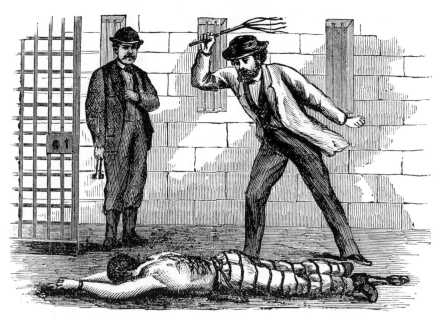

THE CATO'NINE-TAILS.

So long as there remained any of the old convicts that Capt. Lynds had drilled into obedience, and so long as he was active and untrammelled, there was little punishment—but little required —for when punishment was inflicted it came with a will and for a purpose. The "cato'nine-tails" hung by the side of every keeper—a visible reminder of reserved power that was ever potent to keep in subjection the fractious spirits by which he was surrounded.

Until 1819, the only punishment permitted by law was solitary confinement, with a bread-and-water diet. In that year the Legislature authorized the use of the lash, and its occasional use was continued until about 1840, when it was prohibited by legislative enactment.

When the law forbid this mode of enforcing obedience, the discipline soon sensibly demonstrated the necessity for some equally powerful substitute. A shower-bath became that substi-

THE SHOWER-BATH.

tute—not such as is common to the bathing-room, with its gentle, refreshing spray, but one which held the offender in a close embrace, while it poured upon his head a small cataract of water. The above sketch well illustrates the appearance of the first apparatus.

It will be seen that the convict is held as in stocks, by clamps around his ankles, and wrists, and neck, so that it is impossible for him to make the slightest change of position, beyond shaking or turning his head. The water came through a sieve placed four or five feet above the head. The holes in this sieve were a quarter of an inch in diameter, and so close together that before the water struck the head, it had merged into one stream, and, of course, came down with concentrated power. The water came from a tank, and its flow was regulated by a valve, attached to which was a cord.

The first machine was located in an outbuilding near the edge of the dock. There was no supply of water for its use, except what came from the river. In summer it was comparatively warm, and then it had little terrors for those subjected to its embrace. A barrel of water was generally used before the culprit was subdued. It was rare that more was used. There was once one persistent offender—a colored man—who used to take his regular weekly, and seemed to like it. He was never willing to cry enough until about a hogshead had been run through the sieve. Indeed, it used to be said that Jack was so fat and greasy that it took a barrel before the cuticle was reached. The greatest amount of water ever recorded as run on a convict was upon a man named Niles, a lawyer from New York, who was sent up for attempts, in connection with a notorious woman, to blackmail some wealthy citizens. He was found violating one of the rules, and when told of the offence, not only denied his guilt, but charged two others with having been the real offenders. As the evidence of his guilt was in his own handwriting, the Warden had little hesitation in ordering him a bath. It was estimated that three hogsheads of water were run on him before he consented to tell the truth, admit his faults, and promise future good behavior. If he ever again infringed any of the rules he took care not to commit himself in writing. In winter, when the thermometer was near zero, the bath was a menace sufficient to keep the men on their good behavior, and its use was seldom required. But a noted instance occurred in the winter of 1848. Because the ration was beef instead of pork, one entire gang, employed in Humphrey's weaver-shop, refused to resume work on their return from dinner. The keeper, after some talk, sent for the principal officer in charge, who finally, with much reluctance, determined to give them the bath, and so caused them to be marched down under a strong guard to the storehouse, where the machine was located. There were forty-nine of them, and they were all " put through." The temperature was below zero, and men had to be kept pushing the ice from the sieve, so as to permit the flow of water. This was early in January, and it was noticeable that the bath went out of fashion until the warm weather returned.

For mild auxiliaries of the bath, the chain-and-ball and the bishop's mitre were most commonly used. The first is familiar. The second is an open frame of iron, like this.

THE BISHOP'S MITRE.

This is in two parts—hinged at the back and fastened in front with a padlock. When worn night and day, they become exceedingly irksome, but some men have been known to endure them for weeks rather than submit to the rules.

"The Wooden Horse" and "The Yoke," more severe than the "Chain-and-Ball," or the "Mitre"—were at one time quite the fashion. The first required a man to be careful of his balance

—the latter held him in a restraint that in a short time became unendurable.

A few years since, the use of the Bath was prohibited, and following that came the "Spanish Crib," which was probably the most severe instrument of torture ever applied in a prison.

The box has a movable floor, which is raised or lowered by ropes and pulleys at the will of the officer. The neck is in a stock, and of course in a fixed position. The bottom being raised so as to force the culprit to bend his legs at the knees, the entire weight of the body has to be sustained in that position, for of course he cannot settle down without danger of strangulation. Any person can readily realize the terrible strain upon the muscles of the lower limbs, by the simple experiment of assuming this position for two minutes. A short experience prompted the officials to abandon this engine, but in its place came one scarcely less severe. It was called

THE THUMB-STRING AND PULLEY.

This was a modification of the Crib, but still involving intense agony when the time is protracted. Men have fainted before one minute had elapsed.

The Legislature has lately forbidden the infliction of the thumb-string, as it had previously prohibited the lash and the bath; and at the present time the only means of punishment allowed by the law is the old system in vogue previous to 1819—solitary confinement on bread and water. It is claimed by philanthropists that it is more humane than the lash, or the bath, or the thumb-strings. On the other side, officers of experience assert that it is the most barbarous, and liable to inflict injuries from which the convict may never recover. The records show one case where a man was kept three months in a dark cell, on bread and water, and then released because the officers were alarmed at his physical condition. There are many instances where men have remained obdurate until their release was ordered by the surgeon, who feared they might otherwise die of starvation. It is alleged that the system slowly, if ever, recovers from such a shock. The punishment is insidious, and its effects extend far beyond the period intended by the officers ordering it; while the lash or the bath are perceptible and temporary inflictions that speedily subdue the most refractory. This controversy between theory and experience has been long and earnest, and bids fair to be as lasting as crime and imprisonment for crime. By relaxing the rules until the restraint is hardly as much as safety demands, and the system of commutation which lessens the term of imprisonment declared by the court, the necessity for either mode is fast disappearing. The privileges are so many—the discipline so slight—the reward for good behavior so great, that none but a mere brute could be so rash as to bring upon himself even the mildest reprimand.

THE FEMALE PRISON

Was for many years the only place for the incarceration of females within the State. Within a few years a kind of prison for the punishment of those convicted of the lighter grades of crime has been opened in the western part of the State. It is a sort of house of refuge, but is not under the control of the Inspectors of Prisons, although the means for its support come from the State.

That at Sing Sing was constructed and ready for occupation, for the first time, in 1840. It is modelled after the Grecian temples—the front being used by the matron as a residence, and the rear as cells for prisoners. It was originally calculated to room from fifty to sixty, but now has a capacity to hold about one hundred and twenty-five. The old cells are large, and the corridors wide and well finished, so that the interior of the building looks neat and roomy, and is capable of being well ventilated. The prison portion of the structure is surrounded by a high wall, interior space being left for small court-yards.

The workshops are built against the wall on the south, and about one-half of the inmates are employed by contractors at making linen clothing. The price received by the State for their services runs from twenty to thirty cents per day. There is little demand for their labor, and it is difficult to obtain steady employment for them at the lowest rates.

The majority of the female convicts are of the lowest order.

Generally, they are those who, under the guise of servants, committed thefts, and were caught and convicted. Occasionally there is interspersed a bigamist, a dashing shoplifter, a decoy from a panel den, a passer of counterfeit money, or a murderess; but taking out a half-dozen at any time, the remainder would hardly interest you in a second glance, or more than a passing word, except for their repulsive looks, their ignorance and indifference to and disregard of all moral laws.

Three out of the class that have been noted as exceptions to the general character of the convicts, are probably the best representatives of their types. These were Honora Shephard, who was a dealer in counterfeit money; Melinda Hoag, a panel woman; and Henrietta Robinson, generally known as "The Veiled Murderess." They were in the prime of life when they were incarcerated, and noted not so much for their beauty, as for an attractive and commanding presence. Honora so ingratiated herself with the matrons, as to have almost the run of the house. In time she took advantage of the privileges granted, and made her escape, and what was remarkable, never again came to the prison. She was probably the most adroit and polished "shover of the queer," as the slang phrase has it, that had ever up to her time practised in New York. As such, she was the pet and the queen of a large gang of male associates. After, when detected, and the shopman was determined to "hand her over," she would smile him out of his resolve, and eventually he would bow her out of his store, satisfied that she was too much of a lady to wilfully attempt to defraud him.

Melinda Hoag was the legal wife of Alex. Hoag. Together they went into the business of panel-thieving—she doing the decoy when he depleted the gentleman. They were exceedingly successful, for they had plenty of victims, few were willing to proclaim their loss, and still a less number could be induced to prosecute. One haul too many brought them both to grief. They had, at last, a customer who had nothing to lose but his property, and he prosecuted to the bitter end. They were both sentenced to Sing Sing for five years and six months, and the wife was transported at once. Alex., however, obtained a stay of proceedings, but eventually came to prison some six or eight months after Melinda, which brought the date of her discharge a similar period in advance of his. All this previous recital is but the prelude to a strange development of character. Melinda as the decoy, walking Broadway and alluring the unsophisticated, or, perhaps, those who were tempted by a great temptation, was of course well dressed and well bejewelled. In a word, she had all the implements of her calling. Fine dresses—plain heavy silks for the street, and rich brocades for the house—jewelry to match—not sham, but real—were hers, and as she was regal in appearance, she wore them right regally. When she got in trouble, she was too shrewd to give all her finery over to the police, but put it away where it would be at her disposal when time or opportunity should release her from the confines of the prison. One would suppose that thus having husbanded her resources, and being certain of her right to dispose of herself for the time pending when her husband would be discharged and have his marital right to claim her services, she would have resumed her old vocation, and gone it " on her own hook." She did nothing of the kind ; but rather sought and obtained employment as a mere kitchen drudge with a family that lived adjacent to the prison. The family in which she was employed had two little boys— mere children of six or ten years of age, besides the husband and wife, and lived on a small, wild place. The wife was apparently a sacred woman in Melinda's estimation. She was ready and willing to perform all the household work, and when that was done, would take the children and go on a tramp into the fields—bringing them back garlanded with all the wild-flowers that the fields could give, with snatches of song that made one forget what he knew she had been, and think her the innocent, buoyant girl or mother that she so much assumed the semblance of. Then again she would take on the devil, that was evidently her second nature, and if her mistress did but listen, would recite, with flashing eyes and evident glee, the scenes through which her early history had led her. Then on Sunday, she would dress herself in all her recovered finery, walk to church, and seem (in all except her show and glitter) the veriest saint that ever embraced the cross. The end was, that when Aleck was discharged, she discharged herself from further servility, and the two resumed in Philadelphia the old occupation of panel-thieving. They both were caught, prosecuted, convicted, sentenced to prison, and in the prison ended their joint career—almost simultaneously—in death. She "might have been," but like many another, became linked to what could not be, and "could not be" buried "might be."

The third and last of the trio of notabilities has perhaps more of romance grouped about her than any other convict of the later period. She, like the other two, was a bold, dashing, and, when not tasked too long, an entertaining woman. In 1853 she was a resident of Troy, and generally known as the acknowledged mistress of a prominent State officer whose official duties demanded the personal supervision of the public works in that locality. One day she was arrested for the crime of murder— the specific charge being that she had administered some drug in a glass of ale to a man against whom it was supposed she entertained a grudge. He was far below her, even in the degradation to which she had descended, and her motive for committing the crime with which she was charged could be traced to nothing beyond revenge for a casual remark on his part, that possibily she was no better than she should be, or words to that effect. Immediately after her arrest, she assumed the garb of a veiled woman, which she steadily maintained throughout her incarceration in the jail, and subsequent trial. Hence the soubriquet by which she afterwards became known as " The Veiled Murderess." The wearing of this veil became so much a passion (for she was so well known it could serve her no purpose as a disguise) that on her trial she even refused to obey the mandate of the Judge when he commanded her to look unmasked upon the jury when they were rendering their verdict. She escaped the penalty of the charge upon which she was arraigned, and incurred instead the punishment of imprisonment for life. Although she had been notorious previous to her arrest, there was literally nothing, or next to nothing, known in the locality, of her previous history, whence she came or who she was. This or those problems the newspapers endeavored to solve, and in their way assumed as true her mysterious givings out that she bore a close connection to a celebrated and worthy family in Canada. So strongly did she impress the

responsible editor of the first paper in Troy that she was a sister
in the Canada family that the editor took the responsibility of
creating a sensation by proclaiming that fact, and the penalty of
being sued for libel, followed by a retraction and apology when
he found himself unable to substantiate the statement which
Henrietta had rather insinuated than asserted, but yet induced
him to make and so assume. The jury that tried her evidently
believed her guilty of the murder, but compromised somewhat by
giving her so much the benefit of a doubt as to bring in a verdict
which permitted her sentence to be imprisonment for life rather
than the penalty of death. On reflection, writing from memory
only, perhaps they returned as guilty of murder, and her sentence
was commuted through the influence of the State official who had
been "her friend." Be that as it may, she came to the prison as
a life convict. There she assumed, or attempted to assume, the
same mysterious character she had so successfully typified in the
Troy jail. The veil was taken from her, but, unlike the Veiled
Prophet, she was more attractive without than with it. Yet at
the prison, as before, she still assumed the mysterious. When a
visitor came to the prison, she would shield her face with a fold
of her dress, or in some other way.

When MYRON H. CLARK was Governor, in 1856, he came to the
prison, as all governors are in the habit of doing, for the purpose
of examining the workings of the institution, and giving the convicts an opportunity of presenting, in person, their applications
for executive clemency. He was accompanied by Thomas Kirk-
patrick, the Inspector in charge, Alexander H. Wells, ex-Inspector,
Gen. B. F. Bruce, Inspector-General of the State, and a member
of the Governor's staff, and James B. Swain, a former clerk of
the prison, but then State Railroad Commissioner. The Governor
had passed the forenoon in hearing the convicts tell their stories.
By the way, every convict, according to his own story, was innocent. Years before, when Governor Seward visited the prison,
on a similar occasion, he listened patiently, and took notes himself
of all who made applications. Then, as in Governor Clark's
time, every fellow asserted his innocence, except one, who frankly
said he was guilty, but wanted to get out, and was going on to
give his personal assurance that hereafter he would be "a wiser

and a better man," when Seward called his secretary and ordered him at once to make out a pardon for the man who had admitted himself guilty, remarking that if he stayed there any longer he would demoralize all the innocents he had been listening to for the past six hours.   Perhaps it was only an eccentricity of Seward's—a device to get away with importunities—as that was the only pardon following that visit.   It is a matter of fact that the convict who made this happy strike was as guilty as the most guilty, and it is more than surmised that his success was due to the prompting of one of the officers, who knew how to "strike" the Governor.

To return from this diversion.   While Governor Clark and his guests were at dinner, the card of a gentleman was brought to the agent, Mr. Booth, with a request for a personal interview.   The name on the card was that of Mr. P——, well known as a gentleman of mature years, who was at the head of one of the largest importing houses in the city.   It at once secured him the desired interview, at which he stated the object of his coming.   He had read much of the Veiled Murderess, and had become deeply impressed with the belief that she had once been a seamstress or governess in his family.   This impression had been so confirmed by a succession of dreams, and the waking suggestions which will follow dreams, that he had been impelled, or literally compelled, to come to the prison, and, by seeing the woman, test their reality. Such a request from such a source, though strange, was at once complied with, and, after mutual introductions, the assembled parties, accompanied by several ladies—the wives and daughters of the visitors—repaired with Mr. P—— to the parlors of the Matron of the female prison, where she was informed of the object of so extraordinary a convocation, and requested to procure the attendance of Henrietta—being first admonished not to give her any inkling of the purpose for which she was being brought out—which admonition was strictly obeyed.   When she entered the room Mr. P—— rose, and without the slightest hesitation Henrietta met him half-way, and embracing him as if he were her father, threw her arms around his neck, and even shed tears that fell upon his coat, and were perceptible to those looking on.   To them the recognition seemed to be perfect, and promising a quick solution of the problem as to who was the " Veiled Murderess." the Governor, the Inspector, and the half-dozen other officials that were present thought the question settled, but awaited with no little anxiety what should follow. Wondering, too, as well they might, for they had become so deeply interested in the prelude, they could not but be anxious as to the denouement. Mr. P—— took a chair, and invited Henrietta to be seated on one adjoining; but instead, she half-kneeled on the floor by his side, and commenced questioning him as to " his family." It was remembered afterwards that she did not mention names, but so shaped her inquiries as to lead Mr. P—— to give her the names of wife, children, and grandchildren. When she was told that Mr. P—— had lost his wife and a daughter-in-law, Henrietta again assumed the weeping mood, with real tears coursing down her cheeks, and for a period it was thought she was so losing herself in grief as to render her insensible. But she effected a timely recovery, and then all present feeling assured that she was the former seamstress of Mr. P——, a united effort was made to induce her to divulge who and what she was. Mr. Wells was the attorney of the editor who had been sued for libel for asserting that she was a member of the family in Canada, and, of course, felt a deep interest in ascertaining the facts. But all importunities were vain, and perhaps an hour was passed in making them. She would seem to be struggling between a desire to gratify the curiosity of her audience and then suddenly relapse into silence. Finally, she asked the Governor to grant her a private interview, which being accorded, the two retired to the adjoining parlor, and a half hour elapsed before they returned, when, at the suggestion of the Governor, she was remanded to her cell, after bidding Mr. P—— a tearful farewell. It afterwards transpired that she had been as mystical with the Governor as with the rest—her sole anxiety being to learn the then political status of her former paramour and the prospect of his some time being able to exercise the power of executive clemency. She would tell him nothing, only deluged him with questions—a few of which he would not answer, and the remainder he could not, for they apparently had been gathered from all the realms of thought.

A brief chat followed her dismissal to her cell, and Mr. P——'s departure from the prison, but no one of those present who had for several hours witnessed the interview had the slightest doubt as to her being the person Mr. P—— had represented and apparently recognized.

By the request of the Governor, and with the consent of Mr. P——, one of those present at the interview called the next evening at his city residence and had an interview with the family, who all, of course, placed full reliance on the truth of the recognition, with a view to ascertain all the particulars of the departure of the servant for England, her former associations while in their employ, and her habits of life. With one exception she never appeared to have any associates outside of the family. She sang in a choir, and a gentleman, of whom they knew nothing except that he was a machinist, usually accompanied her home, but never entered the house. They always thought her above her station, and that she had reasons for keeping retired. That she was highly accomplished and intelligent was certain. The parlors contained many mementos of her taste and skill, and the letters written shortly after her return exhibit a superior capacity for observation and composition. From some of these the following extracts are made. They show that in the family she was regarded more as an equal than a servant :—

HURST STREET, OLD SWAN, LIVERPOOL.
Tuesday, April 19th, 1853.

MY DEAR MRS. P. : I suppose by the time you get this you will be expecting to hear from me, for you, of course, have seen by the papers that we arrived at Liverpool on Tuesday, the 29th of March.

On our getting into port, there was as usual a whole posse of Custom House officers very soon aboard to search the baggage. On coming to my trunk the first parcel they opened contained Mrs. Sigourney's poems and an engraving of the New York Crystal Palace, that I had purchased in Boston. After handing them from one to another and making what remarks they chose, one of them crammed them both into his pocket, which was large enough to take in the whole trunk, and said "he reckoned I couldn't have 'em again because they were Merikan things." I felt so hurt to lose the book that I could have cried but for the crowd standing around. The next thing was dear little Toney's likeness, and as I expected they would like that too, I snatched it out of the man's hand, something like a tiger I expect, for he turned round and remarked that "the Yankees were pretty fierce about trifles." I suppose my trunk led him to believe I was an American, and I certainly was not disposed to enlighten him on the subject. After waiting till they had upset all that was necessary and unnecessary too, I was allowed to depart in peace with my trunk—minus the book and engraving. On the following morning I went to the Collector of the Port and told him the whole affair—telling him that I should feel very much obliged to him to get the book back, as it was a present; that they might keep the engraving if they wanted it. He promised to do what he could in the matter, and so finally they were both returned to me on Saturday last—the book rather the worse for wear, and the engraving so thumbed and fingered that it is not fit to show any one. So much for the politeness and gentlemanly behavior of my countrymen to females.

It was not so, when two years ago I landed in New York, a stranger in a strange land, with a few dollars only and still fewer friends; when I did not know an inch of the soil I stood on, and when there was not one friendly face to greet me. There I was treated with civility at least, but here it is otherwise.

. . . .

The greatest crowd I ever saw in my life was on the landing stage to see Mrs. Stowe land; men, women, and children knocking each other down to get a sight at her.

It is reported here that the Crystal Palace in New York will not be opened till June.

The Queen had another boy on the 7th of this month. That makes eight. If they all live, John Bull will be out a pretty figure for annuities, for you know each one must have a settlement plum.

I hope Mrs. S—— has got over her sickness well. I dreamed she had a girl on the 13th.

Will you give Toney a kiss from me, and remember me kindly to all the family.　　　　　　　　I remain,

　　　　　　　　　　　Yours very respectfully,

　　　　　　　　　　　　　　　E. M. H.

HURST STREET, Friday, May 20th, 1853.

MY DEAR MISS L. : Instead of receiving your kind letter by the Pacific's mails, last Thursday, the 11th, it only came to hand last evening, owing to a queer kind of a mishap.

It seems the postman for the Old Swan District is *not* noted for his punctuality in delivering letters, nor yet for the soundness and tidiness of his outer garments, and owing to a hole in the pocket of his overcoat, my letter, together with two others, was safely deposited between the lining and the outer part, and might have remained there for ages to come, had it not been that his wife bethought herself to repair it, which was the cause of their being brought to light. She brought the letter to me last night, and was in great trouble about it, and cried so much that I could not say anything to her, for she has five small children to support out of her husband's small earnings, and if the matter had come to the ears of the Post Office authorities, the man would probably have lost his situation, and she begged hard for me not to mention it.

. . . .

Mrs. P—— will get a letter from me by a Mrs. Smith, per Baltic, some days before this, in which I told her what I had done, and what I intended doing. This comes by a lady sailing in the Arabia, and she is expected to reach New York on the first of June. I wrote to Miss B——r, by the Arctic on Wednesday, when I expected to go to London, but was detained on account of the sickness of my brother. I am very sorry to hear of her illness, and hope she is by this time quite well.

I am myself no believer in dreams, but I have of late been much troubled in dreams about her and Mrs. S——l; and mother, who is of the old school, and a believer in dreams, says that night visions foretell a funeral in your family, for I dreamed that Miss B——r and Mrs. S——l were both dressed as brides, and were to be married in your parlors. There was no one in the house but you and I, and we were very busy preparing the rooms for the bridal guests. I think it looks more like a christening than anything else.

I was very glad to hear of Mrs. S——l's having a boy, for I almost feared it would be a girl—though you may remember, I always spoke of it as " him " and " he." I trust she will soon be quite strong again. Poor little R——s, he will stand rather in the background, now there is a younger one, but in his grandma's house he will still be chief. Give him a kiss for me, and tell him that " Johnie Bull " has not seen one like him yet, nor does not expect to while she is here.

I am not quite so well here as in New York. I think it is owing to the want of good water to drink. I cannot drink the water here, and have to put up with milk or ale, and it always flushes my face, and makes me feel uncomfortable.

I quite forgot to say in my letter from Boston, that I saw the towels waving from the windows when the Knickerbocker passed, and answered with my handkerchief, but I suppose you could not see my small flag of truce.

With kind regards to all, and hoping Miss B——r and Mrs. S——l are by this time quite well, I remain,

Yours very respectfully,

E—— M. H——.

Marylebone, London, Friday, May 27.

My Dear Miss S. : I have just received your kind letter of the 14th, forwarded to me from home, and I think I never had such a shock in my life, as the perusal of it gave me. I expected it was an account of your two invalids being so much better, and all going on well, instead of which it was a death. You will, ere this, have received a letter in answer to your first, in which I told you my dreams, and mother's interpretation thereof. At the time I laughed at the idea, but now I really believe a little in what mother says, and *she* will more than ever believe that dreams foretell events. I have wept so much on reading your letter, that my head aches so bad that I can hardly see to write.

Poor, dear Mrs. S —— ! how much, how very much she will be missed, and the dear little motherless baby—how much care it will require! I hope Mrs. A —— may meet with a due reward in health and happiness for her kindness in taking charge of the poor little infant. It will be a great confinement for her through the summer, and I don't think there is another who would have voluntarily done such a thing—for the generality of the aristocracy of New York are like what they are everywhere else, too much devoted to their own pleasure to think of another one's cares.

How much you will all love the baby, for, from the fact of its having no mother to care for it, it will seem bound to you by a still stronger tie. I am very sorry for poor Mr. S——. Such a bereavement, to lose the partner of his joys and sorrows, and at such a time, too. I am glad he has such a house to come to, where he will meet with sympathy on all sides; not but what he would have met with the same at Mrs. A——'s, but in time of sickness or sorrow his mother only would supply his wife's place.

I am very sorry to hear of Miss B——'s still being so poorly, but after so much excitement at your house, it is but to be expected that she will continue weak for some time. I need not ask you to take great care of her. I suppose that "T. B." is still all her comfort and care. Poor little R——'s; if I could just have a good romp with him, hiding away in the pantry, I should feel better.

You will see by my letter that I am in London. I was called here very un-expectedly to make an arrangement which will prevent my being in New York before September or October. On Wednesday I received a letter from the Bishop of London, in which he told me that a daughter of his and two nieces had a wish to go on the Continent, and had in vain been looking for a lady's maid to suit them. He said they had at last thought of me, and he much wished I could go with them for a few months, as if they delayed it much longer the best weather for travelling would slip by. The offer was so unlooked for that I thought a personal interview would serve the purpose better than writing, and as I intended coming here to see my relatives, I shall thus make our journey serve two purposes. I got to the palace about 2 o'clock yesterday morning, and of course found them all in bed. I soon, however, gained an entrance, and after breakfast had a long interview with the ladies and the bishop. They seemed to have fixed their minds on me so much that it would be next to impossible to get away from them, and they at length succeeded in persuading me to go with them. They know all my affairs just as well as I do myself, and I told them exactly how I had left you with the expectation of going back, but when, it was impossible for me to tell at the time, and as no time was fixed I do not think it can be con-sidered quite in the light of breaking a promise, as none was made.

I seem to have the luck of forwarding my letters without charge. This comes by the gentleman to whom my father is gardener. I hope he will see Rutgers Place, for I have been dwelling upon its beauties so much I should like him to see for himself. Most of them here think that because Americans have no titles they are nobodies and do not live in any kind of places fit to put your foot in because they are not styled Castles or Halls.

.   .   .   .

Accept of my kindest love, and please remember me to each one in the house, with much remembrance for Miss B—— and a kiss for R——.

I remain,

Yours very respectfully,

E—— M. H——.

These letters were readily given to Mr. —— to aid him in tracing out the further movements of Miss H., and identifying her with the convict at Sing Sing, or establishing the fact that the former servant of Mr. P—— and the Veiled Murderess were two distinct persons.

Leaving the residence of Mr. P——, the inquirer sought the leader of the choir where Emma and her friend had been assistants. All the leader knew was the surname of the man—further than that, nothing. He had not seen him since the last time Emma was in the choir, and he only knew his name by hearing her address him. Inquiries among other members of the choir were equally fruitless. They knew even less than their leader. The man had been to them a mystery, having no associates, except the girl, who came and went with him. The only hope of tracing him appeared to be melting away, when, in desperation more than from any idea of success, the City Directory was taken up. Such names were there in plenty, but without the Christian name it was difficult to tell which one, if any, of a score or two might be the man. After nearly exhausting the list, and personally satisfying himself that he had yet to hunt further, Mr. —— reached the corner of Canal and Elm, and on the fourth floor came to a door upon which was the name of "—— —— ——, machinist." The door was locked, but in a short time a person appeared, who announced himself as Mr. ——. To the question, Did he ever know Emma M. H——, he frankly answered in the affirmative. Mr. —— then briefly recited the events of the past two days, as they had transpired at the prison and at Mr. P——'s house, and rather sharply demanded to know if the surmises of Mr. P—— were correct. "He never was more mistaken in his life," was the answer. "Emma H—— is living in this city, and has been for nearly two years, and I can bring you to her in a half hour." Accepting this offer, the two took an Eighth Avenue car, and in less than the half hour entered a tenement-house on one of the cross streets, and proceeding up two flights of stairs, came to a front room door, at which the machinist knocked. The knock was answered by a plain, neatly dressed woman, to whom Mr. —— was introduced as the person he was seeking.' After a conversation, during which the woman perfectly identified herself as Emma H——, it was arranged that she should accompany Mr. —— to the residence of Mr. P——; she stipulating that no member of his family should be allowed to question her as to the past.

Singularly enough, the residence of Mr. P—— was within three blocks of where his former servant was found.

The machinist remained behind. When the two others reached the house of Mr. P——, they were invited to the parlor, and a message sent that Mr. —— desired to see that gentleman. He soon entered the room, and Mr. ——, pointing to the woman, said, " Mr. P——, there is your Emma." Without the slightest hesitation, he pronounced her an impostor, and expressed a suspicion that it was a plot to screen the identity of the woman in prison, in which Mr. —— was probably no innocent participant. In vain Emma protested. She pointed him to the portraits on the walls, naming each, and told him the history of many of the articles of furniture and ornament with which the room was filled. Unbelief was written in every line of his face. The ladies of the house were not at home, and the interview was becoming anything but pleasant, when fortunately the lady to whom two of the foregoing letters were addressed, returned. Fancying, in the hall, that she heard Emma's voice, she came into the parlor, and with a cry of joy threw herself into Emma's arms. It was some moments before either could speak, and then came from the one a torrent of questions. The other stood silent, and determined not to answer. She came to put at rest the suspicions of the family as to her whereabouts, and that now having been done, she demanded that Mr. —— should take her from the house, and she departed, the daughter tearfully begging her to stay or to let her come to her. Emma returned home, leaving Mr. —— at the street corner.

Two days after, he was implored by the ladies of the family to tell them where they could find Emma, but he was pledged to silence. Ten days after, he himself sought her in vain. She had moved—no one in the house knew where. The machinist probably knew, but he declined to tell. He had established the fact that she was alive and was not the Veiled Murderess, and no person had a right to question him further.

Mrs. Dewey, the matron, told Henrietta the sequel, and at the same time administered a severe reprimand for the deception she had practised, asking her how she could be guilty of it. Henrietta answered, " The old fellow wanted to know me, and I thought

I would gratify him." Then, with a chuckle and a twinkle of the eyes that spoke volumes, she added, " Didn't I moisten his broadcloth for him," and passed on to her cell, where for some time she disturbed the quiet of the prison with her shouts of laughter.

For years she has given the matrons much trouble by constantly violating the rules, and generally having her own way. Life convicts are rarely subjected to as strict discipline as others, and of this she early and frequently took advantage. For several months past, her eccentricities and outbursts of passion so assimilated insanity that the surgeon in charge at last felt himself justified in giving a certificate that caused her transfer to the asylum for insane convicts at Auburn, where she is now confined. Insane or not, she is but the wreck of the dashing woman who once commanded the admiration of thousands. She never was beautiful, but she was young, symmetrical, showy, and had a devil in her eye that was, to say the least, attractive. Now she is gross and sensual in form and feature, and on the downward slope. A mere mention of her death is all that will probably again recall her name.

CHAPTER XLI.

"It may be discovered that there are even magistrates in town and country who should be taught to shake hands every day with Common-sense and Justice; that even Poor Laws may have mercy on the weak, the aged, and unfortunate; that schools on the broad principles of Christianity are the best adornments for the length and breadth of this civilized land; that prison doors should be barred on the outside no less heavily and carefully than they are barred within; that the universal diffusion of common means of decency and health is as much the right of the poorest of the poor as it is indispensable to the safety of the rich and of the State."—DICKENS, in Preface to *Pickwick*.

BLACKWELL'S Island lies, long and narrow, in the East River, with upper New York on one hand, and the sunny villages of Ravenswood and Astoria on the other. You may get to it by the regular ferry, past the stenches and suggestions of the Morgue, at the foot of 26th street, with convict friends for your company, or convicts themselves, pent in the stifling prison-van unseen; or you can miss the boat, as we did, and make your way to 61st street, where, by signal, the Warden's row-boat shoots across, manned by innocent-faced youth, in striped garments, with shaved heads, who row as swiftly and as noiselessly as Charons, and to almost as grim abodes.

There is a captain at the tiller who enforces obedience by looks, and the accompanying consciousness of deadly weapons, to be put to deadly use, should any too venturesome convict make a bold strike for the freedom that seems so near, and is so far.

We landed opposite the Warden's house, a large, handsome, granite structure, erected in the days of the ten governors, and walked through pleasant paths, past the Penitentiary, of which more anon, to the Charity Hospital, at the lower end of the island, beyond which, at the extremest verge, are only the Small-pox Hospital, and the low, one-story fever wards.

In his office, on the lower floor, we found Dr. Macdonald, the physician in charge, a tall, stalwart, well-bred, courteous Canadian, who, on learning our mission, put his time and services at our disposal during the half hour of our stay; led us from ward to ward, and, with a singular delicacy, gave us brief facts where facts were necessary, and was eloquently silent where eye and imagination told their wordless tale.

The Charity Hospital is an immense building of clean gray granite, of which all the structures on the island are composed, rising story on story, and built on the site of the old hospital, which was destroyed by fire some years ago, and about which there are dark hints of human bones found amid the charred débris.

In the office hung the census for the day, Feb. 14, 1874. Ch. Hospital, 817—Small-pox Hospital, 12—Fever Hospital, 10. The average is, 80 admitted, and the same number discharged, daily.

The lower floor is taken up with the necessary offices and dining-rooms; as, besides the Resident Physician and his family, there is a staff of sixteen doctors on the island, nine of whom reside here. There are twenty-six wards in all, eight on a floor. On one side of the house, males; on the other side, females. So far as externals are concerned, lofty rooms, pleasant outlooks, snowy walls, soft, wholesome beds, generous, and, when necessary, even tempting diet, kindly nursing, and, above all, intense cleanliness; the arrangements are perfect. But who shall speak of the misery, the degradation of conscious, innocent poverty—the inward filth of conscious, blushless shame! the agonies of wasting, incurable disease!

We wandered from ward to ward, reading over and over again, in the wasted faces, the story of pain and poverty and hopelessness; pleasantly varied by finding here and there a convalescent, sitting up in bed, or in the invariable easy-chair beside it, reading a magazine provided by the thoughtfulness of the Lotos Club, playing dominoes with some equally fortunate neighbor, eating oranges, or even smelling a few flowers, sent by some one who remembers that flowers in a sick-room are as sweet as summer, and as welcome as rain upon a thirsting soil.

On the top floor are the wards assigned to the fallen women, who come there to be cured of nameless diseases; who go thence to their brazen haunts of vice, to carry death and desolation in their touch. The heart sinks on the threshold, the eye quails, but the pen must march on. There were girls, with the innocent young look on their faces not yet gone. There were older ones, seamed and scarred and hideous with years of vice. Some with their noses partially eaten off with a nameless canker; some with the hopeless, white death look on their faces, not pathetic, as is the wont of decent dying, but only horrible. Two girls were sitting by the window, evidently convalescents, who flaunted and stared and giggled as we passed; and on a table, near the entrance of the room, a pure white hyacinth raised its innocent bells towards heaven, a silent, fragrant, mocking foil.

We passed on to a ward where children of misery are born to parents of vice; and some, let us hope, within the marriage bond, to decent poverty. Indeed, Dr. Macdonald told us that of the twenty-five or thirty births which occurred during the month, only ten were illegitimate. *Only ten were illegitimate!* We passed on to the chapel, used on Friday nights for concerts, on Sundays for church services—*apropos*, there is here a piano, and an altar for Roman Catholics, seven-tenths of all who enter there being Irish—and on week days for operations, performed by the corps of doctors, witnessed by students from neighboring colleges. There is, in a side room, a sort of iron bed on wheels, awfully suggestive, on which the patient is strapped, and which is then rolled to the centre of the room, from which seats rise, tier on tier, where all may see.

This was all. Then we slipped down, and down, and down, and after good-byes to our courteous doctor, out to the open air, and breathed and were thankful.

I should not omit to say, that where two cases of fever or other disease come under the notice of the Wardens of the Poor in New York city, one will be sent to Bellevue Hospital, the other to the Island—the two institutions thus dividing patients between them, unless it be a case demanding instant surgical attention, when the patient is sent to Bellevue.

Our next visit was to the Penitentiary, in the office of which we waited, while a few necessary preliminaries were gone through with. This office is a large, well-lighted room, with one-half of it railed off, inside of which are the Warden's desk and another for the clerk, on whom two convicts were in attendance, who came and went seemingly at will. There were also books of Register and Reference, and, on a table, dozens of small parcels, carefully labelled, which, we afterwards discovered, contained tobacco, which the convicts' friends are allowed to send or bring them, once a month. The census for the day hung in full view.

Men, 784—Women, 102—Boys, 2.—Total, 888.

The other half of the office is taken up with benches, and on visiting days (Saturday of every week, between the hours of twelve and one) filled with a motley crowd, awaiting their turn to see their friends, and scented with motley smells. The interviews take place in the convicts' hall, and the prisoners are allowed to receive any sort of eatables, under-clothing, and, as has been said, tobacco. They are searched immediately the interview is over, in order to render the concealment of gimlets, files, keys, weapons or poison impossible.

As every one knows, Mr. Tweed has the longest sentence ever heard of, on the Island, being indicted on twelve separate counts of a year each. The next longest term is for five years, on separate counts, unless the convicted is under twenty-one years of age, when, for burglary, house or highway, he may be sentenced on one count for five years. If over twenty-one, the same offence would commit him to Sing Sing.

But the usual sentences are for three months, six months, and a year; offences being assault and battery, petty larceny, and first offences of any sort. All, or most of this we gather, while waiting, from various officials who flit in and out, chat a moment, and are gone. Presently enters the Warden, Mr. Liscomb, a middle-aged, gentle, gentlemanly, tired-looking man, who expresses himself as ready to conduct us through the different departments of the Institution, and leads the way.

The corridor runs in the form of a square, all around the building, between the high outer walls, pierced with tiny windows, and the high inner walls dotted with diminutive cells. These cells are white and clean, and bare as the grave, with room for a bed and a man, and air, and the viewless spirits of good or evil, which? One of the spaces, in the corridor, contains sinks, water faucets and basins, and a little further on are rude wooden tables where the convicts feed with food convenient for them, good in its way—wholesome and plentiful.

It was Saturday afternoon, and, on that day only, the men do not work after three o'clock, being engaged in shaving, cleaning out their cells, and the necessary weekly general clearing up, which all good housekeepers wot of.

The routine for the day is : rise at five, bathe, make.beds, breakfast, away in gangs to work at tailoring, shoe-making, chair-making, stone-breaking, and the building of sea-walls ; back—I had almost said home—for dinner at noon ; to work again, and supper at five, then locked in their narrow cells, to begin all over again to-morrow. It is the history of the Danaides repeating itself.

The Woman's Department is quite unlike a prison, no cells or corridors, but one large lofty well-lighted apartment, cheerful with plants in the grated windows, resonant with the pleasant whirr of sewing-machines, and used for sewing-room by day, sleeping-room at night, and chapel on Sundays. The women sat on chairs, in rows, sewing, presided over by a matron, and can neither speak nor move about, but otherwise seem not unhappy. Other women are engaged outside, doing the washing of the Institution ; the cooking, etc., being performed by men.

We saw neither the Penitentiary Hospital nor Mr. Tweed, who is as invisible as the Man with the Iron Mask, the Emperor of China, or the Veiled Prophet of Khorassan.

Next in turn comes the Almshouse, presided over by Mr. Marshal Vought, tall, plump, warm-haired, rubicund-visaged, cordial and jolly. He strode from ward to ward, throwing a kind word here, a cheerful look there, evidently welcomed and beloved by all, and putting "himself and his extremest means" at our disposal, in his desire to impart all necessary information.

The Almshouse is divided into the building for the males, one for the females, and the two low one-story stone structures for the incurables of both sexes.

It is filled with those poor who, by reason of age, incurable disease, physical debility not amounting to illness, and mental debility not pronounced enough for even a mild madness, are incapacitated for work.

The average number is 1,100. This year it has swelled to 1,530, obviously, because, where many of this class have hitherto been supported by self-sustaining friends or relations, the latter, by reason of high prices and lack of work, have much to do in supporting themselves, and this winter throw their burdens on the city.

We did not go through the building for males; it was not necessary. It had its counterpart in the one opposite, which we entered. At the farthest end are the bath and dressing rooms. Here are received all new-comers, usually filthy beyond expression, and covered with vermin. They are first stripped and bathed again and again, and then anointed with some medicament for the destruction of all crawling things. They are then clad, decently and warmly enough, and their own clothes cleansed and labelled, ready to be returned should any good or *ill* fortune take them back to the world again.

That may seem a strange expression to make use of here; but all who have seen, as all must, pitiful old age, in respectable, even luxurious homes, with well-cared-for and *unwanted* looks, will understand what I mean. Here comfortable buildings are erected, clothes given ungrudgingly, food unsparingly, attendance paid and unceasing, and kindness without stint. As an example, I will cite the case of an old German woman, overjoyed to come home from the hospital to the Almshouse. As we stood by, the attendant helped her dress, and the expression of absolute content with which she fastened on each separate garment, pausing again and again to kiss the hand of the assistant, and ejaculate fervently, "Gut, gut!" was inexpressibly touching.

I hope I shall not be misunderstood. I would only repeat—would to Heaven that some who call themselves Christians would learn from the patient ministrations of despised Almshouse attendants to more despised Almshouse inmates, lessons which it would be well to make real in their own lives and homes.

Thence to the low threshold of the wards for the incurables. First the women. A long, low, narrow room, with a passage between white cots: windows painted green, so the light can come to poor eyes softly. Nearly every bed an occupant; nearly every occupant old, withered, mumbling, imbecile. One woman a hundred and nine years of age, another a hundred and two, many over ninety; a humpback in her chair, blind, eighty. She broke her spine when a little child—has suffered daily, hourly tortures ever since. "How long, O Lord, how long?" A middle-aged, decent, cheerful woman in the corner, sitting upright on her chair, making pin-cushions: is lame, and busy, and happy, she says, and looks so. There are young faces, innocent, with the stamp of death on them; and young faces, guilty, with the same signet— consumption—unmistakable, dissolution inevitable, speedy. Some cover their heads as we pass; the crones mumble; the cheerful, decent, lame woman in the corner says "Good-by," and bids us come again.

We go on to the next low one-story building, the male ward for the incurables. Here the scene is a little different.

There is the same long passage-way between low cots, the same soft light from mercifully painted windows; but the men are mostly up and dressed, playing dominoes, reading, leaning over on their chairs, with their faces in their hands, or staring about gloomily and aimlessly. That man to the right was a bank-teller; farther on is a tailor; yonder a respectable mechanic. Here is the handsome, venerable head of F——k G——r, one of the old sports of New York; and near us a man, only thirty-five years of age, bent, palsied, gray, the victim of sin.

Each face has its own story of toil and baffling misfortune, of profligacy, of wanton recklessness and nature's revenge, or of sorrowful, helpless degradation. We pass, too, from thence.

Farther on is the Workhouse, in the office of which we were introduced to Mr. Keene, who has been Warden here for twenty years. He is a middle-sized, erect, soldierly, venerable-looking gentleman, with no hint in eyes, or voice, or manner, of the hideous sights and sounds of half a lifetime. From him we gleaned the fact that ninety per cent. of the inmates are foreign-ers; that they are sent up for periods of ten days, thirty days, three and six months; that the usual causes are vagrancy and drunkenness; and nine-tenths of them "revolvers." By revolv-ers are meant those who are returned again and again, twenty and forty times a year—for five, ten, thirty, yea, nearly forty years; for there is one woman here who came first in 1837.

Here are the boys, the dock rats, *gamin*; petty filchers of petty things; embryo loafers; infant assassins; baby highway-men, whose mouths are filthy with obscenity, old as sin itself—

who rear their heads as they pass, and strut onwards eying you
in hard, cold, dogged fashion. Five years from now, their
quarters will be yonder in the Penitentiary ; ten years—mayhap,
in Sing Sing ; and beyond that still, imagination paints another
sight—the felon's dock ; the murderer's cell ; the hangman ; the
gibbet ; the fatal noose ; the drop—the swinging, twitching, con-
vulsed form ; silence and an unknown shameful grave. Here,
too, are old men and women, blear-eyed, bent and trembling ;
not feeble enough for the Almshouse, nor diseased enough for
the hospital. Those who waylay one on street corners and ferry-
boats, equally ready to shower unasked blessings for proffered
pennies, or ribald curses for their lack ; and who spend their
poor, ill-gotten substance in the poison that warms and brutalizes,
and is their food and drink, and shelter and rest and solace.
What wonder ! what wonder !

BOYS BOUND FOR THE ISLAND.

The brief dream is hardly over, when a rude policeman hales
them to the Tombs. The Tombs vomits them forth to the Police
Court. The Justice delivers his brief, careless sentence, and the
prison-van receives them ; then the Workhouse ; and anon the
streets, and so this Devil's wheel rolls on.

Here are the young, strong victims of intemperance, the prey of *mania à potu*, for whom mercy has provided a padded cell, where men may scream and writhe and foam, and dash uselessly against soft, baffling walls and yielding floors; while a thousand devils jeer and gibber and menace; and a million snakes glide hissing through the air; and fear and terror, hate, and war, and blood, and murder take wild shapes and hold high carnival; until the heart is paralyzed, the brain reels, and merciful unconsciousness ensues; or more merciful death ushers the poor soul into the presence of his Judge and Maker. Here are the street walkers—soiled doves—*nymphs du pavé*, as they are variously called, whose story may be read in a glance.

From the country they came, fresh, rosy, clean and pure; from a blessed infancy and wholesome childhood in some decent farm-house, where father and mother are rustic, ignorant, and innocent as babes; where the only book is the Bible, and the only newspaper a weekly one, and the simple pleasures an apple-bee, or quilting frolic; and the dress is home-spun, and for Sunday-gear, a calico; and kid gloves are a fiction; and the sinful horrors of the city as far away, as vague, as unreal as hell.

And the ambitious girl comes up to the maelstrom of New York to work in shop or factory and looks about her, a bewildered thing. The cheap hat grows common in her sight, the Sunday calico a thing to be ashamed of, and, instead of hoarding her dimes in some neighboring bank, as was her childish dream, she wastes them on brazen finery and hideous gauds.

By small degrees, evil associations, hints, idle talk, that soon grows shameless; foolish books, to be replaced, gradually, by works and prints obscene; vice, that seemed at first too dreadful, grows familiar, then beautiful, and afterwards necessary. Aye! Necessary. 'Tis an easy thing to fall, easy as breathing, and everywhere some soft, insidious, lurking devil hides, to drag such an one down, but who shall raise her?

There are hells below hells, and lowest depths to every deep, and the first step is only the first. While beauty lasts, or the youth that stands in its stead, these find easy lives, spiced food and wines, rich clothes, fine furniture and liveried equipage; and grow plump, and white, and insolent with pampered sin. But, sooner or later, the poison works. Yonder hospital receives them, cures them in part, and sends them back, broken in health, and cheapened in value, to lower haunts, from whence they come again, are returned again, each time to deeper depths, to resort, finally, with the filthiest of the filthy, the vilest of the vile, or be sneered at, jeered at, flouted, cursed, kicked, and rejected by even the

ONE MORE UNFORTUNATE.

scum, the offscouring of creation. And then with church-doors and brothels closed equally against them; with neither food, nor clothes, nor money, nor shelter, nor friends, nor character, nor health, nor hope, nor anything but life and infinite despair; more lost and homeless than starving cur, or friendless cat, or horse turned out to die, the Workhouse takes them in for a few merciful days, and sends them forth, to receive them again and again and again, revolvers—until death ends the blasted, bitter, shameful life, that might have been so different.

It was nearly five o'clock when we were there, and we found the inmates ranged in files, in the long desolate corridors, receiving their blankets for the night, to be locked, afterwards, four in a cell, like cattle.

As they filed past us, I saw many familiar faces of old women, and others, beggars, whose wont it is, when free, to plead for alms on Fourteenth street and Broadway, and other thoroughfares. These hobbled up-stairs, in an almost cheerful, pleased, familiar way, as though quite at home, as, indeed, no doubt they were. Others passed sullenly, or with averted faces and bowed heads, and others again, indifferent, uncaring, or despairing and desperate.

In a cell in the lower corridor were two young girls, peering curiously at us through intervening bars, like tame animals, caught and caged. They were aged variously, either sixteen and eighteen, or, possibly, eighteen and twenty, not older; and clad decently, in dark stuff dresses, with black coats, and hats with a bright feather or two, and muffs of Alaska sable. Clad decently enough for church or prayer meeting, and with no look of vice or dissipation on their faces, or even of fear, alarm or disquiet. They seemed to be simply waiting for the hours to pass which should bring them their release.

Mr. Keene told us they had been arrested the night before by a policeman, who complained of them as street walkers, that they either had no money to bribe the man to quietness, or were too innocent for his purposes, and so found themselves here, spotted as common drabs. What does this mean? Are they innocent or are they guilty? Poor sewing-girls, virtuous, out of work, homeless and shelterless, walking the streets to prevent the blood from freezing in their veins that bitter winter night, and remaining pure amid a thousand overwhelming temptations to be the contrary; or are they not?

If lost, that they are as yet utterly irreclaimable, I will not believe, but who shall tell the steps? who shall measure the degrees? Lovers of your kind, here is your opportunity; here are brands not wholly consumed, that may still be plucked from the burning; fields white unto the harvest, and the laborers, how few.

There is no definite work carried on here, except shoemaking, and the necessary repairs; but the inmates are kept busy at anything convenient which may be found to give them employment. All the bread used on the island is baked here, consuming fifty-six barrels of flour a day; and all the departments draw their servants, assistants, under nurses, etc., from the Workhouse, with the exception of the Penitentiary, which supplies its own labor from within its own walls.

Owing to the necessity of keeping these people constantly employed, every floor, wall, stairway, window, article of clothing, (bed or personal,) saucepan, platter and utensil on the island, is scoured, swept, bleached, or burnished, with the absolute cleanliness and exactitude found on a man-of-war, until, externally, through all the length and breadth thereof, is matter to wonder at, and be glad over.

Last and farthest, at the extreme upper end of the Island, is the Lunatic Asylum, presided over by Mr. Anthony Allaire, a middle-sized, slender, nervous, kindly gentleman, with straight, intense black hair, who had brewed for us a hospitable cup of tea, which we found refreshing.

In the office was a tall, dark, fresh-cheeked, muscular young man, who, in the harmless belief that he is *Jesus Christ*, condescends to take charge of the books, which would otherwise keep a clerk employed at a cost of $2,000 per annum.

I may say here that, as far as possible, the maniacs are utilized, and any harmless conceit or wayward fancy which they may possess, and which does not injure them or any one else, is treated with due respect and apparent belief. Going up stairs, we found long, pleasant, well-lighted halls, with small bed-rooms opening out of them; with flowers and plants in the windows, and patients sitting about on settees or rocking-chairs, or walking up and down, reading, sewing, knitting, gossiping; and one pleasant-looking, nicely dressed, middle-aged lady came up to us, and asked for a newspaper in such a very sane, polite manner, that it made my heart ache to be obliged to say I had none.

There is observable here, as everywhere else, a marked difference in looks, demeanor, conversation and even dress; some being private patients who have finer food, better clothes, and more comfortable apartments than the others, though all are decent and cleanly, and, with a few exceptions, look even happy— as happy as the majority of people outside of Lunatic Asylums— though, perhaps, that isn't saying much.

The long, slender pillars which support the winding staircase are still festooned with Christmas greens, pleasantly suggestive of past festivities, and a space is left for magic-lantern performances which the patients find amusing. There is an altar at the end of the corridor for Roman Catholic services, and one of the rooms into which I peeped is a perfect oratory in miniature, with crucifix, rosary and a full length wax Madonna in the whitest of virgin attire. Our conductor told us that very many of the inmates, male and female, are crazy on the subject of religion. Poor souls! That is like turning one's daily bread into poison.

There are, besides the Asylum proper, two low, one story wards for patients who are very mildly mad; and, on this side of them, a large building called the Lodge, which is used for women, and is the mad-house *par excellence*, where only the frantic and dangerous ones are confined.

In both of these we found individual cases, singularly interesting, three or four of which I will take occasion to dwell on.

In one of the wards assigned to the mildest patients sat a delicate, lady-like looking woman of about thirty, with peculiar, large, mournful brown eyes of the Evangeline type; a straight nose with delicate nostrils; and lips which, instead of fading indefinably into cheek or chin as most lips do, with nothing to distinguish them therefrom but the different hue—were as cleanly chiselled, as clear cut as a statue's; she sat for a few moments after our entrance with her hands folded idly in her lap, and gazing vaguely, but not staringly straight before her.

Arising as we approached, and wandering towards us, still with the Evangeline look in her eyes, she asked in gentle, hopeless tones—"Have you seen anything of a boy, about so high, I should think?" measuring a space from the ground.

"What sort of eyes had he?" asked one of the party, startled into saying it, I suppose, by the wonderful look in hers.

"I don't know," she answered wearily. "I didn't look at his eyes"—and so saying, wandered back to her place again, and sat down in the same dejected, pathetic way as before.

On inquiry we found her to be a Miss Dupignac, a Southern lady of French extraction, a teacher, and conversant with four or five languages. One who is suffering the penalty of an over-tasked brain.

Another case, from similar causes, quite as interesting, but not so pathetic, is that of a Principal of one of the New York schools, in 40th street. I believe she is an entirely different type of person from Miss Dupignac, quite as well informed, it may be, but not so fine, not of so good blood, perhaps.

Nervous, slender, middle-aged, light-haired, light-eyed, thin-skinned, not at all good-looking, but sprightly and chatty, she rushed towards us, shaking hands most cordially all round, and saying—

"How d'ye do, dear? how d'ye do, dear? how d'ye do, dear? I'm very glad to see you. Come now, what are you here for? what's your business? what's your name?"

"Ah! I see, you are a minister," turning to the Colonel, who is one of the sons of Anak, wears a white neck tie, and whom no one—well, whom no one but a lunatic would ever have accused of belonging to the clerical profession.

The Colonel laughed, turned a shade darker in lieu of blushing, chewed the top of his cane, and would have denied the soft impeachment, but found it useless. The maniac inquisitor had seized pencil and note-book from another member of the party, and with stern persistence went on to ask:

"Presbyterian or Baptist?"

"Presbyterian," faltered the Colonel.

"Church in New York or Brooklyn?"

"Hoboken," answered the heart-broken man.

"Humph!" contemptuously. "That accounts for my not knowing you. I remember now. You belong to the Brown

family, the *Alexander* Brown family," and to what further depths
of humiliation the unfortunate Colonel would have been relegated
is not known ; for suddenly the maniac mood changed, and,
drawing up her figure to its tallest height, she burst upon us with
the astounding announcement—

"*I am the* MOTHER OF GOD.

"I was once as tall, as large, and as grand as that building you
see out there," pointing to the Asylum proper, " but long years of
toil and sorrow have reduced me to my present size, and Satan
has cut off all my elegant back hair, robbed me of my jewels,
satins and velvets, and breaks my back every day. See how
his imps torment me," pointing to imaginary bruises on each side
of her ear; " and, do you know," turning to the Colonel again,
"that Satan has raised seventy thousand new devils, *new devils*,
in Hell ? "

" Is that all ? Why I thought there were a great many more."

" Good gracious ! isn't that enough ? " was the snappish reply.
And then she babbled on about her jewels and her velvets again,
and so we left her. It was sad, but it couldn't help being funny.

In the same ward, a little farther on, is a red-haired girl, evidently of Scotch-Irish or Scotch extraction, with her hands clasped
in the air, in the attitude of prayer, who has not spoken for three
years, and who looks as though she had been frozen in her place by
some awful horror, too terrible for words. I asked the nurse if
she had witnessed battle, murder, or sudden death, and was struck
dumb in some such moment of horrible amazement. But her
answer was, only the old story of a lover untrue, and a brain too
weak, a heart too faithful to bear it.

Between the wards through which we have just passed, and the
Lodge, but quite on the water's edge, is a low, straggling, gro-
tesque-looking building, evidently formed of old bricks, boards
and other débris, and on the door the following, somewhat hos-
pitably inhospitable inscription :

> " I invite the fowls
> And the birds of the air
> To enter."

This place is called, by common courtesy, " The Fort," and was
built some years ago by Thomas Maxey, a mad Irish army officer,

THE FORT AND ITS COMMANDER.

who has fortified it, made additions from time to time, thrown up adjacent breast-works, mounted his Quaker guns, and now patiently stands guard day after day, or marches, sentinel like, to and fro with his wooden bayonet, alert, suspicious, in the firm conviction that to him alone does Blackwell's Island owe her deliverance from threatening steamers, marauding tug-boats, and other piratical craft, with which, as we all know, the East River is lined.

And now we bend our footsteps to the Lodge, the Bedlam, filled with strange, horrible noises, inarticulate babblings, crazy shrieks, maniac laughter; yet even here we find one pleasant spot, and that is associated with Hester Murphy.

" Be sure to let them see Hester Murphy," said the Warden, putting us in the hands of a guide, since he himself was called by business in another direction. And when we asked her story, it was given as follows.

Hester is an English woman, about fifty-six years old, daughter of an aged and most respectable, I might even say, wealthy photographer of Liverpool. She had for many years addicted herself secretly to strong drink, which either caused, or developed in her the lunacy from which she is now suffering, and which, at last, showed itself in an attempt upon her sister's life.

Her father, endeavoring to hush the matter up, gave her money and shipped her off, quietly, to Portland, Maine, whence she gradually worked her way down to New York, and was taken up in the streets for assaulting a policeman, sent to the Workhouse, and there, her madness coming up to the surface again, to the Lodge, where she has been confined three years, most of the time vastly amusing, I dare say, and indeed a perfect god-send to her fellow inmates, and again violent to the last degree, and requiring strait-jacket and close confinement.

A gentleman, one of the first physicians of New York, has taken great interest in her case, and written to her father, who authenticates all I have just stated, and mournfully, but firmly, refuses to have anything more to do with her; and since the Asylum must be her portion until death, either on this side of the ocean or the other, who can blame him?

She caught sight of our party from the other end of the corridor, and rushing towards us, welcomed us with the grace and *empresse-*

ment of a French countess. She is a little, undersized thing, with an intelligent forehead, sanguine complexion and large, burning, blue eyes, and with a manner very un-English, having more of the sparkling vivacity of the race on the other side of the Channel.

Then turning to Jane—a young woman, rosy-cheeked and vacant-looking, who stared at us silently not far off, and who seemed to be her lay figure, her fetish, the thing on which she expended her moods and fancies, as children do theirs on dolls, and who returned the gift in heavy admiration and slavish submission—turning to Jane, she said—

" Oh, what shall I do to entertain this splendid company ? Shall I sing, or shall I recite ? Which shall it be ? " Being incited thereto by a previous hint, we begged for the " Burial of Sir John Moore." Upon which, waving the lunatics imperiously aside, and shrieking " A broom, a broom," she mysteriously disappeared, to return again instantly with the object of her search, which, on perceiving the cane in the Colonel's hand, she rejected for that, taking it from him with a simple imperative, " Your cane, if you please, sir."

This cane became, by turns, a bayonet, a distant random-gun which the foe was sullenly firing, the corpse of the gallant Sir John himself, his narrow bed and lonely pillow, and finally his grave on the ramparts of Corunna. To say that this piece, as rendered by Hester Murphy (half recited and half sung), would be a decided histrionic success on the boards of a first-class theatre, would hardly be saying too much. The dramatic gestures, the wonderful suiting of the word to the action, the action to the word, the steady tramp of the troops, the laying down of their sacred burden with his martial cloak around him, the few short, hasty prayers, and the final hurried tear, were all inimitably given.

After that Hester talked with us awhile, saying in an irresistibly droll manner—" My name is Murphy—awfully Irish, isn't it ? I'm fifty-six years old, and have lost all my front teeth, so that my articulation is defective, but my mastication is perfect—perfect, I assure you."

" Shall I sing something more, I know all Mozart's masses—

Beethoven, Mendelssohn, Gluck, or I'll paint your picture for you. Here's Jane now," pulling the bashful and giggling Jane unwilling forward, " such lovely rosy cheeks as she has, just like mine used to be, but then I'm fifty-six you know—and recites *beautifully*."

On being pressed she herself gave us another song, " The Old Maid," and then, in a low confidential manner, asked our guide for tobacco, and on her request being granted upbraided him with not wrapping it in silver foil, and not giving it to her secretly enough.

" The ladies 'll all know I chew," said she indignantly. Upon which he replied, with some presence of mind, " Oh, no ! They know I gave it to you to wrap your furs in."

After that she gave some quotations from Shakespeare, very wisely and wittily, and bade us a most elegant farewell, with the usual hopes of future meetings, etc.

In short, Hester gives one the idea, both by voice and manner, and also in her well-chosen words, of being the wreck of an exceedingly cultivated, high-bred woman, versed in all the ways of the polite world. Alas ! Alas ! And yet I doubt not, as I have said before, that with her vivacity, and even her imperiousness, she is a real blessing to the darkened minds about her. It was curious to watch the respect with which she was treated by her fellows, and indeed, the melancholy episode of Sir John Moore was pleasantly varied by a free fight in the next room, caused by one impertinent lunatic who tried to walk about during the recital, and was restrained by others, who evidently thought her promenade ill-timed, noisy, and disrespectful to Hester and her guests.

This disturbance was soon quelled, however, by one of the nurses, who, on being asked if she never felt afraid among so many desperate cases, replied :

" Oh, dear, no. It would never do to show fear to the like of them. I was afraid when I first came here, four years ago, but that is all over now—though I was half killed once by that colored girl yonder."

This made us feel rather uncomfortable and not sorry to go, and we escaped from the Lodge with no further adventures, except that an Irish woman peeked through her bars, and, attracted by the Colonel's unfortunate white tie, shrieked after him.

"Sure, you're a clergyman, and I know you'll bring me some whiskey the next time you come"—which was idiotically paradoxical, to say the least.

One scene of suffering more, and then we are free to go our ways; only the Epileptic and Paralytic Hospital, which is an entirely separate department, and where we saw nothing that, after all we had witnessed, seemed either new or strange, with the exception of one poor old woman writhing through the phases of St. Vitus' dance, and which singularly reminded one of the description of some of the tortures in Dante's Inferno, although our guide positively assured us of its utter painlessness. Notwithstanding this, I could not help feeling the awful inconvenience of such intense, protracted and unnecessary gymnastic exercises, and pitied the poor old thing accordingly.

This is all. There are 7,000 inhabitants on the Island, and I might write a separate chapter on at least 6,000 distinct smells which exist there, each equally horrible—but I forbear. For, although, as I have before stated, and again insist upon, everything is done in the way of cleansing and purifying that human agency can do, what can prevent the stenches arising from a vast mass of living but decaying bodies, putrid with the filth of past generations! Nothing.

We stepped into a boat to return, ferried over by the old, silent, striped-clad charons; with steamers and steamboats gliding past us, filled with hopeful human beings, speeding towards happy homes; with the liberal sky above us dotted with dim stars; and the bare black trees on the shore, making silhouettes against the splendid yellow, after-sunset sky; and thanked God that in the city yonder, a thousand household fires burned steadily in pure homes, where noble women were, and good men and pretty prattling children.

Thanked Him, too, that in His infinite mercy there is room, and in His infinite medicine cure for even the festering foulness we left behind us.

CHAPTER XLII.

THE NEW YORK RING—ITS EXTENT, INFLUENCE, AND PURPOSES—
THE GREAT RING MAGNATE, WILLIAM MARCY TWEED—HIS CON-
FEDERATES—BUYING THE LEGISLATURE—RULING NEW YORK—
THE MILLIONS STOLEN FROM THE CITY TREASURY—TRIALS, CON-
VICTIONS, SENTENCES—ESCAPES.

"Such a nursery of statesmen had the department become, in virtue of a
long career of this nature, that several solemn lords had attained the reputation
of being quite unearthly prodigies of business, solely from having practised 'How
not to do it' at the Circumlocution Office."   DICKENS, in *Little Dorrit*.

CORRUPTION and extravagance, twin relics of the Rebellion,
have demoralized more than one municipality in the United
States. But in no city have their blighting effects been more disastrous than in the metropolis. New York has always been the
best field of operation for the professional politician. Here has
graduated the "repeater," the ballot-box "stuffer," the worker
of primaries, the ward "organizer;" in fact all the auxiliaries so
essentially necessary to the successful working of political organizations of the new school. The mutual interests of leaders have
necessitated the formation of various combinations known as
"rings," and the word has become synonymous with corruption
and fraud. Ames in the national capital and Fisk in the
metropolis did more to corrupt men in high places than any
other men of this country. They set a premium on knavery
which started many a man on the road to ruin, and the result
is, bankrupts are as plentiful as blackberries, and beggars crowd
our thoroughfares. The Ring that encircled New York was
most colossal in its proportions and as expansive as rubber. It
was known as the Tammany Ring, and its history, as it is a
record of crime and corruption, must form a chapter of this
volume. Some of the principal actors who figured therein are
men of great ability, who, in their mad ambition for political
power, sapped the exchequer until the credit of the city was
seriously impaired. The Democratic party in New York City
has always been led by a few men, and never was there a leader
that held such undisputed sway over the masses as William M.

Tweed, who was known throughout the city as the "Boss." His magnetic influence was felt in every ward in the city. Each ward had as many organizations as there were election districts, and his retainers or henchmen who presided over them came daily in contact with their chieftain. Never was a party more thoroughly organized, and what wonder is it that such an army should make a city captive! It might be said that William M.

WM. M. TWEED.

Tweed sprang to the helm of the New York Democracy. True, he had been chosen to several high offices from his own district, but his influence did not extend beyond the section in which he had lived from boyhood. He was born on the East Side in the year 1823, of poor parents, and early thrown on his own resources. He learned the trade of a chairmaker and worked at it for many years. He soon became ambitious of political distinction, and to increase his qualifications and improve his chances he entered the

University Law School, from which he graduated as a member of the bar. It was more than twenty years ago when he began to make himself known as a politician. At that time Mike Walsh, then Member of Congress, was one of the shining lights of the Tammany Hall party, and was recognized as the champion of the unterrified and unwashed element. Mr. Tweed was foreman of "Big Six," a famous fire company of the city, and an organization that was a potent power in local politics. The influence he then possessed over that section of the city in which this company was then located he undoubtedly maintains to this day. They regard his misfortunes as the result of political squabbles, in which he was betrayed, and, notwithstanding the evidence presented at his trial, refuse to regard him as otherwise than a martyr.

In 1851, he was elected Alderman from the Seventh Ward, serving in the Common Council through the years 1852–3. In the fall of 1852 he was elected to Congress from the Fifth District, which then embraced the Seventh and Thirteenth Wards of New York, and the village of Williamsburgh, Long Island. He took his seat in the House in December, 1853, while his term as Alderman was about expiring. He was thirty years old at that time, with the promise of a fair future before him. While in Congress he was elected School Commissioner of the Seventh Ward. The year after his term as Representative expired, he was chosen to the Board of Supervisors, and continued to hold a place there until the day of his overthrow.

In 1861, he ran for Sheriff on the Tammany Ticket. The office was then, as now, the most lucrative in the city. Tweed was very sanguine, and worked for his election with his usual energy. At that time he acquired about $80,000 by hard industry at his business. He spent his money like water, knowing only too well that to be successful it must be distributed freely. Every dollar was spent in the canvass, and he was badly beaten by the Independent Democratic candidate. During the winter that followed it was well known among his friends that he was pecuniarily depressed. It was here that Tweed lost his faith in the promises of politicians, and he started in to mend his fortunes whenever the opportunity should offer.

He was not a fine-grained man nor troubled with many conscientious scruples. He saw himself as the victim of what he looked upon as a conspiracy. He had distributed his money among various ward organizations in return for their promised assistance. They divided his fortune and withheld their support. He resolved to " get even " with the public who had preferred another to him, and he set about the undertaking with the coolness of a great general about to besiege an enemy's stronghold. In 1862 he was appointed Deputy Street Commissioner under McLean, yet Tweed was virtually the head of the Department. Here he controlled immense patronage, and, through the giving out of street contracts, must have become rich. It was about this time that he made himself the leading spirit in the Tammany Hall organization.

He showed soon that his power as an organizer was very great. He drew men around him usually by appeals to their selfish natures. To one he gave money; to another, some place of honor and trust. He proceeded on the theory that every man had his price. If a rival arose to dispute his authority he crushed that rival if he could, and if he couldn't, he crushed the rivalry by supporting the man for some office, and thus making him his ally. In this way he spiked the guns of Fernando Wood and called a truce with his most popular enemy, the " Big Judge," Michael Connolly.

There were none now to dispute his power. He drew about him his early associates, and they shared in his political fortune. It was a common expression among the boys that Tweed never forsook a friend. It was this trait in his character, more than any other, that so endeared him to his henchmen and made him the idol of the ward politician. Tweed would not accept a county nomination. He would always remark, when pressed to run for some of the important offices, " I had one nomination, and I never want another."

In 1867 Richard B. Connolly became Comptroller of New York. With him Tweed formed an alliance. Connolly did not possess the popularity of Tweed, and it was always understood that he owed his office to Tweed's influence. That same year, 1867, Tweed was elected to the State Senate from the Fourth District by a large majority. In the Senate he found a majority opposed to him politically, and it was during this session that Senator Tweed ascertained the virtue of money in securing legislation for New York City.

In 1869 Tweed found a trusty counsellor in the person of Peter B. Sweeny, who was to Tammany Hall what Bismarck is to the German empire.

A. Oakey Hall, who was then Mayor of the city, also joined his political fortunes to those of Tweed. When these four men—Tweed, Sweeny, Connolly, and Hall—united their various forces and talents, the Tammany "Ring" was formed. Shortly after the Legislature of 1870 convened, it was discovered there was some disaffection among the New York Senators, and by the latter part of the session Senators Genet, Creamer, and Norton were in open revolt, and in due time James O'Brien, then Sheriff, George W. McLean, John Morrissey, John Fox, and James Hayes, joined the ranks. This was the first revolt against the concentrated power of the Ring. But it was badly planned and bunglingly managed. The Young Democracy had their organ in New York; and in the beginning it was generally believed that the Ring would be overthrown.

On the 24th of March a call for the meeting of the Tammany Hall General Committee was issued by Mr. Tweed, pursuant to a petition signed by the number of members required for that purpose by the constitution of the organization. Among the signers to this petition were Judge Cardozo and other prominent politicians. The meeting was to take place at Tammany Hall on Monday, March 28, 1870. The greatest excitement prevailed as to the result of the attempt of the Young Democracy to capture the organization. The leaders of Tammany now took prompt and decisive measures, especially as Mr. Tweed had been removed from the Street Department. They knew that the Young Democracy were very strong in the General Committee, and might succeed, by dint of hard work and promises, in securing a majority. The Tammany leaders were also aware that, with the exception of the bosses in the several wards, the members of the General Committee were a mercenary class, who were ready to link their fortunes with whatever faction displayed the most strength.

On the same day the organ of the Young Democracy contained the following editorial :—

" WHY NOT TAKE TAMMANY ?

" The Ring have opened a treacherous war on the Young Democracy, and the champions of the people have taken up the challenge like men. The removal of William M. Tweed, Henry Smith, and A. D. Barber, as agents of the corrupt Tammany Ring, shows that the combat will be sharp and decisive, and without useless parley.

" Why do not the Young Democracy take possession of Tammany Hall ? They have a vast majority of the Democratic voters in this city. Why not, then, turn out the corruptionists and traitors who occupy the ancient wigwam ? That is the first duty to be done. It is the only way to restore genuine Democracy to the time-honored stronghold of the party."

This appeal to the Young Democracy had the desired effect, and the members of the Legislature who had revolted from the ranks of Tammany Hall came to New York and made arrangements for the capture of the Democratic General Committee. The organ of the Young Democracy again came out on the following day with another philippic against the Tammany Ring :—

" THE LODI OF THE YOUNG DEMOCRACY.

" This is the auspicious hour for the Young Democracy. They are right, they desire reform, and they aim at progress. We trust they mean business. By exercising a courage that shall border on audacity, they can now take control of the party in this city and State, and ultimately in the whole Union. They have learned that concessions to their enemies yield only bitter fruits. To gratify their grasping, grumbling foes of the Ring, they abandoned a good deal of ground in framing the bills defeated on Tuesday, and all they got by it was betrayal, desertion, and overthrow. They were sold out for money by the very man they had tried to conciliate. Let them shoot down the traitors.

" The Young Democracy must take the lead of the party, at whatever sacrifice of distinguished chiefs, old associates, and even seemingly temporary success. It is a safe battle to fight. As the case now stands, the party in the State is ruined. It can be no more than ruined through efforts made to save it, and such efforts it is the duty of the Young Democracy to put forth. As to the Republicans who belong to the Ring in this city, they, of course, will do all they can to prevent a reorganization and change of leadership of the Democratic party. But they are open enemies, and the reform Democrats know how and where to meet them. As to the twenty Democratic deserters who, in consideration of the money of the Ring, sold out the party in the Assembly on Tuesday, let the Young Democracy put a brand on their foreheads, and their hay-loft and cheese-press constituents will dispose of them.   They have pocketed the bribes of the corrupt combination of Democrats and Republicans which bought them, and they will sink into contempt.   This must be a war in earnest.   The Young Democracy must conquer or die.   But they will not die, for the whole mass of the party is with them.   All they need do is to move right onward and grasp the standard of the party.   Don't let them listen too much to the advice of the bevy of old fogies who want to see them triumph, but dread the fight.   Let them alone.   They mean well enough, and will count when the voting comes along.   But they are too timid and slow to give counsel in a hand-to-hand contest like this.

" The Young Democracy are situated as young Bonaparte was at the bridge of Lodi, with the Austrians thundering at him in front, and a portion of his troops skulking under cover, while whole regiments actually deserted the flag in the red heat of the battle, and refused to cross the bridge.   The young leader of twenty-six summers seized a standard, rushed upon the bridge in the face of a tempest of shot and shell, waved his sword and shouted, " Soldiers, follow your General ! "   The whole army, excepting a few cowards and deserters, who were pitched into the mire of the Adda, plunged pell-mell upon the bridge and carried the Austrian position at the point of the bayonet.   Lodi made Napoleon Bonaparte First Consul, then Emperor and ruler of France, and ultimately of Europe.

" Let the Young Democracy seize the standard, throw cowards and traitors into the mire, move forward, dislodge the Republicans, and save the Democratic party of this State, and ultimately of the nation."

But the Young Democracy did not seize the standard, nor anything else.   Mr. Tweed was equal to the emergency.   He bought off the organ that had urged the Young Democracy to the fight, and on the next day the following editorial opened the eyes of the leaders of the new movement.

". . . The Grand Sachem of Tammany proclaims himself the champion of municipal reform !   Such is the virtue of a little adversity.   It has converted Tweed himself. . . .

" The opportunity of the Young Democracy is to stand by judiciously and help the Grand Sachem in his novel line of business.   It matters not so much to them what individual proposes the necessary measures, as that they should be radical and comprehensive.   The gallant men who have so far led this memorable combat in the Legislature need not fear that they will be forgotten by the people because they have forced the foe of all reform to come forth as the advocate of the very changes he detests.   Let Mr. Tweed hurry up his vaunted charter, and let it be made a law as soon as it is examined and found to contain the features he has promised."

On the Monday following the Young Democracy organ showed its hand more plainly.   It published interviews with Tweed and Sweeny, which were in reality but manifestoes to the public.

That evening the Tammany Hall General Committee were to meet in Tammany Hall, but when the hour arrived for the doors to open, one hundred policemen were found guarding the portals, and a placard announcing that the Hall would not be opened was posted on the door. Thus ended the revolt against the Tammany Ring.

Mr. Tweed did not lose sight of Albany. His associates were working their points in the Legislature. The Young Democracy charter which had passed the Senate was defeated in the Assembly, and the next week Tweed's charter was introduced in the Senate, and, receiving the support of every Republican Senator but Thayer of Rensselaer, it passed. This was quickly followed by other measures, which made the power of the Ring in New York City well-nigh absolute. The process by which these wonderful results were brought about still remains a secret with Mr. Tweed, and those who know him best say it will never be divulged. He never dealt with lobbyists, but transacted his business in person, and we are not hazarding anything when we say that there are hundreds of men throughout the State who have received the moneys belonging to the tax-payers of the metropolis, and who, when speaking of the fate of Tweed, roll their eyes in pious horror.

One member of the Legislature of 1870, a prominent church member from the western part of the State, was overheard praying aloud one night in the Delavan House. He had been approached with the offer of $20,000 for his vote, and was endeavoring to make his conscience easy by seeking counsel from the Throne of Grace. How many satisfied their consciences is not known, but it is known which way they voted.

Tweed was again master of the situation. His rivals surrendered at discretion, and they were taken back into the fold.

It was now that the enormous bills approved by the Board of Audit began to receive attention. Vouchers against the city for hundreds grew to thousands, and from thousands to millions. It is said that Sweeny remonstrated, but to no purpose, and the depletion of the Treasury went on. Prominent capitalists examined the accounts of the Comptroller and certified to their correctness, and, for a time, nothing more was said.

Fate, unswerving and unalterable Fate, here stepped in and laid bare the frauds. James Watson, the Deputy Comptroller, possessed the secrets of the Comptroller's office, and while he was alive no one could get access to the vouchers.

Among those who claimed that the Treasury was indebted to them was ex-Sheriff James O'Brien. He claimed that there was due him for fees $200,000. The Board of Audit refused to consider it, although Mr. Tweed strongly urged its payment, and even went so far (so it is reported) as to give him $70,000 from his own bank account. Sweeny opposed the payment, and refused to allow the claim to be placed on the annual tax levy. Finally, Mr. Watson, of the Comptroller's office, appointed a meeting with O'Brien, at the solicitation of Mr. Tweed, to effect a settlement of the claim ; and it was while he was driving to the place of meeting, on Harlem Lane, in a sleigh drawn by a spirited team of horses, that he was run into by the horse that was driven by an inebriated Teuton, and kicked to death. Afterwards, to strengthen the chances of getting the money, one of O'Brien's confidential clerks in the Comptroller's office secured transcripts of the fraudulent vouchers therein contained. Armed with these evidences of the guilt of the Ring, he again demanded his money. It was again refused; and the Ring stood ready to brave the exposure. Thereupon O'Brien turned his evidence over to the *New York Times*, and that paper printed it. The effect was startling. With one voice the people demanded the punishment of those men who had betrayed so great a trust. Consternation and dismay seized all but Tweed, and he defied all the powers arrayed against him.

Tammany Hall sent its delegates to the State Convention which met at Rochester in the fall of 1871, and Tweed went in person to run the machine. The Reform Democracy sent its delegates to contest the seats of the Tammanyites. The seats were declared vacant, and the last power of the Ring departed. It was here that the Albany regency, headed by Tilden, Seymour, and others, began the crusade against the Ring, and the scene of operations was removed to New York, where Tilden, assisted by O'Conor and the Committee of Seventy, devoted weeks and months of toil in ferreting out the fraudulent transactions in the Comptroller's office, and ascertaining from the bank accounts what had been done with the funds that were fraudulently obtained from the city. When it was ascertained that these gentlemen were preparing to lay bare the transactions of the Ring, all who had in any way shared in the plunder fled from the city. One of the first against whom an indictment was obtained was Connolly.

Messrs. Tilden and Peckham, of the Board of Municipal Corrections, began to investigate the transactions of the Ring in the fall of 1871. They examined the accounts of Tweed, Woodward, Ingersoll, Garvey, and the New York Printing Company in the Broadway Bank, and made a table of the debits and credits of these accounts, and of certain relations which they bore to each other. Tweed saw the coming storm, but his courage did not desert him, and he determined to stay and fight it out.

On the 27th of October, 1871, Mr. Tweed sat in his office at the Department of Public Works, anticipating the order for his arrest. About noon, Sheriff Brennan called on him and exhibited the warrant. Mr. Tweed accompanied the Sheriff to the Court-House, where several of his friends were awaiting his arrival. Bail being required in the amount of $1,000,000, the bonds were drawn up, the sureties signed the papers, and Mr. Tweed returned to his office. The other parties named on the order could not be found. It was subsequently ascertained that they had fled from the city.

On December 16th of the same year, Mr. Tweed was again arrested on the charge of felony. An attempt was made to commit him to the Tombs, but, before it could be effected, Judge Barnard granted a writ of *habeas corpus*. All these trials did not disturb his equanimity. He retained his position as Commissioner of Public Works until the 30th of December, on which day he forwarded his resignation to the Mayor.

Public attention was now attracted towards the situation of affairs in the Comptroller's office. Mayor Hall requested Comptroller Connolly to resign. The Comptroller declined. Connolly appointed Andrew H. Green, the present Comptroller, his deputy, hoping thereby to quiet the apprehensions of the public regarding the safety of the official documents in his possession. The vouchers on which the fraudulent claims were paid were removed one night, and afterwards their ashes were found in the attic of the Court-House.

On November 20th, Comptroller Connolly resigned, and Andrew H. Green was appointed his successor. On the 25th of the same month he was arrested, but was permitted to take up his quarters at the New York Hotel, where he remained in custody of several of the Sheriff's deputies, while endeavoring to obtain bail. The amount required was $1,000,000. Several days were spent by his friends hunting up bail, but without success, and on the 29th he was removed to Ludlow Street Jail.

On the 16th of December he was indicted for misdemeanor. His bail being reduced one-half, his relatives became his bondsmen, and he was released from arrest. Subsequently he left the country for foreign parts, where he will undoubtedly remain.

Ex-Mayor Hall was also indicted, and he and Mr. Tweed were placed on trial. In the case of the former, a juryman died during the progress of the trial, and in the latter the jury disagreed.

During the first week in November, 1873, William M. Tweed was again placed on trial in the Court of Oyer and Terminer, Judge Noah Davis, presiding. The prosecution was conducted by the Assistant District Attorney, assisted by Lyman Tremain and Wheeler H. Peckham. The defence was conducted by John Graham, William Fullerton, Willard O. Bartlett, Willard Bartlett, Jr., and Elihu Root. Several days were taken up in obtaining a jury. In fact, one of the jurymen was excluded after having been sworn in. It appears that the District Attorney, believing that it was next to impossible to obtain a jury among which there would not be some of Mr. Tweed's friends, secured the services of three of Pinkerton's detectives to watch the jury. While the jury was being empanelled, one of the detectives saw the eighth juror in conversation with a captain of police, who was a friend of Mr. Tweed's of many years' standing. On motion of the District Attorney to discharge the juror, Judge Davis said:

I cannot bring my mind to the conclusion that this transaction was entirely innocent. On the contrary, it is covered all over with suspicion. Captain Walsh, a friend of many years' standing, and meeting him, is not a circumstance of grave importance; but that he should chance to be located at the time with particular friends of the defendant, such as his private secretary, and hanging around the antechamber, and talking with a party implicated in the loss of the vouchers, and be there until the jury left their seats, and then, without any intention of going home, shaking hands with the juror, and going down with him to the foot of the stairs, and anxious to know whether he was making plenty of money, and then, coming back to the antechamber, covers the case with such suspicion that whatever verdict would be rendered it would never be regarded by the public mind as an honest one. The juror, besides, has not, in my judgment, acted with frankness in disclosing information that it was proper he should give. He has been the intimate friend of a distinguished politician, and he never told us. It is my duty, which I discharge with more pain than pleasure, to discharge this man from the jury, and get in his place one more likely not to be accosted by any one as to his peculiar success in business.

No. 8 juror being relieved, at once vacated his chair and left the court-room.

The principal evidence for the prosecution was the table of accounts prepared by Samuel J. Tilden, which were obtained from the books of the Broadway Bank and the Comptroller's office.

The first column contained the date of the warrant; the next the date of the deposit; the date of the warrant and of the deposit generally corresponded, but not always; the next column showed the number of the warrant, and the next the name of the last indorser, who is generally the depositor; the next showed the amount of the warrant.

Mr. Graham, on summing up for the defence, claimed that the defendant could not be held accountable for the frauds, as he had the audit of Watson and the approval of the Comptroller, and, more than that, of the Mayor, before he certified the checks.

Mr. Tremain, in his summing up for the prosecution, claimed that the Commissioners of Audit, Messrs. Tweed, Hall and Connolly, had no power to commit these duties to James Watson, the clerk of the Board, and that at the only meeting of the Board of Audit, of which there was any record, they delegated their powers to Watson.

Judge Davis, in his charge to the jury, explained the duties of the Board of Audit as follows:

To audit accounts is to ascertain their justness and correctness, whether they have been paid and if anything remains due on them, and when a body of men are appointed to audit, they are to take cognizance of the accounts and see if they are existing liabilities, and how much has been paid or is due on them. This power was not given to individuals, but to a body of officers, and the claims were not against them, but the tax-payers, and it became an official duty of trust to see to it that the claims presented were justly due. This power was given to them not individually, but in their collective capacity, and they were to pass upon the bills and bring to bear upon them their joint determination. When the law imposes a duty on a body, it imposes the duty to meet and apply their concurrent determination. The majority may determine, where there is not an actual meeting of all; but the law requires the concurrent action of three minds, that they shall convene, organize, sit somewhere, and take up the liabilities, and apply their concurrent capacity to see that the county is not asked to pay on false claims. They cannot delegate their powers, but they may employ clerical help to bring the accounts before them. The indictment charges that these defendants had no meeting but one, and then, instead of auditing, delegated their power to officers and clerks, and then had the certificates sent around to them individually ; and if you are satisfied that the defendants did this, neglecting to audit and taking the amounts from officials, auditors or clerks, you are to convict them under the three first counts in each set. The law presumes every officer to know his duty, and if they certified, knowing they had not passed upon the bills collectively, thus furnishing the basis on which the Comptroller was bound to pay, the offence was committed. The people claim that what the law required was not done ; that the minds of three men were not brought to bear collectively on the claims.

The jury retired on the evening of the 18th of November, and on the morning of the 19th came into court with a verdict of guilty of misdemeanor. The announcement of the verdict was quite unexpected. It was the general impression that no jury could be found in New York City to convict a man who had held the high positions that Mr. Tweed had occupied. The silence that reigned in the court when the verdict was announced, was positively oppressive. Mr. Tweed was perfectly self-possessed, not betraying the slightest emotion. Judge Davis gave him into the custody of the Sheriff, and that officer handed him over to the keeping of his deputies, who immediately left the Court-House and proceeded to the prisoner's office, where he remained the entire day arranging his affairs. The District Attorney objected to the privileges that were being extended to Mr. Tweed by the Sheriff, but that official declared that he was responsible for Mr. Tweed's appearance in court, to receive his sentence, and, until then, he would take to himself the right to take his prisoner where he pleased.

There were those, unacquainted with the fallen chieftain, who believed that he would never appear in court to receive his sentence. But on the morning of the 22d, when the Court of Oyer and Terminer opened, he was there, accompanied by his son, awaiting the sentence of Court. It was, that he was to be imprisoned for twelve years and pay a fine of $12,500.

The same evening Mr. Tweed was taken to the Tombs and confined in a cell, but on the following day a room was fitted up, and there he remained for a week, which enabled him to settle his affairs before leaving for his final place of imprisonment.

BLACKWELL'S ISLAND.

Some correspondence took place between the Attorney-General and Sheriff Brennan, which undoubtedly expedited the removal of Tweed from the Tombs, for, on the morning of the 29th, he left for Blackwell's Island, accompanied by his son William. We need not allude to the parting with his family. It was a sad scene, witnessed by few, but those who saw a loving wife and affectionate daughters taking their farewell under such circumstances, of a father who had always been close by them, may be pardoned for any expressions of sympathy by the most oppressed of tax-payers.

Arriving at the Penitentiary, he fared the same as all others. A legion of reporters had reached the island by a circuitous route to graphically describe every incident of the humiliating ordeal through which he was to pass. But for this information they were compelled to draw on their imagination, for not one of them saw him after he left the Warden's office. It is undoubtedly true that Mr. Tweed, on his arrival, was subjected to the same treatment as the most hardened desperado, and it was this that broke him down and necessitated his removal to the hospital. There he now is, faithfully attending the sick, sustained by the hope that his counsel may succeed in obtaining for him a new trial. Since his incarceration he has been invisible to visitors. Only the officials, his relatives and counsel see him. The rumor that he was writing his autobiography, or that a friend was preparing a history of his political career, occasioned considerable consternation among many whose names appear in his political diary. So many stories having been circulated, some of which are founded on facts and many more being pure fiction, we called on Mr. Tweed to ascertain the truth or falsity of the countless rumors. We stated the purpose of our visit in a brief note, in reply to which he said :

" If any person is preparing a history of my life, it is not from material furnished by me. I am obliged to you for your call, but I feel that, in order not to be either misrepresented, or what is worse, misunderstood, I must decline any conversation in reference to myself. You, therefore, will please excuse my desire not to see any person, and regret that I must decline to see you."

The assurance of the reticence of the late chief of the New York Democracy will quiet the fear of many a politician between New York and Buffalo, but it will not ease their conscience.

Ex-Mayor Hall was the next member of the Board of Audit arraigned for trial. He was charged with wilful neglect in the performance of his official duties.

The proceedings of the last day (Dec. 24, 1873) of the trial were divided into three great acts—the summing up of Mr. Stoughton, the address of Mr. Tremain, and Judge Daniels's charge to the jury. The first speech, that of Mr. Stoughton, was begun at 10 o'clock in the morning, and finished at 12.30. Those present, who had been familiar with Mr. Stoughton's style of delivery, and the eloquence which characterizes his efforts, imagined they noticed in his manner a confidence which pleaded against unnecessary effort and weariness. Certainly his speech lacked much of the length which characterized the one delivered on the other trial, which resulted in a disagreement. Some

A. OAKEY HALL.

were surprised when he took his seat, expecting as they did the customary burst of feeling, and there were not wanting those who thought that the speaker should have said much more on such a doubtful issue. When Mr. Tremain concluded his speech, it was evident that he had spared no pains to put before the jury every possible argument likely to affect, in favor of the people, the silent listeners before him.

Judge Daniels charged the jury for over an hour, reviewing closely the evidence and impressed his views of the meaning of the law emphatically and carefully upon their minds. He practically told them to throw aside all consideration of the meaning of the now famous word " audit," advising them that the statute was plain enough to convince all reasonable men that it meant to examine and pass upon. This left, as the only question for the jury, whether the ex-Mayor neglected wilfully to audit. The jury returned from their room at 8 o'clock to inquire whether they must find wilful neglect, when they could find simple neglect. Judge Daniels informed them that it must be " wilful," and they again retired, with an intimation from the Judge that if they did not find a verdict in an hour or so they would be locked up for the night. At 10.30 they returned with a verdict of " not guilty," and the spectators almost universally testified their approbation by repeated and unrestrained cheers.

The trial of James H. Ingersoll, one of the Court-House Commissioners, and his clerk, John D. Farrington, for forgery, began Nov. 24th, 1873, in the Court of Oyer and Terminer, before Judge Davis. The case was concluded in two days, and Ingersoll was convicted and sentenced to five years in Sing Sing, while his confederate, who was also convicted, received but a sentence of one year and a half, Ingersoll having confessed that he did not share in the proceeds. On the 4th of December they were taken to Sing Sing prison, and after a few weeks transferred to Auburn prison, where they now are.

Henry W. Genet was indicted, Feb. 3d, 1872, for forgery in the third degree, and again on Nov. 22d, 1873, was indicted for grand larceny. He was arrested on the 24th November, and his trial began in the Court of Oyer and Terminer, Dec. 16th, before Judge Daniels. The indictment was for procuring, by false representations, the signature of Mayor Hall to a warrant on a false bill for supplies and work on the Harlem Court-House. Genet was convicted, after a three days' trial, and given into the custody of Sheriff Brennan, who detailed Deputy Sheriffs William H. Shields and Michael Cahill to see that the prisoner was produced in court at the time designated by his Honor to receive the judgment of the Court. There was no particular friendship existing between the Sheriff and Genet, but Genet's friends claimed the same privileges for him that had been extended to Tweed.

It was thought by many that he might escape the officers under whose care he was, and an Assistant District Attorney, acting on what he believed to be trustworthy information, wrote to Sheriff Brennan upon the subject. Subsequently this letter, or a copy, fell into the hands of Genet, and he, in the presence of his guardian, exhibited it to United States District Attorney Bliss. How Genet obtained that letter is a mystery. He scoffed at it. On Saturday, in the court-room, he was as gay as ever. He was permitted to go wherever he chose with the officer, and he visited his old haunts and made merry. He played a game of "draw" as blithely as in other days, and bade his companions not to think he was a "dead cock in the pit." On Saturday night he sat in the reception room of his residence until a late hour, chatting with the deputy sheriffs and some friends. His grief-stricken wife had retired to bed on the floor above, and long after midnight he asked permission to see her. The request was granted by the deputy sheriffs, and he returned to where they were sitting an hour or two afterwards. On Sunday he and the deputy sheriffs rode out together and visited many public resorts, among others well known to sporting men, Remson's, Stetson's, and Barker's. Genet's ostensible object in visiting some of these places was to obtain money due him. It is said that the party drank much wine and became very jolly. In Stetson's Genet boasted that his legal opinion was always considered much better than that of ex-Judge Fullerton, and that he thought a stay might well be argued in his (Genet's) absence. Some reference was made to the return of Woodward, and to a rumor that some of the old members of the Court-House Commission were urging the statute of limitation in their favor, should action be taken against them. Politics were then touched upon, and it was said by an outsider that Genet was to lend his assistance in the Assembly to the present Board of Police Commissioners. On the return of the party to Genet's residence they spent the evening merrily. Deputy Sheriff Cahill was unwell and went to his home, leaving Mr. Shields with the prisoner. About 2 o'clock, while Genet and Shields were smoking in the reception room, the prisoner said he would like to go up-stairs and talk a little while with his wife, as he could not have much further opportunity before being sent to prison, and promised soon to return. Shields assented, and Genet went from the room. The deputy sheriff lay back in his chair and dozed. When he awoke at 7 o'clock he glanced around the room, but his prisoner was not there. Thinking that he might be sleeping in the room above, the deputy sheriff ascended the staircase and knocked at the door of Mrs. Genet's bed-chamber. Mrs. Genet answered the knock. Shields asked for Genet, and was startled by the reply that he had not been in the room that night. The deputy sheriff, scarcely able to control himself, searched every room in the house and then the grounds, but his prisoner could not be found. Then he hurried to the police station in 126th street, and then to the Police Central Office in Mulberry street. Encountering Superintendent Matsell, he told in a few words of the escape of Genet, and the Superintendent ordered a general alarm to be sent out. The news of the flight of Prince Harry was soon in everybody's mouth. The Superintendent had a long talk with Deputy Shields, who wept while he related his story. He said that he had great confidence in Genet, and that when the prisoner asked to be allowed to see his wife, he had no doubt whatever about his returning to the reception room.

Every effort was made to discover Genet's whereabouts, but without success.

Whatever may be the opinion of the public, all who knew Shields were satisfied that he could not be bribed to betray the trust reposed in him by Sheriff Brennan. For three years he had conveyed prisoners to Sing Sing without a single mishap. This unfortunate termination to his official duties was deplored by the sheriff, who took the responsibility on himself. The result of it was that Sheriff Brennan and Shields were adjudged guilty of contempt of court, and they were committed to Ludlow Street Jail for thirty days. It is supposed that Genet escaped to Europe, where he was afterwards joined by his wife.

The remnants of the Ring have gone to parts unknown, where they will remain exiled from their homes and friends.

The New Court-House, which they ostensibly built to perpetu-
ate the power and greatness of their administration, should be
completed, that, with its dome raised heavenward, and surmounted
by the goddess of Justice, it would present a perfect symmetry and
be no longer a reminder of its painful history.

THE NEW COURT-HOUSE.

Regenerated by the victory achieved at last by justice sitting
within its halls, and calling to account the despoilers of its virgin
purity—make it in truth a dwelling-place for law and order,
rather than the monument of a profligate and corrupt, but now
broken Ring.

APPENDIX.

STATEMENT OF EDWARD S. STOKES.

IN the years 1869 and 1870 the oil business in which I was engaged was lucrative, yielding net profits each year exceeding $100,000. The refinery was consuming 15,000 barrels of crude petroleum per month, and Fisk desired to get an interest in its profits, and also control the business for the Erie Railroad. At this time I was unacquainted with Fisk. He sought the interview, and telegraphed me at Saratoga Springs to meet him at the Opera House. This was in the summer of 1870. I met him and entered into business relations through his agent, Henry Harley. It was previous to this, in the fall of 1869, while on a visit to Philadelphia on business, that I was first introduced to Miss Mansfield. The general belief that Fisk introduced me is incorrect. At the time of the arrival of Mad. Monteland, Fisk gave her a banquet at the Erie Office. Miss Mansfield and several others of Fisk's friends were present. Fisk, elated with the brilliant surroundings, through an interpreter, a well-known operatic leader, informed Mad. Monteland that "if she had previously enjoyed the friendship of foreign nobility, she had now struck a prince indeed ; that he owned everything, and that if she so desired, the name of New York City should be changed to Fiskville." The interpreter was astonished. Miss Mansfield was offended, and left the supper-table, and refused to be reconciled to Fisk. This was the real cause of their first estrangement. I was not present at the banquet, and knew nothing about it until I heard it from Fisk. A week or so after this Fisk wrote me a letter asking me to meet him at the Fifth Avenue Hotel. I did so, and in that interview he related all his troubles with Miss Mansfield, and begged me to go to her residence and see if matters could not be amicably arranged. The result was that Fisk was reinstated, and they immediately took a cottage at Long Branch. So far from desiring in any way to interfere with Fisk's private affairs, *I entirely avoided them*, and during that summer I never once visited Long Branch. Towards the close of the season, for reasons which I know nothing of, they quarrelled the second time, and Miss Mansfield came to the city, leaving Fisk at the Branch. I visited the residence of Miss Mansfield, as did hundreds of noted politicians and public men at this time. I never resided there. My home was with my family, at the Worth House, corner of Fifth avenue and 25th street; and when my family went to Europe I went to the Hoffman House, and was a regular boarder in the hotel. I never abandoned my wife and family, and the wicked reports to the contrary are false and heartless. I accompanied my wife and child to the steamer, and saw them safely on board, and under the care of the sister of Mr. J. W. Southack, whom I desired should accompany them as protection.

By every steamer I received the most affectionate letters from my wife, the last one being dated the very day before the tragedy. I paid all their expenses while abroad; and every one that knows me will say that I never neglected, but, on the contrary, provided my family with everything necessary, and afforded them every luxury.

But to my story. Fisk, on finding that Miss Mansfield was determined not to receive him again, sought another interview with me, and besought me to try and bring about a reconciliation. God knows I would gladly have done so, and did everything in my power, but was unsuccessful, and told Fisk so. Hereupon angry words followed—and from this time Fisk began to persecute me. He issued an order through the agent cancelling all my contracts for low freight, and as he had control of the lion's share of the business he soon ran the Company almost into bankruptcy. Matters were in such a serious shape that I wrote to him on the 26th of October, 1870, expostulating with him against this injustice. The next day he sent Mr. Hicks to ask me to meet him at Delmonico's that evening at 6 o'clock. I did so, and at his request adjourned the meeting to Mansfield's house. A reconciliation was effected, he promising to do right and make amends for all that he had done wrong. During the evening, after all had been satisfactorily adjusted, he said, "Ed., this interview saves you from State Prison." He added, "I was at the bottom of that difficulty you had with Morehead, and, when you assaulted him as you did, *I had you, my boy, sure.* It made my blood fly to fever-heat."

I rather ridiculed the idea, and he said, "Ed., you don't know what power we hold here in this city. *We rule New York to-day as absolutely as Robespierre ever ruled France. Our touch is cold and clammy to those who cross our path. When we have the power to drive corporations with millions and millions in terror out of the State, we can easily put up a job to get you in State Prison.*" "Why," he said, "I have the indictment already drawn against you for felonious assault with intent to kill, and to-morrow you were to be indicted. Learning that the witnesses to the affray were all *poor*—that was all I wanted to know—*I had them.*" I inquired what judge he would get, saying, "Judge —— will not do it?"

Fisk laughed and replied, "That would be too apparent. We do not want him. It was to come off in the General Sessions." The interview lasted until the next morning. I called the next evening to carry out the settlement, when Fisk, upon some pretext, put it off until the next week, and kept putting it off and off—in the interim desiring me to arrange that there should be no further difficulty with Miss Mansfield. When I understood this to be the object of his delay, I left the Erie Office disgusted, declining to have anything to do with such business. The consequence was that Fisk renewed his attacks on my oil business, and finally caused me to be arrested upon a trumped-up charge of embezzling the company's money. I was arrested on Sunday, when I could not give bail. While I was locked up, Fisk published a most scandalous article, stating that the officers in arresting me had chased me from disreputable houses, and other damaging attacks in several of the papers.

This was mortifying to my family and friends, and I made an affidavit stating its falsity, as my only redress. I employed counsel, was examined, and clearly showed that the company was heavily indebted to me. Still I was held in the sum of $50,-000 bail.

Mr. Fisk now proposed to settle by paying me some $15,000 in addition to the $30,000 he claimed I had appropriated—and have the judge discharge me. Otherwise I was to be tried in the Supreme Court. By advice of counsel I accepted the terms —having no alternative. I found that it was, indeed, true that Fisk owned the Courts, the Legislature and the City. By this settlement Fisk promised to desist from all attacks upon me, and while thus pretending to smoke the pipe of peace, was really writing infamous articles against me which appeared the next morning, and by his continued and persistent attacks succeeded in making my name as notorious as his own.

My only redress was to prove the bitter malice that existed in the breast of Fisk against me, and this my counsel could readily do by inserting in my affidavit letters written by Fisk to Mansfield, in which were disclosed the manner in which the Erie stockholders were being defrauded—the names of the parties among whom the spoils were being divided. These revelations would have spread consternation in *the Tammany Ring* and startle the world. Alarmed lest it should be published, Fisk sent to me to effect a settlement and suppress the publication. By this settlement I was to receive the sum of $200,000—$50,000 in cash, and $50,000 in cash every year for three years. The agreement was drawn up and awaited my signature. Although the sum named was much less than I was justly entitled to receive, I accepted the settlement. In the mean time, upon assurances that my rights should not suffer, I submitted the whole matter to arbitration, and under the advice of supposed legal friends I confidingly discontinued all suits against Fisk, surrendered all my valuable papers, affidavits, etc., into the hands of the arbitrators, and patiently and hopefully awaited the issue, having the most implicit confidence in the promises and assurances of counsel that my interests would be fully protected. After delays and postponements thirty and sixty days passed, and at last on shipboard, just as the steamer was to leave for Europe, the arbitrator awarded me $10,000—not enough to pay my counsel fees. Sympathizing legal advisers said they were surprised—"it was too bad,"—but advised me to take the $10,000 —pay counsel $5,000—and then commence another action. I now asked to have award opened and the matter investigated by Mr. Wm. M. Evarts, offering to give the $10,000 awarded to any charity Mr. Evarts might propose if he found the award just and not made in the interest of the Erie and Tammany Ring. To this I received no reply.

Shortly after this transaction, affidavits were used in sequent suits in which it was charged that $250,000 was paid for negotiating a decision in the interest of Fisk and Gould, in the U. S. Court, and adverse to the English stockholders in the famous Heath and Raphel suit of 1870. These affidavits were among the suppressed papers.

When this injunction suit was tried, Fisk hired a negro named King to swear that in his (the negro's) presence, Miss Mansfield, Mrs. Williams and myself engaged in a conspiracy to extort a large sum of money from Fisk and Gould. This affidavit was upon its face false; besides, I held the proof that Fisk had suborned this witness, and had paid him $500.

I therefore applied for an order for arrest of this negro, when Fisk spirited him away to parts unknown, and I have never heard from him since.

This is a fair sample of the way Fisk conducted legal tactics.

Fisk was unquestionably the most dangerous man that ever lived in New York City, for the reason no one so depraved ever wielded such immense power. He was desperate, vindictive, unscrupulous, and revengeful; would carry his purpose at all hazards, and would not even stop at murder.

In using this vile affidavit of this boy it was only a repetition of his conduct.

When Mr. Dorman B. Eaton was prosecuting Fisk and Gould, and exposing their rascalities, and endeavoring to turn them out as officers of the Erie Railroad Company, Fisk, first by offers of money, endeavored to persuade Mr. Eaton to desist. Failing in this, Fisk had Mr. Eaton tracked day and night, for the purpose, if possible, in some manner to blacken his character; and as a *dernier ressort*, knowing that Mr. Eaton was a gentleman of high social standing and spotless character, thought to deter him from taking further legal proceedings by a threatened publication of certain affidavits he had suborned witnesses to make, charging Mr. Eaton with visiting improper places, etc.

I read the affidavits, and know them to be as false as they were infamous.

Instead of intimidating Mr. Eaton, they only urged him to still greater activity.

Thwarted, Fisk determined to have him waylaid.

Within two weeks, Mr. Eaton was struck a murderous blow on the head, as he was about entering his home at midnight, which almost deprived him of life. Although he was for months almost in an unconscious condition, by the intervention of a kind providence his life was spared.

There were others implicated in this outrageous plot to waylay Mr. Eaton, but I shall say nothing more on that subject now.

On the afternoon of the 6th of January, I was a witness in the libel suit at Bixby's Court.

The Court adjourned at 2 o'clock, and I left in company of Hon. John McKeon and John R. Fellows, and proceeded to Delmonico's, partook of some refreshments, and immediately proceeded to the offices of Rufus F. Andrews and Francis M. Bixby, and from there I took a cab directly to the Hoffman House, to my room, to get some papers in reference to a disputed turf matter that was to be argued before the Trotting Congress, on Tuesday, January 9th, involving some $10,000.

I ordered the driver to the residence of Miss Mansfield, No. 359 West 23d street, intending to get the original agreement I left there accidentally some weeks previously.

Upon arriving at the door, I noticed the house closed, and remembering that she had been sick, concluded not to disturb her. The story that I followed Fisk's carriage down to the Grand Central Hotel is clearly false.

When I left 23d street, it was only past 3 o'clock.

Fisk, it appears, entered his carriage about 4 o'clock.

I went directly to the store of Dodge's, Broadway and Washington Place, and, for some 15 or 20 minutes remained there in conversation with Mr. David Smith, the gentleman I was in search of, and also with the son of Judge Ingraham, and Mr. Polyhamus, and, God knows, the thought of meeting Jim Fisk never entered my mind. After leaving Mr. Ingraham, I proceeded down Broadway on the opposite side from the Grand Central. At Broadway and Amity street I met a friend, Geo. W. Bailey, with whom I walked a block, and left to speak with a lady in the hotel who recognized me from the parlor window, and with whom I thought I had a previous acquaintance. These facts were indisputably proven.

It is the most absurd idea that any one could for a moment conjecture that I was looking for Fisk.

In the first place, Fisk had been sick for the past two weeks.

Second, he rarely visited the Grand Central Hotel. It was proven that he had only called there four times in as many months.

Third, it was impossible for me to know of his visit, because his own servants and friends were ignorant of it, and testified that when he left the Opera House he did not state where he was going.

Had I had any intention of assaulting Fisk, I would have done so when I was in the vicinity of the Opera House, and not left the locality he was in for another he rarely visited.

Fourth, I should suppose any one committing a cold-blooded murder, as I have been accused of, would desire to escape.

The affray took place within a few feet of Broadway. I could easily have escaped into Broadway.

Instead of which, I walked directly into the heart of the hotel and quietly surrendered myself.

The general impression that Miss Mansfield was responsible for the shooting of Jas. Fisk, Jr., is absurdly false.

She had no more idea of any such occurrence than she would have had if President Grant had been shot.

You can judge of the extent of the intimacy between Miss Mansfield and myself, when I assert I have never seen her since the 6th of January, 1871, have never written to her, and have never received but one letter from her, and that was after my conviction, expressing sympathy, and trusting I did not feel that she had acted wrong in not remaining to testify; that had my lawyers written, she would have returned from Europe, etc.

Had my associations with her been such as have been stated, the prosecution were unaware of it, or they would have proved it; and although the most careful examination of my entire history, I may say from the day of my birth, was rigidly examined into for three consecutive trials—I was for days a witness upon the stand—I left it without a single aspersion being made derogatory to me, and I am proud of it. It speaks louder than anything I can say in my vindication, and brands the slanders that have been so persistently printed about me.

After all, my case is determined by the public upon the same identical theory. Those that believe the evidence of the hall boys, believe I am guilty of murder; and those that believe their story wickedly manufactured, believe I am innocent—that's all there is to it. The theory is correct; I admit, if one-tenth part of what Hart testified be true, a more cold-blooded assassination never was committed, and that any jury believing their evidence and failing to convict of murder in the first degree, were recreant to their oaths. But the jury believed those boys perjured; why are they not tried for the perjury the jury say they have committed? The evidence against them is overwhelming, their guilt is as clear as the noonday sun. I only ask, let them be tried, and upon the result of their trial let the public determine my guilt or innocence.

Erie Ring lawyers and Tammany Ring judges came near destroying me. It was their intention at the outset to make short and quick work, but the tactics of my counsel in a measure prevented it. But the glorious music of reform drove them from power and prevented the forcing on my trial.

It is my decided opinion, that my first counsel made a sad mistake in not allowing at once a public statement of my encounter with Fisk. The public knew nothing concerning it—heard nothing—except the manufactured story of Thomas Hart and his accomplices, and my silence was regarded as conclusive evidence of guilt, and the general impression was that there could be only one defence, and that *insanity*. I was so prejudiced thereby at the time of my trial, that such a thing as a fair trial was impossible. All my witnesses were looked upon with disfavor and distrust. I should perhaps state that Mr. William O. Bartlett, one of my counsel, favored a public statement, but was overruled.

In conclusion, I can only state, on my honor as a man, that Fisk brought about the conflict; otherwise I should have passed him quietly by, on the stairs. EDWARD S. STOKES.

SING SING, Feb. 24, 1874.

PRISON MANAGEMENT AND REFORMATION.

A S the wheels of time have rolled along, and the population of our State has increased, crime, which is ever-present, has kept pace year by year with every advanced step, and our prisons, which were once small and scarcely full, are now large and crowded. Auburn, Clinton, and Sing Sing have a cell-capacity of 3,200, into which are placed 3,313 inmates.

Running the mind back over the past, it is sad to think that, while the world has made rapid strides in mechanics, arts, science, and literature, so little has been accomplished in the formation of systems to prevent and repress crime or reform the criminal. Millions of money have been spent to educate the youth of our land; every description of property is taxed to raise funds to support Public Schools; children of the poorest parents may and must be educated. And if you ask the most stupid man why this outlay, he will tell you the country cannot afford to have its boys and girls grow up in ignorance.

By means of Primary and Public Schools, Academies, and Colleges, society of every grade is passing through a series of great screens; first the indifferent and good members are sifted out, and vast multitudes yearly take their places in society to carry forward the important interests of our State. In this sifting there is a certain amount of refuse, some dwarfed, others misshaped, still others light and vain, and some bad and worthless.

The House of Refuge forms another in the series of screens by which some of the refuse is saved; but, alas! here the effort of society stops as though all that material which passes this screen is worthless, and all must pass in a promiscuous mass to State Prison. It would be well, perhaps, if all here could be obliterated and forgotten; but this cannot be. Most of these men are destined to live on to old age. There is no stopping-place in State Prison. The man who cannot resist temptation and form new resolutions to be better, will yield to surrounding influences and grow hardened in sin and wickedness. Established as our prisons are upon a system without order or design, beyond the packing of a large number of human beings together for safe-keeping, the opportunities for wholesome reflection and reform are nowhere visible.

It is an interesting fact that our State Prisons are filled with young men and boys, a majority of them under twenty-five years of age, and mostly committed for the first time. Is it not well to pause and inquire who is responsible for this state of things? Are these boys sinners above all others; has society no duty to perform for them, or some of the blame to share; must all be given up as lost; is not moral obligation still holding society to its trust; because these boys are in prison, must all natural means to reclaim them be reversed? All good men will say No! The necessity for the formation of an established system that will take hold of these boys between the House of Refuge and State Prison, is staring us in the face from the eyes of every boy who is looking through the grated door of our prison cells. Are these boys very bad? Have they long defied the laws of God and man? Is it a gigantic task to reform them? Then let the effort be equally powerful and the work be pressed forward with unflagging vigor. Under our present system the young boy and the novice in crime are thrown into prison with shrewd, accomplished thieves; lifelong burglars, who have turned a good education and large mechanical skill to the greatest account; light-fingered pickpockets and practised highway robbers, and from them they must receive their first and only lessons of prison life.

At this prison, when they enter, their names, ages, nativity, whether before in prison, married or single, parents dead or alive, temperate or intemperate, are all duly registered, as answered to questions put by the clerk; then all are marched in a squad to the dressing-room, and attired in convict stripes; if the garments fit or not, it is all the same. From this they are marched to the main hall, and on their way take their first lessons in the lock-step. Now they are installed in their little cell, 3 ft. 2 in. wide, 6 ft. 3 in. high, by 7 ft. long, furnished with a plank, narrow bed of straw, pillow the same, with coarse prison blankets. Supper (in a tin basin), a piece of bread and spoonful of molasses. The sobs, tears, and moans tell plainly how intensely some of them suffer; while the coarse ribaldry, grum voices and profanity are unmistakable evidences that human fiends are among them: the former are fit subjects for the reformatory; the latter should be hastened to some strong prison to be incarcerated for life. At the cell-door the contractor appears, and will ply his questions till he thinks he is able to select as many of the new-comers as are best suited to his kind of work. The following day they are found in the workshop, good, bad, and indifferent jumbled together, and their day's labor charged to the contractor at forty cents. And now the monotony of prison life begins; *tramp, tramp, tramp* from the cell to the mess-room, the workshop, the dock, and return. There is one boy here now who has done this twelve years, and all that time worked in one shop, and is reduced to a mere machine; he was worth saving at one time, but now it is doubtful if anything can be made of him. Located so near the city of New York as this prison is, it naturally becomes the receptacle of a majority of the convicts condemned to penal servitude; from here many of these are transferred to other prisons; for this reason, coupled with the fact that the buildings are badly constructed and the large number of prisoners crowded together in a heterogeneous mass, renders it morally impossible to apply reformatory agencies with any chance of success.

From the foregoing statements it is easy to discern the urgent necessity of increased prison accommodations at the earliest day possible. Our rulers have made very grave mistakes, when they enlarged this and Auburn prison beyond the capacity of five or six hundred cells. If only the pecuniary interest is taken into account, it requires little argument to show that employment can be found to advantage for five hundred men, when no profitable work can be had for an additional five hundred. The small establishment is compact, easy to handle; a market may readily be found for its products, and abundant supplies to satisfy every want may be drawn from a cheap market near at hand; while on the other hand the large prison is clumsy, unwieldy, expensive.

It is gratifying to learn that the world is waking slowly, but surely, to the long-neglected subject of Penalogy, and the question comes from every quarter, *What shall we do with our convicts?* And happily the answer comes from the noble Alexander Maconochie, of England, Colonel Monucenas, of Spain, Sir Walter Crofton, the father of the far-famed Irish system, from Meteia, in France, and many others who tell us of success worthy of our admiration and imitation; and yet the Empire State, which can boast of commerce, wealth, learning, climate, soil, and other interests unsurpassed by any community in the world, will still allow the State Prison system within her borders to go neglected and her prisons branded as political playthings.

All wise men admit that our system is bad; all know that society is deeply suffering for want of increased accommodations for criminal classes and modern appliances to conduct the work of reformation; and now who will take the first step in advance and give effect to wisely selected principles to meet this pressing demand?

If convicts can be better and more reliably trained in small numbers than in large, why will not our law-makers begin at once to prepare the means, by taking advantage of well-settled principles and systems, such as have been successful in other parts of the world? By selecting the best parts from each, a plan may be compiled that will meet our necessities and go far to lead us out of our chaotic situation.

It is a well-settled fact that the object of penal servitude is to protect the honest and virtuous members of society, while in the pursuit of happiness, from the depredations and villany of criminals of every form; and, second, to reform the transgressor, if possible. It is well to look at the work in hand, and first to inquire who these villains are, and how they came to be such characters. The history of many of these individuals, if written, would make thrilling narratives. One would tell that he was taught to steal from infancy; another, that he was allowed to run wild under the bad influence of dishonest companions; a third, that he indulged a bad disposition by being disobedient to parents, and nearly all have contracted bad habits of intemperance and gambling. The rules of society are not so formed as to throw a shield around every youth; human nature is naturally jealous, and in its weakness seems better pleased to see a neighbor stumble and fall than to prosper. It is very easy to say, "I told you so; I knew he he would go astray." Men who boast of their integrity are quite willing to sneer and rejoice when fellow-beings fall in disgrace, and, when fallen, are more ready to kick them for falling than to aid them to rise again. Many men may be found now in our community who would not steal or appropriate property of others to their own use on any account; but they seem to take pleasure in using all underhanded means to rob their fellow-beings of character, reputation and position; they will crawl into any hole, watch late and early, in order to decoy the widow's son into dishonest acts, and then glory in seeing him degraded as a thief, while, if that same boy had been taken in time and advised to shun all bad influences, he might have been raised an honest man.

Miss Mary Carpenter has related the following story of an English boy which is no isolated case of neglect: Said the boy, " I have been told a thousand times to go and get work, but it was never said to me during twenty years, while in or out of prison, I'll give you work, hence I have cost the country some two thousand pounds, and I expect to cost a great deal more yet. I was sent to jail for two months when a boy for stealing a loaf of bread, and no one cared for me. I walked to the seaports, but in vain; I tramped, sore-footed, thousands of miles when I was a lad, in order to get honest employment, but it did not answer. I was tempted to steal; I stole, I was imprisoned, I was sent to Bermuda. I have learned the trade of a professional thief, and now I intend to follow it. I believe all philanthropy to be a mockery, and religion to be a delusion, and I care neither for God nor man. The jail, penal servitude, and the gallows are all the same to me."

But how shall we begin to reform these bad boys? First let us beg our rulers to place our Penal Institutions entirely beyond the reach of party politics. Divide our system into three series of prisons, the first for the incarceration of young men sentenced the first time; in this division all the appliances that skill can devise to carry on the work of reformation should be had. Classes should be formed so that the prisoner can advance from one to the other for meritorious conduct. Let the prisoner share in his earnings, and let the percentage of his earnings increase at every stage of advance; make the rules of conduct so stringent that it will cost great effort to gain all the credit marks. Introduce many of the most useful trades, let the prisoner have his choice to learn; make the discipline rigid and firm; for disobedience let the punishment be sure and severe; take time to eradicate all bad habits, and establish honesty, industry, and virtue in their stead; cause the prisoner to heartily co-operate in his own reform by showing him that those placed over him are his friends, and that their best efforts are enlisted for his welfare.

After a prisoner has once had the advantages of this division and, if he then return to crime, he must not be allowed to enter here the second time.

A second division should be arranged for the incarceration of the milder cases of second offence and older criminals; here the system should be different, discipline stern and exacting. A chance should here be offered to reform, but the privileges should be few and labor constant without task or reward.

For cases that have failed here a third division should be arranged. In this I would imprison all cases for third convictions, long-term burglars, cases of manslaughter, arson, robbery, murder. This prison should be very secure, so that escapes would be impossible; the fare should be simple, coarse and regular; the system of labor should be constant, and all the surroundings of the plainest kind. Let as many such prisons as are needed be added to those now in use; let them be wisely located where supplies can be cheaply obtained, and a ready market found for the wares produced, and it is not unreasonable to believe that large advances would be made in the way of reforming criminals, and at very little cost to the public treasury.

GEORGE B. HUBBELL, Warden.

SING SING PRISON, February 28, 1874.

PRISON SUNSHINE.

MISS FLORA FOSTER, Matron of the Tombs, may be justly considered as of the Institution, the best of her life having been spent there. For upwards of thirty years has she ably performed the duties of her responsible position. A practical as well as theoretical Christian, possessed of " the chiefest of virtues, charity." She is firm where firmness is demanded—yet kind and sympathetic to those poor creatures who are too often consigned to her care, because, alas, they can find no better. Her patience has been time and again sorely tried—yet has she ever the cheerful voice and the kindly smile for those poor wretches who are unused to aught save the jibes, the sneers and the insults of a cold, cruel, heartless world. She is ever on the alert to discover the wrongs of her sex, and many are the cases where her timely intercession has saved from further ignominy and disgrace the unhappy victim of some heartless libertine, who, to cover up his

MISS FLORA FOSTER.

crime, trumped up some frivolous charge, that he might thus be spared the consequences. For the little boys and girls—waifs of humanity—she has a *mother's feelings*—and what more could be said ?

May the good lady be spared yet many years to labor in her chosen field ; but when at length, as in the natural course of events must be, she is summoned hence to receive her hire, may her place be filled by one who is worthy to follow in her footsteps ! Such is the wish and the hope of all who know her.

MISS LINDA GILBERT, the Prisoner's Friend, was born in New York city, May 13th, 1846. Her parents moved to Chicago when she was only five years old. Her father's house was directly opposite the old block prison in that city, and thus early she became familiar with all the sights and sounds and miseries of prison life; and thus early felt her heart moved to pity within her; and then and there made the childish resolution, persistently adhered to in maturer years, of devoting her life to raising and ennobling criminals.

Miss Gilbert is a member of the National Prison Congress, and devotes herself, principally to the work of founding libraries in the various Penitentiaries and

Penal Institutions of the land, for which purpose she has visited every large city of the United States.

The "Gilbert Library" in the St. Louis County Jail, and another one, of the same name, in the Chicago Penitentiary, have been founded by the indomitable perseverance, energy and self-sacrifice of Miss Gilbert, and inaugurated under the most honorable auspices.

Nor is this all. She enters the prisoners' cells, reads with them, talks with them, gains their confidence, listens to their confessions, enters into their hopes and fears, their regrets for the past, and plans for the future; and when they finish their allotted term, and go forth into the world, broken and disgraced, homeless and more than often friendless and destitute, Miss Gilbert meets them at the door of their cells with good wishes and good words, and helps them, if need there be, from her

MISS LINDA GILBERT.

own substance, and has obtained permanent homes for three hundred such, of whom only ten per cent. have proved ungrateful and unworthy—a record of which any woman might be proud.

Miss Gilbert is now located in New York, with the special and avowed purpose of founding libraries in all the institutions on Blackwell's Island and at the Tombs—a work so noble in itself that we cannot help bidding her " good speed."

Those who have witnessed invalids poring over old magazines or novels; lunatics asking plaintively for something to read, and even aged Incurables utterly engrossed in the light literature of the day, provided by some thoughtful hand, will see at once what a blessing such a library would be to those who, cursed and unsinning, are condemned to pass their days where excitement and pleasure are unknown.

INDEX.

A

Abortionists, 359
Adams, Samuel, murdered by J. C. Colt, 65
Allan, Col. Ethan, 25
Andrews, the Pirate, hanging of, 150
Astor Place Riot, 340

B

Babe, the Pirate, 286
Baker, the Privateer, 285
Baker, Lewis, his trial for killing Poole, 145
Barnum, P. T., his interview with Hicks, the Pirate, 212
Bartlett, Willard O., Stokes case, 546
Beach, Ex-Judge, defended Maggie Jourdan, 492
Beach, Wm. A., Stokes case, 546, 548
Beecher, Henry Ward, 510
Bellevue, Penitentiary at, 25
Bennett, James Gordon, his description of Jewett, 116
Bishop's Mitre, 594
Blackwell's Island, Penitentiary on, 25
    as seen by a lady, 610
Blood, Col. Jas., 508
Board of Ten Governors, 49
Bond-street Tragedy, 156
Booth, Junius Brutus; see Babe the Pirate, 286
Bowery Theatre, 179
Bowlsby, Alice Augusta, 369
Brady, James T., the Poole case, 145
    defended Restell, 364
    defended Jeffards, 451
Bridewell, origin of name, 27; west of City Hall Park, 29
Bummers' Hall, 51
    an incident at, 283
Buntline, Ned, 353
Burdell, Dr. Harvey, 162
Burdett, the Lunatic, 280
Burglary, 250
Butler, Roes, hanging of, 150

C

Calhoun Letters, McFarland trial, 418
Canter, John, counterfeiter, 258
Cap, the Frank Rivers, 120
Car-Hook Murder, 457
Carnell, Henry, killed Louis Rouseau, 454
City Hall, Wall Street, 23
Clark, Horace F., the Poole case, 145
Claflin, Tennie C., 506
Collect Pond, original site of the Tombs, 44
    first attempt at Steam Navigation, 47
    when filled up, 47
Colt, John C., his office at Broadway and Chambers street, 64
    his confession, 68
    shipping the body of Adams, 68
    his trial, 68
    his marriage in the cell, 75
    his suicide, 77
Confidence Men, 236
Conklin, W. F., Bowlsby case, 373
Cook, James H., Commissioner of Tombs, 1845, 49
Cooper, Richard, Public Whipper, 36
Counterfeiting, 258
Cosher, Catharine, hanging of, 151
Crimmons, John, execution of, 465
Crittenden, Hon. J. J., Monroe Edwards case, 262
Cunningham, Capt. Wm., Provost Marshal, 1775, 25
Cunningham, Dan'l, alias Dad, kills "Paudeen," 146
Cunningham, Mrs. Emma Augusta, 160
    her trial for the murder of Burdell, 159
    her baby, 166

D

Daily, Henry, Jr., Stokes case, 546
Davis, Judge Noah, McFarland case, 404

Davis, Judge Noah, Stokes case, 552
    Tweed case, 639
Debt, Imprisonment for, 31
Dos Passos, John R., Stokes case, 548
Draper, Simeon, benevolence of, 87
Ducking Stool, 40
Duel, the Webb-Marshall, 269
Dunn, James, alias Foster, 291
Dunn, Rob't S., killed by Sharkey, 497

E

Eckel, John J., 161
Edwards, Monroe, forger, 261
    his trial, 263
        the forged Andrew Jackson let-
        ter, 268
Emmett, Robert, Colt case, 76
    Monroe Edwards case, 263
Escapes from the Tombs, 289
    from officers, 292
Evarts, W. M., Monroe Edwards case,
    263
Executions, 148
    list of, 152
    story of a Frenchman, 168

F

Fellows, Assistant District Attorney,
    McFarland case, 404
    Stokes case, 548
Fire of 1776, 150
Fisk-Stokes Tragedy, 520
Fisk, Col. Jas., Jr., shooting of, 524
    his will, 527
    funeral of, 530
    life of, 533
    his love-life, 541
Fly Market, 32
Forrest, Edwin, 341
Foster, Miss Flora, Matron of the
    Tombs, 663
Foster, Wm., killed Avery D. Putnam,
    457
    execution of, 462
Fullerton, Ex-Judge, Stokes case, 546
Furlong, Robert, the perjured witness
    in the Jewett case, 127

G

Gallaudet, Dr. Theodore, escape of, 293
Gambling, 53
    a Gambler's view of, 54
Garvin, S. B., Dist. Attorney, Jack
    Reynolds case, 318

Garvin, S. B., Dist. Attorney, McFar-
    land case, 404
    Stokes case, 546
Genet, Henry W., his trial and convic-
    tion, 645
    escape, 647
Gerry, Elbridge T., McFarland case, 404
    Stokes case, 546
Gibbons, a Philanthropic Butcher, 32
Gilbert, Miss Linda, the Prisoners'
    Friend, 663
Gordon, Capt. Nathaniel, the Slave
    Trader, 295
    attempted suicide, 300
    his execution, 302
Graham, David, defended Restell, 364
Graham, John, McFarland case, 404
    Stokes case, 545
Greenwich, State Prison at, 25

H

Hall, A. Oakey, the Poole case, 145
    his trial and acquittal, 645
Hall, J. Prescott, Monroe Edwards case,
    263
Haunted Cell, 273
Heinrich, Dutch, burglar, 256
Henshaw, Caroline, Colt's mistress, 75
Herald, New York, editorial on Colt's
    death, 77
Hicks, the Pirate, 210
    his confession, 212
    his execution, 214
Hicks, Whitehead, Mayor of New York,
    30
Hoag, Melinda, panel woman, 597
Hoffman, Ogden, his address in the
    Jewett case, 126
    the Poole case, 144
    the Monroe Edwards case, 263
    prosecuted Restell, 364
House of Refuge, 33
    John Mahony's account of, 175
Howe, Wm. F., defended Jack Rey-
    nolds, 305
    defended Rosenzweig, 374
    defended Maggie Jourdan, 492
Howlett and Saul, River Thieves, exe-
    cution of, 470
Huntington, Chas. B., at Sing Sing, 189
Hyer, Tom, attacked by Jas. Turner
    and Lewis Baker, 139

I

Ingersoll, James H., his trial and convic-
    tion, 645

J

Jackson, Richard C., hanging of, 152
Jeffards, Charles, kills his step-father, 449
Jewett, Helen, 97
    early life of, 98
    description of, 99
    correspondence, 101–105, 109
    the house at 41 Thomas street, 107
    the murder, 112
    J. Gordon Bennett's description of the body, 116
Johnson, Chauncey, burglar, 254
Johnson, John, hanging of, 150
Johnson, Richard, hanging of, 151
Josie, Naughty, 542
Jourdan, Maggie, the Sharkey case, 497
Judson, E. Z. C. (Ned Buntline), 353

K

Kent, Judge, Monroe Edwards case, 263
Kidd, Capt., 152
Know-Nothing Party, 137

L

Leonard, Moses G., 49
    Commissioner of the Tombs, 46 to 49
Lewinburg, Moses, murderer, 465
Liberty, Sons of, 29
Lynds, Capt. Elam, superintends building of prison at Sing Sing, 584

M

McCready, Wm. C., 340
McDonald, Robert C., killed Virginia Stewart, 232
    his suicide, 235
McFarland, Daniel, his trial, 404
    story of his life, 406
    his acquittal, 448
McKeon, John, Astor Place Riot, 357
    Stokes case, 546
Maguire, Mark, king of the newsboys, 141
Mahony, John, the American Jack Sheppard, 170
    his escape from the Tombs, 182
    his escape from Mulberry Street Station, 203
    his poetry, 207
Mansfield, Helen Josephine Lawlor, 539
Marshall, Thos. F., Monroe Edwards case, 263

Matsell, Superintendent, 491
Maxwell, Hugh, District Attorney, 33
Mercantile transaction, a, 251
Mickiweez, Eugene, confidence man, 236
Morris, Robert, see Jewett case, 126
Morrissey, John, difficulty with Poole, 140
    his letter on retiring from the prize ring, 146
Mott, John O., defended Maggie Jourdan, 492
Mulligan, Billy, 62
Murder, 209

N

Negro Plots, 149
Noah, Major, 263

O

O'Brien, Jerry, 61
O'Conor, Charles, defended Walworth, 502
Opera House, Astor Place, 349

P

"Paudeen," McLaughlin, 141
    his murder, 146
Payne, J. Howard, see Colt case, 80
Pettis, Spencer, counterfeiter, 260
Phelps, Benj. K., District Attorney, prosecuted Walworth, 502
    prosecuted Stokes, 559
Pintard, John, of N. Y. Historical Society, 24
Piracy, 284
Poole, Bill, 138
    killed in Stanwix Hall, 142
    his funeral, 144
Prevost, 24
Price, W. M., Counsel for Robinson, 119
    Monroe Edwards case, 263
Prison Discipline, 591
    Management and Reformation, 657
    Sunshine, 663
Putnam, Avery D., 457

R

Ransom, Daniel, hanging of, 151
Restell, Madame, 362
Reeves, Col. Marmaduke, confidence man, 239
Reynolds, Jack, killed Wm. Townsend, 303

Richardson, Albert D., a history of, 410
  his intercepted letter, 414
Richardson, Abby Sage, her statement, 379
Ring, the New York, 629
Riot, the Astor Place, 355
River Thieves, 467, 470
Robinson, Henrietta, the veiled murderess, 599
Robinson, Richard P., murderer of Helen Jewett, 101
  his arrest in Dey Street, 115
  his trial, 121
  not guilty, 132
  the Illinois lawsuit, 134
  death in Texas, 135
Rosenzweig, 372
  his trial, 374

S

Sanchez, Felix, 227
  killed his father-in-law, 463
Scandal, the Beecher, 511
Sedgwick, John, prosecuted Dad Cunningham, 146
Sharkey, Wm. J., killed Robert S. Dunn, 482
  escape of, 487
  life of, 496
Shephard, Honora, dealer in counterfeit money, 597
Shower Bath, 592
Sing Sing, punishment at, 185
  State Prison at, 582
Smith, Conrad, alias Schrader, escape and recapture, 291
Snodgrass, Geo. V., witness in Burdell case, 161
Spencer, Chas. S., 404
  address in McFarland trial, 406
Stadt-Huys (first jail in N. Y.), 21
Stadt-Herberg, 21
Stanford, Rev. John, 32
Stanwix Hall Tragedy, 137
Stephens, John L., his plan of the Tombs, 48
Stephens, John, wife murderer, 222
  attempt to escape, 229
Stewart, Virginia, killed at the Brandreth House, 232
Stokes, Edward S., sketch of his life, 536

Stokes, Edward S., his first trial, 546
  his second trial, 548
  his third trial, 558
  statement, 649
Stuart, Judge, the Walters case, 220

T

Tammany Hall, 629
Thumb-string and Pulley, 595
Tombs, when completed, 25
  officers of, 49
  capacity of, 50
  on fire, 77
  Murderer's Row, 94
  escapes from, 289
  ten days in the, 328
Townsend, John D., Stokes case, 548
Townsend, Wm., killed by Reynolds, 303
Train, Geo. Francis, 515
Treadmill, first introduced, 25
  description of, 42
Tremain, Lyman, Stokes case, 548, 573
Tribune Office, murder in the, 376
Turner, James, 138
Tweed, Wm. M., life of, 630
  trial of, 639
  sentence of, 642

V

Vagrancy, 81
Veiled Murderess, 599

W

Walters, Chas., wife murderer, 216
Walworth, Frank H., killed his father, 499
Walworth, Mansfield Tracy, killed by his son, 501
Waterbury, Nelson J., Stephens case, 226
Webb, Genl. James Watson, article on Monroe Edwards, 263
Webb-Marshall duel, 269
Whipping Post, 37
Whiting, Jas. R., prosecuted Colt, 68
  the Poole case, 145
  defended Dad Cunningham, 146
  Monroe Edwards case, 263
Wooden Horse, 43
Woodhull, Victoria C., 506

PATTERSON SMITH SERIES IN
CRIMINOLOGY, LAW ENFORCEMENT, AND SOCIAL PROBLEMS

1. *Lewis: *The Development of American Prisons and Prison Customs, 1776–1845*
2. Carpenter: *Reformatory Prison Discipline*
3. Brace: *The Dangerous Classes of New York*
4. *Dix: *Remarks on Prisons and Prison Discipline in the United States*
5. Bruce *et al.*: *The Workings of the Indeterminate-Sentence Law and the Parole System in Illinois*
6. *Wickersham Commission: *Complete Reports, Including the Mooney-Billings Report.* 14 vols.
7. Livingston: *Complete Works on Criminal Jurisprudence.* 2 vols.
8. Cleveland Foundation: *Criminal Justice in Cleveland*
9. Illinois Association for Criminal Justice: *The Illinois Crime Survey*
10. Missouri Association for Criminal Justice: *The Missouri Crime Survey*
11. Aschaffenburg: *Crime and Its Repression*
12. Garofalo: *Criminology*
13. Gross: *Criminal Psychology*
14. Lombroso: *Crime, Its Causes and Remedies*
15. Saleilles: *The Individualization of Punishment*
16. Tarde: *Penal Philosophy*
17. McKelvey: *American Prisons*
18. Sanders: *Negro Child Welfare in North Carolina*
19. Pike: *A History of Crime in England.* 2 vols.
20. Herring: *Welfare Work in Mill Villages*
21. Barnes: *The Evolution of Penology in Pennsylvania*
22. Puckett: *Folk Beliefs of the Southern Negro*
23. Fernald *et al.*: *A Study of Women Delinquents in New York State*
24. Wines: *The State of Prisons and of Child-Saving Institutions*
25. *Raper: *The Tragedy of Lynching*
26. Thomas: *The Unadjusted Girl*
27. Jorns: *The Quakers as Pioneers in Social Work*
28. Owings: *Women Police*
29. Woolston: *Prostitution in the United States*
30. Flexner: *Prostitution in Europe*
31. Kelso: *The History of Public Poor Relief in Massachusetts, 1820–1920*
32. Spivak: *Georgia Nigger*
33. Earle: *Curious Punishments of Bygone Days*
34. Bonger: *Race and Crime*
35. Fishman: *Crucibles of Crime*
36. Brearley: *Homicide in the United States*
37. *Graper: *American Police Administration*
38. Hichborn: *"The System"*
39. Steiner & Brown: *The North Carolina Chain Gang*
40. Cherrington: *The Evolution of Prohibition in the United States of America*
41. Colquhoun: *A Treatise on the Commerce and Police of the River Thames*
42. Colquhoun: *A Treatise on the Police of the Metropolis*
43. Abrahamsen: *Crime and the Human Mind*
44. Schneider: *The History of Public Welfare in New York State, 1609–1866*
45. Schneider & Deutsch: *The History of Public Welfare in New York State, 1867–1940*
46. Crapsey: *The Nether Side of New York*
47. Young: *Social Treatment in Probation and Delinquency*
48. Quinn: *Gambling and Gambling Devices*
49. McCord & McCord: *Origins of Crime*
50. Worthington & Topping: *Specialized Courts Dealing with Sex Delinquency*
51. Asbury: *Sucker's Progress*
52. Kneeland: *Commercialized Prostitution in New York City*

* new material added

PATTERSON SMITH SERIES IN
CRIMINOLOGY, LAW ENFORCEMENT, AND SOCIAL PROBLEMS

53. *Fosdick: *American Police Systems*
54. *Fosdick: *European Police Systems*
55. *Shay: *Judge Lynch: His First Hundred Years*
56. Barnes: *The Repression of Crime*
57. †Cable: *The Silent South*
58. Kammerer: *The Unmarried Mother*
59. Doshay: *The Boy Sex Offender and His Later Career*
60. Spaulding: *An Experimental Study of Psychopathic Delinquent Women*
61. Brockway: *Fifty Years of Prison Service*
62. Lawes: *Man's Judgment of Death*
63. Healy & Healy: *Pathological Lying, Accusation, and Swindling*
64. Smith: *The State Police*
65. Adams: *Interracial Marriage in Hawaii*
66. *Halpern: *A Decade of Probation*
67. Tappan: *Delinquent Girls in Court*
68. Alexander & Healy: *Roots of Crime*
69. *Healy & Bronner: *Delinquents and Criminals*
70. Cutler: *Lynch-Law*
71. Gillin: *Taming the Criminal*
72. Osborne: *Within Prison Walls*
73. Ashton: *The History of Gambling in England*
74. Whitlock: *On the Enforcement of Law in Cities*
75. Goldberg: *Child Offenders*
76. *Cressey: *The Taxi-Dance Hall*
77. Riis: *The Battle with the Slum*
78. Larson: *Lying and Its Detection*
79. Comstock: *Frauds Exposed*
80. Carpenter: *Our Convicts. 2 vols. in one*
81. †Horn: *Invisible Empire: The Story of the Ku Klux Klan, 1866–1871*
82. Faris *et al.*: *Intelligent Philanthropy*
83. Robinson: *History and Organization of Criminal Statistics in the U. S.*
84. Reckless: *Vice in Chicago*
85. Healy: *The Individual Delinquent*
86. *Bogen: *Jewish Philanthropy*
87. *Clinard: *The Black Market: A Study of White Collar Crime*
88. Healy: *Mental Conflicts and Misconduct*
89. Citizens' Police Committee: *Chicago Police Problems*
90. *Clay: *The Prison Chaplain*
91. *Peirce: *A Half Century with Juvenile Delinquents*
92. *Richmond: *Friendly Visiting Among the Poor*
93. Brasol: *Elements of Crime*
94. Strong: *Public Welfare Administration in Canada*
95. Beard: *Juvenile Probation*
96. Steinmetz: *The Gaming Table. 2 vols.*
97. *Crawford: *Report on the Penitentiaries of the United States*
98. *Kuhlman: *A Guide to Material on Crime and Criminal Justice*
99. Culver: *Bibliography of Crime and Criminal Justice, 1927–1931*
100. Culver: *Bibliography of Crime and Criminal Justice, 1932–1937*
101. Tompkins: *Administration of Criminal Justice, 1938–1948*
102. Tompkins: *Administration of Criminal Justice, 1949–1956*
103. Cumming: *Bibliography Dealing with Crime and Cognate Subjects*
104. *Addams *et al.*: *Philanthropy and Social Progress*
105. *Powell: *The American Siberia*
106. *Carpenter: *Reformatory Schools*
107. *Carpenter: *Juvenile Delinquents*
108. *Montague: *Sixty Years in Waifdom*

* new material added   † new edition, revised or enlarged

PATTERSON SMITH SERIES IN
CRIMINOLOGY, LAW ENFORCEMENT, AND SOCIAL PROBLEMS

109. *Mannheim: *Juvenile Delinquency in an English Middletown*
110. Semmes: *Crime and Punishment in Early Maryland*
111. *National Conference of Charities & Correction: *History of Child Saving in the United States*
112. †Barnes: *The Story of Punishment*
113. Phillipson: *Three Criminal Law Reformers*
114. *Drähms: *The Criminal*
115. *Terry & Pellens: *The Opium Problem*
116. *Ewing: *The Morality of Punishment*
117. †Mannheim: *Group Problems in Crime and Punishment*
118. *Michael & Adler: *Crime, Law and Social Science*
119. *Lee: *A History of Police in England*
120. †Schafer: *Compensation and Restitution to Victims of Crime*
121. †Mannheim: *Pioneers in Criminology*
122. Goebel & Naughton: *Law Enforcement in Colonial New York*
123. *Savage: *Police Records and Recollections*
124. Ives: *A History of Penal Methods*
125. *Bernard (ed.): *Americanization Studies*. 10 vols.:
　　　Thompson: *Schooling of the Immigrant*
　　　Daniels: *America via the Neighborhood*
　　　Thomas: *Old World Traits Transplanted*
　　　Speek: *A Stake in the Land*
　　　Davis: *Immigrant Health and the Community*
　　　Breckinridge: *New Homes for Old*
　　　Park: *The Immigrant Press and Its Control*
　　　Gavit: *Americans by Choice*
　　　Claghorn: *The Immigrant's Day in Court*
　　　Leiserson: *Adjusting Immigrant and Industry*
126. *Dai: *Opium Addiction in Chicago*
127. *Costello: *Our Police Protectors*
128. *Wade: *A Treatise on the Police and Crimes of the Metropolis*
129. *Robison: *Can Delinquency Be Measured?*
130. *Augustus: *John Augustus, First Probation Officer*
131. *Vollmer: *The Police and Modern Society*
132. Jessel & Horr: *Bibliographies of Works on Playing Cards and Gaming*
133. *Walling: *Recollections of a New York Chief of Police;* & Kaufmann: *Supplement on the Denver Police*
134. *Lombroso-Ferrero: *Criminal Man*
135. *Howard: *Prisons and Lazarettos*. 2 vols.:
　　　The State of the Prisons in England and Wales
　　　An Account of the Principal Lazarettos in Europe
136. *Fitzgerald: *Chronicles of Bow Street Police-Office*. 2 vols. in one
137. *Goring: *The English Convict*
138. Ribton-Turner: *A History of Vagrants and Vagrancy*
139. *Smith: *Justice and the Poor*
140. *Willard: *Tramping with Tramps*
141. *Fuld: *Police Administration*
142. *Booth: *In Darkest England and the Way Out*
143. *Darrow: *Crime, Its Cause and Treatment*
144. *Henderson (ed.): *Correction and Prevention*. 4 vols.:
　　　Henderson (ed.): *Prison Reform;* & Smith: *Criminal Law in the U. S.*
　　　Henderson (ed.): *Penal and Reformatory Institutions*
　　　Henderson: *Preventive Agencies and Methods*
　　　Hart: *Preventive Treatment of Neglected Children*
145. *Carpenter: *The Life and Work of Mary Carpenter*
146. *Proal: *Political Crime*

* new material added　† new edition, revised or enlarged

PATTERSON SMITH SERIES IN
CRIMINOLOGY, LAW ENFORCEMENT, AND SOCIAL PROBLEMS

147. *von Hentig: *Punishment*
148. *Darrow: *Resist Not Evil*
149. Grünhut: *Penal Reform*
150. *Guthrie: *Seed-Time and Harvest of Ragged Schools*
151. *Sprogle: *The Philadelphia Police*
152. †Blumer & Hauser: *Movies, Delinquency, and Crime*
153. *Calvert: *Capital Punishment in the Twentieth Century & The Death Penalty Enquiry*
154. *Pinkerton: *Thirty Years a Detective*
155. *Prison Discipline Society [Boston] Reports 1826–1854.* 6 vols.
156. *Woods (ed.): *The City Wilderness*
157. *Woods (ed.): *Americans in Process*
158. *Woods: *The Neighborhood in Nation-Building*
159. Powers & Witmer: *An Experiment in the Prevention of Delinquency*
160. *Andrews: *Bygone Punishments*
161. *Debs: *Walls and Bars*
162. *Hill: *Children of the State*
163. Stewart: *The Philanthropic Work of Josephine Shaw Lowell*
164. *Flinn: *History of the Chicago Police*
165. *Constabulary Force Commissioners: *First Report*
166. *Eldridge & Watts: *Our Rival the Rascal*
167. *Oppenheimer: *The Rationale of Punishment*
168. *Fenner: *Raising the Veil*
169. *Hill: *Suggestions for the Repression of Crime*
170. *Bleackley: *The Hangmen of England*
171. *Altgeld: *Complete Works*
172. *Watson: *The Charity Organization Movement in the United States*
173. *Woods et al.: *The Poor in Great Cities*
174. *Sampson: *Rationale of Crime*
175. *Folsom: *Our Police [Baltimore]*
176. Schmidt: *A Hangman's Diary*
177. *Osborne: *Society and Prisons*
178. *Sutton: *The New York Tombs*
179. *Morrison: *Juvenile Offenders*
180. *Parry: *The History of Torture in England*
181. Henderson: *Modern Methods of Charity*
182. Larned: *The Life and Work of William Pryor Letchworth*
183. *Coleman: *Humane Society Leaders in America*
184. *Duke: *Celebrated Criminal Cases of America*
185. *George: *The Junior Republic*
186. *Hackwood: *The Good Old Times*
187. *Fry & Cresswell: *Memoir of the Life of Elizabeth Fry.* 2 vols. in one
188. *McAdoo: *Guarding a Great City*
189. *Gray: *Prison Discipline in America*
190. *Robinson: *Should Prisoners Work?*
191. *Mayo: *Justice to All*
192. *Winter: *The New York State Reformatory in Elmira*
193. *Green: *Gambling Exposed*
194. *Woods: *Policeman and Public*
195. *Johnson: *Adventures in Social Welfare*
196. *Wines & Dwight: *Report on the Prisons and Reformatories of the United States and Canada*
197. *Salt: *The Flogging Craze*
198. *MacDonald: *Abnormal Man*
199. *Shalloo: *Private Police*
200. *Ellis: *The Criminal*

* new material added   † new edition, revised or enlarged